A Nation of
Home Owners

A Nation of Home Owners

Peter Saunders

London
UNWIN HYMAN
Boston   Sydney   Wellington

Published by the Academic Division of
Unwin Hyman Ltd
15/17 Broadwick Street, London W1V 1FP, UK

Unwin Hyman Inc.,
8 Winchester Place, Winchester, Mass. 01890, USA

Allen & Unwin (Australia) Ltd,
8 Napier Street, North Sydney, NSW 2060, Australia

Allen & Unwin (New Zealand) Ltd in association with the
Port Nicholson Press Ltd,
Compusales Building, 75 Ghuznee Street, Wellington 1, New Zealand

First published in 1990

British Library Cataloguing in Publication Data

Saunders, Peter, *1950–*
    A nation of home owners.
    1. Great Britain. Residencies. Ownership by occupiers.
    Policies of government
    I. Title
    333.33′8′0941

ISBN 0–04–445488–0

Library of Congress Cataloging in Publication Data

Saunders, Peter R.
    A nation of home owners / Peter Saunders.
        p.   cm.
    Includes bibliographical references.
    ISBN 0–04–445488–0. — ISBN 0–04–445489–9 (pbk.)
    1. Home ownership—Great Britain.   I. Title.
HD7287.82.G7S28   1990   89-36016
333.33′8′0941—dc20   CIP

Typeset by Columns of Reading in 10/12pt Times and
printed in Great Britain at the University Press, Cambridge

For Bert, Joan and
their journey to Inyanga

Contents

Acknowledgements

I would like to express my thanks to the following for permission to reproduce cartoons in this book: Bryan McAllister (p. 111), *Private Eye* (pp. 138, 197), *Punch* (p. 294), Hector Breege (p. 228).

Prologue

When I was born, my parents were living in rented rooms on the first floor of a small Victorian terraced house. Whether or not my arrival into this world brought them great joy and happiness I do not know, but it did bring them the offer of a maisonette from the local council. The family moved to a huge, modern council estate three miles out of town, and there we stayed while my parents began saving to buy a house. My father, who taught in a secondary modern school during the day, took on additional evening class teaching for three nights each week, while my mother found part-time employment as a shorthand typist and somehow fitted in cleaning, shopping, cooking, washing and child-rearing around that. At last, some time in the mid-1950s, their efforts culminated in the purchase of their own home.

They bought this house for £1,950, having raised most of the money on a building society mortgage. It was a modest terraced house which had been built between the wars – one of nearly 3 million built in that period. The design will be familiar to anybody who has lived in Britain: bay windows at the front, two living rooms and a small kitchen downstairs, two main bedrooms, a 'box room', a bathroom and a separate w.c. upstairs, and a garden at front and rear. It was the sort of house which has proved enormously popular in Britain yet which has often incurred the displeasure of intellectuals who have never understood the attractions of suburbia and who so often seem to distrust anything which is not designed, planned and provided by professional 'experts'. Most of these houses were built by small companies following plans published in trade magazines, although builders often added their own individual touch to the final product with the help of a 'pebble-dash' finish or leaded light glazing.

A few years later we moved again. My parents sold their first house for just over £3,000 and bought a three-bedroom semi-detached property in a higher-status part of town for £4,150. This house had a 'study' downstairs off the entrance hall, it had a garage to shelter the car which had been purchased some time earlier, and it had a larger rear garden which could be used for growing an impressive array of vegetables. My father told me how, as a boy before the war, he had sometimes visited this part of town and had watched these houses being built. He had dreamed that one day he might live in one of them. In 1961 this dream was realized.

I left home while my parents were still living in that house. My father was still teaching evening classes, and my mother was still fitting in her part-time secretarial job between her domestic chores, but life was becoming easier.

1

The car in the garage changed from a 1936 Morris to a Ford Popular to a second-hand Peugeot 504 which was unfortunately too wide to go up the narrow driveway. I went off to university, leaving them to enjoy their middle age.

Having married and had our first child, my wife and I began our housing career much as my parents had done, living first with my in-laws before moving into rented property. Unlike them, however, we were able to borrow the deposit for our first purchase from my parents-in-law, for they were home owners and, having virtually paid off their mortgage, they had been able to build up some savings. Unfortunately, however, we chose to purchase in 1973 at the height of the first major house price boom in Britain. We paid £7,000 for a property which would have cost us half that amount had we bought it two years earlier. I had learned my first lesson in what has become a national game of housing roulette.

The house was what might be described in estate agents' parlance as 'quaint'. This meant that the windows fell out of their frames when you went to open them, and that there was no bathroom. We replaced the windows, had an extension built for a bathroom, injected a damp-proof course, sprayed the joists and floorboards with woodworm killer, got gas laid on and redecorated all the rooms. We sold it three years later when I was offered a job at Sussex University. We received £8,600 for it, barely enough to recover the money we had paid out, and certainly not enough to compensate for the time and labour which we had devoted to making the place habitable.

We have had two more houses since then. Both of them have been Victorian properties which required extensive renovation, and we have made a fortune from them. We bought the first in 1976 for £11,000 with the help of a £9,000 mortgage. We sold this in 1983 following the second of the national house price booms and got £33,000 for it. We then purchased our present home, a large and elegant semi-detached place, for £49,000 with a mortgage of £30,000. This house is currently valued at around £170,000.

The point of outlining this short and unremarkable life history is twofold. First, it is possible to detect in this story the traces of a major change which has occurred in British society over the last fifty years. When my parents first bought a house in the 1950s, they were one of millions of households who were making the transition from renting to owning. Less than one-third of households lived in owner-occupied housing in 1950. Today, this proportion has risen to two-thirds and is still rising. One reason for writing this book is that I am convinced that this shift marks one of the most important and fundamental social changes to have occurred during this century. Mass home ownership is associated with a strong popular desire to own personal property and is underpinned by deeply cherished and widespread values which emphasize independence, security and the importance of home as a base from which to venture out into the world. It is impossible to understand British popular culture today without understanding the crucial role which home ownership has played in shaping it.

The second lesson to be drawn from this story is that millions of people have accumulated a substantial amount of wealth from their participation in the housing market. Since I left home my parents have moved between a number of different houses and they now own a detached bungalow on the outskirts of London valued at around £130,000. My wife's parents also live in the south-east and own a house worth well over £200,000. As an only child I expect eventually to inherit most of my parents' wealth, although they may be well advised to cash in on some of it to supplement their pensions. My wife is one of five children and may therefore anticipate a legacy of around £50,000 at today's prices. Add these sums to the net value of our own house once the mortgage has been redeemed, and we can expect later in middle age to find ourselves worth around one-third of a million pounds, not counting the value of insurances and pension contributions. Needless to say, our own children's prospects look even brighter.

Now we may not be considered 'typical'. We are a middle-class household living in the south-east with two sets of parents who are themselves home owners. Nevertheless, we are not atypical. Home owners in the north are likely to hold assets of a lower value; working-class owners may live in cheaper houses, and first-generation buyers are one step behind us in what is referred to in Chapter 3 as the process of 'familial accumulation' through the housing market, but all of these people are still making money out of owner occupation, and the sums involved are large. In my own family, less than forty years in the housing market have, in just two generations, produced a capital sum of one third of a million pounds. Some will have made less than this; others will have made more. The point, however, is that sums like this have never been available to ordinary people in Britain before now, and they could never have been accumulated through traditional forms of saving.

Nearly two centuries ago, Napoleon is said to have referred dismissively to the English as a 'nation of shopkeepers'. Today we are a nation of home owners. This book sets out to show how this has come about, the effect which it has had on people's lives, the impact which it has had on British society and its implications for those who, hitherto, have been excluded.

Like all sociological analyses, the book is informed by a particular viewpoint. This does not mean that it is 'biased', for it is quite possible to analyse evidence from a particular perspective without thereby distorting or tampering with it. My approach is one which is generally favourable towards the spread of home ownership. This is because I am committed to a set of values which holds that ordinary people are the best judges of their own interests and that, by and large, it is worth supporting trends and policies which enable such people to express and realize their preferences. Like my parents and like me, most people in Britain would prefer to own their homes rather than rent them, and I consider the reasons for this in Chapter 2. As a sociologist I find it exciting that these desires are slowly being fulfilled, and I find it challenging to work out a way in which more of those who wish to buy may be enabled to do so. Equally, I am aware that not

3

everybody wants to own a home, and that there is nothing 'odd' about those who prefer to rent. My enthusiasm for owner-occupation does not blind me to its problems, nor does it lead me to wish to impose owner-occupation on those who do not want it. In this sense, the perspective which informs this book is not so much one of support for home ownership as one of support for the freedom of households to choose for themselves the housing arrangements which best suit them – it just so happens that when they are able to choose for themselves, the overwhelming majority of them choose to own.

The problem I have had in writing the book, however, is that most of the existing sociological literature on home ownership is written from a very different perspective. The socialist left may have been in retreat politically these last ten years, but its influence in our universities remains as strong as ever. As Peter Williams and I have suggested elsewhere, research and teaching on urban issues are strongly embedded in a socialist and collectivist orthodoxy which still sets most of the academic agenda, which restricts debate and which represents a major obstacle to fresh thinking (see Saunders and Williams, 1986). Although many of those left academics who have written on home ownership claim that they are not opposed to it *in principle*, the tone and content of much of this literature are unmistakably critical, and the policy prescriptions which flow out of it seem designed to strip owner-occupiers of most or all the benefits and advantages which attracted them to this tenure in the first place. There is something about mass home ownership in Britain which deeply disturbs and offends the sensibilities of the academic left, and for all their protestations to the contrary (and notwithstanding the fact that most of them are themselves home owners), it is clear from what they write that they do not like it.

For me, the attraction and the promise of sociology have always been its capacity for illuminating aspects of our lives which we rarely stop to examine for ourselves. Personal experiences can be reinterpreted, and our understanding of them enriched, by setting them in a broader social context which helps make sense of why we do certain things, how other things happen to us and what the unforeseen consequences of our actions are likely to have been. Sociology at its best is the ideal vehicle for achieving such an understanding, but it has to relate in some way to how we experience these things for ourselves. Too often, sociology has failed to make this link and has indulged itself in theoretical flights of fancy which end up portraying the world in the way that sociologists would like it to be rather than as it is felt and lived by those they claim to be studying. This kind of sociology becomes arrogant, detached and often wilfully obscure. It sets up its imaginary version of the world as an objective reality and is dismissive of evidence which suggests that most people see things in a rather different way. It is this brand of sociology which has often come to dominate the literature on home ownership, for what people say they want is subordinated to what they ought to want, and the way they live is explained away by an implicit theory of how they ought to live. In this way, a wedge is driven between personal experience and sociological analysis, and it becomes impossible to square the former with the latter.

As part of the research for this book, I and others sat in many different living rooms in many different houses in three towns scattered across England and listened to what home owners and council tenants had to say about their housing and their aspirations. For most of the time it was impossible to relate what I was hearing to what I was reading. Left academics told me that millions of people have been coerced or cajoled into buying their homes, yet home owners themselves insisted that this is what they had wanted all along. Left academics told me that public-sector renting was 'in principle' a better and more rational way of housing people, yet most council tenants insisted that they would prefer to buy given half a chance. Left academics told me that ordinary people cannot make capital gains from home ownership and that most of them suffer from buying a house, yet the figures which home owners provided of their various purchases and the way they had financed them clearly demonstrated that virtually all of them had made at least some money from the housing market and that, like me, many of them were accumulating small fortunes. Left academics told me that the spread of owner-occupation was undermining collective social life and was fostering a mean-spirited culture of privatism, yet most of the home owners with whom we spoke led full and active lives outside the home as well as within it. The more these interviews went on, the more I felt that most of those we were meeting would have been either amused or appalled to learn of how the academic establishment was misrepresenting their lives. A few months of sitting in other people's living rooms rather than in their own studies would, I feel, help many of these academics to shake off some of the illusions which they seem so intent on perpetuating.

How has the academic left become so divorced from the lived reality of most people's everyday existence? Why are these writers so resolutely hostile to a form of housing which most people seem to want and from which so many have benefited? There appear to be at least four answers to these questions.

The first has to do with a 'cultural lag'. Nineteenth-century radical thought has bequeathed to the British left a deep hatred for private landlordism which persists to this day. Before the First World War, the only feasible alternative to a system of private renting seemed to be a system of state renting, and through its formative years British socialism therefore became unswervingly committed to council housing as its preferred form of tenure. Today, however, private landlordism has dwindled, and council housing now faces a stronger challenge from the spread of owner-occupation. The Labour Party leadership has recognized that this is a battle which cannot be won and has belatedly and reluctantly come to accept policies, such as those giving council tenants the right to buy their homes, which will further erode the size and significance of the public sector. Many left academics have never accepted this move, however, for they have grown up to believe that there is something intrinsically socialist in a system of state renting, although they would be hard-pushed to articulate what it is.

The second factor is intellectual snobbery. Intellectuals on both the right and the left have traditionally reacted with distaste to all forms of 'petty property' and have reserved particular scorn for that class in society whom they designate the 'petty bourgeoisie'. What the right has demanded of the proletariat is respect and deference. What the left has demanded of the proletariat is revolutionary zeal and discipline. What both camps dislike in the 'petty bourgeoisie' are signs of individualism (not to mention anti-intellectualism), and they fear that the extension of home ownership to the 'proletariat' will infect this class too with a spirit of independence and autonomy which will undercut the futures they have planned for it. As André Gorz disarmingly observes, 'Autonomy is not a proletarian virtue' (1982, p. 35). Seen in this way, the emergence of a nation of home owners represents for the left a strengthening of values which they despise and which they see as the antithesis to the virtues of collectivism which they seek to foster.

The third reason is to be found in the left's commitment to social engineering. For them, as for Marx, the only point in analysing the world is to change it, but like all visionaries they want change on their own terms. A nation of public-sector renters, like a nation of public-sector workers, is a country which can be controlled and directed in accordance with master-plans. Millions of households owning their own homes make grand-scale social engineering much more problematic. Widespread home ownership also undermines the social homogeneity of 'the masses' and makes it that much more difficult to 'mobilize' them and to 'raise their consciousness' in pursuit of a common cause. Ray Pahl and Claire Wallace have captured the point nicely when they write:

Radicals of the left have typically scorned aspirations towards respect-ability by working people, since these are often perceived to undermine collective action for collectivist goals. Radical socialists in Britain do not express their goals in terms of *petit bourgeois* respectability, even if that is what most workers seem to want. The stereotype of traditional workers as tatooed beer-drinking machos with clenched fists raised high is out of phase with the reality of the world of the men and women who shop in the British Home Stores, Habitat or Marks and Spencer.

(1988, p. 147)

Respectability, consumerism, individualism, all seem to be associated with the desire for home ownership, and this is a desire against which the academic left therefore sets its face most resolutely.

The fourth reason has to do with the values of left academics themselves. Many of them are products of the 1960s and have never been able to bring themselves to transcend the counter-culture spawned in those exciting yet frivolous years. They still seek to reject the 'bourgeois' way of life of their parents' generation, even though most of their own generation and the one behind that have now come to embrace it more strongly than ever their parents did. They rail against status distinctions and see in home ownership a fundamental basis of the status order. They reject the striving which is inherent to the bourgeois work ethic and find in the pursuit of home ownership a major cause of continued and redoubled individual effort and ambition. They view materialism and money-making with a puritanical horror and recognize in home ownership a property system through which people may try to accumulate wealth. Like Canute on the beach, they sit enthroned in their universities commanding and entreating this tide to recede, and all the while they feel a growing discomfort as the water laps unresponsively around their ankles.

This book represents a deliberate attempt to confront this left academic orthodoxy. It is not, I hope, a polemical confrontation; nor is it a theoretical one. Rather, I have selected what I take to be some of the key sociological questions raised by the growth of home ownership in Britain, and in each case I review evidence collected in my own research and in other studies to evaluate the claims which have been advanced in the academic literature.

Chapter 1 contains a brief history of the growth of owner-occupation in Britain, and the historical evidence is used to refute the view that governments or big business have in some way sponsored or encouraged this growth in an attempt to undermine working-class solidarism. The chapter also outlines the background to my own research in the three towns of Burnley, Derby and Slough, although technical details of how this study was carried out are reserved for two appendices at the end of the book.

In Chapter 2 I consider the evidence on the popularity of owning as opposed to renting and I attempt to explain why so many people now desire to buy their own homes. One section of the chapter considers whether this desire could in any sense be a product of 'natural' inclinations in human beings (an idea which is guaranteed to provoke the indignation and horror of most sociologists wherever they happen to be located on the political spectrum), but most of it is devoted to an analysis of the significance of social and cultural factors in people's motivations. For the left, evidence of a widespread desire to own is explained as the product of ideological conditioning, financial inducements and political coercion, and these arguments are inspected in the light of the evidence and firmly rejected.

Chapter 3 considers whether and how owner-occupiers accumulate wealth from their housing. It is found that the sums involved are considerable, and five arguments from the academic critics of owner-occupation are then considered in turn. One suggests that these gains are achieved at the expense of other home owners. A second forecasts that they are a temporary phenomenon and that the good fortune of home owners cannot last. A third holds that this wealth is not realizable as cash and is therefore insignificant. A fourth believes that only affluent owners make money and that groups like the working class and ethnic minorities may actually lose. A fifth claims that home owners are not interested in their houses as investments and that the possibility of accruing capital gains thus has no

7

effect on their attitudes or behaviour. With the aid of a unique data set providing information on every move made by the households interviewed in the three towns survey, all five of these assertions are shown to be false.

In Chapter 4 I consider the evidence on the political implications of the growth of owner-occupation. Social scientists are divided over the question of whether housing tenure influences political alignments or the way people vote, and some have recently suggested that new cleavages are arising which are cutting across the traditional class bases of political behaviour. The chapter concludes that mass home ownership has had some significant effects on political mobilization and voting, but there is no simple pattern, and for most working-class people, occupation still appears more salient than housing tenure in influencing how they vote.

In Chapter 5 we turn to consider how buying a house may influence the way people experience their homes. Two hypotheses in particular are examined, one from the left and one not. The first suggests that home ownership encourages privatized life-styles in which households withdraw from participation in collective life. This is found to be almost entirely untrue. The second proposes that home ownership enhances people's sense of security and psychological well-being, and some evidence is found to support this view. The chapter also takes issue with feminist critics of home ownership who see in it a vehicle for reproducing patriarchal domination, for there is no evidence that women value the private home any less than men do.

Finally, Chapter 6 considers some of the sociological implications of our evidence as regards the analysis of social inequalities in contemporary Britain and finds that conventional class theories of social stratification are no longer adequate. The chapter shows that a major division has been opening up in Britain between a 'middle mass' and a 'marginalized minority', and much of the ensuing discussion is devoted to reviewing and evaluating various policy prescriptions which have been suggested or adopted as solutions to this problem. The major policy challenge for the 1990s and beyond is to enable the poorest one-third of the population to enjoy the sort of choice over its housing which the more affluent two-thirds now takes for granted, and at the end of the chapter a skeleton housing voucher or allowance scheme is outlined which could go a long way to achieving this objective.

For me, this book represents the fruition of a long period of interest in the sociological questions which home ownership raises. I first developed an interest in this while researching for my doctoral thesis in the early 1970s, for there I became aware of how active suburban owner-occupiers could be in defending their property interests. Having taken up a lectureship at the University of Sussex in the mid-1970s, I was drawn back to the issue from a different direction as I began to encounter what seemed then (and what still seems now) an extraordinary Marxist literature which resolutely refused to accept that housing tenure could represent an important sociological variable. I was moved to write something on this when I came across a booklet produced by the Community Development Project team (who were funded by the Home Office, no less) which proclaimed across its back cover the unlikely slogan: 'I rent, you buy, we lose, they profit' (CDP, 1976b). This slogan epitomizes all that is misguided in left analyses of home ownership, and I still treasure this booklet as an example of one of the worst excesses of blinkered sociological reasoning.

There is, however, a limit to how far one can go in criticizing this sort of work without going out and generating some empirical findings of one's own. So it was that, in 1985, I and some research colleagues began work on what became the three towns survey. We carried out the interviews for this project in 1986, and the results were analysed through 1987. Most of the book was then finally written in 1988. This book is, then, the culmination of four years of research, and of ten years of interest before that, although it could be argued that the seeds of it were first planted back in the mid-1950s when my family first moved from its council maisonette into an inter-war terraced house which we were able to call our own. It seems fitting, therefore, that I should dedicate the book to my parents.

Four years of research pile up many obligations, and a prologue offers the opportunity to acknowledge if not repay them. First, of course, my sincere thanks are owed to the 522 people in Burnley, Derby and Slough who invited us into their homes to interview them. Doing these interviews was, for the most part, a thoroughly enjoyable, rewarding and educative experience, but one is aware of its exploitative character, for at the end of an hour and a half or more, the interviewer disappears out of the door, invaluable data clutched firmly to the bosom, and the respondents are left wondering what, if anything, is to come of what they have said. An academic book is a poor sort of a thank-you, but I hope that those of our interviewees who may come across it find that the time they spent talking with us was in some sense worthwhile.

The interviews themselves were done mainly by Mike Savage, Mark Bhatti and myself. Mark was employed for a year as Research Fellow attached to this project and did much else apart from interviewing to help make it a success. When he left in pursuit of more secure employment, Colin Harris ably filled his place and helped steer the study through to completion by taking on interviewing, coding and data analysis. Mike Savage was throughout this period employed at Sussex as a Senior Research Fellow and research co-ordinator. He was under no obligation to help out on this particular project, and I owe him a special debt of gratitude for all the hard work he put into it.

Conducting hundreds of in-depth interviews in three widely separated towns is a daunting task, and I was fortunate to be able to draw on the help of a number of other people to get the job completed. Additional thanks, then, to Lisa Adkins, James Barlow, Linda Beanlands, Christine Boom, Susan Halford, Chris Howlett and Andrea Jones, all of whom shared with us at one stage or another the exhilaration of interviewing, the delights of afternoon cream teas and late-night curries, and the frustrations of knocking

9

at empty houses and killing time between calls.

A key condition of conducting a survey like this is access to money and to institutional back-up. I am grateful to the Economic and Social Research Council for providing the former as part of a programme grant awarded to four linked projects at Sussex of which this was one. Sussex University provided the latter, and I should mention the particular help I received from David Hitchin in the Computing Centre, Mike Lewis in the library and my secretary, Joyce Smart. I am also grateful to the university for providing me with a term's study leave to help me find the time to write the book.

Other friends and colleagues have helped in all sorts of different ways. Gordon Marshall offered help and guidance on coding social class categories and on log-linear models, and he also commented on a draft of Chapter 4. Clive Payne provided look-up tables for the Goldthorpe social class schema. Dawn Collard took on the laborious task of data punching, and Chris Hamnett and Arlene Graves provided me with copies of various documents as well as with comments on different parts of the book. Peter Williams originally collaborated with me in producing a paper which forms the basis of the first part of Chapter 5, and I am grateful to him for all the advice and criticism which he has offered on my thinking about home ownership over the last six or seven years. Susan Saunders did her best to explain recent developments in molecular biology which were important for part of the analysis in Chapter 2, and Ray Barrell, Rob Carter and Jan Van Weesep helped me sort out various technical problems as regards the analysis in Chapter 3. Mike Barrow, Tim Brindley, Peter Dickens, John Doling, Simon Duncan, Joe Flood, Ray Forrest, Adrian Franklin, Anne Haila, Alan Murie, Lionel Orchard, Andrew Sayer, Hilary Silver and Peter Taylor-Gooby all provided helpful ideas or comments at various points along the way, and David Harrison has had to put up with more boring conversations about home ownership over the last few years than I had any right to inflict upon him.

Various organizations helped in different ways as well. The local authorities in the three towns were most obliging in providing information on their areas. The Alliance & Leicester Building Society provided mortgage payment look-up tables, and the Nationwide Building Society sent us a carton-full of computer print-out when we approached them for information on house price movements in the three towns.

Finally, I should thank the participants at all the different conferences and seminars where I have tested out the various chapters of this book since the autumn of 1987. The left may dominate the academic agenda in this field, but when this agenda is challenged, the ensuing debate can, I have found, still be courteous yet stimulating.

Pete Saunders,
Brighton, March 1989

1   How the meek inherited the earth

Private property is as old as human civilization for human societies developed on the basis of private property systems. As Rousseau observed 'The first man who, after enclosing a piece of ground, bethought himself of saying, "This is mine", and found people simple enough to believe him, was the true founder of civil society' (1973, p. 76).

The first pre-emptive act must have occurred many thousands of years ago. Human beings have been settled upon the land, growing crops and herding animals, for over 10,000 years, and it is likely that claims to private ownership of land date back just as far. Certainly systems of private property were well established by the time the Ancients came to start recording their history.

Private property and human society have, therefore, evolved and developed in tandem. Furthermore, as Karl Marx recognized in the nineteenth century, the organization of private property has a significant impact on how the rest of a society is organized. In his view, all societies have been marked by a fundamental division between a minority who own property and a majority who do not. What the Roman slave, the feudal serf and the industrial proletarian all share in common is exclusion from ownership of property in their respective societies. It was because of this exclusion of the majority from ownership of property that Marx and Engels believed that every known society has been riven by class antagonisms. As they put it in their famous call to arms to the Western proletariat in 1848: 'The history of all hitherto existing society is the history of class struggles. Freeman and slave, patrician and plebeian, lord and serf, guildmaster and journeyman, in a word, oppressor and oppressed, stood in constant opposition to one another' (1970, pp. 35–6).

This is how things have remained for thousands of years – until recently. One of Marx's more successful predictions was that as capitalism matured, so competition would result in an economy dominated by ever smaller numbers of ever larger enterprises. One of his less successful predictions, however, was that this would sooner or later lead to the emergence of a centrally planned socialist economy. What has actually happened in Britain, as elsewhere in the West, is that the production and finance systems have become concentrated into a relatively small number of huge companies as Marx suggested they would, but that ownership of their assets has become remarkably diffused through the population as a whole. Rather than being owned by a few top-hatted plutocrats, or, indeed, by a few grey-suited commissars, the country's major enterprises have today passed into the ownership of millions of individual workers.

Direct ownership by workers of holdings in banks and major companies is relatively insignificant in Britain, although around 20 per cent of households do now own some shares, mainly as a result of the 'privatization' of companies like BT, British Gas, British Airways and BAA in the years since 1979. More important than this growth in popular shareholding, however, has been the spread of indirect ownership. One of the problems faced by contemporary Marxist theory is that it is now so very difficult to draw the sharp dividing lines between 'oppressor' and 'oppressed' which Marx and Engels identified in 1848. There is no obvious 'capitalist class' in modern Britain. There are boards of directors, fund managers and company chairmen, and these people do often own shares, but the vast bulk of the assets which they manage are now owned, not by individuals, nor even by traditional wealthy families, but by institutions such as pension funds and insurance companies (see, for example, Ingham, 1984, ch. 3).

Most of Britain's capital assets are today owned indirectly by most of the people living in this country. The huge financial institutions invest billions of pounds of workers' money in all sorts of capitalist enterprises and government securities in Britain and abroad. The profits are used to pay people their pensions, to redeem endowment and insurance policies when they fall due, and so on.

The system of property relations has been fundamentally transformed over a few short decades. In 1848 Marx and Engels concluded their *Communist Manifesto* with the resounding cry to the workers of the world to unite – 'The proletarians have nothing to lose but their chains. They have a world to win' (1970, p. 63). The slogan made sense then, for it highlighted the lack of any property interest among the masses of the nineteenth century. Even as late as 1929, when the Wall Street stock market collapsed and huge fortunes were lost, most people still lacked any stake in the property system. Many workers were of course badly affected by the closures and redundancies which followed the crash, but few lost their savings as a result of it. Yet when the Western stock markets teetered on the point of collapse in October 1987, millions of workers held their breath, for not only their jobs but their assets and their savings were at stake. Somewhere between 1929 and 1987, the working class finally became incorporated into the capitalist property system.

This incorporation, though significant, is nevertheless still only indirect. Most of us may have a stake in the capitalist property system as a result of our pension schemes, life insurances and endowment mortgages, but few of us even know which investments the stake is bound up with, and provided the cash is paid out at the end of the period, it is doubtful whether many of us even care. Collectively, we own the companies we see listed on the financial pages of our newspapers, but we most certainly do not control them, nor do we really identify with them. If we have purchased a few shares ourselves then we may take a little more notice of what is going on, perhaps checking the price movements of British Gas in much the same way as we might check our Premium Bond numbers, but even here we do not feel any real sense of identity with, or control over, the company. How could it be otherwise in a modern, large-scale economy?

There has, however, been a second major upheaval in the British property system during this century, and this has arguably had far greater *personal* significance for far more people than the expansion of direct and indirect share ownership could ever have had. This second upheaval – let us follow Pawley (1978, p. 7) and call it a 'revolution' – has gone to the heart of our everyday lives. It has entailed a remarkable and dramatic shift in the pattern of property ownership. Nobody planned it – there was no Lenin, no Khomeini – and (somewhat uniquely as revolutions go) nobody has ever been killed or called upon to die for it. As it has proceeded through the twentieth century, so this peaceful revolution has assumed its own momentum, and it has turned out to be one of the most popular revolutions in history. I refer, of course, to the remarkable growth of home ownership.

The principle of home ownership is not new. For most of our history, the ordinary people of Britain have built their own homes and have 'owned' what they built (though not necessarily the land on which it stood). In prehistoric times they built and lived in round huts with timber frames clad in turf, mud, or stone. Two thousand years ago they lived in 'long houses', with the family members eating and sleeping at one end while the animals were kept at the other. The Saxons too built their own homes on individual plots of land marked off by fences (Brindley, 1977, ch. 5), and during the late medieval period, the mass of the people were still housed in single-room huts of their own construction.

It was the enclosures of the countryside and the growth of the towns which together did so much to undermine this long tradition of self-provisioning and independent ownership. As hundreds of thousands of people were uprooted from the land to search for work in the new industrial cities of the eighteenth and nineteenth centuries, so houses were constructed for them by small building firms and were let to them by a new class of urban landlords. The squalor and overcrowding of much of this housing have passed into folklore, although as Engels (1969) noted in his review of working-class conditions of life in 1844, country cottages erected by farmers to house their workforce were often no better and were sometimes much worse than the basements and 'back-to-back' slums to which many urban workers and their families were consigned. It is important to remember, however, that it was not just the poor who rented, and that not all rented accommodation was low in quality and low in price. Private landlords catered for the middle class and working class alike, so that by the nineteenth century it had become the norm for members of all classes except for the rich to live in houses which they did not own. Burnett (1986, p. 147) suggests that by the end of that century there were no more than 14,000 owner-occupier households in the whole of London. For the 'vast majority of people', he says, renting was 'normal' and 'inevitable'.

The home ownership revolution of the twentieth century should perhaps therefore be seen more as a counter-revolution, a reassertion of the independent rights of ownership which for most people withered during and following the period of industrialization and urbanization. Of course, modern owner-occupation is very different in form and quality from its pre-industrial predecessor. Few people today build their own homes (although, as we shall see in Chapter 6, some do), and, in contrast with the labourer's cottage or the peasant's hut, modern housing represents both a means of shelter and a store of wealth. As we shall see in Chapter 3, owner-occupiers today generally enjoy ownership of a high-value tradeable commodity, which was never true of earlier generations of owners. Nevertheless, we should not lose sight of the fact that most people have owned their homes for most of our history and that the twentieth century has in this sense rediscovered a long tradition rather than establishing a new one.

How, then, has this revolution, or counter-revolution, come about? How successful has it been and how many people has it touched? And what have been its consequences for the economic, political and cultural life of contemporary Britain?

The extent of owner-occupation

There are no completely reliable figures on the number of people in owner-occupation in Britain before 1961 when housing tenure was first included in the dicenial Census. Most studies suggest that the home ownership rate at the start of the First World War was probably around 10 per cent, although Swenarton and Taylor have investigated the sources of this claim and conclude that it is little more than a guess. In their view, 'The national level of owner occupation prior to the First World War is still unknown' (1985, p. 376).

Table 1.1 *Housing tenure change in England and Wales, 1914–86*

| | *Percentage of households in tenure* | | | |
Year	Owner-occupied	Public rented	Private rented	Housing association
1914	10	–	90	–
1939	32	10	58	–
1953	32	18	51	–
1961	43	23	34	–
1971	51	28	20	1
1981	58	29	11	2
1986	65	24	8	3

Sources: 1914 estimates – see Swenarton and Taylor, 1985; 1939 and 1953 estimates plus 1961–81 data from Holmans, 1987, table V.1; 1986 estimates from Department of the Environment, 1987a. Percentages may not add up to 100 due to rounding.

The 10 per cent figure is, however, all we have to go on. If correct, it would suggest that nine in every ten British households rented from private landlords during the first decade of this century; for although provisions had been made in various Acts of Parliament from 1866 onwards for local councils to build houses for working-class rental, the size of the public sector remained negligible until 1919 when councils were given subsidies for this purpose from the central Exchequer.

Table 1.1 reveals the extent of the revolution which has taken place since 1914. The three principal trends are clear. First, private renting has collapsed from around 90 per cent to 8 per cent of households in just seventy years.

Second, state housing has grown from nothing to embrace three households in ten by 1981. In Scotland (which is not represented in this table) the proportion of households renting their homes from the state had reached a staggering 55 per cent by 1981. These figures have fallen back somewhat during the 1980s due to reductions in new building coupled with sales of existing stock to sitting tenants. By 1986 the proportion of households renting from local councils or New Town Corporations had dropped to 24 per cent in England and Wales and to 49 per cent in Scotland.

Third, owner-occupation has expanded from around 10 per cent of households in 1914 to 65 per cent (63 per cent in Britain as a whole) in 1986. The first period of expansion came in the inter-war years. By 1939 around one-third of households owned or were buying their homes. This was the period of middle-class expansion into owner-occupation, for by 1939 around 55 per cent of middle-class households were home owners. Ownership was at that time still beyond the financial reach of most working-class people. Swenarton and Taylor (1985) show that average working-class wages in the 1930s were not enough to secure access to home ownership, although both they and Ball (1983, p. 36) accept that nearly 20 per cent of working-class households were nevertheless in this tenure by the time the war broke out.

The second period of expansion began in the 1950s and has continued ever since. In the years during and immediately following the war, owner-occupation rates probably fell back due to bomb damage and the government's decision to direct building labour and materials almost exclusively into the state sector. Swenarton and Taylor calculate that owner-occupation may have fallen from as much as 35 per cent in 1939 to as little as 27 per cent by the late 1940s. Ever since the 1950s, however, owner-occupation has been expanding, first at the expense of private renting, and more recently by eating into the state sector.

In this postwar period, home ownership has spread from the middle class to large sections of the working class. As Table 1.2 shows, all non-manual grades are today overwhelmingly to be found in the owner-occupied sector, but a majority of skilled manual workers too now own their homes, and even one in three unskilled manual workers own or are buying their housing. What this means is that over the last forty years, the basic tenure division between owners and council tenants has come to cut across familiar

Table 1.2 *Housing tenure and socioeconomic group of head of household, 1985*

| | Percentage in each housing tenure | | | |
Socioeconomic group	Outright owner	Mortgaged owner	Council tenant	Other
Professionals	10	78	2	10
Employers and managers	17	70	5	8
Intermediate non-manual	12	67	10	11
Junior non-manual	16	51	20	13
Skilled manual and own account	14	52	28	6
Semi-skilled and personal service	12	34	41	13
Unskilled manual	11	22	57	10
Economically inactive	42	5	41	12

Source: OPCS, *General Household Survey 1985*, 1987.

lines of social class cleavage. It is true that most council tenants are working class – only 1 per cent of 'economically active' council tenants, for example, are to be found in professional or managerial occupations. It is also true, as Table 1.3 shows, that there is still a clear relationship between level of income and housing tenure, for those in the lowest 20 per cent income band are still by and large unable to afford home ownership and therefore often have little choice but to rent from a local authority. But it is no longer true (if ever it was) that the middle class owns and the working class rents, for the 20 per cent of working-class households who owned before the war have now been boosted to at least 50 per cent.

As we shall see in later chapters, this blurring of class cleavages by the spread of home ownership to manual workers may have brought about some significant changes in the character of British society. If it is the case, for example, that home owners have been able to accumulate wealth as a result of rising house prices, then this would suggest that large sections of the working class are today sitting on sizeable capital sums which they will presumably pass on to their children. Similarly, it has been argued that ownership of private property tends to undermine support for socialist politics and for collectivist solutions to social questions, and if this is true,

Table 1.3 *Housing tenure and household income*

| | | Decile group of household income distribution | | | | | | | | | |
Tenure		Lowest 10%	11–20	21–30	31–40	41–50	51–60	61–70	71–80	81–90	Highest 10%	All
Council	No.:	481	380	294	236	191	131	97	64	43	24	1,941
tenants	%:	89	62	48	39	31	20	15	10	6	4	31
Mortgaged	No.:	15	22	70	151	244	342	430	474	530	552	2,830
owners	%:	3	4	11	25	39	53	65	71	78	81	45
Outright	No.:	47	208	253	213	186	172	136	131	105	106	1,557
owners	%:	9	35	41	36	30	27	21	20	15	16	25

Source: Department of Employment, 1987. Percentages may not add to 100 due to rounding.

then the implications of the growth of working-class home ownership for the future of British politics may be quite profound. In short, the home ownership revolution, like the growth of institutional share ownership in industry, has gone a long way to undermine Marx's claim in 1848 that workers have 'nothing to lose but their chains'. Today, many workers have substantial capital assets in the form of housing as well as their stake in private enterprise represented by their pensions and insurances. The implications of this are addressed in later chapters.

The home ownership revolution has not only spread down the class structure, but has also permeated across all regions of the country. We have already seen that Scotland is somewhat unique in the British Isles for its remarkably high rate of council renting, and this reflects both lower average incomes and a strong Labourist and statist tradition of working-class politics in that country. A history of massive public-sector housing schemes ever since the First World War has resulted in more people in Scotland living in state-owned housing than in housing of their own, but in the rest of Britain the owner-occupancy rate is well in excess of 50 per cent in every region, and in the more affluent regions it is over 70 per cent (Table 1.4).

Table 1.4 *Housing tenure in Scotland, Wales and the English regions, 1986*

| | | Percentage in tenure | | |
Region	Owner-occupied	Council rented	Housing association	Other rented
North	55.9	33.6	3.5	7.1
Yorkshire and Humberside	62.6	28.2	1.9	7.3
West Midlands	64.2	27.4	2.5	5.9
South-East	64.9	22.8	3.1	9.2
Greater London	*55.8*	*28.4*	*4.9*	*10.9*
Rest of South-East	*71.1*	*19.1*	*1.8*	*8.0*
North-West	65.8	25.4	2.8	6.0
East Anglia	66.9	21.0	2.2	9.9
East Midlands	67.5	23.2	1.9	7.5
South-West	70.4	17.9	1.9	9.8
England	65.0	24.4	2.6	8.0
Wales	67.5	22.8	1.7	8.0
Scotland	42.1	49.3	2.2	6.3
Great Britain	63.0	26.7	2.5	7.9

Source: Department of the Environment, 1987a.

Judged by international standards, a home ownership rate of 65 per cent is high, but not remarkably so. What is remarkable, however, is the speed with which the tenurial system in Britain has been transformed. To have moved from 10 per cent to 65 per cent home ownership in seventy years is unprecedented in any other country. Many of the nations with higher rates of owner-occupancy are found in the Third World where owner-occupation has a very different meaning than it does in Britain. As in Britain before the

Industrial Revolution, most of the population of these countries live in rudimentary houses which they have built for themselves. As Kemeny points out, it does not therefore make much sense to compare home ownership rates between developed and less developed countries, for we are not comparing like with like: 'Home ownership in peasant societies means something quite different from home ownership in the urban or suburban context' (1981, p. 3).

When we draw comparisons with other advanced industrial nations, Britain's home ownership rate is seen to be one of the highest and is comparable with those of the USA, Canada, Australia and New Zealand (Table 1.5). All four of these countries, however, have a long history of home ownership which reflects their origins in European settlement and immigration. Around the turn of the century, for example, when 90 per cent of British households were still renting from private landlords, nearly one-half of all Canadians and over one-third of all Americans were living in their own houses (Harris and Hamnett, 1987, p. 177). Home ownership has expanded during the twentieth century in all of these countries, but the rate of expansion has been far greater in Britain than in the others.

Table 1.5 *International owner-occupancy rates*

Country	% owner-occupied	GNP per head ($US 1981)	Rank order (tenure)	Rank order (GNP)	Year
Australia	70	11,080	8	8	1981
Bangladesh	90	140	1	19	1981
Brazil	60	2,220	11=	14	1970
Canada	62	11,400	10	7	1978
Eire	74	5,230	6	13	1981
Federal German Republic	37	13,450	18	3	1978
France	47	12,190	16	5	1978
Hungary	76	2,100	5	15	1980
India	85	260	3	18	1971
Italy	59	6,960	13=	12	1981
Japan	60	10,080	11=	9	1978
Netherlands	44	11,790	17	6	1981
New Zealand	71	7,700	7	11	1981
Pakistan	78	350	4	17	1980
Philippines	89	790	2	16	1970
Sweden	57	14,870	15	2	1981
Switzerland	30	17,430	19	1	1980
United Kingdom	59	9,110	13=	10	1981
United States	65	12,820	9	4	1981

Source: Boleat, 1985.

As we shall see when we consider the reasons for this phenomenal rate of growth, one factor has undoubtedly been the rising real incomes of British households through the twentieth century. It is, however, important to recognize that this alone cannot explain it, for there are other countries whose populations are wealthier yet where home ownership rates are considerably lower than in Britain. As Table 1.5 demonstrates, these include

West Germany, the Netherlands, Sweden and Switzerland. It is clear from this that there is no consistent relationship between rates of home ownership and the wealth of a society. Switzerland, the richest country in the world outside of the Middle East, has one of the lowest home ownership rates, but other wealthy nations such as the USA have comparatively high rates. The only consistent pattern which can be detected from the figures in Table 1.5 is the tendency for owner-occupancy to be relatively higher in the English-speaking countries than in other countries with comparable GNPs per capita (Boleat 1985, p. 462), and this would suggest that any explanation for international variations will need to take account of cultural as well as economic or political factors. As we shall see, the origins and causes of the home owner revolution in Britain are many and varied, but among them is probably the emphasis on individualism which is in some ways peculiar to English history.

The modern history of English home ownership

The origins of the twentieth-century home ownership revolution lie in the rich nineteenth-century working-class culture of mutualism and self-help. As David Green has argued, the familiar image of Victorian Britain as committed to the principles and philosophy of *laissez-faire* needs to be complemented by an appreciation of 'a clear working class alternative, aiming to replace the hated Poor Law and the largesse of the well-to-do with the mutual aid of the friendly society and the trade union branch' (1985, p. 1). Integral to this working-class mutualist tradition were the building clubs. These were voluntary organizations of working men who frequently convened their meetings in a public house and who agreed to contribute regular subscriptions into a common fund from which each would eventually draw (the order being determined by lot or bidding) to build or buy a house. The clubs would stay in existence until the last member had been housed, after which they would be wound up. For this reason they were known as 'terminating societies'. The first recorded terminating building club was in Birmingham in 1775, and in the fifty years after that we know of the formation of 250 more which between them built or bought some 2,000 houses (Boddy, 1980, pp. 5–6).

Like other forms of working-class mutual aid, the building clubs tended to recruit from the higher strata of that class. Crossick (1978) tells us that the level of subscriptions required ruled out those who could not command a regular income above subsistence level. He also suggests that one motive which impelled the skilled artisans of Victorian England to seek home ownership was precisely their concern to distance themselves spatially as well as socially as far away as possible from the rest of the working class: 'The desire for home ownership was itself seen as a criterion for being a respectable and superior working man' (1978, p. 149).

Although the search for respectability and status certainly was one factor in the growth of working-class home ownership, there were others, and it would be misleading to pretend that only the skilled artisans were involved in the nascent movement to own. As Mackenzie and Rose (1983, p. 166) suggest, another key motive was the desire for security against unemployment or old age. In Cornwall, for example, the tin miners saw a cottage property and a smallholding as the best available means for securing future family income (Rose, 1987, p. 137). And for some members of building clubs, housing represented an investment, for it was not unusual for more affluent working-class and lower-middle-class home owners to own more than one house with a view to securing an income in retirement (Daunton, 1987, p. 34). Kemp (1987, p. 5) finds that most members of the Leeds Permanent Society in the 1880s were working men owning on average five houses each.

The spread of the building clubs was uneven across the country. In South Wales they accounted for one-quarter of all new houses built on the coalfield before 1914, and in Merthyr Tydfil this proportion reached 58 per cent (Daunton, 1983). In the Potteries there were more than forty building societies by the late 1870s, and working-class home ownership was relatively common (Burnett, 1986, p. 147). Other areas where a strong tradition of mutual aid sustained relatively high levels of working-class owner-occupation included the Lancashire cotton towns, railway towns such as Crewe and Swindon (Kemp, 1987) and parts of the north-east such as Sunderland (where home ownership by the late nineteenth century had reached 27 per cent – Daunton, 1983).

From the mid-nineteenth century onwards, however, the terminating building clubs began to give way to permanent building societies. The first permanent society was founded in 1845, and by 1873 there were 540 of them (Boddy, 1980, p. 7). Despite their legal status as corporations (confirmed in an Act of 1874), these permanent societies began to look more and more like banks (though they were non-profit-making) than friendly societies. The advantage of the permanent societies was that anybody could join at any time, for like banks they split the two functions of lending and borrowing. As the volume of business increased, so the new-style building societies moved away from their origins in working-class mutual aid. People invested in them, not as a way of buying a house, but simply in order to gain interest, and their managements became more professionalized and more distinctively middle class. Williams (1987, p. 199) suggests that most of the societies soon fell into the control of middle-class directors, and Boddy (1980, p. 7) quotes from a Royal Commission of 1872 which found that the growth of the permanent societies 'had altogether changed the character and altered the sphere of the building society movement'.

By the start of the twentieth century, over 2,000 permanent societies controlling assets of £60 million had virtually eclipsed the mutualist terminating clubs from which they had sprung. For the first twenty years of the century, their numbers gradually shrank (as a result of mergers and the occasional spectacular collapse) while their financial power slowly increased.

By 1920 there were 1,271 societies with £87 million of assets and three-quarters of a million shareholders (Building Societies Association, 1988, table 1).

Although the building clubs had originated in the desire of working people to own their homes, it became common for the building societies to lend much of the money deposited with them to landlords, thereby supporting rental rather than owner-occupation. Holmans (1987, pp. 218–19) estimates that before the First World War over half of all building society lending went to landlords or commercial interests. The early growth of the permanent societies did not, therefore, contribute greatly to the spread of owner-occupation. On Holmans's estimates it seems that there were around three-quarters of a million mortgaged owner-occupiers in 1911 of whom no more than 150,000 had secured finance from building societies. It was not until the 1930s that the societies began to lend on a large scale for owner-occupation. The explanation for why this happened is bound up with the sorry fate of private landlordism in Britain.

Britain today has the smallest private rented sector (and the largest directly owned state rented sector) in the Western world (Coleman, 1988, p. 37). The decline of the private landlord can be dated back to the 1880s when rising local property taxes (following the extension of the franchise) and static wage levels (which limited the rents which tenants could afford to pay) combined to squeeze landlords' profits (Daunton, 1987, pp. 24–5). Furthermore, declining profits from housing investment contrasted with new sources of investment income which were opening up elsewhere. These included the building societies as well as stocks and shares and investment trusts (Hamnett and Randolph, 1988, pp. 51–2). These new investment opportunities undoubtedly syphoned off much of the lower-middle-class money which a few years earlier would have gone into investment in housing. As Hamnett and Randolph point out, not only did prospective landlords often find these alternative outlets more attractive, but so too did small savers who had often advanced cash to landlords through private mortgage arrangements. In other words, the growth of the building societies and other financial institutions both induced people away from housing investment and made it more expensive for those who still wanted to invest in housing to borrow the money.

In 1915 the 'push' of the profits squeeze and the 'pull' of better investment opportunities elsewhere were reinforced by government action to control rents. Introduced as a 'temporary' measure, rent controls in one form or another have been in force ever since. Although such controls were not the only factor leading to the demise of the private landlord in Britain, many commentators (particularly but not exclusively those on the political right) have seen them as the major factor. Combined with legislation which has progressively increased the security of tenure enjoyed by tenants, rent controls are seen to have choked off profitability and encouraged landlords to withdraw their investments from housing. Minford, for example, argues that 'rent regulation has suppressed rental returns below what is sufficient to stimulate new lets or to maintain the present stock through relets' (Minford, Peal and Ashton, 1987, p. 41). Similarly Butler, Pirie and Young suggest that 'Government intervention in the form of rent control and security of tenure has ensured that the landlords were impoverished and their property effectively destroyed' (1985, p. 342). And for Donnison (1967, p. 175), 'No other country in western Europe [has] so consistently discouraged private investment in rented property.' The question, of course, is why have governments apparently attacked private landlordism so single-mindedly over the course of this century?

Some writers on the left have interpreted the 1915 legislation as a 'working-class victory' over a 'bourgeois state' representing the interests of a 'capitalist class'. Noting that rent controls were prompted by tenants' agitation over rising rents, notably in Glasgow, those who hold this view (for example, Damer, 1980) explain the state's attack on private landlords simply as the result of the working class flexing its muscle. Other Marxists, however, have disputed this claim, arguing instead that controls were brought in on behalf of industrialists and other 'dominant fractions' of the 'ruling class' who were concerned to dampen social unrest and to maintain low costs of living, and hence low wages (for example, Ball, 1978; Dickens, 1977). Neither position is especially convincing. It seems more likely that rent controls, like the controls on mortgage interest which were introduced at the same time, were simply a short-term response to the exigencies of running a semi-controlled war economy (see Holmans, 1987, p. 397; also Hamnett and Randolph, 1988, p. 55).

What is more puzzling than the question of why controls were introduced is why they were never subsequently lifted. After all, many other countries legislated to control rents during the war, but they scrapped these controls afterwards, and their private rented sectors have survived to this very day. Why did this not happen in Britain?

Part of the explanation is that landlords were not powerful or influential enough to force British governments to rescind controls. According to Daunton, for example, 'The experience of rent control in the First World War and its maintenance in the 1920s and 1930s, along with the extension of security of tenure, confirmed that the private landlord had become a politically expendable fraction of capital' (1983, p. 122). In other words, urban landlords were treated as unimportant by governments because they were, by and large, small investors drawn from the lower middle class who could easily be stigmatized as uncaring Dickensian characters. As such they found it difficult to find a sympathetic ear in Westminster, Whitehall, or Fleet Street. They were without political friends, for the Liberals saw *rentiers* as parasites to be taxed, while the Conservatives were intent on defending the traditional privileges of rural landed property.

No decision was ever taken to kill off private landlords; they were simply allowed to die out. Rent controls, introduced as a stop-gap emergency measure, were easier left in place than removed. The wartime controls were due to lapse six months after the end of hostilities. However, a postwar shortage of some 600,000 houses (Short, 1982, p. 31) made it certain that immediate decontrol would result in substantial rent rises, so in 1919 the government renewed controls while extending them to 98 per cent of all tenancies. The only rents which were not controlled were those on newly constructed housing. In 1923 relets to new tenants were decontrolled, but by the end of the decade 69 per cent of all private lets were still subject to rent restriction. The effect on profitability was considerable, for by 1930 rents on controlled lets had been allowed to rise 50 per cent over 1914 levels, while free market rents had risen by nearly twice that amount (Daunton, 1987, p. 29). As Daunton argues, even though new lets had never been controlled, landlords were reluctant to invest in new housing given the distortions of the market. Private rental was withering as a result of regulations whose effects had never been intended but from which no government could extricate itself (see Minford, Peel and Ashton, 1987, p. 22).

There was a brief respite in 1933 when new legislation proposed to remove rent controls by stages on all but the lowest-value properties. This resulted in some return of confidence in the future of housing investment, and landlords began to borrow again against the security of future rental income. Thirty-nine thousand dwellings for rent were built for private landlords in 1934, and by 1938 this had risen to over 74,000 (Holmans, 1987, p. 400). But the confidence proved to be misplaced. With the outbreak of the Second World War, rents were again frozen, and this time they stayed frozen at their pre-war levels for eighteen years. A further brief period of partial decontrol (1957 to 1965) came too late to revive profitability, and since the 1960s increased security of tenure and rent regulation by means of local tribunals have together killed off the small landlord. Given the long-standing hostility of governments, it is now extremely doubtful whether individuals can ever again be induced to invest in rental housing.

The decline of private renting between the wars is one of the main factors which explains the growth of owner-occupation. Between 1914 and 1939 over one million privately rented houses (14 per cent of the total 1914 housing stock) were sold into owner-occupation (Ball, 1983, p. 23; Merrett, 1982, p. 16), an average of 46,000 every year. Most of these were sold to sitting tenants at substantial discounts. Before the First World War, a house with sitting tenants had been worth as much as (or possibly even more than) one without, for the value of housing was calculated according to how much rent it was likely to generate. Rent controls and security of tenure changed all that. Sitting tenants were now more of a liability than an asset, for even after 1923 it was impossible to raise rents for existing tenants beyond a level stipulated by law, and the increased security of tenure which they enjoyed made it increasingly difficult for landlords to replace them with new tenants at higher rents. Those landlords who decided to cut their losses therefore found that they could not sell tenanted houses at anything approaching their vacant possession value. Not only had their rental income been hit, but so too had their capital assets! Those who decided to get out had little option but to sell to their sitting tenants at below market values. So it was that, as private landlordism declined from the 1920s, owner-occupation expanded.

The plight of landlords selling out to sitting tenants is not, however, the only explanation for the remarkable growth of owner-occupation in this period. A second factor was the availability of mortgage funds.

The building societies expanded rapidly during the 1920s, as small investors, deterred from putting their money into housing and attracted by favourable tax arrangements, flocked to deposit their savings. Between 1920 and 1930 the number of shareholders doubled to nearly one and a half million, while total assets rose from £87 million to £371 million (Building Societies Association, 1988). The problem, however, was what to do with the money. The societies existed in order to lend for house purchase, but one reason why so much money was being deposited with them at this time was precisely that so few people wanted to borrow to invest in housing. There was, as Hamnett and Randolph (1988, p. 63) suggest, an embarrassing build-up of funds with nobody to lend them to. The dilemma was finally resolved in the 1930s when the societies went out to attract owner-occupiers.

Faced with their build-up of surpluses, the building societies deliberately set out to nurture this new market to soak up their funds. They entered into arrangements with builders, they reduced the size of deposit they required and they extended the term over which mortgages could be repaid. Many analysts claim that mortgages were also relatively cheap at this time, but this does not seem to have been the case. Mortgages were cheaper than they had been during the 1920s, but interest charges of 5 per cent meant that money was still relatively expensive at a time when general prices were falling (Holmans, 1987, p. 225). Indeed, as Holmans points out, mortgages cost more in real terms in the 1930s than they did either before 1914 or in the thirty years from 1950.

The fact that so many people could afford to pay relatively high charges on their housing loans reflects the fact that real incomes for those in employment were rising steadily by over 1 per cent per year during the 1930s (Holmans, 1987, p. 58). Not only this, but the cost of housing was falling at the same time. Primary commodity prices fell by two-thirds between 1925 and 1934, land prices were depressed, and technical innovations in brickmaking, cement and roof tiles also reduced costs (Ball, 1983, p. 30). The index of building costs (1930 = 100) fell from 140 in 1921 to 90 in 1934 (Daunton, 1987, p. 105), and although costs rose slowly in the latter part of the decade, house prices remained at very low levels.

The availability of funds, the rising real level of incomes and the falling cost of housing construction all combined to stimulate the biggest private-sector building boom ever seen in Britain. To the 1.1 million households who moved into owner-occupation by buying from their landlords were added another 1.8 million who bought new housing built for the owner-occupied market. Those private landlords who remained in business could hardly compete with this new wave of home ownership. The average level of mortgage repayments fell from 15s to just 10s per week between the 1920s and the mid-1930s, while average rents rose from 6*s* in 1914 to 9*s* (in controlled lets) and 11*s* 6*d* (in uncontrolled lets) in 1930. As Hamnett and Randolph recognize, 'The cost of buying a new house was little different from the cost of renting a pre-war, rent-controlled property' (1988, p. 67). To have made profit, landlords would have needed to charge rents which were uncompetitive with mortgage repayments on owner-occupied homes. Not only, therefore, were they often prevented by law from levying full market rents, but they were also effectively prevented from doing so by the brute logic of competition from building societies offering mortgages.

Nor was the expansion of cheap owner-occupation the only competition faced by private landlords, for following the First World War they were also challenged by the growth of local authority rental housing which attracted many of the more affluent and reliable households among the pool of potential tenants. Council housing (as it has come to be known) owes its origins to legislation in 1866 which allowed local authorities to erect or improve dwellings for 'the labouring classes', although little happened until after the consolidating Act of 1890. By 1914 some 24,000 dwellings had been built, 90 per cent of them since 1890 (Merrett, 1982, p. 3), but in no year did the public sector build as many as 1,000 units (Short, 1982, p. 28).

Three Acts passed by Parliament in the first five years after the war stimulated the growth of this nascent public sector. The first, introduced in 1919 by Lloyd George's coalition government, imposed a duty on local councils to survey their housing needs and to make provision for them. The Act bound the central Exchequer to meet all costs above the product of a penny rate, and this proved to be its Achilles' heel. Completions of new council houses rose from just 576 units in 1920 to over 16,000 in 1921 and 85,000 in 1922 (Merrett, 1979, p. 37); but as the legislation took effect, so did the open-ended subsidy. In 1924–5 the Act cost the central Exchequer nearly £8 million pounds. As Robinson observes, 'The principle of subsidy having been conceded in the 1919 Act, the history of most of the remaining interwar period is of governments desperately trying to limit the considerable sums of money paid through subsidies to local authorities' (1983, pp. 78–9).

The next major Act came in 1923 following the election of a Conservative government. The level of subsidies was reduced, and subsidies were made available to private-sector builders as well as local authorities. Under this Act local councils were allowed to build only if they could demonstrate that private enterprise was not meeting a specific need. Over 300,000 houses were built by private builders under this Act, most of them for owner-occupation, while local authorities built another 74,000.

Finally, in 1924 the first ever Labour government introduced another housing Act in which central government subsidies to local authorities were increased on housing built for rent. Although the succeeding Conservative administration cut the level of subsidy in 1927, this legislation (together with the 1923 Act) remained in force until 1933 when the National Government abolished subsidies to local authorities. In the ten years to 1935, over 500,000 council houses were built as a result of the 1924 Act.

Table 1.6 *Houses built in England and Wales, 1919–39*

Public sector	
Housing and Town Planning Act 1919	170,100
Housing Act 1923	75,300
Housing (Financial Provisions)Act 1924	504,500
Housing Act 1930	265,500
Other Acts	96,300
Total public sector	1,111,700
Private sector	
Built without subsidy	2,455,600
Built with subsidy under 1923 Act	362,700
Built with other subsidies	67,700
Total private sector	2,886,000
Grand total =	3,997,700

Source: CDP, 1976a, p. 16.

Just as rent controls were introduced as a temporary measure in 1915, so it seems that the flurry of legislation providing for council housing after the war was similarly understood by many of those involved as a 'one-off' pragmatic effort to house the war heroes and their families quickly. Few of those in the postwar coalition government which did so much to boost council housing wanted or expected it to grow to house nearly one-third of the population. The 1919 Act 'was clearly conceived as a result of a short-term economic malaise and moral obligations incurred at the end of the First World War' (Robinson, 1983, pp. 77–8). Addison, the minister responsible for the Act, saw the legislation in broader terms than this, but few of his Cabinet colleagues shared his vision. As Lloyd George observed of his departing minister when offered his resignation in 1921, 'He was rather too anxious to build houses' (quoted in Merrett, 1979, p. 41).

Daunton (1987, pp. 47–58) points out that the Liberal Party had never believed in municipal housing, for it threatened to undermine people's independence and their spirit of self-help. In a 1914 report the party had backed voluntary co-operative enterprise as the means for meeting working-class housing need. Nor were the Conservatives particularly favourable towards a massive extension of state provision, although there had long been some in the party who had recognized that private enterprise unaided was unlikely to fulfil the nation's housing requirements. The 1919 and 1923 Acts were, therefore, the product of short-term pragmatism. It was not until the Labour Party briefly assumed power in 1924 that council housing was pursued as a matter of political principle.

As Thane (1984) has demonstrated, many working-class people and socialist leaders before the First World War shared with the Liberals considerable reservations about state provision of housing and other services, but by 1924 the *étatistes* within the Labour Party had prevailed, and the voluntarist tradition of the friendly societies had been submerged. By the 1920s the Labour Party had come to see the choice in housing simply in terms of private as against state landlordism. Alternative forms of provision, such as co-operative housing, were not considered, and owner-occupation was ruled out as impractical for working-class people. Council housing was embraced with the same intensity with which private landlords were reviled, and it was hatred of the latter which led to the view that *all* working-class housing should in principle be supplied by local authorities (Daunton, 1987, p. 61). John Wheatley, who as Minister of Health introduced the 1924 Housing Act, 'wished to see the total replacement of privately rented accommodation for the working class by council housing' (Merrett, 1979, p. 45).

Labour's single-minded commitment to abolishing private landlordism and housing the whole of the working class in state-owned accommodation lingered in the party's collective subconscious for many decades. Indeed, by the time Labour next came to power in 1945, it had moved to a position where council housing was seen in much the same universalistic terms as the new National Health Service and state education system. As Lundqvist observes, 'The 1945–51 Labour government launched a comprehensive housing policy . . . Public rental housing – council housing – was to be the core . . . In Labour's view, the public rental sector should provide good housing for all at reasonable cost' (1986, p. 84).

For six years, this government controlled virtually all building through a strict licensing system which enabled it to direct both materials and labour into boosting the public sector while allowing both owner-occupation and private landlordism to dwindle. Private-sector builders and landowners were also hit by the nationalization of development land values, while private landlords were squeezed by the continued imposition of the prewar rents freeze. In the public sector, by contrast, the 1949 Housing Act enabled local authorities to build, not only for 'the working class' (as stipulated by all previous Acts) but for anybody in their area who wanted to rent. In this way, council housing was promoted as housing for all. For the minister responsible, Aneurin Bevan, 'council housing was for everyone' (CDP, 1976a, p. 16). Although Bevan went on record as saying that it was 'wrong to own somebody else's [house]' (quoted by Forrest, 1983, p. 206), he only ever applied this principle to private landlords, whom he despised. It apparently never occurred to him to apply the same principle to local authority landlords, whom he supported through a 167 per cent increase in subsidies and a new provision for raising loans at favourable terms.

The result of all of this support was the construction of just over 800,000 council dwellings between 1946 and 1951, compared with a total of just 180,000 private-sector completions (Merrett, 1979, p. 239). The relation between the two sectors had been reversed, for it was now council renting which was in the mainstream and owner-occupation which had become marginalized. However, the average of around 130,000 new council homes each year fell a long way short of the government's original target, and by 1951, when Labour left office, there were still 700,000 more households in England and Wales than there were units to accommodate them (Merrett, 1982, p. 25).

27

This deficit was cleared in the 1950s. The new Conservative government actually succeeded in building more council houses each year than Labour had done – only in four years between 1952 and 1964 did local authority completions dip below 130,000 and they never fell below 100,000. Meanwhile, abolition of licensing restrictions in 1954 resulted in a steady rise in the number of private-sector completions, from 90,000 in 1954 to over 200,000 in 1964 (see Merrett, 1979, p. 247). Both sectors, therefore, expanded dramatically in the twenty years after the war, and they did so at the expense of private landlords, whose numbers continued to fall at an even faster rate due to the combined effect of sales to sitting tenants and demolitions in slum clearance schemes. Between 1938 and 1960, two million privately rented houses disappeared, 400,000 through demolition and the rest through sales. Meanwhile, owner-occupation grew from 3.7 to 6.4 million dwellings in this period, while local authority renting also expanded from 1.1 to 3.6 million homes. By 1960, 44 per cent of households were owner-occupiers, 31 per cent were private tenants, and 25 per cent were council tenants (Merrett, 1982, p. 33).

A major factor behind the postwar expansion of owner-occupation was undoubtedly the rise in real incomes coupled with low interest charges and low inflation. In the thirteen years of Conservative government to 1964, real disposable incomes rose by 54 per cent, and this, together with the increased number of women going out to work, brought home ownership within the reach of many more households. If the 1930s were the period when owner-occupation was extended to the middle classes, then the 1950s and 1960s were the time when it came within reach of large sections of the working class.

As we shall see in Chapter 4, the growth of working-class affluence reflected in the spread of home ownership led some observers at this time to speak of a process of *embourgeoisement* in which old familiar class identities were breaking down and the traditional proletariat was fast disappearing. It was this fear that the traditional working class was disappearing which eventually persuaded the Labour Party leadership to endorse the aim of mass home ownership, although the party still retained its support for council renting (manifested in the 1960s by the massive and disastrous programme of industrialized high-rise building) and, of course, its opposition to private landlordism (which it smothered in a new system of rent tribunals and security of tenure for furnished as well as unfurnished tenants).

Richard Crossman, the Housing Minister in the new Labour government elected in 1964, wrote in his diary that the party should switch to clear support for home ownership and that this would help it win the next election. The primary aim, he wrote, should be 'to increase the production of owner occupied houses; we only build council houses where it is clear they are needed' (quoted in Boddy, 1980, p. 19). It was this thinking which led Labour to exempt housing from its Capital Gains Tax, introduced in 1965; to bring in the Option Mortgage Scheme in 1967 aimed at subsidizing low-income house buyers; and to exempt mortgage interest payments when it abolished tax relief on other interest payments in 1969. By the mid-1960s, therefore, all major political parties were committed to supporting the spread of home ownership.

With the collapse of private renting, however, it became increasingly obvious during the 1970s that the future expansion of owner-occupation could only be achieved at the expense of council renting. As we shall see in Chapter 2, a number of Conservative-controlled local authorities in the 1970s launched enthusiastic sales drives aimed at their own tenants, and this fed through to the national party, which fought the 1979 election on a policy of forcing councils to sell their houses at discount to any sitting tenants who wished to buy. This proved too much for most members of the Labour Party, who strenuously opposed council house sales in areas where there was still unmet housing need. Forced to choose between its traditional principled commitment to state housing and its more recent pragmatic acceptance of private ownership, the party opted for the former.

In the years since 1979, however, the pressure from council tenants wishing to buy their homes has proved so strong that the Labour Party has now revised even this position and has reconciled itself to seeing owner-occupation grow at the expense of the public sector. Just as in the 1960s it belatedly accepted the goal of mass home ownership, so in the 1980s it swallowed hard and fell in with a strategy which for the first time ever is resulting in a reduction in the size of the public rented stock. With private landlords killed off and co-operative housing (such as through housing associations) never more than marginal, the titanic struggle for tenure supremacy has been fought since the war between council housing and owner-occupation, and the latter has now emerged triumphant. At 65 per cent of households and rising, the only question remaining appears to be when, if at all, owner-occupation will reach saturation point. This is an issue we shall consider in Chapter 6.

The causes of the growth of home ownership

Why has owner-occupation prevailed? It is always tempting to search for evidence of intentionality to explain historical change. Sometimes, of course, such 'teleological' explanations of history are valid, for particular individuals or groups may successfully set out to bring about a certain change. More often, however, changes occur without anybody actually planning or even anticipating them. Such was the case with the twentieth-century expansion of home ownership in Britain.

Many commentators have denied this. Marxist writers in particular have often insisted that owner-occupation was deliberately and intentionally fostered by governments or by capitalist interests in an attempt to bolster the bourgeois social order. These theorists have between them identified five reasons why the 'capitalist class', aided and abetted by the 'capitalist state',

29

" IT WAS ORIGINALLY BUILT AS A LABOURER'S COTTAGE. "

sought to draw the working class into home ownership. None of these five reasons, however, are convincing.

The first concerns the supposed ideological effects of home ownership. In John Short's view, for example, it has long been the conscious strategy of the Conservative Party to try to secure working-class support for the private property system by making every worker a small owner: 'This tenure forms an important part of the Conservative strategy of ensuring social harmony by widening the basis of property ownership and legitimating the concept of such ownership. Moreover, owner-occupiers are seen as potential Tory supporters. It is believed that the encouragement of owner-occupation assures both social stability and future political support' (1982, p. 118). Similarly, Cynthia Cockburn thinks that all governments have encouraged owner-occupation out of ideological motives: 'Successive governments have used owner-occupation purposively as an inducement to workers to identify with bourgeois values' (1977, p. 45 n).

What Short and Cockburn are essentially arguing is that working-class people have been fooled by cunning capitalist governments. Their argument is based on the assumption that the working class is generally too stupid to understand the difference between private property in the form of a two-up, two-down terraced house, and private property in the form of the worldwide holdings of a multinational conglomerate. In this view, the home-owning proletariat has been led to believe that if private ownership is legitimate in the first case, then it must also be legitimate in the second, and this has the effect of justifying capitalist social relations and undermining popular support for socialist alternatives.

Short and Cockburn are not alone in thinking this. According to Cowley, for example, 'The advantages of this tenure for capital are . . . of immense ideological importance. Home ownership helps underpin and legitimize the possession of private property so dear to the heart of every capitalist' (1979, p. 93). Berry agrees: 'At the ideological level, widespread owner-occupation has been instrumental in diffusing values and attitudes favourable to private ownership in general, and private ownership of land in particular' (1983, p. 100). Ball too believes that the spread of domestic property has helped underpin the capitalist property system as a whole: 'Ideologically, home ownership emphasizes the desirability of the private ownership of property and the philosophy of individual "self-help" and generates a group with a vested interest in maintenance of private property' (1976, p. 29). And in Harvey's view, mass ownership of small-scale property insulates large-scale holdings against any threat of nationalization:

> Extended individualized ownership is, therefore, seen as advantageous to the capitalist class because it promotes: the alliegance of at least a segment of the working class to the principle of private property; an ethic of 'possessive individualism'; and a fragmentation of the working class into 'housing classes' of homeowners and tenants. This gives the capitalist class a handy ideological lever to use against public ownership and nationalization demands because it is easy to make these proposals sound as if their intent were to take workers' privately owned houses away from them.
>
> (1978, p. 15)

This belief that home ownership encourages working-class people to identify with capitalist corporations is linked to the second argument found within the Marxist literature. This holds that owner-occupation has been encouraged in order to create or reinforce divisions within the working class. In particular, it is held that, by helping the higher strata of that class to achieve home ownership, they are effectively detached from others of their class, thereby weakening proletarian solidarity and defusing the threat to capital.

We have already seen that some of the nineteenth-century artisans were attracted to owner-occupation as a way of expressing their difference from lower strata within the working class. Such evidence is used by left analysts to argue that home ownership has provided governments and employers with a convenient 'divide-and-rule' strategy ever since. Boddy, for example, argues that 'The position of mortgaged owner occupiers has never formed a focus or provoked political activity of a radical nature. On the contrary, the rise of working class owner occupation tends to fragment class consciousness arising from the common position of the labour force in relation to the production process by overlaying groups arising from differentiated tenure categories' (1976, p. 34). Much the same idea is expressed by Bassett and Short: 'Owner occupation tends to divide and fragment the working class. Access to owner occupation is usually open only to the more privileged strata of the working class, typically driving a wedge between skilled manual workers and white collar workers on one side and less skilled manual workers in more unstable employment on the other' (1980, p. 210). A similar argument has also been developed in the case of the USA by Edel, Sclar and Luria (1984, p. 14).

A third part of the Marxist view that working-class home ownership was deliberately stimulated by other more powerful classes concerns the likely effects of long-term debt. In her work on the USA, for example, Hayden argues that, after the First World War, 'Industrialists began to consider the strategy of offering white male skilled workers small suburban homes, to be purchased on home mortgages, as a way of achieving greater industrial order' (1981, p. 283). Much the same sort of assertion has been made in the case of Britain too. The mortgage system, it is argued, ties house buyers into a twenty- or thirty-year financial commitment which discourages any activity, such as strike action, which is liable to place their regular income in jeopardy. Revolutionary fervour is thus dissipated out of fear of losing one's home. This for Harvey helps explain why industrial relations in the postwar years have been calmer than in the inter-war period: 'The evident social discontent of the 1930s has, to a great degree, been successfully defused by a governmental policy which has created a large wedge of debt-encumbered home owners who are unlikely to rock the boat' (1977, p. 125). Similarly Berry suggests that mass home ownership has encouraged a narrow set of attitudes in which a concern with the size of the wage packet eclipses broader political issues: 'Widespread owner-occupation encourages the spread of economistic orientations among workers and functions as a mechanism of social control. A long term mortgage ties the material interests of the owner occupier to conditions favourable for the steady receipt of wage income' (Berry, 1983, p. 100). And for Bassett and Short, ownership of a home inculcates discipline at work: 'Owner-occupation is basically a form of debt-encumbrance for the mass of households in this sector. Repayment of the debt demands work discipline and job stability' (1980, pp. 209–10).

A fourth argument also commonly found in socialist academic writing holds that home ownership was fostered because it encourages workers to withdraw from collective life and turn their attentions inwards on home and family. The basic idea here is that the working class has been bought off with trifles. Workers, who in Marx's words had 'a world to win', have settled instead for a few square metres of freehold. With homes of their own, their concerns and efforts come to be focused on their own parochial patch of real estate, to the neglect of the public realm. As Colin Ward puts it, Marxists 'fear that the workers will be at home papering the parlour when they ought to be out in the streets making a revolution' (1983, p. 186). Owner-occupation, in other words, is thought to have individualized and privatized the working class.

This is a claim which we shall consider in some depth in Chapter 5, for it is by no means peculiar to the Marxist tradition. Within this tradition, however, it has been used specifically to suggest that home ownership has been engineered as a way of breaking working-class solidaristic communities. The authors of the Community Development Project booklet *Profits against Houses* complain that home ownership 'defuses class action, rewards personal sacrifice with relative comfort later, puts a premium on acquiescence, privatizes hardship and gain' (CDP, 1976b, p. 42); while Agnew similarly argues that 'Homeownership creates a circumstance in which the capitalist ethic of "possessive individualism" can develop and flourish . . . homeownership encourages a consciousness of local events that effectively precludes much in the way of a "larger" social consciousness' (Agnew, 1981, p. 466).

The fifth and final theme in the Marxist analysis of the growth of home ownership is that owner-occupation has been encouraged as a way of creating a mass market for consumer goods. The privately owned home is at the basis of contemporary consumerism. According to David Harvey (1977, pp. 123–4), for example, the postwar economic boom depended upon an expansion of demand for the products of the new light industries, and this was achieved in the USA and elsewhere by encouraging suburban expansion. Not only did the spread of owner-occupied housing stimulate demand for building materials, but it also fed through into enhanced demand for cars, energy, consumer goods and so on. Similarly, Linda McDowell believes that in Britain owner-occupation was encouraged in order to create a population of compliant consumers: 'Home ownership and state suburbanization have opened up a new lifestyle based on family possession of consumer durables, thereby supporting the rise of vast new industries. The domestic ethic has been manipulated since the Second War to encourage the consumption of a new range of products' (1983, p. 157).

This Marxian version of Keynesian demand management theory has in recent years been coupled up with left-feminist thinking to generate a full-blown conspiracy theory. Watson, for example, asserts that 'Individual housing units clearly do act as an outlet for capital to first build and then to penetrate. Row upon row of family houses and flats are duplicated, each with their own washing machines, dishwashers, vacuum cleaners, ovens and freezers' (1986b, p. 22). This argument, which seems implicitly to assume that working people would prefer to share their freezers and go without their own washing machines, has now entered into left-feminist orthodox thinking. Marcuse, for example, sees in the spread of individual units of owner-occupied housing clear evidence of a patriarchal capitalist conspiracy:

> What used to be provided as one item collectively now is sold in plural copies to multiple individual households. Not one laundry center but a washing machine and dryer in every basement; not one movie but a television set in every living room; not a concert hall but a hi-fi into every new home. And not efficient brick multi-storey apartment buildings, but free standing individual houses using more materials, more labor, more land, more maintenance, more heating, more financing.
>
> (1987, pp. 238–9)

33

Whether people would actually prefer to live in 'efficient multi-storey' blocks is something Marcuse neglects to consider.

What is immediately striking about all five of these assertions is the lack of evidence to back them up. All five arguments are variants on the same theme – namely, that governments and capitalist interests worked in unison to incorporate or weaken the working class by enticing workers into individual home ownership. Yet rarely is any evidence produced to show, first, that working-class home owners have been successfully incorporated or, second, that this was the government's intention.

On the first issue, there are good grounds for believing that many of the effects attributed to owner-occupation are non-existent. The argument that home ownership has created political passivity is difficult to sustain, for example, in the face of evidence of extremely high rates of owner-occupancy in areas of traditional working-class militancy, such as the Welsh mining valleys (Ball, 1983, p. 28). Indeed, industrial militancy may be exacerbated rather than reduced by widespread home ownership, for workers with some degree of independence may prove more difficult to control than those who are dependent on the state for their accommodation. Furthermore, if workers now have a 'stake in the system' it also follows that they will fight that much more tenaciously so as not to lose it. The bitterness of the 1984–5 miners' strike may partly be explained by the fact that pit closures threatened to devalue miners' houses as well as strip them of their jobs.

Much the same sort of point can be made as regards arguments about indebtedness. As Ginsberg suggests, a mortgage 'ties the worker to a debt, but equally it can be the spur to greater militancy in the wages struggle' (1983, p. 47). The only attempt to assess the effects of debt empirically is Pratt's work in Vancouver where respondents were asked whether they *believed* that a mortgage was likely to make someone a more stable employee (Pratt, 1986c). Most did, but such evidence is of limited value since it tells us only about what people think is likely to be the case and says nothing of whether it actually is the case.

Not only is the evidence on working-class incorporation shaky, but so too is that on the intentions and objectives of governments. As regards the period up to the Second World War, the only evidence which Marxists have produced to support their claims that home ownership was used in order to secure the social order consists of a few quotations from prominent politicians and others which show that some political leaders were aware of the possible or likely sociological and political effects of the spread of home ownership. Some writers quote Neville Chamberlain, who as Minister of Health was responsible for the 1923 Housing Act, and who defended owner-occupation in an article in *The Times* in 1920 by suggesting that 'every spadeful of manure dug in, every fruit tree planted' undermined the appeal of revolution (Merrett, 1982, p. 6). Others cite the Conservative peer Viscount Cecil who suggested in the 1930s that the spread of home ownership 'must contribute appreciably to national stability' by giving people a conscious 'stake in the country' (Short, 1982, p. 40).

These and other comments like them are not without significance, of course, but they do not constitute convincing evidence for the arguments which have been based upon them. As Michael Ball (1983, p. 283) has noted, analysts who at other times would give little credence to the utterances of politicians have nevertheless assumed that these scattered comments are an authentic guide to the motives impelling governments during this period.

There are, in fact, two compelling reasons for believing that owner-occupation in Britain *could not have been* deliberately brought about in the inter-war years in order to bolster the capitalist social and economic order by incorporating the working class.

The first is that government had precious little to do with the growth of home ownership before the Second World War. The only direct stimulus which it provided was in the form of subsidies to builders under the 1923 Act, but as we have seen, these were available for housing built for rent as well as for purchase, they had in any case been phased out by the 1930s when the home ownership boom took off, and two and a half million houses (85 per cent of the total built by the private sector between the wars) were constructed without benefit of subsidy. Financial support in the form of tax relief for home owners only became significant in the 1960s, so this cannot have had much effect either. From the formation of the building clubs in the late eighteenth century through to the owner-occupier boom of the 1930s, it is possible to find Conservatives and industrialists applauding the growth of home ownership, but they never did much to bring it about.

The second reason for rejecting these claims about owner-occupation as a strategy for securing capitalism is that before the war it was the middle class rather than the working class which moved into home ownership, and the middle class never did pose a threat to social stability and the economic order. As Swenarton and Taylor point out, the growth of owner-occupation sharpened rather than blurred lines of class cleavage: 'By 1939 owner occupation had become more, not less, middle class; less, not more, working class. If any class was successfully "incorporated" by owner occupation in this period, it was not the working class' (1985, p. 392).

Taken together, these two simple historical facts are sufficient to demolish many of the left-wing myths about the origins of the home ownership revolution. By the time government *did* begin to support home ownership and the working class *did* begin to move into owner-occupation in large numbers, such a momentum had been established (not least by the continuing sale of private rented housing to sitting tenants) that there was no need for anybody to set out to encourage the trend. This is not to deny that recent governments *have* done much to support home ownership, nor that one motive in this may well have been a desire to incorporate the working class into bourgeois values about property, thrift, hard work and the rest. But this has not been a primary factor in explaining the spread of home ownership during the twentieth century.

Marxist explanations for the growth of home ownership are, then, found wanting on a number of empirical grounds. The evidence suggests that mass owner-occupation did not develop in response to a plan to ensnare the working class, and that it has not in any case had many of the effects which Marxist analysis attributes to it. Like so many other social changes, the expansion of home ownership was planned by nobody, and its consequences have been largely unintended and often unforeseen. Clearly, certain people or groups – such as the building societies in the 1930s – have made a significant impact on the expansion of owner-occupation at particular crucial moments in its history, but even they were responding to events as much as they were shaping them.

Anthony Giddens has argued that people's actions are not always consciously motivated, and that even when they are, they do not necessarily produce the consequences they intend. This means that 'Human history is created by intentional activities but is not an intended project; it persistently eludes efforts to bring it under conscious direction' (1984, p. 27). This insight has a clear application to any analysis of the growth of home ownership over the last one hundred years. When working men founded the early building clubs they could never have envisaged that they would evolve into permanent societies controlling £140,000 million worth of assets by 1986. Similarly, when Parliament introduced 'temporary' rent controls in 1915 it was never the intention that they would still be in force seventy years later, nor that private rented housing would be whittled down from 90 to 8 per cent of the total housing stock. Yet we have seen that, although nobody intended them to happen, the growth of the building societies and the squeeze on private landlords are two of the key factors which have stimulated and sustained the spread of owner-occupancy in Britain. Clearly the growth of home ownership has been a largely unintended outcome of a complex and interrelated series of human actions.

From the evidence already outlined in this chapter it is possible to unravel six of the main factors which together helped to produce the dramatic shift to a home-owning society. Two of them, as we have seen, were the growth of the building societies and the collapse of private renting. The other four were demographic change, rising affluence, government financial support and popular values and expectations. Britain's home owner revolution can adequately (though not fully) be explained as the outcome of the interaction of these six factors.

The importance of the *building societies* lies in the relative ease with which people in Britain have been able to achieve access to credit for house purchase. Oxley (1988) has demonstrated the significance of this by comparing the system of housing finance in the United Kingdom with those found in West Germany, the Netherlands, France, Denmark and Ireland. Employing econometric modelling techniques, he is able to show that 'Differences in the cost and availability of mortgages are vital in explaining variations in home ownership rates between countries' (1988, p. 3). In Denmark, Ireland and the UK it is possible to buy a house with a small initial deposit and a long-term credit arrangement, and it is in these countries that owner-occupation is highest. Elsewhere prospective purchasers have to spend longer saving for a bigger deposit, while less time is allowed for repayment of mortgages.

The reason for the difference lies in differences in the historical development of housing financial institutions in the six countries. In West Germany, for example, the *Bausparkassen* operate a contract system under which borrowers must first save for a number of years before a loan is granted, and this 'closed' system of housing finance tends to be far more restrictive than the 'savings bank' system which has developed in the building society movement.

The second important factor is the collapse of the *private rental system* in Britain, for as we have seen, owner-occupation has expanded both through new building and through large-scale transfers from private landlords to their erstwhile tenants. Oxley's analysis is again relevant here, for he shows that the sticks and carrots which drove British landlords to sell up have not generally been present in other countries where the owner-occupancy rate has remained lower. Again taking West Germany as our example, there has not in that country been the sort of legislation which has crippled private renting in Britain, nor has there been the buoyancy of house prices which has encouraged landlords to cash in on their assets.

These two factors – the availability of credit and the ready supply of housing for sale – were necessary but not sufficient conditions for the phenomenal growth of owner-occupation in Britain since the First World War. It still remains to explain why so many people came to seek this credit in order to buy these houses.

One reason can be found in *demographic trends* through the twentieth century; for, as Merrett recognizes, 'One of the most potentially powerful motors in accelerating the effective demand for owner occupied dwellings is population growth' (1982, p. 45). In fact, raw rates of population increase since 1918 have been sluggish, but what has changed is the average size of households following the virtual disappearance of domestic service and the reduction in average family size. Furthermore, people have been marrying younger, and this too has had an impact on aggregate demand for housing. Between 1921 and 1938 the number of families in the UK increased by three and a half million, thereby increasing the demand for the smaller suburban houses which thousands of speculative builders began to provide at that time (Daunton, 1987, p. 105). After the war, too, the demand continued to rise. Between 1951 and 1981 the number of potential households increased by nearly four and a half million, or 32 per cent (Holmans, 1987, p. 103).

It was not inevitable, of course, that this increased demand for housing should have been met by an expansion of owner-occupation. One reason why so many of these new households did, in fact, end up buying their homes was that they, unlike their parents or grandparents, could afford to do so. As we shall see in Chapter 3, ordinary people have become much better off over the last fifty years – *average real incomes* after tax doubled in the thirty years from 1954, for example (Nationwide Building Society, 1985).

Harris and Hamnett suggest that it was rising incomes, coupled with availability of mortgage finance, which were of 'decisive importance' in stimulating the growth of owner-occupation on both sides of the Atlantic (1987, p. 180), and they are almost certainly right. Also crucial, however, has been the rise in the number of women earners; for, while *individual* incomes have risen considerably in real terms during this period, *household incomes* have probably risen even faster owing to the growth in the number of dual- and multi-earner households. As Pahl (1984, p. 231) has suggested, differences of income based on class may well be eclipsed by differences of income between households with varying numbers of earners. It is the growth of household incomes, and not just of individual incomes, which has enabled such a rapid spread of owner-occupation beyond the middle class since the Second World War.

The enhanced capacity of people to buy their homes also reflects the impact of *government policies* such as provision of tax relief on mortgage payments and exemption from taxation on imputed rental value. State financial aid like this has some effect (how much effect is disputed) in boosting people's spending power and thus helping them to meet the costs of house purchase.

As we have seen, the existence of such state support does not mean that governments deliberately set out to foster owner-occupation. As Duncan Maclennan observes, 'The growth of owner occupation is . . . a dominant and long-standing feature of the housing system in Britain. However it is only really in the 1970s that there has been a conscious government policy for expanding the sector' (1982, p. 173). What seems to have happened is that policies which originated with no intention of supporting home ownership have nevertheless over time come to have this effect, and as owner-occupation has spread, so governments have found it difficult to amend them.

Mortgage tax relief is a classic example of this process. Until 1969 all interest on loans was tax deductible – there was nothing special about mortgage lending. When this general concession was abolished, however, the Labour government at the time could not bring itself to remove tax relief on housing loans, since so many people were by then benefiting from it. Nobody ever intended that those buying their homes should benefit to the tune of £5 billion per annum by the late 1980s, and most politicians and their advisers would like to dismantle this subsidy, but as yet nobody dares to. So it is that government has come to be stuck with an increasingly expensive commitment which nobody planned and few politicians support (we discuss mortgage tax relief and associated fiscal issues in more detail in Chapter 6).

These five factors were all important, but a sixth was still necessary if the home ownership revolution was to take place. More households were demanding houses; people's incomes were rising; they could get credit; the housing was coming on to the market due to the collapse of private landlordism; and government subsidies increasingly provided an additional inducement to buy; but without the *desire to own*, it is unlikely that so many households would have switched tenures in so short a time. The scale and pace of this change are unparalleled in any other country this century. It could not have happened without an insistent 'pressure from below', for this was above all a popular revolution.

Perhaps the most distressing aspect of the Marxist accounts of the growth of home ownership discussed earlier is their consistent denial of the authentic spirit and determination of generations of working people who have struggled to achieve a house of their own. This spirit has been captured in the work of Damaris Rose (1980, 1981, 1987), who, with specific reference to Northamptonshire shoemakers and Cornish tin-miners, has shown how working-class people in the nineteenth century often tried to buy a house (or several in the case of many Northampton workers) as a means of increasing their financial security and as a way of establishing an area of their lives free from domination by employers and landlords. Her studies document 'the emergence and development of desires and pressures for home ownership by working people themselves . . . this way of occupying housing was historically created, actively sought after, fought for' (1981, pp. 3–4). As she says, little attention has been paid to this push from below, yet it was a crucial sixth factor in bringing about the move to a home-owning society.

The popular desire to own a house has always reflected a number of different factors. One is economic rationality – a straightforward financial calculation that in the long term it is cheaper or more beneficial to buy than to rent. As Hamnett and Randolph (1988, pp. 88–90) point out, many of those who bought from private landlords in the 1930s and the 1950s had to be convinced that it was in their financial interests to do so; for they had long since lost the culture of independent ownership bequeathed by the generations who lived before the Industrial Revolution, and their decision was shaped by a calculus of financial advantage more than by any other factor.

Such calculative instrumentalism is not, however, the only explanation for why people have bought when offered the opportunity. As we shall see in Chapter 2, home ownership may also be desired for its own sake, as an emotional expression of autonomy, security, or personal identity. It can even be argued that the desire to own is one manifestation of a deep-seated and 'natural' disposition to possess key objects in the immediate and personal environment, although such explanations are rarely even considered in the social science literature in Britain today.

Somewhere between these two kinds of explanation – the coldly rational and the deeply emotional – lies a third. Whatever else it is, and whatever the other causes which produced it, the desire to own a house is an expression of a specific set of cultural values. We saw in Table 1.5 that the countries in the developed world which were originally settled by the British – the USA, Canada, Australia and New Zealand – all share with Britain high rates of home ownership, while many continental European countries have much lower rates. It was suggested in our earlier discussion of these figures that this pattern could probably be explained by an analysis of the different cultural traditions of these various nations. To achieve this it is necessary to appreciate the significance which has long been attached to ownership and individualism in the English-speaking cultures. My focus here will be on England itself, but for a useful discussion of American individualism (which, of course, has the same historic roots), see Gans (1988).

The popularity of the twentieth-century tenurial revolution in Britain is testimony to the strength of 800 years of a cultural tradition which is distinctive from that of mainland Europe. This is not to suggest that continental European cultures do not also carry strong individualistic values, nor that their peoples have not desired to own their homes. Before the First World War, for example, German factory workers apparently 'yearned' for small private houses of their own (Moore, 1984, p. 285). However, only around 40 per cent of the West German population has even today fulfilled this yearning, and this does suggest that the desire for individual private property may run deeper in English culture than it does in the German.

The working men in England who set up the first building clubs in the eighteenth century, the skilled artisans who sought a home of their own in Victorian times, the clerks who purchased the suburban semis in the 1930s and the council tenants who are buying their homes from their local authority landlords today all stand in a long tradition of English individualism. Their striving for a home of their own reflects and helps keep alive an ethic of individualism which dates back at least as far as the thirteenth century and which is in many ways distinctive to this country.

According to Macfarlane, 'A central and basic feature of English social structure has for long been the stress on the rights and privileges of the individual as against the wider group or the State' (1978, p. 5). He argues that the social, economic and legal institutions which developed from the thirteenth century onwards in England were very different from those which developed in Asia, eastern Europe, the continental countries and the Celtic nations. He denies the conventional view (found, for example, in both Weber and Marx) that England was a peasant country which somehow stumbled into industrial capitalism around 1700. Rather, according to Macfarlane, a fully developed system of individual private ownership was present by the sixteenth century, and the peasantry had to all intents and purposes disappeared as early as the fourteenth. He concludes that individualism in England has its roots long before the Renaissance, the Reformation, or the Enlightenment: 'The majority of ordinary people in England from at least the thirteenth century were rampant individualists, highly mobile both geographically and socially, economically "rational", market-oriented and acquisitive, ego-centred in kinship and social life' (1978, p. 163). Individualism and a concern with private property and acquisition have, therefore, been a key feature of English culture for seven centuries, although Macfarlane admits that he has no idea how these values took root in the first place.

Macfarlane's argument is not without its critics (for a review, see Abercrombie, Hill and Turner, 1986, pp. 99–104), but it is now widely accepted that individual rights and liberties – such as the right to sell land and the freedom to bequeath as one saw fit – were more developed in medieval England than has often been acknowledged. It is also generally accepted that English history exhibits some marked 'peculiarities' – the smashing of Catholicism, the intellectual tradition of dissent, the political economy of the market – which reflect and have sustained a distinctive cultural tradition (for example, see Thompson, 1965).

It is impossible to understand why home ownership has grown so far and so fast in Britain during the twentieth century if we fail to understand this cultural tradition. As we shall see in Chapter 2, there is a strong popular desire to own, and this was an essential factor in the mushrooming of the owner-occupied sector. Once people have been able to afford to buy, so they have bought. Rising incomes, the availability of credit, the exodus of the private landlords and so on were all important factors contributing to the growth of owner-occupation, but these seeds were sown in the rich soil of an English cultural tradition which nurtured and sustained them.

Commenting on their research among working-class families on the Isle of Sheppey, Pahl and Wallace write: 'There was a strong element of working class individualism among our sample . . . That people's primary concern is with their homes, their families and the individual life events of themselves and others accords with the particularism of the individualistic English . . . the English may be seen to be more individualistic than most of their fellow Europeans' (1988, pp. 138, 147). The desire to own a house has deep roots in English popular history. To try to explain it away as some ideological mystification conjured up by capitalist interests over the last few decades is to ignore the evidence of seven centuries.

The three towns survey

In this chapter we have outlined the evidence regarding the growth of home ownership in Britain and we have considered the main factors which together help to explain why and how it happened. In the chapters which follow, our focus will shift from the problem of causes to the question of consequences. Our aim is to investigate the effects of the home ownership revolution on three main areas of contemporary British society – the distribution of wealth and material life chances, political attitudes and alignments, and ways of life and cultural values – and in this way to come to some conclusions regarding the changing character of the British social structure.

In the course of our analysis, we shall be drawing upon two types of evidence. First, we shall bring together existing data from government statistics, academic surveys and other secondary sources. Second, we shall be reporting on the results of a new household survey conducted by the author and a team of colleagues in three English towns in 1986. In this final section of this chapter, the background to this survey is outlined and explained, although technical details of sampling method, sample size, questionnaire design and so on have been reserved to the appendices at the back of the book.

Many social scientific surveys are based on national samples in the sense that they try to identify a group of one or two thousand people across the country who are in some way representative of the population as a whole. The three towns survey did not attempt to achieve this. For a start, it included only owner-occupier and council tenant households – private tenants, tenants of housing associations, people living in tied cottages and residential institutions were all excluded from the sample. Moreover, no attempt was made to gather a nationwide sample. Instead, the research was concentrated on just three English towns – Slough, to the west of London, Derby, in the East Midlands, and Burney, in the North-West.

The reason for excluding private tenants was simply that our theoretical interest is concentrated on the two main tenures which have come to dominate the housing system since the war – owner-occupation and council renting. As we have seen, the private rented sector has been squeezed to a point where it can no longer act as a residual pool feeding the expansion of the other two tenures. Today, owner-occupation and council renting confront each other in a 'zero-sum' relation such that one can grow only at the expense of the other. This relation is structured by two sets of dichotomies – ownership against renting, and private sector against public sector. These are the basic parameters of the contemporary housing system, and they are the dimensions which inform our analysis in this book.

The decision to focus on three towns, rather than to spread interviews more thinly across a wider area of the country, reflects a growing recognition in urban sociology in recent years of the significance of locality variations. The social sciences are concerned to develop generalizations. We talk, for example, of changes in 'the' working class while all the time recognizing that such a term glosses over many individual differences between members of that class. Similarly, we rarely hesitate to talk of developments in 'British society', yet a moment's reflection reveals to us that British society is far from homogeneous and that developments may be going off in one direction in one part of the country but taking an entirely different direction in another.

None of this is to deny the usefulness of such generalizations. Indeed, social science would be impossible if we had all the time to take account of differences at the individual level. There does come a point, however, where generalizations can become so broad and ill defined as to be misleading. This is a particular danger when dealing with high levels of aggregation such as nation states. When we begin to break down national-level data, we swiftly discover important regional and local divergences. We came across one example of this earlier in this chapter where we saw (Table 1.4) that the owner-occupation rate in Britain as a whole stands at 63 per cent, yet this average figure disguises a range from just 42 per cent in Scotland to 71 per cent in the South-East of England. And of course, it is possible to find equally wide variations within regions as well.

Sometimes, social differences between areas or regions simply reflect differences in their social composition. We know, for example, that middle-class people are more likely to own their homes than are working-class people, and it should therefore come as no surprise if we find that areas with a high proportion of middle-class residents also exhibit high owner-occupation rates. In cases like these, generalizing at a high level of aggregation need not be misleading. If, for example, middle-class people tend to buy their homes no matter which part of the country they live in, then we are presumably justified in searching for general explanations for this correlation without worrying too much about locality effects.

Variations between areas are not, however, always so simply explained. Consider, for example, the traditionally high rates of working-class home ownership in South Wales as compared with the very low rates in Scotland. Both areas have substantial working-class populations based in a heritage of heavy industry, but it seems that these populations have been behaving very differently according to which part of Britain they happen to live in. People sharing similar social characteristics nevertheless exhibit very different styles of life according to where they happen to live. The Welsh tradition of home ownership, which was apparent as early as the nineteenth century in the spread of the building clubs, has no parallel in Scotland. In cases like these, it seems that there are important *cultural* variations which can only be explained by analysing the distinctive histories of different places. As Allen recognized some years ago, 'Each of the regions of Britain has at bottom a detectable set of interwoven attitudes, a distinctive trend in its underlying psychology, which is long-enduring and which imparts a certain special look or direction to virtually every kind of human activity carried on by its inhabitants' (1968, p. 8).

It can, therefore, be very misleading to talk simply of 'British society', for the whole consists of an aggregate of diverse parts. Increasingly in recent years, researchers have become sensitized to the importance of these locality variations. This is certainly the case in the analysis of housing questions, for housing markets vary widely across different parts of the country, and the desire for this or that type of accommodation tends to vary with them.

It seems, for example, that tenure preferences vary quite widely between different areas and regions. To some extent, these differences reflect factors such as housing costs and the quality of the housing stock – in a low-price area, low-income households can more easily achieve access to owner-occupation. But there is more to it than this, for, as Forrest and Murie (1986, p. 58) have argued, there are local cultural differences in the degree to which people want, hope and expect to buy their own homes. There is a popular tradition of home ownership in some parts of the country, and not in others, and it is the transmission of this culture across the generations which helps reproduce differential patterns of regional housing tenure. The low rate of home ownership in Scotland, for example, has more to do with local culture and history than with present-day property prices.

Not only may the desire for home ownership vary in different places, but so do its sociological effects. The arrival of mass home ownership has undoubtedly affected British society in many ways, but these effects are mediated through different local cultures. We shall see in Chapter 4, for example, that home ownership may influence political attitudes, at least among certain social groups, but this may well happen differently in different places. Mike Savage (1987) has recently suggested that owner-occupation may strengthen support for the Conservative Party in the more affluent parts of the country while reinforcing support for the Labour Party in less affluent regions. He shows that in towns like Barnsley, St Helens and Bury, Labour's vote in 1983 was up to 19 per cent higher than would have been predicted from statistics on the class composition of the local populations, while in southern towns like Bournemouth and Plymouth, Labour did 13 per cent worse than would have been predicted. His explanation is that northern home owners who wish to safeguard their investment may vote Labour in the hope of stimulating the local economy and the local housing market, whereas in the south they are more likely to support the Conservatives in an attempt to prevent new development and keep property taxes down.

Location, then, seems to make a difference to what kind of housing people want and to how they respond when they get it. This then raises the question of *how* location influences the way people think and behave.

The simple answer is that different places have different histories which are reflected today in different local cultures. Doreen Massey (1984) uses a metaphor of 'layers' to express this idea – particular patterns of development and investment get 'laid down' at different times in different places, and each leaves its historical mark, a residue, which can be detected in the physical landscape and the culture and ways of life of these places today. This means that our actions inevitably carry the imprint of our location. All social life is embedded in geographical contexts which help shape it.

The implications of this argument are highly significant. It means, for example, that there is no such thing as a national 'working-class culture', for the norms and values which have developed over 200 years in, say, a Yorkshire mining village will be very different from those which have been shaped by the conditions of life in a Lancashire textile town or a Cornish farming community. As Massey puts it, 'The reproduction of social and economic relations and of the social structure takes place over space, and that conditions its nature' (1984, p. 58).

Social life in Britain today has, of course, been 'nationalized' to a considerable extent. Local economies often depend upon decisions taken by company head offices in London, Tokyo, or Detroit. Local political decisions are subject to the constraints and determinations of governments and administrators in Whitehall and in Brussels. Local education is subject to a national curriculum, and mass media take the form of national newspapers and TV companies. Town centres, municipal housing estates and local railway stations all look increasingly similar whether we are standing in Birmingham, Glasgow, or Southampton. It would be a mistake to overemphasize the significance of locality variation.

Nor, however, can we afford to ignore it. How, for example, could we begin to understand the bitter conflict between the Nottinghamshire and Yorkshire miners during the 1984–5 strike without recognizing that men working in different pits and living in different areas carry with them very different sets of values and social identities? As John Urry warns in his consideration of class relations across Britain, 'There is a danger of committing the fallacy of composition if one does not investigate the diverse forms of local class structure. When added together there may be a "national class structure" which is not in fact pertinent to anybody's specifically local class experience' (1981, p. 464).

What Urry says of social class is true also of housing tenure. We should expect the experience and meaning of home ownership to vary across different parts of the country, in which case any analysis of the sociology of British home ownership must recognize location as an important variable. It was for this reason that the research on which this book is based was carried out in three different towns in England, each with a very different history. A national survey was ruled out, since no nationally representative sample could hope to take account of the specific local factors which help shape people's housing experiences. Nor was it possible to identify any particular towns or areas which could be taken as 'microcosms' of the wider society, for every town has its own unique history and character. There is no such place as 'Middletown'.

As we have already noted, the three towns selected for this study were Burnley, Derby and Slough. They were chosen according to two key principles.

The first was that the research should include towns which developed in different phases of industrialization and which are today experiencing different patterns of prosperity or decline. It was important, in other words, not to skew the research findings in favour of one kind of local economy or to bias them by looking only at prosperous or poor localities. It was also deemed desirable to avoid dramatic or 'extreme' cases.

Many of the old industrial towns of England which grew up around industries such as coal, shipbuilding and textiles have for most of this century been experiencing relative economic decline as revealed in above-average rates of unemployment, below-average wage levels and net population loss. Most of these towns are to be found in the northern regions, and their housing stock often includes a large number of old and relatively cheap properties. In parts of the South-East and East Anglia, by contrast, local economies have been buoyant in recent years as new service and 'high-tech' industries have grown up or moved in which offer high wages and good conditions of employment. In these areas, new house building has

Fig 1.2 Study areas.

been expanding, and property prices are high. Between these two extremes are those areas, many of them in the Midlands, which developed around engineering, electronics, motor manufacturing and so on in the period between the mid-nineteenth century and the 1930s. These were often relatively prosperous towns until the oil crisis and world recession of the post-1973 period, but in recent years they have begun to register rising unemployment rates and factory closures or rationalizations. The housing stock here is generally more mixed, and house prices are considerably lower than in the South-East.

The research design was structured so as to include one old industrial town which has been in long-term decline (Burnley), one new industrial town which is riding the wave of economic growth and prosperity (Slough) and one mature industrial town which has encountered recent problems of economic slow-down or recession (Derby). In the case of Derby (which is approximately twice the size of the other two towns), a decision was made to focus on the southern part of the town (defined by the Derby South parliamentary constituency), since this is where the major industries are located.

House prices in these three towns vary markedly. Slough's location on the booming 'M4 corridor' between London and Bristol is reflected in its high house prices, which at the time of the survey averaged approximately twice those in the other two towns (see Table 1.7). Table 1.7 also reveals the high rate of new building taking place in Slough (as compared particularly with

Burnley), and again this is indicative of the relative state of these local economies. In Slough the housing market is buoyant; in Burnley (and to a lesser extent in Derby) it is relatively depressed.

The second principle of selection was that each town should contain a substantial proportion of working-class inhabitants. As we saw earlier in this chapter, the middle class began to achieve access to home ownership in the 1930s and is now overwhelmingly concentrated in this tenure. A study which seeks to analyse the sociological significance of the growth of *mass* home ownership must therefore look beyond this class to those – the skilled manual workers, the routine white-collar workers and increasingly the younger semi- and unskilled manual workers in dual-earner households – who represent the pool from which new generations of owner-occupiers are being drawn.

Table 1.7 *Local housing statistics, Burnley, Derby and Slough*

	Burnley	*Derby*	*Slough*
Housing tenure (1981)			
% owner-occupiers	69.6	57.6	56.9
% council tenants	22.5	27.8	33.3
% other tenures	7.9	14.6	9.7
Average semi-detached house price (1985)	£25,800	£24,250	£48,410
New house building (1986)			
Private-sector starts	110	591	595
Public-sector starts	21	92	90
Total starts per 1,000 population	1.49	3.15	6.98

* Derby figures are for the whole city except housing tenure which is for Derby South constituency.
Sources: Tenure figures from 1981 Census. House prices from figures supplied by Nationwide Building Society. Building figures from Department of the Environment, 1987.

For this reason, it was decided that the research should focus on predominantly working-class towns, for it is the working class which has been moving into home ownership in recent decades. A study which looked at home ownership in strongly 'bourgeois' towns like Tunbridge Wells or Winchester would therefore be of limited interest. Industrial towns with a large local working class are not difficult to find in the Midlands and the North, but they tend to be few and far between in the South-East. Slough is one of the few places which fits the requirement. Furthermore, like Derby, Slough has the additional advantage of a sizeable 'ethnic-minority' population, and this opens up the possibility of examining how predominantly Asian immigrants and their descendants are faring in the local housing system.

As Table 1.8 demonstrates, the three towns all have substantial working-class populations, many of whom are engaged in manufacturing. All three are 'under-represented' in classes I and II as compared with Britain as a whole where 4.5 per cent are in class I and 18.8 per cent are in class II. All three were correspondingly 'over-represented' in classes IIIM and IV where the equivalent figures for Britain are 26.2 per cent and 12.2 per cent. All three towns also reveal a much higher proportion of their populations in manufacturing (British average = 27 per cent) and a much lower proportion in service employment (British average = 34 per cent).

Table 1.8 *Occupational class, employment sector and ethnic composition, Burnley, Derby and Slough*

	Burnley	Derby*	Slough
Occupational class (%)			
I Professional, etc.	2.2	4.6	3.5
II Intermediate	14.4	15.0	16.6
IIIN Skilled non-manual	7.8	7.9	8.3
IIIM Skilled manual	29.2	28.7	28.4
IV Semi-skilled manual	15.6	15.3	18.3
V Unskilled manual	4.9	5.5	4.1
Armed forces or inadequately described	1.6	1.3	1.8
Economically inactive	24.3	21.7	19.0
Employment sector (%)			
Manufacturing	45.5	43.2	39.7
Distribution and catering	18.3	16.5	19.0
Transport	4.2	6.6	9.2
Other services	24.0	25.3	23.5
% born in New Commonwealth and Pakistan	3.6	17.3	20.9

* Data for Derby are for the city as a whole except ethnicity which is for Derby South constituency.
Source: 1981 Census, constituency data and 'key statistics for urban areas'. Data refer to 'heads of household' (see Appendix II for a discussion of this).

These, then, are predominantly working-class manufacturing towns. Clearly they are in no sense 'representative' of the country as a whole, for they have been deliberately selected in order to focus on certain groups in the population in certain kinds of local economies. In particular, they have been selected as towns where we should expect to find distinctively working-class traditions and cultures and where the influence of 'bourgeois' ways of life is unlikely to be marked. All three towns elect Labour councils to run them, and until 1983 all three returned Labour members to represent them in Parliament (local political traditions are outlined in more detail below).

Taken together, these three towns represent ideal 'testing grounds' for examining the impact, if any, of the growth of home ownership on working-class life-styles, standards of living and political values. If in all three towns we find that home ownership has raised living standards, has changed ways of life, or has shifted traditional patterns of political alignment, then we may justly conclude that the growth of mass home ownership is bringing about significant changes, not just among more privileged or affluent sections of the British population, but among large and important sections of what Pahl (1984) has referred to as 'the middle mass' of British society.

Given that the local economy and local housing market are buoyant in only one of these three towns, these research sites represent a severe test for those theories which have suggested that working-class households are now achieving significant material gains as a result of the expansion of owner-occupation. If working-class owners in Derby and Burnley are gaining out of house purchase, then we may be fairly sure that millions of other working-class households in more affluent parts of the country are gaining also. This is an issue which is addressed in Chapter 3.

For the remainder of this chapter we shall sketch a few historical details regarding the three towns in the survey; for, although all three share much in common as predominantly working-class manufacturing areas, their histories and trajectories are very different.

Burnley: 'Fourth Division England'

On 24 February 1988 the *Guardian* newspaper began a series of articles which it called 'Fourth Division England'. The logic of this title was that the growing economic inequalities between the regions are now reflected in the four divisions of the English Football League, the bottom division of which is largely composed of clubs based in declining northern industrial towns. Predictably, the series opened with a feature on Burnley, whose local team won the league championship in 1921 and again in 1960 but which came within one match of being demoted into non-league football at the end of the 1986–7 season. Like its football team, the town is small, has a proud history and has been in decline for years.

Burnley is a town of 70,000 people located in Lancashire, some fifteen miles north of Manchester. Until the 1780s it was a small market town, but it expanded throughout the nineteenth century, reaching a population size of 21,000 in 1851 and peaking at 106,000 in 1911. This growth was based upon three main industries – cotton, coal and ironworking.

Lancashire was, of course, the home of the British cotton industry, and Burnley was one of its major centres. Initially the town concentrated on spinning, and by the mid-nineteenth century there were fifty spinning firms controlling 400,000 spindles (Bennett, 1951, p. 95). Gradually, however, competition from Oldham led many Burnley firms to switch to weaving, and by 1886 the town's 50,000 looms were producing more cloth than any other town in the world. 'It was said that the Burnley weavers clothed Britain before breakfast and spent the rest of the day clothing the world' (the *Guardian*, 24 February 1988).

This level of output was made possible by the giant steam engines which powered the looms. These were fuelled by locally produced coal. In 1850 Burnley had 1,600 men employed in coal-mining, and this rose to 2,400 by the turn of the century when ten pits were being worked (Bennett, 1951, p. 109). This coal also went to produce coke for the iron foundries which grew up through the nineteenth century to make the looms for cotton mills throughout the world. Not only did Burnley produce more cloth than any other town in the world by 1880, but it also produced more looms. By the end of the century there were five firms making power looms, twenty-one machine-makers and ten iron and brass founders (Bennett, 1951, p. 114).

This nineteenth-century industrial base helped create and reproduce a distinctive local culture which persists to this day. According to the standard work of local history, this culture is characterized by a 'spirit of endurance and enterprise', together with 'an independence of thought and action' (Bennett, 1951, p. 249).

Burnley is today a Labour town, and it has returned a Labour MP at every election bar two (1931 and 1935) since the First World War. In 1987 Labour polled 48 per cent of the vote. In the nineteenth century, however, Burnley was a Liberal stronghold, and this reflected a culture which emphasized independence, self-help and mutual aid.

Workers in the cotton industry, for example, made repeated attempts to set up their own co-operative factories in the years between 1848 and 1887. Most of these initiatives ended in failure, but co-operative stores proved much more successful. In the thirty years from its establishment in 1860, the Burnley Co-operative Society expanded to 6,400 members who between them owned twenty-eight shops. Also successful was the Mechanics Institute, founded in 1834, which went on to provide a library and various lectures and courses taught mainly by unpaid volunteers.

As in a number of other cotton towns, Burnley also threw up some early building clubs. The first, a terminating society limited to sixty members, was established in the 1790s, and this was followed by another started in 1815. Following their legalization in 1846, two permanent societies were founded in the mid-nineteenth century and both grew rapidly through the following decades (Bennett, 1951, pp. 215–17). By the 1880s home ownership among Burnley's artisan class was common, and a 1908 Board of Trade inquiry reported that, together with Bolton and Oldham, Burnley was renowned for its high level of working-class owner-occupation (Swenarton and Taylor, 1985, pp. 378–9).

The tradition of home ownership has persisted through the twentieth century – 35 per cent of Burnley households owned their houses in 1939 (Swenarton and Taylor, 1985), and in 1981 the figure was 70 per cent. As Waller notes, 'It is a local tradition that newly marrieds buy their own inexpensive houses, and it doesn't imply affluence' (1987, p. 376). The inner part of the town consists of dozens of streets of two-bedroomed Victorian terraces built with local stone and selling in 1986 for between £6,000 and £8,000. At prices like these, owner-occupation is well within the reach of many working-class families, although the low prices can bring their own problems. In particular, householders may find that it is not worth spending money to repair or modernize their homes, since the outlay exceeds any increase in the value of the house. In nearby Blackburn, where this problem is more marked, houses selling at £5,000 need a further £6,000 spent on them, yet end up still worth only £9,000 (see Walker, 1985, p. 15; also the *Independent*, 20 August 1987; and Forrest and Murie, 1987a, p. 14).

There are three main reasons for the low level of local house prices. The first is relatively low wage rates. The second is the high level of unemployment. The third is the surplus of older housing consequent upon a falling population.

The low wage rates both create and reflect a high level of female participation in the workforce. Low male wages drive wives out to work, and this in turn keeps wage levels down. There was a tradition of low-waged female employment in the textile mills in the nineteenth century, and this has been carried over today into other areas of manufacturing. At the time of the 1981 Census, nearly 70 per cent of Burnley women of working age were 'economically active' – a staggeringly high figure. They are found working in electrical engineering, metal goods, textiles, rubber and plastics and motor vehicle components (Lucas is the town's biggest private employer) as well as in public-sector services.

At 15 per cent in 1986, unemployment in the town is substantially above the national average, and this too tends to depress house prices. This is particularly true at the bottom of the market in the inner areas where most of the unemployed live; some inner-area wards have unemployment rates above 30 per cent (see Burnley Borough Council, 1986). In the five years to 1981 the town lost 8,000 jobs, mainly in manufacturing; and although this trend has slowed since (a further 2,500 were lost between 1981 and 1985), these jobs have not been replaced by equivalent growth elsewhere in the local economy.

The surplus of low-cost housing reflects the falling population since the First World War. The twin pillars of cotton and coal have both collapsed over the course of this century. Many of the cotton mills closed during the inter-war depression and never reopened, while others went into liquidation more recently under the pressure of competition from the Far East. Today, a highly automated mill at Brierfield still employs a few people manufacturing medical gauze and swabs, while the Queen Street mill now functions as an industrial museum. Even these pitiful traces of a once mighty industry are more than now remains of the coal industry. Of the ten pits in 1900, six were still operating in 1950, but none remain today.

Like the mill owners in the 1930s, the Coal Board has sold off its housing to its former employees. This has further boosted the owner-occupancy rate, but young people have been leaving Burnley for years, and the demand for these houses by new purchasers is low.

Not all is gloomy, of course. There are, it seems, two Burnleys; for out in the suburbs where houses change hands for £30,000 or £40,000, life can be sweet. Set in the rolling green countryside, these avenues and closes are where the one-sixth of the population in social classes I and II live. Many of them are public-sector employees enjoying nationally negotiated wage rates. For them, the cost of living seems low, and they enjoy the benefits of low mortgages as compared with their southern counterparts. Nor are these suburbs exclusively middle class in composition, for many working-class people too share in the comparative affluence of this suburban life-style. Burnley may carry clear reminders of its nineteenth-century industrial past, but it also bears witness to some of the major trends of the twentieth century – the expansion of the middle class, the growth of state-sector employment and the rising living standards of ordinary working people.

Derby: 'a middle-of-the-road place'

With a population of over 200,000 in 1981, Derby is by far the largest of our three case study sites, and this is reflected in its official status as a city (granted in 1977). As already noted, however, the research was focused upon the Derby South parliamentary constituency which has a population of just 93,000 – comparable to the other two towns.

Just as Burnley reveals its own distinctive culture, so too does Derby, but it is far from a dramatic or exciting one:

> There is no feeling here of either the North country or the South. Close to the middle of England geographically, it is very much a middle of the road place in politics and attitudes. The absence of the 'pleasure of fancy and folly' in its buildings reflects the spirit of its people, who could be accused of apathy but rarely of unkindness or intolerance. Moderation in all things might be the motto of Derbeians, whose stock reply to enquiries about their health is a cautious 'middling'. It may seem a slightly negative approach to life, but its effect has been an almost complete absence of serious industrial disputes or riots throughout the city's long history.
>
> (Christian, 1978, p. 23)

If Burnley is stoic, Derby is dour.

In the eighteenth century, Derby was primarily a hosiery town. The first silk mill opened in 1702. By 1789 there were twelve such mills in and around the town, and it was their workers who provided the one exception to Christian's observation regarding the lack of major industrial disputes in Derby's history when they went out on prolonged strike in 1833–4. Derby also developed cotton mills in the Derwent valley, but both the silk and cotton industries faded in the nineteenth century when Manchester was able to exploit the advantage secured by the construction of its canal links.

The decline of hosiery was amply compensated by the coming of the railways. Because of its location, Derby had long been a staging post, and once the railway arrived in 1839 it soon became established as a major rail junction. Just as the old cotton masters had patronized the town by building schools and churches, so the railway companies – and especially the Midland Railway – came to make their presence felt in local affairs by endowing orphanages, founding institutes and dominating local politics (Christian, 1978, p. 38). If Burnley's tradition was one of self-help and mutual aid, Derby's was more one of deference and dependence upon company benevolence. Where Burnley's Mechanics Institute was formed in 1839 by local artisans, for example, Derby's institute was provided much later by the Midland Railway for its employees.

The first railway engineering works were opened as early as 1840. In 1851 Derby began building locomotives. Within ten years 2,000 people were employed at the Derby works, and their numbers doubled over the next forty years (Leleux, 1984). At the turn of the century some 12,000 people were employed at the works, and their numbers continued to grow, reaching 20,000 by 1920. Today, British Rail Engineering remains one of the biggest employers in the city, although the workforce has fallen to around 6,500.

Derby had been expanding before the railways arrived – the population rose from 11,000 in 1801 to 24,000 thirty years later (Burnett, 1986, p. 10) – but it was railway engineering which triggered the major population growth of the nineteenth century as workers from Ireland, Wales and Tyneside were attracted into the town. In 1851 the population stood at 41,000. By 1891 it had grown to over 100,000, and unlike Burnley's population (which was not much smaller at that time) it continued to grow into the twentieth century.

The most significant reason for this continued growth was the arrival of Rolls-Royce in 1908. 'Royce's', as it is known locally, has expanded to be the city's main employer. By 1972 it was employing three times as many workers as British Rail Engineering. In that year, however, the company faced impending collapse following its failure to stay within the costings on a major aircraft engine contract, and the Conservative government of the time executed a famous 'U-turn' by deciding to step in to save the firm from bankruptcy by nationalizing it. In the different circumstances of the 1980s, Rolls-Royce has now been returned to the private sector, although more redundancies were declared in the run-up to the re-privatization. Nevertheless, the massive Rolls-Royce factory complex remains by far the biggest employer in the city and it is still the company's centre for the manufacture of its gas turbine aero-engines.

Like Burnley, Derby was suffering an above-average unemployment rate of around 15 per cent at the time of the research in 1986, and this figure reached 30 per cent in some inner-city wards. There is a substantial Asian population in the city, and most of them live in the Derby South constituency in areas like Normanton to the south of the city centre. Derby exhibits a wide range of housing types from the two-up, two-down Victorian terraces in inner neighbourhoods such as Normanton, through inter-war owner-occupied and council-owned suburban semis in areas like Peartree, to postwar suburbia in more outlying areas such as Littleover. At 58 per cent in 1981, the home ownership rate in Derby South was around the average for the country as a whole. There is no strong local tradition of working-class home ownership as there is in Burnley, although, as in Burnley, the Co-operative Society movement has deep roots in the town.

Derby South has consistently returned Labour Members of Parliament since the war, but the city is not a Labour stronghold. In 1987 the party won a slender majority over the Conservatives of just 1,500 votes, while the Derby North constituency was won for the first time by the Conservatives in 1983 and was held by them with an increased majority in 1987. Despite the high profile adopted by Derbyshire County Council's Labour leader, who represents a city ward, this is not fertile ground for political passions or histrionics. Derby is a solid provincial city whose people harbour few illusions or pretensions. It is, one senses, the natural home of those whom Pahl (1984) has dubbed 'the middle mass' of British society.

Slough: 'Mars Bar City'

Nestling just off the M4 motorway, near Heathrow Airport to the west of London, Slough has no history to compare with the tales of Burnley and Derby. At the turn of the century, when the other two towns were each home to over 100,000 people, Slough was still a small country town with a population of around 7,000. It was not until the inter-war years that it began to attract industry and expand in population, and since then it has come to be associated by many with lower-middle-class suburban sprawl and respectable working-class sobriety and dullness. For years, the municipal leaders have had to cope with the sneering legacy of Betjeman's cruel and well-known poetic jibe:

> Come, friendly bombs, and fall on Slough,
> It isn't fit for humans now . . .
> Mess up the mess they call a town –
> A house for ninety-seven down
> And once a week a half-a-crown
> For twenty years.

In fact, the poem says more about Betjeman and the class snobbery of British society than it does about Slough. A better flavour of what the town is like can be gauged from the sadly defensive and rather naïve poetic retort to Betjeman by Eugene Johnson, published in the borough's *Official Guide*:

> A poet once condemned our town,
> Before he got his Laureate's crown.
> He is a wit, I hear you cry,
> And he had a sharp perceptive eye.
>
> But he made a very nasty crack
> About a town that could not talk back.
> We are ordinary people here, by far,
> In a nice town under the morning star.

Like Burnley and Derby, the 'nice town' of Slough is based squarely on a manufacturing economy. The truckers and Ford Capri drivers who relieve the tedium of the M4 motorway by talking with each other on their CB radios refer to the town as 'Mars Bar City', for the largest single employer is the Mars confectionery factory (employing 3,000 people), and much of the industrial estate on which it is located is pervaded with the aroma of cocoa. Many of the 21 per cent of the town's ethnic-minority (mainly Asian) population are employed in shifts at Mars or the surrounding factories.

Unlike Burnley and Derby, however, Slough's industrial growth did not begin until after the First World War (when Burnley's staple industries were already going into steep decline). The population had been growing slowly – from 3,425 in 1861 to 7,400 in 1901 – as the rail link to London enabled early commuters to settle in the town, but there was no local industry in the nineteenth century apart from some small-scale brick-making (Fraser, 1973). The change came when a development company bought up and cleared a 600-acre army mechanical depot and vehicle dump in 1920. Following an Act of Parliament in 1925, the company (which became Slough Estates Ltd) began to develop the land as an industrial and trading estate. It laid roads and drains, provided its own power supply and constructed advance factory buildings. It also set aside land for 2,000 houses and launched a unique Industrial Health Service to which firms were invited to subscribe. By 1930 one hundred firms had moved on to the estate, 8,000 were employed there, and the government had opened an Industrial Training Centre which was attracting young people from the depressed regions, especially South Wales, in large numbers.

Slough's growth since 1930 has been sustained and rapid. There were 33,000 people in the borough in 1931, 55,000 in 1939, 68,000 in 1955. In 1985 the figure was estimated at 98,300 and rising (Slough Borough Council, 1985). The industrial estate is now almost fully developed and accommodates 390 companies in 800 factories employing 25,000 people. The main industry is light engineering, but a wide variety of firms manufacture a diversity of products including food, drugs, clothing and toiletries. In common with the rest of Berkshire, Slough has also been attracting new 'high-tech' industries in recent years including computing and biotechnology firms. It has been estimated that 10 per cent of the county's workforce is employed in the high-tech sector (Barlow, 1987, p. 32).

Slough was for many years after the war a 'red enclave' in the blue suburbia of the Home Counties, and it returned noted left-wing socialist members to Parliament including Fenner Brockway (1950–64) and Joan Lestor (1966–83) (Waller, 1987, p. 240). In 1983, however, the seat was won by the Conservatives, who held it in 1987 with 47 per cent of the vote, giving them a comfortable 4,000 majority over Labour. The Borough Council, however, is Labour-controlled, with 23 Labour members as compared with just 12 Conservatives and 4 Liberals in 1986.

Despite its political leanings, it is tempting to paint Slough as the epitome of what we might call 'Thatchertown'. The local economy is thriving, there is a new town centre which is buoyant, and there seems to be a spirit of entrepreneurship and modernism which Prime Minister Thatcher would most certainly approve of. There is also, by and large, an affluent working class in the town, and on the council estates over 2,500 houses (20 per cent of the 1980 stock) were sold to tenants between 1980 and 1986.

However, just as Burnley is not all gloom, so Slough is not all boom. There were 4,500 people registered as unemployed in the town in 1986, and most of them were to be found living on the depressed and run-down council estates built in the inter-war years to house the influx of new workers. It is on the postwar suburban estates, local authority and private, that Slough's affluent dual-earning working-class households are to be found, but in other parts of the town, as in many other parts of the country, there is a substratum of the population which has been left behind in the rising wages and spiralling consumer spending boom of the 1980s.

Conclusions

For the first time in the country's history, the majority of people in Britain today own a substantial property holding. This is made up in part of the shareholdings in various enterprises held on our behalf by the pension funds and insurance companies to which most of us now subscribe, and in part by personal ownership of domestic land and buildings. Both capitalist property and domestic property have thus become diffused during this century, the one indirectly, the other directly. In terms of the impact which this has had on British society, the spread of home ownership has arguably been the more significant of these two trends, for the growth of owner-occupation has provided nearly two-thirds of households with a personal and tangible property holding.

The spread of home ownership has occurred at a speed unmatched in any other country. First the middle class and then, since the war, the working class have seized the opportunity to buy their housing. Critics of mass home ownership have tried to explain its evident popularity by suggesting that people's wants and preferences have in some way been manipulated by powerful groups. Many Marxist critics down the years have argued, for example, that 'the ruling class' has deliberately fostered home ownership so as to incorporate working people more securely into the bourgeois order. There is, however, no evidence for this. Indeed, for most of the period under discussion, neither governments nor anybody else appear to have pursued a coherent long-term tenure strategy. As with so many other historical transformations, the home ownership revolution was intended by no one.

It was suggested in this chapter that, while there are many factors which explain how and why home ownership spread so swiftly in Britain, six in particular stand out. Demographic change entailing a rise in the number of households was clearly important. So too was the precipitate decline of the private landlords, many of whom chose or were obliged by circumstances to sell out to their sitting tenants at prices well below vacant possession value.

That these households were able to take up the chance to buy their homes itself reflected two further changes. One was the growth of real incomes of most working-class and middle-class employees, which, together with the rise in the number of women going out to work, meant that growing numbers of people could afford to buy. The other was the growth of the building societies, which, from the 1930s onwards, facilitated the switch into owner-occupation by lending for long periods on low initial deposits. In recent years, house purchase has also been supported to some extent by government subsidies such as exemption from tax on interest payments.

None of this, however, is sufficient to explain the home ownership revolution, for in addition we have to understand a sixth factor – the desire of people to own their homes. Ever since the thirteenth century there has been a distinctive spirit of individualism in English society. Its strength has waxed and waned, and it has been sustained more strongly in some parts of the country than in others. Nevertheless, it is this cultural inheritance which goes some way to explain why it is that so many people are so keen to own. Having lost control over their housing during the Industrial Revolution, many ordinary people have seized the opportunity to reclaim it during this century. In recent years, we have seen the meek begin to reinherit the earth.

In this chapter we have, however, also emphasized that the desire to own may be stronger in some areas than in others. In Scotland there is still a strong tradition of public-sector rental which accounts for half of all households, whereas in South Wales working-class home ownership has been strong ever since the nineteenth century. National-level generalizations can be dangerous, and it was for this reason that the original primary research for this study was done in three contrasting towns with their own specific histories.

Slough, Derby and Burnley are all predominantly working-class manufacturing towns, but they vary in their current economic fortunes. The choice of these three towns as our research sites enables us to consider the implications of the spread of home ownership down the class structure while at the same time staying alive to the possibility that home ownership may have a different significance in a declining industrial region than it does in one which is booming. In the chapters which follow we shall draw on over five hundred interviews with householders in these three towns, and together with material assembled from various secondary sources we shall begin to analyse the ways in which Britain's twentieth-century home-owner revolution has touched the lives of ordinary men and women in different walks of life in different parts of the country.

2   The desire to own

It is a commonplace observation of modern sociology that most people for
most of the time take most aspects of social life for granted. We do not
normally question what we do or why we are doing it. Nor do we ordinarily
subject to scrutiny the various institutions, moralities and beliefs which
constitute the society in which we live. Rather, we tend for everyday
practical purposes to assume that our social world is as natural and enduring
as the physical world, and this assumption then enables us to get on with the
business of leading our lives. Despite the fact that modern societies change
dramatically fast, and that (when we stop to think about it) social order
appears remarkably fragile and precarious, we nevertheless spend most of
our waking hours behaving as if our present ways of living were permanent,
pervasive and perfectly natural.

Adopting the terminology of the philosopher Edmund Husserl, sociologists
have referred to this taken-for-granted character of everyday life as the
adoption of a 'natural attitude': 'The natural attitude is the "naive" attitude
of the situated ego and is characterized by the mundane practical reasoning
of everyday life in which his worlds, social and natural, are indubitable,
simply "there", and taken-for-granted' (Filmer *et al.*, 1972, p. 127).
Adoption of such a natural attitude is arguably a necessary condition of
social existence, for a society where everybody questioned everything all the
time would be paralysed. It helps us get through the day to treat the
routines of work, home, law and order and so on as if they were as
unchanging and predictable as the sunrise every morning or the rainstorms
every bank holiday Monday. It is only when we take time out to analyse
some aspect of this social world that it becomes important to question what
for most of the time we take as given.

We saw in Chapter 1 that mass home ownership in England is a product
of the twentieth century. Widespread working-class home ownership goes
back no further than the 1960s, and it was only around 1970 that a majority
of households achieved owner-occupation. We need retrace no more than
three or four generations, therefore, to find a situation where the great
majority of English people presumably accepted private rental housing as
perfectly normal. As late as the 1930s, the desire expressed by newly
married couples to get a 'home of their own' meant securing rental
accommodation away from the parental home. It is only recently that this
commonly expressed aspiration has broadened in meaning to encompass the
ideal of private purchase.

Popular aspirations for home ownership are, then, quite a recent phenomenon. However, as it has become more *normal* for ordinary people to buy their housing rather than rent it, so the idea has developed that this is also more *natural*. Because so many people today do own their homes and so many others would like to, we tend to assume that such a desire is in some way the expression of a natural inclination or instinct. We are not surprised to see young people making considerable sacrifices, taking on extra work and delaying marriage or child-rearing in order to achieve a foothold on the private housing market. *Of course* they want to own their own place.

This idea of the naturalness of owning has sometimes been made quite explicit by those who are involved in one way or another in the housing system. The building societies, for example, have often appealed to it when justifying their role or promoting their image. In 1964 the chairman of the Building Societies Association spoke for many in the movement when he claimed that home ownership 'satisfies a basic human need to surround oneself with something that is absolutely personal and private' (quoted in Dickens *et al.*, 1985, p. 195). More recently, one building society exploited the same idea visually when it ran a televised advertising campaign which equated saving for a home with a beaver gathering branches for its lodge.

Such images have also become increasingly commonplace in the speeches of politicians and the pronouncements of governments. In 1951 the Conservative Housing Minister, Harold Macmillan, justified his decision to allow local authorities to sell council houses to sitting tenants by suggesting that home ownership 'satisfies some deep desire in their hearts' (quoted in Merrett, 1982, p. 119). This idea has resurfaced under Conservative governments ever since. The 1971 White Paper, for example, stated that 'Home ownership . . . satisfies a deep and natural desire on the part of the householder to have independent control of the house that shelters him and his family' (quoted in Merrett, 1982, p. 268). Similarly, nearly thirty years after Macmillan had *allowed* councils to sell houses to sitting tenants, a new Secretary of State for the Environment, Michael Heseltine, explained to the House of Commons in very similar terms why he had decided to *force* them to do so. 'There is in this country', he said, 'a deeply ingrained desire for home ownership' (quoted in Dickens *et al.*, 1985, p. 195). And in 1985 the Prime Minister, Margaret Thatcher, declared that, 'the desire to have and to hold something of one's own is basic to the spirit of man' (quoted in Pahl and Wallace, 1988, p. 145).

This view of home ownership as a natural desire of human beings, and hence as something which cannot and should not be questioned, has been expressed by Labour as well as Conservative governments in the past. In its housing White Paper of 1965, the Wilson Labour government described the spread of owner-occupation as 'normal' (Short, 1982, p. 55). Twelve years later, the Callaghan Labour government's Housing Policy Review went further by suggesting that 'For most people owning one's home is a basic and natural desire', and that the spread of owner-occupation was 'satisfying deep-seated social aspirations' (quoted in Gray, 1982, p. 269). As the party's National Executive Committee complained at the time, the implication seemed to be that living in a council house was in some sense 'unnatural' (Bassett, 1980, p. 305).

The notion which lies behind so many of these comments and images seems to be that ownership of one's home is in some way the realization of a deep and instinctual desire which is thwarted or sublimated by rental systems. Nor is it simply politicians and building society chiefs who seem to think in this way, for such pronouncements evidently resonate and make sense within the popular consciousness. As we have seen, there is a tendency in social life to accept what is normal as natural and to treat what is recent as if it has existed for all time. Widespread home ownership is a remarkably recent feature of British society, but it is today accepted by many as both the normal tenure and the natural way to organize the housing system.

All this raises the question of whether there really is some 'natural' basis to the desire to own, or whether our ideas of home ownership as a natural form of housing are nothing more than taken-for-granted rationalizations of social arrangements which we accept as (in the words of Filmer and his colleagues) 'indubitable' and 'simply there'.

Two logical steps are entailed in the attempt to answer this question. The first is to determine whether the desire for home ownership is generalized and widespread throughout the population. Of particular significance here is the issue of whether tenants, for whom ownership is not normal, nevertheless still express a strong desire to own.

The second step is then to inquire into the possible causes of the desire to own. Evidence that such a desire is widespread cannot of itself be taken to indicate that it is in some way natural in origin. The second step in our analysis must therefore be to address the complex issue of whether such a desire is best explained as the product of biology or ideology, of millions of years of natural evolution or of a few decades of cultural development.

The popularity of owning

Survey and case-study evidence built up over the last twenty years all indicates that home ownership is a widely (though not universally) cherished value among all social groups in Britain, and particularly among younger generations. The evidence also indicates that the vast majority of existing owners are happy in their tenure, while substantial numbers of public- and private-sector renters would prefer to own their homes.

The earliest available survey data date from 1967 when a study sponsored by the Building Societies Association (BSA) reported that 67 per cent of the population preferred owner-occupation (see Littlewood, 1986). At the same time it was also found that home ownership was the preferred tenure of 43 per cent of council tenants (Pawley, 1978, p. 147). A study conducted in the early 1970s in the city of Bath complemented these national findings when it reported that around half of all unfurnished tenants were happy remaining in the private rented sector (Couper and Brindley, 1975). From these studies, it seems that most people in the late 1960s wanted to be home owners but that renting was popular with about half of all council and private tenants.

The next major survey was conducted by the British Market Research Bureau for the National Economic Development Office in 1975. Drawing on 1,590 interviews nationwide, it found that 69 per cent of the population would prefer to be in the owner-occupied sector and that home ownership was preferred by 40 per cent of all council tenants. A preference for renting was expressed by fewer than three in ten respondents, and nearly all of these were existing tenants. Only 2 per cent of owner-occupiers said that they would prefer to rent from the local authority (see Harrison and Lomas, 1980; Jones, 1982; Littlewood, 1986).

Much the same sort of pattern has been repeated in surveys ever since, although, as time has gone by, so the popularity of owner-occupation has perhaps tended to strengthen a little as that of council renting has weakened. Thus in the 1978 *General Household Survey* by the Office of Population Censuses and Surveys (OPCS), 72 per cent of the population were found to prefer owning when given the choice, and just 19 per cent said they would opt for council tenancy. Owner-occupation was the preferred tenure of 97 per cent of those buying a house on mortgage, 84 per cent of outright owners, 49 per cent of council tenants and 47 per cent of unfurnished private tenants. Only 43 per cent of council tenants said that they would choose to rent a council house. Indeed, taking only those tenants under 60 years of age, a staggering 71 per cent said they would prefer to buy. The desire to own was spread through all occupational groups, accounting for 96 per cent of professionals, 93 per cent of intermediate non-manual employees, 85 per cent of skilled manual workers and 56 per cent of unskilled manual workers (see Holmans, 1987; Littlewood, 1986).

Two further national surveys were conducted in the 1980s, one in 1983 and the other in 1986. Both were sponsored by the BSA and both found that around three-quarters of the population expressed a desire to own a home, while council renting was much less in favour with just 16 per cent opting for it in 1983. Nearly half of the council tenants interviewed said that they would prefer to own (see Bailey, 1987; the *Guardian*, 26 June 1986).

Local case study findings bear out the message relayed by the raw figures of the national surveys. In their study of households in London, Young and Wilmott reported that 'Most people . . . wanted to own so that their property could be as securely bonded to themselves as possible' (1973, p. 46). More recently, Madigan (1988, p. 31) writes that 'almost all' of the low-income buyers she studied in Glasgow saw owner-occupation as 'an overwhelmingly advantageous form of tenure', although she also found that 59 per cent of them would have been happy to rent in the first instance had a good-quality council house been offered to them. In their longitudinal study of young married couples in Wandsworth, Nottingham and Hertfordshire,

Madge and Brown (1981) found that some 90 per cent of the sample consistently expressed a preference for home ownership even though only 55 per cent of them had actually achieved it over the two and a half years that the study lasted. Council renting, on the other hand, was widely held in low regard, with only 5 per cent of the couples selecting it as the tenure of their choice (although 23 per cent had become council tenants by the end of the study). Studies in Manchester and in Southwark in the 1970s also reported the relative unpopularity of council renting, with a majority of council tenants in both studies preferring to buy (Jones, 1982).

My own findings from the three towns survey reinforce all that has already been reported from earlier studies. Table 2.1 reveals a strong desire for owner-occupation in all three towns. The data reported in this and the following table are taken from responses to question 13 (see Appendix III) which asked: 'On balance, would you prefer to buy or rent the house you live in?' The question specifically mentioned respondents' present house so as to focus attention solely on tenure, for it has been suggested by some analysts (for example, Shlay, 1985) that some people who express a preference for owner-occupation do so because they associate owner-occupied housing with higher-quality accommodation or more desirable locations. This is not the case in the findings presented here, for people were thinking solely in terms of their tenure of their current house.

The question followed a series of questions in which people were asked for their housing histories, the reasons why they had come to buy or rent and their views of the advantages and disadvantages of their current tenure. Question 13, therefore, was a summary question in which respondents were invited to arrive at an overall judgement on their tenure preferences given all that they had said about the merits and problems of different tenures. Only 2 per cent of people were unable to express such a judgement.

Table 2.1 shows that people buying their homes on mortgage reveal an almost universal preference for owning (98 per cent), and this preference is also overwhelmingly strong (91 per cent) among outright owners. The latter group has consistently been found to be less supportive of home ownership than mortgagees since it tends to include elderly people (for whom upkeep and repairs are more likely to be a problem) and some of the cheapest and poorest-quality housing stock. Nevertheless, the preference for owning is clearly widespread among outright owners as well as mortgagees, and, taking all owner-occupiers together, 96 per cent say they would prefer to own, while only 3 per cent say they would prefer to rent.

What' is' perhaps more surprising, however, is the level of desire for owner-occupation among public-sector renters. Table 2.1 shows that while the preference for owning is understandably widespread among existing owners, it is also shared by over three-quarters of council tenants. Less than one in five council tenants would choose to rent from the local authority if they could afford to purchase privately. In Slough just 14 per cent of council tenants said that they preferred that tenure, and in Burnley it was 16 per cent. Council renting seems rather less unpopular among Derby tenants, 27

THE DESIRE TO OWN

Table 2.1   *Tenure preferences of owners and tenants in Burnley, Derby and Slough*

| | Prefer owner-occupation | | Tenure preference Prefer council renting | | DK/NA | | Total | |
Tenure	No.	%	No.	%	No.	%	No.	%
Burnley								
Council tenants	35	78	7	16	3	7	45	29
Outright owners	28	85	3	9	2	6	33	21
Mortgaged owners	77	99	1	1	–	–	78	50
Derby								
Council tenants	34	71	13	27	1	2	48	29
Outright owners	45	92	1	2	3	6	49	29
Mortgaged owners	70	100	–	–	–	–	70	42
Slough								
Council tenants	32	87	5	14	–	–	37	23
Outright owners	31	97	1	3	–	–	32	20
Mortgaged owners	89	95	4	5	1	1	94	58
Total	441	91	35	7	10	2	486	

per cent of whom said they preferred it, but even here 71 per cent said they would prefer to own.

Table 2.2 provides data on the same question, this time broken down by occupational and social class (the two class schema represented in this table are explained in Appendix I). What is apparent here is that the preference for home ownership spreads throughout the classes, although there is a noticeable break between Registrar-General's classes IV (semi-skilled) and V (unskilled). Put another way, the only pocket of any significant support for council renting is within the stratum of unskilled manual workers, yet even here three-quarters say they prefer to own! The pattern is fairly even across the three towns, although in Burnley unskilled manual worker support for council renting (22 per cent) is somewhat higher than in Derby (13 per cent) and Slough (15 per cent). The figures when broken down to this extent are, however, very small, and such variations should therefore be treated with some caution.

The findings of my case study show that the preference for home ownership is high and is widespread. The old are just as much in favour of owning as the young (89 per cent of over-65s prefer to own, compared with 92 per cent of under-35s); men (92 per cent) prefer to own just as women do (89 per cent); and Asians (87 per cent) seem as keen as whites (91 per cent). The results indicate even more widespread support for owner-occupation than has been found in earlier studies, although an equivalent level of antipathy towards council tenancies was also reported by Madge and Brown. The fact that my research has found even stronger support for owner-occupation than has generally been found in earlier studies is partly

Table 2.2 *Tenure preferences of different occupational and social class groups*

	Prefer owner-occupation		Tenure preference Prefer council renting		DK/NA		Total	
	No.	%	No.	%	No.	%	No.	%
Reg.-Gen. classes								
I Professional, etc.	20	100	–	–	–	–	20	4
II Intermediate	99	93	5	5	2	2	106	22
IIIN Skilled non-manual	92	96	4	4	–	–	96	22
IIIM Skilled manual	99	91	9	9	1	1	109	23
IV Partly skilled	87	89	8	8	3	3	98	20
V Unskilled	42	76	9	16	4	7	55	11
Goldthorpe classes								
Service class	113	94	5	4	2	2	120	25
Intermediate class	138	95	7	5	–	–	145	30
Working class	188	86	23	11	8	4	219	45
Total	439	91	35	7	10	2	484	

accounted for by differences in sampling, for mine is not a national representative survey. The sampling strategy was designed to produce an over-representation of home owners while excluding private-sector tenants altogether. Given that existing owners favour owner-occupation most strongly while private tenants may see council renting as an improvement on their present circumstances, the sample was bound to generate a higher overall level of support for home ownership than a simple random sample drawn from the population as a whole would have done.

Even allowing for sampling differences, however, it is noticeable that certain groups *within* the sample are more favourably disposed towards home ownership than might have been expected from the results of earlier studies. In particular, the council tenants with whom we spoke in all three towns appear less attached to council renting and more in favour of owning than council tenants interviewed in most earlier studies. Where research conducted in the 1970s found that around half of all council tenants would prefer to own, my research suggests that the figure now stands at around three-quarters.

If such a shift in values and attitudes has taken place among council tenants, it probably reflects the major changes which have affected the public sector over recent years. As we shall see later in this chapter, rents have risen quite steeply in real terms, and financial controls on local government spending have resulted in reductions in repair and maintenance programmes on many council estates. In addition to this, over one million council houses were sold in the ten years from 1979, and this is likely to have encouraged remaining tenants at least to consider the possibility of purchasing their homes. It is therefore entirely plausible to suggest that most council tenants today, like the vast majority of owner-occupiers, have come to see home ownership as their preferred tenure.

The evidence, then, is clear and compelling. National surveys and local case studies conducted at different times over the last twenty years all agree that, given the opportunity, the great majority of British households would prefer to buy and that large numbers of council tenants are renting their homes out of necessity or inertia rather than as a positive choice.

Such findings are not limited to Britain, for it seems that the desire to own a home is just as strong in many other countries. Studies in Australia have shown that 90 per cent or more of the population expresses a preference for owning (Kilmartin, 1988, p. 3). In Canada a 1971 Toronto survey found that 80 per cent of all households would rather buy than rent (Harris and Hamnett, 1987, p. 175). In Finland, where 65 per cent of dwellings are owner-occupied, various surveys in the 1960s and 1970s have demonstrated levels of preference for owner-occupation varying between 80 per cent and 95 per cent (Ruonavaara, 1988, p. 28).

Clearly the desire to own is not unique to Britain, nor even to the Anglo-Saxon countries. Why, then, do so many people in so many parts of the developed world express a desire to own the homes they live in?

A home ownership ideology?

We saw in Chapter 1 that mass home ownership has long been anathema to the political left in Britain. This hostility has made many left academics reluctant to accept research results which indicate that owner-occupation is the preferred tenure of most ordinary people. The evidence of an overwhelming aspiration to own is, of course, too compelling to deny. Instead, critics have attempted to devalue these research findings by suggesting that people's expressed preferences are the product of dominant ideologies and manipulated choices. The evidence on popular preferences is not therefore challenged, but is set aside as irrelevant. As the Marxist author of one key text puts it, 'The existing literature on tenure preference is marred by an excess of unstructured empiricism or ideological rubbish' (Merrett, 1982, p. 56). Having disposed of all this research effort with a stroke of the pen, such critics assert that the important question for research to address is not what people say they want, but how the political and economic system in which they live makes them think they want it.

The left's solution to why so many people apparently want to own is twofold. One part of the answer is that popular preferences have been structured by an artificial system of inducements and subsidies. As we saw in Chapter 1, Marxist analysis has generally held that home ownership has been more or less deliberately encouraged in order to fragment working-class collective organization and incorporate individual workers into the ethos and discipline of the capitalist social order. This has only been possible by constructing a system of housing provision and finance which strongly encourages working-class households to buy rather than to rent. State policy down the years has therefore dangled a carrot of subsidized home ownership while wielding a stick of stigmatized public rental. Ignoring the fact that Britain has one of the largest public-sector rental systems in the Western world, the argument is that workers and their families have effectively been coerced into buying through lack of alternatives. The desire to own has therefore been manipulated and constructed by making people an offer they cannot refuse. As Kemeny puts it, 'Current tenure preferences are the product and not the cause of tenure systems' (1981, p. 63).

We consider this idea of a 'coerced demand' for home ownership in more detail later in this chapter. It is, however, only part of the left's answer to why so many people want to buy. The second strand in the argument is that material inducements have been reinforced by ideological control. The housing which people *believe* they want is not the housing they *really* want. According to Peter Marcuse, for example, what people 'really want' is a housing system which supports 'shared' rather than 'competitive' aspirations, a housing system 'in which people help each other without regard to payment or profit' (1987, p. 233). Marcuse offers no evidence for these assertions which he takes as self-evident. In the absence of dominant ideologies, he is confident that people would choose collective living arrangements and socialized provision and would shun the individualized and competitive system of owner-occupation which they currently embrace. 'The typical suburban middle class home', Marcuse assures us, 'often represents more a commercial, artificial, profit-induced, exclusionary picture of conspicuous housing consumption sold to its occupants as the ultimate "dream", than what those occupants would really want if they had a choice' (1987, p. 232).

The preference for owner-occupation, then, is not the product of genuine choice. It has been massaged by government housing policies and moulded by commercial pressures. The system of home ownership is a system of oppression, for it divides people one from another, encourages conformity and inhibits rather than enables human capacities. It is a system in which capitalists oppress workers and men oppress women (Hayden, 1981, p. 295; Marcuse, 1987, p. 247). The popular desire for home ownership is thus evidence of people's enslavement to the means of their own oppression. It is, in short, an example of 'false consciousness' (Fletcher, 1976, p. 464).

This breathtakingly arrogant form of analysis, in which writers claim to know what people really want better than they know themselves, has a long lineage in the Marxist intellectual tradition. Its claims to knowledge are, of course, entirely unfalsifiable either by empirical evidence or by rational argument, for they rest on the assertion of 'real interests' and 'genuine wants' which exist only in the wishful thinking and fevered imaginations of the theorists themselves. To believe that most people would really prefer to live in feminist collectives and socialist communes, sharing their kitchens and cultivating their common gardens, is to betray a frightening ignorance of the hopes, fears and aspirations of the majority of households. In work like this, the utopian dreams of intellectuals have been allowed to eclipse the more mundane aspirations of those of whom they purport to write. We might also add that work like this is little short of an insult to the efforts and the intelligence of millions of people who work and save and struggle to fulfil their desire to buy a home of their own. It is one of the ironies of the Marxist intellectual tradition that it consistently shows such little respect for the values and aspirations of the very people whose interests it claims to represent and whose futures it seeks to determine.

Given their belief that popular demands for owner-occupation are the product of ideological contamination, it is hardly surprising that left-wing writers react entirely negatively to any suggestion that there may be a natural basis to the desire to own. The 'natural desire' to own one's home is dismissed as nothing more than a 'myth' (Cox and McCarthy, 1982, p. 212; Gray, 1982, p. 271; Kemeny, 1981, p. 11). Martin Boddy argues that this 'myth' treats a capitalist system of property relations as if it were the product of human nature: 'The myth of an innate desire for private property functions by projecting on to *individuals* the characteristics of the particular socio-economic system in which they are located . . . The "desire" for private property springs not from individuals but from the socio-economic system' (1980, p. 25, original emphasis). Similarly, John Short suggests that the notion that home ownership is natural is nothing more than a device for justifying the very policies which continue to encourage people to want it: 'There is a neat logical trick involved here: people desire owner occupation as it is more financially attractive because state policies have made it so; this desire is seen as natural; it is thus up to the government to meet this natural desire. What could be more natural?' (1982, p. 119).

Although the idea of a natural desire for home ownership has often been ridiculed in the left literature, it has never been critically examined. There is in much of British social science a deep distrust of biological explanation. The possibility of a biological basis to human behaviour is often ruled out at the start of sociological analyses; indeed, it is rarely even considered. Thus, when biological arguments or assertions are encountered, they are treated as self-evidently absurd and are relegated to the status of ideologies.

This deep antipathy to biological explanation is particularly marked on the left. Reformers and revolutionaries alike have long refused to countenance explanations of human behaviour which make reference to the biological and genetic features of human beings. Pierre van den Berghe, a rare example of a left-wing sociologist who does take biology seriously, notes how 'The mere mention of biology in connection with human behaviour often elicits passionate rejection, not least among those who share with me a liberal outlook' (1981, p. x). The reason for the passion is not difficult to fathom, for to cede the possibility of a biological basis to social phenomena is to accept limits on the extent to which human actions and social institutions can be changed and moulded to fit in with blueprints of some future egalitarian or socialist order.

There is, however, an irony in the readiness with which biological accounts of human behaviour are dismissed by the left as ideological. As van den Berghe points out, the social sciences themselves are 'riddled with ideology' as a result of the attempt to separate human behaviour from the human organism which produces it. One of the few British academics on the left to have recognized this is Paul Hirst. In his book with Woolley, he notes that 'Sociologists have on the whole energetically denied the importance of genetic, physical and individual psychological factors in human social life. In so doing they have reinforced and theorized a traditional Western cultural opposition between nature and culture' (1982, p. 23). In other words, social science has created its own obstacles to understanding the world by imposing a rigid division between social behaviour which is thought to be the product of cultural systems, and natural behaviour which is seen to be the product of biological systems. We have to go back over thirty years to discover the last sociologist (Talcott Parsons) who seriously attempted to integrate these two systems within a single theory of human action.

Contemporary sociology's concern to perpetuate the artificial division between nature and culture reflects a long tradition in Judaeo-Christian thinking which seeks to separate human beings from the rest of the animal world by asserting the 'uniqueness of man'. It is from the Old Testament that we derive the idea that 'man' is set off from the beasts, for the former is distinguished by the possession of a soul. It was this kind of thinking which produced the intense resistance to Darwinian evolutionary theory in the nineteenth century, for the creationists considered it a heresy to postulate an evolutionary continuity between human beings and other soulless primates. Yet it is essentially the same idea of human uniqueness which in the twentieth century has sustained sociologists and cultural anthropologists in their attempt to deny the relevance of human biology in the determination of human behaviour. As Ardrey (1967) has suggested, the twentieth century denies evolution by asserting culture in the same way that the nineteenth century denied evolution by asserting creation.

This is not to deny that human beings *are* in many senses unique. For Reynolds (1980) this uniqueness consists in the development of human language and the capacity for conceptual thought. As Max Weber also argued many decades ago, our behaviour is not simply 'caused', it is motivated, and this allows us to control and monitor our actions. Furthermore, as Dawkins (1976) and Lorenz (1981, p. 343) both recognize, we enjoy the ability to pass on our conceptual knowledge to the next generation, thereby swiftly building up a cultural heritage which has enabled us to develop from cave dwelling to moon landing in the space of a few thousand years.

But to accept that we are much more than our genes is not to deny that we are nevertheless animals. We share 99 per cent of our genes with our closest relatives among the higher primates: 'Man is an animal. He is a remarkable and in many respects unique species, but he is an animal nevertheless' (Tinbergen, 1951, p. 205). To accept the biological basis of animal behaviour while denying it in humans thus makes no logical sense.

As Tiger and Fox put it, 'Again and yet again, man *is* an animal. He has evolved as other animals: he is a vertebrate, a mammal, a member of the order Primates. How, then, can the same principles of analysis that we apply to the study of the animal kingdom at large not be applied to him?' (1972, p. 7).

It seems clear that no coherent understanding of patterns of human behaviour will be possible if biological factors are excluded from our analysis. As Halsey suggests, '*All* characteristics are *both* acquired *and* genetic. Genotypes determine potentialities. Environment determines which or how much of these potentialities should be realized in living human beings' (1977, p. 2, original emphasis). We need, says Halsey, to abandon the dualism of nature versus culture and instead to think in terms of 'interactive causation'.

Interactive causation is based on the recognition that environment and heredity are inseparable. In the course of human evolution we have adapted our behaviour to suit the environment with the result that the best-adapted have survived to pass on to the next generation the very genes which enabled them to adapt in the first place. When some of our forebears first developed the capacity to use rudimentary tools, for example, they not only passed on this cultural knowledge to later generations, but they also proved more adept at surviving and thus disproportionately passed on their DNA as well. Natural and cultural development thus go hand in hand. To try to break this cycle apart by privileging one factor while denying the other is a recipe for intellectual futility (Hirst and Woolley, 1982).

It follows from this that the resolute refusal on the political left to countenance the idea that the desire for home ownership may reflect some natural disposition may itself be criticized as 'ideological'. The mainstream sociological literature on home ownership has shut out a whole area of knowledge and scientific research from its considerations. Every time it is suggested that there may be a natural basis to the desire to own, the very idea is closed off with the retort that such thinking is ideological. The fear of biology has shrunk the imagination of the social sciences and, in Hirst and Woolley's terms, has made us 'prisoners of our own ignorance' (1982, p. 71). It is time to break out.

A deep and natural desire?

There is a literal sense in which the desire for home ownership cannot be 'natural', for owner-occupation is a distinct cultural-legal phenomenon of recent origin, whereas 'natural inclinations' or 'instincts' are the products of millions of years of evolution. The question, therefore, is whether there is some need or disposition in human beings which, in the contemporary era, comes in some circumstances to be expressed through the specific cultural phenomenon of house ownership.

There are two principal candidates for such a disposition. One is *territoriality*. If it can be shown that human beings are by nature territorial animals, then it could be argued that the desire to own a house is an expression of this aspect of our nature. The second is *possessiveness*. If we are by nature possessive creatures, then the desire to own our own homes would be readily understandable given the central role which housing plays in our everyday lives.

Before considering each of these factors, it is first necessary to establish what it means to say that some aspect of human behaviour such as the defence of territory or the accumulation of possessions is 'natural'. What is generally inferred by such terminology is the idea that such behaviour derives from certain 'instincts'. So what is an instinct?

According to Robert Ardrey (1967), instinctive behaviour is behaviour which is genetically programmed. Sometimes this programming entails 'closed' instincts in which animals always behave in the same way under the same conditions. A good example of closed instinctive behaviour is provided by those strains of honey bee in which workers locate infected grubs before they hatch and pull them out of the nest (see Dawkins, 1976, pp. 64–5). It has been shown that this behaviour is carried in specific genes, for by genetic experiments it is possible to produce worker bees which perform one part of the operation without performing the rest. In an example like this, there is a direct causal connection between the presence or absence of genetic material and the presence or absence of specific behaviours.

Ardrey distinguishes such 'closed' instinctive behaviour from what he terms 'open' instincts. By these he means general dispositions to act in a given way once adequate learning has taken place. An obvious example is the human disposition or capacity for speech which is only realized through the process of learning a language. It is Ardrey's belief that much of human behaviour can be explained as the expression of open instincts, although this is not unique to humans. In some species of birds, for example, the young are only capable of producing the appropriate songs once they have heard them from other birds.

It is important to clarify exactly what is entailed in the claim that human behaviour is the product of open instincts. It is not suggested that specific examples of human behaviour can be explained as the direct manifestations of natural instincts. To take an example from Tiger and Fox (1972), many human societies have developed initiation ceremonies to mark the transition of young males into adulthood, but there is obviously no human instinct which produces such initiation ceremonies. What there may be, however, is a genetic tendency (triggered by biochemical changes in adolescence) for young men to behave in rebellious and uncontrollable ways, in which case this may have brought forth different cultural responses in different societies, many of which entail marking a ritual passage into mature adulthood.

There is a direct parallel here with the claim that the desire for home ownership is based in instinct. Such a claim would not hold that there is a human instinct which produces owner-occupied housing, but it would suggest that there is a genetic tendency for human beings to establish separate territories, or to seek security, or whatever, and that this instinct has brought forth the institution of home ownership in some societies while it has been expressed through other cultural forms in others.

Now there is one very obvious objection to this sort of reasoning, and that is that it does not actually explain very much. As Reynolds complains, 'The demonstration that there are innate predispositions underlying behaviour is not, unfortunately, enough to explain more than a fraction of what we do' (1980, p. 16). What we have here is what philosophers would recognize as a 'realist' mode of explanation in which phenomena are explained as the manifestation of some deeper essential tendency. Like any realist mode of explanation, however, the problem lies in the positing of underlying causes which may become manifest in any number of different ways and which under some conditions may not become manifest at all (see Saunders, 1986, appendix, for a critique of this mode of reasoning in the social sciences). To argue convincingly for an instinctive yet 'open' basis to some aspect of human behaviour, it is necessary to go beyond simply claiming that there is a natural disposition which may be expressed in many different cultural forms; for, as it stands, such an argument brings us dangerously close to a self-confirming and unfalsifiable statement of faith. Almost anything we do could be said to be an expression of such an ill-defined natural disposition, in which case the theory of open instincts ends up explaining nothing.

To sharpen up the theory, we need to know something about how the hidden 'essence' causes the manifest 'appearance'. In other words, we need to know how the posited instinct is translated into observed behaviour. Ardrey does not consider that this is an important issue. He admits that we do not understand how instincts operate or where they are located, but he insists that they obviously exist and that a theory of instinctual behaviour cannot be dismissed simply because we are unable to explain how it works.

This is not good enough. Hirst and Woolley point out that human behaviour seems to have changed quite dramatically over the last 30,000 years, yet human instincts have presumably hardly changed at all in that time. If there is a causal connection between instinct and behaviour, we need to know how it works and how flexible these instincts can be.

Ardrey himself speculates that instincts may turn out to be genetic codes carried in the DNA molecules of our cells. In 1967 he could go no further, but molecular biology has developed dramatically since then, and it is now considered very likely that genes (which are simply segments of DNA arranged in a particular sequence) do carry behavioural as well as physical codes. The example of the honey bees which we considered earlier clearly shows 'that it can be perfectly proper to speak of "a gene for behaviour so-and-so" even if we haven't the faintest idea of the chemical chain of embryonic causes leading from gene to behaviour' (Dawkins, 1976, pp. 65–6). And what is true of honey bees is true also of human beings.

Consider, for example, recent advances in our understanding of schizophrenia. Less than twenty years ago, radical sociologists and psychoanalysts such as Laing, Cooper and Szas were confidently locating the causes of schizophrenia in the family or were even suggesting that it was nothing more than a label invented by the psychiatric profession to account for socially unconventional behaviour. Recent research, however, has demonstrated beyond question that at least some forms of schizophrenia are genetically based and genetically transmitted, and this work has relegated the writings of Laing and Szas to the status of antiquated curiosities.

Our understanding of genetics is still rudimentary, for although we understand how genes are transmitted in chromosomes, our understanding of the causal connection between chemical sequences in the DNA and observed characteristics in the organism is in its infancy. As Reynolds correctly points out, 'The whole question of how genetic instructions are transformed into behavioural outcomes is largely unsolved' (1980, p. 28). Nevertheless, our understanding of this process is growing such that we may predict with some confidence that developments in neurobiology and molecular biology are likely to force a major reappraisal of some of the basic assumptions of the cultural sciences over the years ahead. Having identified the genes for schizophrenia, there is no reason to believe that researchers will not also go on to identify genes for other sources of variation in patterns of human behaviour.

For the moment, however, much of our understanding is inevitably still speculative. Bearing this in mind, let us proceed to consider such evidence as we have for the existence of a genetic disposition which could underpin the desire for home ownership in the contemporary period.

A territorial imperative?

The first possibility to consider is whether there may be a territorial disposition in human beings. 'Territory' is defined in sociobiology as 'An area occupied more or less exclusively by an animal or group of animals by means of repulsion through overt defence or advertisement' (Wilson, 1975, p. 256). A territorial species is therefore one 'in which all males, and sometimes females too, bear an inherent drive to gain and defend and exclusive property' (Ardrey, 1967, p. 3).

When considering whether *Homo sapiens* is an inherently territorial animal, three kinds of evidence may be appropriate. The first concerns the behaviour of other animals which are close to us in evolutionary time. The second concerns the question of whether territorial behaviour could have proved an evolutionary advantage in the development of human beings. The third involves comparative anthropological evidence on the role of territorial defence in different human societies.

Not all species are territorial. Ethologists have documented strong territorial instincts in some animals such as birds, but others appear to display very little if any sign of the appropriate defensive behaviour. It has also been found that closely related species may differ markedly in their degree of territoriality. The scrub jay, for example, is aggressively territorial, whereas the Mexican jay establishes only weakly defended territories (Klopfer, 1969). So too among the primates, the picture is confused. Some of the higher primates, like gibbons and baboons, exhibit strong territorial behaviour (Ardrey, 1967). Gibbons live in small groups and they will aggressively defend their area of forest against intruders. Other higher primates, however, appear largely unconcerned about establishing territorial claims. Chimpanzees and gorillas, for example, are non-territorial (Montague, 1976; Reynolds, 1980) for they do not normally chase off interlopers when they encounter them in their home range. Given that chimps and gorillas are closer to us than gibbons are, comparative ethological evidence clearly cannot bear out Ardrey's argument that it indicates the likelihood of our own territorial inclinations.

A second way of approaching this question is to ask whether human evolution is likely to have favoured those of our ancestors who exhibited aggression in defence of a territory. Ardrey is in no doubt: 'Man's territorial nature is inherent and of evolutionary origin' (1967, p. 102). Such an argument assumes that territoriality in humans has been selected for, just as it has in various other species. What, then, are likely to have been its evolutionary advantages?

Ethologists have suggested that territoriality may enhance survival chances by performing several positive functions for those species in which it is found. One clear function appears to be that of spreading the species across space and thereby avoiding over-exploitation of localized resources. As Lorenz argues, 'The most important function of intra-specific aggression is the even distribution of the animals of a particular species over an inhabitable area' (1966, p. 30). Such spacing is advantageous because it helps regulate competition. Recognition of territorial boundaries allows animals to expend much less energy than if they had constantly to compete anew for access to basic resources (Wilson, 1975).

Other positive advantages are also said to follow from territorial arrangements. Hediger (1962), for example, believes that a sense of territory prevents animals of the same species from moving too far apart and is therefore important in enhancing their chances of locating a mate for reproduction. It has also been argued that territoriality may form the basis for pair bonding in those species where building a nest and rearing the young require the participation of the male as well as the female. Indeed, Ardrey suggests that it is a territorial instinct rather than a paternal instinct which keeps males attached to their mates during the period when they are jointly raising their offspring (1967, p. 100); but this claim is weakened by evidence that some species form enduring pairs without territories (Klopfer, 1969).

One problem with such arguments lies in their assertion of group selection as the basis of evolutionary development. Ardrey, for example, argues that selection favours 'those innate behavioural patterns and capacities in the individual, however extraordinary, which in turn favour the population's good' (1967, p. 173). Seen in this way, individual altruism may be explained by the contribution it makes to the good of the species as a whole. It favours the population as a whole, for example, when only the fittest individuals are able to establish territories prior to breeding, for this ensures that only the strongest genes are transmitted to the next generation. Similarly, we have seen that Lorenz holds that territoriality benefits the population as a whole by spacing it out, thereby maximizing the efficient use of natural resources. For Ardrey and other ethologists, the unit of evolutionary analysis is therefore the population, not the individuals which comprise it.

The problem with this is that it altogether fails to explain how this beneficial state of affairs comes about. What leads the unsuccessful suitor to stand back and allow his rival to mate? Why should one individual respect another's territory and happily wander off to another patch where the grass is sparser? All this may be in the long-term interests of the group as a whole, but are we to believe that the individuals understand this?

As Dawkins (1976) has shown, the theory of group selection is unsustainable, for the 'good of the whole' is always likely to be undermined by selfish individuals cashing in on all the others' altruism. Such free-riders will be able to enhance their survival chances and therefore spread their (more selfish) genes into the next generation. Individuals carrying other, more altruistic genes which encouraged selfless behaviour for the good of the wider population would, by definition, soon die out. The only form of altruism which is likely to prove stable in evolutionary time is one which favours closely related individuals, for altruism towards kin will result in the successful reproduction of like genes.

None of this is to deny the possibility that a genetic tendency to territoriality may have evolved in humans, but if it has done, it would have to be because of the contribution which it has made to the survival chances of the individuals carrying such genes, and it could not be explained in terms of any supposed wider benefits to the species as a whole. Ardrey, Lorenz and others may be right when they posit the existence of a territorial instinct in humanity, but the explanations they offer for how this could have evolved are most certainly wrong.

There is, in addition, a second problem with the argument that such an instinct is likely to have evolved in our past, and that is simply that our forebears were almost certainly mobile. Advocates of the existence of human territoriality recognize that early human societies were based on hunting and gathering, but they argue that this was compatible with, and even necessitated, territorial defence. Tinbergen, for example, argues that 'As a social, hunting primate, man must originally have been organized on the principle of group territories' (1972, p. 129). Against this, however, it can be argued that any instinct favouring homing and territorial attachment would have proved disadvantageous in our early evolution, since the need was to exploit the natural environment wherever the pickings were richest. As Leach has suggested, it is precisely one of the evolutionary advantages of *Homo sapiens* that it proved so adaptable to diverse environments: 'No other species can adjust so readily to drastic variations of temperature, humidity and diet. And this highly advantageous plasticity is tied in with the fact that man, as a species, is almost entirely free from territorial limitations and attachments' (1973, pp. 155–6).

The problem with this sort of argument, of course, is that ultimately we lack the evidence to indicate whether or not our immediate predecessor (*Australopithecus*) was organized in defensible territories. The argument is based almost entirely on extrapolation back in time from what we know of hunters and gatherers today.

It is this anthropological evidence which forms the basis of the third (and most direct) approach which has been taken in addressing the question of human territoriality. If there is a territorial instinct in human beings, then presumably we should be able to find different manifestations of it in different kinds of societies.

According to Suttles, 'In no human community is totally unselective movement permitted. There always seem to be sharp differences between individuals according to the territories to which they have rightful access' (1972, p. 156). This, however, is a very weak indicator of territoriality. As Suttles himself recognizes, virtually all human activity has a territorial basis. It could hardly be otherwise, for every known human society (with the sole exception of the Malayan sea gypsies – Tuan, 1976) conducts its affairs on land and must therefore exhibit some means of organizing access to and use of land. Every human group has some sort of home area, no matter how large or ill defined, but something more than this is entailed in the argument that we carry a territorial disposition encoded in our DNA.

Earlier we saw that territorial behaviour in animals may be identified by the willingness to defend an area and to mark it off as exclusive. On this tighter definition, it seems that some human societies do not exhibit territorial behaviour or institutions, although many do.

Given Ardrey's theory of open instincts, we should not necessarily expect to find territorial behaviour everywhere, for it may be that the conditions necessary to trigger the disposition will not be found everywhere. Frequent references in the literature to the non-territoriality of the Eskimos, for example, need not invalidate Ardrey's argument, for it may be that the environmental conditions of life in the Arctic circle have never brought forth the underlying capacity for territorial behaviour and may never have selected for genes favouring such behaviour.

Nevertheless, we should presumably expect to discover some generalizable pattern across different societies, especially where environmental conditions are similar. According to Montagu (1976), however, this is precisely what we do not find: 'Some peoples are territorial, some only partially so, while others are thoroughly non-territorial' (1976, p. 249). Groups such as the tribes of New Guinea and the clans of Australian Aborigines manifest strong attachments to particular areas of land. The Aranda in Australia, for example, invest high symbolic significance in sacred sites, and their myths reveal an intense concern with home as a highly valued and emotionally charged place (Sopher, 1979, p. 132). Yet it is also possible to point to other groups of hunters and gatherers such as the Vaupes of the Amazon basin or the Kung Bushmen of south-western Africa who seem to place little emphasis on attachments to particular places and who, like the Eskimos, are unperturbed when visitors make use of their land (Altman and Chemers, 1980; Sopher, 1979). Indeed, strong territorial attachments appear somewhat unusual among hunter-gatherer peoples, and this would tend to reinforce our earlier argument that geographical mobility is likely to undermine strong commitments to specific places.

About 12,000 years ago, of course, human beings began to abandon this more mobile mode of living in favour of a settled system of agriculture. Ever since then, territorial behaviour such as the marking and defence of boundaries has become common (Montagu, 1976). It is highly implausible to suggest that this relatively recent behaviour has an instinctive or genetic basis, for the time scale is far too short to have enabled the necessary gene selection to have occurred. Widespread territorial behaviour in agricultural and urbanized societies can therefore only be explained as a cultural adaptation. This is not to say that territorial sentiments and attachments may not be strongly felt, but it is to suggest that they are unlikely to have a basis in human nature as governed by our genes.

The evidence discussed in this section does not finally refute the possibility of a territorial disposition in humans, but the balance of probability does not favour it. We may conclude with Reynolds that 'Ardrey's claim . . . that human and non-human territoriality are basically one and the same process remains an unproven speculation and one that . . . is probably wrong' (1980, pp. 11–12). If the desire for home ownership has natural origins, it seems wise to search elsewhere for the evidence.

An instinct to possess?

If home ownership is not an expression of a human need for territory, could it be a manifestation of our need to possess objects in our environment? If such a need existed, housing would certainly be its principal target, for the home that we live in is on many criteria the most significant object in most of our lives.

Malmberg is one observer who is in no doubt that human possessiveness is a naturally evolved instinct: 'Taking together available facts it seems quite clear that there is in many vertebrates, including man, a basic property instinct, which implies a desire to collect moveable things, probably originating in feeding, and to secure vitally necessary, non-moveable objects in the form of real estate' (1980, p. 90). As in our discussion of territoriality, this claim to an instinctive basis of possessiveness may be evaluated with reference to both animal and human behaviour.

Ethologists and sociobiologists have often emphasized the advantage which accrues to the possessor of a territory when threatened by an intruder. This seems to have nothing to do with inequalities of knowledge of the territory, but is rather a function simply of prior possession. It is a widespread phenomenon in nature that energy and aggression increase as an individual gets nearer to its home base. As Lorenz observes, animals will fight most strongly and will be least inclined to flee when they are at the heart of their territories where they seem to feel safest and most secure: 'In nearing the centre of the territory, the aggressive urge increases in geometrical ratio to the decrease in distance from the centre' (1966, p. 28). Indeed, Lorenz argues that it is possible to predict the winner of an encounter simply by calculating which animal is nearer home.

Clearly we need to exercise some caution in reading into this any lessons about human society. Edney (1972) has shown that ownership of a territory (in this case, private housing) is not necessarily associated with any greater tendency towards defending it. There are in any case obvious dangers in extrapolating from animal territories to human property systems. Lorenz's insight has sometimes been used to develop quite preposterous analogies (a classic example is Ardrey's explanation of the Allied victory over Germany in the Second World War as due to the enhanced energy of the nation under attack). Nevertheless, there are some interesting parallels between Lorenz's sticklebacks, whose energy and commitment are enhanced in their own territory, and evidence about how human beings behave in relation to land or property that they own as opposed to that which belongs to somebody else.

Consider, for example, figures on labour productivity as an indicator of the human energy and commitment released on collective farms as compared with those under family proprietorship. The *Soviet Economic Year Book* for 1973 shows that just 1 per cent of all cultivated land in the Soviet Union was in private ownership at that time, yet this land produced a staggering 27 per cent of the country's total agricultural production (Malmberg, 1980). This tiny fraction of privately cultivated land generated 32 per cent of the country's vegetables, 34 per cent of the milk and meat, 47 per cent of the eggs and 62 per cent of the potatoes! In the 1960s, when the average American farm worker was producing enough food to feed thirteen other people, the average Soviet farm worker was producing enough for only two, and these differences again seem to have something to do with different levels of productivity on private and state-owned holdings (Ardrey, 1967). Indeed, recent reforms in the Soviet Union seem precisely to have been prompted by the recognition that human motivation is ultimately related to private ownership and possession of material resources.

Or, to take a rather different example, consider the growing weight of evidence which suggests that people who own their housing expend much more time and energy in looking after it than those who rent. Alice Coleman (1985) has shown that litter, graffiti, excrement and other such indicators of antisocial behaviour are twice as common in council-owned blocks of flats than in comparable blocks which are owner-occupied. Similarly, John Turner (1976, p. 135) makes the point that virtually all cases of vandalized buildings and estates in Britain and the United States occur with respect to rental housing.

Even more compelling than this is evidence on rates of deterioration of public and private housing. As long ago as 1929–30, a government report commented on 'the improvement in the standard of upkeep of homes' on estates containing higher proportions of owner-occupiers (quoted in Merrett, 1982, p. 11). Since then research has confirmed, not surprisingly, that owner-occupiers spend more money and time on their homes than either landlords or tenants (see, for example, the *English House Condition Survey 1981*, Department of the Environment, 1982, pt 2; also Madge and Brown, 1981; Pahl, 1984; Yates, 1982). The result is that even poor-quality owner-occupied stock goes on for years, while public housing, even when built to high standards, often deteriorates through neglect. Colin Ward has posed the question: 'Why is it that on one side of town the speculative builder's sub-Parker Morris houses are enhanced from the moment they are occupied, while on the other side of town, the high quality council development declines from the time the tenants move in?' He goes on to provide the obvious answer: 'The difference relates to the situation they find themselves in – the fact that some people have a vested interest in the survival of the estate and are in control of their own environment' (1985, p. 18).

So is there a parallel between the triumphant stickleback, defending its territory against a stronger aggressor, and the proud owner-occupier enhancing his or her house while the more expensive council property down the road slowly crumbles? One major difference between the energy of animals released in their home territories and the energy of humans directed at their own property is that human property, including land and housing, is routinely exchanged in market societies. Tiger and Fox recognize this when they write:

> The analogy of property and territory has been taken very far and used to explain a great deal about human behaviour. But most of this analogizing misses the important point: an animal simply *defends* its territory and would never give it up unless forced; humans use property to *exchange* for other property . . . This an animal would never do . . . no animal territory can have the characteristics of human property – that it can be exchanged.
>
> (1972, p. 119, original emphasis)

If there is a property instinct, or a natural disposition to possessive behaviour, then it must be something distinct from territoriality since it is not violated when we keep exchanging the objects we own. This means that analysis of animal behaviour is of limited use when investigating human proprietorship, for animal possessiveness is expressed almost entirely through territorial defence, and these territories are not exchanged. To take the analysis any further, therefore, we must rely on anthropological and psychological evidence relating specifically to human beings.

If there is a possessive instinct then we should expect it to be manifest in different societies across different time periods. It has often been argued, however, that property in the most primitive stage of social evolution was communally owned (to the extent that it existed at all) and that individual possession must therefore be a product of social rather than biological development. Marx's son-in-law, Paul Lafargue, tried to reinforce this claim when he suggested back in the nineteenth century that 'There are savages at present in existence who have no conception of landed property, whether private or collective, and who have barely arrived at a notion of individual ownership of the objects which they personally appropriate' (no date, p. 13). Lafargue may or may not have been correct in his assertion about his 'savages' ' lack of interest in landownership, although Malmberg (1980) suggests that even in primitive societies, ownership of land has normally been vested in families and not in the collectivity. Lafargue's assertion about the virtual absence of personal possessions, however, was almost certainly exaggerated. What he referred to as 'property of personal appropriation' seems to have been pervasive in human societies – a 'culturally universal function of consumption' (Wallendorf and Arnould, 1988). Even highly mobile hunting bands are likely to have developed specific forms of ownership of tools and weapons as well as clothing, ornaments and so on. Indeed, Tiger and Fox speculate that ownership of tools and weapons was the foundation of our modern sense of property.

Further grounds for believing that the drive to possess may be inherent to human beings are provided by evidence of possessive behaviour among young babies. Research has shown that 70 per cent of 6-month-old babies demonstrate a preference for some favourite object (Wallendorf and Arnould), and many infants form attachments to a particular very personal possession during their first two years of life. By the age of 4, most children have a 'strongly developed property sense' which makes them loath to discard any of their own possessions while also displaying a clear concern to accumulate as big a share as possible of other people's (Trasler, 1982, pp. 38–43). Given that children have painstakingly to be taught not to behave in such an aggressively selfish manner, we may safely assume that such possessiveness is a product of genetically based dispositions rather than of cultural learning. Indeed, evolution is likely to have selected for those genes favouring such behaviour. As Dawkins says, 'We must *teach* our children altruism, for we cannot expect it to be part of their biological nature' (1976, p. 150, original emphasis).

In adults too we can identify a disposition to possessiveness, even in those situations where the individuals themselves try to suppress it. On the Israeli kibbutzim people often try to cultivate a little patch of private garden (Malmberg, 1980), and in communes even the most committed members may attempt to retain control over the use of what had previously been their personal property (Bryant, 1978, p. 63). On new housing estates, one of the first actions on taking possession of a house is to mark out the garden boundaries (Hayward, 1975, p. 5), while open-plan developments have proved unpopular and often unworkable as occupiers have agitated to be allowed to erect walls and fences around their properties. It seems that we feel the need for clear demarcation between what is ours and what is not, space that is private and space that is public (see Coleman, 1985, pp. 114–16; Jacobs, 1962, p. 46).

One aspect of this need is the importance of a feeling of security. Like awareness of pain, sensitivity to situations of insecurity has obvious benefits in maximizing evolutionary survival chances, for an individual who is unaware of danger is unlikely to live long enough to pass on its genes. As with pain, we are led to seek relief of distress when sensations of insecurity are awakened in us. Possessions are one way in which we may avoid or alleviate a sense of insecurity.

We shall see in Chapter 5 that the house seems to fulfil a particularly important role in providing for a sense of security. Attachment to the home can, as a result, be very strong. Malmberg gives the example of civilians in the Second World War who stayed in their homes and committed suicide when enemy troops arrived rather than leave the place to which they felt they belonged. Enforced stays away from home can produce both psychological and physical distress; migrants, for example, tend to suffer higher rates of mental illness than natives, and homesickness is common from about the age of 6 or 7. As Rapoport suggests: 'People, like animals, feel more secure and better able to defend themselves on their home ground. This need for security may be one of the reasons why man has to define place, and Anglo-Saxon law, as well as other legal systems, recognizes this by protecting the home from intrusion, even permitting killing in its defence' (1969, pp. 80–1; see also Tuan, 1974).

We may, of course, feel secure in our homes even if we do not own them. There is, however, another feature of possessiveness besides its contribution to a feeling of security, and that is its association with the establishment of privacy and the maintenance of a sense of self and identity. Unlike a sense of security, a sense of identity may well necessitate full legal ownership.

Privacy has been defined by Altman as 'Selective control of access to the self or to one's group' (1975, p. 18). It involves exclusion of others or withdrawal of oneself from the presence of others. When taken to extremes (for example, in the case of the recluse or the hermit) privacy may be judged 'unhealthy' or pathological, for we generally think of ourselves as social animals who need human contact and who owe each other certain limited obligations (but for an alternative view, see Rand, 1964). To say that we also need privacy is not to deny our sociability, however, but is to recognize our need to regulate the claims which others make upon us.

There is some dispute in the literature as to whether mechanisms for ensuring privacy are a universal feature of human societies. Altman and Chemers assert that '*All* cultures have mechanisms that permit their members to regulate privacy' (1980, p. 84, original emphasis), though they emphasize that this is achieved in different ways in different societies. Against this, Madge (1950) points out that the value of personal privacy seems to have developed quite late in human history, and that activities like excretion and sexual intercourse have often been conducted in public. An extreme example of a society apparently lacking mechanisms for ensuring the privacy of its members is that of the Sirino Indians, but closer analysis reveals that even they tend to express dissatisfaction about the lack of opportunities for privacy, and avail themselves of the chance to escape the surveillance of the group whenever it arises. As Barrington Moore concludes, 'Since the Sirino constitute an extreme case, it seems safe to posit at least a desire for privacy as a panhuman trait' (1984, p. 276).

In his book with Chemers, Altman suggests that the universal desire for privacy reflects the vital role it plays in individual and societal functioning: 'The psychological viability or well-being of people and groups centers on the successful management of privacy. That is, success or failure at privacy regulation may well have implications for self-identity, self-esteem and self-worth – or the very well-being or survival capability of people and groups' (1980, p. 81). They go on to suggest that an inability to control one's own boundaries undermines a sense of self-worth and constitutes 'a serious affront to the psychological well-being of a person or group' (p. 130). When rape victims report a feeling of personal degradation, or even when victims of house-breaking say that they feel they have been violated, we begin to glimpse the psychological significance which attaches to our need to maintain personal privacy and to control access by others to our bodily and personal space.

It is at this point that the need for privacy shades into the related concern with establishing and maintaining personal identity. Regimes which have sought to mould individual behaviour so as to render it more manageable and predictable have long recognized that an autonomous sense of self can be destroyed by attacking the right to privacy. In totalitarian societies such as Nazi Germany or the Soviet Union, a state assault on privacy has been the means for dismantling individual identities. As Lenin announced in 1920, 'We recognize nothing private' (quoted in Bryant, 1978, p. 76). Similarly in total institutions such as prisons or mental hospitals, denial of privacy is an essential part of the process of 'mortification of self'. Cut off from an outside world which helped sustain their sense of self, inmates are 'processed' by 'photographing, weighing, fingerprinting, assigning numbers, searching, listing personal possessions for storage, undressing, bathing, disinfecting, haircutting' (Goffman, 1961, pp. 25–6). Personal possessions are confiscated, and the inmate is exposed to 'contamination' from other inmates and staff, whom he or she cannot exclude. Inmates are obliged to sleep together; they defecate in toilets without doors; they are subject to random searches; doors to rooms contain spy-holes; personal mail is opened.

Crucial to the mortification of self is the removal of personal possessions. Admission to total institutions 'entails a dispossession of property, important because persons invest self-feelings in their possessions' (Goffman, 1961, p. 27). In everyday life the self is constructed through interaction with others, but it is externalized in the possession and display of objects. Taken together, our possessions add up to an integrated expression of ourselves. This process seems to be universal in human societies. Wallendorf and Arnould (1988) conducted comparative research on a group of American city dwellers and a sample of peasant villagers in Niger and found that objects sustained people's sense of self in both societies. 'Objects', they say, 'situate an individual's character or personality in a context . . . Although the meaning of self differs cross-culturally and varies in its link with individualism, the fact that these conceptions of self are expressed to some degree through objects seems to be universal' (1988, pp. 3–4).

Possessiveness cannot, therefore, be explained away as some perversion of the human spirit inflicted by modernity or by capitalism, for it is widespread in human societies and is pervasive in human conduct from a very young age. It is true that the drive for possession takes on a specific form in modern capitalism, for, as Campbell (1987) has argued, the characteristic feature of modern consumerism appears to be the instability of wants: 'Rarely can an inhabitant of modern society, no matter how privileged or wealthy, declare that there is nothing that they want. That this should be so is a matter of wonder' (1987, p. 37). This constant search for novelty has only developed since the mid-eighteenth century and is explained by Campbell as the product of growing affluence; for when we are regularly provided with things that we need, the satisfaction of basic needs ceases to be pleasurable. Instead, we derive pleasure from anticipating the consumption of new objects. Campbell sees it as one of the ironic legacies of the Puritan period that it taught us to control our emotions, for this has enabled the fantasizing and daydreaming through which we come to enjoy the anticipation of new possessions: 'The essential activity of consumption is thus not the actual selection, purchase or use of products, but the imaginative pleasure seeking to which the product image lends itself' (1987, p. 89). Measured against these fantasies, however, the use of the object must always appear disappointing. The result is that we immediately begin to desire something else.

Campbell's theory is compelling but it does not undermine the argument that the basic drive to possess is rooted deep within our evolutionary past. He himself argues against instinctivist theory by equating it with Maslow's hierarchy of needs. According to Maslow (1943), human beings have basic needs for air, food, water and relief from pain. When these are satisfied, a need for safety and security arises, and when this has been met, further needs for self-respect, prestige and self-fulfilment appear. Campbell takes issue with this hierarchy on three grounds. First, people sometimes override apparently basic needs (for example, they will sacrifice their lives in pursuit of prestige). Second, human desires change in different social contexts. And third, if these needs were instinctive, people would continue to experience them even when they have been satisfied, yet this is often not the case. Campbell therefore concludes that 'The instinctivist position is quite unsupportable' (1987, p. 45).

The conclusion, however, does not follow. It is quite possible to argue that there is a human instinct disposing us towards possessive behaviour without specifying what it is that people want to possess. Such an instinct is quite likely to have arisen when our primal ancestors were foraging for food, but this does not mean that we are today by nature gluttons. As Trasler (1982) suggests, the possessions which we treasure or desire need have no intrinsic qualities or worth, for their value to us is symbolic.

Trasler himself gives a different reason for rejecting an instinctivist explanation of possession. The sentiments attaching to possession, he says, involve complex cognitive and emotional processes which almost certainly derive from many different instincts – for example, an instinct to seek food, an instinct to assert oneself, a defensive instinct and so on. Once we accept this complexity of causation, however, the power of the explanation is all but lost: 'The notion of an instinct as an inherited disposition to behave in particular ways in certain circumstances, which convincingly describes the complex, apparently unlearned activities of the squirrel or the mason wasp, must necessarily be so diluted and qualified before it can be made to fit human social behaviour that it loses its explanatory value' (1982, p. 35). We are back, in other words, at the problem of employing a concept of open instincts.

As with territoriality, so with possessiveness, we can only conclude by judging a balance of probability, for in the absence of research pinpointing the genes which are generating a given behaviour, we have only indirect evidence to go on. In the case of territoriality, this evidence is far from convincing, but as regards possession, there do seem to be strong grounds for arguing the plausibility of a genetic basis to our behaviour. The peasant farmers tilling their personal plots in the Soviet Union, the 3-year-olds squabbling over the bucket and spade in the sandpit, the home owners spending every weekend improving their houses and the proto-hominids clutching their rudimentary weapons as they roamed across the African plains all speak to the generic quality of human possessiveness. On the balance of the argument and the evidence, it is difficult to accept that there is no natural foundation for such behaviour.

Does this mean that the contemporary desire for home ownership is natural after all? As we shall see below, there is a variety of reasons why people express a preference for owning their home. Many of these reflect conscious calculation of the relative financial and other benefits and costs associated with the different tenures and seem to have very little to do with any genetically based dispositions. Yet in many cases there is something else going on as well. Some people at least evidently *feel* differently about living in a house of their own as opposed to one owned by somebody or something else. The analysis of these 'feelings' must wait until Chapter 5. For now, we may draw the general conclusion from the evidence already discussed that a widespread desire for owner-occupation is likely to be fuelled by certain natural dispositions as well as by economic and cultural factors. To deny the existence of such dispositions by insisting that they are ideological fictions in the minds of politicians and building-society managers is to fail to understand one of the forces behind the spread of home ownership in recent decades.

The advantages of owning

Two principal motives are mentioned time and again when people are asked why they prefer to own rather than rent their homes. One is financial – buying is seen as cheaper in the long run, or rent is seen as a waste of money, or rising house prices are seen as a means of saving for the future or accumulating capital. The other has to do with the sense of independence and autonomy which ownership confers – the freedom from control and surveillance by a landlord and the ability to personalize the property according to one's tastes. Most studies indicate that, while both factors are important, the first probably outweighs the second in most people's thinking.

In their longitudinal study of newly married couples, Madge and Brown asked respondents to name the principal benefit of owner-occupation. Twenty-four per cent mentioned its asset value or investment potential. Taking all their answers together, they found that 43 per cent of couples saw the major benefits of owner-occupation as financial, while 17 per cent saw them in terms of values such as independence, freedom of action, privacy and choice. They concluded, 'The most spontaneous and overt reasons related primarily to finance and secondly to the aspects of independence and security associated with ownership' (1981, p. 76).

Other research generally concurs with this, although a desire for independence has often figured more prominently. Research on inner-area home owners in Birmingham, for example, found that while economic factors were certainly important, so too was the desire for autonomy: 'When we asked for their reasons for buying, we found the owners relishing their freedom' (Karn, Kemeny and Williams, 1985, p. 56). This work showed that 23 per cent bought as an investment, while 22 per cent simply wanted to own their own house. Fifteen per cent said it was cheaper to buy than to rent, and 14 per cent gave reasons of freedom, privacy, security, or independence. Significantly, 11 per cent claimed that they had no option but to buy – a claim which we shall consider in some detail later in this chapter.

Much the same findings are recorded in the 1977 NEDO national study. Here, saving or investment was the main reason given in 26 per cent of cases, and it was closely followed by non-financial factors such as the desire for independence (23 per cent), the freedom to decorate (22 per cent), a feeling of security (17 per cent), the freedom to choose where to live (10 per cent) and the desire simply to live in a place of one's own (10 per cent) (see Jones, 1982). In Glasgow, owner-occupation is favoured because it is seen as cheaper than renting, but advantages of 'choice, mobility, freedom and autonomy' are also emphasized (Madigan, 1988, p. 38). Similar results have also been recorded in other countries (for example, by Halle, 1984, in his study of working-class home owners in New Jersey).

In the three towns survey we asked all those who had ever owned a house why they had decided to move into owner-occupation in the first place, and all those who had ever rented from the council were similarly asked why they had first moved into local authority renting. We also asked owner-occupiers and council tenants to name the main advantages and disadvantages of their present tenure. All of these questions were 'open-ended'. Respondents, that is, were encouraged to provide their own replies rather than choosing from a list offered by the interviewer. The replies they gave are summarized for each of the three towns in Tables 2.3, 2.4 and 2.5.

Table 2.3   *Reasons for first house purchase*

| | Town | | | | | | | |
| | Burnley | | Derby | | Slough | | Total | |
Reason for buying	No.	%	No.	%	No.	%	No.	%
Get something for your money	31	27	39	32	34	27	104	29
Investment	31	27	16	13	26	21	73	20
Desire to own	17	15	25	21	21	17	63	18
No choice	15	13	14	12	34	27	63	18
Automatic, parents own, etc.	16	14	11	9	11	9	38	11
Could afford it so bought	4	4	12	10	14	11	30	8
Security	6	5	12	10	9	7	27	8
Autonomy, independence	7	4	7	6	11	9	25	7
Other reasons	29	26	36	30	45	36	110	31

Total number of respondents = 359 (Burnley 113, Derby 121, Slough 125)

Table 2.3 clearly demonstrates that the initial decision to buy is strongly motivated by financial considerations. Effectively there appear to be three principal reasons why people choose to move into owner-occupation in the first place, and two of them – the desire to get something back for the money they lay out each month and the expectation of building up a capital investment – are entirely motivated by economic calculation. The third is the vague but deeply felt sentiment that they simply want to own their own house:

When somebody owns his house, it gives a nice feeling – it's my own property – doing the decorating and the gardening . . . I'm a family man. It's a nice way of living for the children.

(Male semi-skilled manual worker, Slough)

Owning is a big incentive. It's your own. It's up to you to make something of it . . . A general pleasure.

(Male retired skilled non-manual worker, Slough)

We shall consider the economics of owner-occupation in detail in the next chapter. Here we may simply note that many purchasers clearly consider house buying as an investment, and that their decision to buy must therefore reflect to some extent the financial inducements set before them by governments. The data presented in Table 2.3 would support Jones's contention that 'A change in the structure of housing subsidies could be expected to alter significantly the demand for home ownership' (1982, p. 127). This is something to which we shall return in the discussion of tax relief and other housing subsidies in Chapter 6.

There are three further points to note about Table 2.3. First, relatively high numbers of people see house purchase as an 'automatic' decision, something they did not even think about. Indeed, if we include those who say that they bought because they could afford to (which is itself an implicit appeal to the idea that purchase is an 'obvious' decision to make) then 19 per cent of the total sample can be said to have selected owner-occupation almost unthinkingly. These people tend to come from owner-occupier families, or their friends and work colleagues are mainly home owners. This is significant for it indicates the importance of 'comparative reference groups' in shaping housing decisions. People will tend to aspire to what they see around them and to go after what they grow up to think of as normal (Couper and Brindley, 1975, p. 567; Littlewood, 1986, p. 99). It follows from this that as owner-occupation spreads, so the proportion of people seeking to buy because they cannot think of themselves doing otherwise is likely to rise.

Second, we should again note the relatively high numbers of people (18 per cent of the total) who say that they first purchased because they had no other choice. The assumption here has to be that these households could not find private rental accommodation and were denied access to the public sector, although 'lack of choice' is, of course, always relative. What these respondents presumably meant was that they could not find the sort of housing they wanted at a price they could afford within the rental sectors. We shall consider this further later in this chapter.

Third, we should note the virtual absence of some of those motives which have often been considered important by observers. Although the 'others' category in Table 2.3 is large, it is remarkably diverse and includes no single reason cited by more than 3 per cent of the sample. In 1979, for example, Margaret Thatcher claimed that the sale of council houses 'will give to more of our people that freedom and mobility and that prospect of handing something on to their children and grandchildren which owner occupation provides' (quoted in Forrest and Murie, 1984, p. 5), yet only 5 out of 359 owner-occupiers we spoke to mentioned greater ease of mobility as a reason for buying, and only 5 mentioned the desire to build up a bequest for their children. The motives for buying are much more straightforward than has often been supposed.

When we turn to consider what owners feel are the advantages of having bought their homes (Table 2.4), then many more factors come into play, and the emphasis on the value of independence and autonomy rises sharply:

You can do what you like with it. It's worth decorating – I'm going to

Table 2.4 *Perceived advantages and disadvantages of owner-occupation*

	Burnley		Derby		Slough		Total	
	No.	%	No.	%	No.	%	No.	%
Perceived advantages								
Can do what you like	41	39	47	39	50	39	138	39
An appreciating asset	42	39	38	31	55	43	135	38
Get something for your money	14	13	16	13	25	19	55	15
Security of tenure	19	18	9	7	17	13	45	13
Pride of ownership	15	14	14	12	14	11	43	12
Legacy for the children	10	9	17	14	14	11	41	12
Choice of location	8	8	11	9	14	11	33	9
No advantages	3	3	9	7	9	7	21	6
Others	15	14	21	17	18	14	54	15
Don't know	2	2	2	2	1	1	5	1
Perceived disadvantages								
Responsible for own repairs	49	47	45	38	56	46	150	43
No disadvantages	27	26	39	33	33	27	99	29
Costs more than renting	7	7	11	9	26	21	44	13
Have to pay rates	8	8	18	15	4	3	30	9
Money is tied up	1	1	7	6	5	4	13	4
Others	9	9	11	9	14	11	34	10
Don't know	6	6	4	3	2	2	12	4

Total number of respondents = 358 (advantages) and 347 (disadvantages)

knock that wall out. It's a feeling of freedom to do what you like in it and have who you want in it.

(Male, intermediate occupation, Slough)

You can do what you want with it. And it gives you that bit of security. I've never rented ever since I've been married. I'd feel very uncomfortable in a rented house . . . It gives you pride in yourself. You're not reliant on other people. If I was in a council house I'd feel other people were paying for me. Completely independent, that's me!

(Female skilled non-manual worker, Derby)

People often spoke too of their 'pride of ownership':

We can say, 'This is ours.' It's what we've achieved.

(Male intermediate occupation, Derby)

We often sit down and say, 'Just think, ten years ago we were in a council house and now we've got a £50,000 bungalow which we own.' It's an achievement. There's a sense of achievement when we sit down and think what we've got. We both worked hard for this and now we can sit down and we're comfortable. All our hard work has come to fruition. I feel proud of what we've done.

(Female intermediate occupation, Derby)

Owning a house gave many people a feeling of security, both financial and emotional, and this was often associated with the desire to pass some material benefits on to one's children in order to ensure their security too:

It's a sense of security. And if you've got children you've got something to leave them.
(Female skilled manual worker, Derby)

It's yours and you can please yourself what you do with it. Lots of people in Burnley don't believe in it, but I think you feel more secure when it's yours.
(Female skilled manual worker, Burnley)

We would still like to have bought this house, old as we are. We all like to say, 'This stone is mine', that sort of thing. We've done so much to it – it would be nice to think the grandchildren could inherit it.
(Male retired semi-skilled manual worker in council accommodation, Slough)

It seems, then, that housing finance weighs heavily on people's minds when deciding whether to move into owner-occupation, but that other concerns come to the fore once the decision has been made. This is not, perhaps, surprising, for when people have been in home ownership for a while the concern with the economic costs they are incurring and the gains they may be making will become less immediate. Put another way, in the daily round of living in a house, as opposed to the special occasion of moving into or out of it, it is the 'use value' rather than the 'exchange value' which is likely to be of greatest concern. It is for this reason that factors like the ability to do what you want with the place and the choice over where you will live figure so much more prominently in Table 2.4 than in Table 2.3. These, of course, are the sort of advantage we would expect people to mention if the preference for home ownership does have any basis in the genetic disposition to possession.

As regards the disadvantages of owner-occupation, most respondents seemed to have trouble thinking of one. The high numbers replying in terms of responsibility for repairs should not be taken to indicate a major perceived problem in the owner-occupied sector, for many of those who gave this answer did so because they could think of nothing else, and some even added that they would in any case rather be responsible for their own repairs than be dependent upon a landlord. The one group of owners for whom repairs could be a real problem is the elderly, but we shall delay consideration of this until Chapter 3.

The cost of buying is also mentioned by a few people as a disadvantage of home ownership, but it is not seen as a major problem. Not surprisingly, however, it is mentioned by many more people in Slough than in the other two towns; for, as we saw in Chapter 1, property prices in Slough at the time of the survey were much higher than in Derby or Burnley.

The mention of rates (that is, the local property taxes which were imposed on households before the introduction of the Community Charge) is in some ways misleading, since tenants also paid rates indirectly as an element of their rent. If home owners paid more rates, it was because they often lived in more valuable or desirable housing. The disproportionate numbers of Derby home owners who cited rates as a disadvantage of owning reflect both the relatively high rate levels set by the Labour-controlled council in that city, and the fact that low property prices made the rates issue more visible in Derby since rates represented a higher proportion of most households' total housing costs there than in many other towns.

Table 2.5 *Perceived advantages and disadvantages of council house renting*

	Burnley No.	Burnley %	Derby No.	Derby %	Slough No.	Slough %	Total No.	Total %
Perceived advantages								
No advantages	16	36	17	36	21	57	54	42
Get repairs done	15	34	13	28	9	26	37	29
Cheaper than buying	4	9	5	11	5	14	15	12
Others	10	22	11	24	5	14	26	21
Don't know	3	7	2	4	2	6	7	6
Perceived disadvantages								
Lack of personal control	6	15	13	29	8	26	27	24
Money down the drain	5	12	6	13	14	45	25	21
No disadvantages	10	24	13	29	1	3	24	20
Repairs don't get done	6	15	7	16	6	19	19	17
More expensive than buying	6	15	2	4	4	13	12	10
Others	13	32	10	22	9	29	32	27
Don't know	2	5	3	7	2	7	7	6

Total number of respondents = 125 (advantages), 118 (disadvantages)

The main point to note about Table 2.4, however, is the high number of home owners (29 per cent) who can think of no disadvantage attached to owning a house, and the low number (6 per cent) who deny that there are any advantages. The true significance of these figures can only be appreciated when compared with the responses of council tenants to comparable questions (Table 2.5). While 20 per cent of tenants can think of no disadvantages in renting, a massive 42 per cent say that there are no advantages. Indeed, by far the most common response to our question about the advantages of council renting was a simple denial that there were any.

The main reason why people become council tenants is a simple lack of alternatives – 62 per cent of the tenants in our sample said that they had first entered the tenure because they had no effective choice:

It was beyond my thinking to buy. I came from the north. Just to get a council house was something worthwhile. With hindsight I would have bought my house.

(Male retired semi-skilled manual worker, council tenant, Slough)

We put us name down. No way we could afford to buy. No such thing as a 100 per cent mortgage in them days. We were on the waiting list for two years.

(Female skilled manual worker, council tenant, Burnley)

Many council tenants are in this sense reluctant consumers, for we have already seen that three in every four would prefer to be buying their home. It is not, therefore, surprising that over four in ten of them can think of nothing positive to say about their situation.

There is, of course, nothing new or startling in a finding which tells us that levels of satisfaction are higher among owners than among council tenants. Madge and Brown found in their study that 92 per cent of owners were very or fairly satisfied with their housing situation compared with just 61 per cent of council tenants, and that 20 per cent of tenants were dissatisfied compared with only 1 per cent of owners. A National Consumer Council survey similarly found dissatisfaction among 19 per cent of council tenants (compared with 5 per cent of owner-occupiers), while the 1978 *General Household Survey* reported similar figures of 16 per cent and 5 per cent respectively (see Henney, 1985, pp. 15–16).

What is more important than overall levels of dissatisfaction, however, is analysis of the reasons for them. The 1977 NEDO survey suggested three main causes – the lack of freedom to decorate (mentioned by 14 per cent of tenants), lack of choice in housing (15 per cent) and the indefinite payment of rent with no prospect of final ownership (20 per cent). Other commentators and researchers have added to this list. Dissatisfaction with repairs is frequently mentioned – the National Consumer Council survey, for example, found 43 per cent of tenants complaining about delays and 34 per cent bemoaning the quality of the work (see Henney, 1985, p. 15). Ginsburg (1983, p. 49) identifies housing design and problems in exchanging dwellings as sources of discontent, while Madigan (1988, p. 38) tells us that her informants in Glasgow focused mainly on neighbourhood quality and high-handed management. In addition to all this, most observers also emphasize the lack of control allowed to tenants as a major source of grievance. Although the provisions of the 1980 Housing Act with its introduction of a 'tenants' charter' increased the rights of tenants, this lack of control over the dwelling is still a familiar complaint. In their Plymouth study, Hyde and Deacon (1986) found that 54 per cent of tenants felt that they were treated as 'second-class citizens' by their local authority landlords. As Colin Ward suggests, 'The whole tragedy of publicly provided non-profit housing for rent and the evolution of this form of tenure in Britain is that the local authorities have simply taken over, though less flexibly, the role of

90

the landlord, together with the syndrome of dependency and resentment that it engenders' (1983, p. 184).

Table 2.5 enables us to evaluate these various claims about the sources of tenant dissatisfaction. Poor neighbourhoods and problems of housing design were not major sources of complaint – 3 per cent of tenants identified poor neighbourhoods as a drawback with council renting, 2 per cent mentioned the original quality or design of the housing, and 2 per cent spoke of the low status of council tenancy. It should be remembered that this sample was drawn entirely from tenants of whole houses and that the pattern of grievances may well have looked rather different had we included those living in high-rise or deck access blocks.

For these tenants of whole houses, the problems lay not so much in the bricks and mortar as in the social organization of the tenure. A major concern for many was the continuing lack of control they had over their homes. This sometimes took the form of their vulnerability to unresponsive allocation policies, and a number of tenants remarked on the difficulty in getting a house where they wanted it:

> I'd love to move from this house! I don't like Slough . . . One day I'd like the choice of where I live rather than have someone tell me . . . Someone who owns their house can move when they want to. In a council house you're stuck there.
> (Female council tenant, semi-skilled manual worker, Slough)

> After we moved here we found this area was very rough. You never know when you'll get a brick through the window or a break-in . . . I don't think the council wants to give us another house, but we're not staying here . . . You can never get what you want. If we had the money we'd buy a property.
> (Male unskilled manual worker, council tenant, Slough Asian)

> You took what you were given . . . It's not the sort of home you'd buy if you had the money and went around looking. We were on the waiting list for seven years with four of us sleeping in one room . . . You wouldn't dare refuse what you were offered because you'd go to the bottom of the list.
> (Semi-skilled manual worker couple, now buying their Slough council house)

Sometimes the lack of autonomy was felt more in respect of restrictions on their desire to decorate or modify their homes:

> We wanted to combine the bathroom and the outside toilet but they wouldn't agree. We wanted to rip a fireplace out and they wouldn't agree. We ripped a hedge out to make a driveway without asking because it's a waste of time – the answer's always 'no'.
> (Male unskilled manual worker, council tenant, Derby)

I do believe in asking permission. I wanted to put a patio door in but they wouldn't let us so we're not bothering now. But it would have been nice to have had patio doors out onto the patio.

(Male skilled manual worker, council tenant, Derby)

We don't ask! We did ask once and got turned down. Someone said, 'Don't bother asking, they never check.' So we do it anyway.

(Housewife married to unskilled manual worker, Slough)

A second area of grievance was that council renting was seen as a waste of money. Rent was 'money wasted':

You're paying out every week and don't own a brick. A few years ago they were offering these houses for £3,000. We should have bought. We were stupid. We went on holidays abroad instead.

(Male council tenant, unskilled manual worker, Slough)

There are no advantages in renting. You pay more in this day and age. The rent was 32s a week when I came here. Now it's £28 a week. It's a vast difference. Owning your own house you'd be paying a lot less. That was my grave mistake – not buying years ago when it was £3,000.

(Male council tenant, semi-skilled manual worker, Slough)

It's not your own. We've lived here thirty years and we've been paying all that rent and now you've got nothing . . . There's nothing at the end of the rainbow.

(Housewife married to unskilled manual worker, council tenant, Slough)

Money was also 'wasted' in decorating and modernizing the home, for it was understood that such improvements were being done on someone else's property. Tenants thus faced the dilemma of whether or not to spend money to make their homes more comfortable:

We've done all the repairs to this house – the council's been here once in thirty years. We might as well have bought. My husband's built a garage and put central heating in and it all goes back to the council.

(Female retired skilled manual worker, Slough)

For me to start spending money, I'd have to leave everything I've done. The kitchen needs modernizing but I'd have to leave it for someone else if I did it.

(Female skilled manual worker, Burnley)

The main disadvantage is if you want to do anything structural like an extension. We wouldn't put money into a council house that wasn't our own. We'd like a patio, but we wouldn't spend money on a council house.

(Female unskilled manual worker, Slough)

A third type of complaint concerned the repairs service, which was the one item where tenants could see what they were getting for their money. Although only 17 per cent of tenants specifically cited repairs as one of the disadvantages of renting, direct questions on this issue revealed widespread dissatisfaction. A staggering 65 per cent of all tenants said that their council was unresponsive as a landlord. The complaints, which concerned both the standard of repair work and the tardiness of councils in responding to problems, came thick and fast:

> The front door jams tight – we can't use it. The council never want to do repairs. You have to keep on at them. As we are now, I can't repair it and they won't do it. The window's leaking like hell but it's no good asking the council, they won't do it . . . You have to beg and pray for them to do things. We have to put up with rough bodge-up jobs.
>
> (Male unskilled manual worker, Slough)

> It's shocking! They're robbing the ratepayer. Six or seven times they came to look at the guttering and all they did was put putty round the joints . . . It's worse now than it was before. I'm fed up. I just won't ask them ever again. In the booklet it says you should tell them if things need doing but I'm fed up with it.
>
> (Male retired semi-skilled manual worker, Slough)

> We do [repairs]. I'll tell you why. Because you'd wait for ever for the council to do it . . . We tried to get a new fence and I was told we'd be lucky to get one – we're at the end of a queue of 500 people! The girls in the office are rude to you.
>
> (Female retired skilled manual worker, Slough)

> It's damp. All the carpets go mouldy. The kid's bedroom is a right mess. The council say it's condensation and they won't do it. They say it's our fault. They say we should keep the heating on, but all we've got is a fire in one room. The health people wrote to the council – the baby had woodlice crawling all over him – and they still took no notice. The council said woodlice won't hurt you.
>
> (Housewife married to unskilled manual worker, Derby)

> When we first moved in we decorated and then they rewired and wrecked it all. They left the skirting boards hanging off. The plastering is pretty awful. They left a hell of a mess. They put sockets where we expressly told them not to.
>
> (Female skilled non-manual worker, Derby)

> Sometimes we've had to wait. We had to wait a while for the sink. They said there was twenty houses that required new sinks but we'd have to wait till they got twenty names so they could all be done together.

93

Sometimes you do get the feeling things could be done quicker, like.
(Male semi-skilled manual worker, Derby)

Two years ago they came to paint the outside. They filled some great big cracks down the back wall. A fortnight later the cracks were there again. They were supposed to put in new windows. I could put my fingernail through the wood. They eventually did it, but they patched up my back window rather than replacing it. I reported me troughings went wrong. I reported it three times. Finally they came and cleaned them out but they were still no better. Eventually three months after that they came and put new ones in. Next door's been trying to get hers done for six years.
(Housewife married to skilled manual worker, Burnley)

It is undoubtedly true that some of these complaints (and there are many others like them) are unjustified, and the councils concerned may well have legitimate explanations for many of the rest. It is also certainly the case that some of this dissatisfaction can be explained as a response to a decline in the quality of the public housing service as a result of government expenditure cuts and limits on local government budgets imposed during the Thatcher years. But when all that has been said, the overwhelming impression remains that the basic problem is a crippling and frustrating sense of powerlessness felt by many tenants. Many of those to whom we spoke felt unable to do anything when the clerks in the office ignored them or when the workers who came to their homes did a bodged job, and it was this inability to control factors affecting their own domestic environment which drove so many of them to anger, fatalism, or despair.

It is interesting that although rents have risen steeply in recent years, most of our respondents did not focus on this as the main source of their unhappiness. Rather, they complained at the inability to influence decisions about where they live, what kind of house they live in, the deterioration of their accommodation and so on. It would, of course, be possible to find owner-occupiers who have been treated shabbily by builders or who have been unable to get the right house in the right neighbourhood. The difference, however, is that home owners can normally *do* something if they are dissatisfied with some aspect of their housing. Most of the council tenants we spoke with, by contrast, felt that they could do little more than 'beg and pray' their landlords to do something for them. The complaints listed above are complaints born of the frustration of dependency.

It is probably the case that public-sector renting has always been like this. Indeed, things have possibly improved since the introduction of the tenants' charter in 1980. Tenant dissatisfaction, however, is almost certainly higher than it has ever been. The reason for this is simple. As increasing numbers of households have moved into owner-occupation, so popular aspirations and expectations have been rising.

Before the Second World War, a Mass Observation survey found that 80 per cent of people living on council housing estates expressed satisfaction with their housing situation (Burnett, 1986, p. 237). As some of our older respondents told us, they were glad to get offered council accommodation. The comparison then was with private-sector renting (the same survey found that only 62 per cent of private-sector tenants were satisfied). The comparison today, however, is with home ownership. Tenants now compare their situation with other people who have bought their homes rather than with those who rent old houses from private landlords. Very often the people next door have bought their council house, personalized it inside and out and accumulated considerable capital sums in the process. One reason why so many council tenants are unhappy with their housing is therefore that they are no longer grateful simply to escape from poor-quality private rented housing, but are instead increasingly resentful at being trapped within the paternalistic embrace of the local authority. Comparative reference groups have changed over the last fifty years, and willingness to accept council renting has changed with them.

The inherent advantages of private ownership

We normally think of property as defining our relationship to things – *my* car, *your* house, *his* company and so on. It is, however, more fruitful if we think of property as defining sets of relationships between people. To claim that this is my car, for example, is to assert that I have a right to use it (and, of course, an obligation to tax and insure it) which is denied to you. Similarly, if he owns the company, then it follows that he can make certain kinds of decision about the use of company resources which I have no right to be involved in unless invited. Property, therefore, is one aspect of the organization of social relations between people. Encoded and enforced through law, it specifies rights and duties governing the behaviour of those with title and those without. These rights and duties enable and constrain our actions. Put another way, property relations are relations of power between people: 'The possession of exclusive rights to something that is scarce and valuable necessarily implies the possession of power over others who also desire the scarce and valuable things' (Davis, 1948, p. 454).

The relationship between council tenants, who do not own their homes, and their local authority landlords, who do, is one such relationship of power and domination. Sometimes local housing departments use their power benignly, sometimes they do not, but always they are the dominant partners. Colin Ward has provided an inventory of some of the 'well meant but insufferably inquisitive and inquisitorial' regulations imposed by housing authorities on their tenants:

No washing on the line after 12 noon (Essex), compulsory to burn coke (Notts.), no dogs (Middlesex), evicted for painting his house cream – all the rest were red (Warrington), forbidden to paint doorstep (Bardwell), evicted for keeping pigeons if tenant is not a member of National Homing

Union (Staffs.), tenants graded according to cleanliness – lowest grade must go (Ely), no trees to be planted in garden without permission (Lancs.).

(1983, p. 40)

It may be thought that such examples belong to the past and that things now are different. Yet in 1987 the Housing Director of the London Borough of Brent sent a letter to all tenants threatening them with eviction without the option of rehousing if they were shown to have made racist, sexist, anti-gay, or anti-lesbian remarks to their neighbours (*London Standard*, 27 August 1987). To be a non-owner is to be subordinate, is to be vulnerable to whatever whims happen to motivate the politicians and managers who determine how you shall live. Owner-occupiers who are insulting towards their black or homosexual neighbours may be ostracized or punched on the nose or arrested for behaviour likely to cause a breach of the peace, but they will not be threatened with eviction from their home.

Those who seek to defend the public sector often argue that relations of dependency are not inherent to state rental systems. They also often go on to suggest that the advantages of owning and disadvantages of renting outlined in the previous section are not inherent to these tenures either. In their view, owner-occupation could be made to seem a lot less attractive, while council renting could become highly appealing.

Michael Ball, for example, sees the principal features of each of the two major tenures as 'products of long historical struggles' (1985, p. 24) which are not yet over and which may still reshape them in the future. 'There is', he adds, 'nothing inherently superior in either owning or renting despite frequent protestations to the contrary' (1986, p. 52). Chris Hamnett agrees: 'It cannot be too strongly stressed that whilst these inter-tenurial differences are very real they are socially constructed and, as such, are neither inevitable nor immutable' (1984a, p. 398). And Doling, Karn and Stafford make much the same point when they suggest that the association between renting and insecurity is 'spurious' because 'Insecurity is not inherent in the nature of the sectors themselves' (1986, p. 56).

What these writers are basically suggesting is that ownership need have nothing to do with control. In their view, it is quite possible for a local authority to own houses while those who live in them enjoy all the benefits and advantages we usually associate with owner-occupation. Their arguments are important because they enable the opponents of mass home ownership to suggest that owner-occupation is not inherently attractive. Thus, Oriel Sullivan (1987, p. 33) explains away the survey evidence indicating a widespread desire to own by arguing that what people really want are the advantages which have come to be associated with home ownership but which are not an essential feature of that tenure. According to Gray (1982, p. 244), for example, people think of owner-occupied housing as being of a higher quality. It follows from this that expression of a desire to own is 'in reality' an indication of a desire for better-quality accommodation irrespective of tenure. Similarly, Shlay (1985, 1986) argues in a North American context that aspirations for home ownership can be explained almost entirely in terms of the search for better-quality housing and neighbourhoods.

The most serious attempt to consider whether owner-occupation has any intrinsic merits over council renting can be found in an article by Christine Whitehead (1979). She argues that many of the advantages which people see in home ownership are 'independent' of the tenure *per se*. What she means is that such advantages derive from the social and economic situation of the owners themselves rather than from their mode of consuming housing. Choice, for example, is only possible for those owner-occupiers who can afford to exercise it, and tenants could in any case be offered more choice by relaxing eligibility criteria, improving information on housing availability and introducing greater flexibility into payment systems. Similarly, Whitehead believes that capital growth on housing investment is more readily achieved by those in more expensive properties and that poor home owners may not gain at all (we consider the evidence on this issue in Chapter 3). While recognizing that tenants could not easily be allowed to share in the rising equity value of their homes, she goes on to ague that they could be helped and encouraged to invest in the gilt and share markets instead (something which has, of course, begun to happen as a result of the privatization policies adopted since this article was written).

Whitehead does, however, accept that not all of the benefits associated with owner-occupation are 'independent' of tenure, and that there are some advantages which could not easily be extended to tenants. There are, she recognizes, some advantages of owning which follow directly from rights established through title to property. Her list includes: the right to indefinite use; the right to give away or bequeath; the right to modify; the ability to choose an appropriate price and method of payment; security of tenure; the right to do what one wills with the property; and the advantage of investing in something one controls. However, having recognized these intrinsic rights, she still insists that many poorer home owners do not enjoy them and that much could be done to extend at least some of them to council tenants. Tenants could, for example, be given greater security of tenure, a right to bequeath and a right to repair (some of these rights have subsequently been granted as a result of the 1980 legislation). She concludes: 'There are undoubtedly advantages to being an owner occupier, but there are a lot more to being a relatively rich owner occupier' (1979, p. 41).

Whitehead's paper is both helpful and misleading. It is helpful because it recognizes that some of the advantages of owner-occupation *are* inherent to it, and that these reflect the exclusive rights which derive from title to private property. It is, however, misleading for two reasons. First, Whitehead still insists that what she calls the 'intrinsic' benefits of ownership are not necessarily enjoyed by all owners. Second, she indulges the wishful thinking of the supporters of state housing in suggesting that the intrinsic benefits of ownership can in principle be extended to tenants. Neither argument can be accepted, as we shall see.

The first argument is wrong because, if benefits are intrinsic to ownership, then they must by definition be enjoyed by all owners – that is what it means to say they are intrinsic! This is no mere semantic quibble, for the rights of property ownership *are* enjoyed equally by all owners, and it is to these rights that Whitehead refers when she specifies the intrinsic benefits of owning a house.

There is much confusion in the literature over this issue. Dickens and his colleagues, for example, point out that 'A badly maintained owner occupied house in a depressed area with little demand for house purchase may be impossible to dispose of', and for this reason they conclude that rights of property, such as the right of disposal, 'may be unobtainable in practice' (Dickens *et al.*, 1985, p. 198). The argument is, however, fallacious. The owner of a house may dispose of it by giving it away (for example, through a bequest) or by selling it for whatever price it can command on the market. A tenant enjoys neither option. To say that some owners cannot dispose of their houses is neither true (for even in the most depressed market a buyer can always be found, provided the price is low enough) nor relevant (for the right to dispose is unaffected by the question of whether the owner deems it beneficial to exercise it in any given context).

It is essential to understand that owner-occupation and council renting are defined by the different legal rights attached to them. All owners enjoy the same rights, since the law of property is indifferent to both the identity of the owner and the character of the object (see Renner, 1949, p. 90). Because owners enjoy a different set of rights from those enjoyed by tenants, it follows that people may well aspire to one tenure rather than the other simply because they want rights, such as the right of disposal, which are guaranteed by one but not by the other. As Maclennan puts it,

> The concept of tenure essentially relates to the legal arrangements existing between properties and their owners and inhabitants. Thus tenure differences are essentially variations in the property rights and obligations of property owners and inhabitants. That is, tenure may influence the ways in which households acquire, use, alter and then ultimately dispose of housing. Tenure *per se* can therefore influence housing satisfactions.
>
> (1982, p. 183)

Given that tenurial rights are established through law, it is obviously the case that they may vary over time. Council tenants, for example, today enjoy rights of repair, exchange and purchase which they did not enjoy prior to legislation passed by Parliament in 1980 (Kemp, 1987, p. 4). Similarly, rights of ownership have changed through, for example, the introduction of a system of planning controls in 1947 which limits what owner-occupiers can do with their homes and which even allows the state to expropriate them by means of Compulsory Purchase Orders. Nevertheless, there are certain broad rights which may be deemed essential to ownership in the sense that they are normally recognized as a necessary component of any claim to title. Minimally these may be identified as the right to exclusive use and benefit for as long as title is held, the right to control and the right to dispose (see, for example, Reeve, 1986, p. 19; Rose *et al.*, 1976, p. 703).

Two points should be noted about these essential rights of property ownership. The first is that rights of property are never absolute. The same law which grants rights to property holders also limits them. As Giddens (1984) has shown, systems of rules simultaneously enable and constrain action. The same case or statute which establishes the right to keep people out of one's home also establishes the right of various police officers, meter readers and sundry inspectors to enter it. Recognition of the right to sell the house as one chooses is at the same time prohibition of the right not to sell it to someone on the grounds of their race.

According to Reeve, 'It is most difficult to imagine a system of law which places no restrictions *whatever* on rights of use' (1986, p. 18, original emphasis). Nevertheless, it seems clear that restrictions on the rights of property holders have multiplied as the years have passed. As Benn and Peters observe, 'Locke would have been highly indignant had he ever been presented with a CPO' (1959, p. 155). When considering the advantages of owning a house, therefore, it is important to remember that owners are constrained, though not to the same extent as tenants. The key point when comparing the two tenures is that the state generally proscribes but does not prescribe what owners may do (see Dunham, 1972, p. 281; Reeve, 1986, pp. 19–20). You may not be allowed to build an extension in the back garden, but nobody will tell you what you must do with the land. You may be prosecuted if you announce that you are only willing to sell your house to someone of your own race, but nobody will tell you to whom you must sell.

The second point is that rights of property are divisible. In other words, the rights of use, control and disposal are not always vested in the same person and may be shared among different people. This means that property rights are generally ranged on a continuum. In the case of housing, for example, tenants enjoy considerable rights of use which they share in common with owner-occupiers, although their rights of control and disposal are much attenuated. As Merrett puts it, 'The situation of owner occupier and tenant are entirely different from that of the little pig who had all the roast beef and the little pig who had none, for in the case of housing tenure *both* parties possess a dwelling' (1982, p. 70, original emphasis).

Pulling all these points together, we may suggest that one reason for the attraction of home ownership is that it offers *inherent* rights of use, control and disposal which many people seem to want. These rights are not unlimited, and some of them may also be enjoyed to some extent by tenants. Such rights could, of course, be taken away by legislation; but, as we shall see in Chapter 6, this would be tantamount to abolishing private property ownership itself. It is not therefore true to say, as Ball, Hamnett and others do, that owner-occupation has no inherent advantages, or that all of its current advantages could be removed while still leaving the tenure intact, for many of its key advantages are synonymous with its legal status as private property.

What, then, of Christine Whitehead's second argument that the intrinsic benefits of ownership could be extended to tenants in various ways? This is obviously true up to a point, for as we have seen, some of the rights enjoyed by home owners are already shared with council tenants, and the latter have been granted greater autonomy as a result of the 1980 Housing Act. However, it is obvious from what has been said already that the rights of non-owners can never come to balance those of owners, and Robinson (1983, p. 91) is surely right when he argues that all the evidence suggests that the public-sector tenure system cannot be reformed so as to empower its tenants.

There is an understandable reluctance to accept this on the part of supporters of state housing. Kemeny (1981), for example, asserts that there is no inherent reason why collectivized housing should not involve the same security of tenure, freedom of mobility and household autonomy as is found in the owner-occupied sector. Similarly the Shelter Community Action Team (1980) proclaim that council tenants could immediately be granted full security of tenure, the freedom to carry out alterations and improvements, control over internal and external decoration, freedom to carry out minor repairs and more responsibility for their homes through abolishing petty rules and restrictions. There is no doubt that such reforms would be popular with tenants. The problem is that they could not be carried through to the point where tenants are endowed with equivalent rights to those enjoyed by owners. Short of transferring the full title to the house from the local authority to the tenant, attempts to extend tenant powers will always rub up against the legitimate concerns of the council as the owner of the property.

Take, for example, the right of disposal. We saw earlier that 12 per cent of owners in the three towns survey spontaneously mentioned the right to bequeath as an important advantage of their tenure. This right can never be extended to tenants, simply because the house is not theirs to give. Local authorities may agree to allow a tenancy to pass from parents to children where appropriate, but this concession falls a long way short of recognizing the right of the householder to pass on the house at any time to whomsoever he or she chooses. The same argument applies to the right of control. Control will always ultimately be vested in the council, for no landlord can afford to offer a *carte blanche* for its property to be altered without prior permission. The reason for this is that the local authority must take a wider view than that of the tenant alone. The house is public property and must be managed so as to fulfil the objectives of the public authority. If you allow tenants to knock out a chimney, you prevent their successors from lighting coal fires. If you allow them to turn two bedrooms into one, you render the house unsuitable for occupancy by larger families who may have a need for it in the future. Many of the 'petty' rules and regulations of which tenants complain are, from the point of view of the council, necessary if public housing is to retain its social role. Mumby recognized this many years ago in a Fabian pamphlet on home ownership when he wrote:

> People cannot live at ease in an environment which clashes with their personality and in which they are unable to adapt the house to suit their own needs, whether it be a matter of a bicycle shed or a colour scheme on which one has set one's heart. Good landlords will take account of these things, but they will always remain as problems when houses are rented by their occupiers, perhaps particularly where landlords are local authorities.
>
> (1957, p. 23)

Even rights involving access to and exchange of housing will always be restricted within the public sector, for councils will necessarily be concerned to influence or determine what kind of people get allocated to what kind of housing stock. It is quite rational and reasonable for a local housing authority to try to prevent under-use or overcrowding of its accommodation and to maximize the potential of its housing space. It is also to be expected that authorities will restrict tenants in their choice of housing, since it is precisely the rationale for their very existence that they provide housing according to criteria of 'need' which only they themselves can judge. As Whitehead herself recognizes, 'A degree of individual choice comparable to that enjoyed by the average owner occupier . . . could only happen if social objectives were subordinated to individual preferences in local authority housing' (1979, p. 36). In other words, freedom in council renting could only approximate the freedom of private ownership if the very *raison d'être* of the public housing system were abandoned. However flexibly applications for exchange and transfer are processed, the possibilities of mobility for tenants will therefore never come close to the freedom of purchase and sale enjoyed by owners.

The same argument can be developed for most other factors where owner-occupation is generally seen as advantageous relative to council renting. Local authorities cannot allow tenants to reap the benefits of rising property values, for example, for rents on existing stock must be increased with inflation if the 'pooled historic cost' system of housing finance is to be made to work (see Kemeny, 1981). Put another way, a tenant's rent could be allowed to fall in real terms over time, just as the owner's mortgage repayments do, but this would destroy the very system which allows local councils to offer new tenancies at affordable rent levels.

Responsiveness to tenant complaints can be improved through schemes such as the much-vaunted Walsall experiment with devolved neighbourhood offices (see Sharron, 1982), but the right to ask the council to send a carpenter or plumber can never give tenants the same power as that enjoyed by owners who themselves engage the labour they require. The whole logic of devolved management represents an attempt to shift power out of remote town halls and on to council estates, yet this inevitably proves more expensive, it makes central co-ordination of overall housing policy more difficult and it still fails to give tenants the same sort of control which neighbouring owners take for granted. Participation schemes similarly may allow some tenants some say in collective decision-making, but this is a very poor substitute for the right to make one's own decisions for oneself.

In all of these examples, one essential theme comes through time and again. Just as many of the advantages of owning are inherent to private property rights in housing, so too many of the disadvantages of council renting turn out to be inherent to public housing systems. To abolish all the restrictions is to undermine the very purpose of state housing, for the state builds and lets housing in order to fulfil certain collective objectives which by definition have to be imposed on the diverse individuals who apply to live in this sector. The two systems cannot be equalized for they are inherently unequal. The paradox confronting those who seek to popularize state housing is that it is not possible to give council tenants the same rights as those enjoyed by owner-occupiers without destroying the system of council renting!

This essential point has been well expressed by Alan Ryan in an essay on public and private property:

> Of course, publicly owned housing which was humanely organized so that people had security of tenure, to which officials could not gain access without permission, and so on, would meet most of what was needed. However . . . it is quite likely that even humane and rational public ownership of things like houses will leave important needs unfulfilled – unless tenants' rights to decorate as they wish, keep pets, and all the other things that cause contention, are so guaranteed and so taken for granted that the distinction between public and private ownership begins to whither away.
>
> (1983, pp. 241–2)

The logic of any policy which attempts to increase tenant power is the logic of moving to a system of private ownership. The answer to Whitehead's argument that many of the inherent advantages of owner-occupation can be extended to council renting is therefore that this can be achieved precisely to the extent that councils are willing to transfer ownership to their tenants. To liberalize public rental is to dismantle it; to extend tenants' rights is to make tenants more like owners.

But if the aim really is to give tenants the same sort of benefits and rights that are currently enjoyed by owners, then the policy for achieving this is obvious. Rather than arguing for reforms such as tenants' charters and neighbourhood offices, which can only ever achieve partial success, those who seek to empower tenants should presumably be looking for ways to transfer full ownership rights to them. By the end of her paper, even Whitehead recognizes that the principal way of extending the benefits of ownership to tenants is by selling them the house! She goes on: 'Owner occupation is always capable of providing security and control of a kind that is different from anything that can be made available to tenants . . . Unless full ownership is transferred, the tenant will never feel the same about his home as the owner occupier' (1979, p. 41).

Given that many of the perceived benefits of home ownership are inherent to an owner-occupied system, and that many of the irksome irritations of council renting are an essential feature of a public rental system, the desire to move from the latter to the former is not difficult to understand. It is clear that this desire cannot be explained away, as Ball, Hamnett, Doling, Sullivan, Gray and so many others have tried to explain it, as the result of tenants confusing the question of housing tenure with that of housing quality. Indeed, such an argument never really did make much sense when we remember that in recent years around one million households have changed from renting to owning while continuing to live in exactly the same house. These people have not changed the quality of the accommodation they live in, but in exchanging the frustrations of dependency for the independence of proprietorship they have changed their ability to use, control and dispose of it.

Council house sales and the fallacy of 'coerced exchange'

In September 1986 the Housing Minister, John Patten, announced the sale of the one millionth council house in Britain since 1979. Table 2.6 shows the sales figures for England and Wales over the preceeding ten years (Patten's calculations also included Scotland). As can be seen from this table, the sale of public housing to sitting tenants increased steadily through the late 1970s and then exploded following the introduction of the 1980 Housing Act. Sales boomed in the early 1980s but have since been dropping from their peak of over 200,000 in 1982. As at 1985, 11 per cent of the 1978 council stock had been sold (Machon, 1987, p. 170), and this had generated revenue for the government greater than that from any other single privatization up to that time (Dunn, Forrest and Murie, 1987, p. 48).

This pattern of sales is unprecedented in Britain. Back in the nineteenth century, when government first allowed local authorities to build housing, it insisted that dwellings should be sold within ten years, but very little council housing was produced under this legislation, and the obligation to sell was in any case removed in 1909. The first big drive to build council housing came in the early 1920s, but although local authorities were permitted to sell, the volume of sales was negligible throughout the inter-war years, and in 1939 sales were banned altogether. This ban was not lifted until 1952 following the election victory of the Conservatives, yet from 1953 to 1959 local councils sold an annual average of only 2,003 houses, and this figure included houses built for sale as well as those bought by sitting tenants (Merrett, 1982, p. 119).

The rate of sales stayed at around 2,000 to 3,000 per year until the late

Table 2.6 *House sales by local authorities and new towns in England and Wales, 1976–86*

Year	Local authorities	New towns	Total
1976	5,795	100	5,895
1977	13,020	365	13,385
1978	30,045	575	30,620
1979	41,740	855	42,595
1980	81,485	4,225	85,710
1981	102,735	3,800	106,535
1982	202,055	5,315	207,370
1983	141,455	4,835	146,290
1984	103,175	4,310	107,485
1985	92,295	3,110	95,405
1986	88,410	2,415	90,825
Total	902,210	29,905	932,130

Source: Central Statistical Office, 1988.

1960s when a number of Conservative-controlled councils began to mount enthusiastic sales campaigns. In 1968 over 8,000 sales were recorded despite the then Labour government's circular stating that sales should not be permitted in areas where demand for low-rent housing had not been satisfied. With the return of a Conservative government in 1970, sales figures rose by what was then quite a dramatic rate, peaking at 45,000 in 1972 when the government issued a circular stating that applications to buy should only be refused in exceptional local circumstances. In the mid-1970s, however, sales fell back again as the Labour government attempted to prevent councils from selling housing in areas where there was still a need for low-cost rental. As we see in Table 2.6, sales were back at under 6,000 by 1976, although Conservative victories in local elections helped to push this figure up again towards the end of the decade.

Throughout this period, tenants who applied to buy their homes were generally expected to pay the full market value for them, although discounts of 20 per cent were allowed where councils retained pre-emption rights on future resale. The dramatic effect of the 1980 Housing Act is partly explained by the introduction of a new system of discounts of between 33 per cent (for tenants of three years' standing) and 50 per cent (for those with twenty years or more of residence) of market valuation. These discounts were extended in 1984 to a range of between 32 per cent (for those in residence for two years) and 60 per cent (for those occupying the house for thirty years). The Act was also important, however, for the introduction of a 'Right to Buy' which meant that tenants now had a legally enforceable right to purchase their homes and that, with very few exceptions, local councils could no longer refuse to sell to them. As Lundqvist notes, 'What was really new in the 1980 Housing Act was the shifting of the initiative from the local authority to the tenant' (1986, p. 87).

The results of this legislation are plain to see in Table 2.6. The extent of sales since 1980 has far outstripped anything seen before in the history of council housing (Dunn, Forrest and Murie, 1987, p. 48; Forrest and Murie, 1987c, p. 23). With an average discount of around 44 per cent of market value (Machon, 1987, p. 171), hundreds of thousands of mainly working-class households (most of them middle aged and containing more than one earner) have moved into owner-occupation for the first time (see Stubbs, 1988, and Williams, Sewel and Twine, 1986, for survey data on purchasers in Aberdeen and Sunderland respectively). Sales have been concentrated among houses with gardens. Flats, which made up around 30 per cent of the total stock in the late 1970s, account for just 2 or 3 per cent of sales (Lundqvist, 1986).

We shall consider the social implications of this pattern of sales when we analyse the question of tenurial polarization in Chapter 6. Here, however, our focus is not on the consequences of sales but on why so many tenants have chosen to buy. Over one million sales since 1979 add up to a major transfer of property rights from the state to its erstwhile tenants and would seem to represent a significant shift in the ownership of property wealth towards at least some sections of the working class. In his press release issued to mark the sale of the one millionth council home, the housing minister was in no doubt that the Right to Buy policy had fulfilled the 'aspirations of many thousands of people to own their own home' (John Patten, 5 September 1986). The critics of mass home ownership believe, on the contrary, that many of those who have bought their council homes have done so because government policies have left them little effective alternative. The question, therefore, is whether the obvious success of the Conservative government in encouraging tenants to buy their homes can be taken as yet more evidence of the popularity of owner-occupation, or whether it represents the coerced decisions of thousands of reluctant purchasers who would have preferred to have remained in the public sector.

The idea that people may effectively be 'coerced' into buying goods or services for which they previously depended upon state provision has been developed by Patrick Dunleavy in his concept of 'coerced exchange'. As he explains, 'Unlike market exchanges which are undertaken by people actively to increase their welfare, coerced exchanges are purely or partly defensive – people enter into the exchange to prevent their welfare being reduced' (1986, p. 138). Dunleavy cites as examples the move from reliance on public transport to private car purchase and the shift from council renting to owner-occupation, for in both cases he believes that declining standards of service and rising costs have driven people out of the state sector in search of private provision in the hope of maintaining their standards of living. A similar idea has been developed in the USA where Edel, Sclar and Luria identify a process of 'partial mobility' in which ordinary people are obliged to acquire ever more goods just to stay where they are in terms of life chances (1984, p. 16).

Applied specifically to the analysis of council house sales, the concept of coerced exchange would suggest three main reasons why so many tenants have chosen to buy. One is that owner-occupation has been made artificially attractive through selective subsidization. A second is that council renting has at the same time been made considerably less attractive through a policy of increasing rents. And a third is that, if council renting is no longer suitable or available, there is effectively no other choice for most people than to move into home ownership.

As we shall see in Chapter 6, owner-occupiers may be said to enjoy tax subsidies by virtue of their receipt of tax relief on interest payments and their exemption from Capital Gains and Capital Transfer taxes. In addition, council house buyers have, as we have seen, enjoyed substantial discounts when buying their homes. The comments of some of those with whom we spoke during the three towns survey suggest that the prospect of a substantial discount producing an immediate tax-free capital gain was certainly a factor in the decision of some tenants to buy their homes:

> The day we signed we made £12,000! It was valued at £29,000 when we bought it.
>
> (Male semi-skilled manual worker, Slough, who had bought his council house for £17,000)

> We were persuaded to buy by our children. We could have bought a new car but the house is going up all the time whereas a new car is losing value.
>
> (Male, intermediate occupation, Slough)

The second factor was increasing rents in the council sector. The housing programme was cut back by a massive 64 per cent between 1979 and 1988 as the government switched support from provision of low-rent housing to income support through housing benefits. Council rents increased from an average of 6.6 per cent of mean weekly earnings in 1978–9 to 8.8 per cent in 1982–3 (Forrest and Murie, 1987c). While the Retail Price Index rose by 87 per cent between 1979 and 1987, rents increased by 169 per cent (*Inside Housing*, 10 July 1987, p. 2). Figures like these lead Ray Forrest to suggest that 'For public sector tenants who do not qualify for full housing benefit, whose rents are moving nearer market rents, the move into owner occupation may be a reflection of constraint rather than choice – a coping strategy to reduce housing costs' (1987, p. 1623). In other words, council house sales are an example of coerced exchange. Evidence from a study of council house buyers in Sunderland indicates that rising rents were an important stimulus to sales (Stubbs, 1988, p. 152), and in Leeds it was found that 28 per cent of purchasers cited rising rents as their motive (reported in Jones, 1982). Comments from interviewees in the three towns survey also lend some support to this argument:

> We bought because the rent was going up so much – and we liked to own

our own house. It was the only chance we had of owning one.

(Female semi-skilled manual worker, Slough)

Originally I didn't agree with the idea. I think they ought to keep a backbone of council housing for people who do want to rent. I only bought because of continued rent increases. Otherwise we wouldn't have bothered – we were quite happy as we were.

(Male, retired from intermediate occupation, Derby)

The combination of discounted prices and rising rents has produced a situation in some areas where it can under certain circumstances be cheaper for tenants to buy their homes than to continue renting. Forrest and Murie (1986) show that in Derwentside (a town in the North-East with high unemployment) the average council house was valued at under £10,000 in 1982, while in Hackney (a mainly working-class inner area of London) the average valuation was three times that. Yet despite such differences, rent levels hardly vary at all between the two local housing authorities. It follows that rising rents will make purchase look especially attractive in low-priced areas such as Derwentside: 'The costs and meaning of purchase are very different between localities and have varied significantly over time. For some, ownership is achieved and sustained at very considerable expense. For others, council house purchase can mean an immediate reduction in outgoings associated with housing' (1986, p. 57).

Table 2.7 enables us to investigate this more closely with reference to the three towns in our survey. It will be seen from row (a) that rent levels are broadly comparable in all three towns, yet average house prices in Slough at the time of the survey were twice those in Derby and Burnley – row (b). Indeed, by the end of 1987 the gap had grown even wider, for a dramatic inflation in house prices in southern England drove the average price in Slough up to £76,692, while prices in the other two towns remained below £30,000 and did not begin to pick up until 1988–9 (see Nationwide Anglia Building Society, 1988; relative price movements between regions are discussed in Chapter 3). For this analysis, we shall take the less extreme situation pertaining in 1985–6.

Let us now assume that in each town a household of fourteen years' standing seeks to purchase its semi-detached house and that the house is valued at the average price for each town. The 44 per cent discount will result in purchase prices given in row (c). If the households each take out a 100 per cent mortgage over twenty-five years at, say, a 10.5 per cent interest rate, then they will end up repaying around £130 per month in Derby and Burnley, as compared with some £260 in Slough – row (d). In all three cases, mortgage repayments will represent a large increase over rental payments – row (e) – but in the lower-cost areas the increase is substantially less than in Slough, where it involves a rise in costs of two and a half times – row (f).

Of course, the calculations in Table 2.7 are hypothetical. Many buyers

Table 2.7 *Rents, house prices and the sale of council stock in Burnley, Derby and Slough*

	Burnley	Town Derby	Slough
(a) Average monthly council rent, 1986 (£)	69.60	62.40	70.37
(b) Average semi-detached house price, 1985 (£)	25,800	24,250	48,410
(c) – less average discount, 44%	14,450	13,580	27,110
(d) Monthly repayments on 25-year 100% mortgage for average discounted house price at 10.5% interest	137.85	129.55	258.63
(e) Difference between purchase and rental costs: (d) minus (a)	68.25	67.15	188.26
(f) – percentage cost increase	98.1	107.6	267.5
(g) Total council house sales 1980–6	1,091	4,456	2,193
(h) Total council stock 1986	7,305	20,699	10,476
(i) Sales between 1980 and 1986 as % of 1980 stock	13.0	17.7	17.3

Sources: (a) and (h) CIPFA, 1987; (b) data supplied by Nationwide Building Society; (d) calculated from look-up tables supplied by Alliance & Leicester Building Society; (g) Department of the Environment, 1987b.

have bought housing valued at less than the average because council houses are often valued below those on owner-occupied estates and many will have been paying higher than average rents since the average figures given in this table include tenants of flats as well as whole houses. Many have also received bigger discounts and have arranged lower mortgages by paying a deposit accumulated from savings, retirement gratuities, redundancy money, family donations and so on. Table 2.8 may therefore be more realistic, for it provides details of the actual repayments incurred by those former tenants in the three towns survey who have bought their homes with the aid of a mortgage. The numbers here are, however, very small, so considerable caution is required in generalizing from these figures. Nevertheless, the overall pattern is the same as that in Table 2.7, for again we find buyers in Slough paying much more for their homes and incurring double the mortgage repayments compared with those in the other two towns.

It is clear from both tables, therefore, that the financial inducement to buy should be far greater in areas like Burnley and Derby than in a town with a buoyant property market like Slough. Tenants pay more or less the same rent in all towns, but purchase costs are much lower in the former than in the latter. It follows from this that 'coerced exchanges' as a response to rising rents should be more readily apparent in towns like Burnley and Derby than in Slough. The fact that the rate of sales is actually higher in Slough than in Burnley – row (i) in Table 2.7 – is a point to which we shall need to return in a moment.

The third and final factor which could be said to have 'forced' people out of council renting and into owner-occupation is the lack of alternatives. This argument applies less to existing tenants who decide to buy than to new households who may prefer to rent a house but who end up purchasing in the private sector. Part of the problem is the collapse of the private rented sector which was discussed in Chapter 1. Difficulty in finding private rented

Table 2.8 *Monthly mortgage repayments and price paid by council house buyers in Burnley, Derby and Slough*

	Burnley	Town Derby	Slough
Average purchase price (£)	7,457	5,435	16,395
Mean monthly repayments (£)	76.20	71.75	148.93
% reporting difficulty with repayments	0.00	27.3	20.0

N = 45 (Burnley 9, Derby 17, Slough 19)

accommodation means that many people enter owner-occupation earlier than they would otherwise choose to do (Boleat, 1985). Added to this is the decline in availability of council renting due to the sharp reduction in building in the 1980s and the sale of housing to existing tenants. The result is that some people who, twenty or thirty years ago, might have expected to be allocated a council house may today no longer be considered eligible or will be expected to wait longer. This leads Ball to suggest that effective choice has been curtailed: 'A choice of housing tenure for most households is now non-existent . . . If you can afford to buy, you have to buy; if you cannot you can only hope to be housed by the council' (1983, p. 277).

Support for Ball's contention can be assembled from various case studies. Maclennan found in a study of first-time buyers in Glasgow in the mid-1970s that 15 to 20 per cent were 'reluctant purchasers' who would have preferred to have rented in the public sector but who were deterred by long waiting lists (Maclennan, 1982). In the same city ten years later, Madigan (1988) found that 43 per cent of low-income buyers would have been happy to have rented a council house if accommodation of a good quality had been available. And in Burnley, Walker suggests that 'The economically active have little choice but to buy' (1985, p. 14).

It is clear from all this evidence and argument that *some* of the one million tenants who have bought their homes in recent years have done so not out of any desire to own but in reluctant response to the financial sticks and carrots of the housing tenure system. The idea of 'coerced exchange' is important, for it alerts us to the limits of voluntarism and free choice. The fact that so many people do buy their homes does not necessarily mean that they want to. However, there are problems with the concept of 'coerced exchange' and with its application to the specific case of council house sales. Five points in particular should make us wary of those who seek to argue that tenants have not jumped, but have been pushed, into owner-occupation.

The first point is simply to query the terminology. It is one thing to say that choices are constrained, but quite another to talk, as Dunleavy does, of 'coercion', or as Ball does, of 'non-existent choice'. The 1980 Housing Act forces local authorities to agree to sell housing to sitting tenants, but it does not force tenants to buy it. In Romania the government obliged tenants to buy their state-owned houses and flats (Ward, 1983, p. 187). This is not what has happened in Britain, for there is an important distinction between allowing or even encouraging people to buy and obliging them to do so.

The academic left has often confused this issue by eliding the question of capacity (what people *can* do) with that of liberty (what they are *allowed* to do), yet the two concepts are very different. As Hayek argues, 'Whether or not I am my own master and can follow my own choice and whether the possibilities from which I must choose are many or few are two entirely different questions' (1960, p. 17). Neither subsidies to owner-occupation nor rising rents in the public sector *force* council tenants to buy. Many, indeed, have not bought. Many others (55 per cent in Slough and 70 per cent in Derby; Burnley data are not available) are in receipt of state allowances which shield them from rent increases, so for them there is no question of rent rises 'pushing' them to act in any given manner. Every one of those one million council house purchasers freely chose to buy. Many may have been *influenced* by financial inducements and constraints, but not one was *coerced*. It is, therefore, better to drop Dunleavy's terminology of 'coerced exchange' in favour of some less emotive phrase such as 'constrained choice'.

The second point is that it is important to remember that, just as some of those who buy may have preferred to have continued renting under earlier arrangements, so too some of those who continue to rent might have preferred to buy if circumstances were different. Constrained choices rub both ways. We have already seen that three-quarters of the council tenants interviewed in the three towns survey identified home ownership as their preferred tenure. Some of them are too poor to consider purchase and some are too old, but in some cases tenants would like to buy but do not want to purchase the council house in which they are currently living:

> I would never buy a council house because they're always council houses. You're on a council estate. If you buy your own house you can have it anywhere.
> (Female council tenant, retired semi-skilled manual worker, Derby)

> People are buying rubbish. Even with discounts they are too expensive. People get stuck next to you if you buy a council house. Ninety-five per cent of council tenants would sooner buy a private house.
> (Male council tenant, retired unskilled manual worker, Burnley)

To say that these people are 'forced' to continue renting would be as absurd as arguing that those who have bought have been forced into purchasing. In both cases, households see their circumstances in such a way that they continue to follow a course of action which is not their preferred option. What is clear is that the number of 'reluctant renters' is at least as great as the number of 'reluctant buyers', for the three towns survey is not the only study to uncover such sentiments. The 1985 *General Household Survey* found that 25 per cent of tenants who did not wish to buy gave as their reason their dislike of their accommodation. Similar results have been reported in local case studies. In Aberdeen, 38 per cent of tenants who had decided not to buy said that this was because they were unhappy with the accommodation or the neighbourhood (Williams, Sewel and Twine, 1986, p. 288). In the London Borough of Southwark, 44 per cent of tenants who said they would prefer to own explained that they had not bought because they did not wish to purchase the house they were currently living in. In Dundee, 17 per cent of council tenants said they were interested in buying their present house, whereas 26 per cent said they would only buy a different one. In Manchester, 30 per cent of those tenants who said they would like to buy had enough income to enable them to do so, yet they were reluctant to purchase their existing council housing. As Jones (who reports these three cases) concludes, 'The demand for home ownership is not always a demand to buy council houses' (1982, p. 121).

It follows from this that there is almost certainly a large 'latent demand' for house purchase among council tenants, and that far from feeling forced to buy, many feel that they are 'prevented' from doing so by their distaste for the house to which they were originally allocated. Williams, Sewel and Twine suggest that 'The desire to purchase is more widespread than would appear from the stated intention to purchase, and is being frustrated because of dissatisfaction with either or both the tenant's existing dwelling and area' (1986, p. 289). These reluctant renters would be the main beneficiaries if new 'transferable discount' schemes which have been piloted in Bromley and Brent were to become widely available. Under these schemes, tenants are paid a lump sum to vacate their council houses in lieu of the discount which would otherwise have been available had they chosen to buy them (see White, 1987). These schemes are considered further in Chapter 6.

" But what if the Smiths at No. 3 don't buy theirs ? I. don't fancy living next door to council tenants."

A third point to note about the argument that council house sales are a product of constrained or 'coerced' choices is that people still seem to buy when the cost of so doing far exceeds their current rental outgoings. While it is true that some people may find that buying is as cheap as renting, most do not. As can be seen from Tables 2.7 and 2.8, even in low-priced housing areas, buyers are likely to end up paying more each month in mortgage repayments than they previously did in rent, and this is virtually certain in towns like Slough where prices are much higher. In Aberdeen, Williams, Sewel and Twine found that purchasers took on average monthly mortgage repayments of £82 when average rents were just £36 (1986, p. 283), and this suggests that, as in Slough, people are making deliberate choices to buy and are prepared to pay a lot more as a result.

What is also interesting is that most sales have occurred in the more expensive regions. Table 2.7 shows that 17 per cent of Slough's council housing has been sold since 1980, compared with only 13 per cent of Burnley's, yet it is much cheaper for tenants to buy in Burnley than in Slough. This difference in rates of sale reflects wider inter-regional differences. Forrest and Murie (1986, p. 52) show that twenty out of the top twenty-five selling authorities are located in the South-East, East and East Midlands regions, while none are to be found in the North. And in a paper written with Richard Dunn they provide figures showing that, by the end of 1985, 17 per cent of the council stock in the South-East had been sold, compared with just 11 per cent in the North and North-West regions and 10 per cent in Yorkshire and Humberside (Dunn, Forrest and Murie, 1987, p. 50). In the light of these patterns, it hardly makes sense to claim that many tenants have been 'forced' to buy by rising rents, for sales have been highest where the gap between rent and mortgage payments has remained greatest.

A fourth point to consider is whether those who have bought can afford it. If large numbers of tenants have been 'forced' into purchase, then we might expect to find widespread evidence of subsequent financial hardship and distress, especially since most buyers will have found home ownership considerably more expensive than renting. Table 2.8 reveals that around one in five of those with whom we spoke claimed to have experienced some difficulty in meeting mortgage repayments at some time since they first purchased their house. This compares with 14 per cent of all owners in our survey who said this. However, the question was very general, and we discovered very little evidence of serious hardship resulting, for example, in sustained arrears. Furthermore, other studies of council house buyers have found that if anything they are more financially secure than other buyers! Forrest and Murie, for example, conclude that 'In most areas and cases council purchasers are less marginal than private sector purchasers' (1984, p. 42). Similarly, Nellis and Fleming (1987, p. 19) show that, even if discounts are ignored, council house buyers are 'much less stretched financially' than other groups entering owner-occupation for the first time, and that when discounts (which averaged 43 per cent in their study) are counted in, their financial situation looks highly favourable in comparative terms. There is, then, no sign of former tenants struggling to meet the repayments which some observers believe have been thrust upon them.

The final reason for doubting whether council house sales are the product of 'coerced exchange' is simply that most of those who have bought tell us that they did so freely and gladly. Out of forty council house buyers who answered our question about why they had decided to buy, only two said that they felt they had had little choice. Five said that they had simply wanted to own, and five said that they wanted the autonomy and independence which ownership represents, but by far the most common reason, mentioned by twenty-four of them, was the desire to get something back for the money that they were paying out. What this suggests is that rising rents may have hardened their resolve to get out, but that their motive was to escape from what they saw as the futility of paying 'money for nothing'. They bought, not because they were driven to it, but because they wanted to establish a property stake in the house they were paying for. A handful of tenants may have been 'pushed' into owner-occupation, therefore, but the great majority 'jumped' of their own free will.

Social marginality and the desire to own: the case of Asian home ownership

If council house buyers are one principal group often held to have been 'forced' into owner-occupation, then the other consists of home owners among the ethnic minorities. As Table 2.9 reveals, home ownership rates are relatively low among the West Indian population. This is consistent with the social class distribution of West Indians in Britain, for most are in lower-grade and lower-paid manual occupations. Owner-occupancy is also low among Bangladeshis. The *Labour Force Survey* (OPCS, 1987) explains this as partly a reflection of the availability of housing in the areas in which this group has settled. The remarkable feature about Table 2.9, however, is the extremely high rate of home ownership among Indians and Pakistanis who turn out to be *more likely* than whites to own their homes, and correspondingly much less likely to rent from a local council.

Table 2.9 *Ethnicity and housing tenure*

Ethnic group of head of household	Outright owner	Mortgaged owner	Council tenant
White	25	34	28
West Indian	7	32	47
Indian	23	54	11
Pakistani	29	45	16
Bangladeshi	8	27	45

Source: OPCS, 1987.

There are two ways of explaining these patterns. The first and most common is to argue that Asians have been excluded from council renting on racial grounds and have therefore been obliged to seek accommodation through house purchase. Like council house buyers, therefore, the ethnic minorities are seen as a group of reluctant owners who have had little choice but to buy. Why local housing authorities should have been much less racist towards West Indians and Bangladeshis than towards Indians and Pakistanis is a question which is rarely asked and never answered by those who adopt such an explanation.

The second and more straightforward explanation is that Indians and Pakistanis have placed a particularly strong value on property ownership and have battled against the odds to achieve it. This is a much less popular view among commentators and analysts, for it involves a recognition of Pakistanis and Indians as successful and thus suggests that they may not be as feeble and downtrodden as their self-appointed academic defenders have sought to paint them.

The first view has become something of an orthodoxy in the housing literature. Rex and Tomlinson tell us that the 'immigrant community' in Handsworth, Birmingham, has been 'forced to buy' (1979, p. 146). Papadakis and Taylor-Gooby suggest that ownership is 'the only available option' for some immigrant households (1987, p. 158). Gray announces that 'black' households 'are pushed into certain sections of the market' and often 'have no choice at all in determining their tenure' since they are 'forced into . . . owner occupation' (1982, p. 277). And despite the fact that half of all West Indian and Bangladeshi households are located on council estates, Ginsburg confidently asserts that 'black people' have been kept out of council renting by 'institutional racism' (1983, p. 42).

The intellectual fountainhead for these claims is Rex and Moore's study of housing and race in Sparkbrook, Birmingham, conducted in the early 1960s. In their book, Rex and Moore (1967) argued that there was a generalized aspiration to live either in suburban owner-occupied housing or on suburban council estates. Recent immigrants to Birmingham were, however, excluded from both. They could not achieve access to suburban home ownership since they generally lacked the size and security of income necessary to gain a conventional mortgage, and they could not get access to public-sector rental because they failed to fulfil residence requirements which effectively operated as a race barrier. They were therefore *forced* into inner-city areas where they bought cheap, old housing with a limited life, financing the purchase through short-term expensive loans which they paid off by taking in lodgers. Many of the Asian immigrants in particular owned housing in Sparkbrook, and many were landlords – 18 out of 47 multi-occupied houses in Rex and Moore's sample were owned by Pakistani landlords. But the essence of Rex and Moore's explanation for this phenomenon was that these people were reluctant owners and reluctant landlords, reacting to their exclusion from more desirable forms of housing such as council renting: 'What we did observe was a process of discriminative and *de facto*

114

segregation which compelled coloured people to live in certain typical conditions' (1967, p. 20). The emphasis of the analysis is on 'compulsion' rather than choice; the ethnic minorities are the victims of exclusion, not the agents of their own enterprise.

Rex and Moore's book swiftly entered into the sociological folk wisdom despite the fact that it contains very little evidence to support its claims. No data are presented to demonstrate that there was in fact a widespread desire for suburban owner-occupation and council renting, and this claim has subsequently been questioned by research elsewhere which indicates that at least some of those who live in inner areas or who rent from private landlords actually prefer it that way (Couper and Brindley, 1975). Nor is there any evidence in the book that ethnic-minority groups, and in particular the southern Asians, wanted the council tenancies from which they were apparently being excluded. At one point Rex and Moore do admit that only one of their 39 Pakistani informants had applied for a council house, but they explain this in terms of an anticipation of failure among the other 38 (1967, p. 127). In short, most of Rex and Moore's arguments are unsupported: 'The factual basis of *Race, Community and Conflict* is extraordinarily, indeed, deplorably thin: no one will ever know whether its assertions about immigrant housing in Birmingham are true or false because there are no data in the book to which to refer' (Davies, 1985, p. 4).

Davies himself has done much to undermine Rex and Moore's thesis as a result of his research in Newcastle upon Tyne. There he found that most Asians had positively *rejected* council renting. He could find no Indian or Pakistani family who had ever applied for a council house or who wanted one, and he reports that many of his Asian informants despised the very idea of paying rent (1972, pp. 29–30). Later research confirms this. A 1982 Cleveland County Council survey found that 90 per cent of Asian households owned their homes, that only 12 per cent had ever considered applying for a council house and that none of those contacted believed that their chances of getting allocated a council house were diminished because of their race (reported in Davies, 1985, p. 8). Similarly, Sullivan and Murphy argue on the basis of 1981 national data that council tenancies would have been available to many of those Asian households who nevertheless can be found in cheap owner-occupied housing (1987, p. 189).

It seems from this that high rates of Asian owner-occupancy are more a reflection of choice than of coercion. In Newcastle, Davies found 'a very strong propensity to own property' (1972, p. 26) among Indians and Pakistanis, and he suggests that 'the houses and areas in which they live are the result of their choice and not of discrimination based on the colour of their skin' (1985, p. 12). Similarly Sarre reports from his research in Bedford that many Indian households were so strongly committed to home ownership that they were 'willing to override all other preferences for the privilege' (1986, p. 83).

It is unclear from the literature whether this desire to own is more a product of a need for security in a new country or of an emphasis on the value of property ownership within Indian and Pakistani cultures. In all probability it is both. It is not unusual for immigrants to seek property ownership as a way of enhancing their security in a somewhat uncertain and socially marginalized existence. Migrants to nineteenth-century America, for example, very often made every effort to establish ownership of their home as a way of ensuring some sense of security (Harris and Hamnett, 1987). The same is still true in Australia today. Seventy-two per cent of those born in the country own or are buying their homes, as compared with 76 per cent of West Germans, 79 per cent of Yugoslavs, 84 per cent of Dutch, 89 per cent of Greeks and 92 per cent of Italians, yet average wages among these immigrant groups are considerably lower than those of native-born Australians (Badcock, 1984, p. 186; Kilmartin, 1988, p. 19). Given the low rates of owner-occupation in many of the countries (such as West Germany and the Netherlands) from which these people have come, these figures seem to suggest that it is the act of immigration itself which heightens the desire to own. This would make sense in the context of our earlier discussion of the role of possessions in maintaining a stable sense of self, for it is precisely when we move countries that we are most likely to develop an acute awareness of this need for security. It is also an argument which is consistent with various studies of Asians in Britain which find that the desire for security and the need to counter feelings of vulnerability are a major motive behind the commitment to owner-occupation (for example, Davies, 1972, p. 37; Sullivan and Murphy, 1987, p. 189).

There is also, however, a cultural dimension to Asian home ownership in Britain. After all, West Indian immigrants presumably felt the same sort of need to establish a secure base in their new country, yet owner-occupancy rates among West Indians are only half those of Indians and Pakistanis. There is, it seems, an ethic of independence and a spirit of entrepreneurship in south Asian culture which has achieved expression through owner-occupation (as well as through small business activity) in this country. In Birmingham, for example, Valerie Karn and her co-researchers found a strong commitment to the very principle of ownership (which is the corollary of Davies's finding about the despise of renting). 'When we asked for their reasons for buying,' they say, 'we saw the owners relishing their freedom' (Karn, Kemeny and Williams, 1985, p. 56). Where white owners of cheap inner-city housing tended to emphasize the advantages of housing as an investment, the Asians stressed values of independence and autonomy, although as in Newcastle (Davies, 1972, p. 39) many were also alive to the economic advantages of owning.

In the three towns survey, we found that patterns of Asian home ownership were not dissimilar from those of whites. The total numbers involved are small – there were 37 Asians in the sample of whom 29 were owner-occupiers – and the usual caution is therefore required in considering the data. The tenure composition of households was almost exactly the same in each group – 22 per cent of Asians owned outright (23 per cent of whites), 53 per cent were buying with the aid of a loan (50 per cent of whites), and 25 per cent were renting from the council (26 per cent of whites). Tenure preferences were also similar. Eighty-seven per cent of Asians said that they would prefer to buy than to rent, the equivalent figure among whites being 91 per cent.

When we asked the 29 Asian owners in the sample why they had bought in the first place, seven said that they simply wanted to own, and five emphasized the desire for autonomy and independence. Financial motives did not seem particularly important – only four said that they wanted something for their money, and three spoke of housing as an investment. However, nine out of the 29 made some comment indicating restriction of choice, and this would seem to suggest that home ownership may for some be a product of constraint as well as choice.

In a particularly useful paper on ethnic minority housing, Philip Sarre (1986) has suggested that the polarity between explanations which emphasize choice and those which focus on constraint is misleading. In his view, ethnic-minority housing patterns are the product of an interaction between five variables – the cultural predispositions of the people themselves, the economic resources at their command, their knowledge of the housing system, the 'fit' between household structure and housing availability and the practice of intentional or unintentional racial discrimination. Seen in this way, neither of the explanations outlined at the start of this section can be deemed adequate on its own. Asians have not been forced into home ownership, for most of them wanted it from the outset. Equally, they have pursued this objective within a context of resource and other constraints which has resulted in most Asian households occupying older and cheaper properties in inner urban areas. Whether or not this means that Asian home owners face higher repair and maintenance costs, can achieve lower rates of capital gain and must suffer poor or inadequate conditions of living are questions we shall consider in the next chapter. For now it is enough to note that the 'exclusion' of Asians from council renting has been as much a product of their reluctance to rent as of the attempts of white tenants or housing departments to keep them out. Asian owner-occupiers have often had to struggle for what they have, and what they have may not look very much, but for most of them it is infinitely preferable to a state-sector alternative for which they harbour no aspirations or ambitions.

Conclusions

That the great majority of households in Britain would prefer to own their homes than to rent them is not seriously in dispute. Nor can it be denied that substantial numbers of council tenants – at least half, possibly as many as three-quarters – would rather be owner-occupiers. There is clear evidence that home owners are generally much happier with their housing situation than council tenants are. Home owners tend to buy in the first place out of financial considerations, but having bought they stress the pleasures to be derived from the autonomous control of their own home. Tenants, by contrast, tend to enter public rental housing because they have no other option, and they express deep dissatisfaction about the restrictions which are imposed upon them. They complain of the lack of choice about where they live, of wasting money in a lifetime of rent-paying and of their inability to get repairs done or to get them done properly.

All of this is well documented in my own as well as in other research studies. To the extent that social science can hope to deal in indisputable facts, these are hard facts. Where the argument arises is *why* people want to own and why non-owners find the experience so alienating.

There still lingers a belief on the political left that the popular desire to own is the product of political and ideological manipulation. Given a 'genuine' choice, people would not choose such an individualized and personal form of housing. Those who argue in this way are particularly troubled by evidence that groups whom they fondly term 'the dispossessed' seem just as keen to buy a house as more privileged (and despised) strata. Given half a chance, the underdogs of the Marxist imagination – working-class council tenants and 'black' (actually Asian) immigrants – shun the paternalistic embrace of the local authority housing department and take their chance in the 'shark-infested seas' (Stretton, 1976, p. 208) of the private property system. Such mass rejection of collectivist solutions is taken by the huddled ranks of academic Marxist observers as evidence of coercion – tenants must have been forced to buy by rising rents, and Asians must have been forced to buy by the institutionalized racism of housing allocation systems.

Such arguments are nonsense. Nobody, of course, enjoys unrestricted free choice, and most people aspire to live in a house a little bit better than the one they actually have. But one million council tenants have not been bamboozled into home ownership any more than hundreds of thousands of Asian immigrants have been kept out of council renting. This conclusion holds on a more general level too, for there is no evidence that nearly two-thirds of British households have been fooled or trapped or cajoled into buying. As we have seen, possessive inclinations run deep and are easily expressed through ownership of one's home. Financial supports and inducements are of course important in enabling people to buy, but in most cases they are probably not a sufficient reason for purchase. If there is a possessive instinct within us, carried and honed through genetic transmission down thousands of generations, then it is revealed today in the desire for security, privacy and personal identity which owners articulate when they talk about their experience of their housing.

Few of the left-wing critics of mass home ownership will even countenance such arguments, for talk of instincts is anathema to them. They prefer to cling to their unsustainable theories of ideology as the explanation for the popular desire to own. A few, however, have recognized that owner-occupation does seem to provide people with opportunities which public rental systems deny, and they have then argued that public housing could become equally attractive given an Act of Parliament or two. This is wishful thinking, for the relative benefits and disadvantages of the two tenure systems are to a large extent inherent to them. The advantages of owner-occupation are grounded in the rights of private property and cannot therefore be extended equally to those who are obliged to remain propertyless. A state housing system is by definition a system of power in which those who control the state also ultimately control the tenants of that state. They may allow them to 'participate' in the collective management of their own homes and they may even dispense a few privileges, but council tenants will never enjoy the rights which owner-occupiers take for granted until such time as they are handed the title to their properties. That, in a nutshell, is why so many would prefer to own.

3   A stake in the country

For most of this century, one of the main attractions of home ownership has been the opportunity which it offers for building up savings. As we saw in Chapter 2, motives for house purchase often reflect a belief that rent is money wasted while mortgage payments result eventually in ownership of a valuable asset. Confidence in housing as a means of saving has generally been high in Britain, so much so that we often refer to other secure forms of saving as being 'as safe as houses'. The injunction to 'put your money into bricks and mortar' has long been part of popular folk wisdom, for not only has the price of housing more than kept up with inflation (thereby functioning as an ideal means of personal saving), but ownership has also offered the prospect of a rent-free old age and the advantage of bequeathing a significant legacy to one's heirs. Most people are well aware that savings kept under the mattress, or even money deposited in banks and building societies, can lose value in inflationary times. We have all heard stories of how people's savings were wiped out during the hyper-inflation which afflicted the German economy during the 1920s, and many of us vividly remember the steep increase in the rate of inflation in Britain in the 1970s when interest on savings lagged far behind the erosion in the purchasing power of money. Property has traditionally been seen as an ideal 'hedge against inflation', and home ownership has thus been a popular way of safeguarding personal savings.

In the last twenty years, this image of housing as a secure form of saving has come to be complemented by a newer notion of house purchase as a highly lucrative form of investment. In the eyes of many commentators and home owners, owner-occupation is no longer simply a means of maintaining the value of savings, but has become an attractive and remunerative way of accumulating wealth. Purchase of a house is today widely seen, not as a way of safeguarding money, but as a way of making it. This shift in popular perceptions reflects a history of three dramatic house price booms since the early 1970s.

For twenty-five years after the war, house prices in Britain rose regularly but unspectacularly. In the first ten years they rose at an average of 4.5 per cent per annum. During the 1960s they rose at an average annual rate of 7 per cent. From 1971 to 1973, however, they suddenly and spectacularly doubled as the average house price rose from £5,000 to £10,000 pounds in just three years. Five years later there followed a second boom with prices rising by 50 per cent between 1978 and 1980. And then in 1986 (the year when the three towns survey was carried out) a third boom began. Prices rose by 16 per cent in 1986, by a further 15 per cent in 1987 and then by a hefty 34 per cent in 1988. At the peak of this third boom, in August 1988, the average house price in Britain had risen by more than £55,000 (*Building Societies Association Bulletin*, no. 56, October 1988).

Of course, all other prices have also been rising over this period. Indeed, there have been years (usually following each house price boom) when the general rate of inflation has run ahead of house price rises, and at these times owner-occupiers have suffered a fall in the value of their homes in real terms. Clearly, then, it is necessary to compare movements of house prices against changes in the Retail Price Index (RPI) in order to gauge whether housing has lived up to its image as a secure hedge against inflation and as a lucrative form of investment.

Figure 3.1 charts the rate of inflation of house prices between 1966 and 1986 against both the rise in disposable incomes before tax and increases in the RPI. All three sets of figures have been adjusted to a common index of 100 in the base year of 1966. This means that the percentage rise for each measure can be read off against the vertical axis of the graph.

It is clear from Figure 3.1 that house prices and incomes have tended to keep pace with each other. During the three boom periods since 1971, house prices increased faster than incomes but on each occasion they have fallen back into line in the years that followed. When we look at changes in the RPI over this period, however, it is apparent that both house prices and incomes have greatly outstripped the general rate of inflation in retail prices. What this means is that, on average, people's incomes have been rising in real terms (wages now buy more goods and services than they did in the mid-1960s), and home owners have enjoyed a real increase in the value of

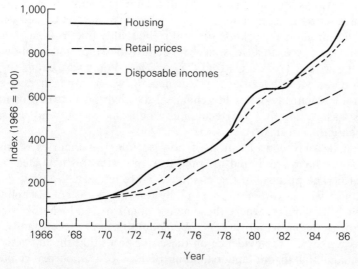

Sources: BSA, 1988; Central Statistical Office, 1987.

Fig 3.1 House prices, retail prices and personal disposable income, 1966–86.

their houses (house prices are now higher relative to other prices than they were in the mid-1960s). As we shall see, these two pieces of evidence – the rise in the real value of incomes and the rise in the real value of houses – are crucial to any understanding of *how* owner-occupiers accumulate wealth. For the moment, however, we need only note that house prices have been rising in real terms and that owners of housing have over this period therefore become wealthier.

The fact that home ownership has provided people with windfall capital gains is of crucial sociological significance when we remember that nearly two-thirds of the British population have now achieved access to owner-occupation. One of the first sociologists to grasp the importance of this was Ray Pahl. In an essay written some time after the first boom and before the second, he suggested: 'For the first time in our history, the majority of our domestic properties are owner-occupied. The maintenance of property values and the possibility of making appreciable capital gains has become a dominant value. *A family may gain more from the housing market in a few years than would be possible in savings from a lifetime of earnings*' (1975, p. 291, my emphasis). In other words, the labour market is no longer the sole or even key determinant of people's life chances. Wages and salaries affect people's material well-being, but so too does their housing tenure, for owners may accumulate wealth in a way that tenants cannot. Two employees on the same income could therefore end up in very different economic situations according to whether or not they own their homes.

For Pahl, the implication of this was that economic inequalities arising out of the occupational division of labour are becoming blurred and confused by the emergence of other sources of inequality based in the housing system. As he put it, 'As long as it is possible to accumulate substantial capital gains through housing careers, and as long as this possibility is denied to a large proportion of manual workers, the major inequality in our urban system will remain . . . I see this tension between ownership and non-ownership increasing in the years ahead' (1975, p. 298). What was being suggested, therefore, was that because house ownership was coming to play a major part in influencing people's life chances, the division between owners and tenants was taking on a new economic significance as a major cleavage in late-twentieth-century British society.

We shall delay consideration of how sociological theories of class and stratification have attempted to come to terms with this new cleavage until Chapter 6. The purpose of this chapter is more modest. We shall simply try to establish whether home owners really do make substantial capital gains, how much they make, where these gains come from and whether significant gains are available to all owners. We should, however, constantly bear in mind as we review the evidence on these questions that the answers we find are fundamental to our understanding of how contemporary capitalism is operating in Britain. The evidence in Figure 3.1, for example, would seem to indicate that many ordinary people have been doing rather well out of their participation in Britain's capitalist system, for not only have their incomes been rising in real terms, but so too have their wealth holdings. If it is indeed the case that widespread ownership of housing is enabling millions of ordinary British households to accumulate large sums of capital, then this would pose a strong challenge to all those who believe that capitalism merely operates in the interests of the capitalist class and that ordinary people stand to gain little or nothing from its continued expansion. It is in this sense that the material to be reviewed in this chapter should help us to determine the extent to which the majority of people now have a real stake in the economic system in which they live.

Measuring capital gains

Before analysing whether or not different groups of owner-occupiers have made substantial capital gains out of their housing, it is necessary to consider a range of problems entailed in calculating such gains. Inevitably this takes us into a discussion of various technical and statistical issues. Although an understanding of these issues is important in order to evaluate the evidence presented later in the chapter, the reader who is only concerned with the results and who is prepared to take figures on trust may choose to skip this section.

Most of the evidence relating to the capital gains which may or may not be made from home ownership is based on analysis of aggregate house price movements over time. Such studies, while interesting, are rarely satisfactory and are often contradictory in their findings.

One study which attracted considerable press comment when it was released was that by Peter Spencer (1987) for the Credit Suisse First Boston Bank. He calculated that returns to housing investment in Britain since 1980 amounted to minus 2 per cent per year, and he contrasted that with a 20 per cent yield on shares and a 10 per cent return on building society deposits. Home owners, in other words, had been losing rather than gaining and would have been better off investing their money elsewhere than in housing.

Spencer's calculations were extremely thorough and in many ways very sophisticated. First he calculated the rate of house price inflation taking account of added value as a result of expenditure on improvements. He then subtracted this figure from the sum of net interest payments, maintenance costs and rates to arrive at a calculation of net cost. This in turn was subtracted from a figure representing the imputed rental income enjoyed by owner-occupiers (that is, the amount they save by not having to rent an equivalent property – the exact figure was taken from the Central Statistical Office *Blue Book* which calculates imputed rent of owner-occupied dwellings by comparing their rateable values with those of houses which are actually rented). On these figures, the net return enjoyed by owner-occupiers was found to have been positive only once in the six years between 1981 and 1986. Spencer concluded, 'An average owner-occupation represented an attractive financial proposition during the 1960s and 1970s but not during the 1980s' (1987, p. 9).

One weakness of this particular study is that it seems to have assumed that owner-occupiers buy houses outright from their existing assets, just as they might buy shares or other investments. Even on this assumption the arithmetic is wrong, for people buying outright would not then have to pay interest on a housing loan. The key point, however, is that most buyers do not purchase outright from their existing resources. In 1987 the average first-time buyer met only 15 per cent of the purchase price from his or her own resources and borrowed the rest. Even existing owners, who have built up some equity, only put down an average deposit of 42 per cent of the purchase price of a new property when they move (figures from *BSA Bulletin*, 1988, tables 12 and 13). Most house buyers, then, put a relatively small amount of their own money into their purchase and they borrow the rest. This means that *rates of return on housing investment have to be calculated on the rate of capital appreciation as a percentage of the original deposit rather than as a percentage of the entire purchase price*. Had Spencer calculated his figures on this basis, his results would have looked very different.

The point is well expressed by Edel, Sclar and Luria in their historical analysis of house prices in Boston, Mass. Figures on house price changes, they say 'may not present the rate of return to the owner's equity if a portion of the purchase price is covered by a mortgage. In this case, the owner's capital gain on equity will be at a higher rate than the rate of appreciation of the property' (1984, p. 131). This is because people who take out a mortgage on a house initially pay for only a fraction of it out of their own money, yet they receive capital growth on the full value of the property.

Unfortunately, having noted this crucial point, Edel and his colleagues ignore it, just as Spencer does. Like Spencer, they are then able to conclude that returns to home ownership are moderate and do not compare with returns to other types of investment.

Other analysts have been more careful. Farmer and Barrell (1981), for example, base their calculations on returns to the amount of money originally invested (that is, the deposit) rather than returns on the full purchase price. Assuming an original investment of £1,000 in 1965, they show that by 1979 non-movers had made nominal gains of 23 per cent p.a. (12 per cent in real terms), while those who traded up made nominal gains of 27 per cent p.a. (16 per cent in real terms).

More recently, the Nationwide Building Society (1986) has calculated rates of return taking account of transaction costs (for example, solicitors' and agents' fees) and mortgage repayments while also allowing for imputed rental income. The figures range from 13 per cent p.a. nominal returns for someone who purchased in 1980 (immediately after the second house price boom) to 25 per cent p.a. for someone who purchased just ten years earlier (immediately before the first house price boom). If imputed rental value (which Nationwide calculates at 3 per cent of capital value) is left out of these calculations, rates of return are still attractive, varying from 5 per cent p.a. for a 1980 buyer to 17 per cent for one who bought in 1970. Interestingly in the light of the Farmer and Barrell study, this analysis finds that people make more if they stay put than if they trade up, since the non-movers save more on transaction costs than they would gain in additional capital growth.

Irrespective of their varying conclusions and methodologies, the basic problem in all of these studies is that they are based on aggregate data. The best they can offer is an analysis of how a mythical 'average' buyer might have fared over a given period, but they have no idea how real households have actually fared for they have no information on individual budgets and housing histories. As David Thorns suggests, analysis based on aggregate data 'masks the true position and does not allow for a clear picture to emerge of the range of gains and losses sustained by owner-occupiers' (1981a, p. 708).

Thorns himself suggests that we need to trace transactions involving individual properties over time – something which he himself has done in Christchurch, New Zealand, and which has also been accomplished in Glasgow (Munro and Maclennan, 1987) and in Boston (Edel, Sclar and Luria, 1984). While this is certainly preferable to using aggregate figures, it is still far from satisfactory. Leaving aside the problem that such research is not possible in England (for there is no register of transactions on individual properties over time as there is in some other countries), the basic objection remains that this sort of approach still only provides indirect evidence. Given that we are interested in the wealth accumulated by particular households as they move through different houses, research on the selling price of particular houses as different households move through them clearly leaves much to be desired.

Clearly what is needed is information which would enable us to follow through the purchases and sales made by a sample of households. Until now, this has not been possible. As Jim Kemeny and Andrew Thomas complained in 1984, 'Data are not available on the purchase price, selling price, present and previous mortgage for a set of individual transactions' (1984, p. 16). This, however, is precisely what the three towns survey set out to collect. Each interview gathered detailed information on individual household movements over time. We asked questions relating to each move since our respondents first set up their own home, and in the case of owner-occupiers we recorded information on the purchase price, the deposit, the loan and the selling price for every property they had owned.

This data set offers a unique opportunity for analysing the question of capital gains from owner-occupation, although there are inevitably some problems and weaknesses of which it is important to be aware.

One problem is that not all respondents could remember full details for every transaction they had been through, although most of those who were interviewed displayed sharp recall on most of the details of their housing

125

histories. Where there are gaps in people's housing histories, certain assumptions have been made so as not to lose the entire case from the analysis.

Where people could not remember the purchase price of a particular property, for example, the price has been estimated at 1.15 times the sale price of their previous property. This multiple of 1.15 represents the average 'trading-up ratio' for the sample as a whole, and it has similarly been used to calculate an unknown sale price in cases where we have information on the subsequent purchase.

Where information is lacking on both the size of deposit and the size of mortgage for any given purchase, it has been assumed in the case of a first purchase that it was financed by an 18 per cent deposit and an 82 per cent loan (the average ratio for first purchases in the sample as a whole), and in the case of second and subsequent purchases that it was financed by a 37 per cent deposit and a 63 per cent loan (again, this is the average proportion in the sample as a whole). The only exceptions here are those cases where proceeds from the previous sale (after redeeming the mortgage) are lower than the assumed deposit on the subsequent purchase. In these cases it has been assumed that the net proceeds were used to finance the subsequent deposit.

A second problem is that it was necessary to estimate the current value of each respondent's house. All interviewees were asked to estimate the market value of their houses, but their answers were not always reliable. Current values are thus based on interviewers' estimates. These should be reasonably accurate, since we checked prices in the different streets and neighbourhoods in which we were working against newspaper advertisements and estate agents' particulars. Nevertheless, interviewers were not trained valuers and did not look over every room in every house on which they called. These figures should therefore be treated as approximations subject to, say, a 10 per cent margin of error either way.

A third problem is that the calculations of respondents' housing costs take no account of repair costs or money spent on improvements and modernization unless these costs were covered by an additional loan or supplement to an existing mortgage. Nor do calculations take account of removal and transaction expenses such as solicitors' fees and estate agents' commissions. We did collect information on the cost of repairs and improvements, but the data here are so incomplete as to be misleading had they been included. Most people could remember what a new roof had cost them two or three years ago, or the cost of installing double glazing one or two autumns back, but most were hard-pressed to come up with any meaningful figure for smaller items, recurrent items, or expenditures incurred ten or twenty years earlier. Similarly, it was unrealistic to expect respondents to recall transaction and removal expenses for each occasion when they had moved house.

Faced with such problems (which are arguably inherent to survey research), two options present themselves. One is to include a notional average cost for repairs and maintenance and transaction costs for each household. According to the 1986 *Family Expenditure Survey* (Department of Employment, 1987), for example, outright owners spend an average of £6.05 per week on repairs, maintenance and decoration, while mortgaged buyers spend an average of £9.86. The problem, however, is that these are averages. Some owners spend much more and some spend much less. To have included such figures in the calculations for different respondents would, therefore, have resulted in extremely misleading results at an individual level. Transaction costs present less of a problem in that they could be assumed at, say, 3 per cent of each sale price, although this too is somewhat arbitrary.

The alternative is to omit these various costs altogether while recognizing that this will have the effect of inflating the calculations of net capital gains. This is the strategy adopted in this study. As we shall see, the overestimation which results may be counteracted by other omissions (notably tax relief on mortgage interest) which produce a corresponding underestimation of gains.

The fourth problem concerns the calculation of mortgage repayments. Few respondents could have told us how much they had paid out in interest since first moving into the owner-occupied sector, and we did not ask them to try. Instead we have calculated total repayments of interest and principal on the assumption that each buyer has always taken out ordinary repayment mortgages at variable interest rates over an average 25-year term (or, in the case of older buyers, up to age 65). Using BSA data on mortgage interest rates for the last fifty years and a 'look-up' table supplied by the Alliance & Leicester Building Society, the total amount paid by each household throughout its time in owner-occupation has been computed according to the size of its loan/s. The rate of amortization of each loan taken out was calculated in the same way, the additional assumption being made here that house moves took place in the middle of the year in which the sale or purchase occurred.

In fact, these figures are almost certainly a very accurate approximation to actual repayments incurred, although some households may have paid off loans more quickly, taken out fixed interest loans, repaid through endowment schemes and so on.

A further point to note about the calculations of mortgage interest payments is that they have not taken account of the tax relief which is available to house purchasers. This probably counteracts the effect of neglecting repair and maintenance costs and transaction expenses. Following the *Family Expenditure Survey* figures, for example, we may assume that repairs, decoration and maintenance cost an average of between £300 and £500 per annum per household in 1986 prices. The same survey shows that tax relief is worth an average of £550 per year to each purchaser. Obviously, just as repair and transaction costs vary between households, so too does the value of mortgage interest tax relief, and it does not necessarily follow that they balance each other out in any given case. Nevertheless, the net result of

127

ignoring both of them in calculating capital gains of households in the three towns survey is that the exaggeration caused by the former is counteracted by the underestimation produced by the latter.

Payment of domestic rates has also been ignored for the purposes of these calculations. There is a debate among housing analysts over whether rates should be seen as a tax on housing (Merrett, 1986). For our purposes they have not been treated as such for two reasons. First, they are levied on all heads of households irrespective of tenure and cannot therefore be seen as a cost specific to owner-occupiers. Second, domestic rates are in any case currently being replaced by a flat rate per capita Community Charge which completely divorces local taxation from housing.

One final problem which should be noted concerns calculations of rates of return. We have already seen in commenting on Spencer's 1987 study that rates of return should be calculated on the basis of the amount of money which buyers themselves advance rather than on the total value of their housing. This creates a problem, however, as regards purchasers with 100 per cent mortgages, for their rates of return are infinite since their initial investment is zero. One possibility would be to treat them as if they had advanced £1 of their own resources, but this is a meaningless assumption which generates meaningless statistics (the most extreme case being that of a council house buyer in Slough who purchased a discounted property on a 100 per cent mortgage and whose rate of return on a notional £1 initial investment works out at 146 million per cent per annum!). Buyers with 100 per cent mortgages are thus excluded from calculations of percentage rates of return, but have been included in all other calculations.

It is clear from all of the above that the figures to be presented in this chapter should be treated with some caution. Nevertheless, the data do have a validity and applicability greater than that achieved in analyses based on averages from aggregate national statistics; for although they are subject to error and to some extent reflect certain working assumptions which in some cases may turn out to be misleading, they are based on real payments and receipts made by real households in the course of their housing careers. Future research will hopefully overcome some of the weaknesses in this data set and will refine some of the measurement techniques, but what is presented here is a first attempt at representing capital gains from the owner-occupied housing system as accurately as is possible given the problems of a survey methodology.

There are a number of different ways in which these capital gains can be represented, and this chapter will use six different measures, each of which can itself be expressed in current or real (that is, 1986) prices.

The first and most obvious measure is of *gross capital gain*. This is calculated as the *value of the house* currently owned (v) plus the *value of any equity withdrawn* at any time (e), less the *mortgage debt* still owing (m), the amount of *deposit first advanced* by the household (d) and any *additional money injected* by the household at subsequent purchases (i). Thus:

Gross capital gain (GCG) = (v + e) − (m + d + i).

This figure can be expressed in real terms (real gross capital gain) by expressing the equity withdrawn, the initial deposit and later injections of capital in 1986 prices (the value of the house and the debt outstanding are already expressed in 1986 prices).

The second measure is of *net capital gain*. This is calculated as for GCG except that *total mortgage repayments* (r) – both interest and principal – have also to be deducted from the total value of the house:

Net capital gain (NCG) = (v + e) − (m + d + i + r).

Again this can be expressed in real terms by converting all figures to a 1986 base.

The third measure is of *annual gross gain* – that is, the amount of capital accumulated per year in owner-occupation. This is a useful measure for comparing gains between different groups of owner-occupiers while controlling for the amount of time spent in home ownership, for total gains tend to rise over time. It is derived by dividing the gross capital gain by the number of *years spent in owner-occupation* (y):

$$\text{Annual gross gain (AGG)} = \frac{[(v + e] - [m + d + i)]}{y}.$$

The real annual gross gain will then be found by dividing the real gross capital gain by the years spent as a home owner.

The fourth measure is of *annual net gain* which is calculated as the net capital gain per annum. In other words, this figure expresses the capital gain made each year after mortgage costs have been deducted:

$$\text{Annual net gain (ANG)} = \frac{[(v + e) - (m + d + i + r)]}{y}.$$

As with the other measures, this can be expressed in real terms by converting all figures to 1986 prices.

The final two measures which we shall be using treat house ownership as an investment and involve calculations of the annual rate of return on the original capital advanced by the household. As we have seen, previous studies have frequently tried to compare rates of return to home ownership with rates of return available on other investments such as shares, bank deposits and bonds. We too shall draw such comparisons, although (as has already been explained) this can only be done in those cases where buyers have not purchased on 100 per cent mortgages.

One measure of the rate of return to home owners in the three towns survey will be the *gross rate of return*. This is calculated by computing the gross capital gain as an annual percentage return on the capital which home owners originally advanced out of their own resources. The formula by which this figure is derived is:

$$\text{Gross rate of return (GRR)} = \left(\frac{(v + e - m - d - i)}{d}\right)^{1/y} - 1 \times 100.$$

Where the sum inside the brackets is a negative figure, the rate of return is computed as if it were positive and is then reconverted to a negative value following the exponentiation. The real gross rate of return is found by expressing the equity withdrawn (e), the original deposit (d) and subsequent injections of new capital (i) in 1986 prices.

The alternative measure of rates of return is that of *net rate of return*. This measure deducts mortgage costs from the calculation of capital gains before computing the annual return or loss on capital invested. The formula in this case is:

$$\text{Net rate of return (NRR)} = \left(\frac{(v + e - m - d - i - r)}{d}\right)^{1/y} - 1 \times 100.$$

Again, this figure can be expressed in real prices by converting all figures to a 1986 base year.

Both gross and net rate of return calculations are expressed in terms of the return on original capital invested. Later injections of capital (other than those rolled forward from the proceeds of previous sales), like later withdrawals of equity, are counted as subtractions from/additions to the total return – that is, they are included in the numerator of the equation but not in the denominator. As explained above, buyers who originally bought on 100 per cent mortgages are excluded from these calculations.

A further point to note about these calculations is that, other things being equal, the rate of return will tend to fall over time. The reason for this is that buyers in the early years of a mortgage own very little equity, and their proportionate gain as house prices rise will therefore be greater than that achieved by more mature purchasers who have acquired a higher percentage equity in their property. Unless caution is exercised in interpreting these figures, this factor can produce quite misleading results. For example, Asians have on average spent less time in owner-occupation than whites, for most Asians first came to Britain some time after the mid-1960s. Similarly, working-class home owners tend to have shorter histories of ownership than middle-class home owners, since working-class owner-occupation is a more recent phenomenon, and many working-class owners are former council tenants who have purchased since the 1980 Act which introduced the Right to Buy. Clearly, then, failure to control for the period of time spent in owner-occupation is likely to result in misleading comparisons between these groups, since later arrivals will tend to reveal higher rates of return, other things being equal.

A further point related to this is that rates of return will be depressed the higher the proportion of the purchase price which is paid for out of people's own resources. If we again compare Asians and whites, for example, we shall see later that there is a tendency for Asian buyers to advance a higher initial deposit, and this will have the effect of reducing the rate of return on their investment since they own a greater share of the equity from the outset. The limiting case here, of course, is that of purchasers who pay for their house outright and do not raise a loan. Their rates of return will tend to be lower than average since they fail to reap any rewards from inflation on that part of the house for which they have yet to pay.

What all of this means is that rates of return calculations should not be analysed in isolation from the other measures discussed above. In particular, comparisons between different groups of owners should not be made purely on the basis of rates of return, but should also involve analysis of measures such as annual gross or net gain. Analysis of rates of return can be illuminating if, for example, we seek to compare the performance of owner-occupied housing with that of other investments, but it can be misleading as a measure of how different groups of owners have fared relative to each other. The various measures used in this chapter have different strengths and weaknesses, and different measures will be appropriate for different analytical purposes.

One major issue remains to be discussed before proceeding to analyse our results. We have seen that capital gains, annual capital gains and rates of gain can be calculated either gross or net. Gross calculations ignore mortgage costs, while net figures include them. Which is the more valid or appropriate guide in understanding wealth accumulation from home ownership?

There is a strong case for arguing for the use of gross figures if the intention is to compare the situation of home owners with that of non-owners. The reason for this is that mortgage costs may be equated with the rent which owners would otherwise have to pay if they chose to put their money into some other form of investment. Both owners and tenants have to live somewhere, and both have therefore to devote a certain portion of income to buying the use of a dwelling. Tenants buy this use value through their rents, while purchasers buy it through their mortgage payments. Put differently, mortgage costs may be equated with 'imputed rental income' (the concept of imputed rent is explained in Chapter 6). What this means is that, while mortgagees pay for borrowing money, they can also be said to receive an 'income' which is equivalent to the money which they would have to pay to a landlord in order to rent the equivalent house. Seen in this way, mortgage costs are cancelled out by imputed rental income (or, if you prefer, by the fact that mortgagees would still have to pay rent had they decided not to buy), in which case they can be ignored for the purposes of calculating capital gains.

The logic of this argument depends, of course, on the assumption that owner-occupiers' outgoings must on average and in the long term be no greater than the rent they would have to pay as tenants in the equivalent house. There are good a priori grounds for believing that this is likely to be the case. As Hugh Stretton points out:

> Over time the tenants pay all the costs of making and maintaining the housing they live in, but their landlords take rent above these costs and also any capital gains which come with urban growth and rising property prices. Over their lifetimes many tenants pay for their housing several times over . . . their rents already buy and maintain it and provide profits for their landlords.
>
> (1978a, p. 40)

For a landlord to stay in business, the rent must presumably cover interest charges, maintenance costs and rates. It is therefore justifiable to equate owner-occupiers' outgoings with their imputed rental income, in which case both can be ignored in calculating returns on their investment.

But is this really true in practice? It is possible, for example, that landlords are content to let houses to tenants at a loss and to cover this in the long term by reaping the capital gain on the rising value of the property. Clearly we need to consider the empirical evidence.

Predictably, perhaps, the evidence is confusing and contradictory, and the balance of financial advantage between owning and renting appears to be different in different countries in different periods. In Ottawa in the 1970s, for example, McFadyen and Hobart (1978) calculated that landlords would need to have charged rents equivalent to 15 per cent of the value of their housing in order to secure a return on capital comparable to that available through other investments, yet they found average rent levels at only 7 per cent of property values, and they concluded from this that house price inflation was making up the shortfall. It followed from their analysis that rental housing was available to households at a price considerably below the real costs of purchasing. Although capital gains made up the difference within five years of moving into owner-occupation, it would seem from these figures that mortgage payments tend to exceed imputed rental income, in which case the logic of using gross rather than net figures when analysing capital gains is severely weakened.

Other evidence points in a different direction, however. In Australia, for example, Badcock's data demonstrate that housing costs of owner-occupiers are lower than those for tenants at all but the lowest income levels (Badcock, 1984, pp. 184, 217), and this would support the view that such costs should at least be seen as equivalent to imputed rental income.

In Britain, it can certainly be shown that average housing costs *over a lifetime* are much greater for tenants than for owners. Using data from the *Family Expenditure Survey* and the Nationwide Anglia Building Society (1987) as the basis for our calculations, let us assume that two 25-year-old males enter the housing market in 1986. One purchases a house and incurs the average initial mortgage repayments in that year of £3,236 p.a. over twenty-five years. The other rents a house at the average rent of £26.15 p.w.

(which will certainly not get him accommodation as good as the buyer's, but we let that pass). We also assume that inflation stays at a modest rate of 5 per cent, that mortgage interest rates stay steady at around 10 per cent and that rents rise by an inflation supplement of 5 per cent each year (the owner's mortgage payments, of course, remain constant in money terms). Finally, we assume that both men live to the average age of 71 and that neither moves house again.

The owner will have paid for his house by the time he is 50, and it will have cost him a total of £80,900. By the time he is 50, the tenant will have paid £64,839 in rent. His annual rental payments will have passed the owner's mortgage payments in the nineteenth year. He continues paying rent until his death in the year 2032 when he will be paying a weekly rent of £234.72. His total rental payments will amount to £229,182 – £148,282 more than the owner has paid to purchase his house. Even allowing for repair and maintenance costs incurred by the owner, it is clear from this simple example that owners' costs are considerably less than their imputed rental income.

Of course, *in the early years* the tenant will enjoy lower housing costs than the buyer. It is only as time passes that the buyer's outgoings drop below those of the tenant. This means that the tenant could in principle not only invest the equivalent of the owner's initial deposit in some other asset, but could also each year invest the difference between what he is paying in rent and what the owner is paying in mortgage. In this way, the tenant could achieve a sizeable capital gain (Murie, Forrest and Williams, 1990, ch. 6). However, while this may need to be taken into account when comparing the capital gains achieved by owners with the returns which tenants could have achieved by investing in other things (that is, the 'opportunity cost' of investing in a house), it does nothing to alter the fact that owners' housing costs will work out cheaper in the long run. It is true that tenants will have more money available for alternative investments in the early years, but once their rents catch up and overtake owners' mortgage payments they would need to start disinvesting in order to make up the difference. In the long term there can be little doubt that they would lose substantially relative to owners. It is for this reason that gross rates of return, ignoring mortgage costs, represent a legitimate basis for judging the performance of owner-occupiers' housing investments.

The case for analysing net rates of return is simply that these reflect actual cash inputs and outflows. This measure is arguably less useful than that of gross rates, for it calculates the return on capital while assuming that owners are living 'rent free'. Calculation of net rates depresses the scale of returns artificially by ignoring the fact that much or all of purchasers' mortgage repayments represent a charge for the use of the dwelling rather than instalments on an investment. Net rate calculations thus mix up payments for use with capital invested. Nevertheless, they do provide us with an interesting 'bottom line' by which to gauge the economics of home ownership. If owners manage to make positive net rates of return, then home ownership really can be described as a golden goose which lays golden eggs, for it means that they are getting a return on their capital even allowing for the cost of servicing their housing loan. As we shall see, the great majority of home owners have achieved precisely that.

Home ownership, the distribution of wealth and the accumulation of capital

Home ownership is a socially heterogeneous form of housing tenure. The contrasts within this tenure – such as between the owner of a Victorian terraced house in the inner area of Burnley and the owner of a detached house in one of the suburban areas around Slough – can be every bit as striking as those which separate owners from renters. Average figures on capital gains are therefore likely to conceal as much as they reveal, and as this analysis proceeds, so we shall begin to break the statistics down in order to investigate the differences between various groups of home owners.

We begin, however, with an overview based on the aggregated results from the three towns survey. Table 3.1 presents the data on total capital gains, net capital gains (after mortgage payments have been deducted) and annual gross and net gains for each owner-occupier household in the survey. The figures in each case are expressed in both money and real (that is, 1986 prices) terms. So as to avoid double-counting, the table is based on only one respondent per household (in the great majority of cases where we interviewed two respondents from the same household, their housing histories as owner-occupiers coincided, and it would therefore produce misleading results if they were counted twice). The results have been broken

Table 3.1 *Capital gains and annual gains by home owners in the three towns survey*

| | | | | Measure of gain (£) | | | | |
Decile	GCG	Real GCG	NCG	Real NCG	AGG	Real AGG	ANG	Real ANG
Lowest 10%	2,216	2,047	−161	−1,925	441	366	−16	−329
20%	7,844	7,525	2,164	1,420	845	810	409	272
30%	12,061	11,282	6,957	6,056	1,196	1,172	676	627
40%	17,239	17,453	10,303	9,523	1,503	1,538	940	913
50% (median)	22,750	22,159	13,527	13,517	2,000	1,987	1,273	1,253
60%	27,597	27,848	19,282	19,343	2,409	2,508	1,594	1,639
70%	33,755	37,231	24,268	26,963	2,956	3,039	2,142	2,054
80%	41,092	46,788	33,255	35,808	3,625	4,004	2,606	2,539
90%	54,999	64,604	45,965	54,950	5,203	5,477	3,210	3,882
Mean	25,823	28,089	18,195	19,697	2,570	2,563	1,696	1,557
N = 289								

Key to column headings: GCG = gross capital gain; NCG = net capital gain; AGG = annual gross gain; ANG = annual net gain. The formulae for calculating these figures are outlined in the previous section.

down into decile groups so as to reveal the range of variation between the lowest and highest gainers.

The figures presented in Table 3.1 are astonishing. The average sum accumulated from home ownership among households in the three towns survey was £28,000 at 1986 prices, and even when mortgage payments are deducted the average still comes out at little short of £20,000. Calculated as an annual return, this means that these households have enjoyed an average capital growth of £2,500 each year, or an average of £1,500 after deducting the cost of mortgage payments averaged over their entire period in owner-occupation. Such averages conceal variations, of course. There are a few extreme cases of gainers and losers at each end of the distribution – for example, people who have experienced unusual good or bad fortune – and there is considerable variation even within the main body of the sample. Nevertheless, even households nine-tenths the way down the distribution have still succeeded in making a real gain before mortgage payments of £2,000 or £366 per year (although these figures turn into losses of nearly £2,000 and £329 respectively when mortgage payments are deducted).

These figures offer strong confirmation of Pahl's argument that many owners can make more from the housing market in a few years than they could save from earnings over a lifetime. Figures compiled by the Building Societies Association (1988) indicate that the average income of first-time buyers in 1986 was just £11,901. If such buyers were to receive the average real net annual capital gain of £1,557, they would effectively be supplementing their income by 13 per cent per year after meeting their housing costs. Expressed a different way, the average real annual gross capital gain of £2,570 would represent a supplement of nearly 22 per cent to the average income of first-time buyers, and it is doubtful whether any tenant on this income could save this much each year even allowing for the lower initial cost of renting. As Murie suggests, 'Few households who do not own dwellings can accumulate wealth on a scale comparable with the house owner' (1983, p. 178).

Clearly, if home owners have been recording gains on the sort of scale indicated by Table 3.1, then the spread of owner-occupation must have had a significant impact on the overall distribution of wealth in Britain. The Royal Commission on the Distribution of Income and Wealth certainly believed that this was the case. Reporting in 1975, it found that housing had grown as a proportion of gross personal wealth from 19 per cent to 39 per cent since 1960 and that the value of dwellings as a percentage of all wealth had risen in this time from 18 per cent to 34 per cent (see Donnison and Ungerson, 1982; Murie, 1983; Murie and Forrest, 1980). This would suggest that the spread of home ownership has spread the share of the nation's wealth more widely. Given that around half of all households owned their homes in the mid-1970s, the Royal Commission's findings indicate that relative shares have shifted away from the richest strata and towards the middle as a result of the growth of owner-occupation.

Trends since the Royal Commission reported are difficult to determine.

Forrest and Murie (1989) suggest that the significance of housing as a percentage of all personal wealth is no longer increasing, and they back up this claim with figures indicating that residential buildings accounted for 42 per cent of net individual wealth in 1979 compared with 41 per cent in 1984. This may turn out only to have been a temporary lull, however, for as we saw earlier, house prices in the early 1980s were falling in real terms following the end of the late 1970s boom, and Forrest and Murie's cut-off date of 1984 may therefore produce a misleading impression of longer-term trends. The share of net personal wealth accounted for by dwellings rose to 48 per cent in 1985 (Hamnett, 1988a), and the start of a new wave of housing inflation in 1986 almost certainly pushed this figure above 50 per cent since then. Between 1979 and the peak of this most recent boom in 1988, the total value of houses rose by 225 per cent (from £270 to £880 billion), and only a fraction of this increase is accounted for by new building (*Sunday Times*, 28 August 1988). It seems likely, therefore, that the tendency for the growth of home ownership to increase the share of wealth held by the home-owning 'middle mass' (Pahl, 1984) is still in evidence.

This trend has two important implications. One is that a new gap is opening up between the majority of households who own property and the minority who do not. The redistribution of wealth which has occurred has been between the top and the middle of the distribution, and those at the bottom still own virtually nothing of any great value. As Alan Murie explains, 'The increase in the value of houses compared with other assets has meant that the gap in wealth between house owners with few other assets and those with substantial other assets has narrowed. However, at the same time, the gap between houseowners and households with few assets of any kind, and not including a house, has widened' (1983, p. 178). When we remember that this same pattern has also been reproduced through the spread of occupational pension schemes (Lowe, 1988), it is clear that a minority stratum is in danger of becoming marginalized as the rest of the population enhances its share of the nation's wealth. This is an issue to which we shall return in Chapter 6.

The second implication is that for the first time in our history millions of people now own a substantial wealth holding. Mass home ownership has achieved what no government redistribution programme has ever achieved. As Hugh Stretton notes, 'The diffusion of house ownership has been the main and almost the only means of diffusing capital ownership in this century' (1975, p. 15). With each wave of house price inflation since the early 1970s, the growing army of home owners has seen its share of national wealth increase. Bracewell-Milnes (1989) estimates that rises in house prices widen and deepen personal ownership of capital ten or even twenty times more rapidly than all other factors combined. Owner-occupied housing has thus today become not only a major source and store of personal wealth for a majority of the population (Thorns, 1982, p. 757), but also the most significant motor for spreading the ownership of capital.

Some critics, however, remain sceptical of such arguments. Michael Ball, for example, argues that although home owners do accumulate wealth, their assets are tied up in their homes and cannot therefore be equated with the more liquid holdings of the richest strata (Ball, 1983, p. 281). Ray Forrest similarly argues that owner-occupied property does not bring economic power such as that enjoyed by large-scale owners of land or productive assets and should not therefore be seen as a diffusion of capital: 'A nation of home owners would not necessarily mean anything in terms of the distribution of property rights in the production of social wealth or in the exercise of social power . . . The property owning democracy is a false promise; the stake in the system is illusory' (1983, pp. 209 and 214).

What both of these writers are concerned to demonstrate is that domestic property is different from capitalist property and that the spread of the former to nearly two-thirds of the population has done nothing to spread the latter more widely. The argument is grounded in Marxist theory which holds that capital is the product of exploiting the labour power of others. This theory believes that capitalists make profit by employing workers and paying them less in wages than the value of the commodities which they produce. It follows from this that the owner-occupier's house does not represent capital, since owners do not employ workers from whom they can extract 'surplus value' (home owners, of course, do sometimes employ others to clean, repair, or decorate their houses, but because this does not result in a commodity sold for profit in the market, this does not qualify as a capital–labour relation).

The argument is, however, fallacious. Even if we accept Marxist theory on its own terms, there are good reasons for identifying owner-occupied housing as capital. Marxists recognize that not all capitalists make profit by directly employing labour and extracting its surplus value. Landowners, bankers and merchants, for example, are treated by Marx as capitalists on the grounds that they claim a share of the value which is extracted by industrialists even though they do not themselves employ the workers who are producing it (see Marx, 1959). Seen in this way, the essence of capital is that it entitles its owner to a share of the value being created in the economy. As we shall see, this is precisely the role played by owner-occupied housing, for it has come to represent a title to a share in the growth of the nation's wealth.

Even if it were not possible to reconcile owner-occupied housing with the Marxist concept of capital, however, it would still be legitimate to see the spread of home ownership as evidence of a diffusion of capital. The inconsistencies and illogicalities of the labour theory of value from which Marxist definitions of capital derive have often been exposed (not least by Marxists themselves – see, for example, Cutler et al., 1977), and there is no need to rehearse these arguments again here. More to the point is evidence that home owners have achieved rates of return on their initial resources which more than match those achieved by owners of property which writers like Ball and Forrest would unhesitatingly recognize as 'capitalist'. If those who own housing achieve higher rates of return on their investments than

137

those who own assets like shares, then it makes little sense to insist that only the latter 'really' own capital, nor that the gains enjoyed by the former are 'illusory'.

We saw earlier that some commentators have suggested that rates of return to home ownership do not compare with those on other forms of investment. Spencer in Britain and Edel, Sclar and Luria in the USA have both argued this. Edel and his co-authors found that although house prices in Boston inflated faster than the RPI between 1950 and 1970, they were outstripped by the Dow Jones index over this period. Spencer found that house prices in Britain out-performed many other investments during the 1970s but compared badly with shares and bank deposits in the 1980s.

Other observers disagree. Tim Congdon of Shearson Lehmann calculates that house buyers on mortgages averaged a 200 per cent return on their investments between 1966 and 1988 (cited in the *Independent*, 1 August 1988); and Moira Munro similarly calculates that 'Over the last twenty years houses have shown an average appreciation in price much in excess of most other forms of investment and certainly far in excess of the return on most popular forms of savings that might be realistic alternatives for tenants' (1988, p. 418). The Nationwide Building Society (1986) confirms this by comparing returns on housing with those on building society accounts, bank deposits, National Savings certificates, unit trusts, gold and shares (measured by the FT Ordinary Share Index). This analysis concluded that 'In the longer term even the gross rates of return on housing are higher than those on most financial investments.' If imputed rent is included in the calculations there is no other type of investment which could have provided as good a rate of return on money invested between 1960 and 1980, and only shares and unit trusts outperformed housing between 1980 and 1985 despite the relative slump in house prices in the early 1980s.

Much the same picture emerges from a 1987 Consumers' Association report which found that 'Over the last twenty years, housing has done better than many other kinds of investment, and far better than inflation. Only shares have done anything like as well – but they're a much riskier investment' (*Which?*, 1987, p. 152). On these figures, a main home bought on an 80 per cent mortgage has shown an annual rate of return of 14 per cent since 1966. This compares with 13 per cent for shares, 8 per cent for unit trusts and 6 per cent for money invested in a building society share account. Inflation over this period has averaged 10 per cent.

As has already been explained, one reason why analysts like Edel and Spencer have recorded comparatively low rates of return on housing investment is that they base their calculations on average house prices rather than on how much money house buyers actually put into their original purchase. Table 3.2 rectifies this error by presenting the gross and net rates of return achieved by home owners in the three towns survey expressed on the basis of their original investments.

As with the findings on capital gains, the results have been broken down by deciles to give an indication of the range across the sample. Caution is needed in interpreting this table, since the mean figures have been inflated by the presence of two sub-groups of very high gainers. The first consists of a small number of recent purchasers, many of them buyers of heavily discounted council houses. We saw earlier that recent buyers will tend to make the highest rates of gain given the relatively small proportion of the equity which they own, and this tendency is exacerbated in this table by the fact that interviews were conducted in 1986 when house prices began to climb following a relatively depressed five-year period. Those who had bought within the last couple of years (nineteen in all) are therefore likely to have recorded abnormally high rates of gain (especially if they bought a council house at a discounted price), and this has skewed the sample mean figures (we consider the relation between rates of gain and time spent in owner-occupation in more detail later in the chapter).

Table 3.2 *Gross and net rates of return on housing investment in the three towns survey*

				Rates of return (%)				
		Real deposit > £1				*Real deposit > £500*		
		Real		*Real*		*Real*		*Real*
Decile	*GRR*	*GRR*	*NRR*	*NRR*	*GRR*	*GRR*	*NRR*	*NRR*
Lowest 10%	12.3	4.3	−6.9	−8.1	12.3	4.0	−6.1	−7.3
20%	15.4	6.7	11.4	2.3	15.3	6.6	11.5	2.1
30%	18.4	8.6	14.6	5.4	18.1	8.6	14.6	5.4
40%	21.9	11.6	17.2	7.6	21.6	11.4	17.0	7.3
50% (median)	25.1	14.5	20.3	10.4	24.4	14.0	19.9	9.8
60%	29.4	18.1	22.6	12.6	29.0	17.4	22.3	11.9
70%	34.5	21.8	27.0	16.6	33.0	21.1	26.2	15.4
80%	44.0	30.7	34.6	23.5	41.5	29.6	32.1	21.7
90%	81.0	68.6	54.5	44.4	68.1	56.6	48.5	34.5
Mean	67.2	53.8	48.6	31.4	52.1	38.8	37.5	21.6

N = 248 cols 1–4; 236 cols 5–8 (41 buyers with initial zero deposits excluded)

Key to column headings: GRR = gross rate of return; NRR = net rate of return. The formulae for calculating these figures are outlined in the previous section.

The second group of abnormally high gainers consists of a dozen buyers in the sample who advanced a very small initial deposit (under £500 in 1986 prices) and who have therefore secured abnormally high returns on a small original stake. Table 3.2 sets out figures both including and excluding this group, but although their exclusion makes a considerable difference to the mean figures, it has little effect across most of the range.

Given these peculiarities, attention should clearly be focused not on the overall mean figures but on the range over, say, the lowest 80 per cent of the distribution. Even when we make this adjustment, however, it is readily apparent that most (though not all) owners have secured rates of return on their original investments which easily stand comparison with those which would have been available to them had they put their money elsewhere.

Ignoring the extremes at each end of the distribution and focusing on those who originally invested at least £500 of their own money in real terms, the middle 80 per cent of home owners have made nominal rates of return on their capital of between 4 and 30 per cent per annum. These figures should be compared with the returns offered by alternative investments which would have been open to them had they chosen to rent and to invest their savings in some other way. Building society interest paid on share accounts has varied between 4 and 10½ per cent since the mid-1960s; interest on bank deposits has ranged from 2½ to 15 per cent over the same period. The FT Ordinary Share Index rose from 337 to 855 in the twenty years from 1966 – an annual rate of increase of less than 4 per cent a year (figures from Central Statistical Office, *Economic Trends Annual Supplement*, 1986). Compared with these, a median real rate of return of 14 per cent per year for owner-occupiers is clearly quite favourable, and the fact that more than 80 per cent of owners have managed to show a positive rate of return even after deducting their mortgage payments is little short of remarkable.

Again, however, the critics on the political left are apparently unimpressed by such evidence. As was noted in the Prologue to this book, there is throughout the academic literature on owner-occupation a marked antipathy to mass home ownership. Critics have for years sought to demonstrate that a capitalist system which has brought owner-occupation within the grasp of ordinary working people has nevertheless done them no favours. This is why there is such a deep resistance to the notion that home owners may actually be making money from their housing, for this sort of evidence suggests that even working-class people may accumulate capital within a capitalist system. Neat theories of class struggle and class exploitation are threatened by the possibility that between half and two-thirds of the population is sharing in the benefits of rapid capital accumulation. Those who have sought to challenge this proposition, even in the face of the evidence we have already reviewed, have generally done so on the basis of one or more of five arguments.

The first holds that the gains accruing through the housing market are illusory in the sense that they are achieved at the expense of other ordinary households. The logic here is that if one set of people is making money, another set must be losing it, in which case the mass of the population taken as a whole is no better off.

The second argument holds that capital gains from owner-occupation are a temporary phenomenon of the 1970s and 1980s and that owner-occupiers may well begin to lose in the future. Theories are adduced to show that house prices 'must' fall back in the long run, and evidence is selectively cited from other countries where prices have fallen or stagnated to show that home owners in Britain are destined to lose all or much of what they have gained.

The third argument suggests that capital gains are only paper gains and cannot generally be realized in the form of cash. Growing evidence that owner-occupiers are converting some of their equity into liquid form has recently led to a modification (actually a reversal) of this argument, for some critics now suggest that the capital which owners accumulate over a lifetime is being eaten away by equity withdrawals in old age. Either way, home ownership is portrayed negatively – it is wealth that cannot be spent, or it is wealth which will disappear because it is being spent!

The fourth, and probably most important, argument claims that only affluent home owners are in a position to generate gains and that poorer purchasers may actually lose as a result of buying. This argument is developed in two stages. First it is suggested that home ownership has proved to be a financial burden for poorer households who are forced to live in substandard housing and who struggle to meet the mortgage repayments. To this is added the belief that capital gains are proportional to the existing income and wealth of different households such that they exacerbate social class divisions rather than ameliorating them.

The fifth argument holds that owners are generally indifferent to the investment potential of their housing and that it therefore makes no sense to analyse owner-occupation as a form of wealth accumulation.

All five arguments are fallacious. This is not to say that none of them could be true under certain conditions, for it is not my intention to argue that home ownership is always and necessarily an effective source of wealth accumulation. The point, however, is that all five arguments rest essentially on empirical claims, and in the context of postwar Britain these claims simply do not hold up in the face of the evidence.

For the remainder of this chapter we shall consider these five arguments one by one, drawing upon the evidence from the three towns survey and on other empirical sources as appropriate. We begin with the claim that capital gains from home ownership are illusory.

Where do capital gains come from?

There is no disputing that house prices have risen in the postwar period in Britain and in other Western capitalist countries. It may even be accepted that rates of return have matched or outstripped those on other forms of investment. What many critics do not accept, however, is that these price rises have benefited anybody other than large landowners, lending institutions and the construction industry. Home owners taken as a whole have not benefited. The argument turns on the question of where capital growth in owner-occupation comes from, for it is held that if some owners gain, others must have lost, in which case home owners as a whole are no better off.

Over the last twenty years or so, home owners have accumulated capital from a number of different sources. Tax relief on mortgage interest payments is one obvious source, for the cost of borrowing money has been subsidized. The cost of this tax relief had risen by the late 1980s to around £5 billion each year, although failure to raise the maximum limit in line with inflation has recently begun to erode its value for those with larger mortgages. As we shall see in Chapter 6, some of this subsidy has been capitalized into higher house prices, since tax relief enables buyers to bid a higher price for housing than they would otherwise be able to afford. Tax relief has thus benefited those with mortgages partly by increasing the value of their assets and partly by lowering their housing costs.

A second source of accumulation has been negative real interest rates. There was a period during the 1970s when inflation was running at over 20 per cent yet mortgage interest rates were down at 12 or 13 per cent. This meant that lending institutions were at that time effectively paying house buyers to borrow their money! However, during the 1980s government has sought to control inflation by relying primarily on a policy of high interest rates, and this has reversed the situation of ten years earlier. By the late 1980s inflation was down to between 6 and 8 per cent, yet mortgage rates were nearly twice this figure.

A third way in which home owners accumulate wealth is through improving their properties, particularly where they use their own labour. Bossons notes that 'The use of leisure time for home production of house improvements (carpentry, gardening, etc.) results in capital improvements whose market value can generally be realized only through home ownership' (1978, p. 92). It is not uncommon for households to buy an unimproved house, use their own labour to renovate it and then sell at a profit in order to move up-market. In his study of working-class owners on the Isle of Sheppey, for example, Pahl writes of 'a particular kind of household work strategy which depends on home renovation and improvement as a means of raising the value of the property, selling with a capital gain and gradually moving up the housing market and acquiring capital at the same time' (1984, p. 183). This, of course, is a strategy which is not available to tenants.

Two points should be noted about these three sources of wealth accumulation. The first is that it is obvious in each case where capital gains have originated. If owners make money through tax relief, this is at the expense of other taxpayers. If they make money as a result of negative real interest rates, this is at the expense of the lenders, many of whom are small savers on low or fixed incomes. And if they make money through DIY improvements, this is no more than a return on their own labour which itself incurs an 'opportunity cost' in terms of alternatives forgone.

The second point is that none of these three strategies of wealth accumulation really goes to the heart of the explanation of where capital gains come from. Tax relief is only available to those who are buying on a mortgage, yet outright owners also secure capital gains. Were tax relief to be ended, home owners could still accumulate wealth, and the fact that the figures presented in Tables 3.1 and 3.2 ignore this subsidy demonstrates that it is not the fundamental explanation for capital gains. Similarly, negative interest rates were important for a period in the 1970s but are now a thing of the past, yet home owners are still making money. As for DIY improvements, they may enable particular households to raise their rate of accumulation, but even home owners who do not possess a paintbrush or a screwdriver still evidently amass wealth through their housing. Tax relief, negative interest rates and DIY may all contribute to capital gains, but to assume that they provide us with the fundamental explanation (as Badcock, 1984, p. 178, suggests) is clearly mistaken. The key source of these gains lies elsewhere.

One possibility which has often been suggested is that owners simply make in capital gains what they pay in financing their purchase. If, for example, there is a uniform rate of inflation of 10 per cent, then owners will see their housing rise in value by 10 per cent each year (their 'capital gain'), but they will pay for this through the interest charged on their loans which will be 10 per cent higher than if there were no inflation. Seen in this way, the more home owners accumulate, the more they have to pay – capital gains are no more than their own 'forced savings'.

We have already seen, however, that this is not empirically the case. Home owners in the three towns survey have been accumulating capital *over and above* what they have been paying to finance their house purchase. We saw in Table 3.1 that the median real annual gain net of mortgage costs is £1,253. Although a few owners have sustained real net annual losses, the great majority have been making money. It is true that part of their gain is explained by their own 'enforced savings' – this is, roughly speaking, the difference between the net and gross figures – but most owners have been making substantial gains on top of this.

The explanation for this is, quite simply, that inflation has not been uniform. As we saw in Figure 3.1, house prices have been rising faster than other commodity prices. This appears to have been the case for most of this century (the 1930s were an exception). Martin Boddy (1980, p. 105) finds that between 1900 and 1970 the price of consumer goods rose by 700 per cent, while the price of housing rose by 1,550 per cent – more than double. Holmans (1987, p. 142) calculates that between 1956 and 1979 house prices rose faster than the general price level by a factor of 2.9 per cent per year; and the Nationwide Building Society (1985) estimates that house prices increased nearly twice as fast as the RPI over the period from 1954 to 1984. As for the years since then, the Halifax Index shows a 60 per cent increase in house prices from 1983 to 1987 compared with a 22 per cent increase in the RPI (Halifax Building Society, 1987).

It seems from these figures that house prices over time have tended to inflate by as much as twice the rate of other commodities. Part of the difference is undoubtedly due to improved housing standards (that is, houses become more expensive because their quality has increased – see BSA, 1976), but most of the difference is a real shift in the price ratio. Put in simple terms, housing is constantly becoming more expensive, and this explains why it is that home owners have been able to record such impressive capital gains.

But if capital gains are primarily a product of housing becoming more expensive relative to other prices, does this not confirm the view of the critics that home owners as a *whole* do not really benefit? After all, individual owners only accumulate wealth at the expense of later buyers entering the market. Each generation, it seems, finances the capital gains of its parents by paying more for its housing than they did. One generation of Peters is simply robbing the next generation of Pauls, and seen in this way, capital gains are no more than an inter-generational redistribution of income.

This has long been a popular argument in the left literature on owner-occupation since it suggests that the only social group which really makes profit out of housing consists of those capitalists who supply it. They benefit because the price of the commodity they are selling keeps rising. Those who buy housing, however, are no better off. Clarke and Ginsburg, for example, are in no doubt that 'The gain is achieved at the expense of another owner occupier who purchases the house . . . The important point is that from the point of view of the sector as a whole, capital gains do not represent a benefit' (1975, p. 19). Similarly Kemeny tells us that 'The phenomenon of "capital gains" is largely illusory . . . The "capital gain" . . . does not represent a free windfall. It is paid for through higher housing costs for remaining or new owner occupiers' (1981, pp. 37–8).

Now there is something odd about this argument. Clarke and Ginsburg, Kemeny and others are certainly right to claim that the basic source of capital gains lies in the rising real value of houses. Their analyses, however, leave two key questions unexplained. First, if each generation has to pay more for houses than its predecessors did, then how is it that more people than ever before can afford to enter owner-occupation? The logic of their argument is surely that rates of home ownership should fall over time as housing becomes more expensive. Second, and related to this, if each generation is indeed paying more for housing, then why are capital gains of existing owners still dismissed as 'illusory'? If more money is going into the housing market and prices are rising in real terms, it clearly makes no sense to insist that the sector as a whole is not gaining. If new buyers are paying more, then somewhere along the line, existing owners must be making real gains.

The source of the confusion is that these writers focus exclusively on the relation between house prices and the general price level and neglect to consider incomes. As we saw in Figure 3.1, it is true that houses have become more expensive relative to other goods, but it is also the case that incomes have tended to rise in line with house prices. This pattern has been in evidence over many years – Daunton (1987, p. 108), for example, shows that the ratio of earnings and house prices remained relatively constant between 1938 and 1975. Similarly, the Nationwide Building Society (1985) shows that real personal disposable incomes (that is, incomes after tax) doubled between 1954 and 1984 and therefore matched the movement of house prices, although periods of marked income inflation did not necessarily match those of marked house price inflation. This study found that the house price/earnings ratio stood at 3.35 in 1954 and at 3.34 in 1984, although in between times it fluctuated between 2.86 and 4.18. At the peak of the late-1980s house price boom, the house price/earnings ratio had been stretched to 4.9 (Halifax Building Society, *National Bulletin*, no. 34, 1988), but this again began to fall back as house prices stalled in the autumn of 1988. Although it is possible that the increased number of multi-earner households buying houses may result in a higher stable ratio in the future, it is clear that earnings and house prices are intimately related and that price rises are always eventually checked by the rate of increase in disposable household incomes.

This finding is crucially significant. What it means is that *in real terms housing has risen in price (relative to all other commodities) but has stayed constant in cost (relative to real disposable earnings)*. This explains the puzzle of how existing owners make money while new buyers can still afford to enter the market. It is not true (as Kemeny and others suggest) that home owners gain at the expense of the next generation of buyers, for the next generation pays no more in real terms for its housing than the previous generation did. It is certainly not true (as Ball suggests) that home ownership is 'a way of making money for a lucky few at the expense of others' (1986, p. 55), for we have seen that the great majority of owners makes substantial gains while new buyers lose nothing.

The truth of the matter, however unpalatable it may be to left academics, is that the capital gains made by home owners represent a share in the growing real wealth of the capitalist society in which they live. For reasons we shall explore in the next section, house prices do not fall as other commodity prices tend to do when the society becomes richer. Rather, the value of housing increases to match the rise in real spending power. Economic growth benefits wage earners (whose wages buy more goods over time) and home owners (whose asset increases in value over time). The result is that home ownership has come to represent the equivalent of a certificate of entitlement to share in the fruits of economic growth. It is, despite all the critics' claims to the contrary, quite literally a 'stake in the capitalist system'.

Will owner-occupiers continue to gain?

Confronted with evidence that capital gains in the housing market are real and are not achieved at the expense of new buyers, critics resort to a second line of attack. The gains, they claim, are temporary. The argument is developed theoretically and with reference to evidence from other countries.

The theoretical argument derives, predictably, from Marx's 'law of value'. According to this 'law', commodity prices are governed ultimately by their value which is determined by the socially necessary labour time which is devoted to producing them. Marx recognizes that in the real world prices diverge from values, but he insists that, if the price of a commodity moves markedly above its value, then new producers will be attracted into the

145

market, and this increased supply will drive the price back down again.

Matthew Edel (1982) is one of those who has drawn upon this theory to argue that rising real house prices cannot be sustained in the long term. 'In a capitalist system', he confidently proclaims, 'housing is a commodity produced for profit. If housing prices rise, eventually this will affect the profitability of supplying more houses, and increasing new supplies will drive price increases back towards the general inflation level' (1982, p. 216). If real house prices rise because of a temporary shortage of supply, house builders will step up production. If real house prices rise because productivity lags behind that in other sectors of the economy, innovators will seize the chance to increase their market share by introducing new building methods and lowering costs. In any event, prices must fall. As Edel concludes, 'A continuing situation in which housing prices rise faster than other prices is thus improbable' (1982, p. 217).

Improbable it may be, but such a situation persists. Edel himself found in his subsequent study of Boston that real house prices had risen in every Boston neighbourhood in the postwar period (Edel, Sclar and Luria, 1984, p. 88), yet despite his own evidence he still insisted that this was unlikely to continue in the future (1984, p. 337). He is, of course, entitled to hold to his theory, for the theory is not necessarily disproved by such evidence. It may be, for example, that house prices would fall back in line with the theory's predictions were it not for the intervention of some other factor (planning controls are one obvious candidate, for these are likely to prevent new suppliers from entering the market in sufficient numbers to reduce prices). Nevertheless, it is apparent that the theory itself cannot help us to resolve the question of whether real house prices are likely to continue rising. The fact that the theory is out of line with the evidence suggests either that the theory is wrong, or that something else is also happening which the theory does not explain. Either way, Edel's theoretical speculations are unlikely to take us very far.

An alternative approach to this issue is through comparative analysis. According to Ball, the British owner-occupied housing market has been leading a 'charmed life' (1986, p. 48). Elsewhere in Europe, home owners have suffered real and substantial falls in the value of their housing. In West Germany urban second-hand house prices fell by 20 per cent between 1982 and 1984, and Italy and Denmark have also witnessed price reductions (Ball, 1985, p. 29). The most dramatic (and most frequently discussed) collapse, however, occurred in the Netherlands, and it is this experience which is often cited as evidence that the same thing could happen in Britain.

The Dutch owner-occupied housing market entered a boom period in 1976. Median house prices rose from Hfl. 110,000 in 1976 to Hfl. 160,000 in 1977 and peaked in 1978 at Hfl. 175,000. Prices then collapsed and fell to a median level in 1982 of Hfl. 140,000 (Van Weesep, 1986). This drop resulted in a sharp decline in new building for owner-occupation while trapping recent first-time buyers who found that they were committed to housing loans far in excess of the market value of their houses. This predictably led to an increase in the rate of mortgage defaults as borrowers abandoned their homes and moved back into the rental sector leaving the lending institutions to carry the loss. The question is, why did it happen?

To understand this it is important to recognize two fundamental differences between the Dutch and British housing markets. One major difference is that the Dutch market is very much smaller and is therefore more prone to sudden price fluctuations. In Amsterdam, which was where the problem was centred, only 10 per cent of households own their homes, and the number of transactions in the owner-occupied market in any one year is therefore tiny. The second difference is that speculation in owner-occupied housing is much easier in the Netherlands than in Britain. In Britain, purchase of a house typically takes three months or more to complete, whereas in the Netherlands houses can be bought and sold as easily as stocks and shares (see David Hendry's analysis in the *Guardian*, 19 June 1986).

The sudden house price boom in Amsterdam in 1976 seems to have triggered off a wave of speculative activity involving a small number of buyers backed by some rather careless banks. Because so few houses became available in such a small market, the speculators swiftly bid up prices until the bankers took fright and called in their loans. The result was panic selling and the ensuing house price collapse. This was then exacerbated by income stagnation, which meant that new buyers could not be found to purchase at the inflated prices, and rising real interest rates, which deterred potential buyers from borrowing (Priemus, 1987, p. 22).

It is difficult to see many parallels between this particular case and the operation of the owner-occupied market in Britain which is simply nowhere near as susceptible to sudden bouts of speculative buying or panic selling. Comparative analysis can be helpful, but we need to ensure that we are comparing like with like. In this case clearly we are not.

This is not to deny that a house price collapse could happen in Britain. Four such scenarios (which are not mutually exclusive) may be considered.

The first is simply a massive and sustained loss of confidence in the market. As we have seen, each of the three major house price booms since the early 1970s has been followed by a fall in real prices until disposable incomes have caught up. The slumps which followed the first two booms were, however, disguised by a high general rate of inflation; real house prices fell, but money prices did not. The aftermath of the 1986–8 boom is, however, rather different, for with inflation at around 6 or 8 per cent, nominal prices of some housing in the highest-priced regions began to fall from the autumn of 1988. Indeed, a report by an adviser to Midland Montagu suggested in December of that year that a fall on the scale of the post-1973 slump could result in nominal house prices dropping by as much as 20 per cent (*Financial Times*, 12 November 1988).

If such a decline were to occur, it is possible that it would feed off itself and develop into a deflationary spiral as buyers and sellers convince themselves that future trends are downward. Such a spiral could be reinforced by a spate of repossessions and defaults as recent buyers discover that their mortgages exceed the value of their homes (see the *Guardian*, 10 September 1988). Against this, however, it seems more likely that, as in previous slumps, existing owners will simply sit tight and delay moving until prices recover with the steady rise in incomes. This would then depress supply, thereby hastening the recovery.

The second scenario is longer term and has to do with the falling population. The same *Guardian* report suggests that the number of new households demanding accommodation in the year 2000 could be half that of the 1980s. Other things being equal, we would expect this to result in a fall in house prices. Whether or not this actually occurs depends, of course, on whether other things will stay equal. In the 1980s, for example, the children of the birth bulge often delayed forming new households because of the intense market competition for cheap accommodation. Just as household formation was suppressed then, so it may be released at the turn of the century – as we saw in Chapter 1, the rate of household formation does not necessarily reflect the rate of population growth. If children leave home earlier or if more marriages split up, demand for housing need not fall dramatically, and geographical shifts in any case suggest that different regions will fare differently according to the pattern of population movement.

The third scenario is that government policies could, intentionally or otherwise, drive house prices downwards. A long period of very high interest rates, for example, could depress demand and reduce prices. This is a fear which has been expressed by the building societies in submissions to the government. Similarly, any decision to withdraw mortgage tax relief, to tax owner-occupiers' capital gains, or to reintroduce a tax on imputed rental values of owner-occupied housing would presumably exert a downward influence on house prices, as would a successful drive to expand low-cost public or private rental. None of this seems very probable, however, for as we shall see in Chapter 4, all political parties are extremely sensitive to the interests of home owners, and long-term policies resulting in a major reduction in their wealth holdings are unlikely to be electorally sustainable.

The final scenario is that the economy itself crashes and brings house prices tumbling down with it. It is not difficult to find pundits willing to predict such an eventuality. Edel, Sclar and Luria foresee a deepening crisis in the capitalist economies in which 'Homeownership values will be threatened by more general economic collapse, and homeowners' equities and living standards will be imperilled by reductions in labor earnings' (1984, p. 348). Ball too seems to share this apocalyptic vision for he warns that 'economic crisis' could produce a 'collapse' in the owner-occupied market, thereby fundamentally altering the current economic advantages accruing to home owners (1985, p. 29). In July 1986 the press carried reports of comments made by Robert Beckman, who predicted at a Shelter conference that prices would fall by as much as 80 per cent over the next ten years and that 'The British dream of home ownership could turn out to be a nightmare in the year ahead' (*Financial Times*, 21 July 1986). In fact, house prices rose by around 15 per cent over the next twelve months and by 34 per cent the following year, and nothing more was heard of Mr Beckman and his prophecies.

It is, of course, the case that any long-term recession involving a sustained fall in real incomes across the board would undoubtedly lead to a collapse in house prices. This is not the place to debate the likelihood of such a dramatic slump, and if it happened the effect on house prices would in any case be of relatively minor consequence when compared with the massive rise in unemployment and poverty which it would entail. All that need be noted here is that even during periods which Marxist commentators deem to be 'crises', British capitalism has proved remarkably resilient. According to the 1988 edition of *Social Trends*, for example, real spending power in Britain increased by 20 per cent over the years from the mid-1970s, yet this period covered what by general consent was the worst economic slump since the 1930s! By the mid-1980s economic growth was running at 4 per cent per annum.

More interesting than the question of what would happen if incomes fell is the question of why house prices seem in the long term to reflect income shifts. We can agree that, if incomes fell sharply with an economic recession, house prices would follow them down, just as house prices rise as real incomes rise. But why does the owner-occupied housing market respond differently from other commodity markets to changes in personal spending power?

In most other commodity markets, rising real incomes are reflected in falling real prices. As British society has become wealthier, so people's incomes have outpaced commodity prices and they have been able to purchase more goods for the same number of hours worked. This is the essence of Hayek's metaphor of the 'moving column' – the argument that capitalism is unequal yet dynamic and that those at the back of the column will in time come to enjoy the standard of living which those at the front enjoy today (Hayek, 1960). It is this that explains how it is that two-thirds of British households could afford a car in 1987 compared with only one-third in 1960; how 16 million Britons could afford to take foreign holidays in 1987 when foreign travel was beyond most people's dreams just thirty years earlier; and so on.

The housing market, however, is different. To some extent, housing has become 'cheaper' in the sense that people have been able to demand more space and better amenities for their money. Peter Berger quotes McCracken as pointing out that although slums still exist, 'The poor live in what would have been thought of in the pre-capitalist period as ill-maintained castles' (1987, p. 42). As recently as 1951, 7½ million households lived in dwellings classed as 'unfit' (a term which is itself relative in a context of rising standards and prosperity). By 1976 this figure had fallen to less than 2 million. Two million households were sharing accommodation and half a million were living at more than 1.5 persons per room in 1951. Twenty-five years later, these figures had fallen to half a million and around one hundred thousand (see Short, 1982, p. 224). As with other commodities, therefore, rising incomes have led to increased consumption. People now enjoy better housing for their money than they used to.

Nevertheless, as we have seen, the price of housing has not fallen relative to incomes, and the improved quality cannot explain this stickiness in the market. After all, the quality of TV sets, holidays and ballpoint pens has improved as well, but their prices have also fallen in real terms. Why, then, is housing different?

Various explanations have been put forward. Some focus on the nature of demand for housing, others on the characteristics of supply.

Two factors on the demand side which have often been cited as explanations for the long-term rise in house prices are demographic change and government subsidies. There are now more households demanding accommodation than in the past (Spencer, 1987), and subsidies like mortgage interest tax relief enable each household to pay more for its housing than it would otherwise be able to do. Neither factor on its own, however, can explain why house prices have risen at a faster rate than other prices. An increase in the number of households seeking housing may push prices up in the short run (especially if it is a sudden increase produced by the maturation of a birth bulge), but we would expect supply to rise in response to this and prices to stabilize in the longer term. Similarly, subsidies to demand will only have a one-off effect. The introduction of a subsidy may raise prices, but it will not push them higher and higher each year.

Another factor on the demand side which is often advanced as an explanation for rising real house prices is the expansion of mortgage lending. Rising real incomes on their own will not produce rising house prices unless buyers can borrow more money on the strength of their incomes to finance their purchases (Holmans, 1987, pp. 263–4), and it is clear that more loans of a higher real value are arranged today than ever before. Lending institutions now commonly advance loans on a higher multiple of earnings and on a lower percentage deposit, and it is argued that this increased effective demand translates into inflated prices (for example, Boddy, 1980, pp. 95–6; Spencer, 1987, pp. 19–20). Indeed, some analysts go on to argue from this that by forcing up house prices through their liberal lending practices, the banks and building societies have stoked the general rate of inflation as workers have increased pressure for wage rises to cover their spiralling housing costs (Ball, 1983, pp. 355, 366; the *Guardian*, 21 July 1987).

This line of argument fails to stand up to close scrutiny, however. For one thing, it is quite possible for a house price boom to occur on the basis of very little additional mortgage funding, for a large number of transactions can be financed by relatively small injections of new money (Ball, 1983, p. 321). More importantly, econometric analysis indicates that the key influence on house prices is the level of real income, not the willingness of building societies to lend (Nellis and Longbottom, 1981; Styles, Marsh and Crossley, 1987). Certainly, restrictions on lending may hold back housing inflation, and any sudden loosening of lending restrictions is likely to release a short-lived price boom as in the period from 1971 to 1973 (Boddy, 1980, p. 99). Liberalization of lending can hardly be said to cause a long-term rise in prices, however, for people will not borrow what they cannot afford to repay. The lending institutions are the means by which rising real incomes are transmitted into rising real house prices, but they are not the cause of it (BSA, 1976).

Indeed, there is a sense in which liberalization of the home loans market may have slowed the rate of house price inflation. Since the late 1970s it has become easier to get access to a mortgage, largely due to the increased competition between building societies and the clearing banks (Davis and Saville, 1982). But in order to lend more, the institutions have had to attract more savings, and this has necessitated a general rise in interest rates (White and White, 1977, p. 114). The liberalization of lending, therefore, has increased housing costs by pushing up mortgage rates (Ball, Martens and Harloe, 1986; Karn, Doling and Stafford, 1986). This means that, although it may be easier to get a loan, it costs more to service it, and this is likely to have reduced the level of effective demand in the housing market and thus dampened the rate of increase in house prices.

It is apparent from all of this that the key explanation for why house prices rise faster than other commodity prices as disposable incomes rise must lie in the peculiar features of housing supply as compared with other industries. Three points are relevant to this.

The first is that, unlike most other commodities, most housing that is traded is second-hand. Only around 15 per cent of housing transactions in any one year involve new houses, and new dwellings only add 1 to 2 per cent to the housing stock each year (Ball, 1983). What this means is that, if the building industry responds to increased demand by increasing its number of fresh starts, the supply will only begin to rise a year or two later (given the length of the planning, land acquisition and construction cycle), and even then will only make a faint impression on the overall number of dwellings available for sale. Michelle and Lawrence White (1977) calculate that it would take ten to twenty years for the building industry to meet a doubling in housing demand. In the meantime, of course, prices would rise. As Davis and Saville conclude, 'The long-lived nature of the housing stock, and the slowness with which it can change, suggest that any increase in the demand for owner-occupied housing will be reflected, initially at least, principally in higher house prices' (1982, p. 392).

This factor explains the 'stickiness' in the housing market, but it does not explain why prices still rise in the long term, even after the building industry has had time to raise its level of output. The real causes of long-term house price rises lie in two other factors on the supply side.

The first has to do with the limits on increasing productivity. Most commodities fall in price in real terms as technological change reduces their

151

marginal cost of production. This has also happened in housing, of course, for as we saw in Chapter 1, there were important innovations in brick-making, roof tile manufacture and cement production in the inter-war years, and further innovations since then (notably in off-site pre-assembly of items like window frames and internal fixtures) have continued to raise the level of productivity. However, as Taylor (1983, p. 438) has suggested, it has proved difficult to reduce unit costs in the construction industry to the same extent as in other sectors of the economy. Experiments with prefabrication and 'system building' do not have a happy history in Britain, and factors such as the survival of many small firms, the speculative nature of much housing production and the persistence of casualized labour practices may all have hindered the introduction of more efficient production methods (Dickens *et al.*, 1985, ch. 3). The key problem, however, is that, short of increasing densities (such as by building upwards), it is not possible to raise the technical productivity of land, yet land costs represent a major item in overall housing costs.

This brings us to the second, and in my view most important, supply-side constraint – namely, the existence of planning controls and their effect on the availability of building land. In recent years the demand for housing in regions such as the South-East has been intensifying, but planning controls, and in particular the 'green belt' policy, have prevented the construction industry from increasing supply to match more than a fraction of this demand. The result, inevitably, has been a marked increase in the price of any development land which does become available, as well as inflation of house prices in the second-hand market. The problem is most marked in the South-East, but it is also in evidence throughout the rest of the country. Figures cited by Evans (1988) show that the price of building land (that is, land with planning permission) has been rising much faster than the price of agricultural land (where new building is prohibited). By 1987 the price of land for housing in the South-East had reached nearly £1 million per hectare – a staggering 230 times higher than the price of agricultural land. Even in Wales, where housing land is the cheapest in the country, the average price of building land was £145,000 per hectare, or thirty-seven times the price of farmland. As Evans concludes, 'If planning controls were relaxed, many owners of agricultural land would be able to sell it for development. As a result, the price of development land would fall to a level closer to that of agricultural land. The difference in prices in the two markets, at the margin, is maintained only by restricting the transfer of land from one market to the other' (1988, pp. 17–19).

The argument that artificial constraints on the supply of new building land have been the major factor in maintaining the rise in house prices can be reinforced by long-term historical evidence. According to Holmans (1987, p. 84) there has been only one period since the early nineteenth century when house prices in England have failed to rise faster than other commodity prices, and that was during the inter-war years. In the nineteenth century prices rose because escalating demand from a rapidly rising urban population encountered technical limits on the supply of new land. The relatively rudimentary state of transportation and communication technologies at that time effectively restricted suburban expansion and thus intensified demand for sites within a limited geographical area. After the First World War, however, the electrification of the railways and the spread of the internal combustion engine enabled new land to be opened up on the periphery of the cities. This eased the supply-side constraints, and house prices fell back to (or even below) the general price level despite an overall improvement in housing standards. Following the Second World War, however, a tight system of planning controls was introduced designed to prevent what was referred to as 'suburban sprawl'. The result, ever since, has been that house prices have risen to soak up any increase in people's capacity to pay.

Drawing together the arguments reviewed in this section, it is apparent that, far from falling in the future, the real price of owner-occupied housing is likely to continue to rise, just as it has in the past. This trend will only be halted or reversed if one of three things happens.

The first is that house prices could fall if the rate of household formation drops and remains at a lower level. We have seen that this could happen from the turn of the century following the maturation of the 1960s birth bulge, for the numbers of young adults seeking accommodation are certain to drop off over the next couple of decades. However, other trends are likely to counteract the effect of this. One is that people are forming their own households at a younger age, and there is a steady increase in the numbers of single-person households. A falling population need not mean that the number of households will fall. Another is that many households now contain more than one earner, and they can therefore bid up the price of housing even if its availability increases. Similarly (as we shall see in the next section), increasing numbers of people are likely to purchase houses aided with the proceeds of an inheritance from parents who themselves owned their homes, and this too may be expected to push prices upwards. Although the overall picture is extremely unclear and difficult to predict, there therefore seems to be no good reason to believe that current demographic trends spell an end to rising real house prices.

The second way in which this trend could be halted is if real incomes fell across the board, for as we have seen, rising disposable real incomes are the main force on the demand side leading to rising real house prices. A dramatic collapse of the economy can never be ruled out, and many Marxists have long been convinced that the next downturn will be the last. All that can be said about this is that, for as long as the capitalist economy keeps growing, house prices are likely to keep rising, and there are few good grounds for believing that such long-term growth is not still a realistic prospect.

The third way in which rising real house prices could come to an end is through political intervention. This could come from the political right or left. A move from the right would involve dramatic easing of planning controls which would allow supply to rise to meet effective demand, thereby lowering prices. In the late 1980s the Conservative government came under mounting pressure to release more green belt land in the South-East, but any serious moves in this direction were checked by the influence of the environmental lobby and of existing home owners in the targeted areas. A move from the left would entail the nationalization of development land and possibly nationalization or regulation of the financial institutions. This would enable the state to regulate the price of land and to control the flow of mortgage funds into owner-occupation, either of which could result in falling house prices. We consider arguments in favour of such a strategy in Chapter 6. Here we need only note that the anticipated electoral repercussions from existing home owners are probably enough to ensure that such plans never get further than the pages of academic journals and textbooks.

Our conclusion is self-evident. The extent to which home owners have been able to make gains from rising real house prices in recent years may prove exceptional, but their ability to derive real and significant gains is not. Real house prices have risen over a long period in the past, and the likelihood is that they will continue to rise in the future. There is no reason to accept the arguments of those who claim that the gains will prove temporary and that owner-occupiers are about to get their come-uppance.

Are capital gains realizable?

Some critics of home ownership accept that owner-occupiers may make real gains in the sense that their housing rises in value, but they argue that this is of little consequence since most owners cannot turn their assets into cash. Kemeny, for example, writes:

> For most owner-occupiers it is not possible to realize any capital gains which might be made by selling the home. The vast majority of owner-occupiers sell their homes in order to buy another one . . . Since the prices of all houses inflate at approximately the same rate . . . the capital gain made on the sale of one home must generally be spent in order to acquire another home . . . Curiously, then, the capital gains made on owner-occupied housing do not generally accrue to anyone: they are simply passed from one owner-occupier to another.
> (1981, pp. 36–7; for a similar argument see Clarke and Ginsburg, 1975)

This is a familiar argument. Even if it were true, of course, it would not justify the view that capital gains are unimportant, for it would still imply that the distribution of wealth is shifting. Michael Ball expresses the point well when he writes:

> It is often argued that such increases in property values are not gains to the owner as they are unrealizable, given that another house of similar

price has to be purchased. The argument is obviously fallacious; the correct comparison is between owning and not owning at one point in time . . . Whether this wealth is ever realized by owners is immaterial; it still exists.

(1976, p. 25)

Compared with non-owners, in other words, owners gain irrespective of whether or not they can turn their assets into cash.

The key point, however, is that increasingly these capital gains are realizable and are being realized. It is true that at any one time, most of the gains made by owners exist in the form of 'paper wealth' rather than cash (Ball, 1983, p. 280). It does not follow from this, however, that these gains are not realizable, for there are a number of ways in which they can be turned into cash. Strategies for playing what the *Architects' Journal* (24 July 1985) has termed a game of 'reverse monopoly' (because unlike the board game, the object is to turn property into money) include over-mortgaging and remortgaging, equity release schemes and trading down, and inheritance. We shall consider these in more detail below, but first it is important to try to arrive at an estimate of what proportion of housing wealth is translated into income each year.

Let us begin by rectifying a common misconception which has entered into the debate over this issue in recent years. It is not true that all the money which seems to disappear from the housing system each year is extracted by people taking out mortgages and spending the money on other things, yet this is a claim which has been repeated many times in the press, by political organizations and even by financial analysts. According to the *Sunday Times* (10 July 1988), for example, the consumer spending boom of the 1980s can be explained by the 'fact' that 'Half the £15 billion loaned in mortgages last year was used for purposes other than housing purchase.' Similarly, the Association of Metropolitan Authorities (1987) claims in its review of housing finance policy that £6 billion of mortgage lending, much of it tax-relieved, finds its way each year into expenditure on other consumer items. This figure seems to have derived from a report by stockbrokers Quilter Goodison which suggested that £6 billion worth of mortgages in 1985 was used for purposes such as car purchase and payment of school fees, and that this had cost the Treasury at least £1.74 billion in fraudulent claims for tax relief (see *The Times*, 6 and 8 September 1986). This report in turn seems to have taken its cue from an article which appeared in the *Architects' Journal* (24 July 1985) which calculated that 50 per cent of all housing credit, amounting to £6,500 per new borrower, was being diverted each year into spending on holidays and consumer durables.

If any of this were true, it would be difficult to see how borrowers could have afforded the houses which they bought with the funds remaining, still less how demand could have risen to a point where it sparked off the 1986–8 house price boom. These various reports all fall into the error of assuming that the total equity apparently withdrawn from the housing market in any

155

one year can all be explained by new borrowers taking out mortgages which are then spent on other items. As we shall see, such 'over-mortgaging' actually accounts for only around £2 billion each year in 1985 prices. The figures for total equity leakage cited in these reports are more or less correct, but borrowing for purposes other than house purchase accounts for at most one-third of the total sum. In order to understand this it is necessary to understand how equity release is calculated.

A simple method of calculation is to subtract total expenditure on house purchase in any one year from the total net housing loans advanced in that year. This produces a figure of nearly £5½ billion pounds in 1984 (double the figure for 1981), which is equivalent to 3.5 per cent of total consumer expenditure (see Drayson, 1985).

Other analysts arrive at other figures on the basis of different calculations. Kemeny and Thomas (1984) estimate what they term 'capital leakage' by subtracting the increase in value of the owner-occupied sector from the size of net advances for house purchase. They then come up with a figure of between £1.4 and £2.6 billion at 1980 prices (which is actually higher than Drayson's estimate for 1980 of under £1 billion). This works out at between 20 per cent and 35 per cent of total mortgage funds advanced.

Most recently, Holmans (1986) has estimated equity withdrawal on the same principle as that adopted by Kemeny and Thomas (that is, the difference between net lending and the value of gross fixed investment in dwellings), although his calculations draw upon a broader range of sources. Defining equity withdrawal as 'The sum of expenditure on house purchase by first time purchasers, *plus* lending to moving owner-occupiers net of loans redeemed on the houses sold, *plus* new money put in by moving owner-occupiers *less* purchase of new houses' (1986, p. 5), Holmans ends up with a figure of £12 billion.

This figure is in some ways misleading, however, for it includes money advanced to purchase existing housing which has hitherto been rented. This accounts for £3.5 billion of the £12 billion in Holmans's calculations, and this has obviously been growing rapidly during the 1980s as a result of the council house sales drive. Holmans's figures are made up of three further components. First, they include money realized on final sales – normally on the death of owners but also including emigrants, divorced people who move into the rented sector and so on. This accounts for half of the total – around £6 billion. Much of this actually finds its way back into the housing system as heirs either use their inheritance to trade up, or put it in a building society deposit account. Second, a small amount is taken out by people moving house and trading down. Holmans estimates this at £500 million. And finally, around £2 billion is taken by people moving house and taking out larger loans than is necessary given their existing equity, although Holmans points out that some of this apparent surplus is probably used to finance improvements and furnishings in the new house.

Given the way he calculates equity withdrawal, Holmans's figures exclude altogether remortgaging by people who stay put in their existing houses.

This category of lending has in fact expanded tenfold since the 1960s (Drayson, 1985, p. 89), and this reflects the expansion of spending on home improvements and extensions in that period. It probably accounted for a further £1.2 billion in 1983 at 1980 prices, or 7.5 per cent of all new mortgage advances (the *Guardian*, 17 September 1986; Lowe, 1988, p. 161).

It is clear that some of the money calculated as part of the total sum of equity withdrawal is never actually taken out of the housing system at all. Loans for purchasing rented properties, for example, appear in the calculations because they represent new advances which are not balanced by any increase in the total stock of housing, but these loans are nevertheless used to buy properties. There are, in fact, three major sources of genuine equity withdrawal which we need to consider. These are, first, over-mortgaging and remortgaging; second, inheritance; and third, trading down and equity release.

Over-mortgaging occurs when existing owners buy a new house and take out a larger loan than they require, thereby realizing some or all of the equity which has built up in their previous house. According to Holmans it accounts for some £2 billion. *Remortgaging* is undertaken by non-movers who increase their mortgage debt in order to raise funds, usually with the purpose of carrying out home repairs or improvements. It accounts for another £1½ billion in Holmans's calculations, but it has been increasing rapidly in the late 1980s as building societies have competed to provide mortgage lending for non-housing purposes. In addition, of course, home owners are generally in a position to raise other more conventional loans secured on the value of their houses (see Pawley, 1978, p. 143; Whitehead, 1979, p. 39), and banks now routinely offer such loans at favourable rates of interest to home owners (Hamnett, 1988a, p. 3).

Over-mortgaging appears to be a significant way in which owner-occupiers turn their equity into cash. A 1983 OPCS survey of a sample of 8,000 moving households over the eighteen months from October 1976 found that 44 per cent of them had made positive net cash proceeds as a result of the move (net proceeds were defined as the sale price minus the loan outstanding *less* the purchase price minus the amount of the new loan). Twelve per cent of these cases only made enough money to cover their transaction costs, but the rest extracted more than this, and 10 per cent of them took out £5,000 pounds or more. It is not clear what this money was spent on, although we may assume that much of it was used to furnish or decorate the new home.

In the three towns survey we calculated equity withdrawals for each move made by each owner-occupied household on the same basis as in the OPCS survey, and we added to this any additional mortgages raised on an existing home. Around one-third of the sample had taken money out at some stage through over-mortgaging or remortgaging, and the mean value of the total sum extracted in 1986 prices amounted to just over £10,000.

This strategy for raising cash from housing was more common in the middle class and among owners of higher-value housing. Over 40 per cent of people in the service class had extracted money at some point compared with around one-quarter of those in the intermediate classes and 20 per cent of working-class owners. The average value of the sum extracted (1986 prices) also varied by class from nearly £16,000 in the service class and over £11,000 in the intermediate classes to just £2,374 in the working class, although these variations are partly explained by the shorter average length of time spent in home ownership by working-class households.

Interestingly, over-mortgaging and remortgaging were less common in Slough than in Derby or Burnley, and the mean sums involved were substantially lower there despite the higher average value of housing. This can probably be explained by the need of purchasers in high-priced regions to use every penny they can borrow to put towards house purchase, and in this sense it may be that supplementary mortgaging is a luxury which is mainly indulged when housing costs are relatively low.

Where respondents had remortgaged an existing house, we asked how they had used the money. The vast majority (87 per cent) had used it entirely for financing home improvements or repairs. We also asked all home owners in the sample whether they had ever raised a loan using their house as security. Nine per cent of them had, and in half of these cases the money had been spent on things unconnected with the house. It would seem from these findings that owner-occupiers do commonly use their house as a means of raising cash, but that much of this money is then ploughed back into the home.

The second main way in which the equity tied up in owner-occupiers' housing is released is through *inheritance*. On Holmans's figures, this accounts for £6 billion each year, although Inland Revenue figures for 1981–2 indicate that £3.2 billion of housing (net of debts) was bequeathed in that year (Munro, 1988, p. 422). The difference between these two sets of figures may be explained by the inflation in the housing market since 1981, by the steady increase in the proportion of wills which include houses and by the fact that Holmans's calculations also include sales by people moving abroad or switching into the rented sector.

Ray Forrest and Alan Murie have pointed out that 'Despite the apparent importance of housing wealth and inheritance in the shaping of contemporary social divisions, it remains a relatively under-researched issue' (1989, p. 25). They explain this neglect as the product of the extreme difficulty of researching inheritance, although the lack of data also reflects the fact that the first wave of purchasers from the inter-war years are only now beginning to die. It is therefore still rather early to assess the patterns of inheritance which may be emerging, although the value of housing in estates has been rising sharply in recent years (partly, of course, because the value of housing has been rising). Residential property accounted for 24 per cent of the total capital value of estates in 1968–9, for 29 per cent in 1973–4 and for 42 per cent in 1982–3 (Hamnett, 1988a; Mintel, 1987). The growing significance of housing inheritance during the 1980s can be seen in the emergence of a new acronym coined by the advertising industry. After giving us the 'yuppies' and the 'dinkies', the industry has now identified the 'pippies' ('people inheriting parents' property') as a potentially affluent consumer group (the *Observer*, 17 July 1988).

Just who the pippies are, and how much money they are likely to inherit, is a matter of some speculation. One of the best available calculations is that by Morgan Grenfell Economics (1987). This report suggests that some 155,000 owner-occupied houses are being inherited in Britain each year (Kemeny and Thomas, 1984, put the figure at between 138,000 and 240,000). Virtually all of this housing is fully owned, for 95 per cent of owner-occupiers over 65 have paid off their mortgage (Drayson, 1985, p. 88). The heirs are therefore receiving an average of around £44,000 per house – a national annual figure of £6.8 billion, or 3 per cent of household disposable income. Morgan Grenfell point out that legacies have to be divided between surviving children, and they calculate that half the population therefore stands to inherit something approaching £20,000 each at some point in their lives. Of course, some households include partners who can both expect to inherit, and in these cases the boost to household income could be twice this sum or more (Hamnett, 1988a).

All commentators agree that housing inheritance is going to grow in significance in the years ahead. Morgan Grenfell believe that, by the year 2000, over 200,000 owner-occupied houses will be inherited each year. Assuming 8 per cent p.a. housing inflation, this will amount to £24 billion in legacies from housing at the turn of the century. The report refers to this trend as 'familial accumulation' (1987, p. 20), a process whereby existing owner-occupiers not only accumulate wealth from their own housing but inherit it from their parents and, in time, pass the whole lot on to their children.

Other forecasters are slightly more cautious. Assuming a 4.5 per cent inflation rate, Mintel (1987) calculates that the proportion of estate value made up of housing will rise to 51 per cent by 1996–7. This would represent nearly £16 billion worth of housing, half of which is likely to be bequeathed to children.

Most people who inherit housing or a portion of it are middle-aged – the Mintel Report found the average age at which children inherit from the last surviving parent to be 50. Most already own their own homes (Munro, 1988). This raises the question of what they are likely to do with their inheritance. A survey conducted by the Henley Centre for Forecasting found that 82 per cent of those who expected to inherit a house intended to sell it (Elgie Stewart Smith, 1988), and this is probably inevitable in most cases where a legacy has to be divided between several children. This means that somewhere between £15 billion and £24 billion will be realized as cash from housing inheritance each year by the turn of the century. How will this money be spent?

The *Economist* (28 November 1987, p. 26) has suggested that this cash could do more to build 'popular capitalism' than all the government's privatization share issues, for much of it is likely to be invested. Returning to this question in a later editorial (9 April 1988), the same magazine speculates that much of this money may also go towards private health or education, thereby undermining support for statism and universalism in welfare services. Murie and Forrest (1980) suggest that some of it could even go into investment in private rental housing – something which has become more likely with the extension of the Business Expansion Scheme in 1988 to include rental housing (see Chapter 6).

Such evidence as we have confirms that most of this money is likely to be invested in one way or another rather than spent on consumer goods or services. The Henley Centre asked a sample of 300 people how they would use a £20,000 legacy, and it found that 60 per cent of them would invest at least some of it, 27 per cent would use it for their own housing purposes, and 11 per cent would take the opportunity to start a business. Mintel offered its respondents different hypothetical legacies and found that the propensities to invest, to buy better housing and to purchase private education all rose as the size of the bequest increased. At around £10,000, 30 per cent of people would spend the money on home improvements, 23 per cent would invest it, 19 per cent would repay debts (normally the mortgage), and 8 per cent (13 per cent among 35- to 44-year-olds) would buy private education. At around £60,000, by contrast, 46 per cent said they would invest in shares, 44 per cent would buy a new house, and 12 per cent (17 per cent in the relevant age group) would place their children in a private school.

Whatever happens to this money, the gap between those whose parents owned their homes and those whose parents rented is likely to become increasingly significant. The Mintel Report concludes prophetically:

> This report confirms the impression of a class that is left out, an 'underclass' because its parents live in council homes and leave so little on death that estates very often do not need to be admitted to probate. The chief result of the patterns of inheritance is not necessarily to make the rich richer – most of the people this report discusses are not rich – but it does make the poor – relatively – poorer.
>
> (1987, p. 123)

This is a crucial insight and one to which we shall return in Chapter 7.

Of course, some people will inherit more than others – Forrest and Murie (1989) point out that there will be a substantial difference between the amount received by an only child of middle-class home owners in the South-East and that gained by one of several children of working-class owners in the North. Nevertheless, we may expect that many households across different classes and regions will inherit significant amounts. Furthermore, it is quite possible that some of this money will get passed on to the third generation to help them get a start in owner-occupation (Ward, 1982, p. 12). Mike Harmer (1988) found that out of sixteen families who had recently inherited, five had used the money to help with their children's first purchases (another four had children who were too young to set up their own homes, and seven had children who had already left home).

In the three towns survey, only 4 per cent of home owners had secured their first deposit as a result of a legacy, although many more stood to inherit later in their lives. More important than inheritance for most people in our sample, however, were cash transfers from parents who were still alive. Previous work has shown how the children of home owners are often helped by their parents to gain access to owner-occupation. Madge and Brown found in their study of newly married couples that over a quarter of those who bought early on in their marriage used a family gift or loan to help with the initial deposit. Similarly, Colin Bell's ethnographic research on a Swansea housing estate demonstrated the significance of cash transfers at two crucial stages in the family life cycle – home-making and child rearing (Bell, 1968).

Thirty-one per cent of the home owners in the three towns survey had received outside help with raising their initial deposit (and 28 per cent of those whose children had left home had in turn helped the next generation with their housing costs). In addition to the 4 per cent of our sample who inherited their deposit, another 10 per cent got at least part of it as a loan from their family (a pattern which was particularly marked among Asian households where 36 per cent of owner-occupiers had received family loans), and 10 per cent received at least part as a family gift. Of those receiving family help with the deposit, two-thirds had the entire deposit paid for them, and the average value of family help received was £3,524. The significance of parents' tenure is revealed by the fact that 60 per cent of those receiving gifts or family loans were the children of outright owners. The significant factor here is tenure, not social class, for working-class owners were just as likely as middle-class owners to have passed some cash to their children. Overall, a quarter of home owners had had help from their parents or parents-in-law, and in the great majority of cases, they were the children of outright owners.

A third way in which housing equity is turned into cash is by *trading down* (accounting for £0.5 billion per year according to Holmans) and through participation in various old-age *equity release schemes*.

In our sample, 11 per cent of owner-occupier households had at some point bought a house for less than they had received on their previous sale, and in most cases this happened after children had left home and as the householders themselves were approaching or preparing for retirement. Trading down was more common in the lower-priced areas (Derby 13 per cent and Burnley 14 per cent) than in Slough (7 per cent), and this probably reflects the fact that those in London and the South-East who trade down tend to move out to lower-priced regions and would not therefore have appeared in our Slough sample.

Trading down is not the only avenue open to older owner-occupiers who wish to cash in on the value of their housing asset. Recently, various schemes have made it possible to raise money in old age without moving house (Hinton, 1987). Home income plans (also known as mortgage annuity schemes) allow elderly home owners to take out loans which are then invested in annuity schemes designed to pay both the interest and an annual income. The loan itself is redeemed out of the proceeds of the house when the owner dies. Alternatively, home reversion schemes involve the sale of the house to a company at a below-value price, thereby realizing a cash sum which can be spent or invested at will. The erstwhile owner then rents the accommodation for a nominal amount, and at death, the house reverts to the company.

There has also in recent years been a significant expansion of private sheltered housing schemes, which are thought to have a potential market of between 250,000 and 400,000 in Britain (Taylor, 1986, p. 22), and of private residential homes, which trebled in capacity between 1975 and 1984 (Means, 1987, p. 90). The significance of growth in these sectors is that it indicates how home ownership may come to underpin privatized consumption in other areas of life (this is a theme to which we shall return in Chapter 4). Its significance has certainly not been lost on the political right, for in 1988 both the Prime Minister and the Junior Health Minister encouraged elderly home owners to consider raising cash from their houses to enable them to enjoy greater financial independence. The political controversy which followed left us with yet another telling acronym of our age as the pundits began debating the issue of the 'woopies' ('well-off old people').

The ability of home owners to raise money to finance a comfortable and privatized old age marks a further crucial division between tenure groups. Home owners 'have a saleable and generally appreciating asset which can at any point be sold and the proceeds used to gain access to private nursing homes or aged people's housing facilities' (Berry, 1986, p. 116). Tenants, by contrast, are likely to reach retirement with few assets and little choice but to rely on the state to care for them in their twilight years just as they have depended upon it to house them during their working lives.

Of course, the more home owners cash in their equity to release money for their old age, the less wealth will be left to bequeath to their successors. The Junior Health Minister recognized this in her 1988 speech when she noted that the children of elderly owners stand to lose if their parents took advantage of equity release schemes. She continued: 'Often they need the windfall money less than their parents do now. It cannot be right that their parents have to turn to the state for help when the family stands to gain a small fortune without any effort when they are no longer with us' (quoted in the *Independent*, 23 April 1988). Some commentators on the left are not so sure, however, for they see in the growth of sheltered housing and equity release schemes the sinister sign of capitalist opportunism: 'The construction and financial sectors are adjusting their products and services to profit from the substantial equity stored in dwellings' (Forrest and Murie, 1989, p. 34). The left, of course, faces an awkward dilemma in responding to such trends, for to encourage equity release is to underwrite the growth of privatized care for the elderly while to resist it is to defend large-scale property inheritance. Meanwhile, elderly owners themselves are now enjoying the choice between realizing a portion of their wealth for their own use and preserving it intact for the next generation.

It is not only in old age, however, that people feel the financial benefit of appreciating house values. Owner-occupiers can reduce their spending on pensions and endowments during their working lives knowing that at retirement they will be in a position to live rent free and to trade down to realize capital, and if they can in addition look forward to inheriting from their parents, then they can be fairly confident of their future financial security. As Michael Ball recognizes, 'There is less need to save out of wages for retirement for the strata of the workforce where owner occupation is prevalent. By the age of retirement housing costs are reduced to repairs, maintenance and insurance and the retired household can "trade down" and use the encashed money gain as an ongoing source of income' (1983, p. 365; see also Morgan Grenfell, 1987, p. 16). The prospect of a secure old age thus opens up the possibility of increased consumer spending earlier in life and diminishes enthusiasm for saving, whether voluntarily or through state social security schemes (see Kemeny, 1981, pp. 59–60).

To conclude, it is obviously not the case that home owners cannot realize their capital gains. While it is true that the extent of equity withdrawal has sometimes been exaggerated, it is nevertheless still significant. As Donnison and Ungerson have argued, owners 'can raise further mortgages on their houses (to buy a car or a country cottage perhaps), or they can sell their houses and use the proceeds as down payments on bigger and better houses, or they can purchase annuities when they retire if they move to smaller and cheaper houses at that stage in their lives' (1982, p. 216).

The major source of cash from home ownership is through inheritance, and we have seen that this will grow in importance over the next few years. Critics often argue that inheritance should not be seen as a form of capital realization for existing owners, but such an argument overlooks the number of current owners who can themselves now expect to inherit housing capital. As we saw in the discussion of the Morgan Grenfell analysis, half of the population can today expect to inherit around £20,000 each at some point in their lives, and both the proportion of people and the size of the sums are growing all the time. What has been developing in Britain since the 1930s, and is now coming to fruition, is a new pattern of 'familial accumulation'. The present generation of owners will not simply leave a lot of money to its children, but many of them will themselves inherit substantial sums from their parents. Capital gains from the housing market are in this sense becoming cyclical, for each generation from here on will benefit from its parents while in turn benefiting its children. The seedcorn planted from the 1930s onwards is now being harvested, and the next generation of fruit has already been sown.

Do all owner-occupiers gain?

The fourth line of argument developed by the critics of mass home ownership is that only affluent owner-occupiers make significant gains, while less privileged groups often lose. Home ownership thus magnifies existing inequalities rather than reducing them (an example of the so-called 'Matthew effect' which is so often referred to by left-wing sociologists – 'Unto them that hath shall be given . . .').

The argument is sometimes developed through comparison of different social groups (working class and middle class, black and white, etc.) and sometimes through comparison of geographical areas (inner city and suburb, north and south, etc.). It is an argument which is reinforced by statistics on mortgage foreclosures and housing disrepair, for these figures are used by many critics to suggest that less affluent home buyers lose out in the housing market. Martin Boddy speaks for many of the critics when he writes:

> Despite the popular ideology of home ownership and the property-owning democracy, that 'everybody gains', it is not only those who cannot obtain their own home that lose. It can also be the poor home-owners at the bottom of the scale who lose out in the face of rising maintenance costs, declining asset values and vulnerability to mortgage failure . . . those who lose [are] generally tenants and working class owner-occupiers.
>
> (1980, p. 142)

One indicator which has often been cited as evidence that low-income home owners are in trouble is the rising trend in *mortgage arrears and repossessions*. These quadrupled between 1979 and 1984 (Karn, Doling and Stafford, 1986, p. 131), and the number of repossessions has again doubled since then. The Institute of Housing announced that 10,000 people became homeless in 1987 as a result of repossession of their home – a 500 per cent rise on 1978 – and local authorities have claimed that the proportion of homeless people made up of repossession cases rose from 5 per cent in 1979 to 12 per cent in 1988 (the *Independent*, 22 and 30 December 1988). Figures from *Social Trends* (1988) show that, while the number of housing loans has grown from 5.4 million in 1980 to over 7.1 million in 1987 (an increase of 32 per cent), the number of mortgages in arrears by six to twelve months has risen from 14,000 to 50,000 (an increase of 273 per cent), and the number of repossessions has risen from 3,000 to around 23,000 (an increase of 667 per cent). Some commentators, furthermore, have suggested that these figures probably underestimate the real size of the problem since there are even more borrowers who are less than six months in arrears (Doling, Karn and Stafford, 1985, pp. 28–9), and many repossessions are avoided by 'voluntary' sales when people realize that they cannot clear their debts (Karn, Doling and Stafford, 1986, p. 131).

Clearly, arrears and repossessions represent a serious and growing problem, but it is important to keep it in perspective. Despite the rise in the number of borrowers whose payments have lapsed by six months or more, such arrears still only account for 0.86 per cent of all housing loans, and just 0.32 per cent of loans end in repossession (*BSA Bulletin*, October 1988). The owner-occupancy rate is now beginning to nudge towards the probable 'saturation point' of around 70 per cent (*Financial Times*, 9 July 1986; Stewart, 1984), and as it does so, so it encompasses an ever-larger proportion of marginal borrowers. As more people have taken the opportunity to buy a home, so the risk of default inevitably has risen. We shall consider ways in which this saturation point could be raised while minimizing the risk of arrears in Chapter 6.

Some critics have been swift to blame the lending institutions for over-extending borrowers with large loans on 100 per cent mortgages (Ball, Martens and Harloe, 1986; Took and Ford, 1987). This seems somewhat disingenuous when we remember that just a few years ago, critics regularly attacked the building societies for being too cautious in their lending policies and for discriminating against low-income, high-risk applicants (for example, Short, 1982, p. 128; Townsend, 1979, p. 515). As we saw when discussing likely explanations for housing inflation, blaming the lending institutions is akin to shooting the messenger for relaying the message. Home ownership is overwhelmingly popular, and liberalized lending practices reflect the fact that many non-owners are demanding the chance to buy. To blame the banks and building societies for responding to this demand by providing more people with the loans that they want betrays a paternalistic attitude towards lower income groups and ignores the fact that the great majority of such borrowers manage the repayments perfectly adequately. It also totally ignores the question of whether those in arrears might have encountered similar problems in meeting rental payments had they remained in rented housing.

In the three towns survey, 86 per cent of buyers said they had encountered no problems in meeting their mortgage repayments, while only 2 per cent had actually gone into arrears. It is often thought that the council house sales policy has caused problems, but the council house buyers in our sample were no more likely to have encountered problems in paying the mortgage than any other group, and as we saw in Chapter 2, other studies have found that council house buyers are if anything more financially secure than other marginal purchasers.

The primary explanations for the increasing number of owner-occupiers in financial difficulties lie not in liberal lending practices, but in factors such as the increased number of low-income borrowers who want the chance to buy, the rising divorce rate resulting in more household break-ups and the continuing high rate of unemployment (Doling, Karn and Stafford, 1985, pp. 31–7; Took and Ford, 1987, pp. 216–19). Also significant has been the fall in the rate of inflation coupled with the rise in real interest rates since the end of the 1970s. The lower inflation rate means that new borrowers now have to wait longer before their rising income erodes the real cost of repaying the mortgage, and higher interest rates mean that this cost is greater than it was a few years earlier. An additional hazard is that 44 per cent of mortgagees now have annually reviewed loans where the interest rate is only adjusted once each year. When the interest rates drift upwards over a period of months, this can result in a single jarring increase in payments rather than a more gradual and phased adjustment.

When people do encounter problems in paying their mortgages, it is normally in the early years. In the three towns survey, one-third of those who bought for the first time in 1984–6 claimed that they found the repayments a problem. But this was true across the classes and was not limited to those on low incomes. Each income group tends to buy the best it can afford when it first enters the market, and tight household budgets are therefore found in middle- and working-class homes alike. To interpret the rising arrears figures as a sign that working-class home owners are losing out is, on our evidence, quite unwarranted, especially when we take account of the capital gains they have been making (see below).

A second indicator of possible problems among low-income home owners is provided by data on the *state of repair* of the owner-occupied housing stock. The 1981 *English House Condition Survey* (Department of the Environment, 1982) found that the proportion of 'unfit' dwellings which were owner-occupied had risen from 35 per cent to 53 per cent in five years. Five per cent of all owner-occupied dwellings required repairs costing £7,000 or more, and 13 per cent of pre-1919 owner-occupied dwellings were classified as 'unfit'. Disrepair is particularly concentrated in the pre-1919 housing stock, in housing owned by elderly people and in housing occupied by lower income groups.

As with the data on arrears, we should recognize that there is a serious problem here but we should also take care not to exaggerate it. It is simply hyperbole to suggest, as Karn, Kemeny and Williams do, that 'Very many owners are unable to afford routine repairs and maintenance on their homes' (1985, p. 135), for 'very many' owners actually spend a great deal of money on their houses and are happy to do so. The *House Condition Survey*, for example, found that owners spent £7 billion on repairs and improvements in 1981, and it was in no doubt that 'The owner-occupied stock had received greater expenditure than either of the rented sectors' (DoE, 1982, pt 2, p. 14). It also found that, on an age-for-age and size-for-size comparison, the state of repair of the owner-occupied stock was better than that in either private or public rental (pt 1, p. 9). For example, although 13 per cent of the pre-1919 owner-occupied housing was classed as 'unfit', so too was 18 per cent of council housing and 26 per cent of private rented housing of the same age.

In the three towns survey, interviewers described 71 per cent of houses in the sample as in generally good condition, another 13 per cent as 'mixed' (for example, sound but in need of decoration) and 16 per cent as generally poor. These assessments usually coincided with those of the householders themselves, 54 per cent of whom described their houses as in good or excellent condition, while another 30 per cent used terms like 'OK' or 'reasonable', and 14 per cent described their homes as in 'poor' condition or worse. Breaking these figures down by tenure, we find that most (62 per cent) of those who believe they are living in 'poor' housing conditions are council tenants. While just 6 per cent of mortgagees and 8 per cent of outright owners described their house condition as poor, no fewer than 32 per cent of council tenants did. It may be, of course, that these figures reflect pride of ownership and alienation from council rental as much as actual housing condition (these issues are discussed in Chapter 5). However, interviewers' assessments bear them out, for 24 per cent of council-owned houses were found to be in generally poor condition compared with just 14 per cent of mortgaged properties and 9 per cent of houses owned outright (it should be remembered that half of the tenants in the sample lived on the most popular estates and half on the least popular).

Notwithstanding reports to the contrary (such as DoE, 1982; Karn, Doling and Stafford, 1986), most householders seemed well aware of the deficiencies in their housing. Twenty-five per cent of our respondents reported that at least one major repair (for example, re-roofing, rewiring, damp-proofing, replacement of rotten window frames or woodworm treatment) needed doing, and a further 24 per cent mentioned outstanding minor repairs (for example, replacement of front gates, reglazing a cracked window pane or mending a garden fence). Again, however, it was in the council houses more than the owner-occupied houses that the need for repairs was most widely recognized. Eighteen per cent of outright owners and 22 per cent of mortgagees said that major repairs needed doing, but 34 per cent of council tenants said this.

Of course, when we break these figures down further, it is possible to identify pockets of owner-occupation where housing conditions appear to be a significant problem. In particular, 54 per cent of those living in Victorian terraced housing at the bottom end of the owner-occupied price spectrum reported that major repairs were outstanding, and interviewers identified 32 per cent of these houses as in generally poor condition. The need for repairs does not of itself indicate that people are suffering bad housing conditions, however. It is quite possible for owners of old houses to know that they need a new roof without this meaning that they have to put buckets in the bedrooms every time it rains. It is important, therefore, to consider whether they see themselves as living in poor conditions. The proportion of those in Victorian terraced housing who describe their housing conditions as poor is only 19 per cent, and this compares favourably with figures of 21 per cent on the popular council estates and 25 per cent on the unpopular ones.

Such disjunctures between the judgements of outsiders and the judgements of residents themselves point to an important consideration as regards analysis of housing conditions. We shall see in Chapter 6 that the imposition of formal, bureaucratic standards can (as in the case of self-builders) prevent households from determining for themselves the point at which they trade off housing quality against time or income devoted to other aspects of their

167

lives. An outside toilet may be deemed by the Department of the Environment to represent 'lack of a basic amenity', but many people may be quite content with such a facility and may prefer to use their money for other purposes than plumbing in an internal water closet. The 1981 *House Condition Survey* found that 'Relatively few people in the worst strata of housing consider their homes to be in a bad condition. This was particularly true of owner occupiers' (DoE, 1982, pt 2, p. 3). It reported that 61 per cent of 'significant defects' identified by surveyors were not recognized as such by occupants, over half of whom said either that they had not noticed the faults or that they were not bothered by them. Eighty-two per cent of owner-occupiers living in houses deemed to be 'unfit' and in a 'serious' state of disrepair described their houses as in 'average' or better condition (6 per cent of them described their houses as 'almost perfect'!). It may be that these people are stupid or ignorant, but it may be that they simply have different standards and expectations than those of government, academic researchers and housing professionals.

Most of the literature assumes that repairs do not get done because owner-occupiers lack the money to do them. The cost of repairs has been rising relative to average incomes (Karn, Doling and Stafford, 1986, p. 135), and some groups, such as the elderly, can do very little for themselves. In their study of inner areas of Birmingham and Liverpool, Karn, Kemeny and Williams (1985, ch. 6) found that over half of long-term owners of Victorian terraced properties had postponed repairs, mainly because they could not afford to do them. They also pointed to what they termed a 'valuation gap' which tends to inhibit repair work in low-cost housing areas where the price of an improved house will not cover the cost of the improvements even after grants have been taken into account (see also Forrest and Murie, 1987a; Hughes, 1987; Walker, 1985 – all of whom report on a similar problem in different Lancashire towns).

What survey evidence makes clear, however, is that lack of money is not always the explanation for why housing repairs do not get done. The *House Condition Survey* found that 'Lack of financial resources to tackle the problem was rarely mentioned' (pt 2, p. 9). In the three towns survey we asked all respondents who said that repairs needed doing why they had not been done. The single most important reason, cited in 28 per cent of cases, was indeed lack of money, but 19 per cent said that the work was in hand, 13 per cent said it had not been done for shortage of time, and 9 per cent said that they were not worried about getting it done. Furthermore, in 21 per cent of cases, the answer was that they were council tenants and that their local authority was unresponsive as a landlord. This reflects the fact that repairs in the public sector normally get done only when the council comes to do them (although 20 per cent of tenants had done some repair work themselves), and 74 per cent of tenants whose houses needed repair complained that the local authority either had ignored them or had done the repairs inadequately. The frustration and deprivation experienced as a result of repairs left undone by local authority landlords are likely to be every bit as great as that felt by those who lack the money to do it themselves.

As for the problem of a 'valuation gap', we certainly did find that owners of Victorian terraces were often pessimistic about recouping money spent on repairs and improvements when they came to sell. Forty-two per cent of them thought that this expenditure would not be recovered. However, this does not seem to have acted as a disincentive to home improvement. Owners of old, cheap properties in Burnley, for example, were no more pessimistic than owners of old and relatively expensive houses in Slough. Furthermore, 27 per cent of the owners in our sample had done improvements or repairs even though they believed that they would not recoup the outlay when and if they came to sell. The valuation gap undoubtedly exists and it can be a disincentive to spend money on an old house in a cheap area, but as we shall see in Chapter 5, home ownership can encourage people to look after their homes even if they do not expect to recover the costs later (see also Ward, 1985, pp. 50–1).

The literature on mortgage arrears and housing disrepair attempts to show that low-income home owners either cannot afford their housing loans or cannot afford the upkeep of their properties. This literature forms part of a larger argument in which critics of mass home ownership go on to suggest that marginal home owners do not make capital gains either. In this view, working-class and ethnic-minority home owners find themselves squeezed between crippling housing costs on the one hand and the declining relative value of their property on the other. As we saw in Chapter 2, the aim is to portray them as helpless victims, coerced into home ownership because of the lack of rental alternatives, and the purveyors of this line often end up with a call for renewed public-sector building as the solution to the housing problems of working-class and ethnic-minority groups.

This is a message which is repeated time and again in the sociological literature yet which is largely unsupported by the evidence. We have already seen that the vast majority of lower-income house buyers do not suffer from home ownership, whether through arrears or bad housing conditions. We can now go on to demonstrate more positively that most of them have in fact done very well out of their participation in the domestic property market. We shall consider the evidence on relative capital gains by focusing on five groups which the existing literature suggests are doing badly out of their experience of home ownership – the working class, council house buyers, ethnic minorities, inner-city owners of older, cheaper housing and people living in relatively depressed regions of the country.

Working-class owner-occupiers

The literature on *social class and capital gains* suggests that inequalities arising out of the labour market are reflected and reinforced in the housing market. John Short makes the point quite assertively in terminology which betrays the evident political bias which underpins so much of this writing. 'Owner-occupation', he says, 'is only a highly significant cumulative form of property ownership for the wealthier households . . . If you are a factory worker you are unlikely to be the owner of a prestigious mansion. If you are screwed at work, the likelihood is that you are screwed in your housing construction' (1982, p. 150). Much the same point is developed by Oriel Sullivan:

> The manual classes, whose social disadvantage is rooted firmly in the production sector, have very little effective choice. These groups may in reality become 'trapped' in unpopular locations in unsaleable homes which become increasingly more delapidated since insufficient resources can be devoted to their repair and maintenance. The prospects for wealth generation among this group are negligible.
>
> (1987, pp. 42–3)

This same argument is also developed by Ray Forrest (1983, p. 213) and John Doling and colleagues (Doling, Karn and Stafford, 1986, p. 49), both of whom argue that capital gains from the housing market simply reinforce existing class inequalities.

So frequently are such claims advanced in the literature that there is a danger that we may actually start to believe them. In fact, they represent yet another example of left-wing sociological mythology. They rarely present systematic evidence on the comparative costs and gains of different social classes in owner-occupation (how could they when data at a household level have not hitherto been available?), and they invariably over-generalize from the plight of the worst cases, assuming that what is true for a few unfortunate working-class owners is true for all. Reading these accounts one is struck by how oddly they would sound to the ears of most of those whom we interviewed in the three towns. They almost all believe that they have done very well for themselves out of buying a house, yet John Short insists that they have been 'screwed', and Oriel Sullivan believes that their gains have been 'negligible'. The truth is that they are right, and Short, Sullivan and other academic sceptics are wrong.

There is not much existing empirical evidence with which to evaluate this issue. The Boston study found that housing in more affluent suburbs had inflated at a faster rate than that in poorer areas. This does not, however, justify the conclusion drawn by the authors that 'The more affluent homeowners were reaping higher capital gains than their fellows' (Edel, Sclar and Luria, 1984, p. 128), for the evidence relates to houses rather than households and it also ignores the question of the size of the original sum invested. David Thorns's work in Christchurch, New Zealand, is rather better. He compared the prices paid for houses in different areas against their current valuation and correlated the results against social class and income data. The result was that

> The largest gains are obtained by those in managerial and professional occupations and in the higher, over $300 per week, income categories.

This would seem to indicate that gains from the job and housing markets are in fact quite closely related and to some extent mutually reinforcing. It further shows that owner-occupation has brought greater financial benefits to middle class home-owners than it has to working class home owners.

(1981b, p. 213)

Again, however, these data rely simply on movements of house prices in different areas and pay no attention to household investment strategies over time. Furthermore, when Thorns turns to analyse Britain, he, like Edel in Boston, simply equates household gains with differential rates of house price inflation in different areas. Indeed, as we shall see below when we consider the question of regional inequalities in capital gains, even these figures are questionable! Certainly there is no warrant in Thorns's work for arguing, as he does, that northern working-class home owners have housing assets which are static or even declining in value (see Thorns, 1982, p. 761).

Table 3.3 sets out the pattern of total and annualized gains (or losses) for each of Goldthorpe's three social class groups using data from the three towns survey. Three points are immediately apparent.

The first (and most crucial) is that the great majority of households in all

Table 3.3 *Capital gains and annual gains by social class*

Social class (quintiles)				Measure of gain (£)				
	GCG	Real GCG	NCG	Real NCG	AGG	Real AGG	ANG	Real ANG
Service class (N = 96)								
Lowest 10%	8,125	7,065	741	−200	721	674	57	−99
30%	18,376	18,305	8,585	7,624	1,452	1,375	805	836
50% (median)	27,701	27,094	16,922	15,986	2,198	2,103	1,263	1,196
70%	38,886	40,950	28,482	30,159	3,011	3,035	2,126	1,920
90%	62,635	75,009	53,407	57,326	5,134	5,420	2,886	3,832
Mean	31,989	40,609	22,727	30,523	2,712	3,024	1,729	1,911
Intermediate (N = 94)								
Lowest 10%	2,073	1,151	−20	−5,180	477	365	−44	−701
30%	12,762	12,509	8,396	7,432	1,315	1,281	741	644
50% (median)	25,285	23,502	13,746	16,872	2,324	2,098	1,425	1,489
70%	40,199	44,421	28,443	32,566	3,055	3,337	2,286	2,356
90%	61,513	71,560	48,492	58,353	4,481	5,683	3,613	4,309
Mean	27,529	31,276	18,850	21,662	2,381	2,361	1,448	1,293
Working class (N = 94)								
Lowest 10%	1,494	1,154	−811	−2,407	253	306	−116	−302
30%	7,239	6,583	2,691	2,215	809	809	438	299
50% (median)	13,736	12,971	9,306	8,791	1,442	1,408	1,055	952
70%	26,956	27,245	20,548	19,429	2,465	2,695	1,921	1,987
90%	44,059	45,542	39,124	39,337	5,672	5,592	4,153	4,136
Mean	18,663	12,238	13,706	6,734	2,618	2,277	1,907	1,443

For key to column headings, see Table 3.1.

three classes have made substantial gains out of home ownership. It is clear from the table that no household above the thirtieth decile in any class has sustained nominal or real losses, gross or net, on any measure. In fact (although the figures are not given in the table), no household above the *twentieth* decile in any class has sustained any such losses (even taking the worst case of real net capital gains, the figures at the twentieth decile are £5,598 for the service class, £1,257 for the intermediate classes and just £31. for the working class). A greater range of variation in the figures for the intermediate classes relative to the other two is apparent from the table (this probably reflects the greater social heterogeneity of this stratum), although the variation across all three classes is considerable. This makes a comparison of means of only limited value, and the median figures are probably more helpful as a simple measure of central tendency. Whether we take the means or medians, however, it is clear that on average, home owners in all three classes have been gaining.

The second point is nevertheless to recognize that the table does indicate that there have been some losses when calculations are computed net of mortgage payments. Some households, that is, have paid out more for their housing than they have got back in capital growth, and this is particularly true of the bottom 10 per cent or so in the intermediate and working classes. It is important, however, that we do not leap from this observation to any over-hasty conclusions about home ownership benefiting the middle class and oppressing the working class. For a start, the numbers involved are quite small (in each class the lowest decile comprises only nine or ten households), and their situation is not typical. These households, further-more, have only lost on the net calculations, and as was explained earlier, these are somewhat misleading measures since they take no account of the fact that, had they not owned a house, these people would still have had to meet housing costs by renting. The key point about these net loss-makers, however, is that their losses can be explained mainly by the fact that they tend not to have owned a house for very long. As recent arrivals, their mortgage repayments are high, and they have had little time to see their properties appreciate in value. The reason why they are concentrated mainly in the intermediate and working classes is simply that there is a higher proportion of longer-term owners in the service class than in the other two. We shall demonstrate this relationship between class, duration of ownership and total gains a little later in this analysis.

Third, it is clear that total gains are greatest for the service class and lowest for the working class. Whether we take the mean, the median, or the range, the service class comes out best, and the working class trails behind on all four measures of total gain (that is, the first four columns in the table). The differences are particularly striking as regards the real net capital gain figures where the working-class median is around half that of the service class while the mean is only around a quarter as large.

Again, however, we should not rush to celebrate another example of the beloved Matthew effect. If we consider the figures for *annual* gains, the class differences become much smaller. It appears from the table that each year the median working-class owner has made a gross real gain of about £1,400, or nearly £1,000 net. This does not compare too badly with gains for the median service-class owner of £2,100 gross and £1,200 net. There is still a class difference – the median real annual gross gain in the working class is 67 per cent of that in the service class – and this is to be expected given that the service class tends to live in more expensive houses and therefore owns a bigger asset from which to accumulate capital. However, the service class also has to pay more for such housing, and this squeezes the class differential on net annual real gains from 67 per cent to 80 per cent. This, of course, is much smaller than the wage differential between the two classes, and it suggests (contrary to received wisdom) that in relative terms, home ownership is reducing rather than reproducing or widening existing class inequalities.

The reason why the figures on annual gains are so much more even across the classes than the figures on total gains is simply that the service-class owners have on average owned a house for longer and have therefore had more time to build up their capital. This can readily be seen, albeit rather crudely, in Table 3.4. This table has been constructed by dividing the total sample of 283 households for whom the relevant information is available into thirds on each of the measures of real gross gain and real net gain. High, medium and low gainers are then analysed in terms of their relative class characteristics while controlling for the length of time spent in owner-

Table 3.4 *Real gross and net gains by social class controlling for length of time in owner-occupation*

Scale of gain	Period when first purchased													
	1984–6		1980–3		1974–9		1970–3		1960–9		Pre-1960		Total	
	Gro.	Net	Gro.	Net	Gro.	Net	Gro.	Net	Gro.	Net	Gro.	Net	Gro.	Net
Service class														
High	–	–	–	–	3	1	7	8	17	14	11	14	38	37
Medium	–	–	4	6	11	10	3	2	7	8	11	7	36	33
Low	6	6	11	9	2	5	–	–	1	3	2	3	22	26
Total	6		15		16		10		25		24		96	
Intermediate														
High	–	–	1	1	3	2	7	7	18	18	6	8	35	36
Medium	2	2	5	5	7	6	3	4	8	7	6	6	31	30
Low	3	3	11	11	5	7	1	–	3	4	5	3	28	28
Total	5		17		15		11		29		17		94	
Working class														
High	–	1	2	2	2	1	4	3	4	5	8	10	20	22
Medium	3	2	8	10	6	4	5	6	3	3	6	7	31	32
Low	9	9	11	9	6	9	3	3	3	2	10	7	42	39
Total	12		21		14		12		10		24		93	

N = 283

occupation (the figures for nominal gross and net gains have been omitted for ease of presentation but a similar pattern is evident for these measures as well).

Two points of interest emerge from Table 3.4. One is that, although we picked up just as many pre-1960 buyers among the working class as in other classes (partly because of the long tradition of working-class home ownership in Burnley), there are considerably fewer households from this class who bought between 1960 and 1979, and considerably more who have bought since 1980. The high rate of working-class purchase since 1980 is in part a reflection of the increase in council house sales, and this in turn helps to explain how three of the post-1980 working-class purchasers have managed to make high net gains in such a short period (for people buying council houses have often received substantial discounts on the selling price). We shall consider the specific case of council house buyers shortly.

The second point is that, in general, recent entrants into owner-occupation do not make high total gains. There are no high gross gainers in the most recent cohort of buyers, and only three out of thirty-three post-1980 purchasers have made high gross gains. Two of these are working class, and one is from the intermediate classes. Indeed, there are only eleven high gross gainers (and just eight high net gainers) among the forty-seven households to have purchased since 1974 (that is, after the end of the first house price boom), and they are divided roughly proportionately between the three classes. The break between pre-1974 and post-1974 buyers is quite striking in this table, for while 51 per cent of the former group come into the category of high gainers, only 9 per cent of the latter do. Clearly, the time spent in owner-occupation is a major determinant of capital gains. This partly reflects the way that capital gains accumulate over time, but it also seems that purchase prior to or following the first of the big house price booms has made a significant difference to patterns of household accumulation.

The comparison between total gains and annual gains in Table 3.3, and the analysis of gains over time in Table 3.4, suggests that the relation between social class and capital gains can be explained as the product of two factors. One is the different periods of time spent in owner-occupation by the different social classes. The other is the different values of the houses which the different classes own. Both of these factors are important (and, of course, are to some extent interrelated since a longer period in owner-occupation provides a greater opportunity to trade up to a more expensive house). The relationships between this increasingly complex tangle of variables can best be demonstrated by means of a series of multiple regression models.

The object of multiple regression analysis is to find a way of expressing the relative significance of a set of posited 'independent variables' in influencing a given 'dependent variable'. This expression is derived by constructing a graph of the relationship between the dependent variable and one (normally the 'strongest') of the independent variables. All observations

174

are then plotted on this graph, and a straight line is drawn through them at the point of 'best fit'. The best-fitting line will be that which minimizes the total distance between each observation and the line. It is then possible to measure how well the linear relationship reflects the actual relationship between the variables, or, to put it another way, what percentage of the actual relationship can be explained by the best-fitting model. The other independent variables can then be added one at a time to see how much improvement they bring about in the exactness of fit of the model. In this way, it is possible to gauge the relative power of the different independent variables to explain the dependent variable, and as with any graph, the final result can be expressed in the form of an equation.

Table 3.5 sets out the various steps in constructing a multiple regression model which considers the relative contributions of five 'independent variables' to the explanation of gross capital gains. The variable FIRSTBT refers to the year when households first entered home ownership and is designated by the last two digits of the year. The variables WORCLASS and INTCLASS are what is known as 'dummy variables'. Social class cannot be entered directly into an equation like this because it is what is known as a 'nominal' or 'categorical' variable and cannot be expressed on an interval scale. There is no sense in which the service class, for example, can be said to be 'more' or 'less' than the working class, for the difference between the two categories is not a numerical one. Because multiple regression modelling requires us to use interval scales, we have therefore to construct new binary variables. WORCLASS and INTCLASS each have two values – zero (not working class or not intermediate class) and one. Similarly, BURNLEY and DERBY are new dummy variables, each with two values; for like social classes, different towns are not ordered on any meaningful numerical scale and cannot therefore be entered directly into the model. The reason for including the towns in our model at all will become apparent later when we consider how capital gains vary among households in different parts of the country.

In the construction of this model, FIRSTBT was entered first because the strength of association with GCG was strongest at the first step (the strength of association is measured by the coefficient; this is adjusted to take account

Table 3.5 *A multiple regression model of social class, time in owner-occupation and town on nominal gross capital gains*

Step	Variable	Coeff.	Standard error	Adjusted R-square	Change in R2	Signif.
1	FIRSTBT	−662	91	0.11	–	0.0000
2	BURNLEY	−22,865	2,885	0.18	0.08	0.0000
3	DERBY	−19,012	2,860	0.30	0.12	0.0000
4	WORCLASS	−8,824	2,884	0.31	0.01	0.0024
5	INTCLASS	−5,137	3,178	0.32	0.01	0.1072
	(Constant)	90,935	6,840			0.0000

of the spread of observations, so that, although 662 is actually smaller than the coefficients for all the other variables, it represents a larger effect since it has to be multiplied by a number between 01 and 86, depending on the year when a household bought its first house). The model at this stage suggests that the best prediction which could be made of a household's gross capital gain is that it will equal the constant value (£90,935, plus or minus the standard error of £6,840) minus £662 for each year past 1900 when the household first bought a house (for we saw that the PERIODBT variable is expressed by the last two digits of the year in which a household purchased its first house). The adjusted R-square figure of 0.11 tells us, however, that PERIODBT only explains 11 per cent of the variance in the dependent variable. Finally, the significance level of 0.0000 indicates that it is highly unlikely that the relationship which we have found could have been a product of chance.

At step two BURNLEY was entered as it had the next highest coefficient. This raised the predictive power of the model somewhat, for the R-square figure rose from 0.11 to 0.18, meaning that we are now explaining 18 per cent of the variance, and the association with GCG is again highly significant in statistical terms. At this stage in the model, the best prediction we are able to make is that a household's gross capital gain will be equal to the constant, less the appropriate multiple of the coefficient of PERIODBT, less £22,865 if that household lives in Burnley. Similarly, by the end of step three (when DERBY is entered) we have explained 30 per cent of the variance. This is a big improvement, for the model now fully takes account of the effects of location, and we are now able to estimate the relative effects on capital gains of each of the towns in the survey (Slough has a zero effect, for Derby and Burnley register negative coefficients taking Slough as the base point).

It is only at step four that the first of the social class variables is entered, and neither WORCLASS nor INTCLASS makes much of an improvement to the predictive capacity of the model (the final R-square only rises to 0.32). Indeed, it is arguable whether INTCLASS should be entered into the model at all, for its standard error is very high relative to the value of its coefficient, and the probability score is also weak (although taken together, the probabilities of the two class variables are low enough to warrant their inclusion).

The equation which derives from this final model as the best estimate we can make of gross capital gains given information about the year when a household first bought, the town in which they live and their social class is:

GCG =
£90,935(c) − (662 × y) − 22865(b) − 19012(d) − 8824(w) − 5137(i) + e

where c is a *constant*, y is the last two digits of the *year* in which they bought, and b, d, w and i are the amounts to be subtracted if they are *Burnley, Derby, working-class* and *intermediate-class* people respectively (e is the unknown *error* term). Nothing has to be subtracted in the case of Slough and service-class households. For example, we would estimate from this model that a service-class household in Slough which first bought in 1980 would have made a gross capital gain of £90,935 less (662 × 80) = £37,975 (though remember that this may still turn out to be a poor estimate, for the model as a whole only explains 32 per cent of the variance in gross capital gains – other factors not included in the model are obviously also influencing the gains that people make). This compares with, say, a working-class Slough household buying at the same time which makes £29,151, a working-class Slough household buying twenty years earlier (£42,391), or a service-class Burnley household also buying in 1980 which makes only £15,110. It is obvious from these figures that social class is having some effect but that time and town are having more, and this is, of course, borne out by the R-square readings.

In order to be certain of this, however, we need to investigate whether the social class variables might look more powerful if they were entered into the equation first. In multiple regression models, the increase in the value of R-square will always tend to fall as each successive variable is entered, for there is less variance to be explained at the completion of each step. It may be, therefore, that social class is a stronger influence on GCG than it looks from Table 3.4.

In fact, this does not appear to be the case, for when WORCLASS and INTCLASS are entered as the first and second variables, they together only explain 5.4 per cent of variance. The two town variables then add another 14.6 per cent, while PERIODBT, *even when entered last*, still explains a further 12.8 per cent of the variance or more than twice that explained by social class when entered first. We may conclude from this that the time spent in owner-occupation is indeed a stronger determinant of gross capital gains than is social class.

Three further points need to be emphasized about the analysis of social class and capital gains. The first is that, while class is found to have a small but significant effect on total gross gains, it ceases to be significant when we model annual gross gains. As is clear from Table 3.6, annual real gains reflect time spent in the housing market (more recent buyers tend to make higher annual gains given the increase in house price inflation since the 1970s) and the town in which owners live (people in Slough have made more per year than those in the other two towns), but social class fails to achieve the criteria for entry into the model. This confirms the conclusions drawn earlier in the discussion of Table 3.4 that the higher total gains accruing to the service class are mainly a product of the fact that people in that class have on average been in owner-occupation for longer than members of the working class.

The model derived from Table 3.6 suggests that annual real gains can best be estimated as £82 for each year after 1900 when a household first purchased, less around £2,500 if they live in Burnley or Derby (the constant should be ignored in this case since, like the class variables, it fails to

177

Table 3.6 *A multiple regression model of social class, time in owner-occupation and town on real annual gains (1986 prices)*

Step	Variable	Coeff.	Standard error	Adjusted R-square	Change in R2	Signif.
1	FIRSTBT	82	22	0.05	–	0.0002
2	DERBY	−2,711	696	0.07	0.02	0.0001
3	BURNLEY	−2,552	703	0.11	0.04	0.0003
4	INTCLASS	−811	774	0.11	–	0.2960
5	WORCLASS	−671	702	0.12	0.01	0.3404
	(Constant)	−817	1,666			0.6242

Table 3.7 *Rates of return by social class*

Social class (quintiles)	Measure of rate of return (%)			
	GRR	Real GRR	NRR	Real NRR
Service class (N = 88)				
Lowest 10%	13	3	7	−1
30%	17	8	15	5
50% (median)	25	14	19	10
70%	34	24	27	17
90%	78	69	49	42
Mean	65	55	47	32
Intermediate (N = 83)				
Lowest 10%	6	2	−9	−19
30%	21	10	15	6
50% (median)	24	14	21	11
70%	31	20	26	15
90%	59	50	48	34
Mean	42	33	30	18
Working class (N = 73)				
Lowest 10%	12	5	−14	−14
30%	18	9	14	6
50% (median)	25	15	20	10
70%	38	22	30	18
90%	180	130	141	103
Mean	99	77	74	48

For key to column headings, see Table 3.2.

achieve the required significance level and has an unacceptably high standard error). The relatively low R-square figure of 0.11 further indicates that a large proportion of the variation is left unexplained by this model.

The second point to be made is that class does not appear to be a strong or significant variable in the explanation of other measures of capital gain such as total net gains, annual net gains, or rates of return. Table 3.7 presents the figures for the relation between social class and rates of return on capital advanced, while Table 3.8 summarizes the final equations and

R-square values derived from a series of regression models in which class, town and year of first purchase were entered as independent variables, and various measures of capital gains were entered as dependent variables.

The very high rates of return achieved by the top 10 per cent of working-class gainers in Table 3.7 are explained mainly by council house sales, for households which bought at discounted prices a year or two prior to being interviewed have obviously made very high rates of return on their initial deposits. Indeed, as was explained earlier, recent buyers in all classes will tend to record abnormally high rates of return given the high ratio of deposit to total house value in these cases, and this suggests that rather than inspecting the misleading mean figures for each class, comparisons need to be based on the overall spread within each class. Even on this basis, however, it seems from Table 3.7 that, with the possible exception of households in the bottom 10 per cent of the range, working-class owners have managed to secure rates of return (gross and net) which are directly comparable with those achieved by people in the service class.

This conclusion is borne out by the results of regression models. The summary equations listed in Table 3.8 show that class cannot be entered into

Table 3.8 *Summary regression equations for class, town and year of purchase on various measures of capital gains*

Measure of capital gain	Summary equation	R-square of final model
GCG	$90.9(c) - 0.67(y) - 22.9(b) - 19.0(d) - 8.8(w) + e$	0.31
St. error	$(6.7)\quad(0.09)\quad(2.9)\quad(2.9)\quad(2.9)$	
NCG	$78.0(c) - 0.69(y) - 20.5(b) - 16.8(d) + e$	0.27
St. error	$(6.6)\quad(0.09)\quad(2.8)\quad(2.8)$	
Real GCG	$95.6(c) - 25.6(w) - 0.06(y) + e$	0.03
St. error	$(23.8)\quad(10.0)\quad(0.03)$	
Real NCG	$63.4(c) - 0.06(y) + e$	0.01
St. error	$(21.8)\quad(0.03)$	
Real AGG	$0.08(y) - 2.7(d) - 2.6(b) + e$	0.11
St. error	$(0.02)\quad(0.70)\quad(0.07)$	
GRR	$-0.22(c) + 0.04(y) + e$	0.05
St. error	$(0.08)\quad(0.01)$	
Real GRR	$-0.22(c) + 0.04(y) + e$	0.05
St. error	$(0.08)\quad(0.01)$	
NRR	$-0.15(c) + 0.03(y) + e$	0.04
St. error	$(0.06)\quad(0.01)$	
Real NRR	$-0.12(c) + 0.02(y) + e$	0.04
St. error	$(0.05)\quad(0.01)$	

Note: the measure in each case has been divided by 1,000 to render the equations more readable. The final sum for each equation should therefore be multiplied by 1,000 to discover the estimated gain in pounds.
Key: c = *constant*; y = year first purchased (last two digits); b = Burnley; d = Derby; w = working class.

any of the models of rates of return (indeed, the only equations where it can be entered are those for nominal and real total gains, and even here its predictive power is very weak). All four of the equations for rates of return include only the year of first purchase and a constant. The message of Table 3.8 is clear. There is no significant relationship between social class and net capital gains, annual gains, or rates of return once the effects of location and period in owner-occupation have been taken into account.

The final point to be made about the findings on social class and capital gains is that none of the models generated so far has achieved strong predictive power. Most of the equations in Table 3.8 have very weak R-square figures (the exceptions are the first two equations for total gross and net gains), and this suggests that some other variable or variables could probably explain the data better than those entered into these models. In fact we need search no further for the 'missing factor' than the obvious variable of current house value.

Now it is true that the value of house owned is likely to reflect all three of the variables which we have been analysing. Other things being equal, we would expect middle-class people to own more valuable houses than those in the working class, people in a southern town like Slough to own more expensive houses than people in the Midlands or the North and long-term owners to have more expensive houses than recent purchasers (for they have had longer to accumulate capital and 'trade up-market'). These expectations are borne out by Table 3.9, which shows that location is the strongest influence on house values (the town variables alone explain 39 per cent of the variance), but that the distinction between working-class and other households and the length of time in owner-occupation are also significant influences. The key point, however, is that we cannot reduce the explanation of house values to any one of these three factors. All three are important, and for many of the households in the three towns survey they will pull in different directions. Furthermore, taken together these three factors still only explain 44 per cent of the variance.

When we model capital gains including current house value (HVALUE) as an independent variable, it becomes clear that the other variables have little additional effect. A strong model of total gross gains (R-square =

Table 3.9 *A multiple regression model of social class, town and time in owner-occupation on current house value*

Step	Variable	Coeff.	Standard error	Adjusted R-square	Change in R2	Signif.
1	BURNLEY	−28,982	2,416	0.12	–	0.0000
2	DERBY	−27,274	2,394	0.39	0.27	0.0000
3	WORCLASS	−9,982	2,414	0.42	0.03	0.0000
4	FIRSTBT	−210	76	0.44	0.02	0.0060
5	INTCLASS	−3,601	2,661	0.44	–	0.1771
	(Constant)	75,207	5,727			0.0000

Table 3.10 *A multiple regression model of house value, social class, town and time in owner-occupation on gross nominal gains*

Step	Variable	Coeff.	Standard error	Adjusted R-square	Change in R-square	Signif.
1	HVALUE	0.73	0.06	0.50	–	0.0000
2	FIRSTBT	−507.6	72.5	0.58	0.08	0.0000
3	BURNLEY	−1,600.3	2,810.0	0.58	–	0.5695
4	INTCLASS	−2,495.7	2,520.8	0.58	–	0.3232
5	WORCLASS	−1,500.1	2,348.5	0.57	−0.01	0.5235
6	DERBY	998.4	2,737.7	0.57	–	0.7156
	(Constant)	35,757.2	6,882.6			0.0000

0.58), for example, can be achieved by entering only current house value and time in owner-occupation into the equation – the town and class variables fail to achieve an independent level of significance (Table 3.10). The same is true for total net gains (R-square = 0.43).

Capital gains, then, are primarily a function of the value of the house owned plus time spent in owner-occupation. The value of house owned itself depends mainly on where a household is located, although the social class of the household is a secondary factor. It is true that, on average, working-class owners have made less money from owner-occupation than middle-class households have, but this is due more to their more recent entry into the housing market than to their social class, and the differences pale into insignificance when set against the area of the country in which people live. The vast majority of working-class owner-occupiers have accumulated substantial capital gains out of their participation in the housing market, and their rates of return on original capital invested are every bit as good as those achieved by households in higher social classes. The relative gap between working-class and middle-class capital gains is lower than that between working-class and middle-class average incomes, and this means that owner-occupation is having a 'progressive' effect in the sense that it is narrowing the relative inequalities between the classes (although it is, of course, widening the gap between those who own their homes and those who rent).

Faced with this evidence, it is clearly absurd to claim that working-class households have in any sense lost out as a result of moving into owner-occupation. John Short's belief that they have been 'screwed' and Oriel Sullivan's view that their prospects for generating wealth have been 'negligible' are quite simply wrong. The left has persistently advanced such claims but has never demonstrated an empirical basis for them. The evidence reviewed above exposes these claims for what they are – ideological myths, nothing more.

We saw earlier that working-class households are only one of five groups in the population who have been identified in the academic literature as losers from home ownership. The other four are council house buyers, ethnic minorities, residents in inner-city areas and those who live in less prosperous regions. Having dealt exhaustively with the claim that working-class owners have done badly out of buying their houses, we may now (rather more swiftly) consider each of these remaining groups.

Council house buyers

From the evidence already reviewed it is clear that *council house buyers* represent a most unlikely group of victims, for substantial discounts on sales since 1980 have provided many of them with windfall gains from the very first day of purchase. There were thirty-two households in the three towns sample who had bought council houses and for whom full information was available. Although these numbers are small, there are sufficient cases here to draw comparisons with the rest of the sample. Bearing in mind that virtually all of these households are recent purchasers (post-1980), and that total gains tend to be lowest among recent purchasers (because they have not had the time to accumulate much capital), such comparisons clearly demonstrate that council house buyers have enjoyed the fruits of capital accumulation just as other owner-occupiers have.

We have already seen earlier in this section and in Chapter 2 that tenants who have bought their homes have subsequently encountered no greater financial problems in meeting the mortgage repayments than any other first time buyers. Indeed, as we saw in Chapter 2, most council house buyers are 'less stretched' financially than other first-time buyers. Furthermore, the three towns survey found that, on average, they lived in houses which were in a better state of repair than those around them which had remained in local authority ownership. If council house buyers have lost out in any way, it can therefore only be by sustaining gross or net losses in the value of their properties.

The reality, of course, is that they have virtually all made substantial gains. Their mean gross gain in 1986 prices is over £20,000, the median is over £18,000, and even the least successful of them (the bottom decile of the distribution) have made over £7,000. Real net gains range from over £3,000 at the bottom decile to over £30,000 at the top, with a mean of £15,000 and a median of £12,000. The mean real annual gross gain is £5,000 (median = £3,391), and the mean real annual net gain is over £4,000 (median = £2,647). None of these households has sustained a loss, gross or net. They have, in short, made a lot of money in very little time, and this is reflected in abnormally high rates of return (such as medians of 144, 128, 97 and 81 per cent per annum for nominal gross rates, real gross rates, nominal net rates and real net rates respectively).

Given the relatively short period of time which most of these households have spent in owner-occupation, the most appropriate measure by which to compare their gains with those achieved by the rest of the sample is that of annual real gains. One way of making this comparison is by dividing the whole sample into three equal categories of high, medium and low annual

Table 3.11 *A multiple regression model of real annual capital gains including council house buyers*

Step	Variable	Coeff.	Standard error	Adjusted R-square	Change in R2	Signif.
1	FIRSTBT	72.7	22.2	0.05	–	0.0012
2	DERBY	−2,700.2	690.7	0.07	0.02	0.0001
3	BURNLEY	−2,536.3	696.9	0.11	0.04	0.0003
4	BUYER	2,452.7	1,023.6	0.12	0.01	0.0172
5	INTCLASS	−871.2	768.0	0.12	–	0.2576
6	WORCLASS	−764.0	697.5	0.12	–	0.2743
	(Constant)	−301.5	1,665.9			0.8565

gainers. When we do this, we find that council house buyers are heavily over-represented in the high-gaining group. Sixty-six per cent of them appear in the high gross real annual gains group, as compared with just 30 per cent of the rest of the sample, and this figure rises to 69 per cent (as compared with 29 per cent) on the calculation of net real annual gains.

Another way of demonstrating the same point is by entering a new dummy variable, BUYER, into our earlier multiple regression models. As we can see from Table 3.11, this produces a final equation in which the best estimate of real annual gains is raised by nearly £2,500 per year for those households which have purchased a council house. Indeed, it seems from this model that the fact of being a council house buyer makes almost as much difference to real annual gains as the part of the country in which people happen to live.

It would seem from all these figures that the 1980 Housing Act, which established the Right to Buy, has turned out to be one of the most dramatic redistributive measures ever taken by any British government. One million predominantly working-class households have bought homes from their former council landlords, and if the results of the three towns survey are at all generalizable, it seems likely that the great majority of them have as a result accumulated substantial capital sums which can now be transmitted to the next generation. As we shall see in Chapter 6, the 'problem' is not that council tenants who have bought have thereby lost out, but is rather that those who have not bought have become relatively poorer, and this means that the challenge facing housing policy in the 1990s and beyond is how to extend opportunities for purchase to more of those tenants who would like to buy.

Owner-occupiers in the ethnic minorities

The third group which is said to have been disadvantaged by moving into home ownership comprises *members of the ethnic-minority populations*, and in particular Asian households, for unlike Afro-Caribbeans, their owner-occupancy rate is higher even than that of whites.

Again, the literature is insistent that Asians and Afro-Caribbeans are victims, herded into decaying inner-city housing which is often declining in value. As we saw in Chapter 2, dozens of researchers have over the last twenty years followed the path beaten by Rex and Moore (1967) and Rex and Tomlinson (1979) by arguing that the remarkably high rate of home ownership among Asians is evidence, not of their success, but of their failure. They have been discriminated against by councils who have kept them out of local authority dwellings and by building societies who have kept them out of desirable suburban locations. Their housing is of a low quality, and they are 'trapped in home ownership' and therefore prevented from gaining access to 'more privileged' public-sector rental (Gray, 1982, p. 276). This extraordinary argument is then elaborated by the assertion that Asian home owners face high housing bills and an unbearable mortgage burden (ibid., p. 277) and is rounded off by the totally unsupported assertion that they also have only 'minimal' opportunities to increase the value of their asset (Ward, 1982, p. 8).

This sort of sociological fantasizing has ably been dissected by Jon Gower Davies. He writes of 'the refusal of the Asian population to take on the role of a down-trodden sub-proletariat' (1985, p. 9), and he demonstrates from his own and other studies that most Asian householders certainly do not want council housing, that they do not live in appalling conditions (98 per cent live in houses with exclusive use of all basic amenities) and that they exercise effective choice in determining where they live. Davies does not, however, address the charge that Asian home owners have bought a pig in a poke, and this is probably because he lacks evidence either way. The three towns survey does enable us to consider this issue, however.

The tenure composition of Asian households in the sample was almost identical to that of whites – 22 per cent were outright owners (23 per cent of whites), 53 per cent were buying with a housing loan (50 per cent of whites), and 25 per cent were council tenants (26 per cent of whites). Most of the owner-occupiers (amounting to half of all Asian households in our survey) lived in Victorian terraced housing near the centre of the three towns. Like Davies, we found no evidence that these households had been 'coerced' into this – 14 per cent said they lacked choice in their housing situation, but 17 per cent of whites said the same thing. The real evidence of 'coercion' relates to the allocation of council housing to Asian families, for not one of our Asian respondents lived on a popular council estate, though 22 per cent lived on unpopular estates. Most of the rest lived in inter-war suburban semis; only three Asian households had made it to the higher-priced, high-status housing.

In general, the conditions in which these households lived were no better nor worse than the average for this type of housing profile. Forty-six per cent of Asians said that their housing needed at least one major repair. This compared with only 22 per cent of whites, but 54 per cent of all respondents living in Victorian terraces made this claim. Similarly, 31 per cent of Asian houses were classified as in poor condition by interviewers, but this compares with the 32 per cent of all Victorian terraced housing so designated. It is true that Asians were more likely to say that they lived in poor conditions (29 per cent) than were either whites (12 per cent) or owners of Victorian terraces (19 per cent), but this may reflect higher standards as much as inferior conditions. As for spending on repairs and improvements, this again compared with the average for this type of housing. Sixteen per cent of those living in Victorian terraced houses had spent £3,000 or more on home improvements and renovations (1986 prices), and the equivalent figure among Asian households was 13 per cent (38 per cent among whites). Asian respondents were, however, rather more pessimistic than whites about recouping the money they had spent.

Clearly Asians on average are in worse housing conditions than whites. This reflects the fact that more of them live in Victorian terraced houses where rates of disrepair are highest. Compared with whites living in this kind of housing, however, Asians seem no more nor less deprived.

As for housing costs, we have already seen that Asian households often receive help from other family members in setting up home, and it is therefore no surprise to find that fewer of them (just 14 per cent) say that they have encountered any problems in meeting loan repayments than is the case for the white population (22 per cent).

Like council house buyers, Asians are relative newcomers to owner-occupation. Sixty-one per cent of Asian owners in the sample bought their first house during the 1980s, compared with 34 per cent of whites. Forty-two per cent of whites bought their first home prior to 1970, but there was only one Asian household in our entire sample who had done so. We should therefore expect total capital gains to be lower than for whites, and this is confirmed by the evidence. The mean real capital gain accruing to Asians in the sample was just under £15,000, and the median was just over £16,000. The equivalent figures for whites were £29,000 and £22,000. Similarly, the mean real net capital gain for Asian owners was £9,208 (median £8,954), while for whites the mean figure was in excess of £20,000 with a median of £14,166. Over 20 per cent of Asian owners had made real net losses, although none had made real losses before mortgage payments are deducted.

Given the differences in length of time spent in owner-occupation by these two groups, one basis for comparing them is that provided by figures on annual gains. Here, Asians appear on average to have done rather better than whites. The mean gross real annual gain for Asians is £4,255 compared with £2,452 for whites. The range between the tenth and ninetieth percentiles for the Asian sub-sample is £348 to £10,853 with a median of £3,051, while the same range in the white sub-sample is £353 to £5,372 with a median of £1,978. The lowest annual gains are therefore equivalent, but at the higher end of the distribution, Asian households appear to have made better annual gains than the highest-gaining whites.

We saw earlier, however, that annual gains tend to be rather higher among more recent purchasers given the higher rates of house price inflation since the early 1970s. Nevertheless, if we compare the total gains made by whites and Asians while controlling for time spent in owner-occupation, there is still no evidence to suggest that the latter have fared any worse than the former. Nearly half of all post-1980 Asian buyers are in the lowest third of the distribution of total real gains, but this is also true of more than half of the equivalent cohort of white buyers. As for the 1970–9 cohort, Asians split evenly across low-, medium- and high-gaining groups, while whites tend to cluster mainly in the 'medium' category. There are, quite simply, no significant differences between these two ethnic groups as regards accumulation of wealth from the housing market. Attempts at regression modelling similarly fail to discover a statistically significant ethnicity effect.

We should conclude, therefore, that Asian owner-occupiers have generally shared in the good fortune of owner-occupiers as a whole. They are also firmly committed to the ethic of home ownership, for as we saw in Chapter 2, 87 per cent prefer to buy than to rent, and we also found that all bar one of our Asian respondents supported the policy of selling council houses. As a relatively recent cohort of purchasers they are still concentrated mainly in the cheaper and older housing, but compared with others in the same position they do not appear to be suffering any greater hardship, nor to be losing out on capital accumulation through housing inflation. These results confirm the conclusion drawn by Jon Gower Davies, who suggests that the high rate of home ownership among Asians in Britain presents 'a picture of a community having basically solved the problem of primary emigration, i.e. the securing of sufficient property both to underpin the settlement and to act as realizable capital should either a further internal emigration or re-emigration become convenient or necessary' (1985, p. 12).

Owners of old, inner-city houses

The last two groups which have been identified as victims of the spread of home ownership are distinguished geographically rather than socially. Obviously these two dimensions are related, for certain kinds of social groups tend to live in certain types of areas. Nevertheless, the argument would be that it is their physical location, rather than their social position, which causes them to lose out from home ownership.

The first of these groups consists of *people living in the oldest and generally inner areas* of our towns and cities. Most commentators agree that there is marked variation between local housing markets (Harris, 1986). Even within the same town, house prices may fluctuate as between different neighbourhoods, and Hamnett (1984a) has suggested that such intra-regional variations are probably more significant than those which occur between regions.

Not surprisingly, it has generally been held that owners of housing in the cheapest areas of cities do worse in terms of capital accumulation than those in more affluent neighbourhoods. In his work in Sunderland, Norman Dennis (1970, p. 236) points out that owners of inner-area terraced houses may find their properties condemned as unfit, in which case they can be relocated on to outlying council estates with little financial compensation. Sullivan and Murphy (1987, p. 190) similarly suggest that owners of old, cheap houses are likely to find it difficult to sell their homes if lending institutions believe that the housing is approaching the end of its useful life, and Whitehead (1979) believes that they are also unlikely to be able to use them as security for raising additional loans. Berry (1986, p. 118) draws upon Marxist rent theory to argue that capital gains will reflect the balance of locational advantages and that cheaper housing will therefore generate much lower returns.

These arguments are important in so far as they serve to remind us that houses do eventually 'wear out'. Like the last owner of a car before it goes to the breakers, some owners each year find that their property has reached the end of its life and has exhausted its value, although unlike car owners, they may still be able to recoup the value of the land. However, the period of large-scale demolition in Britain, when whole neighbourhoods were swept away in a modernizing zeal and with little regard for the views of those who lived in them, has now passed. The emphasis today is on refurbishment and repair rather than replacement (Paris and Blackaby, 1979), and most residents of older housing in inner-city areas can be reasonably confident that they are in no immediate danger of receiving a Compulsory Purchase Order through the letter-box.

The question, then, is not whether owners of inner-area housing are likely to lose what little they have got, but rather whether they are likely to accumulate much capital from it. To the extent that evidence is available, it seems that they are not. In New Zealand, Thorns (1981b) shows that owners in wealthier suburbs make greater gains than those in cheaper areas, and in an important study in Birmingham, Karn, Kemeny and Williams (1985) found that inner-city housing had inflated more slowly than housing elsewhere in the West Midlands.

It is important, however, to clarify just exactly what these various studies have actually found. In particular, we need to be clear on whether inner-area owners have lost money, and we need to be careful in distinguishing the question of absolute gains from that of rates of return.

On the first question, both Thorns and Karn and her colleagues found that cheaper areas inflated more slowly than more expensive areas. The latter study, for example, showed that while house prices rose by 70 per cent in nominal terms in the West Midlands region between 1975 and 1979, prices in the inner areas of Birmingham rose much more slowly (by 47 per cent in Saltley, 45 per cent in Handsworth, 40 per cent in Sparkhill and just 8 per cent in Soho). This does indeed imply that 'the inner city areas have lost value relative to their surrounding regional average' (Karn, Kemeny and Williams, 1985, p. 35), although it does not necessarily imply that they have lost value relative to, say, the level of real incomes or the movement of the RPI or the level of house prices elsewhere in the country or even the average returns to other kinds of investment. Given rates of inflation in the late 1970s, the figure for Soho does suggest that housing there fell in real value quite dramatically over this period, but is this also true of the other neighbourhoods, and would it still be true had the authors gone back four more years to include the 1971–3 boom in their calculations?

The point is, then, that even where it can be shown that inner-area housing is inflating more slowly over an extended time period than houses in the suburbs, it need not follow that owners of such housing are losing money. It may be that they are making high gains while those in the suburbs are making very high gains, in which case it would make little sense to talk of any group of owners 'losing'. Yet what tends to happen in discussions of this evidence is that the fall in value of inner-area property relative to other properties gets interpreted to mean that inner-area owners have actually lost money. Thus Karn, Kemeny and Williams conclude, 'Once a house has been bought, *falling or stagnant prices* offer no advantages to the owner. They reduce the value of the financial asset . . . They make the house more difficult to sell because of justifiable doubts on the part of potential buyers and lenders. They make the possibility of trading up to better quality property more problematic' (1985, p. 49, my emphasis). All of this would be true if these house prices really were falling, but (with the possible exception of Soho) this is not what their findings reveal. We need, therefore, to be clear about the difference between uneven gains and actual losses.

We need also to be clear about a second and crucial issue which concerns the distinction between absolute gains and rates of gain. This point was originally picked up by Geraldine Pratt in her discussion of the Thorns data, for she showed that although absolute capital gains are likely to have varied between the five Christchurch neighbourhoods which he analysed, relative increases in capital values appeared remarkably uniform, working out at around 40 per cent in each case (Pratt, 1982, p. 495). This insight has subsequently been developed by Munro and Maclennan (1987) in a study of housing transactions in Glasgow in the period since 1972, for they found that rates of increase were actually highest in the low-priced areas, although absolute gains were highest in high-price areas. Prices in the most expensive housing areas increased by 569 per cent between 1972 and 1984, while those in the least expensive areas rose by over 1,000 per cent in the same period.

The Glasgow study is important for two reasons. First, it shows that Valerie Karn's evidence on inner areas of Birmingham cannot be generalized; for if house prices at the bottom end of the market in Birmingham have lagged behind average rises, those at the bottom end of the market in Glasgow have moved ahead of them.

Second, the Glasgow study also shows that it is quite possible for rates of gain in the housing market to favour the least well-off owners most (a point which we made earlier when considering the evidence on social class differences). The wealthy in Glasgow may accumulate the greatest absolute sum, but the poorer owners make the greatest relative gains. As Munro and Maclennan put it, 'We have no evidence that the owners of the cheapest houses were denied access to capital accumulation. Indeed, the potential for relative capital gain remains greater in the cheaper areas. It should be stressed that the greatest absolute capital gains can be achieved by the owners of the most expensive houses' (1987, p. 77). What this means is that David Thorns is wrong to argue that the operation of the housing market simply exacerbates inequalities arising out of differential returns in the labour market. Rather, proportionate wage and salary differentials may actually be reduced as a result of differential rates of gain from private home ownership.

The findings from the three towns survey tend to bear out the points that Pratt and Munro and Maclennan are making. Owners of small, Victorian terraced houses in the three towns made real capital gains ranging from just £600 at the lowest decile to nearly £40,000 at the highest. The median real gain was £8,309. The equivalent figures for those living on modern suburban estates ranged from nearly £10,000 to nearly £80,000 with a median gain of £31,258. These figures are, however, meaningless unless we take account of the length of time spent in owner-occupation, for owners of Victorian terraced houses have on average been in owner-occupation for a shorter time than those in other housing areas. Forty-one per cent of owners of this type of housing had purchased their first property since 1980, and between 40 per cent (in Burnley) and 57 per cent (in Slough) of them were under the age of 35. In Slough (where 44 per cent of them are in professional or managerial occupations) and to a lesser extent in Derby (where the proportion is 22 per cent), the bottom-of-the-market old terraced property is for many the first staging post to something bigger and better, although this is less true in Burnley where only 6 per cent of such owners are in the top two social classes. In any event, the shorter time spent in owner-occupation would (as we saw in the discussion of lower-class home ownership) tend to depress the absolute capital gain.

This becomes clear when we consider real annual gains. For those in Victorian terraced houses, real annual gains ranged from just over £300 per annum at the lowest decile to £5,500 per annum at the highest with a median figure of £1,758. These figures are still lower than those for the suburban owners, who were making between £730 and £5,179 each year with a median annual real gain of £2,279, but the gap is clearly much narrower. Indeed, when we construct a multiple regression model of annual real gains with town, period in owner-occupation and type of house owned as independent variables, none of the housing types which are entered achieve statistical significance.

The gains to be made from ownership of the cheapest housing are of course smaller than those which can be accumulated from more expensive properties, and they also vary widely between different parts of the country. But there is little evidence to suggest that owners of this type of housing have lost as a result of their purchases. Even when we consider net real annual gains (that is, how much capital people accumulate each year after paying the mortgage) we find that three-quarters of owners of these houses are still in surplus each year, and even the lowest decile has only 'lost' £646 each year in 1986 prices. It should be remembered, of course, that none of these figures include repair and maintenance costs and that these are likely to represent a significant deduction for many of these home owners. Nevertheless, a net housing cost of just £13 per week plus maintenance at the bottom end of the distribution suggests that even the worst-off households in the cheapest housing are still faring reasonably well out of owner-occupation in that the annual increase in the capital value of their homes does not fall far short of their annual outgoings.

What of their rate of gain? We saw earlier that both Pratt and Munro and Maclennan have suggested that owners of cheaper properties may make smaller total gains but higher relative gains than suburban home owners. Two measures seem appropriate in order to evaluate this claim.

The first is represented by the rates of return on initial capital invested by these two groups. Median gross rates of return achieved by owners of Victorian terraced properties work out at 39 per cent per annum (nominal) and 26 per cent p.a. (real), with figures for the lowest decile of 10 per cent and 3 per cent respectively. These compare with median figures of 26 per cent (nominal) and 15 per cent (real) for owners on suburban estates and they suggest that the former group has been accumulating capital at a faster rate, although the figures for the lowest decile of suburban owners (17 per cent and 7 per cent) show that this pattern reverses at the bottom end of the distribution. The problem with comparing the two groups on these figures is, however, that owners of Victorian terraced houses tend to be more recent purchasers, and, as explained earlier, rates of return tend to be higher for more recent buyers. Such comparisons are, therefore, somewhat misleading, although they do demonstrate that investment at the bottom of the housing market can prove highly lucrative relative to the potential returns available from other kinds of investment.

A more direct method of comparing these two groups of owners, and one which is more consistent with the calculations made by Pratt and Munro and Maclennan, is to compute their returns as a proportion of total house values. The median value of Victorian terraced houses in the three towns sample was £14,000, while that of houses on suburban estates was £43,000 (these figures are themselves, of course, of limited value given the enormous variations across the three towns, but we shall consider the significance of these differences in a moment). Given that median real annual gains accruing to owners of these houses were £1,389 and £2,279 respectively, this represents annual rates of accumulation of 0.10 per cent for the former group and 0.05 per cent for the latter. This suggests that Pratt and Munro and Maclennan are probably right, for it seems that the rate of accumulation relative to the value of the properties is twice as great for owners of cheap old houses as for owners of newer more expensive ones.

It is clear from the various types of evidence which we have reviewed that ownership of the cheapest housing can still bring substantial capital gains and rates of return on investment. However, owners of such houses make somewhat smaller annual gains than those in the suburbs (their median annual real gain is worth 61 per cent of that achieved by suburban owners), and their total gains are obviously less given the smaller sums which are invested at the outset. To this extent, the critics are right when they point out that owners of cheaper properties in the older areas of towns do not do so well out of the housing market as suburban owner-occupiers, and if these figures are correct they would suggest that 'trading up' from one to the other is not likely to be possible unless a household's real income is rising sufficiently for it to make the leap. The critics are not, however, right to suggest that owners of these cheaper properties are therefore losing money. They are accumulating significant capital sums each year; it is just that other groups of owners are making even more.

Home owners in declining regions

The disparity in capital gains between different groups of owners is much more marked, however, when we compare *owners in different regions of the country*. With house prices consistently 25 to 50 per cent higher in London and the South-East than in the rest of the country (Hamnett, 1988b, p. 31), it is obvious that higher potential gains are possible there, and we have seen throughout this discussion that location (in this case the distinction between Derby and Burnley on the one hand and Slough on the other) is a major variable in the explanation of variations in the capital gains achieved by different households in the three towns survey. As Table 3.12 demonstrates, the median Slough owner has accumulated over £33,000 in real terms – 58 per cent more than the median Derby owner and 139 per cent more than the median Burnley owner. The total real gain of over £10,000 achieved at the lowest decile of the Slough distribution is only achieved at the third decile in Derby and at the fifth in Burnley. The median annual real gain of £3,360 in Slough is over twice that made in Derby and nearly three times that made in Burnley, and in both cases this figure is only matched when we reach the ninth decile of the distribution.

Of course, higher prices in the South also mean that buyers have to pay more to get housing in the first place. According to the *Family Expenditure Survey* (DoE, 1987), housing cost home buyers in 1985–6 a weekly average of £32.08 if they lived in the East Midlands and £36.25 if they lived in the North-West, but in the South-East outside Greater London it cost them £50.80. Although incomes are higher in the South-East, this differential is outweighed by the house price gap. As Chris Hamnett observes, 'While owner occupiers in London and the South East currently get much greater equity appreciation than elsewhere, they also have to pay far more for it and get far less for their money in terms of space and housing quality. It would appear that the regional differences in the use value of housing are inversely related to accumulation potential' (1987, p. 24).

What this means is that, comparing like with like, people in the South are capitalizing more of their income through house purchase, while those in more northerly towns presumably enjoy a higher disposable income to

191

Table 3.12 *Capital gains and annual gains in Slough, Derby and Burnley*

Town (quintiles)	GCG	Real GCG	NCG	Measure of gain (£) Real NCG	AGG	Real AGG	ANG	Real ANG
Slough (N = 106)								
Lowest 10%	10,261	10,145	5,627	3,503	1,554	1,360	996	486
30%	26,393	22,230	13,975	11,608	2,489	2,310	1,763	1,578
50% (median)	35,501	33,568	25,189	24,383	3,360	3,427	2,319	2,093
70%	49,150	47,908	40,370	38,159	4,452	4,949	2,816	3,018
90%	70,715	80,691	54,941	64,694	8,480	8,425	6,932	6,800
Mean	37,599	37,132	27,946	26,359	4,471	4,326	3,188	2,811
Derby (N = 94)								
Lowest 10%	1,706	957	−482	−2,081	336	336	−123	−385
30%	12,000	10,655	4,926	4,725	910	854	497	479
50% (median)	19,495	21,261	12,672	12,310	1,397	1,408	796	848
70%	27,047	29,716	20,089	21,486	2,091	2,305	1,266	1,483
90%	43,878	58,293	37,135	45,747	3,308	3,555	2,745	2,504
Mean	21,434	26,019	14,772	18,781	1,378	1,439	780	769
Burnley (N = 89)								
Lowest 10%	1,353	391	−1,857	−3,389	191	124	−266	−491
30%	6,885	4,949	1,659	1,420	731	670	335	243
50% (median)	13,788	14,070	8,276	7,701	1,162	1,184	732	783
70%	23,051	22,917	13,527	14,983	2,011	2,067	1,145	1,286
90%	39,638	46,664	29,503	35,808	3,447	3,931	2,489	2,662
Mean	16,433	19,505	10,197	12,730	1,564	1,651	888	897

spend on other things. It is apparent from Table 3.12, however, that higher housing costs in the South are not enough to reduce the gap in net gains, for even taking the real cost of their mortgage repayments into account, owners in Slough are still achieving a median annual real gain of £2,000 – more than twice as much as in the other two towns. When we were preparing to conduct these interviews one Derby informant told us, 'We all think you're daft down South paying those prices for houses!' It turns out, however, that the capital growth being achieved in the South amply compensates for the higher outgoings.

The housing cost differential between the regions is actually wider for working-class buyers than for middle-class ones. As Fleming and Nellis (1985, p. 8) observe, 'Buyers in the Midlands and the northern parts of England . . . buy more cheaply than similar buyers in the South East, *with the difference increasing as one moves down the scale of social classes*' (original emphasis). This reflects the ability and desire of middle-class households in low-cost regions to boost their housing spending, especially when they are on national salary scales (as is the case with most employees in the public sector) or when their companies offer help with house purchase. For those whose career may entail a move back to a higher-priced region in the future, it is essential that they invest in a relatively high-priced house in order to keep their equity up (Forrest and Murie, 1987b, p. 353).

This ability and desire to pay more for housing may help to explain why the price ratio between the top and bottom of the housing market in a town like Burnley appears much greater than in a town like Slough. In Burnley, we interviewed people in housing worth £7,000 and people in housing worth eight times that; but in Slough, the difference between the cheapest (around £40,000) and the most expensive (around £100,000) was only two and a half times. It seems that the housing market in towns like Burnley is bifurcated between low-priced housing bought mainly by locals and higher-priced housing sought mainly by in-migrants (Forrest, 1987, p. 1619). Movement across these different sub-markets may be rare, for the price differential is large, and there may be few 'stepping stones' in between.

There is then no disputing that people in the South-East make higher gains from inflation of housing than do owners in lower-priced regions. The question, however, is whether or not the relative gap between the regions is widening, for if it is, then existing relative inequalities will clearly become exacerbated as time goes on, and movement from cheaper to more expensive regions will become increasingly difficult.

In an influential paper published in 1982, David Thorns suggested that house prices had risen faster in the more prosperous regions with the result that the disadvantages of high unemployment and low wages were being reinforced by a relative decline in the value of the housing which people live in. As he put it:

> The results of such marked changes upon owner occupiers in these declining areas is to reinforce their losses sustained by the labour market change. Not only have they lost their job, but also their main private investment, their own house, is also of declining value and virtually unsellable except at a price which would represent a substantial loss to the household.
>
> (1982, p. 758)

The by now familiar exaggeration found in this statement can swiftly be refuted, for only in exceptional cases (for example, Aberdeen when the bottom fell out of the oil industry) have significant numbers of people actually lost their investments when local economies decline. Even in Consett, which occupies bottom place on an index of urban economic activity rates, house prices have continued to rise at a little above the general rate of inflation (see Forrest and Murie, 1987a, pp. 15–16). The more serious point in Thorns's argument, however, is that rates of increase in house prices have been uneven across the regions. Even here, however, it is by no means clear that he is right.

Analysing house price movements between 1969 and 1981, Hamnett effectively refuted Thorns's claim by showing that house price rises tend to be led by London and the South-East and that other regions catch up later. 'What we find', says Hamnett, 'is a highly lagged pattern of cyclical house price inflation . . . there is no evidence that regional inequalities in house prices have worsened over the period in question . . . If anything, regional house price inequalities between London and elsewhere have tended to narrow slightly' (1984b, pp. 152–3). Thus Hamnett found that average house prices stood at 75 per cent of the Greater London average in 1969 and at 78 per cent in 1981. In between, they had fluctuated on a range from 65 per cent (in 1972) to 82 per cent (in 1976).

Hamnett's argument has been supported by Barlow, whose analysis concluded that 'There is no evidence that house prices have risen more slowly in depressed regions or that regional inequalities have worsened over the last fifteen years' (1986, p. 19). However, it has been suggested that the pattern of the early- and late-1970s booms (when the South led and the North caught up later) may not be repeated in the future. At the height of the late-1980s boom, the *Independent* suggested that 'The chances of price inflation in the South dropping sufficiently to bring absolute prices back in line with the North look remote' (3 June 1988). The reasons given for this pessimism were that most population growth is taking place in the South and that future economic growth is also likely to be concentrated there given the increasing significance of the European Community, the impact of major new investments such as the M25 London orbital motorway and the Channel Tunnel, and the upward pressure on salaries in London brought about by the modernization and expansion of the City financial institutions (for a similar argument, see also Forrest and Murie, 1989, p. 27). Given the significance of real incomes in influencing movements in house prices, it does seem to make sense to suggest that any widening of the regional income gap is likely to be reflected in disproportionate rates of house price inflation between expanding and declining areas.

The evidence, however, suggests that the house price gap has been closing following the peaking of the 1986–8 boom just as it did in the earlier periods. Hamnett (1988b) shows that the price lag in the North produced a lowering of the price/income ratio there, and that this in turn meant that when prices stopped rising in the South, they continued to rise in the North. In the first half of 1989, for example, average house prices in the South remained static or even fell slightly, yet those in the North were still rising by around 4 per cent per month (*Independent*, 1 July 1989). It does seem that the house price 'race' is akin to that between the tortoise and the hare, for in each boom the South rushes off ahead and then pauses while the northern tortoise makes up ground. Where the analogy breaks down, of course, is that, unlike in Aesop's fable, the tortoise never actually catches up or overtakes.

The regional house price gap represents a serious and enduring problem for the British economy for it acts as a disincentive to labour mobility. In the 1980s high rates of unemployment in the country as a whole have to some extent been counteracted by a growth in new job vacancies located primarily (though not, of course, exclusively) in southern areas. Workers, however, have often displayed considerable reluctance to move, and employers in the South have sometimes encountered difficulties in filling jobs and have blamed their problems on high local house prices (Dickens, 1988, p. 111). The disparity of house prices between North and South is certainly not the only explanation for low rates of labour mobility, for research has demonstrated that workers often refuse to move even when housing is available at a price they can afford (Salt, 1985). Nevertheless, part of the rigidity in labour markets can plausibly be accounted for by regional house price differences.

What seems to be happening is that workers in the North cannot afford housing in the South and, faced with a choice between a house but no job and a job but no house, they opt to stay put (Forrest, 1987). Similarly, workers in the South are reluctant to risk future equity growth from their housing by moving to lower-priced regions (the *Guardian*, for example, reported on 24 February 1987 that civil servants were declining promotions which entailed a move north; see also Champion, Green and Owen, 1987). The result is that labour shortages in the South force up wage rates, while labour surpluses in the North depress them (Minford, Peel and Ashton, 1987; Spencer, 1987, p. 24). Given that disposable income levels are the major determinant of house prices, these differences in wage rates then feed through into even higher house prices in the South, thus exacerbating the problem still further.

Given that mobility rates are even lower in the public rented sector than among home owners, it seems that there are only two possible solutions to this log-jam. Either employers have to be forced or induced to relocate in northern regions where unemployment is high (a policy which was tried and which failed in the 1960s and 1970s) or the supply of new housing in the South has to be increased. The second of these strategies implies an easing of planning controls and a resuscitation of private renting (for in principle the existence of a larger private rented sector should enable easier mobility). We shall return to these issues in Chapter 6.

For the moment we may simply conclude that the regional dimension is almost certainly the most important variable contributing to different patterns of capital gains from the housing market. The single most important explanation for why some groups of owners make more money than others from their housing is that they live in different parts of the country. These regional differences certainly outweigh any social class differences, for as the summary equations in Table 3.8 demonstrated, the influence of location on various measures of capital gain is much stronger than that of social class. In other words, controlling for the length of time spent in owner-occupation, most working-class owners in a town like Slough have made higher gains from the housing market than most middle-class owners in a town like Burnley.

It is, however, still important to remember that owners in depressed regions are accumulating wealth. Even in Burnley owner-occupiers have been averaging real gains of over £1,000 per year as a result of owning a house, and their median total capital gain comes out at £14,000 in 1986 prices. These figures may look relatively small when compared with those achieved by owners in Slough, but they look extremely large when compared with the situation of tenants. The median real rate of return on the capital invested by our Burnley home owners works out at a healthy 17 per cent per annum, and this only falls to 11 per cent when we take account of mortgage costs. It is difficult to see how non-owners anywhere in the country could have matched this through alternative investment strategies. It is also difficult to see how, faced with such evidence, the view that large numbers of home owners 'get screwed' in the housing system can any longer retain any credibility.

Do owners see housing as an investment?

The final argument advanced by those who claim that capital gains from home ownership are either non-existent or sociologically insignificant is that home owners themselves do not see their homes in investment terms, are unconcerned about capital gains and rates of return and therefore do not act in the housing market in accordance with criteria of profit maximization. Given the old sociological adage that people act according to how they see social reality, the thrust of this argument is that the reality of home ownership as experienced by owners themselves owes little to the evidence we have been discussing in this chapter, in which case their behaviour is likely to be little changed by it. Millions of people may now own substantial sums of capital but their orientation towards this wealth is a long way from being capitalist.

As with so many of the other claims and assertions which have been advanced in this field, this one actually rests on precious little evidence. The most influential study appears to have been John Agnew's work in the early 1970s in which he compared a sample of home owners in Leicester with a group of owner-occupiers in the American city of Dayton. He found that the American home owners were much more concerned about the exchange values of their homes than were their British counterparts. Seventy-three per cent of the Dayton sample agreed that the profit motive had been an important factor in their decision to purchase their houses, and this seems to confirm other North American research which has suggested that American home owners are 'preoccupied' with the value of their homes (Perin, 1977, p. 134) and that they tend to see housing as 'a commodity or an investment opportunity' (Rakoff, 1977, p. 93). In Agnew's Leicester sample, by contrast, 86 per cent of home owners professed to be unconcerned about making a profit from their housing (1978, p. 131), and this finding has often been cited along with snippets and anecdotes from one or two other pieces of research to demonstrate that home owners do not think of their housing as an investment and are unconcerned about capital gains (for example, Gray, 1982, pp. 285–6).

Whether Agnew got it wrong or whether times have changed since he did his work is difficult to determine. Both seem likely. Indications that he got it

Great Bores of Today

". . .we bought this house for £7000 in 1965 you wouldn't believe it now would you? it seems ludicrous the people next door have just sold theirs for £290.000 and it's got no garden to speak of no double glazing only one bathroom and you should see the state it's in compared to here where we've put in that extension with an extra bedroom and a bathroom en suite and there's the loft conversion no we reckon if we were to put it on the market tomorrow it would fetch 350 I think people would be queuing up to buy it we wouldn't even need an agent not that we want to sell we're very happy here but if we got that kind of offer we'd be fools not to take it. . . ."

wrong can be gleaned from the fact that fifteen years earlier Willmott and Young had found clear evidence for the existence of a profit orientation among home owners in Woodford:

> The house is regarded as a sort of business . . . Owners notice the selling prices of nearby houses – knowledge of these often circulates freely up and down the road. They notice that in the long-sustained inflation of the last twenty years prices have been rising steadily. They know that, provided they maintain it in good condition, the value of their asset is increasing. Add on a bit for improvements and they can at the end feel very content with their one-man business.
>
> (1960, pp. 32–3)

Given this evidence from suburban London in the 1950s, it is difficult to understand how Agnew managed to come to the conclusion that no home owners in Leicester in the 1970s were very interested in the profit potential of their housing. There seems little to choose between home owners in Woodford gossiping about the rising value of their houses and their American cousins whom Perin has dubbed 'small-scale traders' (1977, p. 133) worrying about their property values.

To be fair to Agnew, however, it does seem likely that the profit orientation of British home owners has increased since he completed his study, for the experience of the house price booms of the 1970s may have sharpened people's awareness and concern about asset values in housing.

197

Pawley (1978) believes that the 1971–3 boom certainly had this effect, and Thorns has suggested that the experience of rapidly increasing property values has led owners 'consciously to develop their housing as a form of capital gain' (1982, p. 757). By 1976 a survey of house movers (cited in Murie, 1983) found that 27 per cent identified saving and investment as an advantage of owner-occupation, and it is difficult to square this with Agnew's view of owner-occupiers as innocent of all avarice.

In recent years, however, what may be seen as a modified and more sophisticated version of Agnew's thesis has emerged. This holds that, while home owners are probably aware of the investment potential of their housing, they choose not to act on it. Alan Murie, for example, reports on the basis of his research in Bristol that 'There is little evidence in the statements of home owners or in the circumstances surrounding their housing moves to support a view that home ownership . . . is used to pursue investment or speculative entrepreneurial activity' (1989, p. 5). Most moves, he says, are triggered by job factors and do not reflect a desire to 'trade up'. Furthermore, choice of a house is dictated more by considerations regarding its use than by a concern for future profit. Similar arguments have been expressed by Ruth Madigan, who concludes that first-time buyers in Glasgow 'were not involved in "profit maximization" or "playing the market" ' (1988, p. 42).

The argument which has been advanced by these and other writers has to be evaluated on two levels. First, we should consider the attitudes expressed by home owners. Second, we need to investigate how home owners actually behave. The evidence on both fronts suggests that, while some owner-occupiers are not especially concerned about the investment potential of their homes, many others are and act accordingly.

We considered some of the relevant attitudinal evidence from the three towns survey in Chapter 2. There we saw, for example, that 29 per cent of owners bought in order to 'get something in return' for what they were paying out, and 20 per cent of them made explicit reference to home ownership as an investment. Such answers were common across all three towns. Similarly, in answer to a question on the advantages of home ownership, 15 per cent said that it provided something for their money, and 38 per cent went further and replied that home ownership gave them an appreciating asset. Again, such responses were common in all three towns.

Pressed further on whether they thought that they had made money out of owning a house, 34 per cent (32 per cent in Slough, 33 per cent in Derby and 38 per cent in Burnley) replied unequivocally that they had, while only 11 per cent (5 per cent in Slough) thought they had not:

> It's a good investment. Anyone who doesn't buy is a bit silly . . . I'm doing the house up and I'll get as much as I can for it. I got a valuation two months ago and it's worth fifteen . . . At the end of the day I'll come out on top . . . The house is fetching value all the time.
>
> (Male unskilled manual worker, Derby)

We've accumulated capital value out of all proportion to the amount of money we've paid . . . People have a housing strategy in the back of their minds. We've been here fifteen years and people say to me, 'You've missed a move; you should have traded up seven years ago.'

(Male, intermediate occupation, Burnley)

I haven't got a pension. I intend to have plenty of money by that time. I'll get another house – it's a better investment.

(Male, intermediate occupation, Slough)

If you add up the money I've made buying and selling houses. I've tended to buy shares with it. At 55 I've been pleased to have been made redundant. I've got a property in Spain which we'll be able to go to in the winter . . . There's no way you can avoid making money out of housing.

(Male, intermediate occupation, Burnley)

We have no money in the bank because of making money on houses. The value of this place has increased from fifteen to fifty. You pay more for the next place you buy, of course, but our next move will mean we will have money – that was the whole idea of buying this place in the first place.

(Male professional, Derby)

I bought this as an investment. When you buy rather than rent, you buy as an investment. When the day comes when it gets difficult to keep this place up I'll sell and go into a flat. I'll sell to get the capital to live off.

(Male, intermediate occupation, Burnley)

Apart from the one-third of the sample who had no doubt that they were making money from their housing and the one-tenth who believed that they were not, the rest gave qualified answers. Twenty-seven per cent of them said that they had made a paper gain but that it could not be realized, 19 per cent said that they would have to move house to get hold of the money, 5 per cent thought they had only made money as a result of doing improvements to the house, 4 per cent thought that the money they had made would only be realizable upon their death, 3 per cent said that they had gained relative to people who rented, and 2 per cent thought that they had gained, but only by a small amount. Thirteen per cent of people not only thought they had made money, but also outlined how they planned to cash in on their enhanced equity!

It is evident from all of these answers that Agnew's study must now be disregarded and that later and more sophisticated versions of his original thesis should be treated with some caution. Many home owners bought housing because it seemed a good investment, see asset appreciation as a major advantage of owner-occupation and believe that they have themselves accumulated real gains as a result of buying a house. It would indeed be strange if it were not so, for if people have been accumulating capital at the rate demonstrated in this chapter, then they would need to be extremely unobservant not to have tumbled to the fact.

Behavioural evidence also indicates that many home owners actively use the housing market as a way of accumulating wealth. Murie's contention that most moves are triggered by job changes rather than by a desire to 'trade up' or 'trade down' can certainly be questioned. The *Recently Moving Households* survey conducted on people who moved between 1976 and 1978 found (OPCS, 1983) that just 26 per cent of owner-occupiers had moved for job reasons, while 44 per cent had moved to get 'better accommodation' (that is, had traded up), and 12 per cent wanted cheaper accommodation (trading down). Sixty-one per cent of them had moved less than ten miles. The 1981 Census of Employment found that 69 per cent of those who had moved in the previous year had gone less than ten kilometres; and the 1983 *National Dwelling and Household Survey* found that only 22 per cent of moves were employment-related, while 41 per cent were motivated by a desire to change house (both of these surveys are cited in Champion, Green and Owen, 1987). A 1981 survey by the Nationwide Building Society found that 83 per cent of moves by owner-occupiers took place within a radius of twenty-five miles and that 60 per cent of owners moved just five miles or less. Only 16 per cent of these moves were prompted by a change in employment location, and many of the rest seem simply to have involved trading up (Ball, 1983, p. 324).

Michael Ball (1986, p. 15) has pointed out that British owner-occupiers are among the most mobile in the world. They move house more frequently than North Americans and much more frequently than other West Europeans. The average life of a building society mortgage in Britain is now just four years (Ball, Martens and Harloe, 1986). The fact that so many owner-occupiers now move so frequently, and yet move across such small distances and without any employment-related motivation, can only be explained by the fact that many of them are following a deliberate and coherent investment strategy through the housing market. This is borne out by the three towns survey, which found that 38 per cent of all households had definite plans to move house in the future. Of them, 18 per cent intended to move to a better house, 18 per cent planned to move to a better neighbourhood, and 12 per cent simply intended to move 'up-market'.

Whether all this amounts to the existence of a strong 'profit orientation' or a pervasive 'entrepreneurial ethic' is less easy to determine. Some commentators have expressed the concern that high house price inflation coupled with the spread of home ownership to two-thirds of British households is producing a nation of property speculators and is undermining a more commercial capitalist orientation to investment. It has often been suggested, for example, that the attractive returns available from home ownership are deflecting savings from industrial investment as people recognize that investing in property is likely to be safer and to generate higher returns on their capital (see, for example, Daunton, 1987; Pawley,

1978). It is noticeable in this regard that the self-employed (arguably the most entrepreneurial risk-takers in the economy) tend to avoid mortgage debt and either rent their housing or buy cheaper housing outright (Pratt, 1986c; Sullivan and Murphy, 1987).

Of course, home ownership need not undermine a risk-taking capitalistic ethos. Capital gains from housing can enable people to start their own business or to realize enough money to open a share portfolio. We saw earlier that inheritance of housing capital is likely to increase levels of investment in shares and that a few legatees may use bequests to set up in business on their own. Similarly, in her work in Canada, Geraldine Pratt (1986c) found that a number of the self-employed people with whom she spoke had got started using money accumulated through the housing market. In the three towns survey, however, the signs were that entrepreneurship was more likely to be expressed through petty landlordism than through other forms of business activity:

> I'll move in another four or five years. I won't sell this place. I'll keep it and invest in another house and let this one out.
> (Male semi-skilled manual worker, Slough)

> I'll rent rooms out. That's why I've got this place, as a fall-back. I could survive if I became unemployed because I could rent two rooms out.
> (Male, intermediate occupation, Slough)

> This is just a starter house. I intend to have another place later on. It's an investment. I'm going to buy a second house to live in and let this one out.
> (Male, intermediate occupation, Slough)

Given the remarkable rates of return which owner-occupiers have achieved by investing in housing, it seems plausible to suggest that most owners will remain happy to keep their money tied up in their property and will not be tempted to cash it in and chance their arm on the stock market. If this is the case, then those who see the spread of owner-occupation deflecting investment away from industry probably have a point. This argument is not, however, without political irony. On the one hand the radical right hopes to encourage a new spirit of popular capitalism yet is intent on increasing home ownership which may be a disincentive to risk-taking behaviour. On the other the socialist left deeply distrusts the spread of home ownership and has continually attempted to demonstrate that ordinary people gain little or nothing from it, yet at the same time it bemoans the fact that home owners' gains have been so great as to syphon money away from other more productive forms of investment.

The truth of the matter seems to be that home ownership is widely regarded as a secure form of investment which demands little attention, entails little risk and offers long-term substantial gains. It is not turning home owners into a new breed of entrepreneurs, but nor are its advantages lost on those who benefit from it. Most people are aware of the wealth they are amassing, and many pursue a more or less conscious lifetime strategy which at the very least assumes that this will continue, and which may also involve judicious moves between houses so as to take advantage of the declining real cost of mortgage repayments and the increasing real value of their holding. Go into most pubs in most English towns on most nights of the week and you will likely overhear a conversation about how much people now believe their housing is worth and whether now is the time to trade up or cash in. To believe in the face of all this that home owners have no interest in housing investment strategies is absurd.

Conclusions

We have seen in this chapter that the spread of home ownership in Britain is having major consequences as regards the distribution of wealth and the organization of life chances. The returns which owner-occupiers have been making on their housing compare favourably with all other investments and far outstrip the general rate of inflation. We have also seen that this is likely to continue in the long term.

We have also evaluated five arguments advanced by those who, critical of capitalism, feel unable to welcome the spread of home ownership which capitalism in Britain has brought about. Like the spectre at the feast, these people warn that people who think they are gaining are 'really' losing and that the gains of the present cannot last into the future. They hope to convince us that owner-occupation is having no effect, or even a negative effect, on the material conditions and life chances of working-class households; for they believe that the home-owning working class remains effectively 'propertyless' despite its ownership of housing, and that it is still disadvantaged by capitalism despite its accumulation of substantial amounts of capital. All five of their arguments have been reviewed and rejected in the course of this chapter, for all five are based on false empirical assumptions.

The first argument suggests that gains from house price inflation are not real, or that they are achieved at the expense of other buyers. We have seen, however, that housing increases in value at twice the rate of RPI while staying constant in cost measured against real income levels. This means that owners do make real gains, but that new buyers pay no more for their housing in real terms than earlier generations did. Capital gains are generated because home owners share in the growing wealth of a capitalist economy, and this means that they do in this sense have a very real 'stake in the system'.

The second holds that these gains are temporary, but we have argued that this is untrue historically, for real gains have been made through most of the century and certainly ever since the early 1950s. We have also seen that there is little prospect in Britain of the housing market collapsing as it did in the Netherlands unless the economy itself collapses or political moves are introduced to bring about dramatic changes in the conditions governing supply.

The third suggests that the gains made by owner-occupiers are not realizable, but we have shown that they can be and are realized through a variety of strategies. We also pointed out that a cycle of 'familial accumulation' has now been set in motion whereby a majority of the population will both inherit cash from housing and in turn pass on a housing legacy to the next generation.

The fourth, which is in some ways the heart of the critics' complaints, has it that low-income households often suffer when they move into home ownership and that only affluent home owners make gains from owner-occupation. We refuted the first part of this claim by analysing the evidence on mortgage arrears and on disrepair in the owner-occupied housing stock, and the second by showing that semi- and unskilled manual workers, council house tenants and Asian families have all registered high rates of gain when they get access to house purchase. Gains are, however, lower in cheaper, older properties than in suburbia, and there is a major division between the gains which can be made in the South and those available to owners in the North. Nevertheless, even owners of Victorian terraced houses in towns like Derby and Burnley still make real gains, and the idea that sizeable numbers of home owners are losing from moving into owner-occupation is without foundation.

Finally, the argument that home owners are not concerned about capital gains and do nothing to enhance them was shown to be as ridiculous as it sounds.

I have not attempted in this chapter to draw any theoretical conclusions from all this evidence. In particular, I have avoided addressing the question of how the continued accumulation of capital gains from owner-occupation may be affecting class relations in Britain. This is, of course, a crucial issue for a sociologist to consider, for if nearly two-thirds of the population are now in a position to accumulate and pass on large sums of money through ownership of domestic property, then our theories of social inequality and social stratification may need revising. I shall consider this issue in Chapter 6. For now it is enough to note that the evidence presented here would seem to undermine familiar fairy-tale academic images of 'the masses' as a propertyless, powerless and dependent proletariat with nothing to lose but their chains. On my calculations, the median home owner stands to lose precisely £1,987.90 every year from any attempt to 'liberate the masses' from the contemporary capitalist system of private property ownership.

4   A property-owning democracy

In 1917, when hundreds of thousands of Allied troops were being slaughtered in the French trenches while in Russia the Romanov dynasty was being toppled, Lloyd George's cabinet commissioned a series of reports on industrial unrest in the English regions. From these it seemed clear that poor housing conditions were producing widespread resentment among various sections of the working classes. This was in turn creating fertile ground in which communist propaganda could take root and grow. Once the war ended, the government's fears began to be realized. In 1919, 35 million working days were lost in strikes. According to Glyn and Sutcliffe, 'From 1919 to 1921 the Cabinet was haunted by the possibility that continued strikes, especially from the Triple Alliance of miners, railwaymen and transport workers, would lead to coups in major cities. Lloyd George feared a "Soviet government" if the miners won their proposed strike of 1921' (1970, p. 25).

One response to this mounting sense of crisis was to act on housing costs and conditions. As we saw in Chapter 1, legislation introduced in the years following the First World War extended rent controls, introduced generous subsidies enabling local authorities to build good-quality houses for rent and attempted to stimulate private-sector construction by offering subsidies to builders. In this climate, supporters of home ownership began to suggest that owner-occupation could prove a stabilizing force in society, a force for moderation and conservatism. In particular, the then chairman of the Building Societies Association, Harold Bellman, wrote in 1927 that 'The man who has something to protect and improve – a stake of some sort in the country – naturally turns his thoughts in the direction of sane, ordered and perforce economical government . . . To him revolution is anathema.' He then went on approvingly to quote an MP of the time, G. N. Barnes, who had described the growth of the building societies as 'A bulwark against Bolshevism and all that Bolshevism stands for' (quoted in Boddy, 1980, p. 23).

This idea that home ownership might undermine popular support for socialist parties and revolutionary programmes was often taken up by politicians in the turmoil of the inter-war years. We saw in Chapter 1 that British politicians such as Neville Chamberlain and Viscount Cecil evidently believed it. So too did American Presidents, for Calvin Coolidge suggested that home ownership could make a major contribution to national stability, while Franklin Roosevelt described a nation of home owners as 'unconquerable' (see Perin, 1977, p. 72).

So often were such claims repeated that they appear to have entered into our political folk wisdom. Today, few politicians or political commentators seem to doubt that the spread of owner-occupation tends to conservatize the population. Fifty years after Bellman's comments, for example, one of his successors at the BSA claimed that 'even a small stake in the country does affect political attitudes', and that political extremism would not find support in a nation of home owners (see Boddy, 1980, p. 24). Others are even more assertive. For Hoyt, for example, 'Communism can never win in a nation of home owners' (quoted in Harris and Hamnett, 1987, p. 175). And as we saw in Chapter 1, by the 1970s many Marxists too had come round to the view that owner-occupation had successfully been used to delay or avert socialist revolution. From left and right alike, the belief is firmly expressed that a nation in which a majority of households own their homes does indeed represent a 'bulwark against Bolshevism'.

In this chapter we shall consider the evidence on the relationship between housing tenure and political alignment. We shall focus mainly on the question of voting behaviour although we shall also briefly consider how home ownership may be influencing broader political values and behaviour. Our principal concern will be with the political significance of housing divisions, but we shall also need to consider the political impact of other changes in the pattern of popular consumption such as the growth of car ownership and the spread of private pension plans. This is because one influential body of literature suggests that the apparent link between home ownership and right-wing voting is simply an expression of a wider association between 'consumption sectors' and political alignment. We shall test this and other hypotheses against data from the three towns survey and from other recent studies of electoral behaviour. On their own, the results of the three towns survey are perhaps of restricted value given the limitations of the case study method, but together with other comparable work, these findings should help us to arrive at some reasonably reliable conclusions regarding the relative political significance of housing tenure divisions, social class divisions and wider consumption-based cleavages.

Class dealignment in Britain

Political scientists have often pointed to Britain (along with Scandinavia) as one of the clearest examples of a class-based electoral system. Although the fit has never been perfect, the single best social indicator associated with voting behaviour has long been occupational class. In their influential study of British electoral behaviour, Butler and Stokes (1974) demonstrated the remarkable strength of occupational grade as a predictor of voting behaviour in the early 1960s. Reworking their data using regression techniques (which they did not use), Franklin (1985) has shown that just 2 per cent of people with no 'working-class characteristics' (Labour parents, a manual job, a rented house, a working-class background, trade union membership and minimum schooling) voted Labour at the 1964 general election. Rarely has social science ever achieved such levels of predictive accuracy!

Butler and Stokes explained this link between class and voting through a theory of political socialization. As we grow up, we adopt a party identification from our parents, and this is then confirmed or changed as we come into contact with others at work and in the local neighbourhood. In this way, we come to think of ourselves as supporters of this or that party and we vote accordingly. For Butler and Stokes, it is our party allegiance which shapes our views on specific issues, rather than the other way around.

This sort of approach has always accepted that factors other than occupational class are also related to political alignment, but in most cases, these factors (such as income and level of education) are treated as indicators of class rather than as distinct influences in their own right. Such is also the case with the analysis of housing tenure and other aspects of consumption such as car ownership. This absorption of other factors under the class umbrella has, however, been criticized. Dunleavy (1979), Peake (1984) and others have argued that this tradition of work has failed to analyse consumption cleavages adequately because of its reliance on a wholly inadequate class model. In this model, which is taken from the advertising industry's ABC1 grading schema, housing tenure is subsumed into an overall measure of social position. The result is that political analysts have rarely bothered to consider the specific significance of patterns of consumption such as housing tenure or membership of private pension schemes, since these have generally been seen as derivatives and indicators of people's overall class position.

All this has been changing over the last ten years, however. The main reason why the conventional view has come under critical scrutiny, and that consumption variables such as housing tenure have come to be analysed in their own right, is that the link between occupational class, party identification and voting seems to be breaking down. According to Sarlvik and Crewe (1983, p. 86), Britain has witnessed 'a series of elections at which class voting has fitfully but gradually declined'. To the extent that class cleavages have been losing their electoral significance, analysts have begun to look around for newly emerging cleavages which may be taking their place. As Dunleavy and Husbands argue, 'When an existing line of political cleavage begins to be less important in structuring alignments, we should expect to find that some new fault line has emerged which has cut across the previous cleavage, fragmenting earlier lines of differentiation' (1985, p. 21).

One obvious candidate for such a new fault line is housing tenure, for the decline of class voting seems to coincide with the growth of working-class home ownership. Things are not, however, quite this simple. For a start, this is not the only candidate. Dunleavy himself, for example, believes that the significant change has come, not with the spread of home ownership, but with the growth in the role of the state which has created new and important divisions between those who rely on the public sector (either as consumers or as employees) and those who rely more on the private sector. Furthermore, there is the added complication that it is by no means certain that the old class-based cleavage really has been eroded in the way that Sarlvik and Crewe suggest. Some writers claim that social class is still the major fault line in British politics, in which case neither housing tenure nor sectoral cleavages are as important as they have been made out to be.

The argument revolves around what 'class dealignment' really means. As Dunleavy (1987) points out, so-called 'class dealignment' can be measured in three different ways, and we are likely to come to different conclusions according to which definition we adopt.

The first criterion is simply that absolute class voting declines. This is essentially what Sarlvik and Crewe mean by 'class dealignment'. They recognize that the voting patterns of manual and non-manual workers are still very different (60 per cent of the latter supported the Conservatives in 1979, while 50 per cent of the former voted Labour), but they go on to point out that the association between class and voting has been weakening over the years. Indeed, in a later paper, Crewe (1986, p. 620) points out that, at the 1983 election, 'For the first time since surveys began, the majority of voters declined to vote along class lines.' Just 42 per cent of the working class voted Labour in 1983, while 55 per cent of the middle class voted Conservative (the equivalent proportions in 1945 stood at 62 per cent and 63 per cent respectively). Clearly, if class dealignment is defined as fewer middle-class people voting Conservative, and/or fewer working-class people voting Labour, then such a process has indeed been taking place. As Franklin puts it, 'Is class, then, still the basis of British politics? At the individual level, the answer must be an unequivocal "no" ' (1985, p. 125).

There is, however, a second criterion of class dealignment which takes issue with such reasoning. It sees dealignment as referring not to absolute but to relative class voting. This is the definition adopted by Heath, Jowell and Curtice (1985, 1986) in their analysis of the 1983 election survey, and it is endorsed by Marshall and his colleagues in their recent study of class in Britain (1988). According to this position, class dealignment can only be said to have occurred if cross-class voting increases. A decline in working-class support for the Labour Party, such as occurred in 1983, does not constitute evidence for class dealignment if Labour support also drops in other classes, for all that this indicates is that Labour is performing badly across all classes. As Heath, Jowell and Curtice explain, 'Labour remained a class party in 1983; it was simply a less successful class party than before' (1985, p. 29). Seen in relative terms, there has been no process of class dealignment in postwar Britain. Labour support has been falling, partly due to the shrinkage of its traditional manual working-class base, and partly due to its declining popularity among all classes, but the likelihood of a working-class elector voting Labour *rather than Conservative* is no smaller now than it was twenty or thirty years ago.

The third criterion of class dealignment, favoured by Dunleavy himself, emphasizes the declining difference in the pattern of voting between different classes. With a rise in third-party support, drawing voters from all classes, the distinctiveness of each party's support base has been reduced. This, says Dunleavy, is enough to sustain the class dealignment thesis. His argument is in essence similar to that developed by Crewe (1986), who maintains that a fall in the working-class Labour vote means that the working class *is* becoming detached from the Labour Party, and that this remains true irrespective of whether the Labour vote is also falling among other classes (1986, p. 624; for a reply see Heath, Jowell and Curtice, 1987). For both Dunleavy and Crewe, a rise in support for third parties is evidence that fewer people are now voting for their 'natural class party', in which case class dealignment must be occurring.

There are two points of agreement in this increasingly complex debate. One is that approximately half of the Labour Party's lost votes can be explained by the decline in size of the manual working class. The other is that a smaller proportion of the manual working class has supported Labour during the 1980s than supported it twenty years earlier, and that this decline in absolute class voting must also therefore be a major factor in the party's recent electoral decline. Leaving aside the dispute over whether class dealignment should be defined as a reduction in the working-class Labour vote (Crewe, Dunleavy) or an increase in the working-class anti-Labour vote (Heath, Jowell and Curtice; Marshall *et al.*), it is apparent that all contributors to this debate agree that there is a problem to be explained, namely, why working-class people do not support Labour as strongly as they once did.

There are basically three possible explanations for this. One is that the working class has changed. It could be that workers have become more affluent, for example, and that this has undermined their willingness to support collectivist political programmes. A second is that the parties have changed. The Labour Party, for example, might have alienated its traditional working-class supporters by shifting away from the kinds of policies which appeal to them. A third possibility is the one suggested by Dunleavy – that a new social cleavage has emerged which cuts across traditional class lines of party support. It could be, for example, that the growth of home ownership has created a division within the working class which encourages those who own their housing to vote differently from those who rent from the local authority.

The first type of explanation was originally advanced during the 1950s and has come to be known as the 'embourgeoisement thesis'. This suggests that increasing affluence and enhanced private consumption have changed working-class values and life-styles and have therefore undermined working-class support for parties of the left. This hypothesis was apparently refuted in British sociology in the 1960s when John Goldthorpe and his colleagues studied a sample of relatively affluent working-class families in Luton and found that their work situation was still inferior in terms of conditions and amenities to that of white-collar employees, that their home lives still differed markedly from those of the middle class, who were far more likely to participate in organized societies and to entertain other couples at home, and that their status was still such that they were not accepted by middle-class people as social equals (Goldthorpe *et al.*, 1969, pp. 24–5). The conclusion from this research was clear: the working class still had its own distinctive culture and was not changing dramatically as a result of rising affluence. This conclusion was then borne out by the Labour victories at the 1964 and 1966 general elections which seemed to refute any suggestion that British society was becoming middle class and was turning its back on socialism.

The embourgeoisement thesis has, however, resurfaced in a different guise in the 1980s at a time when Labour has again registered three successive election defeats. At his party's 1987 annual conference, the Labour leader, Neil Kinnock, reminded delegates that they had now to appeal to dockers earning £300 per week and 'owning a villa in Marbella'. Similarly, Peter Kellner suggested in his analysis of the 1987 election defeat that 'Labour has to appeal to voters who have bought their council home, owned a car and had £500 worth of shares in privatized companies. The implications of this line of argument are profound . . . the voters Labour needs to win back believe that markets are better than bureaucrats at securing individual prosperity' (1987, p. 9).

These same sentiments have also appeared in recent sociological literature. In one of their earlier essays, for example, Newby *et al.* (1985) suggested that changing consumption patterns were combining with the collapse of old-style proletarian communities to create privatized values and life-styles which were generating changed patterns of voting behaviour. In a thinly veiled attack on the Conservative government of the time, they argued that moral restraints on acquisitiveness had been weakened and that those in work had seen their standards of living rise such that they had become intent on defending their own interests while caring little about other people's. There is, they claim, a sense of fatalism about changing anything, and this has encouraged the relatively affluent majority to retreat into their homes and to dismiss political participation as pointless and irrelevant.

We shall consider in some detail the evidence on home-centred privatism in Chapter 5. Here we may simply note that this kind of analysis, with its claim that working-class electors have become more individualistic, more private and less inclined to support traditional Labour Party statist strategies, has been questioned by various analysts and has largely been rejected by Newby *et al.* themselves in their later writings.

The thesis is firmly rejected by Heath, Jowell and Curtice. They believe that rising affluence has done nothing to change working-class values, that the working class is no less concerned about its relative material position than it ever has been, and that Labour's loss of working-class support has occurred because the party has moved too far away from the aspirations and values of its traditional support base. In their later work, Marshall and his colleagues agree with this diagnosis, arguing that class is still the basic source of people's social identity and that there is widespread support for policies aimed at achieving what they term 'social justice'. Thus they conclude: 'Labour voters in particular respond to the language of social class and see the world about them structured by class processes. It would seem, then, that Labour gains to the extent that it succeeds in constituting and mobilizing class interests by presenting issues in class terms' (1988, p. 254).

These findings, however, can be queried on both methodological and analytical grounds. The methodological problem is that the data which reveal people's readiness to endorse a class identity are based on replies to a question which followed no fewer than *twelve* successive questions in which the existence of class identities was taken for granted! There are good grounds for believing that people's responses to Marshall and his colleagues may well be a product of their research design. It would be surprising if people's sense of their own identities *really* was based more in class than in, say, their gender, their family position and marital status, their age, their job, their nationality, or their ethnicity, yet this is what this study claims (see, for example, p. 149).

The analytical problem concerns their conclusion that Labour can increase its support by adopting an explicitly class-based programme – an argument which Heath, Jowell and Curtice also propose but which Crewe under-standably describes as 'highly implausible' (1986, p. 621). In fact, the argument rests on a logical contradiction. Both the Heath and Marshall studies claim that relative class voting has not declined. They also claim that the Labour Party has watered down its class appeal, and that this has cost it votes. Yet if they are correct in their belief that the working class wants a strong, class-based programme, then Labour's watered-down platform should have led to a decline in *relative* class voting as well as *absolute* class voting. This is because, if their thesis is correct, then the counterfactual should also hold that a move away from class rhetoric should have lost the party proportionately more working-class votes than middle-class votes. This, however, is precisely what has not happened according to these studies! Either the claim that relative class voting has not declined is wrong, or the claim that working-class voters want a class-based political programme is wrong. Both claims cannot simultaneously be correct.

Where Marshall and his colleagues are undoubtedly right, however, is in their insistence that political factors must be taken seriously in the analysis of voting behaviour. The decline of the Labour Party obviously does have something to do with its policies, its image and its leadership and cannot simply be explained in terms of a change in the social structure. Whiteley (1983), for example, finds that voters' evaluations of how the parties have performed in the past are more significant than their social attributes in shaping their voting intentions. As he also points out, however, the two types of explanation are not mutually exclusive. Indeed, his own analysis of 1979 election data suggests that social attributes such as union membership and home ownership do play an important part in explaining party alignment (although interestingly, he found that class location was not significant).

This brings us to the third possible explanation for the decline in absolute class voting. This suggests that, whatever else has been happening in terms of changes in working-class values or in party programmes, the key development of the last quarter-century has been the emergence of new political cleavages which have cut across social class boundaries. One such cleavage has arisen as a result of the spread of home ownership, but this is not the only factor which now divides worker from worker. In Dunleavy's view, a new cleavage has been constructed around the division between the private and public sectors, and the split between home owners and council tenants is only one expression of this division.

For Dunleavy, it is the increased significance of sectoral cleavages which best explains changes in the pattern of class voting. These cleavages bifurcate the working class in respect of both consumption and production. As regards consumption, the working class has increasingly been split since the war by changes such as the rise in mass home ownership and the increase in private car ownership (up from one-third in 1960 to two-thirds in the 1980s). Similarly in the production sphere, the proportion of the workforce employed in the public sector increased by two-thirds in the fifteen years from 1960. As Whiteley observes, 'These changes are significant by any standards and clearly provide a possible explanation for dealignment' (1983, p. 85).

It is important to remember that argument and evidence in support of the significance of new sectoral cleavages do not entail rejection of the other two types of explanation of political change. It is not entirely fanciful to believe that increasing affluence may influence people's values. Nor should we ignore the role of political parties in increasing or reducing their popularity with electors. For our present purposes, however, the question to be considered is that posed by Dunleavy in his theory of sectoral cleavages, and it is to this that we now turn.

The theory of sectoral cleavages

According to Dunleavy, the growth of state intervention in the provision and financing of consumption has changed the social structure by creating or reinforcing sectoral cleavages which cut through traditional lines of class differentiation: 'Basically, sectors are lines of vertical division in a society, such that certain common interests are shared between social classes in the same sector, while within a social class, sectoral differences reflect a measure of conflict of interests' (Dunleavy, 1979, p. 419). These cleavages are constituted around divisions of consumption and divisions of production. Both can prove highly significant in shaping political alignments.

Consumption-sector cleavages partly reflect class cleavages, for the size and security of one's income obviously affect access to different forms of consumption. Nevertheless, Dunleavy argues that consumption location also reflects the way the state acts to provide or withhold resources:

> The increase in socialized consumption provisions has a potent effect in restructuring the bases of social inequalities. Access both to material and to symbolic 'goods' is no longer a simple linear corollary of income. The linkage between production positions, 'achievement', income and consumption . . . is attenuated by the introduction of criteria related to 'need', 'merit', 'entitlement' and other nonmarket criteria.
>
> (1986, p. 138)

Consumption-sector cleavages are therefore constituted to some extent independently of class location.

Such cleavages may arise around any aspect of consumption where the state intervenes to organize provision or financing. However, Dunleavy argues that such cleavages will become most prominent under two sets of conditions. The first is where cleavages polarize the population. In Britain, for example, health and education are overwhelmingly organized within the public sector, which means that fragmentation between public- and private-sector consumers is minimal, and the political impact of the cleavage is relatively small. Housing and transport, on the other hand, divide the electorate more evenly, and they dramatically polarize working-class consumers. This, according to Dunleavy, provides the most fertile ground for mobilizing consumption-sector cleavages into political alignments. The significance of such divisions will then be magnified where the system of tax and subsidy support is most visible. Generalized income transfers, for example, are less likely to generate consumption-sector cleavages than are specific consumption subsidies. Similarly, subsidies financed through specific taxes such as local property taxes are more likely to become politicized than those financed out of general tax revenue (see Dunleavy, 1986, p. 137).

Where this analysis feeds into the debate over class dealignment is through Dunleavy's recognition that the key consumption cleavages in Britain (which he sees as those arising in housing and transport) fragment the working class far more than they do higher classes. To the extent that consumption location affects voting, we may therefore expect that the spread of owner-occupation and car ownership will have a damaging impact on working-class support for the Labour Party. As he puts it:

> The implications of this for the two major political parties are assymetrical. Given the relatively homogeneous consumption locations of higher non-manual grades and the highly fragmented consumption locations of routine non-manual and manual workers, the Labour Party suffers very large net losses of votes from consumption effects, while the Conservatives gain extensive support in lower social grades.
>
> (Dunleavy, 1980a, p. 79)

But why should consumption location influence voting behaviour? Dunleavy's answer draws uncritically on instrumentalist Marxist theories of ideology. He dismisses any attempt at understanding political alignments from the point of view of the individuals concerned, and argues instead for what he calls a 'radical structural' perspective. What this means is that people come to form and express their values and interests as a result of exposure to 'dominant ideological structures . . . which make available, visible and interpretable socially constructed images of social processes and related interest perceptions' (1979, p. 422). These ideological structures 'systematically reflect the interests of dominant social groups and classes' (ibid., pp. 422–3). They emphasize divisions of consumption within classes, thereby glossing over the far more fundamental divisions which exist between them:

The importance of ideological and political structures lies in their ability to create a politics of interest displacement in which fundamental longer-term, but less visible interests, such as class interests, can be displaced as influences on political alignment by less important but highly visible 'immediate' interests, such as sectoral interests. This is *not* to say that 'immediate' interests are illusory or without an objective economic basis. It is only to say that subjective and objective interest rankings are incongruent and that this lack of congruence arises from processes of structuration rather than from an individual's values.

(1979, p. 423)

What all this means is that working-class home owners and car drivers are wrong-footed by dominant ideologies, promulgated by the dominant class and expressed through dominant class institutions such as the mass media. State intervention thus has the effect of disorganizing the working class. As Dunleavy and Husbands put it, 'The way in which people vote is conditioned by a set of dominant ideological messages formulated by institutions of central social significance. Chief amongst these are the mass media' (1985, p. 19). Newspapers and television perpetuate the myth that council tenants are subsidized while mortgage payers are not, that only home owners pay rates, that public transport is a drain on the public purse while car drivers are heavily over-taxed and so on. Not surprisingly, perhaps, Dunleavy provides not a shred of evidence for all of this.

Once the division between public- and private-sector consumers has been ideologically constituted, it is a simple matter for political parties to mobilize these ideological interests into political alignments. At the local level especially, Conservative councils restrict new housing developments in order to safeguard the perceived interests of suburban owner-occupiers, Labour councils seek to build more council houses and to restrict council house sales, and the political parties clash over new road schemes and fare subsidies to public transport. In this way, consumption-sector interests are made real through political intervention. Voters identify themselves with an

213

ideologically constituted sectoral category, and they vote accordingly.

Dunleavy's approach clearly recognizes the political significance of housing tenure divisions. However, it is important to emphasize that for him, there is nothing unique about *housing* consumption, for the split between car owners and bus users is in principle no less significant. Indeed, it is the essence of Dunleavy's approach that consumption-sectoral locations are additive in their political effects. Home owners without a car, for example, are more likely to vote Labour than the proud owners of a second-hand Ford Escort who live in an identical house next door. Similarly, any spread of private health insurance to sizeable numbers of working-class people will give added impetus to the move into conservatism. The more individualized consumption locations people occupy, the more they are likely to vote for the right. Housing is only one such location.

It is also important to understand that in Dunleavy's view, the political divisions generated around housing tenure have nothing to do with the fact of owning or renting a house. Rather, they reflect the division between two different modes of state-supported consumption. Individualized consumers of housing are subsidized through tax advantages; collectivized consumers of housing are (or were) subsidized through low rents and various targeted benefits. It is the nature of the subsidy, not the difference in property rights, which has the political effect. This is because subsidies to owner-occupiers are provided indirectly through the tax system, and this makes them less visible. As Kemeny notes, 'If home owners can be indirectly subsidized while, say, public housing tenants can be directly subsidized, it both legitimates home ownership and stigmatizes non-owners' (1981, p. 75). Or as Dunleavy and Husbands explain, 'Housing has political importance because of public/private conflicts over tax/subsidy questions' (1985, p. 137).

Much the same point applies to Dunleavy's parallel analysis of production-sector locations (1980b). The very increase in state intervention which has created the basis for consumption-sector cleavages has simultaneously generated sharp production-sector cleavages between state-sector workers (themselves divided into state employees and those working for public corporations) and private-sector workers (who are divided between competitive and corporate-sector firms). As with consumption locations, these sectors are politically and ideologically as well as economically constituted. In particular, the dominant ideology exaggerates the distinction between state- and private-sector employees: 'The main effect of ideological structuration appears to be the systematic exaggeration of the objective basis of non-class interest polarities in a manner which serves to obscure fundamental or long-term class interests' (1980a, p. 530). Public-sector workers have in general been able to maintain wage levels as a result of high levels of unionization, and during the 1970s there was a marked increase in militant action by public-sector unions. This success in keeping their wages up has led to an increase in the cost of public services. Taxation has increased as a result, and it has been a simple matter for the media to foster divisions between the two sectors by mobilizing stereotypes about bureaucratic waste and inefficiency. Because the Labour Party is associated with support for public services and public spending, there has been a tendency for Labour to mobilize political support from those employed in these services, just as it also mobilizes support from those who consume them. The Conservatives, meanwhile, have been able to launch an attack on the welfare state and the nationalized industries which has attracted support from private-sector taxpayers and which has slowed and in some cases reversed the postwar trend to increasing public spending (see Dunleavy, 1986).

There are two ways of evaluating this theoretical approach to the analysis of sectoral cleavages. The first is to consider whether the argument makes sense. The second is to consider whether evidence on voting behaviour conforms to what the theory would predict. On both counts there are good grounds for scepticism regarding Dunleavy's claims.

Dunleavy's work has had a major impact on political science – Franklin and Page (1984) describe it as a new 'paradigm' – and, not surprisingly, it has attracted considerable critical attention. Perhaps the major problem with it, however, has hardly been discussed at all in the secondary literature. This is its unreflexive reliance on a crude and unsupportable instrumentalist theory of ideology.

We saw in Chapter 1 that much of the Marxist literature on home ownership can be criticized for its view of home owners as passive receptacles of a dominant ideology which leads them (falsely) to believe that they have a stake in the capitalist system of private property. It is now apparent that Dunleavy adopts much the same theoretical approach to his analysis of sectoral cleavages. While accepting that sectoral cleavages do have an economic dimension to them, the emphasis of his explanation is entirely on ideological and political structuration. Because he opposes any 'individualistic' mode of analysis, his 'radical structural' approach deliberately neglects the active constitution and reproduction of meaning by individuals. What we end up with is a familiar top-down model in which intelligent and conscious human beings are given no capacity for thinking and reflecting on their 'objective' situation, while the analyst is invested with a monopoly of wisdom in identifying the 'real forces' which impel people to act in the way they do.

Consider, for example, the tension between public- and private-sector employees. Dunleavy himself admits that taxes have increased to pay for higher wages in the public sector, that strikes by public-sector workers increased dramatically in the 1970s and that increased public spending has not generally resulted in improved output of services. All of this, however, is then treated as nothing more than ideological ammunition which can be mobilized by a capitalist press to divide one worker from another. Dunleavy is not concerned with *why* these media messages may resonate so tellingly with so many people. He ignores people's *experience* of being stranded at Waterloo Station when the signalmen walk out on strike, of seeing the deductions on their pay-slip rise in order to finance other people's wage increase, of being treated condescendingly or dismissively by teachers or social workers. The possibility that there may be an objective and significant material basis to production-sector cleavages – that there is a real tension between people who are forced by law to pay taxes and people who live off the fruits of this levy – is one he will not entertain, despite the fact that taxation has for centuries been a major source of conflict between state power and those subject to it.

Much the same point can be made in respect of his analysis of consumption cleavages. The fact that owner-occupiers enjoy property rights which the tenant does not share, and that as a result owners may develop clear economic interests which run counter to those of tenants, is something which for Dunleavy is inconsequential. The division between them is, for him, visible but superficial. He seems incapable of *understanding* how home owners may come to invest so much of their money, effort, time and identity in their homes that issues to do with property taxes or planning become of paramount importance to them. He seems incapable of appreciating why it is that political appeals to owner-occupiers find so ready and enthusiastic a reception.

Nor does Dunleavy consider it necessary to provide any evidence for his dominant ideology thesis. He does not show that the media do in fact transmit material designed to create sectoral cleavages, nor that 'dominant interests' are concerned to foment such divisions, nor even that working-class consumers are influenced by these 'dominant ideas'. All of this is taken for granted by his 'radical structural approach', yet there are good grounds for doubting that dominant ideologies do have the effects on working-class people which Dunleavy believes they do (Abercrombie, Hill & Turner, 1980).

Dunleavy's radical anti-individualism (that is, his refusal to examine sectoral effects through the subjective meanings they have for those involved) lies at the heart of many of the problems which critics have identified in his analysis. Does it really make sense, for example, to analyse the political effects of consumption location in an arithmetically cumulative manner? As we saw in the discussion of the work of Butler and Stokes, political scientists have often added together effects such as occupation, parental occupation and schooling, but this has been justified by a theory of political socialization which holds that party preferences will be stronger, the more they are reinforced by similar contacts across a variety of different situations. Dunleavy, however, rejects this socialization model, and his theory lacks any justification for the construction of such cumulative indexes. As Franklin and Page point out, 'It is not clear why different consumption locations should operate on individual attitudes in an additive fashion' (1984, p. 525).

In fact, the development of such an index makes little sociological sense. Is the meaning of owning a home in any sense comparable to the meaning of owning a car, or paying into a private occupational pension fund? For Dunleavy the question is irrelevant – the meaning of these things is constituted for people by dominant ideological institutions and by political parties, and all that matters in this process is how strongly individualized or collectivized you are (see Taylor-Gooby, 1986b, p. 597). He is therefore happy to construct an index in which 'ownership of a house, household access to a car, family use of private medical care, family use of a private old person's home, and past use by respondent, or prospective family use, of private schooling' (Dunleavy and Husbands, 1985, p. 141) are all sociologically equivalent! We are asked to accept that having a parent in a private nursing home is no more and no less likely to reduce your resistance to the blandishments of bourgeois ideology than purchasing your council house or buying a second-hand car. Despite his attacks on 'empiricism', the result of this sort of additive indexation is itself empiricist, for Dunleavy goes off with his computer in search of correlations without paying any heed to the need to establish what Max Weber termed 'adequacy at the level of meaning'. Yet as Weber warned, 'If adequacy in respect to meaning is lacking, then no matter how high the degree of uniformity and how precisely its probability can be numerically determined, it is still an incomprehensible statistical probability, whether we deal with overt or subjective processes' (Weber, 1968, p. 12).

·Related to all this is the further criticism that consumption locations are not mutually exclusive. As Taylor-Gooby (1986b, p. 595) points out, individuals may find themselves in both the public and private sectors. People with private health insurance still use the National Health Service; those with cars may still commute every morning by train; and so on. Among those interviewed in the three towns survey, for example, 43 per cent of people in one-car households, and 24 per cent of those in two-car households, still used local bus services from time to time. Such people would seem to occupy an uneasy location straddling one of Dunleavy's key lines of cleavage. It is not clear from Dunleavy's analysis how such cross-sector voters are likely to respond to pro- or anti-state ideologies. Furthermore, there are important divisions *within* sectors (such as between popular low-density council estates and unpopular high-rise public housing), and these too may presumably have meaning for consumers such that they respond differently to the same ideological and political messages (see Preteceille, 1986, p. 152).

Dunleavy has also been criticized for failing to explain how consumption locations are translated into voting behaviour (Franklin and Page, 1984), but as we have seen, he does in fact provide an explanation for this. His argument, quite simply, is that political parties address their electoral appeals to sectoral interests, thereby mobilizing sectoral cleavages into political alignments. However, for this argument to be accepted, Dunleavy would need to show that consumption issues are given a high priority by the parties and are salient for the voters. If the political parties ignore consumption issues, then we may assume that they are not mobilizing consumption sectors. Similarly, if voters do not seem to care about consumption issues, then we may assume that they are not being mobilized on the basis of their sectoral location.

In fact, Dunleavy gives no evidence either way on these questions. According to Harrop (1980) and Franklin and Page (1984), however, neither parties nor voters seem to give these issues the prominence that one would expect if Dunleavy's analysis were correct. Housing is perhaps an exception to this – according to Franklin and Page, 9 per cent of voters in 1979 cited housing as the most important issue influencing the way they voted. Transport, however, is hardly ever mentioned by anyone as an issue of concern, and it is difficult to find any evidence from recent elections of parties mobilizing support around the cleavage between car owners and public transport users.

None of this is to deny Dunleavy's argument that housing and transport are important aspects of people's lives. As he points out in his book with Husbands (1985, p. 23), housing and transport absorb over half of average household incomes in Britain, and most people are therefore likely to be concerned about them. The problem for Dunleavy's thesis is simply that there is no evidence that these identities form the basis for political mobilization. There is not even any evidence that car owners and public transport users have different views on transport policy, or that home owners and council tenants disagree fundamentally on housing policy (Harrop, 1980, p. 395). Furthermore, it has been suggested that consumption-sector cleavages may generate pro-state sentiments in one policy area and anti-state sentiments in another (Taylor-Gooby, 1985b). But if, say, car owners do not see transport as an important political issue, and do not even think any differently from non-owners about transport policy, then it is difficult to see how the division between private and public transport users can be mobilized by political parties.

Dunleavy's theory is, therefore, open to serious criticism on a number of counts. It rests on a wholly inadequate theory of ideology, it makes assertions and assumptions about the role of the media and people's receptivity to media output which are crude and unsupportable, it ignores the real economic interests which divide producers and consumers in different sectors, it provides no coherent rationale for seeing the effects of consumption locations as comparable and cumulative, it is unclear on the analysis of inter-sector consumption and intra-sector conflict, and it leads to predictions about party and voter behaviour which are at the very least dubious and unsupported.

There are also problems with Dunleavy's theory as regards its empirical validity, although the picture here is somewhat confused.

In his original 1979 paper, Dunleavy presented findings, based on his analysis of a 1974 election study, which supported his theory that consumption location has become a major influence on voting in Britain. Utilizing a method of calculating 'odds ratios' while controlling for the effects of other variables, he showed that owner-occupiers were 2.35 times more likely to vote Conservative than non-owners, that households owning two cars or more were 1.87 times more likely to vote Conservative than households without a car, and that by combining the effects of these two consumption locations it could be shown that home-owning households with two cars were 4.39 times more likely to vote Conservative than council tenants with no car.

In this paper, Dunleavy took his evidence of the effects of consumption location to draw two important conclusions. The first was that consumption-sector cleavages are as significant as 'social grade' (that is, the ABC1 measure of occupational class) in influencing voting: 'Overall consumption effects are comparable to those of social grade' (1979, p. 442). The second was that it is consumption sector rather than housing tenure which produces this effect: 'The housing cleavage is not the only or the dominant pattern of consumption cleavage in contemporary Britain . . . Housing locations do not have a distinctive influence on alignment; rather housing and transport effects are broadly comparable' (pp. 442–3). The first of these conclusions challenges conventional class theories of British politics by indicating that consumption sectors are no less significant than class location in shaping political alignment. The second challenges all those who have argued that the growth of home ownership tends to conservatize the working class, for in Dunleavy's view it is not the ownership of a house which makes the difference, but rather the nature of one's tax and subsidy relation to the state.

Not surprisingly, both of these conclusions have been subjected to considerable re-examination. For the remainder of this section we shall consider evidence on the first of these claims, leaving to the next section evidence on the relative importance of housing tenure and sectoral cleavages.

Some later work would seem to have reinforced Dunleavy's argument that consumption-sector cleavages are as important as class in shaping political alignments. In his work with Husbands, for example, Dunleavy analyses data collected at the time of the 1983 general election which shows that Labour's lead over the Conservatives among manual workers was 31 per cent for those who were council tenants and 32 per cent for those who did not own cars, but that it fell to just 3 per cent among those who were home owners and to minus 2 per cent among those with access to two cars. When Dunleavy and Husbands then constructed a simple additive index consisting of use of private medicine, private education and private care for the elderly as well as private housing and car ownership, they found a 34 per cent gap in Labour voting between manual workers with a score of zero and those who scored three or more (the comparable figure among non-manual workers was 27 per cent). The same study also indicated a tendency for those who depend most on state benefits to vote Labour.

Further corroboration has come from a study of two areas of Greater Manchester. Looking at people's attitudes to cuts in state welfare spending, Duke and Edgell (1984) found that working-class people in particular are highly segmented by consumption cleavages around housing, transport and health, and that these cleavages have a cumulative effect on their views on public expenditure issues. There was, for example, a 9 per cent margin of approval for cuts among those who were in the private sector on all three dimensions of consumption, but this contrasted with a 37 per cent margin of disapproval among those who relied upon the state for their housing, transport and health care. Duke and Edgell also showed that voting varied by consumption in a way which is consistent with Dunleavy's theory. Indeed, although class (defined on the basis of Wright's neo-Marxist class schema) was a stronger influence than consumption sector on attitudes to spending cuts, consumer sector was a better predictor of voting preference. Duke and Edgell concluded that

> Social class (defined in terms of the social relations of production) is indeed fragmented by consumption sectoral cleavages in the manner suggested by Dunleavy . . . We are confident that our data have confirmed the theoretical relevance and empirical applicability of the concept of consumption sectoral cleavages . . . Most supportive of the Dunleavy model is the evidence that political party alignment is influenced more by overall consumption location than by social class.
>
> (1984, pp. 194–5)

These same authors have continued to provide evidence for the significance of consumption sectors in later papers, although to some extent they seem to have moderated the claims they are making. For example, they have shown that the effect of consumption location on political attitudes is limited. Distinguishing what they confusingly call 'radical' attitudes on state expenditure (by which they mean support for current levels of spending) from what they term 'industrial radicalism' (for example, attitudes to unions and strikes) and 'political radicalism' (such as attitudes to business power, nationalization and income distribution), they find that consumption sectors have little influence on the latter two dimensions of political ideology, which are much more strongly influenced by class (Edgell and Duke, 1986). Similarly, they investigate people's views on government privatization policies and find that, although views vary with both production and consumption location, the effect of consumption sectors appears to be rather weak, and both class and partisanship (though especially the latter) come out as stronger influences in a multiple regression analysis (Duke and Edgell, 1987, p. 278).

The argument that consumption location is just as significant as class receives added support in a study by Whiteley. In his analysis of 1979 election data, he claims that only three social attributes are helpful in predicting voting behaviour – home ownership, car ownership and union membership. Although he also points out that none of these is a particularly strong predictive variable (because voters' evaluations of the parties are far more significant than their social attributes), it is noticeable that in his model, class does not have any independent effect on voting, whereas home ownership and car ownership do play a small role in shaping alignments (Whiteley, 1983, pp. 94–106).

In contrast with these studies, however, other research continues to find that class far outweighs consumption as an influence on voting. Evidence such as that presented by Dunleavy is often rejected by his opponents on methodological or conceptual grounds. For example, Marshall *et al.* (1988, p. 235) suggest that findings by researchers such as Crewe and Dunleavy are a product of an inadequate conceptualization of class in terms of 'social grade'. However, both the Dunleavy and Husbands analysis of 1983 data and Duke and Edgell's Manchester study use class schema based on Wright's theoretical work, yet they still manage to come up with findings pointing to the partially independent significance of consumption location. Of course, as Marshall and his co-authors show, the Wright class model is itself of dubious value, but it is difficult to dismiss Dunleavy's evidence as purely an effect of inadequate operationalization of the class variable when he has reproduced it using both the advertising industry's grading scheme and neo-Marxist class theory!

More serious are criticisms of Dunleavy's interpretation of the results of his odds ratio calculations and log-linear modelling. The odds ratio calculations employed in Dunleavy's 1979 paper, for example, are to some extent misleading since they exaggerate the significance of the voting behaviour of 'extreme' cases. As Franklin and Page (1984, pp. 529–30) argue, only a relatively small proportion of middle-class households have two cars, and by focusing on them as the point of comparison, Dunleavy has identified a powerful effect which actually explains very little. Similarly, Franklin and Page and Franklin (1985) issue a timely warning about the use of log-linear and logistic models. They point out that such models reveal the effects of particular combinations of variables but do not indicate strength of association. Use of multiple regression techniques reveals a much weaker consumption effect than that apparently discovered by Dunleavy's logistic models – the combined effect of house and car ownership, for example, accounts for only 12 per cent of variance in voting at the 1979 general election, whereas the six class-based 'socialization variables' abstracted from Butler and Stokes's work can explain some 25 per cent of variance.

More damaging than criticisms of Dunleavy's data analysis, however, are studies which have produced apparently contradictory findings. It has to be said that there have been few genuine attempts at replicating Dunleavy's work, and the results of other studies are thus far from conclusive. Nevertheless, there is now enough research evidence to lead us seriously to question the empirical validity of Dunleavy's core claims.

Marshall and his co-researchers found in their national survey in England that voting intention does indeed vary by tenure, state dependency and production sector, but they also went on to suggest that these effects were almost entirely explicable as the product of class position. Unfortunately, they did not systematically test the Dunleavy thesis by constructing additive indexes to identify different consumption sectors, and their evidence is therefore only indirectly relevant to this question.

More helpful is Taylor-Gooby's national sample study of public attitudes to welfare (1986b). He found little support for Dunleavy's thesis, and like Marshall and his colleagues, he found strong correlations between party support and class position. He did find that use of private medical insurance and use of private education were strongly related to party preference (although membership of a private pension scheme was not). However, Taylor-Gooby shows that sectoral cleavages are not as important in shaping party preferences as people's class position or their views on specific issues. He also found that the relationship between private consumption and right-wing voting could not easily be explained in terms of perceptions by voters of their self-interest as private health users, private education users, or whatever. The 'ideological' distinction between private and public sectors, which Dunleavy believes is the basis of political mobilization of sectoral cleavages, simply did not seem particularly salient for most people. Taylor-Gooby concludes that the link between consumption sector and voting remains largely unexplained by existing theories.

The view that class is still more important than consumption in shaping political alignments also emerges from a recent study of local election results. Warde *et al.* (1987) found that class composition of wards was by far the best sociological predictor of voting patterns. They also found (as have others) that housing tenure is the strongest consumption variable and that car ownership could often be dropped altogether from their models. Tenure, however, was weaker than class in explaining variance in voting behaviour.

The three towns survey can also provide empirical evidence regarding the adequacy of Dunleavy's consumption-sector theory. There is, however, a problem which any attempt at evaluating the relative political significance of class and consumption sectors has to address. This is that both models may include within them the common element of housing tenure. Housing tenure is one of the six socialization variables in the Butler and Stokes model of class voting as refined and developed by Franklin, for one characteristic of the working class as defined in this model is that it lives on relatively homogeneous council estates. Yet renting a council house is (together with dependence upon public transport) also a fundamental element of consumption location as defined by Dunleavy. It is for this reason that Franklin and Page have argued that, because it is common to both socialization and consumption models of voting, housing situation should be dropped from analyses which seek to compare the two. This, however, would severely weaken the Dunleavy model, for while housing is one of six factors in the class socialization theory, it is one of only two or three key variables in the consumption-sector model. It seems better, therefore, to evaluate Dunleavy's theory both including and excluding housing tenure.

Proceeding first by excluding housing tenure, it is apparent from Table 4.1 that consumption location is, as expected, associated with voting. The table shows the percentage voting figures for each of the main parties correlated with three key consumption variables. Two points should be noted as background to this table. The first is that data were collected between March and September 1986 when the Liberal–Social Democratic Party Alliance was attracting widespread popular support, and this is reflected in the fact that 20 per cent of our respondents indicated that they would vote for the Alliance if a general election were held the next day (this is discussed more fully in Appendix II). The second is that, as noted in Chapter 1, the three towns are all Labour-controlled, and this is reflected in the fact that 35 per cent of our respondents indicated that they would vote for the Labour Party, while only 21 per cent said they would vote Conservative. The remaining 24 per cent would not vote, did not know how they would vote, or would support some other party.

Turning first to car ownership, we see that although there is a difference in Labour and Alliance voting between one-car and no-car households, the most striking division appears to be that between multi-car households and the rest, for it is here that the Conservative vote leaps and the Labour vote slumps. This, of course, is basically what Dunleavy himself found in his original work where he focused on the significant difference in voting between *two-car households* and those with *no car*. However, the logic of Dunleavy's theory is that the political-ideological cleavage should come at the point between state and private provision (that is, between those with one car and those with none) rather than between different sets of private consumers. Furthermore, multi-car households only account for 13 per cent of the total sample, and this would tend to support Franklin's argument against Dunleavy that his emphasis on two-car households does not explain very much since their numbers are so small.

The main point about the electoral significance of car ownership, however, is that it virtually disappears once we control for social class. If class is defined according to the Registrar-General's system of occupational

Table 4.1 *The association between consumption locations and voting intention*

Consumption location	Voting intention										Sig. level (p)
	Con		Lab		Lib–Soc Dem Alliance		Other, NV/DK		Total		
	No.	%	No.	%	No.	%	No.	%	No.	%	
Car ownership (N = 498)											
None	29	18	74	45	16	10	45	27	164	33	
One	54	20	93	34	69	26	54	19	270	54	0.00
Two or more	25	41	10	15	20	30	9	14	64	13	
Private health ins. (N = 463)											
Yes	20	34	11	19	14	24	14	24	59	12	
Had in past	9	28	8	25	9	28	6	19	32	7	0.05
Never covered	73	20	148	40	74	20	77	20	372	78	
Private pension (N = 398)											
Yes	54	27	57	29	56	28	31	16	198	50	0.00
No	31	16	89	45	27	14	53	25	200	50	

Table 4.2 *Car ownership, social class and voting intention*

	Con		Lab		Lib–Soc Dem Alliance		Other, NV/DK		Total		Sig. level (p)
	No.	%	No.	%	No.	%	No.	%	No.	%	
Service class											
No car	6	38	5	31	3	19	2	12	16	13	
One car	19	27	12	17	26	37	14	19	71	60	0.88
2+ cars	13	41	6	19	8	25	5	15	32	27	
Intermed. class											
No car	9	25	9	25	5	14	13	36	36	25	
One car	25	27	28	30	21	23	18	20	92	63	0.22
2+ cars	7	41	0	0	8	47	2	12	17	12	
Working class											
No car	12	12	57	55	8	8	26	25	103	46	
One car	8	8	53	51	21	20	22	21	104	47	0.01
2+ cars	5	33	4	27	4	27	2	13	15	7	

N = 486

classification, the association between car ownership and voting disappears altogether in all classes. If the Goldthorpe class schema is used (Table 4.2), then car ownership is found to have no significant association with voting among the service and intermediate classes, and the association which does still hold ($p < 0.01$) within the working class is explained entirely by the effect of a very small number of two-car households. In short, the association between car ownership and voting appears to be almost entirely a function of social class.

Much the same pattern emerges in the other consumption variables identified in Table 4.1. Membership of a private pension scheme (data here exclude retired people and include respondents and partners) is associated with Conservative and Alliance voting. Controlling for social class, however, this association collapses among the service and intermediate classes, but it remains significant ($p < 0.05$) among the working class where 51 per cent of members vote Labour and 23 per cent Conservative compared with 77 per cent and 9 per cent respectively of non-members. Unlike Taylor-Gooby, therefore, I do find some evidence of a pension effect although it appears to be restricted to the working class.

The association between private health insurance and voting is almost entirely a class effect given that very few working-class respondents subscribed to health schemes. Similarly, only sixteen respondents had been educated privately, and twelve were sending their own children to private schools, so again it is clear that private education (even more than private health) is largely confined to the service class and that its independent effect on voting is likely to be minimal.

Dunleavy, of course, argues that consumption effects on political alignment are cumulative. We have already commented on the problems in

Table 4.3 *The association between an index of privatized consumption (excluding housing) and voting intention (excluding non-votes)*

| Index score | Voting intention | | | | | | | |
| | Con | | Lab | | All | | Total | |
	No.	%	No.	%	No.	%	No.	%
0	4	8	42	81	6	12	52	24
1	16	29	29	52	11	20	56	26
2	30	38	26	33	23	29	79	36
3+	12	37	8	23	13	40	33	15

N = 220
p < 0.01

constructing an additive index, but in order to test the theory on its own terms it is necessary to develop such an index to see whether the combined effects of consumption locations are stronger than their individual effects.

Let us first consider an index excluding housing but including car ownership, membership of a private pension scheme, membership of a private health insurance scheme and payment for education or training of any form (for example, including dancing classes and extra tuition out of school as well as full-time fee-paying). Table 4.3 shows the correlation between scores on this index and voting (excluding non-voters and don't knows). As can readily be seen, Conservative and Alliance voting rises and Labour voting falls as index scores increase. While 81 per cent of those with a zero score vote Labour, only 23 per cent of those scoring three or more do so. When we control for social class, furthermore, a familiar pattern emerges. The association between private consumption and non-Labour voting disappears in the service and intermediate classes but persists (p < 0.01) among the working class. While 87 per cent of working-class voters with a zero score vote Labour, this is true of only 67 per cent of those who score one and 54 per cent of those who score two (only one working-class respondent achieved a score in excess of two).

These findings are replicated when we take account of house ownership in constructing an expanded five-way index (Table 4.4). Here we see that voters who rely entirely upon state provision for their housing, transport, health care, education and old age support are overwhelmingly pro-Labour (91 per cent). The extent of Labour support falls progressively as people gain more extensive access to private consumption. When we control for social class, we again find that the association persists (p < 0.05) only in the working class. Thus, 90 per cent of working-class voters who score zero vote Labour compared with 71 per cent who score one, 58 per cent who score two and 57 per cent who score three.

It would appear from this that consumption location *may be* influencing voting behaviour among the working class but not among other groups. If

225

Table 4.4 *The association between an index of privatized consumption (including housing) and voting intention (excluding non-votes)*

Index score	Con		Lab		All		Total	
	No.	%	No.	%	No.	%	No.	%
0	1	3	32	91	2	6	35	16
1	8	23	21	60	6	17	35	16
2	11	26	18	43	13	31	42	19
3	31	42	24	32	19	26	74	34
4+	11	37	8	26	11	37	30	14

N = 216
p < 0.01

this is the case, then the electoral implications of continuing privatization of consumption could be extremely significant, for as more working-class people aspire to and achieve private provision of pensions, health insurance and so on, so support for the Labour Party would seem likely to ebb away. However, we need to be very cautious in interpreting these findings. Statistical association does not establish causal adequacy.

It is also important to emphasize that these data do not necessarily lend support to Dunleavy's thesis. For a start, Dunleavy's theory would predict the existence of a consumption effect in all classes, not just the working class. Furthermore, his argument that such effects are the product of ideology remains untested by these findings, which could equally well be explained by a model of rational self-interested voting (a point I take up later in the chapter) or, indeed, in terms of the operation of a third factor.

The possibility that a third factor may be at work is indicated by the fact that it is possible to find associations between voting and other aspects of consumption which have nothing to do with the state/private-sector relation. In the three towns survey we gathered information on household ownership of a range of consumer durables including televisions, stereos, dishwashers, video recorders, freezers, microwaves, telephones, home computers and washing machines. Constructing an index of ownership of consumer durables we found (p < 0.01), not surprisingly, that 56 per cent of those who score five or under vote Labour compared with 33 per cent who score six or more (the equivalent figures for Conservative voters are 20 per cent and 37 per cent). What is more interesting, as Table 4.5 shows, is that the association still holds (though not always strongly) when we control for social class. Within each class, those who own more consumer goods are less likely to vote Labour than those who own less.

It is difficult to see how this could have anything to do with ideology. Far more plausible is the possibility that people with particular kinds of values (for example, stressing privatism, personal property, or domesticity) *both* accumulate more consumer goods *and* vote for more right-wing parties. If

Table 4.5 *The association between ownership of consumer goods, class position and voting behaviour (excluding non-voters)*

	Voting intention								
	Con		*Lab*		*All*		*Total*		*Sig.*
	No.	*%*	*No.*	*%*	*No.*	*%*	*No.*	*%*	*level*
Service class									
Owns 5 or less items	8	22	12	33	16	44	36	37	0.03
Owns 6 or more items	30	48	11	18	21	34	62	63	
Intermed. class									
Owns 5 or less items	17	33	22	42	13	25	52	46	0.19
Owns 6 or more items	24	39	16	26	21	34	61	54	
Working class									
Owns 5 or less items	14	12	81	70	20	17	115	67	0.18
Owns 6 or more items	12	21	33	57	13	22	58	33	
N = 384									

this is indeed the explanation, then it is also possible that the same explanation would hold for the association between private consumption of consumer services and voting behaviour. In other words, it may simply be that people who are most interested in buying private *services* (such as in health, pensions, or education) are predisposed to vote Conservative just as those who are most interested in buying private *goods* for the home appear to be.

To conclude, therefore, it seems that there may be some consumption effect on voting but that it is restricted to the working class. We have found in the analysis of the three towns survey that working-class people who subscribe to private pension schemes are less inclined to vote Labour than those who rely on the state scheme, and we have also shown that the more working-class people rely upon state provision of services, the more likely they are to vote for the Labour Party. The explanation for all this remains unclear, however. Dunleavy's own explanation in terms of a dominant ideology remains unconvincing. The possibility that consumption patterns are creating new sets of interests which voters are intent on defending is more plausible, and we shall consider the theoretical significance of this in Chapter 6.

Finally, a note of caution. We have seen that 'the working class' divides politically along a consumption cleavage. This *may* be because consumption has politically significant effects. It may, on the other hand, simply reflect the way 'the working class' has been defined. It is possible that a narrower and more restrictive definition would have reduced or eliminated the 'consumption effect' by reclassifying many of those who can afford private services into a higher class category. As always in sociology, the data are only as good as the concepts used to classify and interpret them. Although Marshall and his colleagues have recently concluded that the Goldthorpe class schema used here enjoys a high degree of empirical validity, there is always the possibility that 'the working class' with the cars and owner-occupied houses is actually in a very different class situation from 'the working class' which ends up waiting for the bus on a municipal housing estate. It may be their patterns of consumption which make the difference in their voting, but it may also simply be that our class concept is insufficiently sensitive to the variations in their material life chances.

Housing tenure and political alignments

Obviously, class position, consumption sectoral location and housing tenure are all closely interrelated. Different class situations tend to offer different levels of income, and the higher the household income, the greater is the likelihood that the home will be owned and that other aspects of consumption will be organized through the private sector. This is why the evidence on the relative effects of these three factors is often so difficult to disentangle. Nobody denies that class, consumption sector and tenure all correlate with voting; the problem is whether they represent partially independent influences.

To the extent that consumption location does affect voting, all the evidence indicates that the single most significant aspect of it is housing. Dunleavy himself accepts this. However, as we saw earlier, he denies that housing tenure is itself an explanatory variable. In his view, it is not ownership of a house which encourages right-wing voting, but rather the creation of an ideological interest around the system of taxation and subsidies within which house ownership is contextualized.

In earlier work (Saunders, 1978, p. 1984) I developed an alternative view. Like Dunleavy, I argued in these papers that the political significance of class cleavages could be cross-cut by divisions created through consumption, but unlike him, I saw these divisions as grounded in real conflicts of material

228

interest, just as class divisions are. This led me to the view that divisions arising out of ownership and non-ownership of housing were crucial, since housing was a unique consumer good which enabled those who owned it to generate wealth through rising property prices. When home owners mobilize to defend the exclusivity of their neighbourhoods, or to reduce property taxes, or to maintain tax advantages, they act in recognition of a common economic interest in just the same way as workers do when they mobilize through trade unions for higher wages or to prevent redundancies. What this means is that tenure divisions cannot be explained away as the products of dominant ideologies, but are expressions of real material divisions of interests. These economic interests are not the only reason why home ownership may generate distinct political alignments, for we may also expect home owners to develop new values and concerns which may also feed through in changed political alignments. Nevertheless, the basic reason why housing tenure is likely to divide people politically has to do with the economic interests which it entails.

It is in this context that the results outlined in Chapter 3 take on an added significance, for there we saw how working-class and middle-class home owners alike may accrue substantial capital gains from their ownership of housing. The economic interest created by domestic property ownership is therefore real and significant. In my 1978 paper, I drew upon Weber's work to define this interest as the basis for a distinct 'property class' formation. I am now less confident of the usefulness of this formulation, but whether or not we choose to conceptualize domestic property ownership in terms of class theory, it is clear that it is an important determinant of life chances in the contemporary period.

The question, however, is whether this real economic interest is the mainspring for political mobilization. As Ball (1983, pp. 288–92) has legitimately argued in respect of my earlier work, it is a mistake to assume that a material interest translates automatically into a political force. To demonstrate that owner-occupiers share common material interests is to say nothing about whether and how these interests are mobilized politically.

For example, although they may share an interest in maintaining property values, home owners in one situation may interpret this interest in quite a different way from those in another. Savage (1987) suggests that home owners in less prosperous regions of the UK might quite rationally vote Labour in the hope of attaining policies which rejuvenate the local economy and help push up house values, whereas those in more affluent parts of the country are more likely to support the Conservatives. This has been borne out by Johnston (1987), who shows that working-class owner-occupiers in the South of England are more likely to vote Conservative than those in the North. My own research offers little support for such theories, however, for in the three towns studied (which range across the South-East, East Midlands and North-West of the country) there was little systematic difference in the voting intentions of owners (33 per cent of owners in Slough voted Labour compared with 41 per cent in Derby and 36 per cent in

Burnley). Furthermore, I can find no evidence that those owners who are most concerned about the investment and asset value of their homes vote any differently from those who care little about making money from their housing, yet such a difference would seem to be implicit in the logic of Savage's argument. Nevertheless, it does seem reasonable to accept that the political significance of tenure divisions (and, for that matter, class divisions) may be mediated through different local situations, and we should therefore be cautious in drawing national-level generalizations about the effects of tenure, sector, or class.

Having said that, the fact remains that there are strong correlations in national-level data between all three of these variables and voting behaviour, and this poses the problem of disentangling their relative effects. Political alignments do vary with tenure, but to what extent should this be seen, not as a tenure effect, but as a sector effect or a class effect?

The evidence against reducing tenure effects to sector effects is now quite compelling. One reason for this is that tenure has by far the strongest influence on voting of all consumption items. Even Dunleavy's own findings show this. As Harrop suggests:

One remains doubtful whether Dunleavy's own preferred theory of consumption sectors is better grounded empirically than the approach of Weberian urban sociology with which the theory is contrasted. This question, on Dunleavy's own analysis, turns on whether the electoral effects of housing are more important than those of other consumption location variables such as transport. Here we have noted the greater salience of housing policy among the mass public and the more consistent effect of housing tenure than of car ownership on middle class voting behaviour. These results, together with the greater importance of a house than a car to the family budget, all suggest a distinctive housing effect as compared with transport.

(1980, p. 398)

One way of testing the relative importance of the two variables is to investigate the effect of tenure on voting in the absence of consumption-sector cleavages. This can best be achieved through international comparisons. In Britain, the major tenure cleavage is that between home owners and public-sector tenants. Owning and renting (the factors deemed important in my earlier work) thus coincide to a high degree with individualized and socialized modes of consumption (the factors deemed important in Dunleavy's theory). In other countries, however, this is not the case. In the USA, Canada and Australia, for example, public-sector renting is a small fragment of the housing system, and the tenure division between ownership and renting thus falls mainly within the private sector. Furthermore, the division between the tenures is not as clearly hierarchical as it is in Britain, and mobility between them is much more common. It follows from all of this, as McAllister notes, that tenure in North America

230

and Australia 'is not a social cleavage that is amenable to exploitation by one or other political party' (1984, p. 513). Put another way, the conditions which Dunleavy's sectoral theory deems necessary for a political cleavage to occur are not present.

This provides us with ideal comparative experimental conditions for evaluating the two competing explanations, and this has been done by Geraldine Pratt through her work in Canada (Pratt, 1986a, 1986b). Basing her argument on an analysis of 1979 national data as well as her own in-depth interviews with home owners and renters in a Vancouver suburb, Pratt shows that tenure affects middle-class voting patterns even when controlling for factors such as income and life cycle. She also demonstrates that home owners do constitute a self-aware and relatively cohesive political interest. None of this can be explained in terms of Dunleavy's theory of consumption sectors, which would have predicted that there would be no tenure effect given that both owners and renters in Canada are located in the private ('individualized') sector. The difference in political alignment, in other words, has nothing to do with dominant ideologies playing up the significance of the division between private- and public-sector consumers, but is entirely consistent with the alternative theory that tenure forms the basis for distinctive political interests. As Pratt concludes:

> Dunleavy's insistence that consumption cleavages become politically salient only when polarized between collective and individualized forms is opened to question by the finding that Canadian homeowners pursue their housing interests politically, quite in isolation and in a context of predominantly individualized housing provision and consumption. The finding that housing consumption sectors form the basis of a significant political cleavage in Canada, where the division between consumption groups lies between the ownership and nonownership of domestic property, fits more comfortably with the Weberian schema of domestic property classes . . . In the Canadian context, the ownership and nonownership of domestic property creates a significant political and economic cleavage.
>
> (1986b, pp. 178–9)

Disentangling the effects of class and tenure is rather more difficult than sorting out the relative importance of consumption sectors and tenure. Nevertheless, there is now considerable evidence from Britain and other countries that tenure divisions are associated with voting patterns even when the effects of social class are taken into account. In France, for example, Preteceille (1986, p. 153) cites findings showing that working-class owners are more sympathetic to the right (44 per cent) than are working-class tenants (29 per cent), but that middle-class owners (63 per cent) and tenants (55 per cent) are much more oriented to the right than either of the working-class groups. This pattern is similar to that reported by Sarlvik and Crewe (1983) for Britain. In their work on the 1979 election study, they showed that class (measured simply by a manual/non-manual division) was the single best predictor of voting but that tenure was not far behind. They calculated an index of association on which the class/vote relation scored 27 while the tenure/vote relation scored 21 (much higher, incidentally, than any other consumption variable). While 61 per cent of outright owners and 53 per cent of mortgagees voted Conservative, only 28 per cent of council tenants did so. They also found that just three variables – class, union membership and housing tenure – could between them explain as much variation in voting behaviour as any other combination of any number of variables. Tenure, in other words, is subsidiary to but independent of class in its effect on political alignments, and like class, it is a necessary component of any comprehensive model of voting.

Much the same conclusion is reported by Robertson (1984) and McAllister (1984), both (like Sarlvik and Crewe) on the basis of 1979 data (although as so often in this literature, the method for establishing association has been questioned – see Marshall *et al.*, 1988, p. 232). McAllister, for example, finds that even when family background, demography, socioeconomic status and self-assigned class are all held constant, tenure still has a 'substantial' effect on voting (1984, p. 516). Similarly, in a study of home owners in Aberdeen, Williams finds that 'Tenure and vote are statistically related even after controlling for social class. For all social classes, the nature of the relationship is the same, with owner occupiers (whether outright owners or mortgagors) tending to vote Conservative or Alliance, and council tenants tending to favour the Labour Party' (1988, p. 4).

The three towns survey bears this out, though not as convincingly as might have been expected. Table 4.6 shows a clear relationship between tenure and voting – 55 per cent of council tenants vote Labour compared with less than 30 per cent of outright owners and mortgagees; just 11 per cent of council tenants vote Conservative as compared with 24 per cent of mortgaged owners and 32 per cent of outright owners.

However, tenure obviously reflects class position to a considerable extent, for access to owner-occupation has generally depended upon a relatively secure and reasonably paid job. In the three towns survey, for example,

Table 4.6 *The relationship between housing tenure and voting intention*

Tenure	Voting intention									
	Con		Lab		All		NV/DK		Total	
	No.	%	No.	%	No.	%	No.	%	No.	%
Outright owner	36	32	32	28	24	21	22	19	114	23
Mortgaged owner	59	24	73	29	62	25	55	21	249	51
Council tenant	14	11	72	55	15	12	29	22	130	26

N = 493
p < 0.01

only 3 per cent of service-class respondents were council tenants compared with 23 per cent of those in the intermediate class and 42 per cent of those in the working class. Put another way, 74 per cent of all council tenants were working class. Given the class basis of the British tenure system, it is obviously important to control for social class, and this is done in Table 4.7.

Clearly tenure plays no role among the service class, virtually all of whom are owner-occupiers. The relationship between tenure and voting is both statistically significant (p < 0.01) and relatively strong (Cramer's V = 0.35; that is, tenure explains 35 per cent of the variance) in the intermediate class, although again, the number of council tenants here is relatively small, and caution is needed in interpreting tests of probability on a data set of this size. The crucial class is the working class, which is divided fairly evenly on tenure lines, but here the relationship is not statistically significant, and the strength of association is much weaker (Cramer's V = 0.17), although the expected pattern is present (59 per cent of tenants and 47 per cent of owners vote Labour).

When non-voters are excluded, the association between voting intention and tenure does achieve significance at or near the 95 per cent level in each class. Nevertheless, these results are not as compelling as might have been envisaged. This is partly because, while council tenants are overwhelmingly Labour, owner-occupiers are divided across all parties (see Ball, 1985, p. 27), and it is partly because unskilled and (to a lesser extent) semi-skilled manual working-class households remain solidly supportive of the Labour Party even if they own a house. Unskilled manual workers in the three towns survey split 68 per cent Labour, 3 per cent Conservative among council tenants and 50 per cent Labour, 12 per cent Conservative among owner-occupiers (most of the remainder are non-voters). There is a tenure effect here, but it is almost stifled by the class-based pattern of party allegiance.

Table 4.7 *The relationship between housing tenure and voting intention, controlling for social class*

	Con		Lab		Voting intention All		NV/DK		Total		Sig.
	No.	%	No.	%	No.	%	No.	%	No.	%	level
Service class											
Owner-occupiers	37	33	20	18	34	30	21	18	112	97	
Council tenants	1	25	3	75	0	0	0	0	4	3	n.a.
Intermediate class											
Owner-occupiers	36	31	24	21	32	27	25	21	117	81	
Council tenants	5	19	12	44	2	7	8	30	27	19	0.01
Working class											
Owner-occupiers	20	16	60	47	19	15	29	23	128	58	
Council tenants	6	7	55	59	13	14	19	20	93	42	0.07
N = 481											

My research, then, would seem to confirm previous studies which claim that the electoral significance of housing tenure is secondary to that of social class and that its effects may be more pronounced in some strata (notably the intermediate class) than in others. While its effects may be secondary and partial, it would nevertheless be foolish to disregard tenure altogether. Even Heath, Jowell and Curtice accept in their analysis of the 1983 election that tenure is significantly associated with voting, yet much of their book is concerned to emphasize the continuing importance of class as the basis of voting in Britain. Reporting that 53 per cent of owners and 23 per cent of council tenants voted Conservative while 19 per cent of owners and 55 per cent of council tenants voted Labour, they conclude: 'Not surprisingly the association between housing and vote persists even when we control for class. We do not disagree with the view . . . that housing cross-cuts class and that working class home owners are more likely to vote Conservative than are working class council tenants' (1985, p. 45).

Where Heath, Jowell and Curtice do sound a note of caution is in the interpretation of such data. They do not dispute that tenure is related to voting, but they do query whether it is tenure which is the causal variable in this association. In their view, it is not home ownership which leads to conservatism, but conservatism which encourages the move into home ownership. In other words, people who are predisposed towards conservative values will make the greatest effort to purchase their own housing: 'It is quite plausible, and perfectly consistent with the data, to argue that social attitudes influence one's choice of housing rather than the other way round' (1985, p. 49). Given their rejection of the class dealignment thesis, this is an important argument for them to advance, for if it could be shown that it is people's political values which lead them to buy a house, rather than the purchase which influences their values, then their argument against class dealignment is not substantially threatened.

The two types of explanation are not, of course, incompatible. It is entirely plausible to argue that conservative-minded people are most likely to want to buy their houses, and that having bought, their conservative values are reaffirmed or strengthened. It is, however, difficult to accept the view expressed by Heath and his colleagues that this association could wholly be explained by the propensity of conservative-minded people to buy their housing. A good test of this claim is provided by evidence on council house buyers, and this tends to suggest that the very act of purchase has at least some impact on political alignments.

The Conservative Party is convinced that its policy of selling council houses at discount to all tenants who wish to buy has won it substantial numbers of working-class votes (see Bassett, 1980, p. 293). This view is shared by a number of political analysts. Bailey, for example, writes that 'The one million "Right to Buy" sales have been duly noted by all political parties anxious to win or retain power' (1987, p. 15). It seems unlikely that any future Labour government would rescind the principle of the Right to Buy for fear of electoral repercussions.

Table 4.8   *The relationship between council house purchase and voting intention (excluding non-votes)*

	Con		Lab		All		Total	
	No.	*%*	*No.*	*%*	*No.*	*%*	*No.*	*%*
Non-buyers	18	17	74	69	16	15	108	81
Purchasers	9	35	11	42	6	23	26	19

N = 134
p < 0.05

Academic research too suggests that sales have favoured the Conservatives. At the 1983 general election (the first since the 1980 Housing Act which introduced the Right to Buy), 56 per cent of council house buyers voted Conservative, while only 18 per cent voted Labour (Crewe, 1983). More significantly, 59 per cent of former Labour voters who bought their council houses switched to the Conservative Party at this election (Marshall *et al.*, 1985, p. 274). Similarly, Dunleavy and Husbands found that council house buyers were somewhat more Conservative than a comparable group of non-buyers (1985, p. 137); while in her study of buyers in Sunderland, Stubbs (1988) found that in 1983, 20 per cent of recent purchasers voted Conservative, and a further 25 per cent voted Alliance, as compared with 10 per cent and 12 per cent respectively among non-buyers.

My data reinforce this pattern of findings, although the number of cases is small. As Table 4.8 shows, buyers in the three towns survey are twice as likely as non-buyers to vote Conservative. Social class or occupational status does not appear to make much difference to this; for unskilled, semi-skilled, skilled and white-collar grade purchasers all show less of an inclination to vote Labour than their equivalents among non-purchasers.

In itself, of course, this evidence does not necessarily mean that a change of tenure is the stimulus for a change of vote. Heath, Jowell and Curtice show that most tenants who had bought council houses had already voted Conservative in 1979. They believe that this proves their argument that it is conservative people who buy housing rather than purchasers of housing who develop conservative sympathies (a view also expressed by Marshall *et al.*). They also show that buyers who had voted Labour in 1979 were no more likely to desert the party in 1983 than were Labour voters who did not subsequently buy their homes (1985, p. 49). They conclude from this that a shift from renting to buying does not erode support for the Labour Party, nor does it enhance support for the Conservatives.

However, their evidence that most council house buyers in the 1980s had already voted Conservative in 1979 could simply indicate that home ownership was so important an issue to them that they changed their vote at the 1979 election in order to secure the return of a Conservative Party pledged to introducing a Right to Buy. Certainly the swing against Labour in 1979 was widely interpreted at the time as partly a reflection of the sales issue (as we have already seen, 9 per cent of voters at that election saw housing as the most important issue affecting their choice between the parties). It is entirely plausible to suggest that tenants who voted Conservative in 1979 did so, not because they were already Conservative, but because they wanted to own their homes and voting Conservative was the best way to achieve that aim.

Evidence from the three towns survey confirms that the two major parties are still popularly associated with the two major tenures, for only 4 per cent of council tenants believed that the Conservatives supported their interests as tenants, while just 3 per cent of owners nominated Labour as the party which supported their interests as owner-occupiers. This evidence (which is consistent with findings from other studies – for example, Madigan, 1988, p. 49) suggests that tenants aspiring to ownership would certainly have known which party was most likely to advance their cause, and it is not therefore implausible to suggest that some may have switched their votes accordingly.

Anecdotal evidence also points in the same direction. Many of those council tenants or former tenants with whom we spoke recognized that their aspirations to own were more likely to be realized under a Conservative government:

> If I hadn't voted for Margaret Thatcher, we wouldn't own this house now, would we?
> (Female semi-skilled manual worker and council house buyer, Slough)

> You know what they say. People who buy their homes are Tories. They change straight away.
> (Female semi-skilled manual worker and council tenant, Derby)

> I lean towards the Conservatives because they gave me my start. Without the Tories I'd still be a renter. What I wanted was a chance to get out of my council house image and the Conservatives gave me that chance so I'll always vote for them. But don't ask me if they're a good government or not.
> (Female retired from intermediate occupation, council house buyer, Burnley)

> The Conservatives [support home ownership]. Labour would stop people buying their council houses. And they'd stop selling shares.
> (Male semi-skilled manual worker and council house buyer, Slough)

Not only this, but we came across a number of resentful people in Slough who told of how, back in the 1970s, they had been thwarted in their attempt to buy their homes when Labour had regained control of the local council and put an end to sales. Not only does the Conservative support for council house sales appear to have won electoral support, therefore, but Labour's opposition may well have strained the loyalty of many of its traditional supporters on the council estates:

We applied to buy this place ten years ago. They came round. It was all going through and then the council changed from Conservative to Labour and they stopped the sale of council houses. Three or four years later the council changed again and they said we could buy, but by then the price had gone up and there was a reduced time of mortgage. We were keen to buy but we just couldn't afford it. Our friends down the road signed two weeks before us so they let them go through. If we'd bought, we'd be paying less now than we pay in rent.

(Male skilled manual worker and Labour voter)

I was rushed into hospital and by the time I'd come out the council had changed and they wouldn't let us buy. Otherwise we'd have bought. It's unfortunate.

(Female retired unskilled manual worker, non-voter)

My brother was going to buy his house about ten years ago and then Labour won the council and it was all stopped.

(Female retired semi-skilled manual worker and Alliance voter)

We've always voted Labour but they stopped us buying this – they did the dirty on us.

(Male skilled manual worker and Labour voter)

Evidence from other studies also suggests that council house sales have led to a shift in voting patterns. The most convincing and thorough study is that by Williams, Sewel and Twine (1987), who interviewed a sample of former tenants who had bought their homes in Aberdeen. Their data show a significant tendency for purchasers to have changed their vote between 1979 and 1983. These authors agree with Heath, Jowell and Curtice that the Conservatives did not gain from this, but they do argue that Labour lost support to the centre-party Alliance of Liberals and Social Democrats. Explaining the difference between their findings and those of Heath and his colleagues, they point out that Heath's sample of council house buyers (128) was fairly small compared with theirs (500), and that the Heath survey simply compared the percentage of votes cast for each party in 1979 and 1983 and did not analyse the changing behaviour of individual voters. The Aberdeen study, in other words, seems more valid and more reliable on this issue.

Taken as a whole, the evidence pointing to the political significance of tenure divisions is impressive. The only study to deny that tenure is anything more than a surrogate class indicator is that by Marshall et al. (1988), but their evidence on this point is far from compelling, and their argument is

Table 4.9 *The association between social class (Goldthorpe and Registrar-General schema) and voting intention*

	Voting intention									
	Con		Lab		All		NV/DK		Total	
	No.	%	No.	%	No.	%	No.	%	No.	%
Goldthorpe classes										
Service class	38	32	23	19	37	31	21	18	119	24
Intermediate	41	28	38	26	34	23	33	23	146	30
Working class	26	12	117	52	33	15	50	21	226	46
(N = 491, p < 0.01)										
Reg.-General classes										
Prof. and managerial	39	31	24	19	42	33	21	17	126	26
Routine and sk. man.	49	24	77	37	40	19	42	20	208	42
Semi- and unsk. manual	18	12	76	48	22	14	41	26	157	32
(N = 491, p < 0.01)										

confusing. They themselves accept that tenure correlates with voting – in their sample, 44 per cent of owners voted Conservative, while 60 per cent of council tenants voted Labour. Nevertheless, they argue that 'The association that shows up between housing and vote is simply a proxy for the familiar class–vote linkage' (1988, p. 252). This, however, does not square with their own evidence, especially that relating to the effects of tenure on the voting behaviour of council tenants, who 'seem to be more influenced by their housing situation than by objective social class. Indeed, the association between class and vote is not significant among either council or private tenants, with the majority of the former voting Labour whatever their class situation' (Marshall *et al.*, 1988, p. 250).

This is hardly the evidence to support their contention that tenure is simply a surrogate class measure! Furthermore, they are themselves apparently uncertain as to whether tenure has no significance or whether it 'mediates' the effects of class voting (p. 251). All that they succeed in doing is demonstrating that class still influences voting (something which none of the literature discussed above seeks to question), but their data do not really help in determining whether, and to what extent, tenure also influences voting.

It is important to emphasize that none of the evidence or argument presented here has tried to suggest that class is no longer significant in shaping political alignments. Most of the studies discussed seem to agree broadly with Sarlvik and Crewe that class is the main factor but that tenure modifies its influence. Given the data presented in Table 4.9, this is also my conclusion, for it is clear that no matter how class is defined, its significance for voting remains strong. Marshall and his colleagues are tilting at windmills, for few would deny the significance of class. The problem with their study is that they are so concerned to establish the continuing importance of class that they overlook their own findings showing that tenure is also significant and that, in certain cases (such as the council tenants in their sample), it may be extremely significant.

Tenure, voting and the intermediate classes

What is now becoming clear from research in this field is that we need to move away from sterile either/or explanations of voting and instead begin to focus on how different factors interrelate to shape patterns of political alignment. As Geraldine Pratt suggests, 'It seems extremely implausible that homeownership overrides the influence of all other social variables. The interesting and much more complex empirical issue is how the influence of home ownership combines with other, often contradictory influences' (1987a, p. 163). Social class, housing tenure and sectoral locations all have some effect on voting, and they all interrelate to some extent with each other. Rather than arguing which of them is more or less significant, it will be more fruitful to analyse the nature of these interrelationships.

One way of assessing the strength of these variables while taking account of the effects of the other independent variables is through multiple regression analysis. I set out the basic principles of multiple regression models in Chapter 3, and we saw there that the technique can only be used on interval-level data. Most of the variables with which we are concerned here are, of course, nominal, and each has therefore first to be converted to a binary 'dummy variable'. Social class is expressed by the dummy variables WORCLASS and INTCLASS, which refer to the working class and intermediate class categories in Goldthorpe's schema. The service class is not entered into the model, but its affect can be deduced from that of the other two. Similarly, housing tenure is expressed by the dummy variable TENANT with owner-occupiers not entered. The variable CONSECT is, by contrast, an interval level expression with five values ranging from zero to four. It has been constructed by giving respondents one point for each item in the index for which they make private provision, and the index itself consists of car ownership, membership of a private pension scheme, subscription to private health insurance and use of private schooling for one's children now or in the past. The index excludes house ownership in order to avoid confusion with the independent effects of tenure.

These independent variables were entered into multiple regression models with voting behaviour as the dependent variable. Voting too has been expressed as dummy variables. In the first model (Table 4.10) it appears as LABOUR and in the second (Table 4.11) as TORY. Non-voters and supporters of other parties were not entered, and the two models therefore indicate the strength of voters' propensities to support each of the two main political parties.

The model presented in Table 4.10 seems to make it very clear that tenure has virtually no effect on Labour voting once we take account of the effect of the other variables. It falls a long way short of the level of significance

Table 4.10 *A multiple regression model of the effects of class, consumption sector and tenure on Labour voting*

Step	Variable name	Coeff.	Adjusted R-square	Standard error	Signif.
1	WORCLASS	0.39	0.14	0.08	0.0000
2	CONSECT	−0.04	0.15	0.02	0.0503
3	INTCLASS	0.10	0.15	0.09	0.2455
4	TENANT	0.02	0.15	0.03	0.5222
	(Constant)	0.30		0.08	0.0002

normally required; a Beta coefficient of just 0.04 suggests that there is an extremely weak correlation with the dependent variable; and the standard error exceeds the value of the coefficient and suggests that the very weak positive effect of 0.02 can for all practical purposes be treated as zero. Put simply, we can (and on grounds of statistical significance and analytical parsimony should) apparently model Labour voting without reference to housing tenure.

Other points also come out of an inspection of this table. The intermediate-class variable, for example, is also very weak and should not be entered into the final model since it too fails to achieve statistical significance. The index of consumption-sector location more or less just meets the required 95 per cent significance level, but the value of the coefficient here is also very small (−0.04 for each item on the index), and inclusion of this variable only raises the power of the model (adjusted R-square) from 0.14 to 0.16. Furthermore, when this index is disaggregated into its four component variables and these are entered separately into this model, none of them reach the criteria of adequacy.

It seems that the best-fitting adequate model that we are left with is a simple equation including the constant value and the dummy variable WORCLASS. Put another way, the best estimate we can make of the likelihood that somebody in the three towns survey will vote Labour is a probability of 30 per cent (the constant value) plus 39 per cent if they are working class. Even this model, however, only explains 14 per cent of the variance (adjusted R-square = 0.139). We may conclude that Labour voting is associated with being working class, that consumption location and tenure have little effect, but that many other factors which we have not taken into account here seem to influence the decision to support the Labour Party.

Now it could be argued in the face of this evidence that, while interesting, it essentially misses the point of the debate over tenure and voting. Most analyses, like this model, concentrate on Labour voting and find, unsurprisingly, that a working-class identity is still the best single predictive variable for explaining it. The debates we have been discussing in this chapter, however, turn mainly on the question of whether the growth of home ownership and privatized consumption *conservatizes* voters. To gauge

Table 4.11 *A multiple regression model of the effects of class, consumption sector and tenure on Conservative voting*

Step	Variable name	Coeff.	Adjusted R-square	Standard error	Signif.
1	WORCLASS	−0.19	0.06	0.08	0.0175
2	TENANT	−0.04	0.07	0.02	0.0742
3	INTCLASS	0.04	0.07	0.09	0.6742
4	CONSECT	0.01	0.06	0.18	0.6895
	(Constant)	0.37		0.08	0.0000

this, we need to analyse the same variables again, but this time with reference to their influence on Conservative voting. This is done in Table 4.11.

This model turns out to be almost worthless! The consumption-sector variable actually reduces the power of the model when it is entered, its standard error is more than double the value of the coefficient, and, like INTCLASS, it comes nowhere near the required level of significance. Housing tenure does come close to the 95 per cent significance level, but its effect is still weak (−0.04), and it adds only 1 per cent to the power of the model. As in the case of Labour voting, working-class identity seems to be the only variable worth including, and this gives us a final equation suggesting that the likelihood of voting Conservative is 37 per cent for those in the intermediate and service classes as compared with 18 per cent for those in the working class (if tenure were also included, it would suggest that renting a council house would further reduce this figure to 14 per cent). The main point to emerge from this table, however, is that none of the variables is much use for predicting Conservative voting, for the R-square values are tiny. Modelling class against Conservative voting leaves 94 per cent of the variance unexplained!

Multiple regression is not the only method available for modelling this data, for a different way of teasing out the relative effects of variables in complex tables has been provided by the development in recent years of log-linear modelling. The advantage of this technique is that it is designed specifically for use with categorical variables such as those being considered here, and it therefore avoids the necessity of constructing dummy variables. Log-linear models aim to discover the simplest combination of variables which adequately fits the data. Table 4.12 shows how a hierarchical log-linear model was constructed on data from the three towns survey by means of backward elimination starting with a saturated model involving four variables – voting, class, tenure and consumption sector. At each step, that effect is eliminated whose removal results in the smallest change in the likelihood ratio chi square for the model as a whole. Effects continue to be eliminated until the significance level of the next effect to be removed exceeds 0.05. We are then left with the simplest model which fits the data

Table 4.12 *A hierarchical log-linear model of class, tenure, consumption sector and voting by means of backward elimination*

	DF	LR chi² change	Probability of effect	P of model remaining
Saturated model				
V*C*T*S	0	0.000	1.000	
Step 1:				
Delete V*C*T*S	4	4.123	0.3896	
leaves V*C*T V*C*S V*T*S C*T*S				0.390
Step 2:				
Delete V*C*S	12	11.618	0.4768	
leaves V*C*T V*T*S C*T*S				0.471
Step 3:				
Delete V*C*T	5	6.408	0.2685	
leaves V*T*S C*T*S V*C				0.391
Step 4:				
Delete V*T*S	7	6.292	0.5061	
leaves C*T*S V*C V*T V*S				0.441
Step 5:				
Delete C*T*S	12	10.665	0.5578	
leaves V*C V*T V*S C*T C*S T*S				0.510
Step 6:				
Delete V*T	2	3.429	0.1800	
leaves V*C V*S C*T C*S T*S				0.448
Final model:				
V*C	4	22.103	0.0002	
V*S	6	14.466	0.0248	
C*T	2	22.085	0.0000	
C*S	6	26.473	0.0002	
T*S	3	32.638	0.0000	
				0.448

while maintaining a significance level of better than 95 per cent for each association in the model.

The simplest best-fit model as shown in Table 4.12 turns out to be one consisting of five pairs of interaction effects. Not surprisingly, class and tenure both interrelate with consumption sector and with each other. The other two effects show associations between class and voting and sector and voting. It is noticeable, however, that a model can be constructed which fits the data yet which excludes any relation between tenure and voting (the V*T association having been eliminated at Step 6).

The evidence of both the multiple regression and the log-linear models confirms that class is the key variable associated with voting, although its effect seems to be limited to the working class and even then it is a relatively weak predictor (especially of Conservative voting). Consumption-sector location has some effect on Labour voting when it is analysed as a compound variable, but is not significant when disaggregated into its constituent elements, nor when used to model Conservative voting. Finally, housing tenure turns out to have very little effect once other variables are taken into account. This would all seem to indicate that the critics of consumption and tenure theories of voting are correct and that the erosion of the class basis of electoral politics has been exaggerated.

Things, however, are not quite this simple. The regression and log-linear models constructed above are useful for disentangling the relative causal significance of interrelated variables, but they do not tease out the possible significance of specific values within these variables. For example, it is possible that, although tenure does not seem to exert an independent effect on voting, it may still be important for particular social classes. It is possible, therefore, that a variable like tenure is playing a crucial role in influencing *some people's* votes, but that this does not show up in multivariate models because it is limited to one or another social stratum such that its overall effect is dissipated.

There are good grounds for believing that this is indeed the case. The two multiple regression models constructed above showed that the class effect on voting seemed to be limited to the working class, for the intermediate-class category could not be entered into either model. This suggests, as a plausible hypothesis, that some other variable may be confusing the class effect among those in the intermediate classes. Referring back to Table 4.7, we saw there that tenure appears to influence the votes of people in the intermediate classes but that it had a much smaller effect within the working class. In the intermediate classes, Conservatives outnumbered Labour voters by three to two among owner-occupiers, but Labour voters outnumbered Conservatives by more than two to one among council tenants. There are too few tenants among the service class to judge whether tenure is significant there as well, but there does seem to be a clear pattern in this data which suggests that home ownership has its major in-fluence among those who make up Goldthorpe's intermediate classes – routine clerical employees, rank-and-file employees in services, small proprietors, self-employed artisans and lower-grade technicians and supervisors.

This pattern has also been detected in other recent research. In her work in Canada, for example, Pratt finds that tenure generates its own political effects, but that these are different in different classes: 'The relationship between housing tenure and political attitudes is linked . . . to social class in significant ways: housing tenure does not have the same effect on political values across all social classes' (1986a, p. 367). In particular, she finds that in Canada, tenure seems to have its major effect on the political values and behaviour of the lower echelons of the middle class – those in skilled non-manual and lower managerial occupations. It has least effect, by contrast, among skilled manual workers, for whom it seemed virtually irrelevant. Pratt's conclusion is unambiguous: 'While housing tenure is associated with political values for white collar workers and managers, it is *not* associated with the political values of skilled blue collar workers' (1987b, p. 51). As in the three towns survey, therefore, it is the politics of the intermediate classes (to use Goldthorpe's formulation) which seem most strongly influenced by housing tenure.

These findings are also consistent with those reported by Williams (1988, pp. 4–5) in his study of Aberdeen. He found a clear relationship between tenure and voting within every class, but when he considered the association between tenure and political attitudes (for example, on the welfare state and taxation) he discovered that it held only for routine non-manual workers (the Registrar-General's class IIIN). Evidence from three different studies thus concurs that the political significance of home ownership is mainly concentrated on that stratum in society which sits uneasily between the manual working class and the professional–managerial middle or 'service' class.

How can these patterns be explained? Why should tenure mainly influence the votes of the lower middle classes?

One attempt to answer this question has involved analysis of housing tenure as facilitating or inhibiting the tendency of different classes to vote in different ways. This idea is developed by Warde and his colleagues in their study of local election results, and it is also implicit in Harris's analysis of class segregation (Harris, 1984).

Warde and his co-authors argue that tenure does not itself cause political alignments, but that it may inhibit or enable the political effects of social class position. This argument suggests that there is a tendency for, say, working-class people to support the left. This tendency will develop most fully where they live together in class-homogeneous neighbourhoods such as council estates. Tenure therefore reinforces or impedes the realization of class tendencies:

> The considerable range and variety of struggles and political practices are underdetermined by the mere fact of class. Here the most important determinant are [sic] the types of class capacities based in specific local social structure . . . The significance of consumption locations may lie in the way they help generate such capacities. Thus council house tenure may encourage Labour voting among working class people not because they are voting in line with their consumption based interests, but because such areas may be more likely to develop patterns of collective interaction which may serve also as the media for political communication . . . These observations are consistent with our findings that while any measure of class provides a powerful explanation of voting, the power of the model is increased by adding consumption (mainly tenure) variables.
>
> (Warde et al., 1987, pp. 21–2)

Such arguments are interesting, but are open to four counter-arguments. First, if tenure is simply a surrogate for residential homogeneity, then a change in tenure with no change in residence should have no political effect, yet we have already seen that council house sales do seem to result in a shift in patterns of political alignment. Second, if council renting simply enables the expression of working-class collectivist values then it should presumably have no effect on tenants who are not working class, but as we saw above, Marshall and his co-researchers clearly demonstrate that the effect of class on voting disappears among all tenants (no matter what their class), for tenants in different classes tend to vote Labour in equal proportions. Third, the argument rests on the assumption that 'collective interaction' is more developed on council estates than in owner-occupied areas, but as we shall see in Chapter 5, empirical evidence suggests that the reverse is probably the case. And fourth, we may query the very notion of 'class tendencies', a concept which derives from the use of a highly dubious 'realist' epistemology of social science which I have criticized elsewhere (Saunders, 1986).

For all of these reasons we may reject Warde's explanation of the class-specific tenure effect. Tenure is more of an independent variable than Warde is prepared to admit.

A rather different attempt to explain why tenure has its major effect on the lower middle class rather than the working class is found in Pratt's work (see especially 1986a, 1987a, 1987b). She believes that unionization is playing an important mediating role. Membership of a union, she believes, encourages people to identify politically with their roles as producers and thus weakens their political identities as consumers of housing. Because union membership is high among skilled manual workers but low among low-level managers and skilled non-manual employees, the former are relatively uninfluenced by ownership of a house, while the latter are heavily influenced by it.

This is an interesting hypothesis, although Williams's study of Aberdeen failed to find any evidence for it in a British context. In my research I found that the relationship between tenure and voting was much stronger among non-unionists (Cramer's $V = 0.41$) than among unionists ($V = 0.18$), and this could be seen as supporting Pratt's argument that home ownership has its major political effects among non-union members, whose identity is more likely to be caught up in their homes than at their places of employment.

There is, however, a major problem with Pratt's argument. Leaving aside the objection that in Britain many intermediate-class workers are strongly unionized (especially those working in the public sector), the real problem is that union membership actually plays a rather insignificant part in most workers' lives. Why should membership of an organization whose meetings you never attend lead you to construct your identity around your role as a worker rather than as a home owner? As Dunleavy (1980b) has argued in a different context, the strong correlations thrown up in studies of voting between unionization and left voting are likely to be spurious, for few union members take any active interest in union affairs, and it is therefore difficult to see how carrying a card can have such a strong impact on their views of the world. Certainly, Pratt's argument that belonging to a union is enough to direct attention away from one's home and into the workplace seems implausible.

Dunleavy himself believes that union membership is probably a surrogate for production-sector location. Employees in the public sector tend to be aligned to the left, and because the public sector is highly unionized, they tend also to belong to trade unions, but the key factor in explaining their political alignment is the sector, not the union. My data lend some support to his argument. A staggering 84 per cent of public-sector employees belonged to unions or equivalent associations compared with just 32 per cent of those in the private sector, and partial associations between unionism and voting are to some extent explained by sectoral factors (and vice versa).

None of this, however, helps us to explain why tenure has more of an effect on the politics of the intermediate class than on the working class. Production-sector location does not appear to affect the tenure/vote association, nor is there any obvious reason why it should.

Clearly this is a problem which requires further analysis. My own view is that the marked conservatism of intermediate-class owner-occupiers probably has more to do with their marginal social status than with their experiences at work or their membership of unions. We saw in Chapter 1 that housing has long been a means whereby that stratum which perches uneasily between the working and middle classes has tried to identify with the latter while distancing itself from the former. Williams (1987, p. 202) finds that housing has been an important mark of distinction since the eighteenth century, and Crossick (1978) reveals how skilled artisans in the nineteenth century sought to buy their homes so as to distinguish themselves from the working classes below them. Back in 1890 the English economist Alfred Marshall noted that 'Relatively large and well appointed house room is . . . the most convenient and obvious way of advancing a material claim to social distinction' (quoted in Douglas and Isherwood, 1979, p. 190); and in his classic study of status distinction in America, Vance Packard noted how in the 1950s the house was becoming the most important single symbol of family status (1959, p. 61).

Today there can be no doubt that, in Britain at least, housing carries clear symbolic meaning as regards the attribution of status, nor that tenure is a crucial element in this symbolic system. John Short has suggested that 'Owner occupation is a symbol of achievement. Council housing has been denigrated to the role of providing housing for those who cannot afford owner occupation, and to become an owner occupier is a mark of success, while to remain a council tenant is an admission of failure' (1982, p. 233). Council renting is today, and perhaps has always been, a stigmatized tenure because it inflicts upon tenants conditions which run counter to the values by which esteem tends to be attributed. Tenants are sifted and sorted and have no control over where they are to live, and their individuality is negated by the operation of large-scale public bureaucracies (Robinson, 1983, p. 88). By contrast, studies on the Isle of Sheppey (Pahl and Wallace, 1988, p. 140), in Bristol (Franklin, 1986, p. 34) and in Glasgow (Madigan, 1988, p. 11) have all found that home ownership is positively esteemed as a tenure which denotes personal status and achievement.

In the three towns survey, many of those with whom we spoke were clearly sensitive to the status attached to differences in tenure:

I like to be able to say the house is mine. When you go for a job it's an advantage to own your own house. It shows an employer you're ambitious and can be trusted.
> (Male, intermediate occupation, home owner, Slough)

Yes, it makes a difference. Just look around this estate at the houses that have been bought. They call it tarting up. It's keeping up with the Joneses.
> (Male semi-skilled manual worker and council house buyer, Slough)

This neighbourhood has gone down. It's starting to worry us. The council is buying houses. They've closed the X estate and we're getting some of those rehoused here. I'm not a snob, but they're not right bright neighbours.
> (Female skilled non-manual worker and home owner, Burnley)

It is comments like these which help us understand why so many people place so much importance on owning their homes. Indeed, so important is tenure as an expression of status that many households apparently value ownership above housing quality: 'Owning one's own home has a status value which is more important to many couples than the physical conditions of housing' (Murphy and Sullivan, 1985, p. 230).

The relevance of all of this to the question of voting behaviour is that housing status is likely to be most important to those whose employment status position is most marginal. If one's job clearly and unambiguously places one in the middle class, then one's housing may play only a secondary role in contributing to an overall sense of social identity. But if one is in an ambiguous class position at work – that is, if one occupies an 'intermediate' class location – then other status indicators outside of work are likely to take on enhanced importance, and housing tenure will then become crucial.

It has to be admitted, however, that this is no more than a hypothesis, and evidence from the three towns survey neither supports not refutes it. If the hypothesis were true, then we should expect to find, first, that tenure affects people's sense of their own class status and, second, that this then influences the way they vote. While there is some evidence for these propositions, it is too weak to draw any firm conclusions.

As regards the first proposition, there is a slight tendency for owner-occupiers among the intermediate classes to identify more with the middle class and less with the working class than do council tenants in the same class position. Forty-one per cent of intermediate-class tenants think of themselves as 'working class', but this figure falls to 32 per cent among intermediate-class owner-occupiers. This is not, however, a strong enough pattern from which to draw any definitive conclusions. Furthermore, 37 per cent of the sample were either unable or unwilling to place themselves in any class at all, and this suggests (contrary to Marshall *et al.*, 1988) that class identities may not be central to people's social identities and may not be appropriate indicators of how people think about their own social position.

On the second proposition, the findings from the three towns survey do show that subjective class is associated with voting intention within each class grouping. For example, 29 per cent of service-class respondents who thought of themselves as 'working class' voted Labour compared with only 17 per cent of those who thought of themselves as 'middle class'. Similarly, in the intermediate classes, 50 per cent of working-class identifiers voted Labour as compared with 29 per cent of middle-class identifiers, and in the working class the equivalent figures were 69 per cent and 53 per cent. However, these variations are not statistically significant.

The question of why tenure is more strongly associated with voting among the intermediate classes than among the working class must therefore remain open. We can be fairly sure that this pattern does actually exist, for it has been documented now in several studies, but we still cannot say with any degree of certainty why it exists, although a theory couched in terms of status marginality still seems to offer the most likely explanation.

Home ownership and anti-collectivism

When it is claimed that home ownership has conservatised the working class, observers usually mean more than that working-class owner-occupiers may vote for the Conservative Party. Indeed, voting may be a poor guide to whether or not people are conservative in outlook. We may vote for a party despite rather than because of its policies, and it is probably true that millions of basically conservative people vote Labour at every election. Indeed, Williams (1988) found that Labour-voting council tenants in Aberdeen were more likely to hold right-wing views than left-wing views! For them, voting Labour was a way of defending their interests, not expressing their values.

Obviously problems arise in defining what conservative values are and thus in determining whether home owners are more conservative than tenants.

For our purposes, we shall take the conservatism thesis to refer primarily to the view that home ownership encourages a commitment to the principles of private property ownership while discouraging support for principles of collectivism and state provision. If true, this would suggest that a nation of home owners is likely to become more individualistic and more capitalistic as a direct result of the spread of owner-occupation.

This thesis has been developed most explicitly by Jim Kemeny. In his book, *The Myth of Home Ownership* (1981), Kemeny tries to show that housing tenure systems are related to systems of provision of other kinds of goods and services. Much of the argument is based on correlations across three countries – Australia, Britain and Sweden – for Kemeny is able to show that in Australia, where owner-occupancy rates are highest, welfare provision is most minimal, while in Sweden, where home ownership rates are lowest, state welfare is most fully developed. Britain in his view falls midway between the other two countries on both indicators. Although he recognizes that this pattern does not fit all countries – New Zealand, for example, has a high rate of home ownership and high welfare spending, while Switzerland scores low on both dimensions – Kemeny believes that his correlations are nevertheless genuine and are indicative of some sort of causal relation between tenure and welfare systems.

He explains this causal relationship in three ways. The first, and least interesting for our present purposes, involves the introduction into the analysis of a third, mediating variable – namely, housing design. The logic here is that housing tenure is strongly associated with different types of accommodation – houses are often owned, while flats are often rented. In a society like Sweden with a strong collectivistic political culture, many flats are constructed, since these save on infrastructure costs, whereas in more individualistic societies like Australia and Britain there is a greater emphasis on building single family houses. One result of this is that more people come to rent in Sweden, while another is that the state comes to play a more active part in providing public transport, parks, libraries, child-care facilities and so on for the more densely populated areas. In Australia, by contrast, spatial dispersal means that it is impossible to service the suburbs with anything like the same facilities. Instead, suburban home owners buy a car rather than relying on buses, and they spend time in their gardens rather than frequenting public parks. In this way, tenure, design and the level of state services all affect and reinforce each other.

Kemeny's second explanation for the association between tenure and welfare provision is more direct. He begins by noting that home ownership entails high housing costs at an early stage in the life cycle. The result of this is that young households wish both to keep taxes down (and therefore resist increases in welfare spending) and to rein in their own personal expenditure on non-essential items. This leads them to favour voluntary private schemes for health care, pensions and so on as opposed to universal state schemes which make it difficult to reduce premiums or to opt out altogether. Later in life, of course, real housing costs for those who buy tend to fall, and this releases money which can be spent on providing for old age. Furthermore, Kemeny recognizes that (as we saw in Chapter 3) owners may be able to release some or all of their housing equity so as to purchase private medical care, say, or a place in a nursing home. Home ownership thus reduces state welfare by discouraging participation in state schemes early in life while enabling participation in private schemes in later years.

Kemeny's third explanation has less to do with economics than with ideology. There is, he believes, a tendency for home ownership to foster privatized values which undermine popular commitments to state welfare: 'The wider ideological importance of tenure derives mainly from the effect

249

of different forms of tenure on the degree to which life styles and interests become privatized' (1981, p. 64). In other words, as people grow used to owning their own homes, so they are likely to become more receptive to the idea of buying their own health care or purchasing their children's schooling in the private sector.

Kemeny has not been alone in pursuing these sorts of arguments. Michael Ball, for example, supports Kemeny's suggestion that skewed housing costs in the home ownership sector are likely to affect support for state provisions for the elderly. In his view, public support for higher state pensions may be eroded by the spread of owner-occupation:

> Pressures for better state pensions . . . may be weakened by the existence of owner occupation to the benefit of capital. There is less need to save out of wages for retirement for the strata of the workforce where owner occupation is prevalent. By the age of retirement housing costs are reduced to repairs, maintenance and insurance and the retired household can 'trade down' and use the encashed money gain as an ongoing source of income.
>
> (1983, p. 365)

Similarly several observers have recently commented on the way equity release from owner-occupied housing may stimulate private consumption in areas outside of housing. Robin Means (1987) has highlighted the impact on the privatization of care for the elderly, and he charts the growing market for sheltered accommodation and for private residential homes (where numbers of beds trebled between 1975 and 1984) consequent upon the release of equity from owner-occupied housing. Papadakis and Taylor-Gooby (1987, p. 91) indicate that something similar may be happening in education. They quote the Independent Schools Information Service as claiming that 'more parents are using the equity value of owned houses to provide for fees'.

The implicit hypothesis which informs many of these observations is quite simply that, as home ownership expands, so the welfare state may be expected to contract. Kemeny himself puts it thus: 'It may well be that "collective consumption" . . . may decline in importance in some societies as commodification increases in selected but important areas such as housing' (1980, p. 385). Others have been even bolder. Stuart Lowe has no doubt that 'Some of the "new" wealth will sponsor people's flexible use of the public and private sectors of service provision. Examples include the purchase of private health care at a certain stage in treatment; the increased use of private geriatric care for the elderly . . . and the purchase of private education' (1988, p. 164). And according to the *Economist*: 'As they grow richer, many people who never dreamed of a private school for their children or a private visit to the doctor will find they can afford both . . . When more people can afford to buy advantages once regarded as the exclusive privilege of the rich few, it will become even harder to maintain support for universal state provision of education and health care' (9 April 1988, p. 14).

All of this is plausible. But is it true? One way of investigating this is to consider the evidence on the relationship between people's housing tenure and their broader political values and personal preferences as regards state- and private-sector provisions. If Kemeny's thesis is valid, then we should expect to find that home owners are less supportive than tenants of state services and that they express a stronger desire to 'exit' from the state system. Given his emphasis on the importance of housing costs in shaping these values and preferences, we should also expect to discover that younger home owners are less supportive of state services than their older counterparts for whom the costs of supporting the welfare system are less prohibitive while the gains are likely to be more immediate.

Such evidence as is available from other studies indicates that home ownership does tend to be associated with higher than average support for privatized consumption and that it may also influence people's views on more general issues concerning the role of the state in redistributing income and wealth. Williams, Sewel and Twine found in their study of Aberdeen council house buyers that purchase made no difference to the values expressed by non-manual households but that in the manual working class, buyers were 'more likely to express attitudes favourable to a privatized/ individualistic ideology than non-purchasers' (1987, pp. 280–1). Similarly, in the 1983 election study, Heath, Jowell and Curtice found that housing tenure had an effect on attitudes to privatization and income and wealth distribution which was independent of class location. Among working-class respondents, for example, 22 per cent of council tenants favoured privatization compared with 35 per cent of owner-occupiers. Similarly, 17 per cent of working-class council tenants opposed redistribution measures compared with 35 per cent of working-class home owners. From data such as these, the authors conclude that tenure does have an effect on broad political values:

> Housing seems to represent an *additional* source of influence on class values . . . Within social classes, owner-occupiers are markedly more opposed to government intervention than are council tenants. Conversely, among owner-occupiers, members of the salariat are markedly more opposed to intervention than are members of the working class. Both class and housing tenure appear to foster the same attitudes but to do so independently of the other. They may be two sources of values, but they work in much the same direction.
>
> (1985, p. 48, original emphasis)

Data from the three towns survey lend some support to this contention, but the pattern is more confused than these various authors seem to suggest. It is true that on *some* items, owner-occupiers appear less willing to support spending on state provisions, but on others they are clearly more supportive.

251

A NATION OF HOME OWNERS

Table 4.13 *Preferences between rate levels and levels of local service provision by social class and housing tenure*

	Lower rates		Better services		Don't know		Other answers		Total	
	No.	*%*	*No.*	*%*	*No.*	*%*	*No.*	*%*	*No.*	*%*
Service class										
Total	26	23	59	52	17	15	12	10	114	100
Intermediate class										
Owner-occupiers	31	27	57	50	18	16	7	6	113	83
Council tenants	1	4	17	71	5	21	1	4	24	17
Total	32	23	74	54	23	17	8	6	137	100
Working class										
Owner-occupiers	32	25	71	56	24	19	1	1	128	61
Council tenants	12	15	55	66	12	15	4	4	83	40
Total	44	21	126	60	36	17	5	2	211	100

Notes: Service-class respondents have not been divided by tenure since all but four of them are owner-occupiers. Most of those giving 'other answers' argued that efficiency should be increased so as to improve services without raising rates.

Furthermore, a tenure effect sometimes appears only among members of certain social classes.

The clearest tenure effects can be found in the way our respondents answered general questions about taxation and state spending. For example, we asked how they would vote if a local referendum were held offering the choice between higher rates (local property taxes – this was before rates were replaced by the flat-rate Community Charge) with improved services and lower rates with poorer services. The answers, summarized in Table 4.13, demonstrate that, while a majority in all classes and tenures said that they favoured improved services, tenants were slightly more strongly opposed to rate reductions than owners were.

One obvious explanation for this tenure effect is that owner-occupiers pay rates as a separate item in the household budget, whereas council tenants pay a consolidated sum to the local authority to cover both rent and rates. The size of the rates bill is thus more immediately apparent to owners, and this may explain why just 12 per cent of all tenants favoured lower rates as compared with 25 per cent of all owners.

A second general question concerned our respondents' views on government policies aimed at reducing expenditure on the welfare state. Again we found apparently strong opposition to service reductions, while opposition was at its strongest among working-class people and council tenants. Like Heath, Jowell and Curtice, therefore, we may conclude from this that tenure and class reinforce each other, for opposition to 'cuts' is greater among tenants than among owners within each class, and is greater among working-class than among intermediate-class respondents across both tenures (Table 4.14).

This pattern, however, becomes confused when we turn to consider what

252

Table 4.14 *Views on cuts in welfare spending by social class and housing tenure*

	Support cuts		Qualified support		View on cuts Oppose cuts		No opinion		Total	
	No.	%	No.	%	No.	%	No.	%	No.	%
Service class										
Total	11	10	18	16	79	71	4	4	112	100
Intermediate class										
Owner-occupiers	13	12	14	12	77	68	9	8	113	80
Council tenants	1	4	0	0	26	90	2	7	29	20
Total	14	10	14	10	103	73	11	8	142	100
Working class										
Owner-occupiers	8	7	4	3	101	82	10	8	123	58
Council tenants	3	3	1	1	79	90	5	6	88	42
Total	11	5	5	2	180	85	15	7	211	100

Notes: Service-class respondents have not been divided by tenure since only four of them are council tenants. Most of those giving 'qualified support' argued either that cuts are a 'necessary evil', or that cuts were justified in some areas but not in others.

people say about particular areas of state spending. In the course of the three towns survey we investigated people's preferences as between private- and public-sector provision of services such as health care and education and found that many people appear to have somewhat ambivalent attitudes. Many of our informants, for example, say that they would like private health insurance and would support a policy which enabled them to 'contract out' of the National Health Service, yet the same people are also quite likely to say that they are relatively happy with the treatment they have received under the NHS and that they would be willing to pay higher taxes to improve state provision in this area. A similar pattern also emerges in answers to questions about schooling. I have analysed this apparent ambivalence in detail elsewhere (Saunders and Harris, 1989) and shall not repeat that analysis here. The question to be addressed here is simply whether housing tenure appears to influence the way people answer these questions.

If Kemeny's thesis were correct, we should expect home owners to favour private health insurance and private schooling more strongly than tenants do. In fact, no such pattern emerges.

Asked whether they would be prepared to pay higher taxes to enable state expenditure on education to be increased, for example, there was little difference in the replies of owners and tenants in either the working or intermediate classes. Fifty-two per cent of intermediate-class owners agreed with the idea as compared with 43 per cent of intermediate-class tenants, 53 per cent of working-class owners and 61 per cent of working-class tenants. It is difficult to detect in these figures any marked tenure or social class effect.

Even more confusing are our respondents' attitudes to health-care provision. Here there is no tenure effect within the working class – 30 per cent of working-class owners and 28 per cent of working-class tenants say they would not be willing to pay higher taxes in order to enable more to be spent on the National Health Service, while 48 per cent of owners and 53 per cent of tenants say that they would be prepared to pay some (unspecified) extra amount. Within the intermediate class, however, there is a weak tenure difference in people's answers on this question, but counter-intuitively, it is council tenants who are most reluctant to see taxes raised. Thus, 27 per cent of intermediate-class owners would not be willing to pay more in tax to support NHS spending, yet this proportion rises to 45 per cent among intermediate-class tenants. Similarly, 53 per cent of intermediate-class owners would pay more in tax compared with only 38 per cent of tenants in this class.

A similarly surprising pattern emerges from people's answers to a question on whether there should be a right to 'contract out' of NHS payments for those who would prefer to take out private insurance. Again, there is not much difference in people's replies among working-class respondents (38 per cent of working-class owners and 35 per cent of working-class tenants oppose the idea), but in the intermediate class we find a marked and significant ($p < 0.01$) tenure effect. Thus, while 48 per cent of intermediate-class owners oppose contracting out and 43 per cent support it, the proportions among intermediate-class tenants are 17 and 67 per cent respectively.

Two points of interest emerge from these answers on health policy. One is that the tenure effect, where it exists, operates in the opposite direction to that posited by the Kemeny thesis and revealed by more general questions on taxation and state spending. The other is that the tenure effect only seems to be operating within the intermediate class.

Earlier in this chapter we found that the significance of housing tenure in influencing voting was almost certainly limited to the intermediate class. A similar pattern can now be seen to have emerged in respect of attitudes to certain aspects of state provisioning, and this again supports Pratt's view that class and tenure interact and that tenure may have its most significant political impact among the intermediate or 'lower middle' classes. As she puts it, 'Housing tenure tends to be related to a wide range of attitudes for skilled white collar workers and managers but unrelated to political attitudes for skilled blue collar workers' (1987b, p. 46). To the extent that this is the case (and we really require much more evidence drawn from larger samples than this one before we can treat it as anything more than a plausible hypothesis), then it would seem to undermine Kemeny's claim that home ownership weakens support for state welfare.

Kemeny's thesis is also undermined by the lack of any relationship between size of mortgage payments and support for private provision of other services. As noted earlier, Kemeny believes that the high cost of mortgages in the early years of owner-occupation is likely to encourage house buyers to seek to reduce expenditure on social provisions and to favour low tax programmes and optional private welfare schemes. There is, however, no evidence to support this idea. If this explanation were valid then we should expect to find that those with the highest repayments are the least inclined to support state welfare services or to vote for parties associated with high public expenditure. In fact, we find no relationship between the size of mortgage payments and political alignment. In the three towns sample of working-class home owners, for example, 44 per cent of those paying £50 per month or less voted Labour, but so did 46 per cent of those paying £200 per month or more. Similarly in her work in Canada, Pratt found no evidence to support Kemeny's hypothesis that it is their housing costs which lead home owners to withdraw support for state collectivism. There is, for example, no relation between housing cost and views on state policy and expenditure – indeed, those home owners with the highest debt tended to be *most* supportive of government assistance to the poor and of government spending on health and medical care.

Kemeny's thesis cannot, therefore, be supported. To the extent that there is an association between owner-occupation and anti-statist views on social policy questions, it is probably better explained as a reflection of the values of home owners rather than their pragmatism. In other words, it is not shortage of money in the early years which leads owner-occupiers to desire private solutions in other areas of their consumption needs, but it is rather a commitment to general values of autonomy and free choice of which ownership of a house is but one expression.

Home ownership and political mobilization

Home owners do not vote distinctively, nor do they subscribe to a specific set of anti-collectivist political values. Housing tenure does seem to be associated with right-wing voting and with anti-collectivist sentiment among members of intermediate classes, but its influence in the working class is minimal.

There is, however, one area of political life where tenure divisions may become significant across all social classes, and that is in housing policy itself. There is now very strong evidence to suggest that home owners form a distinct and crucial interest in the politics of housing at both local and national levels.

Even this has sometimes been denied, for it has been suggested that tenure is a poor rallying cry for political mobilization because of the lack of any identifiable political opponents. As Alan Warde and his colleagues put it: 'Interests arising out of consumption location are less likely to lead to political mobilization than ones arising out of class position . . . Because of the lack of any clear antagonist, it is more difficult for people to organize around interests deriving from housing tenure' (1987, p. 21). The evidence, however, does not bear this out.

It is true that in the three towns survey, organizations of tenants on council estates were more common than residents' organizations in owner-occupied areas. While 46 per cent of tenants said there was no organization in their neighbourhood, 71 per cent of owner-occupiers reported this, and this would seem to suggest that home ownership does not generate cohesive political organization. However, the greater presence of tenants' organizations is simply explained by the fact that local authorities often encourage and even help in the establishment of such groups on council estates. Residents' associations, by contrast, will only form where householders themselves feel the need to organize in order to express their collective interests. The critical question, therefore, is not whether an organization exists but whether local people bother to join it, and here my findings reveal a very different story.

Of those respondents living in areas where there was a local organization, only 10 per cent of tenants belonged to it compared with 51 per cent of owners. Nor can this be explained as a class effect, for the pattern is reproduced among intermediate-class (14 per cent and 50 per cent respectively) and working-class (8 per cent and 41 per cent) households. Home ownership thus encourages and facilitates widespread participation in local organizations representing householders' interests, but council renting seems to inhibit it.

In Britain and in other countries, home owners frequently act in concert against what they see as a perceived threat to their common interests. In his study of the American working class, Halle suggests that politics come to be segmented between the concerns of work, home and nation and that in issues concerning housing and the local neighbourhood, home owners mobilize on the basis of their tenure, not their class. He writes:

> The situation I have presented makes possible a variety of politics based on issues at work, in the residential setting and in relation to the nation state . . . Outside work, blue collar homeowners, like most American homeowners, will become involved in a 'politics of homeownership' centring on an identity as middle or lower middle class, and on issues such as the level of property taxes, the quality of the items these taxes fund (the school system, local police and fire services) and the quality of the neighbourhood and township, especially insofar as this affects the value of their houses.
>
> (1984, pp. 301–2)

In Halle's view, therefore, a class solidarism at work may go hand in hand with a tenure-based conservatism at home. As pluralist theories have long realized, we all occupy a number of different roles which give us different sets of interests to pursue or defend according to the situation. What Halle has found is simply that no one of these roles is hegemonic. In the workplace our class role is dominant, but in the locality our housing role is likely to come to the fore. In work-based conflicts over wages or conditions of employment we may exhibit a strong sense of class solidarism which then disappears altogether when we get home and find that our neighbourhood is 'threatened' with invasion by low income groups. Similarly many of us are quite capable of resisting higher taxation in our role as workers while at the same time demanding higher state spending in our role as citizens. There is no paradox in such responses. They simply reflect the fact that we are capable of recognizing many sets of interests, and our interests as members of a particular class are only one of them.

In their capacity as home owners, therefore, we should expect people to reveal a keen interest in local issues which affect their domestic property holdings. As Robson observes, 'The local residential environment provides the most common locus of conflict within the city not simply because residential areas comprise the largest single land use, but because of the strong commitment which people have to the immediate area in which they live, a commitment which is reinforced in the case of the owner-occupier by a very direct financial vested interest' (1982, p. 45). It follows from this that there is likely to develop a distinctive 'politics of home ownership' which revolves around the desire to defend current use values and future exchange values.

This argument has been challenged, but the counter-argument is far from persuasive. In his study of Columbus, Ohio, Cox (1982; see also Cox and McCarthy, 1982) found that home owners were more likely than tenants to get involved in local defensive groups, but he explained this not in terms of defence of property values but rather as due to problems entailed in moving. Tenants, he argued, do not organize because if an area begins to change it is easy for them to move away (this, of course, is less true of the British situation and is certainly not true of council tenants in Britain, who are highly immobile). Owners, by contrast, may find it difficult to sell up and move because of prohibitive transaction costs and other obstacles, so they are more likely to stand and fight.

In fact, it seems not to matter whether Cox's analysis is right or wrong, for the result amounts to the same thing. Whether owners mobilize to defend their investment or whether they mobilize because it is difficult to sell up is hardly important. Some owners will seek to defend their investment, others will act so as to avoid the costs of moving; but in both cases, home owners will recognize a common cause grounded in shared economic interests and will act accordingly. As Harris and Hamnett suggest, all the evidence indicates that owner-occupiers tend to act at neighbourhood level like 'militant conservatives' in defence of their property interests (1987, p. 175).

At local level, the issues which tend to spark off home-owner mobilization are those concerned with local taxation and changes in local land uses (see Agnew, 1981, p. 473; Young and Kramer, 1978, p. 240). In a previous publication (Saunders, 1979) I have reviewed a number of studies of local home-owner mobilization around these issues, and I have also reported my own analysis of the power and influence exerted by suburban owner-occupiers in the London Borough of Croydon who successfully organized to maintain low property taxes and low housing densities in their areas. More recently, Lowe (1986) has shown how tenure divisions form the basis of mobilization for many urban movements in Britain and how ratepayer parties can still attract substantial electoral support by addressing the specific interests and concerns of home owners. Indeed, in recent years the specific issue of residential densities and new building has spilled over into national politics in Britain where it has split the Conservative Party between those who defend the property privileges of existing owner-occupiers in the South-East and those who side with the development industry in seeking to open up new sites for housing.

This 'spillage' of the local politics of home ownership on to the national stage should not surprise us, for although explicit political organization by owner-occupiers is less in evidence nationally than locally, home owners still have a significant impact on national politics. As Pawley notes, 'Home owners today are figures of far greater political and economic importance than private landlords ever were: their combined voting power not only determines the housing policy of all governments, but settles the outcome of all general elections' (1978, p. 7).

Nowhere is this clearer than in respect of government policy on housing subsidies. We saw earlier that nearly one in ten voters at the general election in 1979 cited housing as the most important issue influencing their vote. This was at a time when, with the exception of council house sales, the parties fundamentally agreed on basic issues of housing policy. The figure would arguably be much higher if this agreement ever broke down and the privileges of owner-occupation (mortgage interest tax relief and exemption from Capital Gains Tax) were seriously threatened by a major political party.

Most politicians seem convinced that they cannot attack the tax privileges of owner-occupiers without sacrificing significant political support. Margaret Thatcher, who built her reputation as an 'iron lady' by confronting vested interests, was described as 'timorously conservative' when it came to reform of mortgage tax relief (the *Independent*, 13 June 1987), and Labour leaders are said to be convinced of the political impossibility of introducing reform in this area (Ball, 1985, p. 20). Twice in recent years, opposition politicians (Shirley Williams in 1981 and Michael Meacher in 1985) have floated the idea of phasing out mortgage interest tax relief, and twice they have hastily withdrawn it. The Treasury would dearly love to save the £5 billion per annum which this subsidy is now costing, and most Thatcherite politicians deplore the distortion in the housing market which the subsidy causes, yet Britain's Conservative governments have firmly resisted any such move. When the Treasury recently floated the idea of levying Capital Gains Tax on house sales, the chairman of the Conservative Party's finance committee in the House of Commons responded, 'The Tory party will oppose this tooth and nail – they will never get away with it. It would be political suicide' (*Sunday Times*, 10 July 1988).

Most academic observers of the political scene endorse the politicians' caution. Hamnett describes any attempt to reduce mortgage tax relief as 'the political kiss of death to any party' (1983, p. 11). Donnison and Ungerson suggest that 'No party which intends to win an election will suddenly or completely withdraw tax relief on mortgage interest or reimpose a Schedule A tax' (1982, p. 228). Stuart Lowe tells us that 'Parties openly advocating this sort of reform stand to lose millions of votes' (1988, p. 157). And Martin Daunton says that 'It has become very difficult for any government to challenge the principles of taxation upon which commitments have been based' (1987, p. 86). Only Michael Ball has queried this consensus by arguing that a left-wing government could get away with abolishing tax relief if this were coupled to nationalization of the land and the building industry, but this sounds more like utopian withful thinking than serious analysis (Ball, 1983, pp. 11–12).

The three towns survey reveals widespread support for mortgage interest tax relief among tenants as well as owner-occupiers (Table 4.15), although predictably, the strongest support comes from those who are actually paying mortgages and the least support comes from those who rent their homes. This pattern emerges in both the intermediate and working classes and it suggests that politicians are probably right to worry about the electoral implications of taking on the owner-occupiers.

Table 4.15 *Views on mortgage interest tax relief by tenure*

| | Opinion on tax relief | | | | | | | | | |
| | Support | | Oppose | | Ambivalent | | No opinion | | Total | |
Tenure	No.	%	No.	%	No.	%	No.	%	No.	%
Outright owners	70	67	1	1	18	17	15	14	104	22
Buying on mortgage	182	79	12	5	25	11	12	5	231	50
Council tenants	81	63	11	9	19	15	18	14	129	28

N = 464
$p < 0.01$

Does this mean that owner-occupiers are the hidden force in British politics? It does seem that, on certain sensitive housing issues, they are the interest which cannot be challenged. Their power resides in a 'mobilization of bias' and a process of anticipated reactions by governments which ensures that they do not have to flex their collective muscle. For as long as they are seen as unchallengeable, they will not be challenged, and in consequence they will not need to demonstrate their political clout. As Peter Williams observes:

> While there can be no doubt that home ownership is a political issue, its impact on political outcomes is complex and varied . . . There is little evidence of home owners acting in concert to achieve gains through the state. Government commitment and consensus on home ownership has meant that such campaigns have rarely been necessary. We can observe, however, the consequences of neglecting home owner interests . . . This suggests that groups of owners, albeit in the form of numerous

individuals, may act to express their dissatisfaction at elections.

(1984, p. 187)

Similarly, Fred Gray suggests that 'During the post-war period, the majority of home owners have not seen their material housing conditions threatened . . . In general, then, home owners have had little need to engage in housing protest since their material housing conditions have not been threatened' (1982, pp. 280–1).

Most politicians, then, *believe* that the home-owner interest is too strong to be attacked, and this is the source of home owners' power at national level. But what if the bluff were called? What would happen? Could the home-owner vote on a key housing issue swing a general election?

This is, of course, an extremely difficult question to answer. Geraldine Pratt (1986a, 1986b) has attempted to provide a few clues through analysis of her interviews with Canadian home owners. She found that a substantial number of owner-occupiers (52 per cent of her sample) would be willing to change their vote purely on the basis of housing policy (many wanted the introduction of tax concessions on the US model). From this Pratt concluded, 'In the contemporary Canadian context, homeowners (particularly those classified as skilled nonmanual) tend to recognize their interests as homeowners and are keen to pursue these interests through the electoral process' (1986b, p. 177). However, answers to hypothetical questions like this may not be very valid, for there is a long history in sociological research of people saying one thing and doing another.

The truth is that we do not know what impact it would have on voting patterns if one party were to launch an attack on the tax privileges of owner-occupiers. Most people, including most owner-occupiers, are politically apathetic. They have other things in their lives which are more important to them than worrying about political issues or political philosophies. In Glasgow, Madigan found that a majority of new home buyers were 'either uncommitted or ambivalent' (1988, p. 50). On the Isle of Sheppey, Pahl found that 'It was difficult to raise any interest in broader political questions with most people and turn-out at local and national elections was characteristically low' (1984, p. 326). And so too in the three towns survey, most people knew little and cared less about the great political issues of the day.

The question, however, is whether a direct attack on their financial privileges as home owners would be enough to galvanize this quiet majority into concerted and effective action. As Pahl points out, their antipathy towards organized politics often contrasts sharply with their enthusiastic activity around the home. What, then, if the financial basis of this home life were threatened? Given the response at local level when owner-occupiers are threatened, we may suppose that there would be a general sense of outrage if any government ever did move to withdraw tax advantages, but could this opposition by mobilized effectively as a voting block? It will take a brave and committed political party to find out.

Conclusions

It has long been supposed by left and right alike that home ownership tends to conservatize people. This belief has been fed over the last twenty or thirty years as electoral support for the Labour Party has ebbed away at the same time as home ownership has spread among the party's traditional working-class constituency. But are these two trends related?

We have seen in this chapter that three plausible explanations can be put forward for the absolute decline in the level of working-class support for the Labour Party. One is that the working class has changed – for example, it has become more affluent and has lost interest in collectivistic strategies for improving its material circumstances. A second is that the Labour Party has changed – for example, it has lost sight of the issues which are important to its traditional supporters and has forfeited their votes as a result. And a third is that new bases of political alignment have emerged which are cutting across older class allegiances. The belief that home ownership undermines socialist commitment is one example of this third type of explanation, but it is not the only one. An alternative explanation has been offered by Dunleavy, who suggests that production- and consumption-sector cleavages have become increasingly significant in structuring political alignments.

It is possible that all three arguments are valid, but in this chapter we have considered only the third. Dunleavy's version of this argument was rejected, however, for it is susceptible to both theoretical critique and empirical disconfirmation. His analysis is premissed upon an unsupportable theory of ideology; the additive index by which he operationalizes the concept of 'consumption sector' is a crudely empiricist device of little sociological validity; sectoral locations are not mutually exclusive; some of the consumption issues which are fundamental to his index (such as transport policy) have a low political saliency; his use of the method of odds ratios exaggerates the degree of association between sectoral cleavages and voting; and other studies have in any case failed to find a consumption-sector effect when they have controlled for the political significance of social class. Furthermore, testing Dunleavy's theory against data from the three towns survey, we found that, apart from housing, individual consumption variables such as car ownership or membership of a private health insurance scheme were not significant in shaping voting behaviour (although they did have some apparent impact when taken together).

In place of Dunleavy's theory of consumption sectors, it has been suggested that we focus specifically on the significance of housing tenure divisions. Empirical evidence demonstrates that the division between home owners and council tenants is by far the most significant consumption factor associated with voting behaviour. This is not because of the play of dominant ideologies, as Dunleavy claims, but because owners and tenants have different interests which can lead them to support different political parties and to develop different sets of political opinions and values.

All studies support some sort of relationship between tenure and voting, even when controlling for the effects of social class. That this is likely to be a *causal* relationship is indicated by evidence on voting shifts among recent council house buyers. However, most evidence also suggests that tenure is only a secondary effect and that social class remains the primary basis of political cleavages. In the three towns survey, for example, multiple regression and log-linear modelling suggests that the association between class and voting virtually eclipses that between tenure and voting.

This does not mean that home ownership has no political significance, but it does mean that the conservatism thesis needs to be specified much more carefully and that we need to consider the political saliency of housing tenure for people occupying different locations in the social order. In particular, it seems that tenure divisions have their major impact on the socially marginal 'intermediate classes'. It is the white-collar workers and the self-employed who seem most likely to shift their vote when they change their tenure. It is also this same stratum which appears most likely to embrace an anti-collectivist ethos when it moves from renting to owning. If, therefore, the spread of home ownership has had any kind of conservatizing influence, it has been concentrated in the lower middle class rather than the working class. This may be explained by the status marginality of this particular stratum, but such a hypothesis must remain speculative at this stage.

Although voting is important, it is only one isolated aspect of political behaviour. In the final section of this chapter we turned briefly to explore broader questions of political mobilization and we saw that home owners have often organized effectively at local level in defence of their property interests while at national level they are seen by politicians in all parties as a voting block whose privileges cannot be challenged. This suggests that the most dramatic political effects of the growth of home ownership in Britain are revealed in conflicts over housing policy issues. For as long as various agencies of government do not threaten to build a road through their back gardens, or to locate a new council estate in their neighbourhoods, or to remove their tax subsidies, home owners are unlikely to vote as a block, or to endorse a common set of political values, or to organize and mobilize in defence of their shared interests. Left alone to enjoy the privileges of their property, home owners appear as a politically mixed and heterogeneous group. It is only if and when they are challenged that their other political interests and identities fall away and tenure comes to the fore as a common basis for political activity.

5 A home of one's own

The home is one of the core institutions of modern British society. It is the place where we are reared when we are young and in which we tenaciously try to remain when we grow old and frail. In the years in between, home is the place which we 'make' for ourselves, for the definition of maturity in our culture is bound up with the movement out of the parental home into one of our own. It is also the place where we spend most of our lives. We usually start each day from home and end the day by returning to it. It is the fixed place in our lives, a place of familiar routine. Sometimes we experience these routines as tedious and irksome, and we are glad to get away from home for a 'break', but domestic routines can also be a source of comfort and reassurance. When we return from time away we tell ourselves that it is 'nice to be back in our own home'.

The Australian sociologist Hugh Stretton has listed some of the factors which make the home so central to everyday life in modern industrial societies. 'In affluent societies,' he writes,

> much more than half of all waking time is spent at home or near it. More than a third of capital is invested there. More than one-third of work is done there. Depending on what you choose to count as goods, some high proportion of all goods are produced there, and even more are enjoyed there. More than three-quarters of all subsistence, social life, leisure and recreation happen there. Above all, people are produced there and endowed there with the values and capacities which will determine most of the quality of their social life and government away from home . . . It is in the activities of home, neighbourhood and voluntary association that there is . . . the best opportunit[y] for cooperative, generous, self-expressive, *unalienated* work and life.
>
> (1976, p. 183, original emphasis)

Home, in other words, is a key unit of production as well as of consumption. It is a place where various forms of work get done, but it is also a place where we may expect to experience a sense of personal autonomy and freedom.

The central importance of the home in our lives is reflected in the evolution of dozens of clichés, homilies, poems and songs through which we construct and recognize its meaning. Home is a place of independence ('An Englishman's home is his castle'); it is a place of emotional significance ('Home is where the heart is'); it is a unique and personal place ('There's no place like home'); it is a place of warmth and security to which we hope to return ('Keep the home fires burning'). The catalogue of such 'home truths' and 'homespun philosophies' seems endless and bears testimony to the felt need of generations of people to give expression to common sentiments which attach to and arise out of the process of producing and consuming a home.

Home, however, may have a negative as well as a positive connotation, and it has attracted its critics as well as its admirers. Precisely because the home is so central to modern social life, it has become the object of acrimonious argument and political dispute between warring factions. People who see modern society in different ways almost inevitably come to evaluate the home differently too.

Socialists, for example, have often seen the home as an anachronistic obstacle to the fulfilment of collectivism. In communes and kibbutzim, attempts have been made to break down the division between the private world of the home and the public world of 'civil society', for as Lenin recognized, the private realm poses a recurring threat to a collectivistic social order. Socialist critics are supported in their hostility by many present-day *feminists* who see the home as the locus of gender domination, the place where relations of patriarchy are reproduced on a daily basis. For these feminist critics, images of warmth and security commonly associated with 'home and hearth' are male myths which serve to obscure the subordination and servility of women. For most women, it is claimed, the home is a place of drudgery, and for some (as for some children) it is also a place of violence and fear.

Ranged against these various critics are equally passionate supporters of home life and the things it represents. *Liberals*, for example, have generally emphasized the importance of the home as the cornerstone of individual liberty and autonomy, a place where people can still do what they want and fend for themselves. For them, the home represents a last bastion of freedom in opposition to the persistent encroachment of state power in the modern world. Similarly, *conservatives* generally emphasize the positive value of home and family life in inculcating and reproducing traditional values of duty to others, self-discipline, respect for property and authority and observance of moral codes which have proved their worth down the generations.

The home, then, is a political battleground. Its imagery is contested, and its character is disputed. Rarely, however, are these arguments informed by evidence. Assertions are traded against counter-assertions with little regard for what ordinary people feel and say about their homes.

In this chapter, we shall consider what home means to people in Britain today. In particular, given our interest in owner-occupation, we shall consider whether owning a home leads people to feel any differently about the place they live in than those who rent. We shall also evaluate the feminist claim that home may represent a sanctuary for men but is a place of work and subordination for women. First, though, it is important briefly to consider what it is we are referring to when we talk of 'home'.

More than bricks and mortar

The word 'home' seems to carry many different meanings in the English language. It may refer to a specific building, but it can also refer to a town ('my home town') or even to a nation state ('my homeland'). During the Second World War, units of part-time soldiers made up the 'Home Guard', but they were defending the whole country, not just their own houses. Similarly, the 'Home Secretary' is that cabinet minister whose responsibilities focus on internal affairs of state, and he has nothing to do with housing, which is the portfolio of an altogether different minister (Tuan, 1971, p. 189). Unlike in French and Spanish, therefore, it is possible to refer to one's home in English without making any reference to the house in which one lives (Sopher, 1979, p. 130).

According to Hayward (1975), the ambiguity and confusion surrounding the idea of 'home' in the English language arose at the time of rapid urbanization during the seventeenth and eighteenth centuries. Before that, 'home' referred simply to one's place of birth. It could be a village or a country, but what defined it was its natal significance. The meaning of the term was broadened two or three hundred years ago when people's work became dissociated from their places of residence. The separation of the workplace from the domestic sphere then gave rise to the idea of home as the place from which one ventured out to engage in paid labour. The home thus came to be seen as the antithesis to work. In particular, it became associated with a special quality of social relationships. Where people were calculative at work, they were affectionate at home. Work offered 'cold comforts', while home offered the warmth of the hearth and the cosiness of the family unit.

Today, the image of 'home' combines the idea of a particular place – the house in which we live – with the idea of a particular set of social relationships and emotions. As we shall see later, the relationships which are normally associated with home are those based on family ties – home is the place where one's family resides. The two images are intimately interrelated: 'Home may be conceptualized as a social unit with an emphasis on the family' (Hayward, 1975, p. 8). This association is found in many cultures. Perin tells us that in the United States, 'A sacred quality endows both the family and its "home", sacred in the sense of being set apart from the mundane and having a distinctive aura' (1977, p. 47). Gullestad suggests that in Norway, 'For each of the spouses their home symbolizes their identity as members of their particular independent family' (1983, p. 97). And in Britain too, 'The home is the focus of the family unit, the focus for eating and sleeping and loving and caring' (Oliver, Davis and Bentley, 1981, p. 16).

In reality, of course, not all homes entail social units based upon family ties. The nuclear family consisting of husband, wife and dependent children makes up only 29 per cent of all households in Britain today, and the fastest growing household type is that consisting of single people (*Social Trends*,

1988). Important as it undoubtedly is, the family is therefore only one type of household structure. The irreducible social unit on which home life is based has to be understood, not as the family, but as the household.

If the home is the core institution in our society, then the household is its distinctive form of organization. As Ray Pahl has demonstrated, a strong case can be made for arguing that the household is the most basic unit of social organization in the modern world: 'It seems to me to be self-evident that social, cultural and biological reproduction are the central social processes of society and that the household has been the basic instrument for achieving such reproduction at least since the thirteenth century' (1984, pp. 328–9). It is as members of households that we engage in various forms of work, participate in various budgetary strategies and co-operate in resolving problems and crises. Each household is in this sense a 'society in miniature' with its own system of authority, its own mode of production and its own traditions and way of life.

Of course, no household is an island. There is a permeable membrane between the household unit and the wider society, and resources, people and ideas pass constantly between the two. The home may be a castle, but the drawbridge is forever being lowered as household members venture out to shop, earn money, go to school or seek entertainment, while agencies of the 'outside world' pass in the opposite direction and penetrate the home through the television set, the telephone, the letter box and the front door.

The interface between the household and the wider society is a critical boundary in social life, for it marks the distinction between private and public, self and society, the individual and the state. The dark image of the 'knock on the door in the middle of the night' is so terrifying precisely because it negates our belief in the sanctity of our own homes. It is because this boundary is so critical that we have evolved so many rules and rituals marking it out and governing its traversal. We make the boundary as visible and unambiguous as possible by means of fences, porches, privet hedges, gates and net curtains. We then maintain the boundary by observing and enforcing norms regarding 'dropping in', 'good neighbourliness' and so on. There are usually clear rules which govern when people may call, whether they may expect to be invited across the threshold and where in the home they may be received. When we intrude uninvited, such as through a telephone call, we often open the interaction with an apology (we are sorry for disturbing someone at home).

The outside of the house is, then, a barrier of enormous symbolic importance. It is also an identifier which is used to signify to others (and to ourselves) what kind of people we are. The stone-clad walls, the mock-Tudor ornamentation, the stained glass or leaded lights, the brass carriage lamp and the gravel driveway all denote rich shades of meaning to occupant and outsider alike (see Chapman, 1955; Oliver, Davis and Bentley, 1981). The home is a symbolic as well as a material environment: 'Not only is it a place, but it has psychological resonance and social meaning. It is part of the experience of dwelling – something we do, a way of weaving up a life in particular geographical spaces' (Saegert, noted in Lawrence, 1987, p. 155).

It seems likely that dwellings have always represented more than just a means of shelter and personal defence. Mumford, for example, suggests in his history of the city that 'Even in the crudest neolithic village, the house was always more than mere shelter for the physical body: it was the meeting place of a household; its hearth was a centre of religious ceremony as well as an aid to cooking; it was the home of the household god and the locus of a family's being, a repository of moral values not measurable in money' (1961, p. 256). Similarly, Rapoport suggests that 'Very early in recorded time the house became more than shelter for primitive man, and almost from the beginning "function" was much more than a physical or utilitarian concept' (1969, p. 46).

Sociologists and anthropologists have long recognized that symbols play a crucial role in human action and communication. Language itself is symbolic, but so too is much of the environment in which we move. It would not, therefore, be surprising to find that the home provides a set of powerful symbols which may influence our behaviour and our thinking.

Research on this question is still in its infancy. Nevertheless, it is clear that different kinds of designs and spatial arrangements do affect social relations. Alice Coleman (1985) gives one example of this when she shows how children brought up on open-plan estates may find it difficult to understand or recognize boundaries between public and personal space. Fences are not just physical barriers which keep dogs in and people out, but are symbolic markers which convey and reproduce the idea of self and other, private and public.

Because it is symbolically significant, our housing should not be treated simply as a backdrop to our actions, for our actions to some extent reflect the way we are housed. Take, for example, the classic single family house. Most of us aspire to this kind of accommodation and most of us have been brought up in it ourselves. However, the physical form of this type of house constrains and influences the kinds of social arrangements which can successfully be organized within it. For example, each single family house is designed on the expectation that one member of the household will cook for the others – hence every house has its own kitchen, and kitchens are often too small to accommodate several people working at one time. When these houses come to be occupied by unconventional households (such as students sharing), it is normally necessary either to change the physical lay-out (for example, by converting bedrooms into bed-sitters) or to conventionalize the household's life-style (for example, so that one person takes responsibility each day for cooking for everyone else).

What this example illustrates is that households not only reshape their housing, but their housing in a sense helps shape the household. Put another way, there is an interplay between the physical environment of the house and the social activity of the household. Rapoport captures this idea when he defines the home as a 'social unit of space' (1969, p. 46). But it is

Anthony Giddens who has most fully elaborated upon it by identifying the home as a 'locale'.

Giddens defines a 'locale' as 'A physical region involved as part of the setting of interaction, having definite boundaries which help to concentrate interaction in one way or another' (1984, p. 375). The home, he says, is one such locale, for social life within the home comes to be expressed in and expressive of the physical environment of the house. The house, in other words, is not simply the container within which households live their lives, but is the medium through which these lives are realized. The relations between husbands and wives, parents and children, householders and visitors are all sustained and reproduced through the physical setting in which they are situated. Put simply, the setting is part of the interaction (see Giddens, 1984, p. 118; Williams, 1986, p. 248).

At one level, Giddens's observations appear banal. He makes the obvious point, for example, that different parts of the home are reserved for different types of activities; cooking is confined to the kitchen, bathing to the bathroom and sleeping to the bedrooms. But he is also saying more than this, for these situated activities are structured by social roles. Take, for example, North America, where Suttles (1972, pp. 178–9) tells us that the 'master bedroom' is generally out of bounds to children, that the kitchen is a feminine world, while the garage is a masculine preserve, that the living room is the place for entertaining visitors, and so on. Similarly, Altman and Chemers note that the inside of the American home is generally identified as female, while the outside is male:

> Much of the home in middle class American society has the stamp of the female's personality. In fact, visitors usually discuss the qualities of the home with the woman and compliment her on them, since it is known that her energies, imagination and uniqueness are displayed in the interior decor and design. The converse seems to be true for the outside of the American home which is generally recognized as the domain of the senior male.
>
> (1980, p. 192)

Gender divisions, in other words, are expressed and sustained in the physical organization of the house.

Such matters are normally taken for granted. Indeed, we even have sayings and proverbs to reinforce their 'normality': a woman's place is in the home, a woman's work is never done, and so on. But Giddens argues that it is precisely because we take for granted the ways in which we order and use our domestic environments that they play such an important role in social affairs. He believes that the social world is reproduced through routine interaction embedded within physical settings. Our lives follow routine 'time–space paths' which allow us to know with a reasonable degree of certainty which people we are likely to encounter at which times in which places and how we are expected to behave towards them. We rarely have to stop and think about what we are doing, still less why we are doing it. So it is that 'social reproduction' is accomplished almost without our realizing it.

For Giddens, the home is a key aspect of this process of social reproduction. Home life is highly routinized: 'Home is a place where every day is multiplied by days before it' (Stark, quoted by Tuan, 1974, p. 242). Men and women, adults and children, live out their lives by discharging familiar roles in familiar situations – the wife in the kitchen, the husband in the garden, the children sent to bed at a specific time, and so on. In the course of following these routines, we continually recreate them. Every time a woman prepares a meal in the kitchen while her husband potters around in the garden shed, they help reproduce not only their own domestic division of labour, but also the pattern of gender relations in the wider society beyond the garden gate.

It is not only gender relations which come to be reproduced in and through the home. A key organizing principle of the home is the distinction between front and back regions (Goffman, 1959), and this helps structure social relations in terms of status and authority differences. The front of the house is a place of display, and different kinds of people use the front and back entrances – 'domestics, delivery men and children' enter through the rear, while the front is reserved for adult members of the household and their guests' (Goffman, 1959, p. 123). The 'front room' has traditionally been reserved for the entertainment of visitors and may rarely be used at other times, while the kitchen is normally sited at the back of the house away from the public gaze, reflecting the lowly status of domestic work and those who perform it (Williams, 1986, p. 265).

Of course, times change, and housing design changes with them. In many ways it is possible to chart social change in the architectural history of the home. Large families, for example, are a thing of the past, and the Victorian houses which accommodated them are now subdivided into flats. Domestic servants disappeared in the inter-war years, and servants' quarters have disappeared with them. Changing patterns of conjugal roles and child-rearing are reflected in changes such as the evolution of the kitchen-diner and the establishment of a separate bedroom for each child. The through-lounge reflects the erosion of the traditional separation between a place for everyday living and a more formal place for receiving visitors, and there are signs that the kitchen may be moving forward from the back of the house as the traditional role of women and the lowly status of domestic labour begin to change. As social relations evolve, so domestic space evolves with them, thereby facilitating further changes while closing off others.

Seen in this way, the home is the place where the webbing of the social fabric is continually being copied, repaired, or rewoven. It is the carrier of social structure and social change. As Peter Williams suggests, the home is a 'site and situation where social relations, including class, status and gender, are composed and contextualized' (1984, p. 248). It is the crucible of our modern society.

The meaning of home and the significance of home ownership

In his interviews with middle-income householders in Seattle, Robert Rakoff set out to identify the key components of the symbolism of the home in American culture. He found that the family and child-rearing were central to many people's conceptions of home: 'My subjects agreed that it is the presence of children and the activity of family life that makes a house into a home' (1977, p. 93). However, he also showed that there were other equally strong images which commonly attached to the idea of home. One's home was an indicator of personal status and success. It was also a place of permanence and personal security: 'The house, particularly the owner-occupied house, seemed to be a powerful symbol of order, continuity, physical safety, and a sense of place or physical belonging' (p. 94). For many, home was a refuge, a place from which the outside world could be excluded and where one could take control of one's own life. It was a place of freedom and autonomy, especially for home owners: 'Above all, the sense of freedom that people associated with owned houses expressed their belief, if not their experience, that these private spaces were a real and proper realm of self-fulfillment' (p. 94).

Rakoff's findings have been replicated on both sides of the Atlantic. In the USA, Loewy and Snaith found predominant definitions of home entailed references to family life and children, relaxation and comfort, ownership, privacy, retreat, security and autonomy (reported in Hayward, 1975, p. 3). In Britain, Gordon Marshall and his colleagues found that 49 per cent of their national representative sample saw home as a centre of family life, while 43 per cent saw it as a place of relaxation or retreat. The third most popular definition, mentioned by 24 per cent, was of the home as a place of independence and freedom. 'There are', they conclude, 'few who see their homes as providing simply a roof over one's head. For most people . . . home means more than this: it is a centre of family life, a place to retreat where one can relax and "be oneself", a place of freedom and independence' (1988, p. 213). Once again, therefore, we see how the home entails more than simply the house as a physical shelter and location but is also associated for most people with particular kinds and qualities of social relationships and organization.

In the three towns survey, we found much the same sort of pattern as that reported by Marshall and his colleagues. Like them, our results show that the three main themes in popular imagery of the home relate to family life, physical and emotional comfort and ownership of the dwelling.

Table 5.1 shows that these three themes were strongly expressed in all three towns in the survey, although there are some interesting locality variations. The notion of the home as a place of relaxation and comfort, for example, appears more widespread the further south we move, and people in Burnley were correspondingly more likely to equate home with neighbourhood than were households in the other two towns. These findings may lend some support to popular stereotypes of northern life as more

Table 5.1 *The meaning of home across three towns*

Home means:	Burnley No.	Burnley %	Derby No.	Derby %	Slough No.	Slough %	Total No.	Total %
Family, love, children	46	31	58	37	59	39	163	36
Comfort, relaxation	26	18	38	24	49	33	113	25
Place you own or worked for	30	20	30	19	19	13	79	17
Belonging to a neighbourhood	32	22	13	8	17	11	62	14
Personal possessions	18	12	16	10	11	7	45	10
Long residence or memories	10	7	16	10	9	6	35	8
Privacy, a retreat, peace	4	3	6	4	7	5	17	4
Place of sanctuary or safety	7	5	5	3	4	3	16	4
Independence, being your own boss	6	4	3	2	5	3	14	3
Don't know	12	8	9	6	9	6	30	7
Total	147		156		151		454	

community-based than life in the South and there is no doubt that many of our Burnley respondents firmly believed that this was so. The proportion of people who described their neighbourhood as friendly, for example, rose as we went northwards (53 per cent in Slough, 58 per cent in Derby and 68 per cent in Burnley), and people in Burnley were more likely to have at least one close friend living in the immediate vicinity.

Nevertheless, the similarities between the three towns are more striking than the differences. In all three, 'home' is widely associated with family life and children, with images of comfort and relaxation and with the idea of a personal space over which one enjoys some degree of proprietorship or control. The emphasis on the family is widespread and was commonly evoked by our informants as the factor which transformed a house into a home:

> There are houses and there are homes, and it's family makes a house into a home. People who get up in the morning, go off to work, and then come back and go off to bed live in a house, not a home.
>
> (Female semi-skilled manual worker and home owner, Slough)

> Your home is with your family. And the things you do to it. You put part of yourself into your housing, don't you?
>
> (Male home owner, intermediate occupation, Burnley)

> My children used to say when we were camping that home is anywhere where we are. We could make ourselves at home anywhere. It's where we are.
>
> (Female semi-skilled manual worker and home owner, Slough)

> It relates to happiness, not bricks and mortar. As a house this is very plain – a box – but we've had so much happiness here . . . It's lovely to

go away on holiday, but it's lovely to come home again. It's sloppy I suppose.

(Female clerical worker and home owner, Derby)

To feel at home – you never call it your house, it's your home. It's the way you build it up and the people who live in it . . . It's the house you build together. A house isn't just bricks and mortar, it's the love that's in it.

(Female skilled manual worker and home owner, Derby)

Both owner-occupiers and council tenants emphasized the family as the single most important feature of home life, although as Table 5.2 reveals, 43 per cent of tenants gave this answer as compared with only 33 per cent of owners. Owners, by contrast, were far more likely than tenants to identify home as a place of relaxation and comfort. Only 14 per cent of tenants saw their homes in this way compared with 28 per cent of owners:

I can dress how I like and do what I like. The kids always brought home who they liked. Other people's places, you take your shoes off when you go in.

(Male skilled manual worker and home owner, Slough)

It's very free and easy. People come in and kick their shoes off so they must feel at home.

(Female skilled manual worker and home owner, Slough)

It's not having everything regimental. Not feeling it's got to be like a furniture showroom to be comfortable . . . It always annoys me on building sites when it says, 'Wimpey Homes'. They're not homes, they're houses. Home is happiness and family, that sort of thing.

(Female, intermediate occupation and home owner, Burnley)

Table 5.2 reveals other interesting variations between owners' and tenants' images of home. Tenants, for example, are twice as likely to associate home with neighbourhood ties but are only half as likely to equate it with personal possessions. At the risk of over-generalizing, we might say that owners are more likely to identify their house as home, while tenants place greater emphasis on the people around them. Home for many council tenants has to do with family and neighbours. Home for many owner-occupiers has to do with a place where they feel relaxed and where they can surround themselves with familiar and personal possessions.

These tenure-based variations are most sharply revealed in the case of former council tenants who have bought their houses from the local authority. Referring again to Table 5.2, we see that, even more than other owners, council house buyers see home as a place of relaxation, a place which they have worked for and express pride in and a place where they can

Table 5.2 *The meaning of home for owners and tenants*

Home means:	Council tenants No.	%	All owners* No.	%	Council buyers No.	%	Total No.	%
Family, love, children	48	43	111	33	12	27	159	36
Comfort, relaxation	16	14	95	28	16	36	111	25
Place you own or worked for	19	17	60	18	9	20	79	18
Belonging to a neighbourhood	24	21	37	11	5	11	61	14
Personal possessions	6	5	38	11	2	4	44	10
Long residence or memories	10	9	25	8	6	13	35	8
Privacy, a retreat, peace	4	4	12	4	2	4	16	4
Place of sanctuary or safety	2	2	14	4	1	2	16	4
Independence, being your own boss	2	2	12	4	5	11	14	3
Don't know	7	6	22	7	4	9	29	6
Total	113		334		45		447	

* Figures for all owners include council house buyers.

be their own boss. Unlike those who still rent their homes, this group of buyers places relatively little weight on home as family or home as neighbourhood.

Such findings suggest that the meanings which people derive from and invest in their homes may be influenced by whether or not they own them. It seems from the tenants' answers that people may find it difficult to establish a sense of belonging in a house which they do not own. This does not mean that tenants suffer acute anomie and lack any sense of belonging at all, but rather that they find such an identity in other ways. Because the house is not personal to them, they emphasize family and neighbours when they think of home.

The council house purchasers are an interesting group in this respect, for 41 of the 45 of them in the sample are still living in the same house which they previously rented from the local authority. Their family circumstances have not changed, their neighbourhood has not changed, and the house they are living in is still the same house (although many of them have altered its appearance in various ways), yet their orientation to home is dramatically different from that of most of the tenants around them. Whether it is that people with a different orientation to home apply to buy their houses, or whether it is the act of purchase which changes the way they think about their homes, is difficult to judge. Probably both factors operate together. What is clear, however, is that owners are more likely than tenants to express a sense of self and belonging through their houses, and that this difference is related to ownership rather than to the nature of the housing itself.

Many of our respondents had no doubt that ownership affects the way people feel about their homes:

We did [feel differently when we bought it]. There's a dividing line between renting and owning. Having to rent, it's something that's never going to be yours personally. It's not your personal property to dictate what you're going to do with. There always was that dividing line and there always will be.

(Male skilled non-manual worker and council house buyer, Slough)

[*Husband*] 'I liked the place when I rented it but we've put more effort into it since we started buying it. We've got more pride in the place.'
[*Wife*] 'Oh yes, we've improved it so much. It's more liveable now.'
(Skilled and semi-skilled manual worker couple, council house buyers, Slough)

When you own you can do a lot more with it and make it more homely because it's yours. You don't bother too much when it's rented.

(Female semi-skilled manual worker and council tenant, Derby)

If I bought my own house I think I'd feel it actually belonged to me, whereas with a council house you walk along a row of little boxes until you come to a little box that's yours.

(Male semi-skilled manual worker and council tenant, Slough)

I would have a different feeling about a house if I rented it. It's part of you – you put a lot more into it.

(Male, intermediate occupation, home owner, Slough)

Evidence that home owners and tenants do feel differently about their homes leads us to pose two significant questions. The first concerns what may be termed 'privatism' or 'home-centredness'. Owners, we have seen, are less likely to identify home with neighbourhood, and they tend to have fewer friends living nearby. To what extent, therefore, is ownership associated with a withdrawal from involvement in life beyond the garden gate? Does private ownership generate privatized life-styles?

The second question relates to the evidence that tenants are far less likely than owners to see their homes as places of comfort and relaxation. Does this mean that ownership can provide a sense of personal security, identity and autonomy which may be denied to non-owners? Put another way, does private ownership generate greater scope for the expression of self and identity in a private realm?

In addressing these two questions, we need to be alive to the distinction between the three related concepts of *private property* (a socio-legal term denoting rights of exclusive use, control and disposal – see Chapter 2), *privatism* (defined as a withdrawal or detachment from active participation in collective life) and *privacy* or the 'private realm' (denoting freedom from surveillance by others). It has often been assumed that the common etymological root of these three terms implies some real connection between them – that a move into private ownership encourages adoption of a privatized life-style, for example, or that people only feel secure in their own private space if they own the property rights to it. Such assumptions may be intuitively plausible but they are by no means axiomatic.

In the next section we shall explore the relation between private ownership and privatized life-styles. Following that, we shall consider the relation between private ownership and the establishment of a private realm. In both cases we shall need to appeal to empirical evidence, for we cannot assume any inherent connection between these three variables.

Home ownership and privatism

The concept of privatism was developed in British and American sociology in the 1950s in an attempt to identify and explain apparent changes in working-class culture and behaviour. The concept was elaborated in the 1960s through David Lockwood's influential analysis of the different types of working-class social imagery (Lockwood, 1966). Lockwood recognized that growing privatism may be characteristic of some sections of the working class but not of others and he set out to explain why this was.

It is important to note that Lockwood himself never equated privatized life-styles with private ownership of housing. Rather, he believed that privatism arose in response to the social organization of the workplace as well as the neighbourhood. In his view, it was possible to identify three typical patterns of work and neighbourhood organization which were associated with three distinctive sets of working-class values and life-styles.

One group of workers, whom he termed 'traditional proletarians', were to be found working in traditional industries where work groups commonly forged a strong sense of camaraderie and collective identity. This solidaristic culture was then reinforced by a pattern of neighbourhood organization in which male workers spent much of their leisure time together and away from the home in pubs and working men's clubs. The result was a strong sense of common class interests and a dichotomous them-and-us conflict model of the social structure.

A second group of workers, 'deferential traditionalists', worked and lived in small-scale environments such as farms and family firms. Their work situation encouraged vertical identification between them and their employers, and their lives outside work rarely brought them into contact with other workers. These circumstances tend to foster a view of society as comprising a finely graded status hierarchy.

Finally, 'privatized workers' were employed in relatively high-wage modern industries and tended to live in modern, anonymous housing estates. They had an instrumental orientation to their work in the sense that money was the sole object of their employment, and they shared little sense of identification with either their employers or their fellow workmates. The sense of isolation thus engendered was then reinforced by the lack of kin or neighbourhood ties in the localities in which they lived. The result was a

275

withdrawal into the home. Surrounding themselves with material comforts, these workers tended to see themselves as part of a vast middle-income group.

Lockwood followed up this conceptual paper by participating in research on a group of workers employed in the car and chemical industries in Luton whom he expected to reveal privatized attitudes and life-styles. The result was the so-called 'Affluent Worker' study, a classic of British empirical sociology which we have already encountered in our discussion of embourgeoisement in Chapter 4. Essentially this study found that these workers and their wives had few friends and that 'time outside work was time devoted overwhelmingly to home and family life rather than to sociability of any more widely based kind' (Goldthorpe et al., 1969, p. 103). In many cases geographical mobility had disrupted kinship networks and forced couples to rely more on each other for sociability, although the research also found that many of these workers were quite happy to limit their social lives to their homes and immediate families. These workers had values which led them to adopt an 'instrumental' attitude to their work in the sense that time spent in employment was the means to achieve the money which was necessary to enrich time spent at home: 'Work was defined and experienced essentially as a means to the pursuit of ends outside of work and usually ones relating to standards of domestic living' (1969, p. 164). They led privatized lives, therefore, in the sense that their interests centred upon the home to the virtual exclusion of both the workplace and the neighbourhood.

Since the 1960s many sociologists have commented on what they see as the spread and growth of this privatized and home-centred culture in Britain. In their earlier essays, for example, Newby and his co-researchers proclaimed that 'The recession has been associated . . . with a retreat from class politics into a privatized world within the home' (Newby et al., 1985, p. 95; see also Marshall et al., 1985). Allan, similarly, argues that a shift has occurred 'in people's conception of the home and the social relationships within it . . . this shift has been one that has encouraged an orientation best characterized as "home centred" . . . It is now quite acceptable, indeed expected, that people regard their home, and the relationships and activities it entails, as central to their definition of self' (1985, pp. 55–6). Kumar agrees. He identifies 'a general and pervasive tendency towards privatization in British life' and suggests that 'We are rapidly becoming a home-centred society to an extent that must surprise even the sociologists of the 1950s and early 1960s who first discovered the "privatized worker" ' (1986, pp. 356, 359). Perhaps most dramatically of all, Anthea Holme has re-studied life in Bethnal Green, the working-class area of East London first researched in the 1950s by Michael Young and Peter Willmott. The original study had documented a bustling, traditional working-class community, but Holme's re-study suggests that all this has changed: 'One striking difference was how home-centred most Bethnal Green families had now become . . . the corollary in Bethnal Green to this new home-centredness was the emptiness of the streets and corridors and staircases in the housing estates . . . no longer could it be said that people in Bethnal Green were (in Young and Willmott's words) "vigorously at home in the streets" ' (1985, p. 45).

Many of these authors are in no doubt that the growth of home ownership is a – if not *the* – major factor in explaining this retreat into a privatized life-style. Marshall and his co-authors suggest, for example, that home ownership is a 'particularly important feature' of these changes (1985, p. 274). Kumar tells us that, while 'the passion to own one's house is hardly new', its intensity in recent years is indicative of the 'drive to exclude every particle of public experience, every public form, from the general life of society' (1986, p. 356). John Burnett (1986, p. 265) explains patronizingly that the spread of home ownership in the inter-war years led people of 'limited cultural and intellectual horizons' to direct their energies and emotions inwards on to their homes. And Peter Marcuse is in no doubt about the pernicious effects of the spread of owner-occupation in eroding householders' participation in collective life: 'It restricts their opportunities, and even their desires, to engage in other activities, including collective activities, that might involve them in political or social issues. It leads to a privatization and internalization of problems, housing and other' (1987, p. 251).

Of course, few writers see home ownership as the sole cause of the growth of privatism. At least six other contributory factors have been identified in this literature.

The first is the improvement in material home comforts. From the nineteenth century onwards, the home has been transformed in design and technology. Heating, lighting, water supply and sewage disposal were all revolutionized in the Victorian period (Williams, 1987), and in the twentieth century the home has continued to become more attractive as a result of innovations in home furnishing, central heating, consumer electronics and so on. Today's homes are healthier, less crowded, cleaner and more luxurious than in the past (Allan, 1985).

Various writers have identified these material changes as important in encouraging home-centred life-styles. Focusing mainly on the late Victorian period, Daunton suggests that 'These developments entailed a trend towards domestic-based consumption within a more private, internal life which was very different from the experience of the early Victorian city. Daily life become less public and less communal, more private and more introverted' (1983, p. 232). Similarly, in her re-study of households in Luton, Devine (1988) has suggested that improvements in working-class housing since the Second World War have fostered a greater degree of home-centredness.

A second factor which has been identified as tending to encourage home centredness is the growth of mass consumerism. Alt (1977), for example, suggests that the collectivism of the workplace has been eroded by the privatism of consumption. Fuelled by easy credit, ordinary people now demand ever-increasing amounts of consumer goods which they place and use in their homes. The result is that external and communal facilities come to be replaced by internal and private ones. An early example of this is the provision of bathrooms, for this brought to an end the need to leave the house to attend the municipal slipper baths. The arrival of television, and later of video recorders, undermined the tradition of visiting the cinema. Automatic washing machines have brought laundry functions back into the home, the hi-fi has replaced the concert hall, the private car takes us away from public transport, the telephone substitutes for face-to-face visiting, and so on. We withdraw into the home because the home is becoming ever more self-sufficient.

Table 5.3 *Ownership of consumer durables – the national evidence*

Item	General Household Survey (1987 %)	Family Expenditure Survey (1987 %)
Monochrome or colour TV		97
Colour television	86	
Washing machine	81	83
Telephone	81	81
Freezer or fridge-freezer	66	69
Car		62
Video recorder	31	36
Home computer	13	15
Dishwasher	6	

Sources: OPCS, *General Household Survey*, 1987; Department of Employment, *Family Expenditure Survey*, 1987.

Ownership of consumer durables is now widespread. Table 5.3 summarizes evidence from two different national surveys, while Table 5.4 sets out the results from the three towns survey, breaking down the figures by social class categories. It is clear from these tables that ownership of major items of domestic technology has spread right through the class structure: 'A redundant shipbuilder qualifying for welfare payments could possess some or all of them, so too could a wealthy stockbroker, and neither would see any incongruity in their both doing so' (Hardyment, 1988, p. 1). As Table 5.4 shows, the latest domestic innovations such as dishwashers are taken up first by the middle class and only later 'trickle down'. Nevertheless, as Glyptis found in a study in Nottingham, 'Virtually all homes contained a vast array of gadgetry and equipment, both leisure and work related' (1987, p. 20). Not only, therefore, are people's homes now more comfortable than they were, but it is easier to pursue a range of different activities within them which once could only be carried on outside.

A third factor which has been adduced to explain the apparent growth of home-centred privatism is the increase in leisure time, most of which is spent at home. Using interviews and diaries, Glyptis (1987) estimates that four-fifths of leisure time is spent in or near the home. This is borne out by various trends in consumer spending. A family leisure survey conducted by Gallup for Woolworths in 1985 found that two-thirds of households prefer to spend their leisure time at home and that the average household spends £1,800 each year on home-based leisure pursuits (reported in *The Times*, 1 November 1985). Spending on alcohol has been rising – from £8.5 to £14.5 billion between 1978 and 1984 – but most of this increase has occurred through the off-licence trade rather than in pubs, and the home-brew industry has been expanding at 6 per cent per annum (*Sunday Times*, 21 April 1985). Attendances at cinema, theatre, bingo and sport have all been falling, yet the Gallup survey found that over a quarter of men and a fifth of women do some painting and decorating around the home at least once a week!

Table 5.4 *Ownership of consumer durables by different social classes in the three towns survey*

Item	Service class No.	%	Social class (Goldthorpe categories) Intermed. class No.	%	Working class No.	%	Total No.	%
Colour television	86	70	97	63	135	58	318	63
Monochrome TV	47	38	69	45	81	35	197	39
Washing machine	112	91	142	93	201	87	455	90
Telephone	118	96	133	87	159	69	410	81
Freezer	110	89	129	84	180	78	419	83
Stereo	103	84	109	71	138	60	350	69
Video recorder – owned	46	37	49	32	71	31	166	33
Video recorder – rented	16	13	26	17	28	12	70	14
Microwave oven	39	32	47	31	37	16	123	24
Home computer	41	33	36	24	40	17	117	23
Dishwasher	14	11	11	7	9	4	34	7
Total	123		153		230		506	

Time spent in the home seems likely to increase in the future as computer-based home shopping is extended and as at least some forms of employment move back into the home. This then brings us to the fourth factor which is said to have fostered a growing privatism, namely, an increasing aversion to the experience of formal employment.

The basic argument here is that people have looked to their home lives for compensation for the depradations they suffer at work. Daunton, for example, argues that in the nineteenth century 'The stress upon the home as the crucial element in life was in part a defensive retreat from the loss of control over work, a compensation in the home for an increased sense of dependence in the work place' (1983, p. 224; see also Rose, 1981, for a similar argument). The same point has also been made about the inter-war years:

The psychological importance of the home was increased by changes which affected people's working lives. As the Depression began to kill off

many smaller firms, and as "rationalization" affected the largest survivors, work for most people became increasingly a matter of routine. This was as true for the clerk as for the manual worker . . . many people saw their homes as the *only* places over which they could exercise control.
(Oliver, Davis and Bentley, 1981, pp. 71–2)

And exactly the same arguments are still being advanced today: 'Outside the private spheres of family, friends, leisure interests, etc., the worlds of work and bureaucracy loom large as impersonal forces from which individuals somehow need to escape . . . It is in the private sphere that an individual finds meaning and identity, not in the bureaucratized world of work' (Brittan, 1977, pp. 45–6).

For these and other writers, home-centredness is therefore a response to alienation in the workplace. The response takes two forms. The first is passive; as work has become increasingly bureaucratized, routinized and depersonalized, so employees have retreated into their homes to find comfort and solace. This idea surfaces time and again in contemporary sociological literature – workers see home as 'an arena where they can escape the humiliations and constraints of the factory' (Halle, 1984, p. 295); the return home at the end of the working day 'may be an escape from the tensions and worries of the job' (Moore, 1984, p. 270); and home is experienced as 'an attractive haven after tiring work in noisy and dirty factory conditions' (Devine, 1988, p. 11). The second is more active; home is said to be important, not only for recuperation, but also for the opportunities it offers to engage in autonomous and creative activity and thus to realize those aspects of oneself which are closed off in routine employment. 'Many ordinary people', says Pahl (1984, p. 323) in his study on the Isle of Sheppey, 'can express themselves more creatively in their own homes than they can in their employment.' The same idea was advanced a quarter of a century earlier by Willmott and Young, who found in their study of Woodford in the 1950s that home-based activities of the evenings and weekends were becoming increasingly rewarding as compensation for the growing boredom of work during the day (1960, p. 32).

Growing home-centredness is thus seen as a reaction against formal employment. Figures cited by Gorz (1982, p. 140) would seem to bear this out, for he reports that a 1977 survey of nine EC countries found that 55 per cent of people would prefer more free time as compared with 45 per cent who would prefer higher wages. His thesis is that, whereas workers in the past struggled to free themselves in their work, today they struggle to free themselves from their work. While work represents a 'sphere of heteronomy', home provides a 'sphere of autonomy'.

A fifth factor which has been identified as contributing to the spread of a privatized culture is suburbanization. This is essentially what Lockwood had in mind when he argued that privatized workers were likely to live on modern housing estates, and this theme has been resurrected in later work. Alt (1977, p. 56), for example, suggests that suburbs isolate workers by removing them from the daily world of labour into a sanitized and domesticated realm, while Perin argues that the physical-separation characteristic of suburbia has eroded people's capacity to interact with one another. In her view, suburbanites 'are accustomed to using walls but not rules . . . The ready availability of physical avoidance having atrophied tactics of negotiation, mediation and other adjudicative mechanisms, social fright is heightened' (1977, p. 106). Unable to get along, suburbanites retreat behind privet hedges and net curtains in the hope that they will be left alone.

Finally, it has been suggested that privatism has grown as the need for mutual aid has shrunk (for example, Marshall *et al.*, 1985). There is a sense in which solidarism in the community is born out of adversity. As rising affluence and the safety net of the welfare state have eroded the desperate poverty which traditionally afflicted at least some sections of the working class, so the need for close-knit networks of mutual support has declined, and people have disappeared off the streets and behind their own front doors. Where is the need to borrow a cup of sugar if the larder is full? What is the point of setting up a friendly society if the state guarantees to care for you when you are ill and to pay you a pension when you retire?

These, then, are the six factors which have been said to contribute to privatized life-styles in the modern period. Putting them together, we may summarize 'the privatism thesis' as follows. There has been a move away from participation in collective life. Some authors date this to the latter part of the nineteenth century, some see it as a product of the inter-war years, and some see it as a recent phenomenon. The expansion of home ownership is often seen as a key factor in the growth of privatism and home-centredness, although most writers also emphasize such factors as improvements in the material comforts of the home, the expansion of ownership of consumer goods, an increase in home-based leisure, an erosion of the satisfactions available from formal employment, the spread of the suburbs and the decline in the need for mutual aid.

Summarized in this way, the privatism thesis seems intuitively plausible. It is certainly believed by many sociologists, for it is now common to hear pundits complain that British social life is withering and that our culture is every day becoming more like the stereotype of life in New York City. Privatism is generally portrayed in negative terms. It conjures up the image of the family group, huddled around the VCR with the curtains drawn and the doors locked and barred, while out in the streets cries for help go unanswered.

Not only is the thesis intuitively plausible; it is also reflected in the way some people seem to think about their lives. In the three towns survey, for example, the image of 'home' was often associated with the idea of withdrawal:

If I got the chance of a bungalow in an acre of ground, I'd bolt tomorrow! We come home and shut ourselves in. We don't see the neighbours for

months . . . we just sit and watch the idiot's lantern. You come in and
lock the door up.

(Male council tenant, intermediate occupation, Slough)

I don't know any more which way to vote. I've reached the stage where
as long as everything in our little bubble is all right, then okay.

(Female home owner and skilled non-manual worker, Derby)

But how widespread are such privatized and home-centred ways of life? The
privatism thesis may seem plausible, but is it true?

The thesis may be evaluated in two ways. First, we may ask whether there
is any evidence to support the view that home-centredness and a withdrawal
from collective life have actually been increasing. Second, we need to
consider whether the growth of home ownership is in any way linked to
tendencies to privatism. In both cases, we shall see that there is actually very
little evidence to support the claims which have been made.

One reason for doubting that privatism has been on the increase is simply
that historical evidence tells us that people have led home-centred lives for a
long time. There is nothing new about wanting to spend time at home or
with members of one's family. According to Franklin (1986), our image of
the nineteenth-century working-class neighbourhood as a place where social
life centred on the streets is little more than a myth. Neighbourhoods were
often experienced as hostile places, and home was a private realm in which
people could seek refuge from unwanted and undesirable contacts in the
streets. Furthermore, many workers did not live near their workmates, and
the close-knit occupational community always was the exception rather than
the rule. In his study of Bedminster in Bristol, for example, Franklin (1989)
goes on to show how even one hundred years ago, most working men did
not spend much time outside of work with fellow employees. By the 1920s
he is able to show that husbands were *normally* home- and family-centred,
developing close emotional bonds with their children.

Evidence from a variety of other sources supports Franklin's scepticism
about the supposed recent growth of privatism. Allan and Crowe (1988)
reaffirm his argument that home in working-class communities was often
used as a defence against neighbourhood criticism and gossip, and they
argue that working-class home-centredness certainly dates back at least as
far as the prewar years. Most historians, however, place its origins much
earlier than that. Both Crossick (1978) and Lasch (1977) trace the
development of privatized and family-centred values to the second half of
the nineteenth century, and Marshall et al. (1987) also recognize that home
and family took on increasing significance for artisans and skilled workers at
this time. Daunton (1983) traces the shift to the replacement of self-
contained courts and alleys by through-streets during the Victorian period.
Others have gone still further back in time – Pahl, for example, suggests that
the evidence of historical demographers demonstrates that privatized, home-
centred households 'have a long history in pre-industrial England' (1984,

p. 322); and in his work with Wallace, he suggests that 'Domesticity is not a value born of contemporary consumerism but has been an essential element in working class life for as long as we have any historical knowledge of the context and nature of everyday life' (1988, p. 141). It seems from all of this that home-centredness may have been with us for centuries!

These various historical works also remind us that privatism and home-centredness have long *coexisted* with collectivism and working-class organization. Emphasis on the importance of home does not necessarily result in withdrawal from collective life outside the home, for it is possible for people to participate fully in both spheres of life. As we saw in Chapter 1, it was precisely a desire to have homes of their own which led nineteenth-century artisans to join together in building clubs. Individualism and fraternalism often went hand in hand, and it is clear that privatism and sociability may not therefore be incommensurable.

Marshall and his co-authors recognize this when they point out that the home-centred artisans and skilled workers of Victorian England were at the same time active in friendly societies, trade unions and various other locally based initiatives. They go on to suggest that much the same may be true today in the sense that many workers are both privatized and collectively oriented (Marshall *et al.*, 1987, 1988). Certainly it seems from their evidence that home-centredness does not necessarily mean that people are trying to escape from their workplace in the way that Gorz and others have suggested. Seventy-three per cent of their respondents felt that their work was at least as important as any other single aspect of their lives, and even among working-class people, 80 per cent of men and 68 per cent of women described their jobs as rewarding or enjoyable.

These findings are supported by data from the three towns survey where we found that less than one-quarter of our respondents denied any interest in the job that they did. For many, work remained important as a source of social contact (two-thirds valued the social contacts they made at work), and this was confirmed by interviews with retired people, over a quarter of whom said that they missed the social aspects of their former employment. There is little indication in these findings that people are trying to free themselves from work in order to flee to the autonomy of the domestic realm. Rather, home and work both figure centrally in most people's lives, and both bring their compensations as well as their troubles. As Moore suggests, going to work can represent an escape from domesticity in just the same way as returning home can bring relief from one's job. 'There is', he notes sardonically, 'at least some relief in changing the psychological bunions on which life's varied pressures pinch' (1984, p. 270).

What all this suggests is that home-centredness has probably always been in evidence in Britain but that it has not necessarily undermined collective activities, nor does it indicate a withdrawal from the world of formal employment. Such evidence must lead us to question some of the basic assumptions behind the privatism thesis in that privatism seems to be neither new nor all-pervasive. In particular, it leads us to question the view that the expansion of home ownership has produced a society of privatized and home-centred households: for as we saw in Chapter 1, the growth of mass owner-occupation is a relatively recent phenomenon dating only from the 1930s, yet it seems that privatized life-styles go back much further than that.

If the historical evidence casts doubt on the privatism thesis, so too does the contemporary sociological evidence. It is true that there are some grounds for believing that home ownership may erode some aspects of collective life and organization. A recent study of council house buyers in Sunderland, for example, suggests that new owners do withdraw from collective life and begin to feel differently about their homes and neighbourhoods: 'Domestic life was further privatized for this group of people at the same time as tenure was privatized. The home improvements and garden fences are the obvious manifestations; equally important is the withdrawal from a collective experience and an espousal of privatized responsibility for children's futures' (Stubbs, 1988, p. 153; see also Banion and Stubbs, 1986, p. 190). Unfortunately, however, these authors cite no evidence by which to gauge these claims, which appear to rest solely on the researchers' impressions.

Nevertheless, it does seem that council house purchase may affect patterns of social interaction on council estates. In the three towns survey we found that 26 per cent of council tenants volunteered the opinion that house purchase makes people more withdrawn and 'snobby', and many of them believed that the sale of council houses had undermined the quality of social relationships on their estates:

They change! They seem to go a bit snobbish – 'You can't touch me.' They don't want to have a cup of tea with you like they used to. It's the same as with friends at work if they get made manageress – they turn off.
(Female council tenant and unskilled manual worker, Derby)

A lot of people, they buy and the first thing they do is put a wall around it. It's a funny attitude.
(Male council tenant and skilled manual worker, Slough)

They seem to have more to say. The kids were playing ball in the street yesterday and a private owner complained. Some of them get too bigoty over it. If you're going to buy your own house in the midst of a council estate, you're asking for trouble. You've got a lot to put up with on a council estate and private owners see it as a violation.
(Male council tenant and unskilled manual worker, Slough)

There is, furthermore, one cluster of statistical indicators which seems to suggest that home ownership may be related to privatism. These indicators concern the quality of informal neighbourhood networks which on average seem to be denser on the council estates than in the owner-occupied areas. As Table 5.5 shows, tenants were more likely than owners to have at least one close friend living in the same neighbourhood, they were more likely to have first made acquaintance with current friends through neighbourhood interaction, and they were more likely to have retained friendships from school days.

Some caution is required in interpreting this evidence, however. First, these differences may in part be a function of length of residence rather than tenure *per se*, for tenants tend on average to have lived in their current homes or neighbourhoods for longer than owners. Four out of five tenants have never lived in any other town since first setting up their own home, whereas owners seem rather more mobile, just under half having lived in a different town at some time in the past.

Table 5.5 *Housing tenure and neighbourhood relations*

| | Housing tenure | | | |
| | Home owners | | Council tenants | |
Neighbourhood relations	No.	%	No.	%
At least one close friend living in the neighbourhood	89	35	56	56
At least one close friend living in the town	112	44	57	57
At least one close friend met through the neighbourhood	82	35	44	50
At least one close friend known since childhood	71	31	77	90
Has lived in three or more dwellings since first set up home	182	50	60	46
Always lived in the same town since first set up home	205	56	101	79
Thinks neighbourhood is friendly or very friendly	216	60	77	60
No favours or aid for or from neighbours	100	29	37	30
Regular help by or for neighbours	38	11	23	19

Note: Totals differ for each item due to missing data.

Second, the evidence should not be taken to indicate that the council estates are full of happy folk who all know and help each other, while owner-occupiers peep nervously at their neighbours from behind net curtains. It is quite possible to have one or two old friends living nearby yet still feel estranged from the neighbourhood. Just as Damer (1971) found in his work on a Glasgow housing estate, there is a tendency among some tenants to distance themselves from their neighbours, and this was particularly true of those living on the older and least popular estates:

There's some bad 'uns come in. It used to be very nice – beautiful. No violence. You could leave things unlocked. But it's gone very rough now with the people they're putting in them. Why don't they put the rough buggers by themselves? Why mix them up with clean, decent people?
(Female council tenant and retired skilled non-manual worker, Burnley)

It's deteriorating fast. I'd always said this is my home and I'm going to stay here, but now if I get the chance I'll move when I finish work. The environment has changed. We used to visit each other's houses and lock up last thing at night if at all. Now all the windows are barred and locked.
(Male intermediate worker and council house buyer, Slough)

You can't blame the council – it's the people who live in the houses. Rough bloody people up here now.

(Male council tenant and retired skilled non-manual worker, Burnley)

Third, it is important to recognize that some owner-occupiers were clearly active members of neighbourhood networks involving mutual help and reciprocity:

I mow the lawn for next-door and do little jobs for her. Apart from that we tend to do things on a barter system. I fixed the car of the man who moved house for me – it's like a barter system. My friend is a plumber and gas fitter and he races motor-bikes. He gets me to do his welding for him, and when I need the gas boiler servicing, he does it. I take tomatoes from the garden down the pub and they give me my drinks free.

(Male home owner, intermediate class, Derby)

I do lots of things for the ones round here – hanging doors, assembling DIY furniture. And next-door helps me when there's something wrong with the car.

(Male home owner, semi-skilled manual worker, Slough)

Notwithstanding these notes of caution, however, it does still remain the case that neighbourhood networks are on average stronger among council tenants than among owner-occupiers. As Pahl (1984) found in his study on the Isle of Sheppey, so we found in the three towns survey, home owners spend a lot of time working in and on their own homes, but mutual aid and reciprocal labour among neighbours are not widespread. They are not widespread on the council estates either, but they are more common there, especially among women, and this too confirms Pahl's findings in so far as he showed that it tends to be the poorest households which rely most on the unpaid, informal labour of others (1984, p. 222).

Table 5.5 shows that around six in every ten people in each tenure group reported giving or receiving some help or support in relations with neighbours, but on closer inspection it is clear that tenants tend to be involved rather more in regular arrangements such as shopping or child care, while owners were more likely to engage in minor or irregular help such as watering people's house plants when they go away on holiday or taking in a parcel when the postman calls. Patterns of neighbourhood life do, therefore, seem to differ as between the two tenure groups. The neighbourhood plays a more important role for tenants than it does for owners, and this is reflected in the fact that 21 per cent of tenants described 'home' as belonging to a neighbourhood, while only 11 per cent of owners felt this way.

Patterns of friendship and informal aid networks do, therefore, suggest that neighbourhood life is stronger on the council estates than in the owner-occupied areas. On other indicators, however, a very different picture emerges. If we look at Table 5.6, for example, it is apparent that owner-occupiers tend to be *more* rather than less involved in local organizations. If they led privatized lives we would expect them to steer clear of local organizational involvements, yet 56 per cent of owners belong to at least one organization, and this compares with only 34 per cent of tenants.

It is well known that working-class people tend to join fewer organizations than middle-class people do, but when we control for the social class difference between the tenures, the effect still holds. Among skilled non-manual workers, for example, 49 per cent of owners but only 18 per cent of tenants belong to at least one local organization. The same pattern emerges among skilled manual workers, where 59 per cent of owners and 40 per cent of tenants belong to an organization, and among semi-skilled manual workers where the figures are 54 per cent and 32 per cent respectively. There does, therefore, seem to be a genuine tenure effect here – home ownership is associated with organizational activity within each social class.

The same conclusion emerges when we look at membership and participation in residents' organizations. As we saw in Chapter 4, only 29 per cent of owner-occupiers lived in areas covered by residents' associations, whereas 54 per cent of tenants lived in areas which had tenants' associations. This is explained by the role of local authorities in encouraging tenants' associations on council estates. The important figures, however, concern density of membership. Half of all owners who were eligible to join residents' associations did so, yet this was true of only one in ten tenants. Again, therefore, home ownership seems to be more of a stimulus than a hindrance to participation in organizational life beyond the garden gate.

Table 5.6 *Organizational activity by housing tenure*

| | Housing tenure | | | |
| | Home owners | | Council tenants | |
Organizational activity	No.	%	No.	%
Belongs to at least one local organization	209	56	45	34
Belongs to residents' organization (all)	39	11	5	4
Belongs to residents' org'n (where available)	39	50	5	10
Belongs to trade union or other work-based assoc'n	117	33	23	18

Perhaps the most remarkable feature of Table 5.6, however, concerns work-based organizations. If home ownership led people to withdraw within the home and to retreat from involvement in the place of employment, then we would expect tenants to be far more actively involved in trade unions and other similar bodies than owner-occupiers are. In fact, the reverse is true, particularly among clerical and skilled manual workers, where 33 per cent of owners but only 20 per cent of tenants belonged to a union or equivalent body. Such findings make a nonsense of familiar Marxist claims (discussed in Chapter 1) that home ownership has been encouraged in order to break down employee solidarity in the workplace, for if anything it is

287

those who live in state-owned housing who seem least inclined to get involved in unions and other equivalent bodies.

Such findings are not unique to the three towns survey. Some years ago, Bernard Ineichen conducted research in Bristol where he found that manual worker owner-occupiers were more likely than manual worker council tenants to belong to voluntary organizations (1972, p. 399). Indeed, Ineichen went further, for he also found that patterns of sociability were stronger among working-class owners than working-class tenants. He found, for example, that owners were more likely to invite neighbours in for a cup of tea, were much more likely to have neighbours round for a meal and were more likely to have visited neighbours, although he also found that 'popping in' uninvited was more common among tenants. His results have since been replicated in a MORI national survey in 1982 (see Dickens, 1988, p. 130).

Table 5.7 *Home-centred leisure by housing tenure*

| | Housing tenure | | | | | |
| *How free time is spent* | *Home owners* | | *Council tenants* | | *Total* | |
	No.	*%*	*No.*	*%*	*No.*	*%*
Normally stay in, rarely have visitors	39	11	25	19	64	13
Normally stay in but do sometimes have visitors	70	19	35	27	105	21
Go out regularly (e.g. once or twice a week)	204	55	65	49	269	54
Go out frequently	52	14	6	5	58	12

$p < 0.01$

Although we did not collect strictly comparable data in the three towns survey, we did gather some information on sociability by asking our informants about how they spent their leisure time and about their preferences as regards going out or staying at home. As with the data on organizational memberships, the results indicate that home owners are if anything less home-centred and less privatized than tenants. Thus, despite the fact that tenants are more likely to have close friends living nearby, they tend to lead less active social lives.

Table 5.7 shows that home owners tend to go out more than tenants do. No fewer than 70 per cent of owner-occupiers go out regularly or frequently, whereas only just over half of all tenants do so. Of course, when we delve a little deeper, we find that this difference can mainly be explained by differences of income between the two groups. When we compare owners and tenants within the same income bands, the differences between them virtually disappear, and this suggests that it is people's financial situation, and possibly their class culture, which shapes the extent to which they stay at home rather than their housing tenure as such. Nevertheless, the findings are important, for the privatism thesis would lead us to expect that owners would spend more time at home than would tenants with an equivalent level of income, and this is certainly not the case.

The privatism thesis would also lead us to predict that home ownership would prevent people from going out because it soaks up so much more of their income. This, however, is not true either. We did find a few examples of people who became more home-centred in their leisure time as a result of buying a house. Sometimes this was because finances became tighter and sometimes it was because they felt more inclined to stay at home when they owned the place. One young, single white-collar worker in Slough, for example, told us: 'Before I bought the house I used to go out for a drink every night. When I bought this I couldn't afford to any more, but I also didn't want to, I was so happy. People said I was being antisocial, but I just wanted to be in the house.' Such clear examples of owner-occupier privatism were not common, however, and even this informant went on to add that 'I go out whenever I want.'

There is no evidence from the three towns survey that home ownership burdens people with heavy debts such that they cannot afford to go out and socialize. Indeed, home owners were less dissatisfied than tenants with their opportunities for going out – 60 per cent of owners compared with only 48 per cent of tenants said that they had no desire to go out any more than they already did. Twenty-eight per cent of tenants complained that they would like to go out more but were prevented from doing so by lack of money, yet only 16 per cent of owners voiced this complaint. When we take account of the difference in average incomes between the two groups, we find that tenure makes little difference – at each income level, complaints about shortage of cash inhibiting social activities are equally common among owners and tenants. Again, therefore, the privatism thesis is found to be groundless.

There is one group of owners who do tend to find that owner-occupation keeps them indoors more than they might otherwise prefer. Young couples with small children and relatively new mortgages may well have to withdraw into the home for a few years, although this has as much to do with problems in organizing babysitting (cited by 20 per cent of under-35s) as with financial stringency. Adrian Franklin has suggested that one reason why so many commentators have assumed that home ownership leads to home-centred life-styles when the evidence shows quite clearly that it does not is that they have tended to focus on precisely this group: 'Their focus is often on that stage in the life cycle when children are young and demanding and compete with other forms of sociability outside the family. Such households are busy and necessarily home and family centred for ideological and practical reasons' (1989, p. 111). Yet according to Franklin, even this group has developed new forms of sociability within the home, and this is borne out by Ineichen's work, and by data from the three towns survey which shows that less than half of them wanted to go out more often than they did.

The privatism thesis is, therefore, disproved. Owner-occupiers are more actively involved than tenants in local neighbourhood organizations, they are more likely to belong to trade unions or other work-based associations, they tend to go out more socially and they are no more inclined than tenants to stay at home when they have the choice. All of this not only undermines the privatism thesis, but also lends strong support to Hugh Stretton's argument that, rather than privatizing workers, owner-occupation facilitates greater social engagement.

In Stretton's view, domestic privacy and community life reinforce each other, for people are more likely to contribute to collective affairs when they know that they can escape back to a secure private and personal space when and as they please. The idea that private ownership leads automatically to privatism is, in other words, sociologically naïve as well as historically inaccurate; for it is only when people feel secure at home that they are likely to venture out to play an active role in the wider society, whether at work or in the local neighbourhood. Brindley recognizes this in his observation that 'People who have private places always have somewhere to escape' (1977, p. 412). So does Marcuse when he notes that 'The home as refuge, as castle, as shelter is central to most people's ability to survive, and thus also their ability to fight back' (1987, p. 261). Or as Stretton himself puts it, 'There is no way to nourish public social life by starving and overcrowding private life' (1976, p. 191).

The evidence discussed in this section strongly suggests that the private home is more a condition of social participation than it is the antithesis of it. In this sense, the idea that mass home ownership is producing a privatized society is not only groundless, but may even turn out to be the opposite of the truth.

Home ownership, ontological security and the private realm

We saw earlier that private ownership has often been elided not only with privatism, but also with privacy and the private realm. On the one hand it has been assumed that private ownership leads to privatized life-styles; on the other that it is a condition of maintaining an effective private realm by enabling people to construct and develop an independent sense of self and identity. We have seen that the first of these assumptions cannot be sustained, but what of the second? Is home ownership a necessary condition of a secure private realm?

We saw in Chapter 3 that the property rights associated with owner-occupation provide people with a degree of control over their homes which can never be matched by rental arrangements no matter how enlightened they may be. Recognizing this, a number of commentators have accepted that renters are unlikely to derive the same benefits from their homes as owners do. Whitehead, for example, concludes that 'Unless full ownership is transferred, the tenant will never feel the same about his home as the owner occupier' (1979, p. 41). Similarly Ryan suggests that 'Even humane and rational public ownership of things like houses will leave important needs unfulfilled – unless tenants' rights . . . are so guaranteed and so taken for granted that the distinction between public and private ownership begins to wither away' (1983, p. 242).

What is being suggested in these arguments is that the exclusive rights of control which ownership confers are in some way tied up with feelings of psychological security and social well-being. Ryan states the thesis quite explicitly:

> If we do not have rights of exclusion of others of the sort which go along with (though, of course, they neither add up to, nor are only to be had with) private ownership of homes and the like, we suffer insecurity, we constantly need to think about how we appear to an audience, and are ill at ease . . . A concern for ownership of one's own space is one branch of a concern for control of that space.
>
> (1983, p. 241)

Ryan's argument seems to imply two distinct claims about private ownership. One is that ownership is an important condition of personal privacy; without ownership, he says, we have constantly to worry about how we appear to an audience. The second is that ownership contributes to a sense of personal security in that it enables the development of personal identity. The second of these assumptions stands up logically and empirically rather better than the first.

Privacy has been defined as 'freedom from surveillance' (Bryant, 1978). To occupy a private realm is to deny the right of others to enforce demands upon you. Georg Simmel argued that we live in a process of continual competition with society over the ownership of our selves, and privacy is the condition of insulating our selves from the claims of the wider society (see Malmberg, 1980, p. 240). The private realm is where our social roles are dropped and our 'real selves' are allowed to surface (Porteous, 1976). Or as Giddens puts it, privacy implies release from the monitoring of actions and gestures (1984, p. 129).

This idea of privacy appears to be relatively modern. Hannah Arendt argues that in ancient times the private realm was literally a realm of privation and that freedom was sought in the public sphere through participation in the *polis*. The modern image of the private realm as a sphere of intimacy was unknown in the ancient world. What changed all this was the rise of the modern state and the growth of 'mass society'. Arendt shows how, by the eighteenth century, Rousseau and the Romantics had come to fear for the survival of the individual, and they championed the private realm as a bastion against conformism and uniformity. Today, the private realm is defended as the source of personal intimacy, and private property is seen as the means of this defence. As Arendt puts it: 'The four walls of one's private property offer the only reliable hiding place from the common public world . . . The only efficient way to guarantee the darkness of what needs to be hidden against the light of publicity is private property, a privately owned place to hide in' (1958, p. 71).

It is apparent, however, that private ownership does not guarantee privacy and that privacy can be achieved without private ownership. It is not necessary to own one's home before one can relax in it, and tenants and owners alike enjoy the right to control access to their private space. What seems to matter, therefore, is not ownership as such, but the right and ability to control boundaries and regulate access. The intimacy of the self, for which Rousseau feared, is undermined not by lack of ownership but by lack of control. When people are obliged to live in environments which they cannot control, unhappiness and resentment are likely to result. This has been shown in the case of residential homes for elderly people (see Means, 1987, p. 95) and in the case of lower-class tenants of poor-quality public housing in St Louis (Rainwater, 1966). In both cases, people were unable effectively to shut out intrusion from outside.

Home owners, of course, do enjoy more control over their dwellings than tenants do, but both have the right to keep people out. If home ownership contributes to a specific personal sense of well-being which cannot be achieved through renting, it cannot be because it enables greater privacy. More plausible is the second hypothesis – that it enables a greater sense of emotional security and a stronger development of self and identity.

In her study of two private housing estates near London and Manchester, Kuper concluded that 'For many owners the home represents some form of security, not only financially but also emotionally' (1968, p. 8). The feeling of financial security is easy to explain. As Pahl and Wallace (1985) point out, outright owners enjoy a degree of security in their home lives which may well be greater than that which is available to them in the world of formal employment. The job can always be lost, but the house, once paid for, is yours for life. But what does it mean to say that home ownership generates a feeling of emotional security?

Emotional security seems to denote the social psychological notion of durability of and confidence in the self. We can begin to understand what is entailed in this with reference to the work of the radical psychiatrist R. D. Laing. He spoke not of emotional but of 'ontological security', by which he meant 'A feeling that the self can survive whatever it encounters in the world' (Sennett and Cobb, 1973, p. 201). This same concept of 'ontological security' has been taken up more recently by Anthony Giddens, who defines it as 'Confidence or trust that the natural or social worlds are as they appear to be, including the basic existential parameters of self and social identity' (1984, p. 375).

Giddens argues that ontological security has been eroded in the modern world. The enduring ties of kinship and tradition which bind people together and give their lives sense and meaning in pre-capitalist societies have in his view been eroded by a process of 'time–space distanciation'. What he means by this is that both temporal organization and spatial organization have become formalized and divorced from nature. We mark off time, not by the position of the sun or the passing of the seasons, but by clocks and calendars. And we utilize space, not according to the natural contours and boundaries of hills, rivers and plains, but on the basis of created environments and lines drawn on maps. The result is that the content of our actions has been abstracted from its spatial and temporal context, 'a transformation of substance into form' (1981, p. 152). What we do and how we do it are no longer governed by the natural rhythms of the day or the seasons, nor do they depend on the natural resources of the land and the physical environment, but they are set by the human constructs of the timetable and the office block. Furthermore, our actions are divorced in time and space from their purposes and consequences, for we produce goods and services for people we do not know who will consume them in a different place at a future time.

The result, according to Giddens, is a sense of rootlessness and meaningless in modern life: 'Large areas of the time–space organization of day-to-day social life tend to be stripped of both a moral and a rational content for those who participate in it' (1981, p. 154). We lack a sense of belonging and a sense of purpose in our lives. This in turn leads people today to search for something which will give them a renewed sense of ontological security, and according to Giddens, people find this (albeit in a more fragile form than before) in the private realm.

Seen in these terms, we may suggest that home ownership is one expression of the search for ontological security, for a home of one's own offers both a physical (hence spatially rooted) and permanent (hence temporally rooted) location in the world. Our own home is unambiguously a place where we belong, and the things that we do there have an immediacy of presence and purpose. Putting all this in more familiar terminology, it may be suggested that home ownership represents an individual solution to the problem of alienation. As Peter Marcuse suggests, 'Home ownership is so widely favoured because, at a quite deep psychological level, it is a means by which individuals seek to overcome a sense of alienation in their lives as a whole' (1987, p. 251; see also Stretton, 1974, p. 77, for a similar argument).

The concept of ontological security is difficult to operationalize empirically, and to test whether home ownership has any effect on levels of ontological insecurity we should presumably need to utilize sophisticated indicators of people's levels of worry, concern and paranoia as well as measures of self-conception and positive social identity. None of this was addressed in the three towns survey, but we do have access to various indirect indicators, all of which lend support to the hypothesis that ontological security is enhanced by access to owner-occupation.

One indicator is the set of answers given by owners and tenants to our question on the meaning of the home. As we saw in Table 5.2, owners tended to equate the home with the idea of relaxation and personal possession, while tenants were more likely to define home in terms of family or neighbourhood. These differences were most marked in the case of recent council house buyers, who emphasized even more than other owners

"It's nice of you to meet me every night Gladys, but ..."

the idea of home as a place to relax in, a place they have worked for and a place to express pride in. One possible explanation for these variations is that tenants are less able than owners to express a sense of self and belonging through their houses. They can identify with their families and neighbours but not with the house. This has nothing to do with the building itself, but is a function of tenure. That this is the case is confirmed by the data on council house buyers, for once tenants buy their homes, it seems they can begin to identify more readily with them.

A second indirect indicator of the significance of home ownership for feelings of ontological security is provided by data on the strength of attachment which owners and tenants feel to their homes. Emotional attachment to a house can be a source of psychological comfort. Indeed, it has been suggested that people develop 'deep psychological and existential ties' to the places in which they live and that these attachments may be as important psychologically as attachments to other people (Relph, 1976, p. 41). Evidence for such claims can be found in studies showing that rates of mental illness increase when people migrate (Malmberg, 1980) and that symptoms of psychological distress rise sharply among groups who have been forcibly removed from their homes. In Boston, for example, 46 per cent of women and 38 per cent of men felt quite severe grief for at least six months after their relocation in a slum clearance scheme (Fried, 1963).

Yet despite our apparent psychological need to form attachments to places, Table 5.8 shows that tenants in the three towns survey are much less inclined to develop attachments to their houses than are owners. Only around one-quarter of owners denied feeling attached to their houses, yet nearly half of all tenants did. This is a highly significant finding, substantively as well as statistically. It cannot be explained by factors such as length of residence, for as we saw earlier, tenants tend to have lived in their

Table 5.8 *Attachment to the home by housing tenure*

Attachment to home	Council tenants No.	%	Housing tenure Owner-occupiers No.	%	Total No.	%
No strong feeling of attachment	55	46	100	28	155	33
Strong feeling of attachment	48	40	226	64	274	58
Ambivalent or other feelings	17	14	29	8	46	9

p < 0.01

current homes for at least as long as owners. Nor can it be due to differences of geographical mobility, for the two groups show no discernible difference in the number of houses they have lived in. There are important variations by age, for less than half of those under 35 felt attached to their homes compared with 80 per cent of those past retirement age, yet tenants are on average no younger than the owner-occupiers in our sample. In short, nothing except tenure itself can explain these data. Tenants have had just as much opportunity to 'put down roots' in their houses yet they are much less inclined to do so.

A third set of indicators regarding the association between tenure and ontological security concerns the extent to which people personalize their dwellings. In an important article which draws upon Jungian psychology, Clare Cooper has suggested that we grasp at physical symbols to express our sense of self, and that the house is one such symbol. We experience the house as an extension of ourselves: 'It seems as though the personal space bubble which we carry with us and which is an almost tangible extension of our self expands to embrace the house we have designated as ours. As we become accustomed to, and lay claim to, this little niche in the world, we project something of ourselves onto its physical fabric' (1976, p. 436). The self, she says, is an archetype in the collective unconscious which is expressed through a common symbol – the house. 'For most people,' she goes on, 'the self is a fragile and vulnerable entity; we wish therefore to envelop ourselves in a symbol-for-self which is familiar, solid, inviolate, unchanging' (P. 447).

The theory behind Cooper's argument can be challenged, for as Pratt (1981) points out, there is nothing inherent in housing to suggest that it always plays this role in all cultures, and it is important to recognize that even in our own culture, people may find ways of projecting themselves other than through their homes. Nevertheless, it does seem to be the case that, in most Western cultures, domestic space can play an important role in expressing individual identity. Stretton points out that 'When people can influence the design of the spaces they use, they always try to individualize them' (1978a, p. 205). The posters in the student hall of residence, the pin-ups in the prison cell and the banners at the football stadium all indicate how we try to impress our specific identities on even the most institutional of settings. How much more effort, then, do we put into personalizing our housing? As Porteous (1976) shows, we are generally more concerned to personalize the home than any other physical space. Or as Hirschman puts it: 'When owners have the opportunity, as with a house to furnish, arrange and rearrange it, to repair, improve or even to add to it, they in effect make it into a reflection of themselves. The pleasure yielded by the house is immeasurably enhanced by the narcissistic contemplation of the result of their own effort and choices' (quoted by Papadakis and Taylor-Gooby, 1987, p. 177).

Now to some extent council tenancy agreements prevent tenants from engaging in these sorts of activities (Robinson, 1983, p. 86), but what is more significant is that tenants often decline to do so when the opportunity is open to them. Tenants are responsible for internal decoration of their homes, and 80 per cent of those in the three towns survey had in fact carried out some such decoration. Thirteen per cent had also carried out some home improvements. But in many council houses, work often went undone because it was seen as the council's responsibility to do it, and when tenants did do such tasks for themselves, they often did so grudgingly or out of despair at what they saw as the council's lack of interest or concern. Thirty-eight per cent of tenants claimed that jobs needed doing in their homes but that the work had not been done because the council had not got around to doing it.

What this means is that whether or not tenants feel 'alienated' in their employment, many of them do seem to feel 'alienated' from their homes. They deny responsibility for the conditions which they themselves must live in, or if they do make improvements they feel resentment that the value of their labour will end up benefiting the council rather than themselves when and if they move house:

> We need a new tap in the bathroom – my husband won't do it on principle because he thinks the council should do it, but the council plumber won't.
> > (Female skilled non-manual worker and council tenant, Slough)

> They paint the outside every three years, though it's pretty poor when it's done . . . I put a shower in, a toilet, a built-in wardrobe in the bedroom. I thought of putting central heating in but I didn't because if anything happened to me the central heating would belong to the Corporation.
> > (Male skilled manual worker and council tenant, Derby)

> The main disadvantage is if you want to do anything structural like an extension. We wouldn't put money into a council house that wasn't our own. We'd like a patio but we wouldn't spend money on a council house.
> > (Female unskilled manual worker and council tenant, Slough)

> We've done all the repairs to this house. The council's been here once in

thirty years. We might as well have bought it. My husband's built a garage and put central heating in and it all goes back to the council.

    (Female retired skilled manual worker and council tenant, Slough)

For me to have to start spending money, I'd have to leave everything I've done. The kitchen needs modernizing but I'd have to leave it for someone else if I did it.

    (Female skilled manual worker and council tenant, Burnley)

I've a friend who's in a council house and she doesn't even clean it because it's not hers. Her husband doesn't decorate it because it's not his.

    (Female skilled manual worker and owner-occupier, Burnley)

It should have been modernized. The sink should have been changed . . . But I've never approached the council. It's their prerogative. It's their property and they should improve it. If it were mine I'd do it.

    (Male retired semi-skilled manual worker and council tenant, Slough)

One tenant even told us that he had been willing to knock down a garage he had built because the council had refused to compensate him for it when he came to move house.

Karl Marx described alienation as expending one's labour to produce goods whose value accrues to someone else: 'The worker puts his life into the object; but now his life no longer belongs to him but to the object . . . the life which he has conferred on the object confronts him as something hostile and alien' (1964, p. 108). This is precisely the experience described by those tenants who do improve their houses, for they feel that they are putting in effort on somebody else's property for somebody else's benefit. Marx also observed that under such conditions of alienation, unless people are forced to work, 'labour is shunned like the plague' (p. 111). So too we find many council tenants refusing to carry out work on what they see as the council's house. If workers do not like working in somebody else's factory, it is also apparent that they do not like living in somebody else's house. The reaction in both cases is similar.

This alienation of many tenants from their housing is reinforced by the fact that they often have little or no choice over the house in which they are obliged to live. Asked what, if anything, attracted them to their present house, no fewer than 42 per cent of tenants (compared with just 9 per cent of owners) denied that they had enjoyed any choice in the matter. Their homes had been allocated to them rather than chosen by them, and this was an additional source of disillusionment and resentment:

I'd love to move from this house . . . One day I'd like the choice of where I live rather than have someone tell me.

    (Female semi-skilled manual worker and council tenant, Slough)

We never chose this house. We were put here. We want to choose where to live.

> (Male skilled manual worker and council house buyer, Slough)

We didn't have any choice. They allocated it to us. We got a letter saying we'd got number thirty-four.

> (Female retired unskilled manual worker and council tenant, Slough)

We didn't want to be on this estate but as the houses are modernized we took it.

> (Male skilled manual worker and council tenant, Burnley)

The contrast with owner-occupiers could not be sharper. While many tenants express their alienation from their homes, many owners show pride and commitment in working in and on their homes. This seemed to be recognized by owners and tenants alike. Sixty-five per cent in each group believed that tenure makes a difference to how people feel about their homes, and many of them felt that owners were likely to look after their homes better than tenants did and to feel a greater sense of pride and achievement (Table 5.9).

Thirty-seven per cent of owners suggested that ownership leads people to take more care of their homes:

If somebody's paying rent they don't care for the garden or the property. To own is good for the country and the people.

> (Male semi-skilled manual worker and owner-occupier, Slough)

If it's your own you take more care of it. If it's mine I do a job properly no matter what the cost. If I was renting I'd do the cheapest job possible.

> (Male, intermediate occupation and owner-occupier, Slough)

There's a greater desire to take care of it [if you are an owner]. I feel sorry for tenants – they're tied, so many restrictions. Private estates always seem more looked after.

> (Male, intermediate occupation and owner-occupier, Burnley)

A further 32 per cent of owners (44 per cent among those who had bought their council houses) argued that ownership generates pride or a sense of achievement. As one former tenant in Derby put it:

We often sit down and say, 'Just think, ten years ago we were in a council house and now we've got a £50,000 bungalow, which we own.' It's an achievement, a sense of achievement when we sit down and think what we've got. We both worked hard for this, and now we can sit down and we're comfortable. All our hard work has come to fruition. I feel proud of what we've done.

> (Male, intermediate occupation and owner-occupier, Derby)

Table 5.9 *Perceived differences in attitudes of owners and tenants, by tenure*

	Owners		Tenants		Total	
Perceived difference	No.	%	No.	%	No.	%
Owners look after house better	88	37	15	19	103	33
Owners feel pride or sense of achievement	76	32	11	14	87	28
Owners are more snobbish	13	6	20	26	33	11
Owners feel more freedom to do more in the house	19	8	13	17	32	10
Owners invest a greater sense of identity in house	10	4	7	9	17	5
Other differences mentioned	38	16	16	21	54	17

N = 314 (236 owners, 78 tenants)
p < 0.01 on first 3 items; < 0.05 on fourth item; not significant at 95% or better on last two items

Not only do owners *believe* that tenure makes a difference, but there is also considerable evidence to suggest that it really does affect attitudes and behaviour. Back in the 1950s Willmott and Young found that their sample of Woodford home owners were 'preoccupied' with their houses as a result of 'sheer pride of ownership' (1960, p. 31). During the 1970s Madge and Brown (1981) followed through a group of new first-time buyers and found that within thirty months of purchase, 96 per cent of their housing had been put into a good state of repair with remaining defects being mainly decorative. The 1981 *English House Condition Survey* found that 'Generally the owner occupied stock had received greater expenditure than either of the rented sectors' (Department of the Environment, 1982, pt 2, p. 14). Such findings tend to support Colin Ward's contention, discussed in Chapter 2, that ownership does indeed encourage people to spend more time, energy and money on looking after the houses they live in.

Owner-occupiers often devote many hours of every week to working on their houses. Eighty-two per cent of the owners in our sample reported having done some DIY work on their homes, and 16 per cent (compared with only 8 per cent of tenants) mentioned DIY when they were asked about their hobbies and leisure interests. Some owners, of course, do their own repairs and decoration because they cannot afford to buy in professional services – no fewer than 48 per cent said that at least part of their motive was to save money. But 43 per cent said that they derived satisfaction from working on the house, and 13 per cent said that one reason 'for doing it themselves was that they would do a better job than anybody else would. There is, in other words, a sense of pride, satisfaction and self-esteem to be gained from even simple DIY work, and many owners delight in the thought that they are adding to the value of their homes through their own labour. Where tenants often shun such activities, owners often seem to embrace them:

I stood and looked at that kitchen ceiling for quarter of an hour last night after I'd finished it. I know it's silly but it's the satisfaction you get. And I wouldn't feel like that if I didn't own the place.

> (Male, intermediate occupation and owner-occupier, Slough)

I'm too mean to pay anybody else! We must have revalued the bathroom by £2,000. I spent £700 and the value is £2,000 . . . But I do enjoy it as well. I'd feel lost if I didn't have things to do.

> (Male, intermediate class and owner-occupier, Derby)

One obvious reason [for doing it myself] is cost. But I enjoy it. It's a hobby. And the quality of the work you have done. If you want it doing at a price, you get a shoddy job.

> (Male, intermediate class and owner-occupier, Burnley)

These findings strongly support Pahl's conclusion, following his study on the Isle of Sheppey, that while 'some self-provisioning is a coping response for those with insufficient financial resources to hire labour in the market', much of it is done because it 'provides aesthetic satisfactions, pride in workmanship and a sense of domestic solidarity' (1984, p. 105).

Domestic self-provisioning has been defined as 'The production of goods and services outside the market by household members for their own use and enjoyment' (Pahl and Wallace, 1985, p. 379). This sort of activity has been increasing in Britain and other Western countries since the early 1970s. Pahl (1984, p. 101) shows that expenditure on DIY, tools and home decorating in Britain grew by 19 per cent in real terms between 1974 and 1980. In 1986 the Central Statistical Office calculated that consumers spent £5,819 million on housing maintenance, improvement and decoration, 54 per cent of which was accounted for by DIY goods (CSO, 1987, table 4.7). Meanwhile in the USA, Scott Burns (1975) has calculated that American households produce goods and services each year with a total value equal to the GNP of the Soviet Union!

One factor which explains the recent growth of self-provisioning is the expansion in the availability of cheap domestic technology. Nearly 60 per cent of households owned a power drill in 1981 (Pahl, 1984, p. 104); 66 per cent of the households in the three towns survey did so in 1986. The spread of washing machines, freezers, vacuum cleaners, lawnmowers, sewing machines, home computers and so on has meant that the average British householder today commands greater horsepower than the average British factory worker did in 1900 (Stretton, 1978a, p. 53). If the first Industrial Revolution shifted much production from the home to the factory, then the second has shifted much of it back again. As Stretton puts it: 'The most profound achievement of modern industry – of the forty hour week of organized alienated labour – has been to give people at home energy, equipment, materials and communications, and time and space and freedom to produce for themselves' (1976, p. 186). More and more, industry provides households with the goods which enable them to produce services for themselves.

Self-provisioning is normally cheaper than buying the equivalent services commercially. Burns (1975), for example, calculates that ownership of a washing machine produces a rate of return on investment of 20 per cent per annum expressed as the savings on laundry bills. Similarly, car ownership is five times cheaper than buying the equivalent point-to-point transportation by using taxis. Moreover, not only is it cheaper, but as we saw in Chapter 3, home-based self-provisioning can provide households with the opportunity to use their own labour to increase their wealth by augmenting the resale value of their homes.

More significant than the economic advantages, however, is the opportunity which self-provisioning seems to offer for satisfying, non-alienated and uncoerced labour. As Stretton puts it:

> Well equipped and highly-skilled families produce a great many visible and invisible goods for themselves. And in doing so, they do *not* have to be alienated from ownership of their means of production, *or* from choice and control and enjoyment of what they produce, *or* from one another. In other words, the revolutionized domestic sector does away with precisely the aspects of alienation and exploitation that Marx denounced.
>
> (1978a, p. 54)

Now it is important not to push this argument too far. Not all home-based pursuits are productive, nor is all home-based production satisfying. Hardyment (1988) has quite rightly alerted us to the fact that in some cases (she cites clothing manufacture as a prime example), the movement of services out of the home has been liberating rather than debilitating in that it has freed people (normally women) from drudgery and routine. Seen in this way, movement of production back into the home (for example, laundry through the spread of washing machines) may be as much a cause for concern as for celebration. Nevertheless, much of the labour entailed in self-provisioning is voluntary and is experienced by men and women alike as genuinely productive, creative and fulfilling. Work on the house generally falls into this category, and this appears to be true for both sexes. According to market research conducted for Polycell in 1980, for example, 49 per cent of home improvements are carried out by husbands and wives working together, while 38 per cent are done mainly or wholly by men and 13 per cent wholly or mainly by women (Pahl, 1988b, p. 6).

The important point to note about this growth of self-provisioning is that it is tenure-related. In his Sheppey study, Pahl (1984) found that the households which were most active in doing things for themselves tended to be young or middle aged rather than elderly, they usually had more than one person in waged employment and they normally owned their homes rather than rented them. Similarly we have seen that in the three towns survey, self-provisioning was clearly related to ownership of a house, for tenants were often unwilling or unable to use their own labour and resources to improve their housing. Ownership of a dwelling does not necessarily generate self-provisioning activity, but it is in many ways a condition of it. If you do not own your house, you are less likely to be inclined to spend time and money working on it. Thus, while many tenants express a sense of alienation from their homes, many owners find in their homes a means for combating alienation arising from the world of formal employment.

These, then, are the factors which together seem to point to a significant association between home ownership and a sense of ontological security. We have seen that owners and tenants define their homes in different ways and that owners find it easier to equate home with the house they live in. We have also seen that owners are much more strongly attached to their houses and that such a sense of attachment to place can be an important source of psychological comfort. Owners associate home more strongly with values such as personal autonomy and they are more likely to see the home as a place where they can relax and 'be themselves'. Owners experience greater freedom in expressing choice over where they live and they experience greater control over their living space. In many cases they derive a high level of satisfaction from working on their homes, whereas many tenants feel unwilling or unable to perform such labour on a house which they constantly remember is not their own.

Does all this amount to confirmation of the argument that home ownership generates ontological security? Critics of this thesis have sometimes argued that the concept of ontological security is 'obscure' and that the hypothesis suggesting a link between it and housing tenure is impossible to test (see, for example, Harloe, 1984, p. 236). Franklin (1986, p. 39) goes even further, attacking the idea that home ownership may contribute to ontological security as mere 'polemic' and as 'a fantasy of the academic'. Such criticisms are, however, unwarranted. We have seen that the concept itself is difficult to define and awkward to operationalize, but it is possible to identify a set of indicators such as those discussed above which together can provide strong indirect evidence for or against the thesis. Whether we follow Laing in defining ontological security as robustness of the self, or whether we adopt Giddens's formulation in terms of 'basic existential parameters of self and social identity', it is clear that the concept has something to do with expression of self and identity, and the evidence discussed in this section can leave little doubt that home ownership may play a key role in such a process.

Some critics have tried to dispute this claim by showing that non-owners may also feel a sense of ontological security. Forrest and Murie (1986, p. 60), for example, point out that the desire for home ownership varies across different parts of the country, and they conclude from this that ownership can therefore have little to do with the search for ontological security, otherwise everybody would want to be an owner. In similar vein, Peter Kemp (1987) suggests that before 1914 renting was considered perfectly normal, and many households who could have afforded to buy chose not to, and he concludes from this that housing tenure can have little effect on psychological well-being. And in his discussion of housing in the

Soviet Union, Andrusz (1987) accepts that privacy is important for ontological security but he goes on to argue that this need not entail private ownership. For him, it is enough for the state to 'grant individuals private space', the amount being determined by experts such as architects, economists, demographers, sociologists and planners (p. 496).

Such arguments are generally fallacious, however. To suggest that home ownership creates ontological security does not entail denial of the possibility that non-owners may seek and achieve an equivalent sense of security through other channels. The home is a crucial location in social life, but it is not the only one. It is entirely possible that, say, Scottish tenants who have no desire to buy, nineteenth-century renters who chose not to purchase and Soviet flat-dwellers who (prior to 1988) had no choice but to rent from the state all find or found other ways of expressing identity and personal autonomy in their everyday lives. It is also possible, of course, that these groups do or did not achieve a strong feeling of security in the world and that their lives are or were all the more miserable as a result. Either way, the fact that home ownership enables ontological security does not mean that non-ownership prevents it. This type of criticism is, therefore, misplaced.

To my knowledge there has been only one previous attempt to test this thesis empirically, and that is in Cherrie Stubbs's work on council house buyers in Sunderland (Stubbs, 1988). Unfortunately, she seems confused about what the concept entails. Thus she accepts that people 'feel differently about their houses after purchase', yet she denies that this feeling amounts to a sense of ontological security. The reason she gives for this denial is that many of them still think of themselves as working class and are keen not to be regarded any differently by their neighbours (1988, pp. 153–4). Yet how they think of themselves in class terms, and whether they recognize status divisions between themselves and those who continue to rent, are issues which, though interesting, are quite irrelevant to an analysis of ontological security. More relevant is Stubbs's conclusion that 'The significance of tenure change remains personal and is personally and privately celebrated' (1988, p. 154), for this is entirely consistent with the thesis. If the move from renting to owning did produce greater feelings of ontological security, then we would expect such sentiments to get expressed and celebrated privately. Rather than contradicting the thesis, then, the Sunderland study tends to confirm it.

Recent criticisms of the view that home ownership is associated with ontological security are not, therefore, compelling, and the evidence discussed above does seem to indicate that private ownership of a house is for many people the cornerstone of a sense of independence and of their conception of their own place in the world. Anyone who still doubts this need only observe those council estates up and down the country where recent purchasers have celebrated their release into ownership with new front doors and porches, garden fences, replacement picture windows, stone-clad walls, crazy-paved paths and house names fixed to the garden gate. These homes stand out from the uniformity of the state-owned houses around them, and their message to the world is unambiguous. Each newly purchased and newly personalized former council house seems proudly to proclaim: '*This is mine! This is private! This is where I belong!*'

A woman's place?

Thus far I have focused on the question of how tenure affects the experience which people derive from their homes. This whole discussion does, however, beg the very large question of whether males and females within each of these tenure groups feel the same way.

One reason for suspecting that they may not is that they tend to perform very different tasks and duties around the home. Of course, the traditional roles and status of women have been changing quite dramatically during the twentieth century, and the organization of domestic relationships has been changing with them. In particular, the growth in the number of women employed outside the home has inevitably forced changes in the way household tasks are organized and allocated. Pahl (1984, p. 275), for example, has shown that 'The more hours the female partner is in employment, the less conventional is the domestic division of labour.'

Nevertheless, domestic work is still patterned to an extraordinary degree by gender. Despite the increased number of women who now leave the home each day to go to a place of paid employment, and despite some evidence that traditional divisions of responsibility for work within the home may be weakening in some households, there is no doubt that gender remains a key factor in shaping domestic activity. A survey by Research Bureau Ltd in 1985 found that just over half of married men had done some washing-up in the previous week, while only one in three had cooked a meal or used a vacuum cleaner, and just one in ten had washed or ironed clothes (see *Marketing Week*, 11 October 1985). Similarly, a survey conducted for the *Sunday Times* Colour Supplement (8 March 1987) found that women were mainly responsible for washing and ironing in 88 per cent of households, with a further 9 per cent sharing; for cooking the evening meal (77 per cent with 16 per cent sharing); for cleaning the house (72 per cent and 23 per cent sharing); and for shopping (54 per cent with 39 per cent sharing). Washing-up and running the household budget tended to be shared or spread more evenly, while tasks like repairing household equipment were overwhelmingly male (true of 83 per cent of households). As Hardyment suggests, 'Men's participation in housework and parenthood [is] still staggeringly low according to surveys' (1988, p. 194).

This is borne out by findings from the three towns survey, outlined in Table 5.10. From this it is obvious that the domestic division of tasks within the households in our sample is strongly patterned by gender, with laundry, cooking and house cleaning being strongly associated with women, while gardening and looking after the car tend to be predominantly male

Table 5.10 *The domestic division of labour by gender and occupational class*

Task	Reg.-Gen. class I/II	Male III	IV/V	Female I/II	III	IV/V	Joint I/II	III	IV/V
				Household member who is mainly responsible *(% figures in parentheses)*					
Cooking	8(6)	24(11)	11(7)	104(80)	164(77)	126(78)	16(12)	23(11)	22(14)
Washing-up	25(19)	36(17)	13(8)	56(43)	97(45)	102(63)	43(33)	76(35)	40(25)
Shopping	14(11)	27(13)	15(9)	74(57)	106(49)	79(49)	41(32)	79(37)	58(36)
Laundry	6(5)	16(7)	9(6)	110(85)	168(78)	132(83)	10(8)	25(12)	13(8)
Clean house	7(5)	14(7)	9(6)	90(69)	140(65)	101(63)	27(21)	54(25)	44(28)
Garden	54(42)	91(42)	67(42)	31(24)	42(20)	41(26)	35(27)	58(27)	26(16)
Maintain car	73(57)	96(45)	54(34)	15(12)	22(11)	14(9)	12(9)	14(7)	5(3)
Clean windows	28(22)	59(28)	42(26)	33(26)	54(25)	49(31)	14(11)	29(14)	11(7)
Budget	59(45)	82(38)	51(32)	44(34)	85(40)	73(46)	24(19)	42(20)	33(21)

Note: Where percentages add up to less than 100, the shortfall is accounted for by the task being done by other people (either in or outside the household) or not being done at all (e.g. car cleaning and maintenance in households without a car).

activities. It is important to recognize that work is *divided* in the sense that women do not do everything. As Pahl reminds us, 'The notion that one gender systematically and universally benefits from the way housework is divided is unsatisfactory' (1984, p. 255). Men do perform domestic tasks, but they tend to be of a specific kind.

In an earlier paper, Peter Williams and I suggested that at least three patterns could be detected in the way domestic work is divided between men and women (Saunders and Williams, 1988, p. 85). First, domestic tasks *within* the home often turn out to be feminized, while those outside it (digging the garden, cleaning the car, clearing the gutters, painting) are often taken on by or (as in the case of shopping) shared by men. Second, those tasks which are symbolically most 'polluting' (such as those – like laundering, changing nappies, caring for sick children, or cleaning the toilet – which have to do with bodily excretions) are overwhelmingly still women's chores. And third, tasks which are high on energy and low on information tend to be female, while those low on energy and high on information tend to be male. For example, although few men do the cooking, many of them take over to carve the Sunday joint or to open and serve the wine when entertaining guests. Such tasks symbolically imply knowledgeability but entail little effort, and they indicate what Parsons (1977) has referred to as a 'cybernetic hierarchy' of functions based on gender divisions.

One interesting exception to this cybernetic hierarchy of control is provided by the data on budget management. As in previous studies, the three towns survey found that women are often solely or partially in control of the household budget. As Table 5.10 shows, responsibility for organizing the money is just as likely to lie with the woman as the man, and on the council estates (where 51 per cent of women are solely responsible for the household budget compared with just 22 per cent of men) this pattern is even more pronounced. This responsibility may, of course, be experienced by some women (especially those on tight budgets) as irksome, but the fact remains that control over spending is a major power resource within household units as much as within any other social groupings.

What all this amounts to is that women do most of the work in the home, but do not do all of it, and that although they generally get left with some of the least attractive and most repetitious tasks, they also often play a major role in key control tasks such as budget management.

In his Sheppey study, Pahl found that patterns of domestic labour varied very little across the social classes (1984, p. 272). The results of the three towns survey confirm this. From Table 5.10 it is clear that, with just one exception (male semi- and unskilled manual workers are much less likely to be found washing up than are men from higher social class groups), the pattern of domestic work appears fairly similar across professional, managerial, white-collar and manual working-class households. It should also be said at this point that there is no difference in the organization of domestic labour in the different tenure groups – cross-tabulation of tenure with the sexual division of tasks within the home failed to achieve statistical significance on any item except for budget management (discussed earlier).

The fact that women tend to do more of the less pleasant work around the home has led many feminists to argue that they are therefore likely to experience the home in a very different way than men. Men, it is suggested, experience the home as a retreat, as an emotional refuge from work and as a place where they can exert power. Such positive emotions, it is argued, are not shared by women since it is they who cook the meals, iron the shirts and hoover up the dog hairs from the hearthrug.

Davidoff, L'Esperance and Newby, for example, criticize what they see as the 'fantasy' of the home as haven, and urge us to 'lay aside the rosy spectacles' and to recognize that the cosy domestic imagery associated with the home is premissed upon long and unrewarding hours of female labour (1976, p. 173). Suzanne MacKenzie and Damaris Rose similarly argue that 'For women in their domestic role, the ideal single-family home has always been primarily a *workplace* for their reproductive work, and often a very oppressive and isolating one, rather than a haven' (1983, p. 159, original emphasis). Linda McDowell agrees: 'Women clean, prepare food, mend clothes and generally put things in order for their husbands and children for whom the home is more normally regarded as a place of rest and respite from work' (1983a, p. 142). The image of the home as offering relaxation and recuperation is dismissed in this literature as a 'male view of the home' (Allan, 1985, p. 56), or even as a 'male myth' (Sopher, 1979, p. 133). While men experience home as haven, their wives experience it as an oppressive workplace which drives them into 'serious states of depression . . . drug-dependency and alcoholism' (Cowley, 1979, p. 42). For women, we are told, the home is 'a spatial component of their economic oppression' (Hayden, 1981, p. 295). Home for the woman is experienced as a place of confinement and oppression (Marcuse, 1987, p. 247). The female householder is, in short, a 'captive wife' (the title of a much-quoted book by Hannah Gavron).

Some feminist critics of the home have attacked home ownership in particular, arguing that it is the most oppressive form of housing for women. Austerberry and Watson, for example, announce that 'As socialist-feminists it is important to challenge owner occupation as a form of tenure' (1985, p. 98). This is because, first, the autonomy of ownership only advantages the male householder; second, the cost of house purchase means that women have to increase their dependency on male 'bread-winners' in order to get housed; and, third, the pressure on the wife to keep the home spotless is even greater in an owner-occupied house 'where standards are seen to be the individual responsibility of the owners' (1985, p. 106). Watson has elsewhere added to this catalogue of evils by further suggesting that home ownership perpetuates patriarchy by idealizing home life:

The promotion of owner occupation has particular implications for women, since there is a close ideological association between owner occupation, or rather 'owning your own home', and an implied domestic role for women. The ideal home with the ideal housewife choosing the furniture and fittings, and providing a warm and comfortable environment for her family is an all pervasive scenario reflected in the popular media and literature.

(Watson, 1986a, pp. 22–3; see also Watson, 1986b)

In the view of these and many other writers, male home comforts are achieved at the expense of females, and the positive images of home life which pervade our culture – what Linda McDowell dismissively refers to as 'the ideology of the home as haven rather than as workplace' (1983b, p. 69) – are thus representative only of the male experience. For women, home is more of a 'prison' than a 'haven', more of a 'cage' than a 'castle' (Allan and Crowe, 1988, p. 5).

What is remarkable about much of this literature (apart from its repetitive character) is how rarely these writers feel any need to back up their assertions with evidence. As we have seen, there is no doubt that women do perform much of the work in the home, but it seems all too often to be assumed from this that they therefore experience home negatively as an oppressive and alienative environment. Judging by what women told us during the three towns survey, this seems not to be the case.

Let us begin with the issue of home ownership. In the three towns survey, 89 per cent of women and 92 per cent of men said that they would prefer to own rather than rent. If owner-occupation were really experienced by women as the most oppressive form of tenure, we should hardly expect nine out of ten of them to give it as their first preference. In their work on council house buyers, Banion and Stubbs found that women purchasers were apt to express 'pride in ownership and control of the home, seeing owner occupation as offering real gains in security as a woman . . . There was certainly little to indicate that this was perceived as anything but a gain in the minds of the women involved' (1986, p. 190). Yet Sophie Watson would have it that the 89 per cent of the women in the three towns survey are sadly misguided, and that the women householders who bought their council homes in Sunderland had taken a step backwards into the clutches of male oppression. Either the academic feminists have got their theories wrong or millions of ordinary women are too stupid to recognize their own best interests.

This is not the only example of where feminist dogma and empirical evidence part company. There is, for example, no evidence from the three towns survey that women feel any more tied to the home than men do. Men and women go out socially – to the pub, to visit friends, to meetings, or whatever – in roughly the same proportion (53 per cent of women and 56 per cent of men go out on a regular basis, while a further 11 per cent of women and 12 per cent of men go out frequently). Even more significant than this is the fact that men and women are equally contented about the opportunities they enjoy for going out. Fifty-six per cent of women and 57 per cent of men said they had no desire to go out any more than they already do. Most of those who would have liked to have gone out more often cited lack of money as the major obstacle (mentioned by 23 per cent of men and 16 per cent of women). The other major factor was babysitting problems, which, predictably perhaps, were mentioned more by women (10 per cent) than by men (6 per cent).

There is no reason to believe that these sorts of findings are in any way peculiar – in Bristol, for example, Franklin found that 'few women reported feelings of isolation and boredom in the home' (1989, p. 108). Yet such findings cast considerable doubt on the dark images conjured up in the feminist literature of the home as a female prison.

Not only do women feel no more tied to the home than men do, but they also feel equally positive about the benefits of home life. As Table 5.11 shows, there is simply no evidence from the three towns survey to support the view that home is experienced as a haven by men but as a place of oppression by women. The association of home with images of comfort, relaxation, warmth, love and affection is no male myth, for it is shared by men and women alike. In her study of a group of young working-class mothers in Bergen (Norway), Gullestad (1983, p. 85) argues that the home has a central significance as a source of identity and a means of expressing autonomy for husbands and wives alike. The data reported in Table 5.11 suggest that the same is true in Britain.

These findings are crucially important for they must lead us to question the sorts of assertions being made in the feminist literature. While it is certainly true that the home is more of a 'workplace' for women than for men, it is equally certainly true that this has little effect on the positive sentiments which they attach to it. The evidence on this point is compelling, and it is reinforced by similar findings from the recent national survey conducted by Marshall and his colleagues, who report that, 'somewhat surprisingly', there was no difference between male and female views of the

Table 5.11 *The meaning of the home for men and women*

Home means:	Men No.	Men %	Women No.	Women %	Total No.	Total %
Family, love, children	83	35	81	37	164	36
Comfort, relaxation	53	23	60	27	113	25
Place you own or worked for	38	16	41	19	79	17
Belonging to a neighbourhood	35	15	28	13	63	14
Personal possessions	20	9	25	11	45	10
Long residence or memories	13	6	22	10	35	8
Privacy, a retreat, peace	9	4	8	4	17	4
Place of sanctuary or safety	6	3	10	5	16	4
Independence, being your own boss	8	3	6	3	14	3
Don't know	10	4	20	9	30	7
Total	235		220		455	

meaning of the home (1988, p. 213). This same study also found that, of over 3,000 replies to their question on the meaning of the home, just six mentioned the idea of the home as a place of work or a place which has to be kept clean and tidy. Rarely in the history of social science can there have been so glaring a disparity between the view of reality emphasized by academics and the view of reality held by those of whom they purport to write. The orthodox feminist image of the home as an oppressive institution simply does not square with what women themselves say and feel about it.

At this point, feminist critics may be tempted to argue that patriarchy is a structural relationship which operates whether or not women are aware of it. This seems to be what Oakley has in mind, for example, when she dismisses evidence of female endorsement of home life as simply 'a rationalization of inferior status' (1974, p. 233). Similarly Brittan (1977, p. 75) argues with breathtaking arrogance that 'the illusion of personal fulfillment' is an ideological stumbling block which prevents women from recognizing the need for their own liberation from the home. Such responses should, however, be rejected with all the derision they deserve, for they entail the familiar subterfuge of denying the validity of what people tell us whenever we do not like what we hear. If feminist critics of the home were right, and patriarchal relations were indeed so oppressive as to make the home a place of comfort for men but a place of oppression for women, then we should expect this to show up in people's comments. The fact is that it does not. *None* of the women in our sample spontaneously referred to home as a place of work or oppression; and as we have seen, this figured in 0.002 per cent of answers in the Marshall survey. Women are just as enthusiastic as men in volunteering images of warmth, love and comfort when asked what the home means to them, and their answers should be respected as valid representations of their everyday experiences.

Other indicators all reinforce this conclusion. We asked people whether they felt attached to their homes and whether they entertained hopes of moving to somewhere else at some point in the future. Men and women answered in roughly similar terms. Indeed, more women (61 per cent) than men (54 per cent) said that they felt attached to their houses and would be unhappy to leave them, while exactly half of all men and half of all women said that they had no intention to move. If women's experience of the home were as alienative, as 'oppressive and isolating', as is often suggested, we should surely expect to find much higher levels of emotional detachment and restlessness.

Similarly, we asked whether our respondents harboured some image of an 'ideal home', and again women responded in much the same way as men, telling us how they would like a cottage in the country (22 per cent of women and 23 per cent of men), how they dream of a place with a large garden (14 per cent of men and women) and so on. According to Davidoff and her co-authors, such idyllic imagery of thatched cottages and rural retreats – what they term the 'beau ideal' – serves only to mystify and disguise the tensions and power relations which are maintained within the home. Perhaps – but few of the women in our sample would agree.

What all this suggests is the need to distinguish the question of the work which people do in the home from the different question of the emotional significance which the home has for them. It may be, of course, that these two aspects of experience of home are to some extent contradictory (Matrix, 1984, p. 2). In other words, we may experience the home as a place where we can express our individuality and where we can relax and 'be ourselves', but if it is our responsibility to perform most of the domestic labour, then we may also feel at the same time that instead of sitting in front of the television and relaxing we 'should' be clearing the dishes or getting on with the laundry. Some years ago, Relph recognized that emotional commitments to places can be simultaneously central to our lives and constricting on our actions: 'Drudgery is always a part of profound commitment to a place . . . Our experience of place, and especially of home, is a dialectical one – balancing a need to stay with a desire to escape' (1976, p. 42). This tension may arise for men and women, but to the extent that women continue to do most of the work in the home, this contradiction is likely to be most acutely felt by them.

Be that as it may, the evidence from this survey suggests that the image of the 'home as haven' is not a peculiarly male one, and that for both men and women, the home may be experienced in a positive way as a realm where they can relax, 'be themselves', establish their own rules of conduct and feel relatively secure. Pahl has written of an 'overall set of values concerned with homeliness, cosiness, domesticity and a belief that, if one can control just a small part of this large and threatening world, then one has achieved something worthwhile' (1984, p. 324). These are values which are not limited to any one gender.

Conclusions

The home is a core institution in modern society. It shelters the smallest viable unit of social organization – the household – and basic patterns of social relations are forged, reproduced and changed within it. It is the place with which individuals can most readily identify and it easily lends itself to the symbolic expression of personal identity. It offers both physical and psychological shelter and comfort. It is the place where the self can be expressed outside of social roles and where the individual can exert autonomy away from the coercive gaze of the employer and the state. It is the private realm in an increasingly public and intrusive world. For many of us, its integrity is of the utmost value in our lives.

Given that the home is such a crucial and central institution, it would be surprising if its ownership made no difference to its enjoyment and significance. Ownership not only guarantees certain rights which may be denied to tenants, but it also ensures permanency, even across generations. In a world where change is rapid and expectations are forever being turned upside down, the privately owned home seems to represent a secure anchor point where the nerves can be rested and the senses allowed to relax.

In this chapter we have explored the relationship between ownership and the way people experience their homes. In the process, we have unpacked three commonly identified sets of associations having to do with the home. The first was that between ownership and privatized values and life-styles. The second was that between ownership and psychological well-being. The third was that between gender and autonomy or oppression. On inspection, only the second of these apparent associations turned out to be empirically supported.

In respect of the first, we saw that many observers have suggested that ways of life in Britain are becoming more privatized in the sense of more home-centred. This is often explained as the product of the spread of owner-occupation, although other factors are also thought to have contributed, among them the improvement in home comforts, the expansion of home-based consumer durables, the increase in leisure time, the growing disillusionment with formal employment, the spread of the suburbs and the decline in the necessity for neighbourhood-based mutual aid. We saw, however, that this privatism thesis is dubious historically (for home-centredness goes back for well over one hundred years and has in any case tended to coexist with social activity) and almost certainly unsupported sociologically. Drawing on the findings of the three towns survey, it was shown that owner-occupiers are often *more* actively engaged in social life than are tenants. Even controlling for class and income differences, owner-occupiers are *more* likely than tenants to participate in clubs and organizations outside the home, to belong to neighbourhood-based residents' groups and to be members of work-based bodies such as trade unions or professional associations. They also tend to go out more socially and to be more satisfied with their social lives. For all these reasons, the belief that

311

home ownership leads to privatism was firmly rejected, and we followed Hugh Stretton in suggesting instead that owner-occupation may enable rather than constrain social activity of various sorts.

The other familiar association for which there was no evidence was that between gender and positive or negative experiences of home life. We saw that tasks within the home do reveal a clear pattern based on familiar stereotypes of male and female work, but we also found that this does not mean that women find the home any more oppressive or less supportive than their menfolk. Women do not generally feel that they are tied to the home, most of them go out as often as men, and they are happy with their opportunities for getting out of the house whenever they wish. They see the home in the same positive light as men do – as a place to relax, a place of comfort, a place of warmth and love – and they are just as emotionally committed to their homes as men are. There is, quite simply, no evidence to support feminist claims that women experience the home as oppressive or that notions of the home as haven are a male myth. Indeed, much of the feminist literature in this area seems to have developed through assertion rather than research, and the stereotypes which it peddles owe more to images of nineteenth-century domestic drudgery and sexual exploitation than to home life as it is lived by most men and women in the 1980s.

The one association which was borne out by the evidence was that between home ownership and what was termed, following Laing and Giddens, a sense of 'ontological security'. The thesis that home ownership may generate ontological security has been subject to some scepticism in recent years, but by identifying a series of indicators it was possible to assemble a strong set of evidence to support the thesis. In particular, we found that owners are much more strongly attached to their homes in emotional terms than tenants are. We also showed that owners invest a different meaning in their homes than tenants, such that they tend to equate their houses with images of comfort and relaxation, whereas tenants generally find it difficult to draw such an association. Many tenants feel what can only be described as 'alienation' from their homes. They seemed constantly aware that they were living in someone else's house, and this often inhibited them from doing work and making improvements which they would like to have done and which would have made their lives more comfortable and fulfilling. Owners, by contrast, felt free to engage in a wide variety of self-provisioning activity in and through their homes, and this was often experienced as a way of expressing their identity through uncoerced and non-alienative labour.

What we have seen in this chapter, then, is that the growth of home ownership in Britain may be having profound cultural – as well as economic and political – consequences. When ordinary men and women own their homes, they seem to feel more confident and self-reliant. Because they have a base which they feel is financially and emotionally secure, they are more willing to venture out into social activities beyond the home as well as to devote considerable time and energy to improving the living environment within their own boundaries. A home-owning society is likely to be one where people are quietly proud of their achievements and fiercely jealous of their rights and privileges. It is one where people will fight tenaciously to defend what they have got, but where, if they do not feel threatened, they will join in collective life, thereby sustaining rather than undermining the vitality of civil society. It is almost as if the vanished independent yeomanry of England is gradually being remade behind the hedgerows of Acacia Avenue.

6 The marginalized minority

In Chapter 1 we saw that Britain has been through a housing revolution in the twentieth century. Before the First World War, 90 per cent of the population lived in houses or flats which belonged to somebody else; today this is true for only one-third of the population, most of whom are now tenants of the state. For the majority of people, the house that they live in is now the home which they own.

The consequences of this move to a home-owning society have been reviewed in the various chapters of this book. We have seen that home ownership is widely desired, while council renting is preferred by few. One reason why so many people want to own is that they see better financial prospects in owning as opposed to renting. Many believe that buying a house costs less in the long run, and many also cherish the opportunity to build up a valuable capital asset which may be drawn upon later in life and which can be passed on to their children. For the first time in its history, Britain is becoming a genuine property-owning democracy. The market value of privately owned housing now amounts to £739 billion, equivalent to nearly twice the value of the nation's gross domestic product (Bracewell-Milnes, 1989). This capital is widely distributed through the population – ethnic minorities as well as whites, working-class people as well as middle-class people, owners of the cheapest houses as well as owners of expensive ones, all have benefited financially from house purchase. As we saw in Chapter 3, millions of ordinary people have accumulated capital sums through home ownership which would have been inconceivable to their parents or grandparents, and which they themselves could never have hoped to save from earnings from employment.

Financial gain is not the only reason why owner-occupation has become so popular, however, for many people also find in home ownership a means for expressing and realizing values of autonomy, personal independence and emotional security which are deeply cherished. Home ownership enables them to personalize their surroundings and it fosters a stronger sense of belonging and personal achievement. By providing people with a secure home base which they can call their own, it also underpins a greater willingness to become involved in social affairs beyond the garden gate; for as we saw in Chapter 5, a sense of domestic security may well be a necessary condition for participation in wider social and civic affairs.

All of this, however, poses one stark and uncomfortable question. What happens to those who cannot afford to buy? If the home-owning majority are building up their capital assets, enjoying an enhanced sense of autonomy

314

and personal fulfilment, and may even be encouraged in the future to move into private services in other areas of provision, what is to become of those who are too old or too poor to buy? If a home-owning democracy encourages values of self-reliance and independence among a majority of the population, what is to happen to the minority whose voice can be ignored by parties seeking to win political office? We have seen that most tenants would prefer to buy, that most are dissatisfied in one way or another with their local authority landlords and that most are happy to support policies which aid the spread of home ownership, yet under existing arrangements they seem unlikely to realize their preferences. The danger is that their aspirations will go unfulfilled, and that as time goes on they will become less and less able to gain access to house purchase.

The nightmare scenario which this opens up is of a twenty-first-century Britain in which perhaps three-quarters of the population enjoy the benefits of property ownership while the remaining quarter are confined to crumbling and stigmatized estates in which are concentrated the multitude of problems associated with unemployment, broken families, poverty, crime, social malaise and moral disintegration. The signs of such stark polarization are already apparent, and the implications are frightening. On the Broadwater Farm estate in Tottenham, North London, where a lone police officer was surrounded and hacked to death by rioters in 1985, the Post Office has stopped delivering letters for fear of personal assault, and doctors refuse to make house calls because their drugs get stolen when they go to attend patients. The question is whether estates like Broadwater Farm are destined to become the norm rather than the exception. The extension of home ownership to three-quarters of British households will become a Pyrrhic victory if the remaining quarter are to be coralled within isolated islands of state dependency with no prospect of escape or deliverance.

Polarization and residualization

The British class structure is changing. Sociologists, of course, have never agreed on how social class should be defined or conceptualized, still less on what the class system looks like and how it might be changing. Nevertheless, there is widespread recognition, even among Marxists, that simple dichotomous models in which a small class of capitalists is counterposed to a large and exploited class of proletarians are unhelpful, and that any theory or model must take account of the expansion of intermediate positions between these two extremes as well as of divisions within each category. Put simply, the middle class has been growing, the traditional working class has been shrinking, and the line of demarcation between the two has in some respects become less sharp and distinct.

According to some observers, one change of particular significance has involved the expansion of a relatively prosperous stratum together with the emergence of an increasingly deprived one. This process of 'social

315

restratification' has a number of causes including the growth of service occupations, the decline in employment in heavy manufacturing, the introduction of new technologies demanding a highly-skilled and autonomous workforce, the rise in the number of dual-earner households which creates a new division between 'work-rich' and 'work-poor' households, the expansion of managerial and administrative functions in both the public and private sectors, the collapse of Keynesian full-employment strategies and the emergence of large-scale unemployment among specific sections of the population, and the attempts by governments since 1976 to control the growth of social expenditure. According to Ray Pahl (1984, 1988a), the result of such developments has been the growth of what he calls the 'middle mass' on the one hand, and the 'underclass' on the other.

Pahl warns against any uncritical adoption of simplistic conceptions of a new class polarization. Nevertheless, he does suggest that in Britain, the class system is coming to correspond less to the familiar metaphor of a pyramid (that is, a small stratum at the top, a larger middle stratum and the mass of the population at the base), and more to that of an onion (with the majority in the bulging and comfortable middle, while a smaller stratum remains anchored to the bottom). Seen in this way, familiar lines of cleavage drawn between, say, the manual working class and the lower middle class are losing their significance. Far more important is the cleavage that is opening up between the middle mass (which includes large numbers of working-class as well as middle-class households) and the lower stratum or underclass. As Pahl puts it, 'The division between the more affluent home-owning households of ordinary working people and the less advantaged underclass households is coming to be more significant than conventional divisions based on the manual/non-manual distinction . . . The new line of class cleavage is now between the middle mass and the underclass beneath it' (1984, pp. 314, 324).

For Pahl, a number of factors differentiate these two strata. One, certainly, is employment – not so much the kind of jobs which people do, but whether or not they have secure, full-time employment. Another is household structure, for members of the middle mass are likely to live in households where two or more members can expect to have jobs, full or part time, and therefore contribute to the household budget. A third is housing tenure. By and large, the middle mass increasingly owns its housing, while the underclass rents from the state.

I have elsewhere discussed the principal features which go to make up that stratum which may be termed the emerging 'underclass' of British society (Saunders, 1989; see also Dahrendorf, 1987). Four factors are particularly pertinent. First, it suffers multiple deprivations, a culmination of social pathologies and disadvantages. Second, it is socially marginal. Its members do not generally belong to formal organizations such as trade unions, nor do they find it easy to participate in the mainstream society for they are often unemployed and lack everyday means of communication such as cars and telephones. They are also often marginalized or ghettoized by virtue of their race or their family structure. Third, it is characterized by a culture of fatalism which is both a response to hopelessness and a factor which reproduces it. And finally, it is a dependent class. Its members are powerless clients of a patronage state, relying upon state provision not only for their health care and their children's schooling, but for virtually every aspect of their lives including their income and their housing.

Of course, tenurial divisions do not neatly coincide with this distinction between the middle mass and the underclass. Dahrendorf estimates the size of the underclass in Britain at around 5 per cent of the population, but as we saw in Chapter 1, a quarter of the population still live in state housing. Clearly, by no means all council tenants are members of this underclass – many of those interviewed in the three towns survey were relatively affluent and financially secure – although it is probably true to say that very few home owners belong to it. The point, however, is that as more people move into owner-occupation, so council renting is likely to become increasingly reserved for those who cannot participate in the mainstream economy and society by virtue of age, infirmity, or unemployability. As Ray Forrest puts it, 'Although marginal groups such as the long-term unemployed, ethnic minorities, working class youth, single-parent families, are not concentrated exclusively in the state housing sector, the largest spatial concentrations are to be found in the council estates of the inner city or urban periphery' (1987, p. 1620).

The trend, therefore, seems to be that tenure divisions are coming to reinforce and express existing social divisions. As the haves move increasingly into home ownership, the have-nots become geographically concentrated in public renting. To the extent that this happens, then the poorer and least popular council estates (where few tenants want to buy and even fewer can afford to) will increasingly come to be seen as the dumping grounds where the problems and casualties of our society can be concentrated, controlled and forgotten.

There are signs that this process may already be well advanced. According to Yates, 'Public housing is drifting solely towards a residual, welfare role – an ambulance service to carry off the wounded – catering largely for lower income and disadvantaged groups' (1982, p. 218). We saw some of the evidence for this view in Chapter 1. As regards income distribution, for example, we saw in Table 1.3 that 89 per cent of households in the lowest decile of household income are now to be found in council renting. It has long been the case, of course, that low-income households have been concentrated disproportionately in this sector, but this pattern has become increasingly marked over the last thirty years. Forrest and Murie (1987a) show that, while 26 per cent of households in the bottom third of the income distribution rented from local authorities in 1963, this figure had risen to 57 per cent by 1985.

The same pattern is revealed in data on recipients of supplementary benefits. Forrest and Murie show that the proportion of home owners claiming supplementary benefit grew from 4 to 5 per cent between 1979 and

1984 (a period when home ownership expanded from 11.6 to nearly 14 million households), but the proportion of council tenants claiming benefit expanded during this same period from 21 per cent to 34 per cent. Indeed, if rent rebates are included, the proportion of council tenants in receipt of some means-tested benefit stood at 63 per cent in 1986–7.

Such high rates of dependency upon state income support among council tenants are partly a function of disproportionately high rates of unemployment. Figures presented in the *Labour Force Survey 1985* (OPCS, 1987) show that the 27 per cent of households in public-sector renting accounted for 49 per cent of all unemployed adults who had been seeking work for six months or more. The high rates of dependency on state benefits also reflects the large number of council tenants who are classified as 'economically inactive' (a category which includes retired people, the sick and disabled, and adults of working age who are not seeking employment such as housewives and single parents). The *Labour Force Survey* reveals that council tenants account for only 19 per cent of all economically active adults in Britain, and Robinson and O'Sullivan (1983) show that the majority of single-parent families and of low-income single-person households over retirement age now live in council accommodation.

318

Furthermore, those council tenants who are in employment are usually found in semi- and unskilled manual occupations. In Table 1.2 we saw that 41 per cent of semi-skilled workers and 57 per cent of unskilled workers were renting from local authorities in 1985. In a series of important papers, Chris Hamnett has shown that, as the private rented sector has shrunk, so the association between council renting and social class has strengthened. The private rented sector used to be socially heterogeneous, but the council rented sector is overwhelmingly working class in social composition. Hamnett (1984a) shows that, between 1961 and 1981, the decline in the proportion of professional, managerial and skilled manual employees renting privately is almost entirely explained by moves into owner-occupation; but among semi-skilled workers, only half of those leaving private renting went into owner-occupation, and among unskilled manual workers this proportion was only one-third. Thus, although home ownership rates have been rising among semi- and unskilled manual strata, so too have rates of council renting, for the growth of council renting in the 1960s and 1970s was almost entirely confined to these groups. As Hamnett concludes, 'Skilled manual workers have moved increasingly into the owner occupied sector, leaving behind them a council sector increasingly dominated by the semi-skilled, the unskilled and the economically inactive' (1984a, p. 397; see also Hamnett and Randolph, 1986, for an analysis which traces moves across tenures in London between the 1971 and 1981 Censuses).

Hamnett describes this trend as a process of 'socio-tenurial polarization' – that is, a process in which different socioeconomic groups are becoming increasingly associated with different housing tenures. As Berge (1988) has demonstrated, however, this formulation may be somewhat misleading, for 'polarization' implies a clustering at *both* tenure poles. While it is certainly true that council renting is increasingly associated with the lowest socioeconomic groups, Berge shows that it is not true that owner-occupation is correspondingly increasingly associated with the highest groups. Indeed, the relative share of owner-occupied housing held by professional and managerial strata has actually fallen as skilled manual workers have moved into home ownership; and this suggests that, while council renting has become more homogeneous in social class composition, owner-occupation has become more heterogeneous. As Forrest and Murie (1987a, p. 24) recognize, socio-tenurial polarization is therefore becoming *less* marked as home ownership becomes more socially diverse.

This conclusion is entirely consistent with Pahl's contention that a division is opening up between a socially mixed home-owning 'middle mass' and a propertyless 'underclass'. What has been happening is not polarization between classes, but residualization of the bottom stratum. Council renting is being left to a 'residuum' of old, poor and unskilled people who cannot afford anything else, while the rest of the working class makes good its escape into the home-owning middle mass.

As we saw in Chapter 2, this escape has been facilitated since 1980 by the statutory provision for council tenants to buy their homes at discounted

319

prices. This policy has resulted in one million households transferring between the tenures. Those who have bought have, by and large, been the more affluent tenants, and this has in turn given an extra twist to the process of residualization. As Lundqvist (1986, p. 128) notes, those who have bought share many of the social characteristics of existing owners, and sales have therefore sharpened the social differences between the tenures, since those who have been left behind tend to be concentrated in the least advantaged sections of the population.

All studies of council house sales show that buyers have higher incomes than other tenants – Nellis and Fleming (1987) found in their analysis of 55,000 sales in 1985 that the mean income for the heads of households who bought was twice that of those who continued to rent. Studies also show that buyers are disproportionately middle aged and are often drawn from households with more than one earner. In Aberdeen, for example, 75 per cent of sales have been to multiple-earner households, and the mean number of earners in purchasing households is 2.15 as compared with 1.17 among non-purchasers (Williams, Sewel and Twine, 1986; see also Dunn, Forrest and Murie, 1987, and Forrest and Murie, 1984, for similar evidence on other parts of the country). These same studies also demonstrate that sales have been concentrated among households where the principal earner is in secure employment, where he or she is in a skilled manual or a non-manual occupation and where the family is of a conventional nuclear type. Williams, Sewel and Twine conclude on the basis of a logit model fitted to their data, 'Purchasers are more likely to have higher incomes; to come from households with two or more incomes; to come from social classes I, II and III; to be aged between 41 and 64; and to come from households with two or more adults of working age, especially when there are no dependent children' (1986, p. 281).

It follows from this that the sale of council stock has increased the proportion of council tenants who are old, who live in households with one or no earners, who have low incomes, who are in the lowest social classes and who live in single-person households or in single-parent families. Furthermore, there has been a marked tendency for sales to be concentrated among those living in the most desirable parts of the council stock. Nellis and Fleming found that 95 per cent of sales were to tenants living in semi-detached or terraced houses, while only 4 per cent were to those living in flats; and a 1985 BSA survey similarly revealed that while flats account for 28 per cent of the total stock, they represented only 7 per cent of sales (cited in Machon, 1987). This suggests, not only that a distinctive stratum of the British population is being left in the public sector, but also that 'the council sector is becoming more distinct from owner occupation in terms of dwelling type' (Forrest and Murie, 1984, p. 27). When we asked our respondents in the three towns survey to describe their 'ideal home', 28 per cent of council tenants said they would like a larger house than the one they had, 23 per cent spoke of a cottage in the country, 18 per cent said they would like a bungalow, 15 per cent said they would like a house with a big garden, and

10 per cent said they would like to live in a detached house, but nobody said that they would like to live in a block of flats. The reality of their situation, however, is that as more council houses are sold, the likelihood of new tenants being allocated to one of the despised high-rise or deck-access estates is increasing.

All commentators agree that a process of residualization is taking place. Council renting is becoming ever more distinctive in terms of both the people who live in this sector and the kind of accommodation which is found there. Where there is disagreement, however, is over two fundamental questions arising out of this evidence. One concerns the significance of this trend for an understanding of how the British class system is changing. The other relates to the sorts of policies which could or should be pursued to ameliorate the situation of those who remain in the public sector. It is with these two issues that the remainder of this chapter will be concerned.

Housing tenure and the British class structure

Although not everybody would subscribe to Ray Pahl's view that the major social cleavage in contemporary Britain is becoming that between a home-owning middle mass and a propertyless underclass, most analysts do recognize that the division between these two strata is becoming more marked and more significant. The question, however, is whether this division can be explained as an expression of existing class differences.

Now it is obvious that people's class situation has a major influence on whether or not they can get access to home ownership. The reason why most council house buyers are drawn from the Registrar-General's social classes I, II and III is quite simply that these groups tend to enjoy greater security of employment and a higher earning capacity. Lending institutions are understandably reluctant to provide a mortgage for people whose jobs are insecure and low-paid. In this sense, the division between the majority of people who are in home ownership and the minority who remain in council renting is simply an expression of the inequality which already exists between different classes. As Ray Forrest puts it, 'Housing positions reflect and enhance class positions, they do not transform them' (1983, p. 213). If this is the case, then it follows that analysis of housing inequalities should focus not on people's housing situations but on their position in the labour market. Thus Forrest and Murie suggest:

> Divisions in consumption are significant, and notably in housing, but the analytical starting point must be labour market and economic restructuring. Whilst for those in work living standards have continued to rise, the unemployed have experienced a decline in real personal disposable incomes . . . The discussion of housing tenure change should, it is argued,

321

be linked to these changes prior to examination of consumption cleavages.

(1986, p. 49)

There are, however, two reasons for questioning this view that inequalities between housing tenures are simply one expression of existing inequalities between social classes.

The first is that, while class position is obviously one important factor shaping access to home ownership, it is not the only one. As Pahl's work shows, and as the evidence on council house sales underlines, there are other factors which are just as important as social class. One of these is undoubtedly household structure and composition, for in a household where two or more adults are earning, a relatively weak class position is often countered by a relatively high aggregate household income. Similarly, as we saw in Chapter 1, geographical location can be as important as social location in shaping people's life chances, for house prices vary markedly between different parts of the country, and two people occupying similar class positions may find that they enjoy very different opportunities for gaining access to owner-occupation or for accumulating wealth once they have done so. An analysis which focuses solely or even primarily on class differentiation will thus fail to understand some of the most important processes shaping patterns of housing change.

The second reason for rejecting the view that housing inequalities should be analysed as the product of class inequalities is that patterns of consumption of housing may themselves contribute to inequalities of life chances. As we saw in Chapter 3, the home-owning middle mass is accumulating wealth through ownership of its housing. As Hamnett (1988b) has argued, house price inflation is constantly widening the economic gap between owners and non-owners. Existing economic inequalities are thus overlaid by new ones.

The whole argument really turns on this issue of capital gains. To sustain his position, Forrest would need to be able to show that middle-class owner-occupiers accumulate wealth from housing while working-class owner-occupiers do not. He hints that this *may* be the case: 'For many owners, the real appreciation of their asset is not assured. House ownership may be a game we can all play, but the chances of winning are skewed heavily in certain directions' (1983, p. 214). Yet the evidence outlined in Chapter 3 is surely incontrovertible – members of *all* classes secure capital gains through home ownership. This means that class position and housing position have independent effects on people's life chances, in which case the latter cannot be seen simply as an expression of the former. The lifetime income capacity of young people today has to be calculated, not only in terms of their earnings potential from employment, but also in terms of their potential for accumulating wealth through participation in the housing market and through inheritance of housing. The housing system is not simply a reflection of the class system, for it is itself a source of economic advantage.

As Pahl suggests, 'It would be ludicrous to assert that tenure of the domestic dwelling is taking the place of paid work as the main determinant of most people's life chances and sense of social identity in the middle mass. But it would be equally ludicrous to deny the potency of home ownership, both as a source of capital accumulation and as a focus for self-provisioning' (1984, p. 321).

The point is, then, that people's housing and employment situations *interact* to shape patterns of economic inequality and life chances in contemporary Britain. As Peter Dickens (1988, p. 107) argues, we have to understand people's material circumstances as the product of a combination of their housing position, their employment situation and their domestic circumstances. We simply cannot read off from the kind of job which people do the economic position which they are likely to be in, for this is also crucially shaped by the kind of household they belong to and by their housing tenure. This means, as Ray Forrest has himself recognized, that the position of a stratum such as the underclass is structured by *both* its labour market situation and its housing situation, for it is 'doubly excluded' from these two crucial systems of resource generation (see Forrest, 1987, p. 1625; Forrest and Williams, 1980, p. 16).

If we accept that life chances are today a product of access to home ownership as well as of access to secure employment, then the implications for a sociological understanding of class and inequality in Britain are profound. Sociological concepts of class and stratification are still grounded to a remarkable degree in the ideas of Karl Marx and Max Weber, both of whom were writing of societies very different from our own. Not only were nineteenth- and early-twentieth-century capitalist countries characterized by the existence of a mass proletariat which owned no property, but the role of the state in shaping people's lives through provision of resources such as housing, health care and income support was rudimentary. Little wonder, then, that both of these theorists focused in their different ways on the labour process as the fundamental mechanism structuring people's life chances.

In the modern period, such a restrictive perspective is no longer adequate. A focus which is limited purely to people's position in the organization of production will fail to understand why one group of workers is able to accumulate wealth and pass it on to its children while another remains propertyless. It will fail to understand why one group of workers is less likely to support socialist parties than another group. And it will fail to understand why one group of workers feels pride and takes comfort in its achievements outside of work while another feels resentful and powerless. Any analysis of the forces which shape people's life chances in contemporary Britain must therefore take account of their position as consumers as well as their position as producers, and central to any analysis of patterns of consumption is the question of ownership and non-ownership of housing.

There has been a long debate in urban sociology stretching back nearly a quarter of a century over the question of whether and how housing tenure should be integrated into sociological theories of class and social stratification. There are basically three possibilities. One is that home ownership influences class position – for example, a home-owning worker is in a different class situation from one who rents. A second is that home ownership influences the status order – for example, a home-owning worker may still be working class but enjoys a higher status than one who rents. The third is that home ownership is the basis of a sectoral cleavage which cuts across the class system – for example, a home-owning worker is still working class but also has a different interest and identity as a private-sector consumer of housing which drives a wedge between him or her and other workers who rely upon the state for their housing.

Home owners as a distinct property class

The relevance of housing tenure to class analysis was first raised by Rex and Moore (1967) as a result of their research in Birmingham where they found that different groups were engaged in a competitive struggle for access to scarce and desirable housing. The class position of these different groups was certainly important in influencing their success in this competition, for access to owner-occupied housing in the suburbs was dependent upon having a reasonably secure job attracting a reasonably high income, but Rex and Moore argued that this was not the only significant factor. Access to state housing, for example, was governed by an entirely different set of principles laid down by bureaucrats and politicians in the local housing department, and the authors suggested that the rules which they adopted were designed to favour some groups (such as the respectable white working class) while excluding others (notably newly arrived black immigrants). It followed from this that the struggle over housing in Birmingham reflected something more than just existing class differences; as Rex put it, 'Among those who share the same relation to the means of production there may be considerable differences in ease of access to housing' (1968, pp. 214–15). And, crucially, he continued: 'A class struggle between groups differentially placed with regard to the means of housing develops, which may at local level be as acute as the class struggle in industry' (1968, p. 215).

From this insight was born the idea of a 'housing class' system. Essentially it was Rex's view that people occupied two different class positions by virtue of their participation in two different markets. From the labour market they derived their occupational class location; from the housing market they derived their housing class location. These two class systems were obviously related, in that income gained through the first could be used to secure a privileged position in the second, but they were distinct, and it was quite possible for some people to occupy a relatively privileged position in one while suffering relative powerlessness in the other.

The theory of housing classes was, however, fundamentally flawed (see Saunders, 1986, pp. 139–51). There were a number of problems with the theory, but the main one concerned Rex's attempt to define housing classes in terms of a taxonomy of tenure categories. In his view, the basic housing class system comprised, from top to bottom, outright suburban owner-occupiers, mortgaged suburban owner-occupiers, council tenants in good-quality accommodation, council tenants in short-life accommodation, landlords of inner-city subdivided houses and the tenants who rented rooms from these landlords. Leaving aside the fact that this hierarchy clearly reflected Rex's own values rather than any objective evidence of the existence of such a pecking order, the basic problem with the whole approach was that these six groups represented the *outcome* of a struggle over housing rather than the *basis* of it.

The theory of housing classes emphasized inequalities of *access* to housing. It follows from this that the groups which should have been identified as distinct 'classes' were those which shared in common a set of attributes governing access to different types of housing. This would have pointed, for example, to the identification of groups like Asians, single-parent families and the elderly as 'housing classes', rather than to tenure groups. The equation of the theoretical concept of 'housing class' with the empirical category of 'housing tenure' was therefore unwarranted.

This does not necessarily mean, however, that housing tenure divisions cannot be related to a class analysis. Rex claimed to have derived his distinction between occupational class and housing class from the sociology of Max Weber. In his analysis, Weber (1968) took the view that class refers to differences of economic power – that is, people are differentiated according to their capacity to achieve given goals through control of material resources. There were basically two ways in which people could achieve access to material resources. One was by participating in the labour market; the other was through participating in the property market. People are powerful in labour markets if they can command high incomes for the skills that they sell, and inequalities of power in labour markets give rise to a differentiation of what Weber termed 'commercial classes'. People are powerful in property markets, by contrast, if they can secure high returns on property which they own, and Weber referred to different strata here as 'property classes'. Thus, like Rex, Weber ended up with two distinct sets of classes reflecting the two different markets in which people are involved.

Weber then went on, however, to integrate commercial and property classes into a unified theory of social class stratification. He suggested that those who achieve high returns through both markets represent the upper class, and those who lack power in both markets make up the working class. In between these two stand two distinct middle strata. One, the petty bourgeoisie, has few skills through which to dominate labour markets but it lives by exploiting its assets in property such as shops or rented housing. The other, the intelligentsia, owns little in the way of property but is able to command a good standard of living through selling its scarce skills on the labour market.

The importance of Weber's approach lies in the recognition that the life chances of different social classes are shaped, not only by the occupational system and the division of labour, but also by access to private property. In his time, of course, most housing was owned by private landlords and was used to generate profits, and Weber had no doubt that this source of wealth accumulation represented an important component of any analysis of the class situation of these owners. It was not housing tenure as such which shaped class position, but rather the ownership or non-ownership of property (be it housing or any other capital asset) which could generate an economic return.

It is clear from this that Rex's attempt to update and apply Weber's theory was misconceived, for there is nothing in Weber's sociology to suggest that, say, council tenants in good-quality housing and private tenants in inner-city rented rooms occupy different class locations. However, it is also apparent that Weber's analysis of the significance of property ownership for class formation *could* fruitfully be applied to the analysis of contemporary housing tenure divisions if it could be shown that different tenures offer different opportunities for achieving economic returns. In Chapter 3, we saw that this is indeed the case, for like nineteenth-century small landlords, present-day owner-occupiers do own a capital asset which does generate wealth which can be realized and which does affect people's life chances.

This finding opens up the intriguing possibility that Rex's idea of housing classes could be reworked through a more faithful application of Weber's theory, and that in this way, modern class analysis could find a way of taking account of the importance of home ownership in influencing people's material circumstances. In short, ownership of a house could be said to privilege people in respect of the property market. Home owners could then be seen as a distinct 'property class'; and following Weber's logic, this would in turn influence their overall social class position. Seen in this way, a nation of home owners, each of whom generates wealth through ownership of domestic property, could be seen as pre-eminently a 'petty bourgeois' society.

In 1978 I published a paper in which I suggested that home owners should be seen as a distinct property class. Few home owners, of course, can live entirely from the proceeds of the property market, yet most do achieve substantial capital gains from the appreciation of the value of this asset. Home owners could not be seen as capitalists, for they do not live from property income and they employ no workers, but nor could they be seen as part of the 'negatively privileged' propertyless stratum. They therefore constituted an intermediate property class for whom housing represented both a use value and an exchange value. Although this stake in the property system was, I argued, insufficient to transform workers into capitalists, it was significant enough to differentiate them from the working class. It is in this sense that the growth of home ownership in Britain may be said to have contributed to the expansion of a new 'intermediate property class', or a 'petty bourgeois stratum', or what Pahl has subsequently termed a 'middle mass'.

One problem with this formulation, however, is that home owners themselves do not appear to feel that their class identity is any different because of their ownership of domestic property. It is true, as Geraldine Pratt (1982) has argued, that in some situations, home owners do express a distinct identity and pursue a distinct set of interests in relation to other groups. In battles over land use and in conflicts over government taxes, services and subsidies, for example, home owners may find themselves pitched either against capitalist interests or against other groups of workers, yet they may identify with neither of these groups. Pratt concludes from this that 'House ownership as the basis for a middle property class may offer grounds for potentially fruitful theorizing about the theoretically enigmatic middle social class' (1982, p. 495).

It is also true that there is some evidence that home owners have sometimes seen themselves as 'middle class' or 'lower middle class' by virtue of their housing tenure. In his study of American factory workers, for example, Halle found that those who owned houses tended to identify themselves as working class while in the factory, but that they shed this identity when they returned to their homes: 'Many blue-collar workers do not see themselves as basically part of a working class culture when away from their jobs' (1984, p. 295). He concluded from this that 'Outside work, blue collar home owners, like most American home owners, will become involved in a "politics of home ownership" centering on an identity as middle or lower middle class' (1984, p. 302). Similarly, Willmott and Young's study of manual workers in London in the 1950s reported that, while 59 per cent of those who were home owners thought of themselves as middle class, only 43 per cent of tenants did so.

Against this, however, more recent studies in Britain have failed to find any significant tenure effect on people's class identities. In their national survey, Marshall and his colleagues found that most people see class solely as a function of occupation or employment. Only 12 per cent thought of the middle class in terms of home ownership, and just 8 per cent characterized the working class as council tenants (Marshall et al., 1988, p. 146).

Nor does housing tenure appear to have had much impact on the way in which people in the three towns survey thought of their own class position. Many (35 per cent) claimed not to see themselves as members of any social class. Thirty-six per cent said that they were working class, and 12 per cent claimed to be middle class (the remainder gave a wide scatter of responses such as 'ordinary', 'poor', 'comfortable' and so on). These answers correlated significantly with people's 'actual' class positions as determined by both the Registrar-General and Goldthorpe schema (both of which are based upon occupational categories), but there is little evidence that housing tenure influenced people's answers. Indeed, as Table 6.1 indicates, the proportion of working-class owner-occupiers calling themselves 'working class' was higher than the proportion of working-class council tenants giving this answer!

Like most sociologists, therefore, it appears that most ordinary people today think of class (to the extent that they think of it at all) in terms of

Table 6.1 *Subjective class identities by social class and housing tenure*

				Subjective class identity							
			Working		*Middle*						
	None		*class*		*class*		*Other*		*Total*	
	No.	%	No.	%	No.	%	No.	%	No.	%
Owner-occupiers										
Service class	40	36	29	26	24	22	18	16	111	24
Intermediate class	41	38	34	32	12	11	21	19	108	24
Working class	39	31	63	50	10	8	14	11	126	28
Total	120	35	126	37	46	13	53	15	345	75
Council tenants										
Service and										
intermediate class	9	29	9	29	2	6	11	36	31	7
Working class	27	33	32	40	8	10	14	17	81	18
Total	36	32	41	37	10	9	25	22	112	25

Note: The four service-class council tenants have been included with the twenty-seven council tenants from the intermediate class.

occupational position rather than domestic property ownership. Whether this has always been so is difficult to judge. It may be that, as home ownership has been extended down the class system, so its association with specific class identities has been weakened. Marshall and his colleagues (1985, p. 277) suggest that, as home ownership has become commonplace, so it has lost much of its significance as a social demarcator; and Forrest (1983, p. 212) believes that the image of home owners as a privileged class derives from a time before the war when home ownership was generally the mark of a middle-class minority. If images of home ownership have changed as it has become a mass tenure, then this could explain the difference of findings between Willmott and Young's study thirty years ago and more recent work in the 1980s. However, according to Daunton (1987, p. 73), even in the nineteenth century workers who achieved a home of their own still thought of themselves as working class: 'It should not be assumed that the ownership of a small house meant a rejection of a sense of identity as a working man . . . their greatest concern was respectability defined as independence – including independence from a landlord. It did not, however, mean the surrender of working class identity.'

All of this suggests that the influence of home ownership on the British class structure has been rather more subtle than the theory of property classes suggests. Most home owners do not think of themselves as belonging to a different class simply by virtue of holding the title to a dwelling. This does not mean, however, that housing tenure plays no role in shaping people's social identities, for there is little doubt that it does influence self-images. One way of understanding this process is through an analysis of status group formation.

Home owners as a distinct status group

Let us return for a moment to Rex and Moore, who represent the fountainhead of so much of this debate. We have seen that their attempt to equate different tenure groups with Weber's idea of property classes collapsed when it was recognized that tenure is a product of the competitive struggle for housing rather than its basis. Groups like suburban home owners, council tenants, private landlords and tenants living in rented rooms are not 'classes' in Weber's sense of the word, yet the differences between them do seem to have significant effects on the way they live their lives. Tenure may not change people's class position, but it is clearly nevertheless important for an understanding of the system of social stratification.

In an early and important critique of Rex and Moore, Haddon (1970) argued that the groups which they had distinguished in their study of Birmingham's housing system should be understood in Weberian terms not as classes but as status groups. For Weber, power in society is only partly determined by market capacity or social class position. It is certainly true that those who command material resources as a result of power in labour or commodity markets can often use them to realize their objectives in interaction with other less advantaged people, but power also accrues to those who can command prestige and deference irrespective of whether they have money or other assets. Put in Weber's terminology, social power may be a function of class or of status position.

For Weber, the power of status groups rests upon their claim to special esteem, a claim which is reinforced through the adoption of specific styles of consumption. Stratification on the basis of status entails closure and the maintenance of social distance from those deemed inferior. In some societies – feudal Europe, traditional village India and contemporary South Africa, for example – status affiliation is the primary structuring principle of social organization. In others, such as modern Britain, the rise of market systems has eroded traditional status privileges, but even here, stratification on the basis of status groups is still common. In Birmingham, for example, Rex and Moore showed how families which were seen as 'respectable' were allocated to the most desirable public housing, and they also claimed that ethnic-minority status was effectively a bar to entry to the council sector.

Status affiliation is displayed through distinctive styles of consuming goods (see Douglas and Isherwood, 1979). In the modern period, housing in particular has become a key identifier of claims to status. This is true of housing styles, house size, housing areas and, notably, housing tenure, all of which are associated with distinctive social groups with their own styles of life. We saw in Chapter 1 that in Victorian England, home ownership was seen by the middle class (Burnett, 1986, p. 196) and by working-class artisans (Crossick, 1978, p. 149) as a way of demonstrating 'respectability' and thus of maintaining social distance from lower status groups. This remains the case in our own time, especially among those strata that find themselves near but not at the bottom of the status hierarchy.

In Glasgow, for example, Madigan found in her study of low-income buyers that 'For the majority of respondents housing appeared to represent an affirmation of their social status/class position rather than a means of advancement' (1988, p. 11). In their study on the Isle of Sheppey, Pahl and Wallace claim that 'Many of the consumption patterns of those we interviewed appeared to be ways of demonstrating a sense of "respectability" to others in the local area . . . consumption patterns serve to reinforce these status divisions in the community – particularly the purchase of housing' (1988, pp. 140–1). In the working-class Bedminster area of Bristol, Adrian Franklin reports that 'Ownership is associated with high achieved status' and that 'To stay with local authority housing meant one could not afford to buy very cheap terraced villas' (1986, pp. 34, 36).

If home ownership is a sign of achievement, respectability and high status, then council renting represents a stigmatized status of dependency. In Britain, council renting has long been seen by many people as a stigmatized form of tenure – Bentley reports how, during the 1930s, 'The low status accorded to council tenants – by council tenants themselves as well as by owner occupiers – turned home buyers strongly against any suspicion of council house styling in their own homes' (1987, p. 14). Today, this same set of values is revealed in the way so many council house purchasers have set about changing the outward appearance of their homes to set them apart from the council-owned properties around them. As Robinson suggests, 'The policy of encouraging local authorities to build and manage a large housing stock has created a separate, second class and stigmatized status for council tenants' (1983, p. 77). Home ownership has come to be associated with individual success, while council renting is increasingly symbolic of personal failure (see Short, 1982, p. 233).

The reasons for this have to do with the way in which access is achieved to the different tenures. In the United States, where tenure is 'a primary social sign used in categorizing and evaluating people in much the same way that race, income, occupation and education are' (Perin, 1977, p. 32), home ownership confers honour, while public renting implies disgrace. According to Perin, the high status accorded by home ownership is in a sense conferred by the lending institutions, which, by advancing a loan, make a public statement about the mortgagee's credit worthiness and respectability. This contrasts with the low status conferred by public housing authorities which allocate housing to people who 'qualify' by virtue of their poverty. Similarly in Britain, the two tenures have symbolic meanings. Home ownership is a badge which displays to the world the occupier's level of personal achievement, but council renting is a sign which carries connotations of misfortune or even fecklessness.

Analysing housing tenure divisions as status divisions helps to explain how people from the same social class may adopt different values, life-styles and opinions according to their housing situation. Such an approach therefore appears to offer a framework for understanding much of the evidence reviewed in earlier chapters – for example, the pride expressed by those who

330

own, the complaints by tenants that council house buyers become 'snobbish' and 'stand-offish', the resentment felt by many tenants against their landlords, the emphasis placed by owners on values of self-reliance and even perhaps the tendency of many council house buyers to vote Conservative, thereby distancing themselves politically as well as socially from the party which is associated with public renting. As Marcuse (1987, p. 257) suggests, housing tenure is so divisive in class terms precisely because of the strong association between tenure and social status.

There is, however, one crucial difference between home owners and council tenants which cannot be explained by a theory of status stratification, and that is that home owners accumulate wealth by virtue of their tenure. Housing tenure *is* associated with claims to status, but there is more to it than that. As we have seen, it is not just *life-styles*, but *life chances*, which vary with tenure, and if housing is successfully to be integrated into theories of social stratification it is essential that the resulting framework takes account of its economic as well as its social significance.

This leaves us with a problem, for if housing does not change people's class situation, yet affects people's lives in more ways than are revealed through an analysis of status distinctions, then how else can tenure divisions be theorized?

Home owners as a distinct sectoral interest

Weber does recognize a third dimension to the distribution of power in society, for in addition to the command over material resources (class power), and the claim to social honour (the status order), some groups can achieve their objectives through control of, or influence over, the state. Weber refers to these groups as 'parties', a concept which refers to any organization which orients its activities towards the exercise of political power and which therefore encompasses various types of pressure groups and special interest lobbies as well as formal political parties. Can home owners or council tenants therefore be described as 'parties' in Weber's definition of this term?

The division between these two tenure groups can give rise to political organization. Tenants in both public and private sectors have from time to time organized rent strikes (for example, see Moorhouse, Wilson and Chamberlain, 1972), and there were sporadic mortgage strikes in the 1930s organized by the Communist Party to protest against collusion between builders and building societies arising out of the builders' pool system (see Daunton, 1987, p. 84). Home owners have also shown a capacity to organize politically to defend the value of their houses or to fend off taxation. In Chapter 4, for example, we saw that the owner-occupier interest is often organized at local level to fight over planning and local taxation issues, and evidence was given in Chapter 5 which showed that, when such organizations are formed, they tend to attract a high density of membership (50 per cent in the three towns survey).

Home owners appear to be aware of their political interests and are sensitive to any perceived political challenge to their privileges. The two main political parties are clearly associated in many people's minds with support for different tenures – as we saw in Chapter 4, only 4 per cent of tenants believed that the Conservatives supported their tenurial interests, while just 3 per cent of owners believed that Labour supported theirs. And, as the reluctance to reform the system of mortgage interest tax relief indicates, national politicians from all parties see home owners as a significant voting block which should not be alienated or provoked.

There is, however, no specific home owner party, nor are owners or tenants organized on a permanent basis to pressure or lobby national legislators and civil servants. The home owner interest is for the most part the slumbering giant of British politics. Nobody wants to disturb it, but it does not actually do very much while it is sleeping. It is a strong latent interest but only rarely a manifest one. Seen in this way, the Weberian concept of a 'party' seems inappropriate to analysing tenure differences.

It seems that we have exhausted the conceptual armoury of stratification theory. Home owners are not a class, they are more than a status group and they are less than a party. Tenure divisions are important in the organization of social power and inequality, yet we seem to lack the tools which would enable us to explain how and why they have the importance that they do.

This theoretical impotence reflects the continuing reliance of modern-day sociology on nineteenth-century social theories. The social order in Europe before the First World War could perfectly adequately be analysed in terms of the relationships between classes, status groups and parties. The contemporary social order, however, cannot. What has changed in the intervening period is the role of the state in structuring life chances.

In Weber's day, and even more so in Marx's, the idea of a nation state processing up to half of a country's national product and employing perhaps a quarter of the workforce in order to dispense services like health care, education, housing and income support to millions of its citizens was little more than a Utopia (or an anti-Utopia, depending on your point of view). Until the mid-nineteenth century, the role of the state had essentially been limited to the organization of national defence, the securing of domestic order, the relief of acute social distress and the provision of sound money and a legislative framework for contract and trade. Although the liberal order began to crumble during the second half of the nineteenth century, national politics were still at this time primarily the practice of 'statecraft', and most of the issues of the day revolved around what Bulpitt has termed the 'high politics' of defence and foreign policy (1983, p. 82). Pelling (1968) has shown that the role of the state in social provision never featured as a central election issue in Britain until 1911. Little wonder, then, that Marx and Weber had so little to say about it.

Today it is clear that people's life chances depend as much upon the actions of the state as upon their participation in the economy. In this changed context, changed theories are required. The analysis of social stratification, in other words, needs to take into account a fourth dimension of social power and inequality, one which relates to whether and how people's material circumstances and personal lives are shaped by the intervention of the state.

The basic tool for analysing this fourth aspect of social stratification already exists, although it requires careful revision and refinement. We saw in Chapter 4 that Patrick Dunleavy has, in a series of papers, outlined a new theory of 'sectoral cleavages' which takes as central the divisions which are now apparent between those who produce or consume in the public sector and those who produce or consume in the private sector. We also saw in Chapter 4, however, that as it stands, Dunleavy's analysis of these cleavages is unsupportable given the theory of ideology from which it derives. The basic problem is that Dunleavy fails to recognize that sectoral cleavages have a material basis as well as a political and ideological expression. The division between public- and private-sector workers, for example, is grounded in the fact that the former are remunerated out of tax revenues raised from the income of the latter. Sectoral cleavages thus reflect the activities of the state in levying taxes and distributing revenues, activities which produce and sustain real differences of material and political interest. These divisions may be mobilized by political parties and expressed through ideology, but they are not the creations of parties or ideologues.

Taxation – the forcible extraction of revenue from a population to finance expenditure by those who control the state – has always been subject to political conflict and ideological dispute. Whenever the state levies a tax in order to finance a service or benefit, it redistributes resources between different groups in the population and thus creates and reproduces politically charged sets of competing interests. As Habermas (1976, pt 2) has recognized, state intervention politicizes ever-increasing areas of social life and thereby displaces economic conflicts of interest into the political realm. Where previously people sought to realize their goals through economic activity, state intervention encourages them to pursue their interests by political means. As the tax take has escalated through the twentieth century (and particularly since the 1960s), so these conflicts have been sharpened, and new lines of political cleavage have come to the fore.

The relevance of all this to a sociological analysis of housing tenure divisions is that the cleavage between private-sector home owners and state-sector council tenants is underpinned and reproduced by the intervention of the state in the housing system. Both home owners and council tenants receive financial support out of state revenues. The former benefit through tax relief on mortgage interest payments, exemption from Capital Gains Tax, receipt of improvement grants and so on; the latter benefit through receipt of goods and services directly provided by state agencies – that is, through the process of allocating state-owned housing and the back-up services such as repairs and decoration which go with it. These two groups therefore enjoy different relationships to the distribution of state revenues, and this significantly influences their relative life chances. State support of owner-occupation helps a majority of the population to achieve access to a tenure which enables them to accumulate wealth and to enhance control over their personal lives. State support of council renting results in a minority of the population being consigned to a tenure which prevents them from capitalizing their housing payments and which inhibits personal control and autonomy. The two tenures have come to be distinguished by a differentiation of life chances which is grounded as much in the use of state power as in existing class inequalities.

What is true of housing, of course, is also true of other services in which the state is involved. Clearly, housing is not the only area of state intervention where cleavages arise between different groups of consumers, although in contemporary Britain it is certainly the most vivid example of this process. Nevertheless, wherever the state is involved in providing goods or services to one group while another is able to provide or buy them for itself in the private sector, then a sectoral cleavage can arise. The analysis of housing divisions is therefore only one aspect of a wider concern with the distributive effects of state intervention in the sphere of consumption. Seen in this way, housing research cannot sensibly be detached from a broader analysis of how different forms of state intervention structure life chances in the contemporary period.

Jim Kemeny has recently drawn attention to the failure of housing research to relate its analysis to broader sociological questions concerning power and social structure. What is needed, he says, 'are prior analyses which concentrate on making the theoretical links between general theory and housing analysis' (1987, p. 258). The concept of consumption-sector cleavages enables us to make one such link.

I have argued elsewhere that the move from public to private housing, which has achieved increased momentum in recent years, is likely to be repeated in the future in other areas of consumption (Saunders and Harris, 1989). As real household incomes rise, and as opportunities for achieving access to private services like pensions and health care are extended, so more and more consumers seem likely to exit from the state sector. If this analysis is correct, then the emergence of mass home ownership is only the first step towards a mass privatized mode of consumption. The state may still play a role in subsidizing this privatized system through tax allowances or benefit payments, just as today it supports private house purchase, but the decisive change will lie in the move away from direct state provision in kind. Increasingly, therefore, consumers should be able to select and pay for the kind of pension plan they want, the health insurance package which best suits them and the type of schooling they prefer, rather than being obliged to accept whatever is on offer from public-sector agencies.

As this trend unfolds, so the state sector in these various services is likely to become increasingly marginalized. The division which is so apparent today between those in private housing and those in state housing will in this way come to be seen as simply one aspect of a broader consumption cleavage between a majority of private-sector consumers and a minority of public-sector dependants. In other words, it is not *housing tenure* as such which lies at the basis of the distinction drawn by Pahl between the middle mass and the underclass, but it is rather the division between those consumers who can purchase what they want (albeit with the help of state subsidies) and those who must put up with what they are given. Today, this contrast is revealed most starkly in the housing system, but there is no reason to believe that it will be contained there. Those who today find themselves marginalized by the growth of home ownership may tomorrow find themselves marginalized by the growth of private provision across other services as well. The defining feature of the underclass is not so much its exclusion from owner-occupation (although this is important) as its dependency on state provision across *all* aspects of life including its housing.

At present, of course, private health care and private schooling remain out of reach and out of mind for most British consumers. The key consumption cleavage is still that between private home owners and state-sector tenants, for it is here that we find the most pronounced division between choice and constraint, the exercise of consumer power and the experience of consumer powerlessness. Furthermore, access to private housing opens up the possibility for wealth accumulation which is closed off to council tenants, and this too helps to explain why tenure divisions figure so centrally in the determination of social inequality in Britain today.

If, however, the 'middle mass' comes to achieve access to private provision of other consumption services which have hitherto effectively been monopolized by the state, then we may expect the basis of the cleavage to broaden. Housing will always be a crucial factor in influencing the quality of people's life experiences, but so too are other aspects of consumption such as the schools which their children attend or the provision which they are able to make for their old age. We should not allow a justifiable concern with tenure inequalities to eclipse the related issues of emerging inequalities between health sectors, education sectors and so on.

Recently, some housing analysts have suggested that the theoretical importance of housing tenure for the analysis of social stratification has been exaggerated. Barlow and Duncan, for example, believe that tenure categories have little theoretical relevance and they suggest that 'Researchers need to abandon the use of this single, uniform housing shorthand' (1988, p. 229). Stubbs goes even further in arguing that 'The so-called housing class debate . . . now seems a curiously dated controversy, overtaken by events, and only taken seriously by the participants' (1988, p. 156). Such arguments are important in that they alert us to the dangers of focusing exclusively on tenure categories. But to recommend that we abandon the analysis of tenure, and to suggest that the significance of tenure has been overtaken by events, is clearly going too far. What is required is not the abandonment of analysis of tenure, but its integration into a wider analysis of sectoral cleavages; not a denial of the importance of housing as a source of inequality, but an exploration of the importance of all aspects of consumption in influencing and shaping life chances.

Housing tenure, then, remains crucial to an understanding of power and inequality in the contemporary period. The widening gap between a comfortable middle mass and an increasingly marginalized stratum of state-sector clients represents a major challenge to existing sociological conceptions of the British social structure, and this is a cleavage which finds its most acute expression in the division between those who own their homes and those who have no option but to rent from public landlords. Those social analysts who insist on continuing to view the late-twentieth-century world through the blinkers of nineteenth-century social theories will increasingly be at a loss to make sense of the changes going on around them.

Overcoming marginality

The great majority of people in Britain would like to own their homes. Those who already own generally wish to stay in owner-occupation, and between half and three-quarters of council tenants would like to join them. The problem, however, is that those on low incomes, and particularly those in single-earner households and those without employment, often cannot afford to buy. Their aspirations thus go unfulfilled, and with each round of inflation in the housing market, the gap between the tenures widens. Not only do tenants find it increasingly difficult to buy, but existing owners continue to build up their store of personal wealth. This in turn is sharpening the division between the two groups, for owners can use part of their housing equity to finance private purchase in other areas of consumption, while their children and grandchildren stand to inherit substantial sums which will provide them with additional advantages in securing house purchase in the future. The tenure gap is therefore becoming increasingly difficult to cross, with the result that council tenancy is becoming marginalized.

Logically, any attempt to reduce or overcome this tenure gap can only entail one of two strategies. Either the advantages of owning can be attacked so as to erode tenure inequalities by making owners more like public-sector renters, or policies can be adopted which enable those who wish to buy to do so. Not surprisingly, Marxists writing about housing have generally favoured the first of these strategies.

Socializing the housing system

The starting point for left prescriptions is to deny that housing policy should necessarily reflect what most consumers want. As Harrison and Lomas put it, 'In itself, evidence on preferences cannot justify the conclusion that owner occupation should be available to all those who express a desire for it' (1980, p. 20). This is a necessary initial premiss given that most socialist academics have a deep theoretical aversion to the expansion of private ownership (even though they are themselves normally home owners), yet most households would prefer to buy. A strategy designed to thwart such aspirations cannot therefore allow itself to be restricted by evidence on consumer preferences.

Most left academics are willing to tolerate home ownership, but this reflects a pragmatic political judgement rather than a commitment to the principle of private ownership of housing. There was, for example, a debate in the early 1980s in the Marxist journal *Critical Social Policy* between those who sought to develop public rental at the expense of owner-occupiers and those who argued that such a policy would frighten off home owners and was therefore unwise. Norman Ginsburg, who described owner-occupiers as 'a modern peasantry' (1983, p. 35), but who accepted that working-class home ownership is not 'entirely a disastrous development' (1983, p. 47), belonged to the former group. He accepted that most home owners could be left with their property, although he warned that 'plenty of overhoused bourgeois and owners of second homes' deserved to be expropriated and that the wealthiest home owners should be stripped of their assets (1983, pp. 48–9). His main proposals, however, involved giving absolute security of tenure to all households except the most privileged, imposition of minimum and maximum housing standards and an attack on the economic advantages of owner-occupiers by ending mortgage tax relief and introducing capital gains and capital transfer taxes on private house owners. The principle behind all this was clear: 'Council and private tenants should be given far more preferential treatment than all but the poorest homeowners' (1983, p. 51).

Those who joined him in this debate expressed doubts about the political wisdom of such a strategy. Sidney Jacobs, for example, earnestly counselled that 'The infant Socialist Republic of Britain will need as many allies as it can get . . . it is essential to be able to reassure owner occupiers that they have nothing to fear from socialism' (1982, p. 44). Similarly, Cowling and Smith saw the problem as how 'to devise a socialist strategy which will not unduly alienate existing home owners, but will still pursue Ginsburg's egalitarian aims' (1984, p. 65).

This debate between ideologues and pragmatists goes to the heart of current left analyses of housing policy. By and large, home ownership is reluctantly accepted by most socialists, but there is resistance to policies (such as council house sales and mortgage interest tax relief) which are likely to extend owner-occupation, and there is a desire to take into public ownership as much as possible of the housing system in order to reduce the advantages and privileges which owners now take for granted. For the Shelter Community Action Team, for example, the priority is to expand council housing for general needs, enhance democratic control by tenants over their housing and take into public ownership all land, banks, financial institutions and the construction and building industry (1980, p. 6). Stephen Merrett similarly outlines what he terms his 'modest proposals' which include nationalization of the land and of major building companies, the

337

introduction of a licensing system on all new building, municipalization of old private rented stock, expansion of local authority direct labour organizations, zero-interest loans for public housing construction, elimination of subsidies to buyers and tenants, rent-free council housing for the elderly, an end to council house sales and democratization of housing management (1982, pp. 322–3). Michael Ball endorses most of this agenda, particularly the nationalization of land, financial institutions and building firms and the expansion of direct labour organizations, and he adds a few more items of his own including the control of all new and second-hand house prices by local 'Housing Exchange Authorities' and the imposition of sales taxes to syphon off capital gains (see Ball, 1986, pp. 53–5; also Ball, 1983, ch. 13, and his 1982 and 1985 papers published in *Capital and Class*).

What is immediately striking about lists of proposals like these is how, whether intentionally or not, they seek to wrest power from the hands of those who consume housing and to place it in the hands of those who produce or manage it. In particular, they represent concerted attacks on the two key advantages of owner-occupation which are mentioned by most people as their main reasons for wanting to own – the financial benefits and the personal autonomy. Such proposals are not without irony given the left's historic claim to represent the interests of the broad mass of the people.

One of the most obvious ironies is that, at the very moment when a majority of the British people have for the first time in our history secured for themselves a means by which to accumulate some personal wealth, intellectuals who claim to favour wealth redistribution towards 'ordinary working people and their families' are intent on taking it away from them! When home owners attempt to help their children by giving them a slice of the equity value they have accumulated, the capital transfer is to be taxed. When children come to inherit their parents' house, the legacy is to be taxed. When owner-occupiers sell up in order to move, any capital gain they have made will be taxed. Taxation is being used here, not as a necessary means for raising revenue, but as a vindictive instrument of social policy. Nobody is to gain from the housing market, and all gains are to be 'syphoned off' by the state. Indeed, if Ball has his way, people wishing to sell their houses will be obliged to use a centralized and computerized state transfer agency which will fix the price for them! In terms of the three rights of ownership discussed in Chapter 2, the aim is evidently to allow a continued right of use (except for the wealthiest owners or those deemed to be 'overhoused', who may find themselves expropriated if people like Ginsburg ever get control of the state apparatus) while curtailing the rights of control and disposal. The unstated aim is to make owner-occupiers more like council tenants.

The power which is taken away from owner-occupiers will be given to state agencies. House prices will be fixed by the state. Money for new building will be advanced by the state either by borrowing or through increased taxes. Houses themselves will be built by the state according to its own criteria of 'housing need' and 'productive efficiency'. Building land will be owned by the state, and building workers will be employed directly by the state. Small builders who currently undertake much repair and improvement work will be squeezed out by state-run direct labour organizations. Building societies will disappear to be replaced by state-owned housing credit institutions. In short, the private market will disappear.

This scenario betrays a remarkable faith in the wisdom and goodwill of those who run and are employed in these various state agencies. The wisdom is entailed by the fact that they will have to judge what type of housing is 'needed', where it should be built, what proportion of the country's resources is to be allocated to it and which people have the best claim to which accommodation. As analysts as diverse as Max Weber and Milton Friedman have pointed out, free markets are crucial information systems, for relative price movements provide precise guidance to producers and consumers alike about changing patterns of costs and preferences. The sort of system envisaged by writers such as Merrett and Ball would destroy this information system. The system to be put in its place would be run by 'experts' – the same kind of evangelistic bureaucrats whose decisions relocated millions of people into disastrous high-rise monoliths during the 1960s. When the state controls all aspects of housing – its financing, its construction and its exchange – then the potential for getting decisions wrong is enormous, and the likelihood of maximizing consumer satisfaction rapidly approaches zero.

Not only will those who run this system be invested with remarkable intellectual qualities, but they will also be motivated by a pure public-service ethic in which self-interest and self-aggrandizement have no place. In a competitive market, private producers have to take account of the desires of their consumers in order to safeguard and extend their market share. Critics of the volume house builders often express contempt for the quality and style of the houses they develop, but those who buy them enjoy the right to go elsewhere if they are not happy with what they are offered, and it is for this reason that no private builder ever put up a deck access block and lived to tell the tale. Those who run the new socialist housing system will operate under no such constraints. Given that people will only be able to buy or rent such new housing as the state decides to build, and that the price of all existing housing will be fixed by the state, there is no means other than pleading, bribing, or entering into black-market transactions by which consumer demand can influence the kind of housing which is made available. Under this system, house buyers will have no choice but to rely on the good faith of those who have the power to determine what they shall be offered. Like council tenants under existing arrangements, they will have to take what the state decides to make available.

Ball does at least recognize this problem. He warns of the difficulties of controlling a black market and he also accepts that producer interests are quite likely to try to exploit their power for their own ends: 'It would be naive to expect that once the profit motive had been removed as the sole operating criterion of the building industry all social conflicts over the aims and practices of the state building enterprise would cease. It is easy to imagine how the interests of external groupings, like users, may diverge from those of groups inside building production' (1983, p. 383). There would, in other words, be a conflict between state producers and their consumers. Lacking the power of 'exit', the consumers would have to rely upon 'democratic' political procedures to express their views. Despite the fact that most left commentators agree that these 'democratic procedures' have proved woefully inadequate in the existing council house system, they are nevertheless firmly of the opinion that matters can be improved and that the interests of tenants and house purchasers alike could be safeguarded through the adoption of democratic procedures in a new and fully socialized system.

Much play is made in these discussions of the importance of 'devolved management' and 'local organization'. Ball emphasizes that house building is to be accomplished by means of 'publicly accountable bodies organized on a regional and local basis' and that the new housing credit institutions 'should be locally or regionally based' (1986, pp. 53–4). The various proposals for a socialist housing system stand or fall on the effectiveness of such local democratic channels; for in the absence of a market and of competing suppliers of housing and loans, they are the only legitimate means by which consumers can try to exert any influence over what gets produced at what price. Yet these proposals overlook at least three basic problems.

The first is that the capacity for exerting effective control through democratic participatory systems is very unequally distributed through the population. By and large, those who have the most time, money, education and contacts are those who tend to come out on top in such arrangements. As Friedman and Friedman have noted, the disadvantages faced by the poor in such 'political markets' are often even greater than those they face when competing in economic markets (1980, p. 148).

Second, democratic decision-making is a very poor instrument for delivering resources where different people may want different things. As Nove (1983, p. 54) points out, voting systems are hopelessly unwieldy when it comes to responding to a wide variety of preferences, and the principle of majority rule disables minorities who are also entitled to be supplied with what they want even if the majority does not share their preferences. A socialized system would therefore prove to be extremely conservative and highly conformist, for when everyone relies upon the state to organize housing, the scope for innovation is minimal. As Banion and Stubbs argue in their critique of Ball, 'The removal of private tenures would at present mean that sizeable groups of people were less able to lead the lifestyles of their choice – thus reducing the opportunities for future generations to develop alternative forms of living' (1986, p. 188).

Third, there is an inherent tension in socialized systems between what the experts consider necessary for the system as a whole and what particular groups of consumers want for themselves. If a socialized housing system is to be genuinely responsive to what consumers want, then it cannot also provide what planners say is necessary or socially desirable, for the two will often be in conflict. Furthermore, the self-interest of the producers (for example, in maximizing their incomes, guarding their professional autonomy, or imposing their ideas) will almost certainly clash with that of the consumers, and the former will usually prevail over the latter unless there is competition and a right of exit.

None of these issues is seriously addressed in the literature under discussion. The left has belatedly recognized the failures of state rental housing, but rather than assimilating the lessons to be drawn from them, it seeks to generalize them across the whole housing system. The failures of state housing in Britain are assumed to have been accidental and are therefore held to be redeemable next time around. There is no recognition in this literature of the inherent problems in such systems (see, for example, Stretton, 1978a, ch. 12), and no attempt is therefore made to show how these would be confronted. Licensing, price controls and public ownership are all to be endorsed as part of a megalomaniacal solution to current housing problems with the sole aim of dismantling the private housing market. Both analysis and historical experience suggest that the result would almost certainly be an unresponsive, inefficient, standardized and (for all the talk of local democracy) centrally directed system in which few outside the producer agencies manage to manipulate the system to get what they want out of it. The best that can be said of such proposals is that it is most unlikely that those who put them forward will ever be given the chance to put them into effect.

The future of council housing

If one way of overcoming the marginality of council renting is to make home owners more like council tenants, then the alternative strategy is to turn council tenants into owners. A basic problem here, however, is that not all tenants can afford to buy.

Although left prescriptions for housing reform would generate more problems than they solve, socialists are nevertheless right to criticize market systems for their failure to cater adequately for the poorest sections of the population. It may be true that many existing council tenants would prefer to own, but it is also true that many of those in the public sector would not have been able to buy or rent equivalent accommodation in a free market system. Although, as we saw in Chapter 1, state intervention in the housing system has often created problems as much as it has resolved them (notably in undermining private rental), council housing does at least provide accommodation for people who under existing arrangements could ill afford to buy or rent privately. The privatization of council housing must, herefore, be evaluated in terms of the effect on poor households.

Under the Thatcher governments of the 1980s, new council house building

Table 6.2 *Views on the Right to Buy by social class and housing tenure*

| | View on sales policy | | | | | | | | | |
| | Approve | | Disapprove | | Ambivalent | | No opinion | | Total | |
	No.	%	No.	%	No.	%	No.	%	No.	%
Service class										
Total	72	63	23	20	20	17	0	0	115	100
Intermediate class										
Owner-occupiers	80	70	21	18	12	11	1	1	114	79
Council tenants	23	77	6	20	0	0	1	3	30	21
Total	103	72	27	19	12	8	2	1	144	100
Working class										
Owner-occupiers	98	77	14	11·	13	10	2	2	127	58
Council tenants	69	76	17	19	4	4	1	1	91	42
Total	167	77	31	14	17	8	3	1	218	100

Note: Service-class respondents have not been divided by tenure, since only four of them are council tenants.

has declined dramatically, while sales of existing stock have reduced the number of households renting from the state for the first time this century. Furthermore, the Housing Act of 1988 allows ownership of whole estates to be transferred from local authorities to private or other landlords. While the Marxist left harbours dreams of dismantling the private housing market, the Thatcherite right is busy selling off the state rental sector.

The 1980 Local Government and Housing Act obliged local authorities to sell houses at specified discounts to most categories of sitting tenants who wished to buy. The Conservative Party's arguments in favour of this policy all basically reflect the arguments in favour of owner-occupation in general – it is suggested that home ownership is a natural desire, that it enhances individual freedom, that it encourages individual responsibility and that it enables people to accumulate personal wealth (see Bassett, 1980, p. 291). The evidence from earlier chapters suggests that most of these arguments are sound. It is also apparent that most people in Britain agree with the Right to Buy policy.

Taken as a whole, 71 per cent of owner-occupiers and 76 per cent of council tenants interviewed in the three towns survey approved of the sales policy. Of this group of approvers, 17 per cent gave as their reason that home ownership was a good thing and should be encouraged, and 8 per cent felt that it was right that tenants should be able to buy since they had often paid for the house several times over in the rents they had been charged. The main reason given for approval, mentioned by 34 per cent of all those in favour of the policy, was, however, that people should have the choice of whether or not to buy.

Two main reasons were given by those who opposed sales. One (mentioned by 31 per cent of all those opposed to the policy) was that discounts were wrong or unfair. This view was particularly strongly expressed by middle-class opponents of the policy, half of whom gave it as their reason for disapproving, and it is also noticeable that only one council tenant in the whole sample expressed this view. The other argument (mentioned by no fewer than 74 per cent of all those against sales) was that the policy depleted the availability of low-cost housing for low-income families. This argument was advanced by middle-class and working-class opponents alike, although again it was the middle class who were most likely to express such a concern, with 93 per cent of them giving this as a reason for objecting.

When we inspect the data in Table 6.2 more closely, it is apparent that support for council house sales is inversely related to social class. In the service class (where virtually every respondent is a home owner), 63 per cent favour sales and 20 per cent disapprove. In the intermediate class, support rises to 72 per cent with 19 per cent opposed; and in the working class, 77 per cent support sales and just 12 per cent oppose them. This pattern emerges even more clearly if we employ the Registrar-General's social class schema, for then we find that approval of sales rises from 61 per cent among professional and managerial groups, through 70 per cent among routine white-collar grades and 76 per cent among skilled manual workers, to 80 per cent among semi- and unskilled manual workers. It seems from this that the classes which have least contact with the state housing system are the most likely to oppose the right of others to get out of it (and they are especially critical of the discounts which enable them to do so). Putting the same point another way, those at the sharp end are the strongest supporters of legislation designed to aid the privatization of housing.

When we consider the academic literature on council house sales we find that three basic arguments have been advanced against this sales policy. One has to do with the principle of local government autonomy – the argument that it is wrong for central government to force local councils to sell – and although this raises important constitutional issues (see especially Forrest and Murie, 1985), it is not central to our current discussion. The other two have to do with the economics of public-sector renting and the impact of sales on those who remain behind.

One aspect of the economic argument against sales is that they represent a form of public asset-stripping. They raise revenue in the short term, but in the long run they cost money because local councils still have to meet interest repayments on loans raised to build houses but are no longer receiving rents from letting them: 'The net expenditure effect is likely to be a short-run surplus followed by a more-or-less permanent deficit' (Merrett, 1982, p. 124). The calculations here are, however, complex and contested.

A second aspect of this argument is that sales disrupt the system of 'pooled historic cost' on which socialized renting is based (see Kemeny, 1981). The point here is that new housing can be built and let at below-market rents if the total rent pool is being supplemented by receipts from tenants of old houses which have already been paid for. Tenants in old houses, in other words, subsidize the rents paid by tenants in new ones. While it is true that such a system is indeed undermined by sales, it is by no means self-evident that this is to be deplored. As we saw in Chapter 2, one reason why so many tenants want to buy is precisely because they resent paying for the value of their house two or three times over in the course of a lifetime of renting. What observers like Kemeny see as a fair and equitable system of rent pooling is seen by many tenants of older houses as a grossly unfair and inequitable system of rental exploitation. As Ward suggests, 'The tenants of council property, who may well have lived there for decades, are subject to a continually rising rent to help keep down the rents of tenants in new council property. Under no conceivable ethical system can this be considered just, and it presents not an argument against sales but an argument for changing the system of housing finance' (1983, p. 191).

More powerful than the economic argument against sales is the social one, for this focuses on those who are left behind. Sales, it is claimed, exacerbate the process of marginalization of council renting because the more affluent tenants buy and the most desirable housing is sold (for example, Bassett, 1980; Merrett, 1982, p. 124). Not only are the poorest people therefore left living in the worst housing, but the total stock is reduced, thereby making it even more difficult for the next generation to get access to public housing of a reasonable quality. As the Shelter Community Action Team self-righteously observed in its attempt to dissuade people from buying, 'Tenants who buy their council houses, by adopting an attitude of self-interest, directly contribute to a worsening of the housing situation for their children (who will have to seek their own accommodation before they will inherit the house their parents own), friends and relatives and all other council tenants and those seeking and needing a council house' (1980, p. 3).

If such claims were true, then they would represent a major challenge to the sales policy. In fact, such arguments make little sense. If tenants are to enjoy security of tenure and the right to pass their tenancy on to other family members (as most defenders of council renting accept that they should), then selling them the house makes little effective difference to the rate of re-lets. Furthermore, as Ward (1983, p. 189) points out, people still get housed whether as owners or tenants; selling council houses neither increases nor decreases the total stock available for people to live in. Nor does it make any sense to try to block sales on the grounds that those who remain behind will be more residualized, for the logic here seems to be that anything which improves anybody's life is to be resisted unless it also improves everybody else's. The problem of marginality and residualization is important, but it is clearly ridiculous to try to solve it by preventing some members of the minority from bettering their situation.

The arguments against council house sales are, therefore, unconvincing, and in truth, the issue now appears to have been fought and won. No future socialist government would dare try to take back into municipal ownership the million homes which have been sold, and it is doubtful whether any future Labour administration would find it worth the political trouble to introduce anything more than token restrictions on new sales. At a time when even the Soviet Union has authorized the sale of state flats to sitting tenants (*Financial Times*, 7 December 1988), the prospect of any British government seeking to reverse the policy seems slim, although there are still some left academics and activists who oppose sales. Their reasons for doing so, however, seem to have more to do with hostility to private ownership and the market economy than with reasoned arguments about the balance of advantages for tenants or for housing authorities. As one speaker at the 1978 Labour Party Conference opined, council housing is to be supported as 'the greatest challenge to the values of capitalism that this movement has ever posed' (cited in Bassett, 1980, p. 305). Such ideological arguments can still be heard, but the political agenda has moved a long way since 1978.

What is true, of course, is that the Right to Buy has only benefited a minority of tenants. Over 4 million households are still renting from local authorities. Some of these have no desire to own, some would like to own their homes but do not wish to purchase the accommodation in which they are currently living, and some cannot afford to buy, even at discounted prices. It is the future of these groups which is now central to discussions of reform in the public housing sector.

For *those who wish to continue renting*, the issue is whether local authorities are the most appropriate landlords. Under the 1986 Housing Act, local authorities are allowed to sell their houses to new landlords if they can win the consent of sitting tenants in a secret ballot, and this provision was subsequently broadened in 1988 to oblige councils to transfer their houses to a different landlord if an acceptable bid is made and if a majority of tenants do not oppose the change. This legislation is designed to break up the local authority housing sector by introducing the principle of 'tenants' choice', and it is hoped to encourage take-overs by housing associations, housing action trusts, co-operatives, building societies and private institutions. As things stand, however, most transfers are likely to involve only housing associations given the various tax and subsidy advantages which they enjoy and which are denied to other potential landlords (see Coleman, 1989, pp. 54–5). As Coleman points out, this effectively means that tenants are limited to the choice between two types of public-sector landlord.

Despite its limitations, however, this legislation is likely to reduce the number of tenants remaining in the council sector, although it is difficult to judge how many transfers are likely to take place. By the end of 1988, some 130 councils had begun to initiate the transfer process under the 1986 Act, although only a handful had got as far as organizing ballots. The results of these have been mixed – tenants in Sevenoaks and in Chiltern voted by large majorities to transfer to housing associations, but those in Rochford in Kent decided by a substantial majority to remain within the council's control. Coleman cites an opinion poll which found that half of all council tenants preferred to stay with the local authority, while the rest split evenly between those who would transfer to a housing association, a building society, or a co-operative, and those who did not know. These figures suggest that many estates will remain in council hands, although when tenants have become

345

more accustomed to the idea of changing their landlord, and have had a chance to evaluate the success of those transfers which do go ahead, this picture may change. As Coleman suggests, however, any dramatic increase in the number of people renting outside of the council sector is unlikely to occur in the absence of other legislative innovations. We shall consider how private renting may be boosted when we discuss voucher schemes and the problem of mortgage tax relief later in this chapter.

For *those tenants who would like to buy but who have no desire to own their present council accommodation*, there is the possibility that a system of 'transferable discount' could help them to move. In Chapter 2 we saw that council house sales have been depressed by a general unwillingness of tenants living in flats or on unpopular estates to purchase their homes. This reservoir of potential owner-occupiers has been tapped by experimental pilot schemes tested in the London Boroughs of Bromley and Brent where tenants who have not wanted to buy their existing council accommodation but who have been willing to move and buy in the private market have been given cash incentives of around £5,000 in lieu of the discount to which they would have been entitled. Those taking up the offer were mainly young low-income families (average incomes of purchasers were around two-thirds the Greater London average), and most (96 per cent in Brent and 88 per cent in Bromley) were living in flats. There is little doubt that such a scheme introduced nationally could give a major boost to low-income home ownership rates, and some local authorities, such as Wandsworth in south-west London, have already introduced similar schemes (for further details of transferable discount schemes, see Lewis and Platt, 1988; White, 1987).

Transferable discount does not, however, help *those who would like to buy but cannot afford it*. Various ideas have been put forward to overcome this major obstacle. One, a scheme devised by a former Environment Secretary, Peter Walker, would enable council tenants to turn their current rent payments into mortgage instalments. Under this plan, council tenants could cease to pay rent and would instead pay the same amount, index-linked, in mortgage payments until they had achieved full ownership of their home. Those receiving housing benefit could transfer the benefit from rent to mortgage payments. According to the *Sunday Times* (29 May 1988), the scheme was under active consideration by the government in May 1988 and a pilot scheme along these lines was subsequently announced for Scotland.

An even more radical proposal, which was originally floated by Murray Rothbard (1981), is simply to give council accommodation away free to those who live in it. This proposal is clearly designed to wipe out the division between the home-owning middle mass and the marginalized and stigmatized underclass by making everybody a home owner. As Brian Walden explains:

> It is the poor who have not gained from the rise in house prices . . . I do not claim that giving the poor their own homes would eradicate poverty but it is far and away the most constructive step we could take to improve

their lives and enhance their motivation. If we want to act unselfishly towards the poor, let us do the job properly by providing the kind of help that goes to the heart of their alienation from the rest of society.

(*Sunday Times*, 29 May 1988)

The idea is not without its difficulties. Poor owners would need help with repair and maintenance costs, but this could easily be provided through existing arrangements for providing improvement grants. More serious is the justifiable sense of resentment likely to be felt by those who have bought council properties when they discover that the next-door neighbours are to be given their home free of charge! Furthermore, as Robinson (1983) suggests, many of the positive benefits associated with ownership are a product of the sense of pride which comes with personal achievement. To give council properties away is to devalue them in both senses of the term. Peter Walker's rental purchase proposal seems both more feasible politically and more desirable socially.

All of these ideas and initiatives seem to indicate that the division between a substratum of council tenants and a middle mass of home owners could realistically be overcome by extending owner-occupation to all council tenants who want it. Taken together with the continuing significance of the Right to Buy, schemes such as transferable discounts and rental purchase could enable several million existing low-income tenants to switch into home ownership. If the aim of housing policy is to enable as many people as possible to achieve their preferences, then such initiatives are surely to be welcomed.

Such innovative strategies tend, however, to ignore two distinct groups of housing consumers. One consists of those on low incomes who would like to buy but who do not live in council accommodation and who are not therefore eligible for discounts or other help designed to enable council tenants to purchase. Most of the radical thinking on housing policy in the 1980s has revolved around strategies to privatize the council stock. This is fine for those who wish to go private and who are eligible for the special deals which are offered, but something more is required if all consumers are to be helped to realize their preferences.

The other group which still has to be considered consists of those who would still prefer or need to rent rather than to buy. Existing tenants can, of course, continue to rent if they wish, and following the 1988 Act, they have the choice of whether to stay with their local authority or to transfer to a new landlord. But if most of the council stock is sold off or even given away, then some provision will need to be made to enable future generations of renters to find suitable and affordable accommodation in the private sector.

As we shall see, both of these groups could be helped by the introduction of housing allowances or vouchers. Before discussing this, however, we shall consider such schemes and initiatives which already exist to aid low-income prospective purchasers.

347

Low-income home ownership, index-linked mortgages and self-build

It is generally believed that the extension of home ownership in Britain is nearing its saturation point. Kemeny cites unpublished reports by both the Building Societies Association and the Department of the Environment which suggest that 'There is a "natural" home ownership rate of around seventy per cent of households' (1981, p. 144), and a 1986 report from the Nationwide Building Society similarly concluded that 30 per cent of the population could not realistically expect to become home owners (*Financial Times*, 9 July 1986). The main problem identified in all of these reports is low income and irregular employment, although Payne and Payne (1977) have shown that life cycle factors are also pertinent, for even higher income groups often find it impossible to move into owner-occupation once they start having children. The basic argument, however, is that most semi- and unskilled manual workers are excluded from home ownership and will continue to be so.

In the three towns survey, 89 per cent of semi-skilled manual workers and 76 per cent of unskilled manual workers expressed a preference to buy rather than to rent. The argument that home ownership is approaching saturation point suggests that these desires will go unrealized. The challenge, therefore, is to raise this saturation point. As Littlewood suggests, 'One of the challenges of the next decade is to satisfy the still unfulfilled demand for ownership' (1986, p. 100).

Given a gap between the price of even the cheapest housing and the payments which people on low incomes can afford, one of two things can be done. Either an attempt can be made to reduce housing costs, or policies can be adopted to enhance the capacity to pay. Most recent low-income ownership initiatives have followed the first of these strategies. Such policies have achieved some success, but their potential for raising home ownership rates above the saturation point of 70 per cent seems limited.

A wide variety of schemes is available (see Booth and Crook, 1986; Champion, Green and Owen, 1987; Fielder and Imrie, 1986; Merrett, 1982, ch. 7). One is *equity sharing* under which purchasers buy a proportion (normally half) of a property while paying rent on the rest. They then retain the right to buy the remainder of the house, at current market value, at any later date. Such schemes were run mainly by local authorities during the 1970s, but since 1984 they have been picked up more by housing associations. Local authorities are, however, still centrally involved in *partnership schemes* under which they make land available on licence to private builders who can then sell to low-income buyers at below market prices. Fifteen thousand homes were built under this scheme between 1981 and 1986, and half the purchasers were potential or actual council tenants (*Hansard written answers*, 19 March 1986, col. 238). Sometimes local councils and housing associations have *improved housing for sale* without recouping the full cost from purchasers, and at other times hard-to-let or dilapidated council stock has been sold off cheaply to low-income purchasers who then use their own time and labour to improve the property (so-called *homesteading*). There are also *mortgage guarantee schemes*, under which local authorities and the Housing Corporation guarantee mortgages taken out by low-income borrowers.

Virtually all of these special schemes are directed at existing council or housing association tenants, or at those on housing waiting lists, and involve the public sector in one way or another. Other innovations have, by contrast, occurred within the private sector. Private building companies have taken advantage of falling average household sizes to produce small *starter homes*, which are often offered on 100 per cent mortgages (Champion, Green and Owen, 1987). Financial institutions too have devised various *low-start mortgage schemes* which are designed to reduce repayments in the early years while increasing them later when inflation and career advancement can be expected to have increased the capacity to pay. And in 1988 the Nationwide Anglia Building Society launched a new type of loan for National Health Service employees living in the London area. This allows applicants to borrow up to four and a half times their income at just two-thirds of the normal interest rate, in return for which the building society takes 50 per cent of the increased capital value of the property when it comes to be sold (*Nationwide Anglia Newsletter*, Spring 1988; see also *Housing Gazette*, January 1988). If the scheme is successful, it is possible that the government will offer incentives to other lending institutions to offer similar loans to other low-income groups living in high-priced areas such as London and the South-East, although some lenders may be cautious about gambling on future house price increases in this way, and potential borrowers may think twice about sacrificing some of their anticipated capital gains.

All of these initiatives have undoubtedly helped some marginal buyers get access to home ownership, but their impact is limited. A 1983 study of 338 Glasgow households who had bought by means of one or other of the government's schemes found that most buyers were young single people or childless couples with two incomes, and the authors concluded that 'In effect, far from extending home ownership to those with little or no income potential to afford a home, Low Cost Home Ownership was extending home ownership to those who constituted the future demand for private dwellings' (Fielder and Imrie, 1986, p. 271). Similarly Booth and Crook (1986) suggest that these various schemes have had little effect when compared with the Right to Buy, which accounted for three-quarters of all low-income sales between 1980 and 1984; and they conclude that, although equity sharing has had some significance, homesteading, improvement for sale and mortgage guarantees have had little effect. It seems that most of these policies simply help people to buy earlier than they would otherwise have been able to do, but they do not touch many of the households who could never expect to purchase.

Two other initiatives should, however, be mentioned at this point. One, index-linked mortgages, has been introduced with some success in Australia and New Zealand but has not been used much in Britain. The other, self-build, has been expanding in Britain but has received little explicit support from government and has sometimes been hindered rather than helped by officialdom. Both could, under certain circumstances, help raise the 70 per cent saturation level of home ownership, especially when used in conjunction with some of the other strategies discussed above.

The principle of *index-linked mortgages* has been most clearly spelled out in various essays by Hugh Stretton (see especially his 1978b paper). In this work, Stretton has attempted to alert us to what he terms a 'capital mistake' in the organization of housing finance. He suggests that few problems in social affairs are amenable to simple solutions, but he believes that this one could be rectified fairly easily and painlessly to the advantage of all parties.

The mistake has to do with the way lending institutions cope with inflation. Intent on maintaining the value of loans, they have generally increased interest rates. For example, if inflation is expected to run at 10 per cent per year, an institution which seeks a real rate of return on its capital of 4 per cent will try to lend at 14 per cent in order to cover the declining real value of the money advanced.

Stretton's objection to this is that it has the unintended consequence of squeezing out less affluent borrowers from access to housing credit. The reason for this is that borrowers effectively have to repay the bulk of the loan in the earliest years of its term. This is a problem we encountered in Chapter 3 where we saw that many buyers stretch their budgets to the limit in the early years but find that, as time goes on, the burden becomes easier and easier because the real value of the money payments declines with inflation. Stretton calls this the problem of 'sloped credit'; it is perhaps more familiarly referred to as 'front-loading'.

Whatever we call it, it is clear that this way of organizing lending is keeping people out (and in some cases, driving them out) of owner-occupation who, in the absence of inflation, would have been able to afford the initial repayments more easily. Assume, as a somewhat simplified example, a buyer seeking a £20,000 mortgage at 4 per cent p.a. real interest with equal repayments over twenty years. With no inflation, the first annual repayment will be one-twentieth of the capital plus 4 per cent of the total debt – that is, £1,000 capital repayment plus £800 interest, a total of £1,800. But if inflation at, say, 10 per cent is expected, then the first year's payment will be one-twentieth of the capital, plus 4 per cent real interest, plus 10 per cent to allow for inflation – a total of £3,800! At the end of the twenty years, the real value of the capital payments and interest paid to the lending institution will be the same in both cases, but in the second case, more of the loan has been repaid in the early years as a result of inflation-proofing the money rate of interest.

Stretton's simple solution to this problem is to index-link the loan rather than raise the notional interest rate. In other words, if inflation is running at 10 per cent, then interest could still be pegged at just 4 per cent if, at the end of the first year, the sum still outstanding were increased by 10 per cent in order to retain its real value. In effect, this cancels out the impact of inflation, for the first year's payment is the same as it would have been under a situation of nil inflation. The real cost of repayments under this system remains constant over the twenty years of the mortgage, for the money repayments increase each year to take account of the inflated money value of the loan, but the rate of interest remains constant at 4 per cent. Given that incomes can be expected to have risen with inflation, the borrower continues to repay at a constant real level. At the end of the twenty years, the same real amount of capital and interest has been repaid, so in this sense the lender is no worse off. Indeed, people who lend to financial institutions could under this system have the real value of their savings guaranteed. The key effect is on the borrower, for a system of index-linked mortgages would open up mortgage credit to many people on below-average incomes who under existing arrangements cannot afford the initial repayments on even a modest housing loan.

Although index-linked loans have been used in Britain, usually in conjunction with some other low-income home ownership scheme, lending institutions do not seem keen to extend them. One reason for this may be the worry that, in the (albeit unlikely) event of general inflation consistently outstripping housing inflation over a period of years, borrowers would begin to find that the value of the loans outstanding on their homes was growing faster than the value of the property. In such an event, the economically rational borrower might simply default on the loan, leaving the building society to take the loss on the repossessed house.

Lenders can guard against this eventuality by insisting that borrowers insure against it, or by asking for higher initial deposits, but both measures make index-linked mortgages less attractive for the low-income groups they are intended to help. This may indicate the need for public-sector involvement in such schemes, and where this has been forthcoming in other countries, index-linked mortgages have been used with some success to help low-income buyers (see Carter, 1988; Thorns, 1988). In the Australian state of Victoria, for example, the state government issued index-linked Housing Bonds in 1988 to raise funds to finance a new 'Home Opportunity Loans' scheme. Under this scheme, low-income buyers take out full-value index-linked loans at a rate of 6 per cent, which is fixed for five years. Repayments are limited to 27 per cent of gross household income, and any shortfall between revenue (from mortgage repayments) and expenditure (on payments to bond holders) is covered by a state government indemnity. This scheme, which is intended to be self-financing, has enabled households with a gross income as low as three-quarters of the Australian average to buy houses. Furthermore, an additional concessionary scheme appended to the Home Opportunity Loans scheme and funded by the state government has enabled some households on under half the average income to take out these loans, and this group includes many social security recipients.

As Thorns points out, there are problems with such schemes. For example, although buyers can still accumulate equity, they cannot look forward to falling housing costs as those with more conventional mortgages can, and this suggests that index-linking is unlikely to be taken up by any but the most marginal buyers. A further problem is that the pegging of repayments to a set percentage of income can result in extended terms of thirty or forty years before the loan is paid off, and in some cases it is possible that the loan may never be paid off. It is also obviously the case that index-linking becomes more appropriate the higher the rate of inflation, although Boleat's claim that 'Index-linking has operated successfully only in countries with very high inflation rates – above fifty per cent' (1985, p. 5) seems absurd given the Australian evidence. The Victoria scheme is proving popular, there have been few defaults, and it is reaching the lowest income levels. There is no obvious reason why such a scheme should not be reproduced in Britain for those who want it.

The other important initiative to be considered for the future is *self-build*. This, of course, is hardly a new idea, for as we saw in Chapter 1, people have built their own homes through most of Britain's history, and as late as the inter-war years many London working-class families were drawn to the prospect of developing their own houses on the 'plotlands' dotted around south-east England (Hardy and Ward, 1984). These plotland developments were effectively killed off, however, by the postwar planning legislation which was capably used by rural vested interests to bulldoze most of the houses which had been constructed. As Hardy and Ward explain, 'Each new encampment with the promise of a measure of freedom for its proud owners, was at the same time a spur to action amongst an emergent body of preservationists. The very disorder and personal freedom which newcomers sought was anathema to the self-appointed guardians of a more traditional landscape' (1984, p. 35).

Today, despite planning controls, some 12,000 people build their own houses each year in Britain. Indeed, self-build accounts for more new construction than is produced by the country's largest building firm, Tarmac. Much of this self-build activity involves considerable subcontracting, however, and the number of people who themselves dig the foundations and put up the walls is probably much smaller. Nevertheless, use of modern materials and designs (such as the timber-frame construction developed by the radical architect Walter Segal) has made it possible for people with only basic skills to construct their own homes, and groups of self-builders, many of them women and people in late middle age, have successfully used Segal's designs in developments in Lewisham, Brighton and elsewhere (on the Lewisham scheme, see Ward, 1985).

Although self-build is in principle a libertarian housing strategy, for it enables people to construct their own homes with little reliance on either state bureaucrats or big companies, it clearly does require some degree of state support if it is to succeed. In particular, sites need access to services and infrastructure which cannot feasibly be organized on a small scale (Turner, 1976, p. 115); and if self-build is to be taken up by low-income groups, then help will also almost certainly be needed in finding cheap land and cheap sources of finance. This means that self-build will often need to be supplemented by other initiatives discussed earlier. In Lewisham, for example, the site was made available by the local authority under a partnership agreement (it was a small, sloping site, unsuitable for conventional building but ideally suited to Segal's design), and costs were reduced by organizing a shared equity scheme with the local council.

According to Colin Ward, self-build could flourish in Britain if local authorities were willing to support it:

> Imagine that the corporation provided a road, party walls and a service core of plumbing, bath, basin, wc, sink and ring-main terminal, as our equivalent of the site-and-services nucleus, and then encouraged people to do their own thing. Self-building housing societies would spring up, voluntary effort would aid those unable to help themselves, the homeless and unemployed could make homes and make jobs, and in a decade we would see a self-made community, freed from the awful dependency we inflict on the municipal tenant.
>
> (1983, p. 86)

In similar vein, Peter Hall (1988) has called for derelict inner-city sites to be handed over to the poor for them to build their own homes.

Instead of this, however, self-builders generally encounter official delay and hostility. Like the plotlanders, they run foul of planning controls and building regulations – conservative planning departments seem to find it particularly difficult to accept Walter Segal's revolutionary designs, for example, and local councils also insist that houses be completed to bureaucratically imposed standards rather than allowing self-builders to add facilities over a period of years as and when they can afford the time and money to expend upon them (see Turner, 1976, p. 112). Hardy and Ward propose that zones could be established in which these regulations are relaxed, and it seems that unless some such measure is adopted, the potential growth of self-build will continue to be stifled.

Self-builders have also encountered other official obstacles. In Lewisham, for example, the Inland Revenue taxed them on the imputed value of their labour! They encounter the hostility of housing professionals, who dislike the idea that their services can be dispensed with, of local authority unions, who are opposed to the bypassing of the direct labour organization, and of local councillors, who dislike the idea of people escaping from the public sector into an autonomous form of housing provision.

Taken on its own, self-build is no universal panacea. Many people do not want to build their own homes, and although the eventual cost is substantially reduced by the use of one's own labour, the cost of land, finance and materials can still be substantial for those who do. For those who are attracted to it, however, self-build offers not only the prospect of getting a home of one's own more cheaply than through conventional purchase, but also the satisfaction, independence and pride of having achieved this by one's own efforts.

Subsidies, benefits and vouchers

Most people in Britain wish to own their homes, but some would still prefer to rent. Renting is, for example, a particularly appropriate form of tenure for those who need to move around frequently because of their jobs, for young people who do not wish to commit themselves to purchase and for those who find that the advantages of renting (in particular, the freedom from responsibility for repairs) outweigh the advantages offered by ownership. As we noted in Chapter 2, obliging people to buy when they would rather rent is no more sensible or justifiable than obliging them to rent when they would prefer to buy.

If the ultimate objective of housing policy is to enable as many people as possible to realize their housing preferences as far as possible, then it follows that state support should in general be tenure-neutral (Kemeny, 1981). In other words, just because home ownership is desired by the majority does not mean that government is therefore justified in supporting owner-occupation at the expense of renting. As we saw in criticizing Marxist prescriptions, majority voting can result in the tyranny of the majority and is therefore no solution to provision of a resource like housing where different people want different things at different times. The minority who wish to rent therefore have every right to expect that their preferences will be heeded, and given that the various initiatives discussed above all help those who wish to buy, other strategies are obviously required if people are not to be forced into a tenure which does not suit their requirements.

At present in Britain, there are four principal ways in which the state intervenes in the housing system in an attempt to reduce the gap between what consumers can afford to pay and the price at which producers can afford to supply accommodation. Only one of these four strategies is tenure-neutral, and the other three often pull in different directions. The British housing subsidy system is confused, expensive, contradictory and biased.

The first strategy involves state control or regulation of prices. By this means, consumers are able to afford housing because suppliers are forced to reduce the price they charge for it. Although Conservative administrations through the 1980s set their face firmly against the use of price controls in other areas of the economy, such controls still remain in the housing system, the clearest example being the system of rent regulation in the private sector. Although rents for new tenancies have now been deregulated, those on existing tenancies have not – a situation reminiscent of that in the 1930s, outlined in Chapter 1.

The second strategy involves direct state provision of subsidized housing. The most obvious example here is council renting, although initiatives such as homesteading could also be included in this category. This type of strategy enables consumers to pay for housing by providing it directly at below current market prices.

Third, the state offers subsidies in cash or cash equivalents which are tied to particular forms of housing consumption. The most obvious examples here involve support to owner-occupiers – for example, through tax relief on interest paid on housing loans, exemption of home owners from Capital Gains Tax, improvement grants to help pay for repairs, building for sale and so on. Other groups also benefit from targeted tenure subsidies, however. The government makes grants to housing associations through the Housing Corporation, for example, and this feeds through to tenants in lower rent charges. It also subsidizes those council tenants who wish to buy their homes by selling at discounted prices, and new transferable discount schemes involve paying a cash sum to be used for future purchase in the private housing market.

The fourth way that the state intervenes to make housing more affordable is through income support irrespective of tenure. The housing benefit system is an imperfect example of this kind of subsidy, for it is payable to low-income renters in both public and private sectors. In 1988, 45 per cent of private tenants, 60 per cent of council tenants and 70 per cent of tenants of housing associations were in receipt of benefit (Coleman, 1989). Owner-occupiers on supplementary benefit are eligible for help with paying mortgage interest for a limited period, and low-income owners may also qualify for rate rebates. It has often been suggested that all housing consumers could be covered by a single universal benefit or allowance system, and we shall consider this idea (which comes close to proposals for a housing voucher system) in more detail below.

All four of these strategies have their problems, but there is a strong case for arguing that this mixed system of subsidies and support should be simplified, and that effective choice in housing can only be achieved by moving to a tenure-neutral system which only the fourth of these strategies can offer.

The basic problem with strategy one – price regulation – is that, the more effective it is in reducing housing costs to consumers, the more it chokes off new supply. As we saw in Chapter 1, private rental housing in Britain has declined alarmingly through the twentieth century, and although they are not the only cause, rent controls have been a major factor in this collapse. Minford, Peel and Ashton (1987, p. 39) cite evidence to show that regulated 'fair rent' levels in the private sector in 1982 provided an average rate of return to landlords of no more than 1 or 2 per cent on vacant capital values, and that many landlords do not receive enough in rent even to cover their costs. Little wonder, then, that much of the private rental which is still available is in a 'black market' in which landlords and tenants conspire together to circumvent the Rent Acts.

Following decades of hostility and neglect, the government has now moved belatedly to attempt to resuscitate private renting, partly by enabling council tenants to transfer landlords under the 1988 legislation, and partly by stimulating new housing investment under the Business Expansion Scheme which offers tax exemptions to those investing in companies which build housing to rent. Such initiatives may have some effect (the BES system does go some way in counterbalancing the tax advantages of competing tenures, for example), but large-scale new investment is still likely to be deterred by the prospect of some future government switching policies, and existing landlords are still hampered by rent regulation and secure tenancies. The problem, then, is that if rents are regulated, landlords disinvest, and that if they are not regulated, many tenants cannot afford to pay them (Coleman points out that BES tax relief will enable rents under this scheme to be set below market levels but that they are still likely to be above what most low-income households can afford to pay). Clearly, control of prices is no answer to the problem of matching low incomes to high housing costs. .

Nor is strategy two – provision in kind – an appropriate response to this problem. It is true that state housing can in principle be used to accommodate people who could not otherwise afford to rent or buy in a free market. This is only achieved, however, at the expense of other equally important principles. As we have seen throughout this book, council housing is unpopular – few young households want to enter it, and many of those already in this sector would like to get out of it. It is a system which strengthens the power of service producers while disabling and stigmatizing the consumers who are dependent upon them. As Paterson suggests, 'When allocation is by non-market means, discretionary power is *automatically* conferred on somebody to make arbitrary choices between alternative claimants on a given resource' (1975, p. 34, original emphasis). British council housing is a system which encourages political patronage and bureaucratic caprice. Consumers must take what they are given for they are deprived of the power of exit. Where people have no alternative suppliers, they have no choice and no power.

There are other problems, too. Geographical mobility is notoriously sticky in the public rented sector, for like private tenants with regulated rents, council tenants are trapped in this tenure by their subsidy, and transfers between local authorities are difficult to arrange (Minford, Peel and Ashton, 1987, p. 5). State provision of housing also tends to squeeze out competitors, thus attenuating consumer choice even further (Nesslein, 1988). As we saw in Chapter 1, the state began to provide rental housing because the private sector was declining, yet the more it provided, the more private landlords were squeezed out of the market, and the greater the problem became. The result is the near monopoly which the state enjoys today over provision of rental housing. Those who wish to rent often have little option but to put their name down on a local authority waiting list, even if they would prefer to rent privately or through co-operative arrangements.

Some of these arguments can also be applied to the third strategy of subsidizing the housing costs of consumers in specific tenures (in particular, owner-occupiers). This is done in many different ways, and the total sums involved are enormous. The Association of Metropolitan Authorities (1987) estimates that owner-occupiers in 1985–6 received £50 million in various grants, £100 million through low-cost home ownership schemes like improvement for sale and homesteading, £1,000 million in the form of discounted Right to Buy sales, £2,500 million as a result of exemption from Capital Gains Tax, £1,000 million from exemptions from Inheritance Tax and over £500 million through VAT exemption on new private houses. The main subsidy to owner-occupiers, however, is tax relief on mortgage interest payments. This cost the Exchequer some £4.7 billion in 1986–7 and it supplemented the incomes of over 8 million mortgage payers by an average of £565 each (see *Hansard* written answers, 12 May 1986, cols. 341–2, and 30 October 1987, col. 458).

As we saw in Chapter 1, mortgage tax relief was never deliberately introduced as a means of supporting or encouraging owner-occupation, but like so many other parts of the housing finance system, it has evolved in an *ad hoc* manner in the absence of any coherent housing strategy (see Holmans, 1987, ch. 6; Maclennan, 1982, ch. 7). Back in 1799 the government allowed tax relief on interest incurred in buying capital while imposing a tax on the income realized by using that capital. A landlord investing in housing, for example, could deduct tax relief from interest payments incurred on a loan taken out to purchase a house. Equally, of course, landlords also had to pay tax on the income received from the house. This was calculated, not on the actual amount of rent received, but on a figure imputed from the rateable value of the house (rateable value was the amount of annual rent for which the Inland Revenue judged that the house could be let). The reason for imputing income in this way was that owners of capital do not always receive income in the form of cash – the owner of a field, for example, may grow crops which are sold, or may use it for grazing cattle, and to tax the income received from the crops while ignoring the imputed income received from the grazing would generate a bias against the former use.

As owner-occupation expanded through the twentieth century, so home owners came to be taxed in the same way as any other owners of capital. On the one hand, they could set their mortgage interest against tax; on the other, they paid tax (known as Schedule A) on the imputed income from the dwelling calculated on the basis of rateable values. Of course, unlike landlords, owner-occupiers did not actually receive any income from their houses, but the logic of levying Schedule A was that, like the owner of the field who uses it for grazing, they supply services to themselves, and these services have an imputed value (Robinson, 1979, p. 129).

This system of housing taxation began to crumble during the 1960s. Like domestic rates, the Schedule A tax was levied on the rental value of property and therefore depended on regular revaluations. There was, however, no revaluation between 1938 and 1961, and the amounts paid on Schedule A had therefore been steadily falling in real terms. When eventually a full revaluation was carried out, rateable values were found to have tripled. The government decided that rather than raise Schedule A assessments by 300 per cent, it would be easier to abolish the tax altogether. Eligibility for tax relief on mortgage interest was not, however, removed, and when tax relief on interest on other loans was abolished in 1969 in an attempt to discourage consumer borrowing, housing loans were exempted. Home owners were also exempted from Capital Gains Tax when that was introduced in 1965. The result of all this was that, by the late 1980s, owner-occupiers were in a peculiarly favoured tax position.

The exact nature of their tax privilege depends upon whether we see domestic housing as an investment good which generates income, or as a consumer good akin to, say, cars and television sets (see Boddy, 1980; Stafford, 1980). If housing is an investment good, then it makes sense to allow tax relief on the interest paid on housing loans, but it also suggests that both imputed income and capital gains should be taxed. If, on the other hand, we believe with Merrett (1982, p. 329) that domestic housing is a consumption good, then we should accept that the notion of an imputed income is 'a piece of grotesque nonsense' and that 'Since "imputed income" does not exist, it is logically impossible to tax it.' It also follows from this, however, that housing should be treated in the same way as other consumer goods and that there is no rationale for allowing tax relief on housing loans. At present, owner-occupiers are getting the best of both worlds – unlike other investors they pay no tax on their imputed income, yet unlike other consumers they can claim tax relief on their interest payments.

The problem of treating owner-occupied housing differently from all other goods is that the tax system is skewing the housing market, is subsidizing the relatively better off at the expense of the worse off and is pushing up house prices. These three results, none of which were actually intended given the haphazard way in which we have come to find ourselves in this situation, represent compelling arguments for either reintroducing Schedule A or abolishing mortgage interest tax relief.

The tax privileges enjoyed by owner-occupiers skew the demand for housing by making home ownership cheaper than other competing tenures such as private rental. Many other countries also subsidize owner-occupation through the tax system (Boleat, 1985), but most maintain efficiency pricing by treating other tenures in the same way. In Britain, however, the abolition of Schedule A and the continuation of tax relief have created an artificial inducement to buy rather than rent (Coleman, 1988; Paterson, 1975). These subsidies thus undermine any attempt at achieving tenure neutrality and destroy rather than support genuine consumer choice in the housing market.

They also redistribute income in a highly regressive manner. Aughton is only one of many to have noted how 'The incidence of help given by tax relief on mortgage interest is grotesque in its excessive assistance to those least in need' (1981, p. 53; see also Donnison and Ungerson, 1982, ch. 13; Yates, 1982, p. 221). It is the people paying income tax at the highest band

and taking out mortgages for the full amount allowable against tax who gain most from tax relief. Similarly, it is those living in the most expensive houses who benefit most from the absence of Schedule A and the exemption from Capital Gains Tax (the same people, incidentally, also stand to gain most from the replacement of domestic rates by a flat-rate 'community charge'). Figures given in the *Family Expenditure Survey* indicate that in 1985 people with mortgages received an average of £550 each through tax relief, while council tenants received an average subsidy to their rents of £200 (although, of course, council tenants were also eligible for housing benefit averaging around £500 each as compared with just £20 of rates rebates for mortgagees and £50 for outright owners). Clearly, a lot of money is being directed towards people who are already quite well off.

The subsidies to owner-occupiers also have some effect in pushing up house prices. Michael Ball has argued in many different publications that tax subsidies are directly reflected in higher house prices since they simply enable all buyers to bid more for housing than they would otherwise be able to afford (see, for example, Ball, 1982, p. 72, and 1983, p. 367; also Boddy, 1980; Stafford, 1980). If correct, it then follows that house buyers do not really benefit at all and that the real beneficiaries are housing suppliers and landowners who can extract higher prices for their goods (Ball, 1978, p. 94, and 1985, pp. 29–31). The argument is not necessarily correct, of course, for the price effect of these subsidies depends upon the relative elasticity of demand and supply. Ball's argument assumes that supply will not increase in response to the increase in effective demand, and this is an empirical question rather than something which can simply be assumed. Nevertheless, research in the USA (Malatesta and Hess, 1986) and in Britain (Barrow and Robinson, 1986) does seem to indicate that much of the value of this subsidy is in practice capitalized into higher prices. As Barrow and Robinson point out, this still benefits house buyers, for it enhances equity growth, but it disadvantages tenants, for not only do they fail to share in this inflationary windfall, but they are likely to see rents rise owing to the higher prices which landlords will have to pay to purchase the houses they wish to let out.

The case for abolishing the tax advantages currently enjoyed by owner-occupiers is, therefore, overwhelming. This could be done in one of three ways: by extending similar privileges to other tenures, by reintroducing Schedule A, or by ending mortgage interest tax relief.

The first of these, which was essentially the idea of the 'universal housing allowance' proposed by the 1985 Duke of Edinburgh's inquiry and endorsed by others such as Stretton (1974) and the Association of Metropolitan Authorities (1987), would win political popularity but would be extremely expensive. The AMA, for example, calculates the cost of a non-means-tested universal allowance of £30 per week at a staggering £36 billion! Means testing would, of course, reduce the cost substantially, as we shall see when we consider the idea of housing vouchers.

The other two possibilities would save money but appear to be politically impractical. Reintroduction of Schedule A on the basis on which it was levied before 1963 would probably raise around £3.5 billion at an average annual cost to each household of around £250 (the Central Statistical Office *United Kingdom National Accounts* for 1987 calculated the average imputed rent of owner-occupied housing at £979, and Schedule A levied at 25 per cent on £14 million home owners would therefore raise £3.43 billion each year). Abolition of tax relief would save the taxpayer even more money – about £4.7 billion. As we saw in Chapter 4, however, the electoral implications of attacking these privileges appear daunting, and at the time of writing, it seems that the government has no intention of antagonizing so many voters (although it may allow the value of tax relief to be eroded gradually through inflation). As the Housing Minister told the House of Commons in 1987, 'The Government have made it clear on many occasions that they have no intention of abolishing mortgage interest relief' (*Hansard*, 30 April 1987, col. 231). The possibility of reintroducing Schedule A is even more remote.

So far we have considered three of the four ways in which the state in Britain attempts to match the high price of housing to people's ability to pay. First, it regulates prices. This is done mainly in the private rented sector and it has resulted in a precipitate fall in supply. Second, it provides cheap housing itself. This is achieved through council renting and it has resulted in an unresponsive producer-dominated housing system which offers little choice to those trapped within it. Third, it subsidizes housing costs. This occurs mainly in the owner-occupied sector and it has resulted in a skewed pattern of housing demand, a regressive redistribution of income and inflationary pressure on house prices. These three strategies are confused in their objectives and contradictory in their outcomes. The government hopes to resuscitate private renting, for example, yet tax relief to house buyers and subsidized rents in the council sector both militate against this. It also says that it wishes to promote greater choice in the housing system, yet tenure-related subsidies influence and constrain consumer choice rather than extending it.

What is needed if these objectives are to be secured is a simplification of the subsidy system. So as to overcome the problems of present arrangements, any simplified system should avoid stifling supply (as happens when rents are regulated), enable competition between suppliers (which is not possible when the state itself becomes a supplier of housing) and maximize genuine consumer choice (which means avoiding one-sided tenure subsidies).

The basis for such a tenure-neutral system of housing support does, in fact, already exist in the fourth of the state's set of housing policies – housing benefit. Unlike the other three, a housing benefit system need not depend on tenure (the existing system covers private- and public-sector tenants, and although it excludes owner-occupiers, low-income owners may qualify for help with rates, and those on supplementary benefit are helped with mortgage interest payments). Nor does it encourage consumers to move into one tenure rather than another. It is simply an earmarked system of cash support which is made available to those with insufficient income to pay rent or mortgage at a level which is necessary if they are to house themselves adequately.

As it stands, however, the housing benefit system has drawbacks of its own of which four are paramount. The first is that it is restricted to renters, although it would be a relatively simple matter to extend it across all tenures.

The second problem is that, like other means-tested benefits, there is a danger of stigma attaching to claimants, and although tenants on social security are automatically tied into the system, other potential claimants may lack the knowledge necessary to make a claim to which they are entitled.

More serious than this is a third problem which relates to the 'poverty trap'. Because eligibility for benefit declines steeply as income rises, some relatively low-income households can find that an increase in wages is virtually entirely eclipsed by the ensuing reduction in benefit. The result is tantamount to a marginal tax rate on the low paid of anything up to (or even exceeding) 100 per cent, and this acts as a major disincentive to finding better-paid work, putting in overtime, both partners finding employment and so on.

The final problem is that the housing benefits system requires state regulation of the private rental sector so as to prevent landlords from raising rents in line with the enhanced capacity of their tenants to pay. Just as tax relief to owner-occupiers may simply be capitalized in higher house prices, so there is the danger that housing benefit may simply result in higher rents being charged by landlords. Under the 1988 Housing Act, Rent Officers determine a 'reasonable rent' (irrespective of the actual rent charged) and limit benefit to this. They also determine whether claimants are 'over-accommodated' and reserve the right to limit or withdraw benefit where claimants are living in expensive accommodation (Coleman, 1989). While such safeguards are understandable, they entail more rather than less state regulation and, as Coleman notes, they may easily result in a shortfall in many people's ability to pay.

One way in which the advantages of the housing benefit system could be retained while at least some of its disadvantages are avoided or minimized is through the development of a single housing allowance or housing voucher scheme to replace the existing array of housing subsidies and supports. Like housing benefit, allowances and vouchers involve income support rather than subsidies targeted on particular tenures. The problem to which they are addressed is not, therefore, how to reduce the price of renting or buying, but how to enable consumers to meet this price. Subsidies are attached to people, not houses.

We have already noted that the Duke of Edinburgh's *Inquiry into British Housing* came out in favour of a universal housing allowance (see National Federation of Housing Associations, 1985), but that unless it were means-tested, this would be prohibitively expensive if it were to be effective. In an attempt to get round this, the Association of Metropolitan Authorities

(1987) has proposed a low universal flat rate of £10 per week for every household which could then be topped up on a means test for poorer owners and tenants, although even this more modest scheme would still cost £4 billion more than the cost of the current system of mortgage tax relief, housing benefit and supplementary benefit paid on mortgage interest.

The expense is not the only problem with this amended proposal, however. The means-tested element would still fall foul of the problem of the poverty trap and would still run the risk that eligible households may not apply for the top-up allowance. Indeed, this scheme would seem to combine the worst of both worlds, for in addition to means-testing the poor, it would also pay billions of pounds in flat-rate payments to millions of households which had no need of support and would therefore reproduce one of the major problems associated with current mortgage tax relief arrangements. The AMA would also leave intact current controls and restrictions on private renting while retaining state subsidies to council and housing association renting, thereby perpetuating the imbalance between the sectors. And as if all that were not problem enough, the proposal takes no cognizance of the enormous regional differences in house prices. A flat-rate allowance in 1986 would have been worth twice as much in relative terms to a house purchaser in Burnley than to an equivalent purchaser in a town like Slough.

Proposals for housing vouchers are rather more radical in that they entail the replacement of *all* supply-side subsidies with a single subsidy to demand. The aim, in other words, is to leave the market to determine prices while boosting the purchasing capacity of low-income consumers. This implies an end to state support of council house and housing association rents, the scrapping of rent regulation in the private sector and the phasing out of tax subsidies to owner-occupation. It would also probably entail an easing of other controls which impact on the housing market. In particular, security of tenure in private rental would have to be reduced to put rental housing on an equivalent footing with other investments (this need not cause hardship, since, with genuine freedom of choice, most of those electing to rent would do so for the mobility offered by this tenure). There would also need to be an easing of planning controls in areas of high housing demand so as to allow supply to respond more readily to changes in demand.

A major advantage of a free market in housing supplemented by a system of housing vouchers is that it would ensure genuine tenure-neutrality. No government could attempt to boost one tenure or reduce another, since state funding would be limited to supplementing people's incomes. Under such a system, individual ownership, co-operative ownership and various forms of renting would expand or contract solely in response to the aggregate of individual consumer preferences. As Bendick explains,

> Financial subsidies could be provided to low income families themselves to augment their purchasing power. These families could then be allowed to select their own housing (and perhaps even their level of expenditures

on housing relative to other goods) from what is offered without subsidy by private builders and landlords. Such government subsidization of the *demand* for housing would operate through the private housing market, rather than as a substitute for it.

(1982, p. 366, original emphasis)

But how would it work, and how effective would such a system be in ensuring that those on low incomes were able to exercise a real degree of choice and to secure for themselves an adequate level of housing? Critics have often accepted that the principle of a voucher scheme is attractive but have argued that it is unrealistic in practice – Maclennan and Clapham, for example, suggest that 'The argument falls down because it ignores the real politics of income distribution in Britain, and because it adopts an idealized, mythical view of the technical nature of housing markets' (1982, pp. 14–15). To assess this, we need to consider four sets of questions concerning the mechanism for determining the value of the voucher, the response of housing suppliers to subsidized demand, the response of housing consumers to freedom of choice and the political feasibility of the proposed reform.

Clearly any *mechanism for determining the value of a voucher* would need to fix its maximum value at a point at which the least affluent could enter the market. This suggests that its value would have to be determined by the interaction of two factors – household income and prices in local housing markets. As we have seen in respect of proposals for a universal housing allowance, a simple flat-rate payment would be exorbitantly expensive and would in any case be worth more in relative terms to people living in low-price areas than to those who have to pay a higher proportion of their income in housing costs. Given the problem of the poverty trap, one way of taking account of income differences is to treat vouchers as taxable income, although Coleman (1989, p. 51) has suggested an alternative method by which a delay could be allowed between household incomes rising and the subsequent reduction or withdrawal of the voucher. This, however, is clumsy and does not really overcome the problem. As for the problem of regional variations in house prices, Coleman proposes different regional ceilings on the value of vouchers. The problem here, however, is that such a system could reinforce such variations and would possibly be insensitive to intra- as well as inter-regional price differences.

An alternative and more sensitive way of taking both income and regional variations in prices into account would be to set the value of the voucher on a sliding percentage scale. Under this system, eligibility for a voucher of any given percentage value would be determined by household income, while its absolute value would depend upon how much of this income the household chose to allocate to its housing. The germ of this idea can be found in Paterson's proposal for housing subsidies to be fixed at a different percentage of housing costs at different levels of income (Paterson, 1975, p. 35). For example, a household with an income of £150 per week could be given a voucher redeemable for, say, 50 per cent of its housing expenditure.

If it lived in a low-cost area, or chose to limit its spending on housing in favour of some other item, then it might spend £40 per week on housing, £20 of which would be covered by the voucher. If, on the other hand, it lived in a high-cost area, or chose to sacrifice a greater proportion of its income in order to get better housing, then it might spend £100 per week of which £50 would be redeemable through the voucher. Different levels of income would attract different percentage-value vouchers – a household earning £200 per week, for example, might only receive a 30 per cent value voucher, while one on £80 might receive a voucher for, say, 90 per cent of its housing costs.

The attraction of this kind of formula is that it seems to overcome many of the problems associated with flat-rate allowances or means-tested benefits. It reflects people's ability to pay yet avoids the problem of the poverty trap. It takes account of variations in the cost of housing between different areas (including those within regions), but will not exacerbate them. Because it is a percentage payment, it ensures that consumers remain sensitive to the cost of accommodation and it therefore rules out the need for officials to check up on whether people are living in better housing than the rules allow. Yet it also has the flexibility to enable people to choose whether to devote greater or lesser amounts of their income to their housing.

What would be the *response of housing suppliers* to such a change? The danger here lies in capitalization of the subsidy, for we have seen that subsidies like mortgage interest tax relief do seem to generate an increase in price, and critics of voucher schemes are confident that the same thing would happen with them (for example, Stretton, 1978a, p. 119). It is for this reason that any move to a voucher scheme would have to be tied to a loosening of supply-side constraints such as planning controls and security of tenure. If this were done, then there is no reason to believe that enhanced demand in any given sector or area would not bring about an increase in supply, especially since a voucher scheme would open up a major new source of demand from people who have hitherto effectively been limited to the state sector.

The best evidence for this comes from the experience of a major voucher experiment in the USA (see Bendick, 1982; Coleman, 1989; Nesslein, 1988). This scheme involved 30,000 low-income households in twelve cities who were monitored over periods between two and ten years. Different groups were given different kinds of income support (some, for example, were given rent vouchers, while others were given straight income supplements), and a control group was also included in the study.

One finding from this study was that, where they could, many of these households spent much of their income support on things other than housing. British critics such as Maclennan and Clapham (1982) have seized upon this to argue that voucher schemes are an inefficient way of supporting low-income households given the problem of leakage, and that direct provision in kind (that is, council housing) is therefore preferable. Yet in his review of the evidence, Bendick concludes that vouchers are *more efficient* than direct housing provision! This is because most households in the scheme were able to find housing of an equivalent quality to state housing at a lower price. This then freed some of their income for other purposes. Most therefore ended up in housing no better or worse than public housing even though they spent some of their allowances or vouchers on other items.

Given that some of the value of these vouchers never went into increased demand for housing, there was not a major rise in supply. However, Bendick found that the increased demand which did occur did stimulate some rise in supply and did not simply feed through in increased prices. This is confirmed by Nesslein, who reports that, in the two areas where full-scale voucher schemes were operated, rent rises attributable to the schemes amounted to just 1.6 per cent and 0.7 per cent. Given that aggregate demand for rental housing in these areas was boosted by 4.6 per cent and 5.6 per cent respectively, he calculates that full capitalization of the subsidy would have resulted in rent rises of 9.2 per cent and 11.2 per cent (1988, p. 100). In short, increased demand did feed through in increased supply and did not produce a significant increase in price. Obviously adjustments in the housing market occur over a period of years, but Nesslein is confident that demand-side interventions like this are unlikely to cause appreciable inflation in the long run.

The third issue to be addressed concerns the *response of housing consumers* to a voucher scheme. A standard criticism of voucher schemes in any area of social provision is that some people are incapable of acting as effective consumers in a market even when they have the financial means to purchase. State provision in kind is then supported on the dubious grounds that public-sector suppliers have the best interests of their clients at heart, while those in the private-sector are motivated only by self-interest. Hugh Stretton, for example, asserts:

> It does not necessarily do most for freedom and dignity to give the most vulnerable people nothing but shark-bait in shark-infested seas – nothing but money in societies with money-lenders and debt-collectors, landlords who keep rents up to capacities to pay, old folks' homes and hospitals which do likewise, alluring advertisers, hire purchase offers you can't refuse – and any number of bars, betting shops, poker machines, commercial religions, overpriced tranquillizers and other addictive attractions.
>
> (1976, p. 208)

Such extraordinarily élitist arguments against vouchers and similar cash transfer schemes can be answered in three ways. First, there are as many 'sharks' swimming in the public-sector sea as in the private. The difference between them is that consumers are not tied down when they operate in the market, whereas as state-sector clients they have to stay still while bureaucrats, professionals and unionized labour take bites out of them. As we have seen at several points throughout this book, it is a grave mistake to trust in the goodwill and altruism of any producer interest, irrespective of whether it derives its livelihood out of taxes or out of profits, and the fundamental consumer safeguard can only be the right of exit.

Second, Stretton may be right that there are a few genuinely feeble or vulnerable people who cannot function properly in a market. Such people require the protection of institutions – for example, of sheltered housing, mental hospitals, or old people's homes. Their existence does not, however, justify the state in providing mass housing for up to one-third of the population, for people who are relatively poor have not thereby been deprived of their mental faculties. As we saw in Chapter 2, the self-appointed defenders of the poor are only too keen to portray them as victims rather than to allow them to exercise their competence. Yet most of us, rich or poor, *are* competent. The US voucher experiment found, for example, that 'There was very little evidence that participants in the programme had difficulty functioning effectively as housing consumers. They generally could shop for units, negotiate leases and live as tenants without either training or assistance provided by the housing allowance administrative agency' (Bendick, 1982, pp. 371–2). Research showed that these people paid no more than anybody else for equivalent housing – they were astute shoppers and 'provided no indications of the need for government to act as their purchasing agent' (1982, p. 372). If they encountered sharks, they evidently knew how to handle them.

Of course, we have also seen that many of the participants in this scheme did not spend their entire allowance on housing – where they were given the opportunity, they also bought food, dental care, clothing, furniture and fuel. Some may even have indulged in 'bars, betting shops, poker machines and commercial religions'! The point, of course, is that the poor have their own values and preferences just as politicians, bureaucrats and academics do. If they choose to devote large slices of their budget to items other than housing, then neither the state nor Hugh Stretton has any business trying to force them to raise their housing standards to some official and arbitrary norm (although it may retain the right to take children into care if they suffer as a result). As we saw when discussing self-build, people need more freedom to choose and change their standard of housing rather than being coerced by planning regulations and building standards into conforming with the state's idea of what is best for them.

The third response to Stretton is that vouchers are an earmarked cash transfer – they can only be redeemed in exchange for housing services. This provides a safeguard against recipients spending all of their money having their teeth capped or whiling away their time in amusement arcades and thereby ending up living on the streets. There is a school of thought which sees this as an unwarranted and unnecessary restriction on their personal liberty and which would prefer to dispense with vouchers or allowances altogether in favour of a simple minimum income level. Milton Friedman, for example, defends his proposal for a Negative Income Tax by suggesting that 'If funds are to be used to help the poor, would they not be used more effectively by being given in cash rather than in kind? Surely the families being helped would rather have a given sum in cash than in the form of housing. They could themselves spend the money on housing if they so desired' (1962, p. 178). From a different political position, Colin Ward similarly points to 'the appalling difficulty about the expensive business of looking after people. They would be better off if they simply had the cash to look after themselves' (1985, p. 94). And the lesson drawn by Bendick from the US voucher experiment was that vouchers, while preferable to state housing, are nevertheless inferior to a simple system of unrestricted cash transfers: 'Unrestricted income transfers remain the benchmark, the seemingly ideal instrument for aiding the poor' (1982, p. 374). Seen in the light of these arguments, a move to a housing voucher scheme such as that proposed here represents a cautious reform, a stepping stone perhaps, on the route to a genuinely libertarian system for supporting the less well off.

There is, however, one final issue to be considered regarding a transition to a voucher scheme, and that concerns *the political feasibility of the proposed reform*. It is one thing to demonstrate that the system could work, but quite another to conclude that it could therefore be implemented. The current complex, inefficient and contradictory system of housing controls and subsidies has grown up and is perpetuated in response to the power and influence of vested interests. These are to be found among both consumers and suppliers of housing services, and their resistance to change could be enough to strangle any voucher initiative at birth.

The key consumer interest is, of course, the owner-occupier majority. A voucher scheme could presumably win the support of most renters in both public and private sectors for it would enhance their autonomy and scope for choice. It could also enlist the backing of low-income owner-occupiers, who would gain at least as much in voucher entitlement as they would lose in tax privileges. More affluent home owners would, however, lose out in any such change and could be expected to oppose it and perhaps to swing their electoral support behind whichever party was prepared to torpedo reform in an unseemly scramble for votes (see Chapter 4). The fact that the reform could be defended in terms of its fairness might help defuse opposition, for all subsidies would be ended, not just those of home owners. The fact that, over time, house buyers could be expected to gain (in lower house prices) as much as they lose (in tax relief) could also be used to win support, although this is a double-edged sword given that any fall in house prices would entail a reduction in equity held by existing owners.

The conclusion has to be that such a change would lay any governing party open to considerable opposition from the home-owning middle class unless a bipartisan agreement were reached and held firm. For this reason of political pragmatism, it may be that the change would have to be phased in gradually. Low-income buyers could be offered the choice between a voucher or tax relief, the value of tax relief for higher income groups could be allowed to decline as inflation and lower income tax rates gradually erode its significance, and relief could be restricted to the basic rate of tax and limited to a period of twenty-five years from a household's first purchase, as was originally suggested to the 1977 Housing Policy Review (see Aughton, 1981).

Just as significant as the opposition from the home-owning middle class would be the outcry which could be anticipated from the controllers and suppliers of the state housing sector, who would see their power challenged by any attempt to enable 'their' tenants to exercise effective purchasing power in the housing market. The local authority associations, the housing professionals, local socialist politicians and the public-sector unions could all be expected to try to sabotage a voucher scheme, just as these same kinds of interests mobilized to scupper an experimental education vouchers scheme in Kent in 1982 (see Seldon, 1986). Although introduction of the scheme does not depend on these groups (for it could be organized through either the social security or the income tax system), they are in a position to generate a lot of noise and not a little obstruction.

Given the strength of vested interests built up during the evolution of the housing system over the last century, it would be naïve to expect that the whole array of special interest subsidies and petty bureaucratic and professional fiefdoms could be replaced in one dramatic gesture by a new and neutral system of housing vouchers. Realistically we can only demand that old tenurial inequalities are not further strengthened and that new initiatives aim to promote consumer choice and greater tenure-neutrality.

In practice, this means setting our face firmly against those who would try to socialize the private sector rather than liberalizing the state sector, and it implies support for moves (such as rent deregulation and the extension of the Business Expansion Scheme) designed to make rental housing more attractive as an investment. It means welcoming policies (such as the Right to Buy, the right to transfer landlords and the transferable discount experiments) which enhance the choices open to existing council tenants. It means exploring how schemes for index-linked borrowing and self-build can be opened up to more of those who wish to take advantage of them. It means resisting pressures to increase tax thresholds on mortgage interest relief and moving to include all tenures within a single housing benefit system. None of this on its own is ultimately enough, but each of these proposals takes us further towards the goal of a free and fair housing system.

In his celebrated essay on 'Politics as a Vocation', Max Weber warned that what he called 'an ethic of conviction' has to be moderated by 'an ethic of responsibility'. What he meant by this was that, in the real world of politics, the pursuit of pure ends, justified by ultimate values, has always to be tempered by regard for short-term considerations. As he put it, 'If . . . one chases after the ultimate good in a war of beliefs, following a pure ethic of absolute ends, then the goals may be damaged or discredited for generations because responsibility for consequences is lacking' (1948, p. 126). Pragmatism as well as principle is required in successful political programmes, and this means recognizing where we are starting out from as well as where we wish to end up. A tenure-neutral and socially just housing system based on the principle of housing vouchers is technically possible, but to achieve it immediately would involve trampling over many powerful vested interests. In the short run, it may be that to get any worthwhile change at all, we have to settle for a compromise which is less than perfect and which leaves some of the existing array of subsidies and controls in place. If our ultimate commitment is to maximizing consumer choice and control in housing, then future policies need to edge towards the development of a fully fledged voucher scheme such as the one outlined here, and the test of new initiatives such as transferable discount and tenants' choice of landlords will lie in whether they bring us nearer to this objective. We should never forget that we do not live in a comic-book world. For us, it is likely to take more than one bound before we can be free.

Conclusions

There is in Britain a worrying gap opening up between what have been termed the 'middle mass' and the 'underclass'. This division is, of course, generated by factors other than the housing system, but it is coming to be most vividly expressed through housing differences and it is reproduced through tenure-based inequalities. However it is defined, the underclass appears to be concentrated in the least desirable parts of the council housing sector. State rental has today become associated with low incomes, high dependency on state benefits, high rates of unemployment and disproportionate numbers of single parents and single elderly people. When council tenants do have jobs, they are increasingly likely to involve unskilled or semi-skilled employment.

The residualization of the low paid and the economically inactive on what remain of the nation's council estates (for much of the best housing has been sold into owner-occupation) does not simply reflect existing economic inequalities but actually contributes to new ones. While home owners of all social classes share in the expansion of the country's wealth by virtue of their ownership of domestic property, those who remain in the council sector (many of whom would like to buy) are deprived of the chance to benefit from the rising value of the house or flat they live in. Instead, they face the prospect of indefinite rent payments (subsidized where necessary by housing benefit). As the home-owning middle mass gets wealthier, those who are trapped in state housing stay exactly where they are. Socialist defenders of state housing call this 'rent pooling'. Tenants themselves call it 'money down the drain'.

In this chapter we have examined the significance of this widening tenure division for an understanding of how the British social structure is changing.

More importantly, we have also considered the efficacy of different proposals for how the division may be overcome.

As regards the analysis of the impact of tenure cleavages on the British social structure, we have seen that, while they do little to influence people's class location, they clearly do more than simply highlight distinctions of social status. The division between the home-owning middle mass and the state-dependent underclass sustains a growing inequality of life chances as much as it reflects a difference of life-styles. This division is best understood as the product of state intervention in the housing system.

The growth of state intervention through the extraction of taxes and distribution of revenues has given rise to new sectoral cleavages in Britain between those who are able to enter the private market and those who are obliged to become clients of a patronage state. This division generates unequal life chances between the two groups, for the former can accumulate wealth and exercise personal autonomy, while the latter are locked ever more tightly into dependency and powerlessness. This division between the two sectors is, furthermore, one which is likely to grow in significance as members of the middle mass begin in the future to buy into private pensions and private health plans just as in the past they bought into private housing. The marginalized minority are today shut out of home ownership but may tomorrow find themselves shut out of many other areas of private provision as well.

What, then, can be done to reduce or overcome this growing fissure between a majority of private owners and a minority of increasingly marginal and dependent state-sector tenants? The broad answer to this is that the minority have to be enabled just as the majority have been, and this means providing them with the opportunity to escape their dependency and to become active consumers in a market system.

This rules out those recent left-wing prescriptions which, with all their talk of nationalized land and building companies, state licensing and price controls, aim essentially to dismantle the private housing market and to strip owner-occupiers of their property rights to a point where they become little different from existing council tenants. In contrast to all this heavy-handed coercion, policies like the Right to Buy, transferable discount and rental purchase do seem to offer those council tenants who would like to become owner-occupiers the chance to make the switch, and given that between a half and three-quarters of tenants apparently harbour such aspirations, such initiatives could go a long way in helping low-income households to realize their housing preferences.

Other policies are required, however, to help other groups in other situations with other sets of preferences. Most of the current low-income home ownership schemes are worthy but have limited potential, and although more could be done to expand the use of index-linked mortgages (as in the Victoria example in Australia) and to facilitate self-build experiments, the most fruitful strategy in the long term is to move towards a tenure-neutral system of income support in which consumers can choose whether to rent or buy without their decision being influenced by a confusing and often contradictory system of controls and subsidies.

We have seen that the case for phasing out 'bricks and mortar' subsidies is compelling. Price controls on private renting have proved counter-productive, state provision in kind has become dominated by producers and unresponsive to consumers, and subsidies to owner-occupiers through mortgage interest tax relief and other channels distort supply and demand and redistribute income from those who cannot afford it to those who do not need it. A voucher scheme based on household income and sensitive to patterns of housing expenditure would seem to be the most appropriate instrument to replace this confusing array of housing policies and interventions, and the bare details of how such a scheme might work have been sketched in the closing pages of this chapter.

For centuries, ordinary men and women in Britain have cherished the values of personal freedom. The people in Burnley, Derby and Slough who invited us into their homes during the course of 1986 are fortunate to live at a time when it is possible to enable all British citizens to exercise this freedom in respect of that most personal area of their lives, the choice of a place to live. Yet some of those whom we met in the course of our survey did not enjoy such freedom. They wanted one thing but were given another. This book has been written in the belief that the freedom currently enjoyed by the many could, fairly easily, be extended to the few. All that is required is a realistic social vision reinforced by a firm political resolution. Failure to embrace this vision or to hold fast to this resolution will consign a minority of the British population to an unedifying and stigmatized state of dependency, and the cost of such failure in the years to come will be felt by us all.

Appendix I: The Registrar-General and Goldthorpe social class schema and their use in this study

Throughout this book, social class data from the three towns survey and from other sources have been presented using one or both of two systems of classification.

The first, referred to as the 'Registrar-General's class schema', is that used by the Census in 1981 and by many government sources. It is also commonly used by sociologists. The principles which inform this approach, and the method by which it goes about allocating individuals to classes, are set out in OPCS (1980). Basically, it organizes individuals into six social classes on the basis of their occupations. These social classes consist of 'professional occupations' (class I), 'intermediate occupations', including most managers (class II), 'skilled non-manual occupations' (class IIIN), 'skilled manual occupations' (class IIIM), 'partly skilled occupations' (class IV) and 'unskilled occupations' (class V).

The classes are differentiated from each other on the criterion of 'occupational skill'. Unlike earlier versions of this schema, which tried to rank occupations by their 'standing in the community' (that is, a status dimension), the 1980 version is based solely on differences in the nature of work which people perform in different occupations. Although it takes no account of differences of education or qualification within occupational categories, it does take account of employment status and levels of authority. Foremen in manual jobs, for example, are always classified to class III even if the jobs themselves are deemed to be partly skilled or unskilled. Similarly, it is possible for employers or self-employed workers to be allocated to a different class from employees in the same occupational group.

The advantage of the Registrar-General's system of classification is that it is simple, fairly easy to use and widely understood. Its disadvantage is that it fails to correspond with any conception of social class to be found in sociological theory. It was for this reason that John Goldthorpe devised an alternative schema for use in his analysis of social mobility (Goldthorpe, 1980).

Goldthorpe's approach tries to take account of two factors which together determine people's class location. The first is the work situation – principally the autonomy which individuals enjoy in performing their tasks and the authority to which they are subject or which they are able to exert over others. The second is the market situation, which refers to the capacity of people in different positions to achieve economic rewards and security. These two factors are familiar in Weberian analyses of social stratification and can be found in, for example, Goldthorpe's earlier study of 'affluent workers' (Goldthorpe et al., 1969) and in Lockwood's analysis of variations within the working class (discussed in Chapter 5). He uses the OPCS model as the basis for his classification of occupations, but then applies his additional criteria to allocate people to one of several social classes ranging from higher-grade professionals, administrators and managers in class I to semi- and unskilled manual workers, together with agricultural workers, in class VII.

In this book, the Goldthorpe classes have been compressed into three main groups. The 'service class' comprises classes I and II and therefore includes lower- as well as higher-grade professionals, administrators and managers as well as managers in small businesses and supervisors of non-manual workers. The 'intermediate classes' are made up of classes III, IV and V. These include clerical and service workers ('white-collar workers'), small proprietors (the 'petty bourgeoisie') and lower-grade technicians, together with supervisors of manual workers (the 'blue-collar élite'). Finally, the 'working class' consists of classes VI and VII – skilled manual workers and other manual workers respectively.

The great advantage of using the Goldthorpe schema is that its categories are in some sense operationalizations of the categories found in theories of social stratification. In addition to Goldthorpe's own analysis of social mobility rates, this schema has also been employed in the 1983 general election study (Heath, Jowell and Curtice, 1985) and in the analysis of the British class structure by Marshall and his colleagues (1988). Indeed, the latter devote much of their book to a comparison of the Goldthorpe, Registrar-General and Marxist models and conclude that, for all its faults, the Goldthorpe schema seems best to reproduce in practice what many sociologists seem to have in mind when they discuss class divisions in theory.

Of course, any framework for analysing social class is almost bound to involve arbitrary or contentious judgements. The Registrar-General's schema seems to be based on somewhat arbitrary decisions about the amount of skill required by different jobs, and Goldthorpe's approach similarly rests on his personal assessments of how authority relations and levels of remuneration vary between occupations. However, it is important to arrive at some way of operationalizing social class in empirical research, and Goldthorpe's framework seems to be the most useful available at the moment (the OPCS is currently revising its schema for use in analysing the 1991 Census material, while the neo-Marxist approach evaluated by Marshall et al. seems to generate hopelessly confused results).

Given that both the OPCS and Goldthorpe schemata depend upon people having a job in the first place, any survey needs to make the additional decision of how those who are not currently employed are to be classified. One solution to this is simply to leave them out of the analysis. This seems unsatisfactory, however, since social class plays such a pivotal role in so many sociological accounts of human action and social attitudes. Large sections of the population would be excluded from such accounts if only those in current employment were allocated to a class location. One way around this problem is to allocate those who are not 'economically active' on the basis of what Wright (1978, p. 93) terms their 'class trajectory'. Those who are retired, unemployed, or sick can in this way be allocated to a class position on the basis of their last job, and this is the procedure which was adopted in the analysis of the data from the three towns survey.

This still leaves the question of how to classify those conventionally referred to as 'housewives'. Sociology has often classified married women according to the social class of their husbands, even if they are themselves working, and there has been a lively debate in the pages of *Sociology* in recent years over whether this practice should be continued or be replaced by separate classifications for each partner according to the job they do or did in the past. In this book, the latter strategy was adopted. Women who were themselves working (either full- or part-time) were classified on the basis of their occupation, irrespective of that of their partner, while those who were no longer employed were classified according to their most recent job.

The danger in this approach is that some women may be classified on the strength of a job held many years ago, and that their material circumstances and cultural attitudes may have changed dramatically as a result of a long period married to someone who currently occupies a different class position. The logic for holding to this approach even in the face of this problem is, however, twofold. First, it has been found that women in 'cross-class' marriages do not simply absorb the characteristics commonly associated with the social class of their husbands – women's subjective class identification, for example, seems to have as much to do with their own level of education as with their husbands' jobs (Abbott, 1987). Second, it is clear that class, unlike, say, housing tenure, is an attribute of individuals, not households. The logic of both the Registrar-General and the Goldthorpe schema is that people belong to classes as a result of their place in the occupational system, for it is this which determines their income, helps shape their attitudes and so on. It therefore makes little sense to classify them according to somebody else's occupation.

As Table A.1 makes clear, 48 per cent of those interviewed in the three towns survey were 'economically inactive', yet 97 per cent of the total sample was eventually allocated to a social class position (the table breaks the sample down according to the Registrar-General's categories, but the same principles were also followed in constructing Goldthorpe classes). Those who were employed or self-employed were classified according to their current occupations. In addition, 19 per cent of those we interviewed either referred to themselves as 'retired' or were not in employment and were over retirement age, and they were classified according to their most recent occupation; 10 per cent were unemployed, and 3 per cent were sick

Table A.1 *Allocation of respondents to social class categories in the three towns sample*

Employment status	I No.	I %	II No.	II %	IIIN No.	IIIN %	IIIM No.	IIIM %	IV No.	IV %	V No.	V %	Not classified No.	Not classified %	Total No.	Total %
Employee	17	7	71	28	48	19	58	23	40	16	23	9	–	–	257	49
Self-employed	1	7	4	29	1	7	6	43	1	7	1	7	–	–	14	3
Retired	1	1	23	23	19	19	26	26	24	24	8	8	–	–	101	19
Unemployed	–	–	2	4	9	17	12	22	16	30	15	28	–	–	54	10
Sick/disabled	–	–	–	–	3	20	6	40	2	13	4	27	–	–	15	3
Other not emp.	1	2	10	15	21	32	6	9	19	29	8	12	–	–	65	12
Never employed	–	–	–	–	–	–	–	–	–	–	–	–	16	100	16	3
Total	20	4	110	21	101	19	114	22	102	20	59	11	16	3	522	

Registrar-General's classes

or disabled, and they too were classified according to their most recent job; and 12 per cent (nearly all of them women) were also without employment and were similarly classified on the basis of their most recent occupation. Only 3 per cent of the sample was not allocated to a class position, and these were people who had never had a permanent job.

When women are classified by their own jobs rather than by those of their husbands, and when all 'economically non-active' people are classified on the basis of their last job rather than being excluded from the analysis, the pattern of the class system which results can appear rather different from that produced by more traditional methods. Two differences in particular stand out.

The first is that class IIIN becomes much larger, while class IIIM in particular becomes proportionately smaller. This is because many more women than men are employed in clerical and personal service occupations, while skilled manual employment is overwhelmingly male. John Goldthorpe has expressed the concern that, when married women are classified by their own occupations, the findings may become 'spurious or artefactual' (Erikson and Goldthorpe, 1988, p. 545). As we shall see in Appendix II, it is certainly true that the findings are changed when we follow this procedure, but it is not clear that they therefore become spurious, for it can be argued that analyses based solely on the occupations of male 'heads of households' are actually more misleading since they neglect the crucial significance of female labour in the economy.

The second way in which this procedure influences results is that it tends to increase the proportion of people in working-class positions while reducing the proportion in professional, administrative and managerial grades. The reason for this is that people who have been out of the labour market for some time are likely to have occupied lower-class positions on average than those currently in the labour market. Inclusion of retired people, housewives and the unemployed on the basis of the last jobs they held therefore shifts the class distribution towards the lower end. This can be seen from Table A.1 by comparing the column totals against the figures for employees. Thirty-five per cent of those who are currently employed are allocated to classes I or II as compared with only 26 per cent in the sample as a whole. Conversely, 25 per cent of current employees are allocated to classes IV or V as compared with 32 per cent for the whole sample. The figures for class III are, however, virtually identical.

These variations are explained mainly by the fact that, as Goldthorpe's 1980 study demonstrates, the proportion of higher-class jobs relative to working-class jobs has been growing in the British economy over the years. Thus, those who were retired, or who had not held a job for some time, have less chance of having been in a higher-class occupation when they were in work than that available to those who are currently employed. Once we take account of this time factor, it seems that it is quite possible to allocate virtually all members of the adult population to a social class on the basis of their own occupational history without thereby producing spurious or artefactual results.

Appendix II: The samples for the three towns survey

The logic which informed the choice of the three towns as case study areas was explained in Chapter 1. The purpose of this appendix is to outline how the samples were drawn in all three towns.

Our aim was to generate a set of interviews with principal householders (male or female) drawn from a variety of owner-occupied and council rented houses. All other tenure groups – tenants of private landlords, housing association tenants, owners in partnership schemes and so on – were excluded from the final sample. So too were people living in flats, maisonettes, or temporary accommodation, and those who were sharing accommodation with another household. In this way, we ended up only including tenants or owners of whole houses, and the sampling unit was therefore household addresses as opposed to individuals. In single-person households, the interviewee was obviously the sole householder; in multi-person households, interviews were sought with the adult owner or tenant and/or his or her partner (children living in the parental home were therefore excluded). In most cases, one householder was interviewed, but in seventy-two cases full interviews were conducted with two people. This generated a final sample of 522 individuals drawn from 450 households.

The target in each town was 150 households. Interviewing finished when this target was accomplished (that is, not all households originally selected in the sampling procedure were necessarily contacted). This target was in turn structured by quotas for different types of housing areas. Three main types of areas were selected in each town, each with a sampling quota of fifty. These areas were matched as far as was possible across the three towns, and each was made up of several different neighbourhoods.

The first type of area (type A) consisted of suburban neighbourhoods with a high proportion of semi-detached houses located in the upper half of the price range of the local housing market. In all three towns, this first category included both relatively new estates and more established houses built before the war.

The second type of area (type B) tended to be found nearer the town centres and consisted mainly of terraced houses towards the lower end of the local price spectrum. In all three towns, these areas included a substantial proportion of pre-1919 terraced housing, much of it at the bottom' of the housing market, although some neighbourhoods were also included where houses were built in the inter-war period.

Council estates made up the third type of area (type C). In all three towns, households were sampled from both the most and least 'desirable' estates (desirability was assessed by comparing application rates for transfers in and out of estates). The most desirable estates tended to have been built since 1945 and to include few blocks of flats. A high proportion of council house sales in all three towns was concentrated on these estates, and interviews were conducted irrespective of whether households drawn in the sample turned out to be renting or buying. The least desirable estates had generally been built before the war and had a much lower rate of sales.

In each town, the neighbourhoods from which we sampled were first identified through inspection of small area census data which provided information on tenure and socioeconomic composition. This short-list was then developed and amended following interviews with local estate agents (for the owner-occupied neighbourhoods) and local authority housing officials (for the council estates) in which we asked for comments on the relative suitability of different neighbourhoods as examples of 'up-market' and 'down-market' owner-occupation as well as 'desirable' and 'undesirable' council properties. The final selection from this short short-list of potential case study areas was then made visually by visiting the neighbourhoods. This also had the advantage of excluding particular roads where, for example, there appeared to be a high proportion of flats or commercial premises.

An example of how this procedure worked in practice can be provided in the case of Slough. Small area census data (which was organized on the basis of the pre-1983 ward boundaries) indicated that the Upton and Central South wards were more appropriate for type A housing (rates of owner-occupation, for example, were 84 per cent and 93 per cent respectively); that Farnham South would be an appropriate ward for type B (half of the population here were in skilled or semi-skilled manual occupations, yet 87 per cent of skilled manual workers were owner-occupiers); and that Wexham Court was an obvious example of council renting (36 per cent owner-occupation in the ward as a whole). Following discussions with estate agents and local housing officials, Upton was confirmed as an area of type A housing, and part of Langley was added to it; Farnham was confirmed as an example of type B housing, and part of Bayliss ward was added to it; and Wexham Lea (basically the old Wexham Court ward) was confirmed as type C housing, while Stoke ward was added to it. These assessments were checked out against current property prices as advertised by estate agents and in the local press – houses for sale in type B neighbourhoods, for example, were generally priced between £38,000 and £45,000, whereas those in type A were selling for at least half as much again. Finally, visual inspection led to a final selection of seven neighbourhoods representing these three categories of housing, and approximately half a dozen roads were then sampled from each of them.

Much the same procedure was followed in Derby and Burnley with the additional criterion that, when it came to visual inspection, an attempt was made to match up neighbourhoods in terms of types, age and condition of

Table A.2 *Response rates by town and type of area sampled*

| Town | Type of housing area | | | |
	Type A	Type B	Type C	Total
Slough	48%	44%	33%	42%
Derby	60%	38%	57%	52%
Burnley	76%	40%	66%	61%

housing with those already selected in Slough. This was not, of course, always possible given the different histories of the three towns. There was, for example, much less pre-1919 housing in Slough than in the other two towns, and there was no direct equivalent in Slough and Derby to the streets of stone terraced cottages which cluster around the centre of Burnley. Comparability, therefore, was assured more in terms of price bands (for example, housing at the bottom of the market was included in the samples in all three towns) than in terms of the design and type of houses.

Having selected various clusters of roads in each of the three types of housing areas, the final selection of households was made through random selection from the electoral register. The households which were selected were sent letters stating the nature of the research and that an interviewer would be calling.

The response rates were in general disappointing (Table A.2), ranging from just 42% in Slough to 61% per cent in Burnley. The variation in response rates across the three towns may partly reflect changes in our competence in securing interviews as time went on (we interviewed in Slough in the spring of 1986, moved to Derby in July and ended up in Burnley in September), although polling agencies with which we spoke confirmed that it has become increasingly difficult in recent years to achieve interviews around London and the Home Counties.

Response rates were particularly disappointing in the type B areas, although in Slough they were also poor on the council estates. The long questionnaire may have put some people off (naïvely we warned people in the letters which were sent out in Slough that interviews would last for up to one and a half hours!), although there is also evidence that people are now becoming more concerned about invasions of privacy (see Goyder and McKenzie Leiper, 1985) and are distrustful of 'interviewers' who too often nowadays turn out to be selling insurance, double glazing or encyclopaedias (we were ourselves sometimes mistaken for sales representatives despite offering identification). Nor did it help our cause when in Derby a gang of burglars read of our survey in the local newspaper and proceeded to gain entry to various houses while claiming to be from Sussex University!

Relatively low response rates like these inevitably raise questions about the representativeness of the sample which was finally achieved. The problem in assessing this, however, is that there is no obvious yardstick against which to compare the sample, for it was never intended to be representative of the whole populations of these towns given that sampling was structured by pre-set quotas for types of neighbourhood, and that the sampling frame excluded non-principal householders, private renters, flat-dwellers and so on. Table A.3 compares the sample with statistics for social class, housing tenure and voting in each town, but we should not expect the two sets of figures to match up. As was emphasized in Chapter 1, the data from this survey should not be, and were not intended to be, taken as a microcosmic reflection of the three towns as a whole (still less the population of the country as a whole). The logic of the sampling method was to target three socio-tenurial strata – the comfortable home-owning 'middle mass', the more marginal owners at the bottom end of the market and present or former council tenants – which could then be compared with each other in order to address recent sociological debates about home ownership (such as debates over the contrasts between owners and tenants, North and South, working-class and middle-class owners and so on). Nevertheless, Table A.3 is interesting in that it enables us to judge the extent to which this sampling procedure may have placed more or less emphasis on different groups in the population.

Considering first the social class breakdown of the samples, it is clear that in all three towns our sampling strategy produced final samples which quite closely reflected the class composition of the towns as a whole. The exception in all three cases lies in an under-representation of skilled manual workers (class IIIM) – by ten percentage points in Slough, seven in Derby and eight in Burnley. In Slough this was reflected mainly in an over-representation of unskilled manual workers; in Derby it was reflected mainly in an over-representation of workers in intermediate (class II) occupations; and in Burnley it was reflected in a slight over-representation in three other classes (I, IIIN and IV). Overall, though, the samples seem reasonably representative of the populations from which they were drawn.

The data on housing tenure show that owner-occupiers were over-represented relative to council tenants in Slough and Derby, and were under-represented in Burnley. The Burnley ratio of 71:29 owners:tenants (compared with 75:25 in the town as a whole) is explained by the fact that Burnley has historically had high owner-occupation rates and relatively low levels of council renting. A sampling strategy which includes a 33 per cent council estate quota would therefore be expected to generate disproportionate numbers of tenants, especially since council house sales in Burnley have been slower than in the other two towns. The Derby and Slough figures can, by contrast, be explained largely by the expansion of owner-occupation between 1981 (when the Census was carried out) and 1986 (when the interviews took place). Table 2.7 showed that both of these towns sold 17 per cent of their council houses between 1980 and 1986; and when this is taken into account, the disparity between the 'actual' and sample tenure ratios certainly narrows and possibly disappears altogether.

Finally, the figures on voting intentions (adjusted as explained in note 3) show that we apparently underestimated the Conservative vote in Slough

Table A.3 *Social class, tenure and voting in Burnley, Derby and Slough comparing the samples with the whole populations*

Town	Registrar-General class % (controlling for economically non-active)						Tenure % (others excluded in brackets)		Voting % (1987 adjusted in brackets)		
	I	II	IIIN	IIIM	IV	V	Owner-occup.	Council tenant	Con	Lab	Lib/SDP
SLOUGH											
Actual	5	23	11	35	21	5	58 (64)	33 (36)	36	30	10
Sample	6	27	10	25	21	12	(77)	(23)	23 (28)	31 (27)	24 (19)
DERBY											
Actual	6	20	10	37	20	7	59 (66)	30 (34)	28	31	11
Sample	6	26	13	30	17	8	(71)	(29)	20 (25)	39 (30)	23 (23)
BURNLEY											
Actual	3	20	11	40	21	7	70 (75)	23 (25)	27	38	14
Sample	6	16	14	32	24	8	(71)	(29)	22 (29)	38 (31)	15 (13)

Notes and sources:
1 *Social class data*. The 'actual' social class breakdown for each town is taken from the 1981 Census data (*Key statistics for urban areas*). The figures for 'economically inactive' and 'armed forces and inadequately described' have been excluded, and the remaining statistics have been raised to a total of 100% in order to enable comparison with the sample data. The Census figures refer only to 'heads of household', which normally means male heads in households where two adult partners are present (see OPCS, 1986). The class breakdown for the sample data has therefore been presented in the same way. As explained in Appendix I, this produces a very different pattern given that women are over-represented in some classes and under-represented in others. In particular, it reduces the proportion of respondents in class IIIN and raises it in class IIIM. Taking all respondents rather than just 'heads of household', the sample figures for each of the six classes were: Slough (4%, 26%, 20%, 19%, 18% and 13%); Derby (3%, 22%, 21%, 26%, 19% and 9%); and Burnley (5%, 18%, 19%, 22%, 25% and 12%).
2 *Housing tenure data*. The 'actual' tenure figures are again based on the 1981 Census. Figures in brackets express the proportion of owner-occupiers and council tenants excluding other tenures and therefore enable direct comparison with the sample figures. However, the Census data are now seriously out of date given the rate of council house sales since 1981. We saw in Table 1.1 that owner-occupation in England and Wales rose from 58% to 65% between 1981 and 1986 (a rise of 12%), while council renting fell from 29% to 24% over the same period (a fall of 17%). Some adjustment on the 1981 'actual' figures would therefore be required in order to make comparisons with the 1986 sample figures.
3 *Voting data*. When the interviews were conducted, Labour and the Alliance parties had higher levels of support nationally (and the Conservatives were correspondingly less popular) than they eventually achieved at the 1987 general election. On 2 April 1986 (when the Slough interviewing was in progress), MORI gave the Conservatives 34%, Labour 36% and the Alliance 28%. On 2 July, at the time of the Derby interviews, MORI gave the Conservatives 34%, Labour 40% and the Alliance 23%; and on 18 September, when we were interviewing in Burnley, a Gallup poll showed the Conservatives at 33%, Labour at 38% and the Alliance at 28%. The actual result at the 1987 election was 42% Conservative, 31% Labour and 23% Alliance. Comparisons between opinion polls during the interviewing and the final election result enable us to adjust our 1986 sample voting intentions to allow for the shift in public opinion which then occurred, and the adjusted figures are given in brackets for each sample so as to enable direct comparison with the actual voting patterns in 1987.

and the Labour vote in Burnley while overestimating Alliance support in Slough and Derby. This is partly explained by the under-representation of class IIIM in the samples, for our data show that, excluding don't knows, respondents in this class were the most strongly committed to Labour (60 per cent support) and were most lukewarm towards the Alliance (15 per cent support). Alliance support was strongest in class II (39 per cent), and the over-representation of this class in the Slough and Derby samples would also help to explain the inflated Alliance support recorded in these two towns. It also needs to be said, however, that support for the Alliance parties was often far from firm among our respondents, and it therefore came as no surprise when the 1987 election results in the three towns revealed that many potential Alliance voters had in fact returned to their traditional party loyalties. All three of the constituencies covered in these samples were Conservative/Labour marginals as a result of the 1983 election, and this undoubtedly squeezed the Alliance vote as compared with other areas where Liberal or SDP candidates had run second in 1983.

Let it be stressed again that the samples which were drawn for this study were not intended to be representative of the entire populations of the three towns. A simple random sample would have included many households in whom we were not interested while reducing the numbers of those in whom we were particularly interested. Nevertheless, the final samples which were drawn appear fairly representative of owners and council tenants in the three towns. Certainly there are no grounds for believing that those whom we interviewed were in any sense a 'peculiar' group, and we can be fairly confident that the sorts of results presented in this book would broadly be replicated if other researchers went back to Burnley, Derby and Slough and asked the same set of questions to a different sample of home owners and council tenants. The findings, in other words, seem fairly reliable.

Appendix III: The questionnaire

As I noted in the Prologue, the bulk of the interviewing was carried out by three members of the research team at Sussex, although seven other people also helped out at some stage. Most survey work in sociology is contracted out to specialist agencies which then employ interviewers (normally part-time women) to do the actual work. There are at least three advantages to be gained by having done the interviews ourselves.

One is that we were able to develop a 'feel' for the data which would have been impossible had we simply been presented with a computer disk containing the findings. Thus, not only do we know what people said in reply to the questions, but we also know how they said it. Given our interest in the home, it was also useful to meet householders in their home environments.

A second advantage is that all those involved in interviewing were trained social scientists who had an interest in the project and were not simply taking on interviews in order to earn some money. By and large, the interviews were very competently handled by people who knew why the questions were being asked and who could note down (often at some length) verbatim answers where these seemed particularly relevant to the concerns of the research. There is, of course, always the danger that interviewers with a personal interest in the research may in some way bias people's responses, but the use of a number of different interviewers with very different political views and personal opinions about home ownership will have helped guard against this.

The third advantage is that we were able to include in the questionnaire a large number of open-ended questions. These are always difficult when interviewing is contracted out, for commercial interviewers are usually intent on completing interviews as quickly as possible (especially if they are paid on piece rates) and show little inclination either to encourage respondents to elaborate on their answers or to spend much time writing down what they say.

What all this amounts to is that the findings we recorded probably have a higher degree of validity than that achieved in most surveys of this kind.

The questionnaire itself was piloted in ten interviews in Brighton. The final version contained various grids and codes on which answers could be entered. These have been excluded from the schedule reproduced here in order to save space. Various instructions to interviewers and 'show-cards' have also been deleted.

Questions i to x were completed by interviewers after each interview
i. Interview number
ii. Date
iii. Time started and time finished
iv. Interviewer
v. Town and road
vi. Gender of interviewee
vii. Ethnicity of interviewee
viii. Type of house (terraced, semi-detached, etc.)
ix. Estimated house value
x. Condition of house

I would like to begin by asking a few questions about your past and present housing:

1. In what period was this house built?
2. How many bedrooms does the house have?
   How many living rooms (not including kitchen)?
   How many rooms altogether (not including sep. w.c.)?
3. Do you own or rent the house?
4. Who currently lives in this house?
5. Do you have any grown-up children who no longer live here with you? (*Gender, marital status, children, location, tenure.*)
6. Can I trace through with you the different places you have lived in since you first set up your own home. Let's start with the first place. (*When, where, type of accommodation, tenure, price paid, deposit, mortgage, sale price, reason for moving.*)
   Repeat for each move.
7. *If ever owned.* Why did you decide to buy a house in the first place?
   How did you get the deposit together to buy your first place?
8. *If ever council tenant.* Why did you first decide to rent from the council?
9. Where do/did your parents and parents-in-law live?
   Do/did they own or rent their home?
   When you were still living at home, what line of work were they in?
10. Do you have any definite plans to move from this house, either in the short term or the long term?
    If yes When do you think you might move and why?
11. *Tenants* Has there ever been any problem in your experience in getting the sort of council house you want in the place you want it?
12. Comparing yourself with someone who owns/rents their house, what would you say are the main advantages of being a tenant/owner?
    And what are the main disadvantages?
13. On balance, would you prefer to buy or rent the house you live in? Why?

14. *Tenants* Have you ever considered buying this house from the council?
    If yes Why didn't you?
    If no Is there any particular reason why not?

15. *Owners* The price of housing has gone up quite a lot over the years. Would you say you have made money out of owning a house? Roughly, what do you think this house is worth now?

16. *Owners* Have you at any time remortgaged a house, or taken out a second mortgage on one, as a way of raising cash?
    If yes What did you use the cash for?
    Have you ever used a house as security against a loan?
    If yes What did you use the loan for?

17. Have your parents or in-laws ever been able to help you financially with your housing costs. (*Details.*)

18. How would you describe the state of repair of this house?

19. Are there any repairs which you feel need to be done but which have not been done?
    If yes What are they?
    Is there any particular reason why they haven't been done?

20. *Tenants* Have you (or your partner) done much in the way of decorations or repairs to the house since you first moved in?
    Have you ever wanted to do something in the house which your tenancy agreement has prevented you from doing?
    How quickly does the council act when it comes to doing repairs or dealing with problems or complaints?

21. *Owners* Have you received any council grants towards the cost of repairing or improving the property?

22. *Owners* Have you done any of the following things to the house since you moved in? (*For each item note date, cost and who did the work.*) Were any of these things already done?
    (*Central heating, double glazing, wall insulation, rewiring, roof repair or replacement, extensions, damp-proofing, new kitchen, new bathroom, exterior decoration, interior decoration, other.*)
    Would you expect to get back the money you have spent on these things when you sell the house?

23. Why did you choose to do the job/s yourself rather than pay for someone to come in and do it for you?

I would like to ask a few questions about your life up to now.

24. First, can I ask where you were born?
    And which age group do you belong to?

25. What type of school did you attend from the age of eleven?
    How old were you when you left full-time education?

26. I would like to know about the different jobs you have done since

you finished full-time education. (*Dates, full job description, full- or part-time, sector, reason left.*)

27. Do you find the job that you do at the moment interesting and challenging?

Are you satisfied with the level of pay for the work you do?

Do you feel that your employment is fairly secure?

Do you enjoy the social side of the job – being with the people you work with?

28. How many hours do you spend doing your job in an average week?

Would you prefer to increase your hours/income, reduce them, or carry on as present?

Why?

29. *If not in employment* What, if anything, do you miss most about not having a job?

Do you have any problem filling your time or are you kept pretty busy?

30. Thinking of the day-to-day jobs around the house, can you tell me who is mainly responsible for: cooking, washing up, shopping, laundry, cleaning the house, doing the garden, looking after the car, cleaning the outside windows, child minding during school holidays, paying the bills and keeping the accounts?

31. Does anyone in the household ever do any of these sorts of tasks for other people outside your immediate household?

32. In general would you describe this neighbourhood as friendly or unfriendly?

33. Thinking of the people who live nearby, do you ever do favours for them, or do they do favours for you?

34. Is there any organization like a residents' (or tenants') association to represent the people who live in this area?

Do you belong to it?

What sorts of things has it done in recent years?

35. Can you think of the three people you consider your closest friends. For each one, can you tell me where they live, whether they own or rent their house, how you first met them and how often you see them.

I'm interested in getting some idea of how you spend your spare time.

36. Thinking of weekends, what are the main things you normally do? And what do you do in your spare time during the week?

Would you say this is fairly typical of how you spend your spare time?

37. When was the last time you had people come round for a social visit or just for a chat?

38. Would you prefer to go out more often than you do?

If yes What is it that stops you going out more?

39. Do you have any particular hobbies or leisure interests?
40. Do you belong to any clubs or organizations – sports clubs, work clubs, political parties, PTAs, that sort of thing?
41. Have you ever belonged to a trade union, staff association, or professional association of any sort?
    Is there any particular reason why you decided to join/not to join/ leave?

I would now like to go on to ask a few questions about your household's income and outgoings.

42. Thinking of your average gross earnings before tax and other stoppages, which of the following income groups do you (and your partner) belong to?
43. Does anyone else in the household have a job at the moment?
    Do they contribute to the housekeeping?
44. At present do you (and/or your partner) receive any income from: casual, temporary, or freelance employment; rent from lodgers or properties let elsewhere; state pension or pension from former employer; state benefits such as supplementary benefit or housing benefit; family allowances; maintenance payments; interest or dividends from savings or investments; any other source of income?
    Adding up the total value of all these different sources of income, how much are they worth?
45. Have you ever inherited any money or property?
    When was that?
    What was the total value of the legacy/legacies?
    What did you do with the money?
46. *Owners* How many years are left before the mortgage is paid off? (Or: when was the mortgage paid off?)
    In whose name is the house/mortgage registered?
    How much do you pay in mortgage repayments each month?
    Do you experience any difficulties in meeting the cost of the mortgage repayments?
    Do you receive any special help with your housing costs from your employer?
    How much do you pay in rates on this house?
47. *Tenants* Whose name is on the tenancy agreement for this house?
    How much rent do you pay each week?
    Do you experience any difficulty in meeting the cost of the rent?
48. People with mortgages can claim tax relief on their interest payments.
    Do you support the continuation of tax relief to people paying mortgages?
    Why do you think that?

49. Thinking of your total household income, and your total outgoings, would you describe yourself as well off, hard up, or what?

50. Does anyone in the household run a car?
    Do both of you have a car?
    Who has the car during the week?
    Is/are the car/s your own or does it/do they come with the job?
    How much did it/did they cost?
    How did you pay for it/them – cash, HP, bank loan, or what?

51. Do you use the bus services much?

52. Are you generally satisfied or dissatisfied with the level and quality of the local bus services?

53. In some towns the council has kept bus fares very low by increasing subsidies from the rates. Would you like to see the local council here reduce fares by increasing the rates?

54. I shall now read a list of household items. In each case please say whether or not you have one, and whether you own or rent it: colour TV, b&w TV, video recorder, home computer, washing machine, freezer, dishwasher, microwave, stereo, telephone, power drill.

55. In general do you prefer to buy or rent items like telephones, televisions and video machines?
    Why?

56. When you buy major household items like televisions or carpets or furniture, do you generally pay cash or buy through a loan or credit?
    Why?

57. Have you been on holiday away from home in the last twelve months?
    Approximately how much did the holiday/s cost in total?
    If no Is there any particular reason why not?

58. Are you/your partner covered by a private pension scheme?
    Is this a condition of employment or did you choose to join?
    Are you currently paying into any insurance or endowment schemes designed to give you a cash sum later in life?

59. Suppose your household income were to increase in the future, say by a third. How do you think you would use the extra money?
    And now imagine that your household income dropped by a third. What do you think you would have to cut back on?

60. Have you or anyone else in the household ever been covered by private medical insurance?

61. *If yes* Who in the household is/was covered by the scheme?
    Who pays/paid the premiums?
    Do you think that private health insurance is worth the money given that you are already paying for NHS treatment through your taxes?
    Why did you leave the scheme?

62. *If no* Would you choose to take out private health insurance if you could afford it?
    Why/why not?

63. Are you generally satisfied or dissatisfied with the treatment you have received within the NHS?

64. Should people be allowed to stop paying towards the NHS if they want to choose private medical care instead?

65. Would you be prepared to pay higher taxes if that meant that more could be spent on the NHS?

66. Do/did you make use of any pre-school facilities for your child/ren?
    Do/did any of your children go to a fee-paying school after the age of five?
    If yes Why do/did you consider it worth paying for your child's schooling given that you are already paying for the state system through your taxes?
    If no Do/did you pay for any private tuition for your child/ren out of school hours – music lessons, extra coaching, that sort of thing?

67. If you could afford it, would you send your child/ren to a private fee-paying school?
    Why/why not?

68. Have you been generally satisfied or dissatisfied with the education your children have received?

69. Would you be willing to pay increased taxes if that meant more money was spent on state education?

70. The teachers' unions have recently been involved in industrial action to get higher wages. Do you think teachers should be paid more?

71. Do you think teachers were justified in calling one-day strikes as part of their campaign?

72. Suppose the local council held a vote on whether people wanted lower rates with fewer services, or higher rates to maintain or improve services. Which would you vote for?

73. In recent years have you noticed any change in the quality of the public services you use?

74. Do you support or oppose the government's attempts to cut back spending on items like housing, education and social services?

75. Would you support a policy of reducing inequality by increasing the taxes paid by people on higher incomes?

76. In recent years local councils have been obliged by law to sell council houses to any tenants who wish to buy. Do you approve or disapprove of this policy?
    Why?

77. In recent years the government has been selling off a number of state-owned industries such as British Telecom or Jaguar cars, and it plans to sell British Gas and British Airways in the future. Do you support or oppose this policy?
    Why?

78. What in your view should be done to tackle the unemployment problem?
79. Generally speaking do you think of yourself as a supporter of any particular political party?
80. If there were a general election tomorrow, which party do you think you would be most likely to vote for?
    Why is that?
    Have you always voted for that party?
    Is there any party which you think is most likely to benefit owner-occupiers/council tenants such as yourself?
81. Do you think of yourself as belonging to any particular social class?

Finally, returning to the theme of your house and home . . .

82. Can you tell me what (if anything) first attracted you to this particular house?
83. Do you feel particularly attached to this house – for example, would you be unhappy to leave it?
84. People often distinguish between 'house' and 'home'. What does the home mean to you?
    What is it that makes people feel at home in a particular place?
85. Do you think people who buy their home feel any differently about it from those who rent?
86. What would you describe as your 'ideal home'?
    Do you think you'll ever get to live in somewhere like that?

References

Abbott, P. (1987), 'Women's social class identification', *Sociology*, vol. 21, pp. 91–104.

Abercrombie, N., Hill, S., and Turner, B. (1980), *The Dominant Ideology Thesis* (London: Allen & Unwin).

Abercrombie, N., Hill, S., and Turner, B. (1986), *Sovereign Individuals of Capitalism* (London: Allen & Unwin).

Agnew, J. (1978), 'Market relations and locational conflict in cross-national perspective', in K. Cox (ed.), *Urbanization and Conflict in Market Societies* (London: Methuen).

Agnew, J. (1981), 'Homeownership and the capitalist social order', in M. Dear and A. Scott (eds), *Urbanization and Planning in Capitalist Society* (London: Methuen).

Allan, G. (1985), *Family Life: Domestic Roles and Social Organization* (Oxford: Blackwell).

Allan, G., and Crowe, G. (1988), 'Constructing the domestic sphere', paper presented at the British Sociological Association annual conference, Edinburgh, April.

Allen, D. (1968), *British Tastes* (London: Hutchinson).

Alt, J. (1977), 'Beyond class: the decline of industrial labor and leisure', *Telos*, pp. 55–80.

Alt, J., and Turner, J. (1982), 'The case of the silk-stocking socialists and the calculating children of the middle class', *British Journal of Political Science*, vol. 12, pp. 239–48.

Altman, I. (1975), *The Environment and Social Behaviour* (Monterey, Calif.: Brooks/Cole).

Altman, I., and Chemers, M. (1980), *Culture and Environment* (Belmont, Calif.: Wadsworth).

Andrusz, G. (1987), 'The built environment in Soviet theory and practice', *International Journal of Urban and Regional Research*, vol. 11, pp. 478–99.

Ardrey, R. (1967), *The Territorial Imperative* (London: Collins).

Arendt, H. (1958), *The Human Condition* (Chicago: University of Chicago Press).

Association of Metropolitan Authorities (1987), *A New Deal for Home Owners and Tenants* (London: AMA).

Aughton, H. (1981), *Housing Finance: A Basic Guide* (London: Shelter).

Austerberry, H., and Watson, S. (1985), 'A woman's place: a feminist approach to housing in Britain', in C. Ungerson (ed.), *Women and Social Policy* (London: Macmillan).

Badcock, B. (1984), *Unfairly Structured Cities* (Oxford: Blackwell).

Bailey, G. (1987), *New Life for Old Estates* (London: Conservative Political Centre).

Ball, M. (1976), 'Owner-occupation', in M. Edwards, F. Gray, S. Merrett and J. Swann (eds), *Housing and Class in Britain* (London: Political Economy of Housing Workshop).

Ball, M. (1978), 'British housing policy and the house building industry', *Capital and Class*, no. 4, pp. 78–99.

Ball, M. (1982), 'Housing provision and the economic crisis', *Capital and Class*, no. 17, pp. 60–77.

Ball, M. (1983), *Housing Policy and Economic Power* (London: Methuen).
Ball, M. (1985), 'Coming to terms with owner occupation', *Capital and Class*, no. 24, pp. 15–44.
Ball, M. (1986), *Home Ownership: A Suitable Case for Reform* (London: Shelter).
Ball, M., Martens, M., and Harloe, M. (1986), 'Mortgage finance and owner occupation in Britain and West Germany', *Progress in Planning*, vol. 26, pp. 185–260.
Banion, M., and Stubbs, C. (1986), 'Rethinking the terms of tenure: a feminist critique of Michael Ball', *Capital and Class*, no. 29, pp. 182–94.
Barlow, J. (1986), *Economic Restructuring and Housing Provision in Britain*, Urban and Regional Studies Working Paper No. 54 (Brighton: University of Sussex).
Barlow, J. (1987), 'The housing crisis and its local dimensions', *Housing Studies*, vol. 2, pp. 28–41.
Barlow, J., and Duncan, S. (1988), 'The use and abuse of housing tenure', *Housing Studies*, vol. 3, pp. 219–231.
Barrow, M., and Robinson, R. (1986), 'Housing and tax capitalization', *Urban Studies*, vol. 23, pp. 61–6.
Bassett, K. (1980), 'The sale of council houses as a political issue', *Policy and Politics*, vol. 8, pp. 290–307.
Bassett, K., and Short, J. (1980), *Housing and Residential Structure* (London: Routledge & Kegan Paul).
Bell, C. (1968), *Middle Class Families* (London: Routledge & Kegan Paul).
Bendick, M. (1982), 'Vouchers versus income versus services: an American experiment in housing policy', *Journal of Social Policy*, vol. 11, pp. 365–78.
Benn, S., and Peters, R. (1959), *Social Principles and the Democratic State* (London: Allen & Unwin).
Bennett, W. (1951), *The History of Burnley, Part IV* (County Borough of Burnley).
Bentley, I. (1987), 'The social production of housing design', paper presented to the BSA study group on sociology and environment seminar, London School of Economics, February.
Berge, E. (1988), 'Some comments on C. Hamnett's reading of the data on sociotenurial polarization in south east England', *Environment and Planning A*, vol. 20, pp. 973–82.
Berger, P. (1987), *The Capitalist Revolution* (Aldershot: Wildwood House).
Berry, M. (1983), 'Posing the housing question in Australia', in L. Sandercock and M. Berry, *Urban Political Economy* (Sydney: Allen & Unwin).
Berry, M. (1986), 'Housing provision and class relations under capitalism', *Housing Studies*, vol. 1, pp. 109–21.
Boddy, M. (1976), 'Building societies and owner-occupation', in M. Edwards, F. Gray, S. Merrett and J. Swann (eds), *Housing and Class in Britain* (London: Political Economy of Housing Workshop).
Boddy, M. (1980), *The Building Societies* (London: Macmillan).
Boleat, M. (1985), *National Housing Finance Systems* (London: Croom Helm).
Booth, P., and Crook, T. (1986), 'Low cost home ownership initiatives', in P. Booth and T. Crook (eds), *Low Cost Home Ownership* (Aldershot: Gower).
Bossons, J. (1978), 'Housing demand and household wealth', in L. Bourne and J. Hitchcock (eds), *Urban Housing Markets* (Toronto: University of Toronto Press).
Bracewell-Milnes, B. (1989), 'In praise of rising house prices', *Economic Affairs*, vol. 9, pp. 28–9.
Brindley, T. (1977), 'Privacy: a sociological interpretation', D.Phil. thesis, University of Reading.
Brittan, A. (1977), *The Privatized World* (London: Routledge & Kegan Paul).
Bryant, C. (1978), 'Privacy, privatization and self-determination', in T. Young (ed.), *Privacy* (Chichester: Wiley).

Building Societies Association (1976), *Facts and Figures*, no. 7 (July).

Building Societies Association (1988), *A Compendium of Building Society Statistics* (London: BSA).

Building Societies Association (various years), *BSA Bulletin*.

Bulpitt, J. (1983), *Territory and Power in the United Kingdom* (Manchester: Manchester University Press).

Burnett, J. (1986), *A Social History of Housing 1815–1985* (London: Methuen).

Burnley Borough Council (1986), *Burnley: Employment Survey 1985* (Burnley: Borough Council Planning and Estates Department).

Burns, S. (1975), *The Household Economy* (Boston: Beacon Press).

Butler, D., and Stokes, D. (1974), *Political Change in Britain* (Harmondsworth: Penguin).

Butler, E., Pirie, M., and Young, P. (1985), *The Omega File* (London: Adam Smith Institute).

Campbell, C. (1987), *The Romantic Ethic and the Spirit of Modern Consumerism* (Oxford: Blackwell).

Carter, R. (1988), 'Mortgage-backed securities, inflation-adjusted mortgages and real rate funding', paper presented at the International Research Conference on Housing Policy and Innovation, Amsterdam, June.

Central Statistical Office (1987), *United Kingdom National Accounts* (London: HMSO).

Central Statistical Office (1988), *Social Trends* (London: HMSO).

Central Statistical Office (various years), *Economic Trends Annual Supplement* (London: HMSO).

Champion, T., Green, A., and Owen, D. (1987), 'Housing, labour mobility and unemployment', *The Planner*, vol. 73, pp. 11–17.

Chapman, D. (1955), *The Home and Social Status* (London: Routledge & Kegan Paul).

Christian, R. (1978), *Derbyshire* (London: Batsford).

CIPFA (1987), *Housing Rents and Statistics at April 1987* (London: Chartered Institute of Public Finance and Accountancy).

Clarke, S., and Ginsburg, N. (1975), 'The political economy of housing', in Conference of Socialist Economists, *Political Economy and the Housing Question* (London: CSE).

Cockburn, C. (1977), *The Local State* (London: Pluto Press).

Coleman, A. (1985), *Utopia on Trial* (London: Hilary Shipman).

Coleman, D. (1988), 'Housing: conditions for success in government policy', *Economic Affairs*, vol. 8, pp. 37–40.

Coleman, D. (1989), 'The new housing policy: a critique', *Housing Studies*, vol. 4, pp. 44–57.

Community Development Project (1976a), *Whatever Happened to Council Housing?* (London: CDP Information and Intelligence Unit).

Community Development Project (1976b), *Profits against Houses* (London: CDP Information and Intelligence Unit).

Cooper, C. (1976), 'The house as symbol of the self', in H. Proshanksky, W. Ittelson and L. Rivlin (eds), *Environmental Psychology*, 2nd edn. (New York: Holt Rinehart & Winston).

Couper, M., and Brindley, T. (1975), 'Housing classes and housing values', *Sociological Review*, vol. 23, pp. 563–76.

Cowley, J. (1979), *Housing for People or for Profit?* (London: Stage 1).

Cowling, M., and Smith, S. (1984), 'Home ownership, socialism and realistic socialist policy', *Critical Social Policy*, no. 9, pp. 64–8.

Cox, K. (1982), 'Housing tenure and neighbourhood activism', *Urban Affairs Quarterly*, vol. 18, pp. 107–29.

Cox, K., and McCarthy, J. (1982), 'Neighbourhood activism as a politics of turf', in

393

K. Cox and R. Johnston (eds), *Conflict, Politics and the Urban Scene* (London: Longman).

Crewe, I. (1983), 'The disturbing truth behind Labour's rout', *Guardian*, 13 June.

Crewe, I. (1986), 'On the death and resurrection of class voting', *Political Studies*, vol. 34, pp. 620–38.

Crossick, G. (1978), *An Artisan Elite in Victorian Society* (London: Croom Helm).

Cutler, A., Hindess, B., Hirst, P., and Hussain, A. (1977), *Marx's 'Capital' and Capitalism Today*, Vol. 1 (London: Routledge & Kegan Paul).

Dahrendorf, R. (1987), 'The erosion of citizenship and its consequences for us all', *New Statesman*, 12 June.

Damer, S. (1971), 'Wine Alley: the sociology of a dreadful enclosure', *Sociological Review*, vol. 22, pp. 221–48.

Damer, S. (1980), 'State, class and housing: Glasgow 1885–1919' in J. Melling (ed.), *Housing, Social Policy and the State* (London: Croom Helm).

Daunton, M. (1983), *House and Home in the Victorian City* (London: Edward Arnold).

Daunton, M. (1987), *A Property-Owning Democracy?* (London: Faber).

Davidoff, L., L'Esperance, J., and Newby, H. (1976), 'Landscape with figures: home and community in English society', in J. Mitchell and A. Oakley (eds), *The Rights and Wrongs of Women* (Harmondsworth: Penguin).

Davies, J. (1972), *The Evangelistic Bureaucrat* (London: Tavistock).

Davies, J. (1985), 'Asian housing in Britain', *Social Affairs Unit Research Report*, no. 6.

Davis, E., and Saville, I. (1982), 'Mortgage lending and the housing market', *Bank of England Quarterly Bulletin*, vol. 22, pp. 390–8.

Davis, K. (1948), *Human Society* (New York: Collier-Macmillan).

Dawkins, R. (1976), *The Selfish Gene* (Oxford: Oxford University Press).

Dennis, N. (1970), *People and Planning* (London: Faber).

Department of Employment (1987), *Family Expenditure Survey 1986* (London: HMSO).

Department of the Environment (1982), *English House Condition Survey 1981*, parts 1 and 2 (London: HMSO).

Department of the Environment (1987a), *Housing and Construction Statistics 1976–86* (London: HMSO).

Department of the Environment (1987b), *Local Housing Statistics, England and Wales*, no. 83 (London: HMSO).

Devine, F. (1988), 'Sources of privatism', paper presented at the British Sociological Association annual conference, Edinburgh, April.

Dickens, P. (1977), 'Social change, housing and the state', in M. Harloe (ed.), *Proceedings of the Conference on Urban Change and Conflict* (London: Centre for Environmental Studies).

Dickens, P. (1988), *One Nation? Social Change and the Politics of Locality* (London: Pluto Press).

Dickens, P., Duncan, S., Goodwin, M., and Gray, F. (1985), *Housing, States and Localities* (London: Methuen).

Doling, J., Karn, V., and Stafford, B. (1985), *Behind with the Mortgage* (London: National Consumer Council).

Doling, J., Karn, V., and Stafford, B. (1986), 'The impact of unemployment on home ownership', *Housing Studies*, vol. 1, pp. 49–59.

Donnison, D. (1967), *The Government of Housing* (Harmondsworth: Penguin).

Donnison, D., and Ungerson, C. (1982), *Housing Policy* (Harmondsworth: Penguin).

Douglas, M., and Isherwood, B. (1979), *The World of Goods* (London: Allen Lane).

Drayson, S. (1985), 'The housing finance market: recent growth in perspective', *Bank of England Quarterly Bulletin*, vo. 25, pp. 80–91.

Duke, V., and Edgell, S. (1984), 'Public expenditure cuts in Britain and consumption sectoral cleavages', *International Journal of Urban and Regional Research*, vol. 8, pp. 177–201.

Duke, V., and Edgell, S. (1987), 'Attitudes to privatization: the influence of class, sector and partisanship', *Quarterly Journal of Social Affairs*, vol. 3, pp. 253–84.

Dunham, A. (1972), 'Property, city planning and liberty', in M. Stewart (ed.), *The City: Problems of Planning* (Harmondsworth: Penguin).

Dunleavy, P. (1979), 'The urban basis of political alignment', *British Journal of Political Science*, vol. 9, pp. 409–43.

Dunleavy, P. (1980a), *Urban Political Analysis* (London: Macmillan).

Dunleavy, P. (1980b), 'The political implications of sectoral cleavages and the growth of state employment', *Political Studies*, vol. 28, pp. 364–83, 527–49.

Dunleavy, P. (1986), 'The growth of sectoral cleavages and the stabilization of state expenditures', *Society and Space*, vol. 4, pp. 129–44.

Dunleavy, P. (1987), 'Class dealignment in Britain revisited', *West European Politics*, vol. 10, pp. 400–19.

Dunleavy, P., and Husbands, C. (1985), *Democracy at the Cross-Roads* (London: Allen & Unwin).

Dunn, R., Forrest, R., and Murie, A. (1987), 'The geography of council house sales in England 1979–85', *Urban Studies*, vol. 24, pp. 47–59.

Edel, M. (1982), 'Home ownership and working class unity', *International Journal of Urban and Regional Research*, vol. 6, pp. 205–22.

Edel, M., Sclar, E., and Luria, D. (1984), *Shaky Palaces* (New York: Columbia University Press).

Edgell, S., and Duke, V. (1986), 'Radicalism, radicalization and recession', *British Journal of Sociology*, vol. 37, pp. 479–512.

Edney, J. (1972), 'Property, possession and permanence', *Journal of Applied Social Psychology*, vol. 2, pp. 275–82.

Elgie Stewart Smith (1988), *The Inheritance Generation* (London: Elgie Stewart Smith PLC).

Engels, F. (1969), *The Condition of the Working Class in England* (St Albans: Panther).

Erikson, R., and Goldthorpe, J. (1988), 'Women at class crossroads: a critical note', *Sociology*, vol. 22, pp. 545–53.

Evans, A. (1988), *No Room! No Room!: The Costs of the British Town and Country Planning System* Occasional Paper No. 79 (London: Institute of Economic Affairs).

Farmer, M., and Barrell, R. (1981), 'Entrepreneurship and government policy', *Journal of Public Policy*, vol. 1, pp. 307–32.

Fielder, S., and Imrie, R. (1986), 'Low cost home ownership: the extension of owner occupation', *Area*, vol. 18, pp. 265–73.

Filmer, P., Phillipson, M., Silverman, D., and Walsh, D. (1972), *New Directions in Sociological Theory* (London: Collier-Macmillan).

Fleming, M., and Nellis, J. (1985), *Housing Policy and the Future of Home-Ownership in the UK* (Cranfield: Cranfield School of Management).

Fletcher, C. (1976), 'The relevance of domestic property to sociological understanding', *Sociology*, vol. 10, pp. 451–68.

Forrest, R. (1983), 'The meaning of homeownership', *Society and Space*, vol. 1, pp. 205–16.

Forrest, R. (1987), 'Spatial mobility, tenure mobility and emerging social divisions in the UK housing market', *Environment and Planning A*, vol. 19, pp. 1611–30.

Forrest, R., and Murie, A. (1984), *Right to Buy? Issues of Need, Equity and Polarization in the Sale of Council Houses*, School for Advanced Urban Studies Working Paper No. 39 (Bristol: University of Bristol).

Forrest, R., and Murie, A. (1985), *An Unreasonable Act?*, School for Advanced

Urban Studies Study No. 1 (Bristol: University of Bristol).

Forrest, R., and Murie, A. (1986), 'Marginalization and subsidized individualism', *International Journal of Urban and Regional Research*, vol. 10, pp. 46–66.

Forrest, R., and Murie, A. (1987a), 'Social polarization and housing tenure polarization', paper presented at the Sixth Urban Change and Conflict Conference, University of Kent, September.

Forrest, R., and Murie, A. (1987b), 'The affluent homeowner: labour-market position and the shaping of housing histories', in N. Thrift and P. Williams (eds), *Class and Space* (London: Routledge & Kegan Paul).

Forrest, R., and Murie, A. (1987c), 'Fiscal reorientation, centralization and the privatization of council housing', in W. Van Vliet (ed.), *Housing Markets and Policies under Fiscal Austerity* (London: Greenwood Press).

Forrest, R., and Murie, A. (1989), 'Differential accumulation: wealth, inheritance and housing policy reconsidered', *Policy and Politics*, vol. 17, pp. 25–39.

Forrest, R., and Williams, P. (1980), *The Commodification of Housing*, Centre for Urban and Regional Studies Working Paper No. 73 (Birmingham: University of Birmingham).

Franklin, A. (1986), *Owner Occupation, Privatism and Ontological Security: A Critical Reformulation*, School for Advanced Urban Studies Working Paper No. 62 (Bristol: University of Bristol).

Franklin, A. (1989), 'Working class privatism: an historical case study of Bedminster, Bristol', *Society and Space*, vol. 7, pp. 93–113.

Franklin, M. (1985), *The Decline of Class Voting in Britain* (Oxford: Clarendon Press).

Franklin, M., and Page, E. (1984), 'A critique of the consumption cleavage approach in British voting studies', *Political Studies*, vol. 32, pp. 521–36.

Fraser, M. (1973), *The History of Slough* (Slough Corporation).

Fried, M. (1963), 'Grieving for a lost home', in L. Duhl (ed.), *The Urban Condition* (New York: Simon & Schuster).

Friedman, M. (1962), *Capitalism and Freedom* (Chicago: University of Chicago Press).

Friedman, M., and Friedman, R. (1980), *Free to Choose* (London: Secker & Warburg).

Gans, H. (1988), *Middle American Individualism* (New York: Free Press).

Gavron, H. (1966), *The Captive Wife* (Harmondsworth: Penguin).

Giddens, A. (1981), *A Contemporary Critique of Historical Materialism*, Vol. 1 (London: Macmillan).

Giddens, A. (1984), *The Constitution of Society* (Cambridge: Polity Press).

Ginsburg, N. (1983), 'Home ownership and socialism in Britain', *Critical Social Policy*, no. 7, pp. 34–53.

Glyn, A., and Sutcliffe, B. (1970), *British Capitalism, Workers and the Profits Squeeze* (Harmondsworth: Penguin).

Glyptis, S. (1987), 'Leisure and the home', in S. Glyptis (ed.), *Leisure and the Over-Fifties and Leisure and the Home* (London: Leisure Studies Association).

Goffman, E. (1959), *The Presentation of Self in Everyday Life* (New York: Doubleday).

Goffman, E. (1961), *Asylums* (New York: Doubleday).

Goldthorpe, J. (1980), *Social Mobility and Class Structure in Modern Britain* (Oxford: Clarendon Press).

Goldthorpe, D., Lockwood, D., Bechhofer, F., and Platt, J. (1969), *The Affluent Worker in the Class Structure* (Cambridge: Cambridge University Press).

Gorz, A. (1982), *Farewell to the Working Class* (London: Pluto Press).

Goyder, J., and McKenzie Leiper, J. (1985), 'The decline in survey response', *Sociology*, vol. 19, pp. 55–71.

Gray, F. (1982), 'Owner-occupation and social relations', in S. Merrett with F. Gray,

Owner Occupation in Britain (London: Routledge & Kegan Paul).

Green, D. (1985), *Working Class Patients and the Medical Establishment* (Aldershot: Gower).

Gullestad, M. (1983), *Kitchen-Table Society* (Oslo: Universitetsforlaget).

Habermas, J. (1976), *Legitimation Crisis* (London: Heinemann).

Haddon, R. (1970), 'A minority in a welfare state society', *New Atlantis*, vol. 2, pp. 80–133.

Halifax Building Society (1987), *The Halifax House Price Index: National Bulletin*, no. 30.

Hall, P. (1988), 'Arcadia for some: the strange story of autonomous housing', paper presented at the International Research Conference on Housing Policy and Innovation, Amsterdam, June.

Halle, D. (1984), *America's Working Man* (Chicago: University of Chicago Press).

Halsey, A. (1977), 'Introduction', in A. Halsey (ed.), *Heredity and Environment* (London: Methuen).

Hamnett, C. (1983), 'From the foundations up', *New Statesman*, 14 October.

Hamnett, C. (1984a), 'Housing the two nations', *Urban Studies*, vol. 43, pp. 389–405.

Hamnett, C. (1984b), 'The postwar restructuring of the British housing and labour markets', *Environment and Planning A*, vol. 16, pp. 147–61.

Hamnett, C. (1987), 'Accumulation, access and inequality: the owner occupied housing market in Britain in the 1970s and 1980s', paper presented at the 6th Urban Change and Conflict Conference, University of Kent, September.

Hamnett, C. (1988a), 'Housing inheritance and wealth in Britain', paper presented at the International Research Conference on Housing Policy and Innovation, Amsterdam, June.

Hamnett, C. (1988b), 'Regional variations in house prices and house price inflation in Britain 1969–1988', *Royal Bank of Scotland Review*, no. 159, pp. 29–40.

Hamnett, C., and Randolph, W. (1986), *Socio-Tenurial Polarization in London*, Social Statistics Research Unit Working Paper No. 45 (London: University of London).

Hamnett, C., and Randolph, B. (1988), *Cities, Housing and Profits* (London: Hutchinson).

Hardy, D., and Ward, C. (1984), *Arcadia for All: The Legacy of a Makeshift Landscape* (London: Mansell).

Hardyment, C. (1988), *From Mangle to Microwave* (Cambridge: Polity Press).

Harloe, M. (1984), 'Sector and class: a critical comment', *International Journal of Urban and Regional Research*, vol. 8, pp. 228–37.

Harmer, M. (1988), 'As safe as houses', *New Society*, 22 April.

Harris, Richard (1984), 'Residential segregation and class formation in the capitalist city', *Progress in Human Geography*, vol. 8, pp. 26–49.

Harris, Richard (1986), 'Boom and bust', *Canadian Geographer*, vol. 30, pp. 302–15.

Harris, Richard, and Hamnett, C. (1987), 'The myth of the promised land', *Annals of the Association of American Geographers*, vol. 77, pp. 173–90.

Harrison, A., and Lomas, G. (1980), 'Tenure preference: how to interpret the survey evidence', *CES Review*, no. 8, pp. 20–3.

Harrop, M. (1980), 'The urban basis of political alignment: a comment', *British Journal of Political Science*, vol. 10, pp. 388–402.

Harvey, D. (1977), 'Government policies, financial institutions and neighbourhood change in United States cities', in M. Harloe (ed.), *Captive Cities* (London: Wiley).

Harvey, D. (1978), 'Labor, capital and class struggle around the built environment in advanced capitalist societies', in K. Cox (ed.), *Urbanization and Conflict in Market Societies* (London: Methuen).

Hayden, D. (1981), *The Grand Domestic Revolution* (London: MIT Press).

Hayek, F. (1960), *The Constitution of Liberty* (London: Routledge & Kegan Paul).

REFERENCES

Hayward, D. (1975), 'Home as an environmental and psychological concept', *Landscape*, vol. 20, pp. 2–9.

Heath, A., Jowell, R., and Curtice, J. (1985), *How Britain Votes* (Oxford: Pergamon Press).

Heath, A., Jowell, R., and Curtice, J. (1986), 'Understanding electoral change in Britain', *Parliamentary Affairs*, vol. 39, pp. 150–64.

Heath, A., Jowell, R., and Curtice, J. (1987), 'Trendless fluctuation: a reply to Crewe', *Political Studies*, vol. 35, pp. 256–77.

Hediger, H. (1962), 'The evolution of territorial behaviour', in S. Washburn (ed.), *Social Life of Early Man* (London: Methuen).

Henney, A. (1985), *Trust the Tenant*, Policy Study No. 68 (London: Centre for Policy Studies).

Hinton, C. (1987), *Using your Home as Capital* (Mitcham: Age Concern England).

Hirst, P., and Woolley, P. (1982), *Social Relations and Human Attributes* (London: Tavistock).

Holmans, A. (1986), *Flow of Funds Associated with House Purchase for Owner Occupation in the UK 1977–1984 and Equity Withdrawal from House Purchase Finance*, Government Economic Service Working Paper No. 92 (London: DoE and DoT).

Holmans, A. (1987), *Housing Policy in Britain* (London: Croom Helm).

Holme, A. (1985), 'Family and homes in East London', *New Society*, 12 July.

Hughes, C. (1987), 'Homeowners caught in a cycle of chronic deprivation', *Independent*, 20 August.

Hyde, M., and Deacon, B. (1986), 'Working class opinion and welfare strategies', *Critical Social Policy*, no. 18, pp. 15–31.

Ineichen, B. (1972), 'Home ownership and manual workers' life styles', *Sociological Review*, vol. 20, pp. 391–412.

Ingham, G. (1984), *Capitalism Divided?* (London: Macmillan).

Jacobs, J. (1962), *The Death and Life of Great American Cities* (London: Cape).

Jacobs, S. (1982), 'Socialist housing strategy and council house sales', *Critical Social Policy*, vol. 1, no. 3, pp. 40–5.

Johnston, R. (1987), 'A note on housing tenure and voting in Britain, 1983', *Housing Studies*, vol. 2, pp. 112–21.

Jones, C. (1982), 'The demand for home ownership', in J. English (ed.), *The Future of Council Housing* (London: Croom Helm).

Karn, V., Doling, J., and Stafford, B. (1986), 'Growing crisis and contradiction in home ownership', in P. Malpass (ed.), *The Housing Crisis* (London: Croom Helm).

Karn, V., Kemeny, J., and Williams, P. (1985), *Home Ownership in the Inner City* (Aldershot: Gower).

Kellner, P. (1987), 'It wasn't the campaign, it was the product', *New Statesman*, 10 July.

Kemeny, J. (1980), 'Home ownership and privatization', *International Journal of Urban and Regional Research*, vol. 4, pp. 372–88.

Kemeny, J. (1981), *The Myth of Home Ownership* (London: Routledge & Kegan Paul).

Kemeny, J. (1987), 'Towards a theorized housing study', *Housing Studies*, vol. 2, pp. 249–60.

Kemeny, J., and Thomas, A. (1984), 'Capital leakage from owner-occupied housing', *Policy and Politics*, vol. 12, pp. 13–30.

Kemp, P. (1987), 'Some aspects of housing consumption in late nineteenth century England and Wales', *Housing Studies*, vol. 2, pp. 3–16.

Kilmartin, L. (1988), 'Housing: an antipodean perspective', paper presented at the International Research Conference on Housing Policy and Innovation, Amsterdam, June.

Klopfer, P. (1969), *Habitats and Territories* (New York: Basic Books).

Kumar, K. (1986), 'The privatized society', *Universities Quarterly*, vol. 4, pp. 356–64.

Kuper, B. (1968), *Privacy and Private Housing* (London: Building Design Partnership).

Lafargue, P. (no date), *Evolution of Property from Savagery to Civilization* (Calcutta: Sreekali Prakasalaya).

Lasch, C. (1977), *Haven in a Heartless World* (New York: Basic Books).

Lawrence, R. (1987), 'What makes a house a home?', *Environment and Behavior*, vol. 19, pp. 154–68.

Leach, E. (1973), 'Don't say boo to a goose', in A. Montagu (ed.), *Man and Aggression* (Oxford: Oxford University Press).

Leleux, R. (1984), *Regional History of the Railways*, vol. 9, *The East Midlands* (Newton Abbot: David & Charles).

Lewis, J., and Platt, S. (1988), 'Council tenants get cash to go', *New Society*, 26 February.

Littlewood, J. (1986), 'Is home ownership for renters?', in T. Booth and T. Crook (eds), *Low Cost Home Ownership* (Aldershot: Gower).

Lockwood, D. (1966), 'Sources of variation of working class images of society', *Sociological Review*, vol. 14, pp. 249–67.

Lorenz, K. (1966), *On Aggression* (London: Methuen).

Lorenz, K. (1981), *The Foundations of Ethology* (New York: Springer-Verlag).

Lowe, S. (1986), *Urban Social Movements* (London: Macmillan).

Lowe, S. (1988), 'New patterns of wealth: the growth of owner occupation', in R. Walker and G. Parker (eds), *Money Matters* (London: Sage).

Lundqvist, L. (1986), *Housing Policy and Equality* (London: Croom Helm).

Macfarlane, A. (1978), *The Origins of English Individualism* (Oxford: Blackwell).

Machon, P. (1987), 'The sale of local authority houses in Britain', *Geography*, vol. 72, pp. 169–71.

Mackenzie, S., and Rose, D. (1983), 'Industrial change, the domestic economy and home life', in J. Anderson, S. Duncan and R. Hudson (eds), *Redundant Spaces in Cities and Regions*. (London: Academic Press).

Maclennan, D. (1982), *Housing Economics* (London: Longman).

Maclennan, D., and Clapham, D. (1982), 'The social market', *Roof*, November/December, pp. 14–15.

Madge, C. (1950), 'Private and public spaces', *Human Relations*, vol. 3, pp. 187–99.

Madge, J., and Brown, C. (1981), *First Homes: A Survey of the Housing Circumstances of Young Married Couples* (London: Policy Studies Institute).

Madigan, R. (1988), 'A new generation of home owners?', discussion paper (Glasgow: Centre for Housing Research, University of Glasgow).

Malatesta, P., and Hess, A. (1986), 'Discount mortgage financing and house prices', *Housing Finance Review*, vol. 5, pp. 25–41.

Malmberg, T. (1980), *Human Territoriality* (The Hague: Mouton).

Marcuse, P. (1987), 'The other side of housing: oppression and liberation', in B. Turner, J. Kemeny and L. Lundqvist (eds), *Between State and Market: Housing in the Post-Industrial Era* (Almqvist & Wiksell International).

Marshall, G., Rose, D., Vogler, C., and Newby, H. (1985), 'Class, citizenship and distributional conflict in modern Britain', *British Journal of Sociology*, vol. 36, pp. 259–82.

Marshall, G., Vogler, C., Rose, D., and Newby, H. (1987), 'Distributional struggle and moral order in a market society', *Sociology*, vol. 21, pp. 55–74.

Marshall, G., Newby, H., Rose, D., and Vogler, C. (1988), *Social Class in Modern Britain* (London: Hutchinson).

Marx, K. (1959), *Capital*. Vol. III (London: Lawrence & Wishart).

Marx, K. (1964), *Economic and Philosophic Manuscripts of 1844* (New York: International Publishers).

REFERENCES

Marx, K., and Engels, F. (1970), 'Manifesto of the Communist Party', in *Selected Works* (London: Lawrence & Wishart).

Massey, D. (1984), *Spatial Divisions of Labour* (London: Macmillan).

Maslow, A. (1943), 'A theory of human motivation', *Psychological Review*, vol. 50, pp. 371–96.

Matrix (1984), *Making Space: Women and the Man-Made Environment* (London: Pluto Press).

McAllister, I. (1984), 'Housing tenure and party choice in Australia, Britain and the United States', *British Journal of Political Science*, vol. 14, pp. 509–22.

McDowell, L. (1983a), 'City and home: urban housing and the sexual division of space', in M. Evans and C. Ungerson (eds), *Sexual Divisions: Patterns and Processes* (London: Tavistock).

McDowell, L. (1983b), 'Towards an understanding of the gender division of urban space', *Society and Space*, vol. 1, pp. 59–72.

McFadyen, S., and Hobart, R. (1978), 'Inflation and urban home ownership', in L. Bourne and J. Hitchcock (eds), *Urban Housing Markets* (Toronto: University of Toronto Press).

Means, R. (1987), 'Older people in British housing studies', *Housing Studies*, vol. 2, pp. 82–98.

Merrett, S. (1979), *State Housing in Britain* (London: Routledge & Kegan Paul).

Merrett, S. (1982), *Owner Occupation in Britain* (London: Routledge & Kegan Paul).

Merrett, S. (1986), 'The taxation of housing consumption', *Housing Studies*, vol. 1, pp. 220–7.

Minford, P., Peel, M., and Ashton, P. (1987), *The Housing Morass* (London: Institute of Economic Affairs).

Mintel Special Report (1987), *New Wealth and the Individual* (London: Mintel Publications).

Montagu, A. (1976), *The Nature of Human Aggression* (Oxford: Oxford University Press).

Moore, B. (1984), *Privacy* (Armonck, New York: M. E. Sharpe).

Moorhouse, H., Wilson, M., and Chamberlain, C. (1972), 'Rent strikes: direct action and the working class', in R. Miliband and J. Saville (eds), *The Socialist Register* (London: Merlin Press).

Morgan Grenfell Economics (1987), 'Housing inheritance and wealth', *Morgan Grenfell Economic Review*, no. 45.

Mumby, D. (1957), *Home Ownership*, Fabian Research Series No. 188 (London: Fabian Society).

Mumford, L. (1961), *The City in History* (London: Secker & Warburg).

Munro, M. (1988), 'Housing wealth and inheritance', *Journal of Social Policy*, vol. 17, pp. 417–36.

Munro, M., and Maclennan, D. (1987), 'Intra-urban changes in house prices', *Housing Studies*, vol. 2, pp. 65–81.

Murie, A. (1983), *Housing Inequality and Deprivation* (London: Heinemann).

Murie, A. (1989), 'Supply, transition and differentiation: perspectives on home ownership', paper presented at the British Sociological Association Sociology and Environment study group seminar, London School of Economics, February.

Murie, A., and Forrest, R. (1980), 'Wealth, inheritance and housing policy', *Policy and Politics*, vol. 8, pp. 1–19.

Murie, A., Forrest, R., and Williams, P. (1990), *Home Ownership in Transition* (London: Unwin Hyman).

Murphy, M., and Sullivan, O. (1985), 'Housing tenure and family formation in contemporary Britain', *European Sociological Review*, vol. 1, pp. 230–43.

National Federation of Housing Associations (1985), *Inquiry into British Housing* (London: NFHA).

Nationwide Building Society (1985), *House Prices over the Last Thirty Years*, background bulletin, April (London: Nationwide Building Society).

Nationwide Building Society (1986), *Housing as an Investment*, April (London: Nationwide Building Society).

Nationwide Building Society (1987), *The North/South Divide*, August (London: Nationwide Building Society).

Nationwide Anglia Building Society (1987), *House Prices in 1987*, December (London: Nationwide Anglia Building Society).

Nationwide Anglia Building Society (1988), *House Prices Highs and Lows: A Local View* (London: Nationwide Anglia Building Society).

Nellis, J., and Fleming, M. (1987), *Home-Ownership Policy in the UK* (Cranfield: Cranfield School of Management).

Nellis, J., and Longbottom, J. (1981), 'An empirical analysis of the determination of house prices in the United Kingdom', *Urban Studies*, vol. 18, pp. 9–21.

Nesslein, T. (1988), 'Housing: the market versus the welfare state model revisited', *Urban Studies*, vol. 25, pp. 95–108.

Newby, H., Vogler, C., Rose, D., and Marshall, G. (1985), 'From class structure to class action', in B. Roberts, R. Finnegan and D. Gallie (eds), *New Approaches to Economic Life* (Manchester: Manchester University Press).

Nove, A. (1983), *The Economics of Feasible Socialism* (London: Allen & Unwin).

Oakley, A. (1974), *Housewife* (London: Allen Lane).

Office of Population Censuses and Surveys (1980), *Classification of Occupations* (London: HMSO).

Office of Population Censuses and Surveys (1983), *Recently Moving Households* (London: HMSO).

Office of Population Censuses and Surveys (1986), *Britain's Households*, Census Guide No. 4 (London: HMSO).

Office of Population Censuses and Surveys (1987), *Labour Force Survey 1985* (London: HMSO).

Office of Population Censuses and Surveys (various years), *General Household Survey* (London: HMSO).

Oliver, P., Davis, I., and Bentley, I. (1981), *Dunroamin: The Suburban Semi and its Enemies* (London: Barrie & Jenkins).

Oxley, M. (1988), 'Tenure change in western Europe', paper presented at the International Research Conference on Housing Policy and Innovation, Amsterdam, June.

Packard, V. (1959), *The Status Seekers* (London: Longman).

Pahl, R. (1975), *Whose City?*, 2nd edn (Harmondsworth: Penguin).

Pahl, R. (1984), *Divisions of Labour* (Oxford: Blackwell).

Pahl, R. (1988a), 'Some remarks on informal work, social polarization and the social structure', *International Journal of Urban and Regional Research*, vol. 12, pp. 247–67.

Pahl, R. (1988b), 'Housing, work and lifestyle', paper presented at the International Research Conference on Housing Policy and Innovation, Amsterdam, June.

Pahl, R., and Wallace, C. (1985), 'Forms of work and privatization on the Isle of Sheppey', in B. Roberts, R. Finnegan and D. Gallie (eds), *New Approaches to Economic Life* (Manchester: Manchester University Press).

Pahl, R., and Wallace, C. (1988), 'Neither angels in marble nor rebels in red', in D. Rose (ed.), *Social Stratification and Economic Change* (London: Hutchinson).

Papadakis, E., and Taylor-Gooby, P. (1987), *The Private Provision of Public Welfare* (Brighton: Wheatsheaf).

Paris, C., and Blackaby, B. (1979), *Not Much Improvement* (London: Heinemann).

Parsons, T. (1977), *Social Systems and the Evolution of Action Theory* (New York: Free Press).

Paterson, J. (1975), 'Home owning, home renting and income distribution', *Australian Quarterly*, vol. 47, pp. 28–36.

Pawley, M. (1978), *Home Ownership* (London: Architectural Press).

401

Payne, J., and Payne, G. (1977), 'Housing pathways and stratification', *Journal of Social Policy*, vol. 6, pp. 129–56.

Peake, L. (1984), 'How Sarlvik and Crewe fail to explain the Conservative victory of 1979 and electoral trends in the 1970s', *Political Geography Quarterly*, vol. 3, pp. 161–7.

Pelling, H. (1968), *Popular Politics and Society in Late Victorian Britain* (London: Macmillan).

Perin, C. (1977), *Everything in its Place* (Princeton, NJ: Princeton University Press).

Porteous, J. (1976), 'Home: the territorial core', *Geographical Review*, vol. 66, pp. 383–900.

Pratt, G. (1981), 'The house as an expression of social worlds', in J. Duncan (ed.), *Housing and Identity* (London: Croom Helm).

Pratt, G. (1982), 'Class analysis and urban domestic property', *International Journal of Urban and Regional Research*, vol. 6, pp. 481–502.

Pratt, G. (1986a), 'Housing tenure and social cleavages in urban Canada', *Annals of the Association of American Geographers*, vol. 76, pp. 366–80.

Pratt, G. (1986b), 'Housing consumption sectors and political response in urban Canada', *Society and Space*, vol. 4, pp. 165–82.

Pratt, G. (1986c), 'Against reductionism: the relations of consumption as a mode of social structuration', *International Journal of Urban and Regional Research*, vol. 10, pp. 377–400.

Pratt, G. (1987a), 'Class differences in the relationship between housing tenure and political consciousness in urban Canada', in R. Harris and G. Pratt (eds), *Housing Tenure and Social Class* (Gavle: National Swedish Institute for Building Research).

Pratt, G. (1987b), 'Class, home and politics', *Canadian Review of Sociology and Anthropology*, vol. 24, pp. 39–57.

Preteceille, E. (1986), 'Collective consumption, urban segregation and social classes', *Society and Space*, vol. 4, pp. 145–54.

Priemus, H. (1987), 'Economic and demographic stagnation, housing and housing policy', *Housing Studies*, vol. 2, pp. 17–27.

Rainwater, L. (1966), 'Fear and the house-as-haven in the lower class', *AIP Journal*, vol. 32, pp. 23–31.

Rakoff, R. (1977), 'Ideology in everyday life: the meaning of the house', *Politics and Society*, vol. 7, pp. 85–104.

Rand, A. (1964), *The Virtue of Selfishness* (New York: New American Library).

Rapoport, A. (1969), *House Form and Culture* (Englewood Cliffs, NJ: Prentice-Hall).

Reeve, A. (1986), *Property* (London: Macmillan).

Relph, E. (1976), *Place and Placelessness* (London: Pion).

Renner, K. (1949), *The Institutions of Private Law and their Social Functions* (London: Routledge & Kegan Paul).

Rex, J. (1968), 'The sociology of a zone of transition', in R. Pahl (ed.), *Readings in Urban Sociology* (Oxford: Pergamon Press).

Rex, J., and Moore, R. (1967), *Race, Community and Conflict* (Oxford: Oxford University Press).

Rex, J., and Tomlinson, S. (1979), *Colonial Immigrants in a British City* (London: Routledge & Kegan Paul).

Reynolds, V. (1980), *The Biology of Human Action* (San Francisco: W. H. Freeman).

Robertson, D. (1984), *Class and the British Electorate* (Oxford: Blackwell).

Robinson, I. (1983), 'Subsidizing stigma: social consequences of council housing policies', in D. Anderson and D. Marsland (eds), *Home Truths* (London: Social Affairs Unit).

Robinson, R. (1979), *Housing Economics and Public Policy* (London: Macmillan).

Robinson, R., and O'Sullivan, T. (1983), 'Housing tenure polarization', *Housing Review*, July/August, pp. 116–17.

Robson, B. (1982), 'The Bodley barricade: social space and social conflict', in K. Cox and R. Johnston (eds), *Conflict, Politics and the Urban Scene* (London: Longman).

Rose, Damaris (1980), 'Towards a re-evaluation of the political significance of home ownership in Britain', in Conference of Socialist Economists, *Housing, Construction and the State* (London: Political Economy of Housing Workshop).

Rose, Damaris (1981), *Home Ownership and Industrial Change*, Urban and Regional Studies Working Paper No. 25 (Brighton: University of Sussex).

Rose, Damaris (1987), 'Home ownership, subsistence and historical change', in N. Thrift and P. Williams (eds), *Class and Space* (London: Routledge & Kegan Paul).

Rose, David, Saunders, P., Newby, H., and Bell, C. (1976), 'Ideologies of property: a case study', *Sociological Review*, vol. 24, pp. 699–730.

Rothbard, M. (1981), 'Buy out the obstructors', *Journal of Economic Affairs*, vol. 1, p. 159.

Rousseau, J. (1973), 'A dissertation on the origin and foundation of the inequality in mankind', in J. Rousseau, *The Social Contract and Discouses* (London: Dent).

Royal Commission on the Distribution of Income and Wealth (1975), Cmnd 6171 (London: HMSO).

Ruonavaara, H. (1988), *The Growth of Urban Home Ownership in Finland*, Sociological Studies Series A No. 10 (Turku: University of Turku).

Ryan, A. (1983), 'Public and private property' in S. Benn and G. Gaus (eds), *Public and Private in Social Life* (London: Croom Helm).

Salt, J. (1985), 'Labour migration and housing', paper presented at the Conference on Labour and Housing Market Change, London Open University Regional Centre, December.

Sarlvik, B., and Crewe, I. (1983), *Decade of Dealignment* (Cambridge: Cambridge University Press).

Sarre, P. (1986), 'Choice and constraint in ethnic minority housing', *Housing Studies*, vol. 1, pp. 71–86.

Saunders, P. (1978), 'Domestic property and social class', *International Journal of Urban and Regional Research*, vol. 2, pp. 233–51.

Saunders, P. (1979), *Urban Politics: A Sociological Interpretation* (London: Hutchinson).

Saunders, P. (1984), 'Beyond housing classes', *International Journal of Urban and Regional Research*, vol. 8, pp. 202–27.

Saunders, P. (1986), *Social Theory and the Urban Question*, 2nd edn. (London: Hutchinson).

Saunders, P. (1989), *Social Class and Stratification* (London: Tavistock).

Saunders, P., and Harris, C. (1989), *Popular Attitudes to State Welfare Services* Research Report No. 11. (London: Social Affairs Unit).

Saunders, P., and Williams, P. (1986), 'The new conservatism: some thoughts on recent and future developments in urban studies', *Society and Space*, vol. 4, pp. 393–9.

Saunders, P., and Williams, P. (1988), 'The constitution of the home', *Housing Studies*, vol. 3, pp. 81–93.

Savage, M. (1987), 'Understanding political alignments in contemporary Britain', *Political Geography Quarterly*, vol. 6, pp. 53–76.

Seldon, A. (1986), *The Riddle of the Voucher* (London: Institute of Economic Affairs).

Sennett, R., and Cobb, J. (1973), *The Hidden Injuries of Class* (New York: Knopf).

Sharron, H. (1982), 'Walsall: out of the civic centre, into the field', *New Statesman*, 19 March.

Shelter Community Action Team (1980), *The Great Sales Robbery* (London: Shelter).

Shlay, A. (1985), 'Castles in the sky: measuring housing and neighborhood ideology', *Environment and Behavior*, vol. 17, pp. 593–626.

Shlay, A. (1986), 'Who governs housing preferences?', *Environment and Behavior*, vol. 19, pp. 121–36.

Short, J. (1982), *Housing in Britain* (London: Methuen).

Slough Borough Council (1985), *The Borough of Slough Official Guide*, ed. J. Burrow & Co. (Slough Borough Council).

Sopher, D. (1979), 'The landscape of home', in D. Meinig (ed.), *The Interpretation of Ordinary Landscapes* (Oxford: Oxford University Press).

Spencer, P. (1987), *UK House Prices: Not an Inflation Signal* (London: Credit Suisse First Boston Ltd).

Stafford, D. (1980), 'Housing policy: objectives and strategies', in R. Leaper (ed.), *Health, Wealth and Housing* (Oxford: Blackwell & Martin Robertson).

Stewart, J. (1984), 'Home ownership', *Housing Review*, vol. 33, pp. 179–81.

Stretton, H. (1974), *Housing and Government* (Sydney: Australian Broadcasting Commission).

Stretton, H. (1975), 'Class bias in housing', *Community*, 11 June, p. 15.

Stretton, H. (1976), *Capitalism, Socialism and the Environment* (Cambridge: Cambridge University Press).

Stretton, H. (1978a), *Urban Planning in Rich and Poor Countries* (Oxford: Oxford University Press).

Stretton, H. (1978b), 'Capital mistakes', in C. Bell and S. Encel (eds), *Inside the Whale* (Oxford: Pergamon Press).

Stubbs, C. (1988), 'Property rights and relations: the purchase of council housing', *Housing Studies*, vol. 3, pp. 145–58.

Styles, G., Marsh, G., and Crossley, S. (1987), 'House prices, retail prices and earnings', *Halifax Research Briefing* (London: Halifax Building Society).

Sullivan, O. (1987), 'Housing tenure as a consumption sector divide', in R. Harris and G. Pratt (eds), *Housing Tenure and Social Class* (Gavle: National Swedish Institute of Building Research).

Sullivan, O., and Murphy, M. (1987), 'Young outright owner occupiers in Britain', *Housing Studies*, vol. 2, pp. 177–91.

Suttles, G. (1972), *The Social Construction of Communities* (Chicago: University of Chicago Press).

Swenarton, M., and Taylor, S. (1985), 'The scale and nature of the growth of owner occupation in Britain between the wars', *Economic History Review*, vol. 38, pp. 373–92.

Taylor, H. (1986), *Growing Old Together: Elderly Owner Occupiers and their Housing* (London: Centre for Policy on Ageing).

Taylor, T. (1983), 'Accommodation costs fall in a century of housing progress', *Building Societies Gazette*, April, pp. 438–40.

Taylor-Gooby, P. (1985), 'The politics of welfare', in R. Klein and M. O'Higgins (eds), *The Future of Welfare* (Oxford: Blackwell).

Taylor-Gooby, P. (1986a), 'Privatism, power and the welfare state', *Sociology*, vol. 20, pp. 228–46.

Taylor-Gooby, P. (1986b), 'Consumption cleavages and welfare politics', *Political Studies*, vol. 34, pp. 592–606.

Taylor-Gooby, P. (1987), 'Disquiet and state welfare: clinging to Nanny', paper presented at the 6th Urban Change and Conflict Conference, Canterbury, September.

Thane, P. (1984), 'The working class and state welfare in Britain 1880–1914', *The Historical Journal*, vol. 27, pp. 877–900.

Thompson, E. (1965), 'The peculiarities of the English', in R. Miliband and J.

Saville (eds), *The Socialist Register* (London: Merlin Press).

Thorns, D. (1981a), 'Owner-occupation: its significance for wealth transfer and class formation', *Sociological Review*, vol. 29, pp. 705–28.

Thorns, D. (1981b), 'The implications of differential rates of capital gain from owner occupation for the formation and development of housing classes', *International Journal of Urban and Regional Research*, vol. 5, pp. 205–30.

Thorns, D. (1982), 'Industrial restructuring and change in the labour and property markets in Britain', *Environment and Planning A*, vol. 14, pp. 745–63.

Thorns, D. (1988), 'New solutions to old problems: housing affordability and access within Australia and New Zealand', *Environment and Planning A*, vol. 20, pp. 71–82.

Tiger, L., and Fox, R. (1972), *The Imperial Animal* (London: Secker & Warburg).

Tinbergen, N. (1951), *The Study of Instinct* (Oxford: Oxford University Press).

Tinbergen, N. (1972), 'On war and peace in animals and man', in H. Friedrich (ed.), *Man and Animal: Studies in Behaviour* (London: MacGibbon & Kee).

Took, L., and Ford, J. (1987), 'The impact of mortgage arrears on the housing careers of home owners', in A. Bryman, B. Bytheway, P. Allatt and T. Keil (eds), *Rethinking the Life Cycle* (London: Macmillan).

Townsend, P. (1979), *Poverty in the United Kingdom* (Harmondsworth: Penguin).

Trasler, G. (1982), 'The psychology of ownership and possessiveness', in P. Hollowell (ed.), *Property and Social Relations* (London: Heinemann).

Tuan, Y. (1971), 'Geography, phenomenology and the study of human nature', *Canadian Geographer*, vol. 15, pp. 181–92.

Tuan, Y. (1974), 'Space and place: a humanistic perspective', *Progress in Geography*, vol. 6, pp. 211–52.

Tuan, Y. (1976), 'Geopiety: a theme in man's attachment to nature and to place', in D. Lowenthal and M. Bowden (eds), *Geographies of the Mind* (Oxford: Oxford University Press).

Turner, J. (1976), *Housing by People* (London: Marion Boyars).

Urry, J. (1981), 'Localities, regions and social class', *International Journal of Urban and Regional Research*, vol. 5, pp. 455–74.

van den Berghe, P. (1981), *The Ethnic Phenomenon* (New York: Elsevier).

Van Weesep, J. (1986), 'Dutch housing: recent developments and policy issues', *Housing Studies*, vol. 1, pp. 61–6.

Walker, R. (1985), 'Housing in north-east Lancashire', *Housing and Planning Review*, vol. 40, pp. 14–17.

Wallendorf, M., and Arnould, E. (1988), 'My favourite things: a cross-cultural inquiry into object attachment, possessiveness and social linkage', *Journal of Consumer Research*, vol. 14.

Waller, R. (1987), *The Almanac of British Politics* (London: Croom Helm).

Ward, C. (1983), *Housing: An Anarchist Approach* (London: Freedom Press).

Ward, C. (1985), *When We Build Again* (London: Pluto Press).

Ward, R. (1982), 'Race, housing and wealth', *New Community*, vol. 10, pp. 3–15.

Warde, A. (1986), 'Space, class and voting in Britain', K. Hoggart and E. Kofman (eds), *Politics, Geography and Social Stratification* (London: Croom Helm).

Warde, A., Savage, M., Longhurst, B., and Martin, A. (1987), *Class, Consumption and Voting*, Lancaster Regionalism Group Working Paper No. 23 (Lancaster: University of Lancaster).

Watson, S. (1986a), 'Women and housing or feminist housing analysis?', *Housing Studies*, vol. 1, pp. 1–10.

Watson, S. (1986b), 'Housing and the family', *International Journal of Urban and Regional Research*, vol. 10, pp. 8–28.

Weber, M. (1948), 'Politics as a vocation', in H. Gerth and C. Mills (eds), *From Max Weber* (London: Routledge & Kegan Paul).

405

REFERENCES

Weber, M. (1968), *Economy and Society* (Berkeley, Calif.: University of California Press).

Which? (1987), 'The best home for your money?', *Which?*, March.

White, J. (1987), 'Cash: an incentive to move?', *Housing*, vol. 23, pp. 18–20.

White, M., and White, L. (1977), 'The tax subsidy to owner-occupied housing', *Journal of Public Economics*, vol. 3, pp. 111–26.

Whitehead, C. (1979), 'Why owner occupation?', *Centre for Environmental Studies Review*, no. 6, pp. 33–41.

Whiteley, P. (1983), *The Labour Party in Crisis* (London: Methuen).

Williams, N. (1988), 'Housing tenure, political attitudes and voting behaviour', paper presented at the International Research Conference on Housing Policy and Innovation, Amsterdam, June.

Williams, N., Sewel, J., and Twine, F. (1986), 'Council house sales and residualization', *Journal of Social Policy*, vol. 15, pp. 273–92.

Williams, N., Sewel, J., and Twine, F., (1987), 'Council house sales and the electorate', *Housing Studies*, vol. 2, pp. 274–82.

Williams, P. (1984), 'The politics of property: home ownership in Australia', in J. Halligan and C. Paris (eds), *Australian Urban Politics* (Melbourne: Longman Cheshire).

Williams, P. (1986), 'Social relations, residential segregation and the home', in K. Hoggart and E. Hofman (eds), *Politics, Geography and Social Stratification* (London: Croom Helm).

Williams, P. (1987), 'Constituting class and gender: a social history of the home, 1700–1901' in N. Thrift and P. Williams (eds), *Class and Space* (London: Routledge & Kegan Paul).

Willmott, P., and Young, M. (1960), *Family and Class in a London Suburb* (London: Routledge & Kegan Paul).

Wilson, E. (1975), *Sociobiology* (Cambridge, Mass.: Harvard University Press).

Wright, E. (1978), *Class, Crisis and the State* (London: New Left Books).

Yates, D. (1982), 'The English housing experience: an overview', *Urban Law and Policy*, vol. 5, pp. 203–33.

Young, K., and Kramer, J. (1978), 'Local exclusionary policies in Britain', in K. Cox (ed.), *Urbanization and Conflict in Market Societies* (London: Methuen).

Young, M., and Willmott, P. (1973), *The Symmetrical Family* (London: Routledge & Kegan Paul).

Index